COCO

COCO

10 World-Leading Masters choose
100 Contemporary Chefs

Coco is an unprecedented survey of the most significant chefs working today. It presents 100 of the best contemporary chefs from around the world selected by ten of the most internationally recognized masters: Ferran Adrià, Mario Batali, Shannon Bennett, Alain Ducasse, Fergus Henderson, Yoshiro Murata, Gordon Ramsay, René Redzepi, Alice Waters, and Jacky Yu.

From Singapore to New York, Stockholm to London, Hong Kong to Paris, the 100 selected chefs are creating the most innovative and delicious food in the world today. Whether experimenting with new components and adventurous combinations, or producing simple, traditional food made with fresh, locally sourced ingredients, these chefs are pushing their craft to new heights. With its vast and varied selection of recipes, *Coco* is an unrivalled snapshot of what is happening in current gastronomy.

While the 100 selected chefs hail from all over the world, and cook very different styles of food in very different types of restaurants, they take their ingredients and methods equally seriously, perfecting their dishes and gaining more and more international attention for their work. They have been selected not only for their food, or for their skill as chefs, but also for the way they run their kitchens, and the contribution their restaurants make to the world of gastronomy.

Arranged alphabetically, *Coco* presents each selected chef over four pages. The first pages include a sample menu, images of the restaurant, the kitchen, and the chef at work, a brief biography, and an insightful text by the chef-curator explaining his or her choice. These are followed by a selection of recipes accompanied by photographs.

In the back of the book each of the chef-curators discusses a specific dish that has had a particular significance throughout his or her career, accompanied by the recipe and a photograph of the dish.

Part cookbook, part guide to the world's best new restaurants, and part who's who of the international food scene, *Coco* showcases 100 of the best contemporary chefs, as chosen by ten acknowledged world masters.

10
World-Leading Masters

Ferran Adrià
Ferran Adrià is the founder of elBulli restaurant in Roses, Spain. His legendary talent and creativity have inspired chefs and food lovers around the world, making elBulli the preeminent culinary destination, and the best restaurant in the world.

Mario Batali
With fifteen restaurants, seven cookbooks, and a host of television shows, Mario Batali is one of the most recognized and respected chefs working today. His many accolades include a James Beard Outstanding Chef Award.

Shannon Bennett
Shannon Bennett is the chef and owner of Melbourne's award-winning restaurant, Vue de monde, one of Australia's most prized restaurants, celebrated for its theatrical contemporary French fine dining.

Alain Ducasse
Alain Ducasse, one of the most renowned French chefs of his generation, is at the helm of several restaurants around the world, including Le Louis XV in Monte Carlo and Alain Ducasse at the Plaza Athénée in Paris.

Fergus Henderson
Fergus Henderson is a famous British chef and author. He opened London's St. John restaurant in 1994, and later St. John Bread and Wine, to wide critical acclaim. He is well known for his philosophy of "nose to tail eating."

Yoshihiro Murata
Yoshihiro Murata is chef and owner of the famed Kikunoi restaurant in Kyoto, Japan, where he has expanded the vision of traditional Kaiseki cuisine. His books and television appearances have introduced his legendary, exquisitely refined cuisine to audiences worldwide.

Gordon Ramsay
Gordon Ramsay is an internationally celebrated chef and restaurateur. His eponymous restaurant in Chelsea remains the only establishment in London to hold three Michelin stars. Ramsay, along with his protégés, operates a number of restaurants across the UK and abroad.

René Redzepi
René Redzepi is head chef and owner of Noma restaurant in Copenhagen, where he offers his inventive take on Nordic cuisine with a distinctive emphasis on regional specialties. Hailed as one of the most influential chefs worldwide, culinary wunderkind Redzepi has reinvented the Nordic kitchen.

Alice Waters
One of America's most influential chefs, Alice Waters created a revolution in 1971 when she introduced local, organic fare at her restaurant, Chez Panisse, in Berkeley, California. Credited for helping change the food landscape in America, Waters has championed sustainable farms and ranches for more than three decades.

Jacky Yu
Jacky Yu opened the private dining restaurant, Xi Yan, in Hong Kong in 2000 to critical acclaim. With a series of celebrated restaurants, a line of Xi Yan food products, his own television show, and four bestselling cookbooks, Yu is one of China's most famous chefs.

100
Contemporary Chefs

Hugh Acheson
Inaki Aizpitarte
Victor Arguinzoniz
Armand Arnal
Alex Atala
Jason Atherton
Eneko Atxa
José Avillez
Pascal Barbot
Cédric Béchade
Martin Benn
Mark Best
April Bloomfield
Robert Owen Brown
Mario Carbone
Wai Man Chan
David Chang
Ricky Cheung
Ryan Clift
Mauro Colagreco
Chris Cosentino
Enrico Crippa
Mathias Dahlgren
Kevin Davis
Anthony Demetre
Kobe Desramaults
Pascal Devalkeneer
Marcus Eaves
Didier Elena
Andrew Feinberg
John Fraser
Dani García
Cruz Goler
Skye Gyngell

Tommy Habetz
Wassim Hallal
Charlie Hallowell
Anna Hansen
Alberto Herráiz
Benjamin Hirst
Jing-long Huang
Jonathon Jones
Jacob Kenedy
Tom Kitchin
Anatoly Komm
Filip Langhoff
Ka Lun Lau
Alvin Leung
Jereme Leung
Lionel Lévy
Ed Lewis
Josh Lewis
Kelly Liken
Tung-Yuan Lin
Donald Link
Paolo Lopriore
Willin Low
Robert Marchetti
Christophe Martin
Andrew McConnell
Jakob Mielcke
Russell Moore
Marcos Morán
Hisato Nakahigashi
Motokazu Nakamura
Akhtar Nawab
Davide Oldani
Gustav Otterberg

Scott Peacock
Tom Pemberton
Ricardo Perez
Jean-François Piège
Glynn Purnell
Theo Randall
David Rathgeber
Albert Raurich
Lyndy Redding
Mads Refslund
Koji Saito
Chris Salans
Thorsten Schmidt
Amaryll Schwertner
Ben Shewry
Hideki Shimoguchi
Clare Smyth
Yosuke Suga
Takuji Takahashi
Mona Talbott
Kitty Travers
Michael Tusk
Naoya Ueno
Allison Vines-Rushing
Sylvestre Wahid
Tristan Welch
Jody Williams
Martin Wishart
Margaret Xu
JinR Zhang
Yue-Jiau Zhuang
Eric Ziebold

Some of my favorite people have hailed from Athens, Georgia. Although Hugh Acheson comes by way of Canada, he was smart enough to know that the regional Southern cuisine of Georgia can be re-created in exciting new ways if you only think outside the box. His menus boast twists on Southern favorites such as the pimento cheese sandwich that he serves as a snack on crostini, grits and collards to accompany pork cheeks, Maytag blue cheese in his spinach salad, and cornmeal to crust sweetbreads. In particular, his signature dish, Frogmore Stew, takes a Southern classic of low-country boil and reinvents it as a bouillabaisse.

Hugh, like myself, learned about food, culture, and cooking by doing. Rather than sitting in a classroom and hearing about great food, Hugh engaged himself in the kitchens of great restaurants. I respect Hugh as a chef because he can capture as much inspiration from an old travel book as from a recent article on molecular gastronomy. He regularly reads clippings sent to him from around the world as a source of inspiration. This clearly keeps his menus fresh and innovative. His characteristic and unique vision achieves the merging of soul food with Old World cuisine, but he understands and appreciates contemporary cuisine. A true academic and philosopher in his own right, Acheson thinks about what he is doing.

Making great food is only the half of it. Real energy and true talent come through when food is thoughtful. Acheson is thoughtful, but not the least bit contrived. His cooking at both Five & Ten and the National is delicious, smart, and feels like the place where it grows. His aim, for his restaurants to appeal to the community and his menus to present comfort food rather than haute cuisine, suits current trends and the desires of his patrons. The menu and wine list regularly change with the season to ensure wonderful ingredients and a wide appeal which, along with grits, he believes is the future for cuisine.

Mario Batali

Born in 1971 and raised in Ottawa, Hugh Acheson was influenced from an early age by the landscapes of Canada. After spending time as a waiter, he worked under Rob MacDonald at Café Henri Burger, where he gained a solid grasp of stylized French food and a firm foundation in the basics, from butchery to stock-making. A move to San Francisco took him to a number of other restaurants, culminating in 2000 with the opening of his own, the acclaimed Five & Ten in Athens, Georgia. Aspiring to offer a great community restaurant, Acheson takes seminal Southern dishes and injects them with French technique, melding soul food with Old World cuisine. Acheson has also recently opened a casual Mediterranean-inspired restaurant, the National, as well as a wine shop with sommelier Ben Giacchino. Complementing his concern for regional sourcing and sustainability, he hopes to open a series of restaurants focusing on the products of local agriculture, and to begin to brew North Georgia cider.

MENU

Seared scallops with chickpea puree, aleppo, salmoriglio, chopped spinach, and crushed pine nuts
Pinot Gris, Ransom, Willamette Valley, Oregon, USA, 2006

~

Cornmeal-dusted veal sweetbreads with baked grits, succotash, and tarragon jus
Meursault, Jean-Michel Gaumoux, "Les Perrières," Burgundy, France, 2002

~

Red trout with Southern bubble and squeak, lemon emulsion, and a boiled peanut and arugula salad
Condrieu, André Perret, "Chéry," Northern Rhône, France, 2006

~

Braised pork belly with roasted fillet, foie gras dirty rice, citrus, and okra
Pinot Noir, Radio-Coteau, "la Neblina," Sonoma Coast, California, USA, 2006

~

Chess pie, sorghum zabaglione, and spicy mango
Moscato d'Asti, Rinaldi, "Bug Juice," Piedmont, Italy, 2007

Hugh Acheson

1 & 2
Gathering fresh vegetables

3 & 4
Hugh Acheson in the kitchen

5
Preparing garnishes

1
Cornmeal-dusted veal
sweetbreads with baked grits,
succotash, and tarragon jus

2
Chess pie, sorghum
zabaglione, and spicy mango

CORNMEAL-DUSTED VEAL SWEETBREADS WITH BAKED GRITS, SUCCOTASH, AND TARRAGON JUS

Serves 6

For the baked grits
225 ml whole milk • 225 ml water • ¼ tsp salt • 60 g stoneground white hominy grits • 2 tbsp unsalted butter • 3 egg yolks • 1 egg white • 1 tbsp heavy (double) cream

1 In a medium pan combine the milk and water and bring to a boil. Add the salt.
2 Slowly add the grits, stirring with a whisk. When they have all been whisked in, reduce the heat to low and switch to a wooden spoon. Cook for 45 minutes, stirring, or until the grits are fully cooked. Preheat the oven to 375°F (190°C). Remove from the heat and let cool a little.
3 Temper in (slowly add without scrambling them) the butter, egg yolks, egg white, and cream. Butter 6 ramekins and pour an even amount of the custard base into each, filling them about three-quarters full.
4 Bake in a warm water bath for 20 minutes. Remove and let sit for about 15 minutes, still in the water bath, before using.

For the tarragon jus
2 tbsp unsalted butter • 2 shallots, peeled and finely chopped • 125 ml dry vermouth • 1 star anise • 2 bay leaves • 475 ml chicken stock • 225 ml veal stock • 1 tbsp chopped tarragon • salt and pepper

1 In a pan over medium heat melt 1 tbsp of the butter until it foams. Add the shallot and sauté for 3 minutes until translucent. Add the vermouth, anise and bay. Reduce until just about dry.
2 Add the chicken stock and veal stock and reduce by two-thirds (down to 225 ml).
3 Whisk in the remaining butter and the tarragon.
4 Season to taste and keep warm, in a water bath, until ready to serve.

For the succotash
2 tbsp extra-virgin olive oil • 25 g leek, white part only, finely chopped • 85 g corn kernels (sweetcorn), freshly cut • 60 g okra, thinly sliced against the grain • 85 g ripe tomatoes, peeled, seeded, and finely diced • 85 g black-eyed peas (beans), cooked until tender (I like to cook them with a ham hock) • 60 ml chicken stock • 1 tsp thyme leaves • 1 tsp freshly chopped flat-leaf parsley • salt and pepper to taste

1 In a small skillet, warm the olive oil over medium heat and add the leek. Cook until translucent, stirring often, for about 5 minutes.
2 Add the corn, okra and tomato and cook for 5 more minutes, stirring often.
3 Add the peas and stock and cook for 5 more minutes.
4 Finish with the thyme and parsley, season to taste and keep warm until ready to plate.

For the sweetbreads
700 g veal sweetbreads • 2 bay leaves • 1 stalk fresh thyme • 60 g celery, finely chopped • salt and pepper • 225 ml buttermilk • 120 g fine yellow cornmeal • 1 tbsp butter • 1 tbsp olive oil

1 Preheat the oven to 425°F (220°C).
2 Place the sweetbreads in a medium pan and cover with cold water. Add the bay, thyme, and celery. Place over heat and bring to a boil, then turn off the heat. Let the sweetbreads sit in the warm water for 10 minutes.
3 Remove the sweetbreads from the water and carefully extract the connective tissue from around and between them. Then cut the resulting pieces into 4-cm thick slices and place in a bowl.
4 Season the sweetbreads and cover with buttermilk.
5 Warm a skillet over medium heat. Pull the sweetbreads out of the buttermilk and dredge in the cornmeal. Remove and place on a plate.
6 Add the butter and olive oil to the warmed skillet. Add the sweetbreads and cook until golden and crisp, turning after about 2 minutes.
7 Place the skillet in the oven for about 4 minutes to finish roasting the sweetbreads. Leave the oven on for plating.

To serve
1 Arrange 6 plates on the counter.
2 Reheat the grits by placing the ramekins in the still-hot oven for about 3 minutes. Carefully remove, and invert one onto each plate.
3 Spoon 1–2 tbsp of the succotash onto each plate.
4 Arrange 2–3 crisp sweetbread chunks on each plate, and then drizzle with the tarragon jus.

CHESS PIE, SORGHUM ZABAGLIONE, AND SPICY MANGO

Serves 6

For the pie dough
400 g unsalted butter, at room temperature • 175 g granulated sugar • pinch of salt • 1 egg • 1 tsp vanilla extract • 450 g all-purpose (plain) flour

1 Place the butter, sugar, salt, egg, and vanilla in a small mixer bowl and mix at low speed using a paddle attachment until just combined. Some small pieces of butter should be left unincorporated.
2 Switch to the dough hook and slowly add the flour, mixing on low speed until the dough is just smooth. If it is overmixed, it will be difficult to roll out.
3 Place the dough on a parchment-lined baking sheet and press as flat as possible to chill quickly. This will also make the rolling out process quicker and avoid overworking the dough.
4 Refrigerate for about 30 minutes until firm enough to work with.
5 Roll the dough on a lightly floured board to the desired thickness.
6 Cut circles and line clean, ungreased tart pans with dough. Maintain a consistent thickness by not pressing the dough too tightly into the pans. Chill until ready to fill and bake. If you have extra dough, wrap it tightly in plastic wrap (clingfilm) and freeze for later use.

To finish the pie
225 g granulated sugar • 450 g unsalted butter, at room temperature • pinch of salt • 6 egg yolks • 2 egg whites • 75 ml water • 1 tsp white-wine vinegar • 2 tsp vanilla extract • 2–3 tbsp all-purpose (plain) flour

1 Preheat the oven to 375°F (190°C).
2 Using a stand mixer with a paddle attachment, cream the sugar, butter, and salt until light and fluffy. Lower the speed to medium and mix in the egg yolks and whites for about 2 minutes.
3 Add the water, vinegar, and vanilla and mix until fully incorporated.
4 If the batter appears broken or thin, add a little flour to bring it together.
5 Pour the filling into the chilled tart shells and bake for 20–25 minutes. To avoid soggy bases, bake them on oven tiles.

For the sorghum zabaglione
225 ml heavy (double) cream • 4 egg yolks • 60 ml sorghum syrup • grated zest of 2 lemons, juice of 1 • 1 vanilla bean, scraped • 175 ml Champagne

1 Whip the cream to stiff peaks and place in the refrigerator.
2 In a large stainless steel bowl, whisk the egg yolks with the syrup, lemon zest, lemon juice, vanilla, and Champagne. Place over a water bath on the stove top and whisk carefully but vigorously until foamy and thick. Remove from the heat and continue whisking until thick and cool.
3 Fold the zabaglione base into the whipped cream and set aside.

For the spicy mango
150 g peeled and diced mango • 2 tbsp Moscato d'Asti wine • ½ tsp red chili flakes

1 In a small bowl, macerate the mango in the wine.
2 When ready to serve, sprinkle the mango with chili flakes.

To serve
Cut each chilled pie into two and arrange slightly overlapping on each plate. Spoon about 2 tablespoons of mango next to the pies. Spoon zabaglione over the pies and serve.

Hugh Acheson

1 & 2
Outside Le Chateaubriand

3
Assembling a strawberry
meringue

4
Inaki Aizpitarte plating a dish

5
Searing eggplants

6
Wine producers on a
chalkboard in the restaurant

Inaki Aizpitarte

MENU

Fish custards

~

Beef with charred eggplant

~

Strawberries, lemon verbena whipped cream, and bittersweet paprika meringue

Inaki Aizpitarte was born in 1972 in Besançon, in the French Basque Country, and began cooking by accident after working as a dishwasher in a Serbian restaurant in Tel Aviv in 2000. Returning to France, he trained through experience, becoming chef de partie at Paris's Café des Délices. He later moved on to La Famille bistro, an innovative restaurant where Aizpitarte was able to experiment and stretch himself, coming under the influence of Laurent Chareau. In 2005, he began work as a chef at Transversal, the restaurant at Vitry-sur-Seine's museum of contemporary art, moving on after a year to Le Chateaubriand as head chef. Aizpitarte presents ingredients as closely as possible to their natural state, providing an honest encounter between produce, chef, and guest.

Le Chateaubriand is one of the most modern restaurants in Europe right now. It is a restaurant with no tablecloths, no silverware, no restrictions in the way of thinking about gastronomy — it is a bistro.

How can I consider a bistro to be one of the most modern restaurants? The answer is Inaki's cuisine: It is inventive and light. He lives with the seasons, cooks with his intuition, despises recipes, does not seem to care about fame, and has never taken the easy route of simply deconstructing bistro classics. If his food was to be served in more palatial surroundings, I am sure he would have several Michelin stars and all the celebrity that comes with them. But he just wants to serve good food — modern food.

Over the last few years a new term has been coined: bistronomy. Inaki is without a doubt at the forefront of this movement. I think that bistronomy sends out a message to more established gourmet restaurants saying that the way guests want to dine today is different from ten years ago. Today gourmet travelers and chefs from around the world no longer care so much about the extravaganza surrounding the food and wine. They want to experience something honest and real, without all the pretentiousness that often seems to accompany über-gastronomy.

Going to Inaki's restaurant reminds me of how a restaurant experience should be. It is about having a good time, it is about sharing an experience with friends or loved ones, and having taste sensations, being served by professional people with a passion for their trade. It is not about big chandeliers and gold forks, 200 euros apiece. In a way you can say that Inaki's restaurant is the essence of a restaurant today.

I once read that Alain Ducasse said a restaurant should be a reflection of society — perhaps Le Chateaubriand is just that.

René Redzepi

1
Fish custards

2
Beef with charred eggplant

3
Strawberries, lemon
verbena whipped
cream, and bittersweet
paprika meringue

FISH CUSTARDS
Serves 4

trimmings from a good-sized cod (skin, cheeks, throat, belly, bones, cleaned head) • 1 white onion • 15 g fresh ginger • 1 clove garlic • 1 stalk lemongrass • 10 white peppercorns • 500 ml cow's milk • salt • elderflowers, for garnish

1 Wash the cod trimmings thoroughly in cold water. Break up the head and bones, and put them in the bottom of a pan.
2 Add the flavorings: the roughly chopped white onion and ginger, crushed clove of garlic, lemongrass split in two lengthways, and 10 whole white peppercorns.
3 Cover the ingredients with cold milk. Salt lightly and infuse the mixture slowly over a gentle heat about 140°F (60C°) for 6 hours.
4 Strain through a cheesecloth (muslin). Pour the warm liquid into individual dishes and leave to set overnight in the refrigerator. The natural gelatin contained in the fish trimmings will set the mixture.
5 Sprinkle the fish custards with elderflowers and serve quickly.

BEEF WITH CHARRED EGGPLANT
Serves 4

For the charred eggplant
2 good-sized eggplants (aubergines) • 2 tbsp mellow, fruity olive oil

1 Turn the gas burners on full. Place the washed eggplant on the stove, right against the flames. Scorch the eggplant meticulously on all sides (between 8 and 15 minutes each side). Remove the stalk.
2 Put the eggplants in blender to make a smooth mixture. Remove them from the blender and mix in 2 tbsp olive oil with a fork, season, and set aside.

For the new potatoes
250 g baby new potatoes (such as La Bonnotte de Noirmoutier) • 500 ml chicken stock • 50 g slightly salted butter

Wash but do not peel the potatoes. Mix the chicken stock and butter in a pan. Put the potatoes into cold stock and cook, covered, over gentle heat until cooked to your liking.

For the beef
600 g top rump of beef in one piece or boned shoulder blade • 1 tbsp peanut oil

1 Keep the meat whole and take it out of the refrigerator 30 minutes before you cook it.
2 Put the peanut oil in a skillet over moderate heat, salt the beef, and put it in the pan. Continue cooking, gradually raising the temperature. Brown the meat on all sides. Serve rare.

For the scallions
4 scallions (spring onions)

At the same time as the beef, in the same skillet if possible, fry the whole scallions.

To serve
1 bunch chive flowers, for garnish

Reheat the eggplant and carve the meat. Using a spatula, spread the charred eggplant like a relish on the edge of a plate. Place the meat in the center of the plate and pour pan juices over it. Add the scallions, potatoes, and chive flowers.

STRAWBERRIES, LEMON VERBENA WHIPPED CREAM, AND BITTERSWEET PAPRIKA MERINGUE
Serves 4

For the whipped cream
120 g lemon verbena leaves • 750 ml light (single) cream • 330 ml milk • 40 g white sugar

1 Remove the leaves from freshly washed lemon verbena.
2 Put the light cream, milk, and sugar in a heavy-bottomed pan. Bring to a boil, then remove from the heat. Add the lemon verbena leaves.
3 Cover and leave the mixture to infuse for ½ hour. Strain and cool.
4 Pour the mixture into a siphon until two-thirds full. Put on the lid and screw in 2 gas cartridges. Shake the siphon well at each stage.
5 Rest for at least 4 hours in the refrigerator.

For the bittersweet paprika meringue
150 g egg whites • 20 g confectioners' (icing) sugar • 150 g superfine (caster) sugar • 10 g cornstarch (cornflour) • 3 g ground bittersweet paprika

1 Beat the egg whites to stiff peaks. While continuing to whisk, gradually beat in the confectioners' sugar, superfine sugar, cornstarch, and bittersweet paprika.
2 Put the mixture in a pastry (piping) bag. Pipe 2-cm-diameter cylinders on to a nonstick silicone mat. Cook and dry the meringue in the oven at 120°F (50°C) for 8 hours.

To finish
2 baskets strawberries in season (such as Mara des Bois) • 4 pinches popping candy

1 Place halved strawberries with a pinch of popping candy and a large piece of meringue in a soup plate.
2 Shake the siphon vigorously and cover the strawberries evenly with lemon verbena whipped cream.

Inaki Aizpitarte

In 1980 Rafael García Santos invited me to his restaurant, where Victor had just started. Victor is a reserved character, which is reflected in his style of cooking. One of the most personal and innovative to be found in the world of haute cuisine, it embraces the Spanish tradition of grilling, while introducing modern ideas.

Victor has created an entirely new cuisine where he literally grills everything—from caviar, *anguiles* (the very expensive delicacy of baby eels), and eggs, to peas, and ice cream. Furthermore, he has invented various pieces of equipment that he uses to grill the ingredients in his dishes. But the way he raises his cuisine to an art form is by pairing different ingredients with various types of wood and making his own charcoal on site. For instance, black oak is used for fresh seafood, apple wood for caviar. His kitchen operates through a complex series of pulleys that allows the various ingredients to sit above the flame and enables him to control the temperature.

Reflecting this new cuisine's roots in tradition, his restaurant retains the old Basque feel as well. When he bought Etxebarri in 1989 it was a dilapidated wreck, but after major refurbishment it has regained its place at the center of the community.

What is particularly important about Victor is that he has made us think again about food and its possibilities, and he continues to fire the imagination of all the avant-garde chefs who, like me, go to his restaurant to think. Like a lighthouse, this innovative, inspirational chef who sees beauty in simplicity, guides us and reminds us that other, more thematic avant-garde cuisines such as his exist. I have chosen him simply because he is the only contemporary chef that I reference directly in my food.

Ferran Adrià

Victor Arguinzoniz was born in Axpe Atxondo in Spain, in 1969. After pursuing other careers as an electrician and lumberjack, Arguinzoniz began to teach himself to cook. Inspired by the culinary heritage of the Basque Country, Arguinzoniz now influences every process at work in his kitchen, including hand-curing the chorizo himself. The menu at Etxebarri changes daily, reflecting the changing produce of the seasons, which is all sourced as locally as possible—shellfish and glass eels from the nearby shore, vegetables from the kitchen garden, and berries and mushrooms from the mountainside.

MENU

Homemade chorizo

~

Grilled oyster, wakame

~

Grilled Iranian caviar Imperial Beluga 000

~

Grilled bone marrow and *zizas*

~

Hand-churned smoked butter with fresh bread flakes

~

Grilled Palamós shrimp

~

Grilled belly of tuna and slow-roasted tomato

~

Grilled eel and zucchini

~

Grilled Galician beef chop

~

Grilled baby peas and pancetta

~

Zizas ice cream with wild mountain strawberries

~

Torrija with smoked-milk ice cream

~

Wood-fired madeleines

Victor Arguinzoniz

1
Flame-roasting peppers

2–3
Victor Arguinzoniz at the grill

4
Inside the wood burning oven

Asador Etxebarri, Axpe-Marzana, Spain

GRILLED BONE MARROW AND ZIZAS

We use bone marrow from retired Rubia Galician cattle (the same that we use for the *chuleta* or cutlets (chops). The marrow is cut and cleaned to remove the bone, then grilled over grapevines for approximately 8 minutes, turning halfway through cooking. It is then removed, trimmed, and finished with fleur de sel and shavings of wild St. George's mushroom or *zizas*, which are in season between April and June. We serve it on grilled bread.

GRILLED EEL AND ZUCCHINI

Eels are kept live and killed upon request using the Japanese *unagi* method. Each fillet is cut into two and then grilled over holm oak charcoal, skin side down, for approximately 10 minutes, until the skin becomes crispy. It is then turned and grilled for a further 2 minutes alongside the peeled and cut zucchini (courgettes).

GRILLED PALAMÓS SHRIMP

These are freshly caught shrimp (prawns) from the small fishing port of Palamós, in the province of Girona, Catalunya. Taken from depths of more than 1,000 meters, these shrimp are famous for their bright pink hue and the intense soup that can be made from their heads. They are grilled gently over holm oak charcoal for about 6 minutes (depending on the size), turned halfway through and sprinkled with a little fleur de sel.

HAND-CHURNED SMOKED BUTTER WITH FRESH BREAD FLAKES

Depending on the time of year, raw cow's and goat's milk is heated individually in a wood-fired oven, giving it a smoky aroma and helping to separate the cream. The cream is then cold-matured over 24 hours, developing acidity and its crystalline structure before we beat it by hand to form butter. It is then rolled in fresh bread flakes that are formed by grating the dough over the hot stone base of the oven, and we finish it with carbonic sea salt.

GRILLED BABY PEAS WITH PANCETTA

We pick baby peas from the garden and grill them whole, in their pods, over olive wood for approximately 4 minutes, turning halfway through. The peas are then shelled and combined with the juice of the pods. The dish is finished with a thin slice of homemade pancetta.

1
Grilled bone marrow and *zizas*

2
Grilled eel and zucchini

3
Grilled Palamós shrimp

4
Hand-churned smoked butter
with fresh bread flakes

5
Grilled baby peas
with pancetta

Victor Arguinzoniz

1–2
Armand Arnal in the kitchen

3
Preserves at La Chassagnette

4
The restaurant's dining terrace

Armand Arnal

MENU

Bitter herb velouté with
Brousse cheese

~

Escabèche of gray mullet

~

Vaccarès crayfish and carrots
preserved in ginger, arugula

~

Roasted green asparagus,
broccoli, and dandelion
guacamole

~

Glazed zander, marmalade of
scallions, and artichokes with
kaffir lime

~

Suckling lamb on a skewer,
garlic chives, fava beans, and
mangetout peas

~

Seasonal cheese and a relish

~

Camargue rice pudding and
preserved seasonal fruit

~

Chilled bowl of Gariguette
strawberries in green
tea, strawberry sorbet/
fromage blanc

Armand Arnal was born in
Montpellier, France, in 1979,
and started his apprenticeship
as a pastry chef at the world-
famous Fauchon in Paris.
He then worked closely with
Didier Elena at Alain Ducasse's
restaurant the Essex House
in New York for several years;
this apprenticeship, together
with his many travels in Japan
and elsewhere, influenced and
formed his culinary vision.
Since 2006, Arnal has been
head chef at La Chassagnette.
Situated in the heart of the
Camargue in France, the
restaurant is surrounded by a
vast vegetable garden. Cooking
and planting vegetables are
thus in constant symbiosis at
La Chassagnette—an organic
working method that was
rewarded with a Michelin star
in 2009.

Far from all the noise about experimental cooking, a quiet revolution is taking place. Let's call it the "green revolution," to make it clear that it has nothing to do with dogmatic vegetarianism. What's it all about? Quite simply, rehabilitating vegetables. To gauge the scale of the change, you have to remember to what extent vegetables used to be no more than a foil for meat and fish, which were the real stars of the dish. The rest was just a garnish or an accompaniment, treated with a touch of condescension. Today that's all changing. Slowly, but inexorably, we're looking for what's authentic, simple, and healthy.

Armand is one of the pioneers of this revolution. To talk about his cooking, you have to start by talking about his vegetable garden. It covers almost five acres, employs three gardeners, and offers 180 varieties of vegetables, citrus fruits, and herbs. The tomatoes are just one example: In season, there are fifty varieties, including the legendary "Téton de Venus," or "Venus's Nipple."

When the garden is only a few meters from the table, the notion of freshness takes on a whole new dimension. And the taste buds respond: "Aha! Now *that's* what you could call a vegetable!" This is where Armand's skill comes in. His cooking is still Mediterranean, naturally, because we're in Arles. It brings out a chorus of flavors, textures, and colors. Everything is just right, not in the least bit fussy, and is bursting with life. You discover that vegetables are joyful. Even the desserts, marrying citrus fruits with herbs and spices, make generous use of the resources of the garden. But as I've said, this isn't vegetarian cuisine. There's meat, and not just any old meat: beef from Camargue bulls, pork from Mont Ventoux pigs and Marseille pigeons. And there are creatures from the nearby sea: little sea snails, cuttlefish, and many more.

Armand isn't a "green" cook. He's a cook, no more, no less. In other words, a man who pays attention to nature. Some people had just forgotten that that is an avant-garde outlook.

Alain Ducasse

La Chassagnette, Arles, France

1
Bitter herb velouté
with Brousse cheese

2
Escabèche of gray mullet

3
Camargue rice pudding and
preserved seasonal fruit

24

BITTER HERB VELOUTÉ WITH BROUSSE CHEESE
Serves 4

20 g chives • 10 g mint • 20 g flat-leaf parsley • 10 g chervil • 1.5 kg mixed green salad (spinach, mixed salad leaves, watercress, dandelion, wild arugula (rocket) • 1 bunch scallions (spring onions) • olive oil, for sweating and drizzling • 1 liter vegetable stock • fleur de sel • a little pepper • Fernet Branca, heated, to taste • 80 g Brousse, or other fresh soft cheese

1 Trim, wash and dry the herbs.
2 Remove the coarse stems from the salad leaves and wash them.
3 Peel and finely chop the scallions, then sweat them, without allowing them to brown, in a dribble of olive oil. Once they are soft, add the salad leaves, season with fleur de sel and pepper, and moisten with very hot stock and Fernet Branca.
4 Bring to a boil and cook for 3 minutes, then add the herbs and continue to cook for 1 minute. Mix with a hand-held beater, strain through a conical sieve and chill quickly on ice to fix the chlorophyll and preserve the bright green color.
5 Serve with the Brousse and a dash of olive oil.

ESCABÈCHE OF GRAY MULLET
Serves 4

For the marinade
3 oranges • 2 lemons • 50 ml white balsamic vinegar • 1 tsp coriander seeds • ½ tsp peppercorns • 2 sprigs fresh cilantro (coriander) • 1 clove garlic • matured olive oil, for drizzling

Blanch 1 orange and 1 lemon in separate pans, and then make a marinade using the balsamic vinegar, the juice of 2 oranges and 1 lemon and the zests of the blanched orange and lemon. Add 1 tsp coriander seeds and ½ tsp peppercorns, 2 sprigs of cilantro, a clove of garlic, chopped, and a drizzle of olive oil.

For the mullet escabèche
2 good (700-g) gray mullets • 40 g orange carrots • 1 clove garlic • 2 oranges • 1 lemon • 3 sprigs fresh cilantro (coriander) • matured olive oil, for drizzling • 1 red onion • ½ tsp peppercorns • 1 tsp coriander seeds • salt and pepper to taste

1 Fillet and bone the mullet. Cut in half lengthwise, not too thin, not too thick.
2 To make the escabèche, first cut the carrots and a clove of garlic into slices 3 mm thick. Remove the zest from 2 oranges and 1 lemon. Cut both zests into fine julienne strips and blanch twice. Mix 2 sprigs of cilantro with a drizzle of olive oil. Cut the onion into small pieces.
3 Sweat the carrots and garlic without letting them color, then add the onions and the peppercorns and coriander seeds. Deglaze with the white wine and reduce by half. Add the juices of one orange and half a lemon. Add salt and pepper.
4 The vegetables should be slightly crunchy. Put them aside and add a sprig of fresh cilantro, which will infuse while the vegetables are cooling, a drizzle of olive oil and the blanched zests.
5 Pour the marinade over the strips of mullet 20 minutes before serving.

To serve
coriander oil, to finish • crushed cilantro (coriander) leaves

Arrange the prepared fillets on a plate, in a rosette. Arrange the escabèche garnish neatly over the fish. Pour a little coriander oil over the plates and the fish, with some crushed cilantro leaves.

CAMARGUE RICE PUDDING AND PRESERVED SEASONAL FRUIT
Serves 8

For the pudding and the fruit
1 kg Camargue short-grain rice • 4 liters semi-skimmed organic milk • 1 Madagascar vanilla bean • 300 g sugar • 20 g crystallized strawberries • 20 g crystallized figs • 20 g crystallized angelica

1 Put the rice, with 1 liter of milk and the vanilla bean, into a large saucepan.
2 Heat the remaining 3 liters of milk in a separate large pan. Once it has boiled, gradually add it to the pan containing the rice, stirring until it is completely absorbed.
3 Pour the mixture into a large bowl to stop the cooking process, and stir in the sugar. Remove the vanilla bean.
4 Cut the crystallized fruit into large cubes.

For the crème anglaise
1 liter organic milk • 600 ml organic light (single) cream • 1 Madagascar vanilla bean • 17 egg yolks • 120 g superfine (caster) sugar

1 Bring the milk, cream, and vanilla bean slowly to a boil.
2 Beat the egg yolks with the sugar in a bowl.
3 Remove the vanilla bean from the milk and cream mixture, then pour the mixture onto the egg yolks, stirring continuously.
4 Return the mixture to the pan and stir over low heat until it is thick enough to coat the back of a spoon. Strain.

To serve
1 Carefully mix the rice and the crème anglaise together, then add the crystallized fruit.
2 Pour the rice pudding into whisky tumblers—putting it in a glass gives it a gourmet look.

1–4
Alex Atala perfecting
a dish in kitchen

Alex Atala

MENU

Sea scallops with coconut milk, aromatic pepper, crispy mango, and Brazil nuts
Grand Cru Gewürztraminer, Alsace, France

~

Liquid coconut risotto with dendê oil, mint, and nori
Vaem Chardonnay Reserve, Argentina

~

Banana royal with coconut ice cream and cocoa chips
Vintage Port, Douro, Portugal

Born in 1968 in São Paulo, Alex Atala has forged a career from exploring the national ingredients of Brazil. Atala began his career at 19, at the Namur Hotel School in Belgium. From there he joined Jean-Pierre Bruneau's restaurant in Brussels, later moving to the Hotel la Côte d'Or, owned by Bernard Loiseau. After that, Atala broadened his horizons in the kitchens of Montpellier and Milan, before returning to São Paulo in 1994. There he quickly gained the attention of the food community with his technical flair, which Atala says aspires to the balance of simplicity and complexity found in the cuisine of chefs such as Michel Bras. In 1999 Atala opened D.O.M., where he offers dishes that showcase the traditional ingredients of Brazil, brought to a new level of expression through rigorous French techniques.

A journalist once referred to the components of the dishes served at D.O.M. as "humble ingredients." The review was very complimentary and they enjoyed the dishes; but there was a clear misunderstanding of food here. When I met Alex I was intrigued by his use of a root vegetable called cassava, which I had seen in a documentary a few years earlier being prepared by a group of women in an indigenous Amazonian tribe. The film-makers highlighted the fact that the root can be deadly poisonous when not prepared correctly. Alex turned this ingredient into a white, velvety puree. I don't see this as humble food—I see this as an experience. Other ingredients such as hearts of palm and Amazonian herbs, are turned into works of art in Alex's talented hands, which have trained in some of the best Michelin three-star restaurants in France. After meeting Alex I have changed my focus to the heritage of the ingredients that I use. I too want to know the full story of where my food and recipes come from, and to present them in a way that transforms humility into exhilaration.

D.O.M. is important to South America because when it opened in 1999 it raised the bar. The onus is now on other chefs to live up to and continue what Alex is doing. He is giving the Brazilian melting pot of amazing ingredients and cultural blends a clear identity. More importantly, he now realizes the responsibility he has to world cuisine to continue and become an even better chef and creator than he already is.

Shannon Bennett

SEA SCALLOPS WITH COCONUT MILK, AROMATIC PEPPER, CRISPY MANGO, AND BRAZIL NUTS
Serves 4

For the aromatic pepper oil
200 g aromatic pepper • 30 ml cachaça • 15 ml white-wine vinegar • 1 rosemary stalk • 1 bay leaf • 1 clove garlic • 750 ml canola (rapeseed) oil

Mix all the ingredients and let them infuse in a vacuum-pack bag for 30 days at below 15ºF (8ºC).

For the scallops
8 Brazil nuts • 12 sea scallops, cleaned • 25 ml lemon juice • salt • 150 ml coconut milk • 6 mint leaves

1   Grate the Brazil nuts on a microplane and set aside.
2   Place the scallops in a bowl on top of a bain-marie filled with ice. Add the lemon juice and a little salt and let them marinate for 1 minute.
3   Add the coconut milk and the aromatic pepper oil. Mix well.
4   Chiffonade the mint leaves and add to the mixture.

For the crispy mango
300 g mango flesh • 1 vanilla bean • 100 ml glucose

1   In a blender, blend the mango with the seeds from the vanilla bean. Pass it through a sieve, and reserve.
2   Heat the glucose until it melts and mix it with the mango.
3   Preheat the oven to 230ºF (130ºC).
4   On a nonstick silicone baking mat, make very thin layers of the mango mixture and bake in the oven for 35–40 minutes until crunchy.
5   Keep in a cool, dry place until needed.

To assemble
cilantro (coriander) sprouts

1   In each soup plate, arrange 3 scallops and a little of the marinade.
2   Place the grated Brazil nuts, 1 piece of crispy mango and a cilantro sprout in each bowl.

LIQUID COCONUT RISOTTO WITH DENDÊ OIL, MINT, AND NORI
Serves 12

For the risotto
50 g unsalted butter • 50 g onion • 500 g Arborio rice • 350 ml dry white wine • 700 ml vegetable stock • 500 ml coconut milk • salt

1   Melt the butter in a pan and cut the onion into brunoise. Sweat the onion in the pan for a few minutes.
2   Stir in the rice. Continue sweating for a few minutes and then add the wine.
3   Let the wine evaporate completely and then add the warm vegetable stock. Let it simmer on low heat, stirring occasionally, until it has turned into a thick paste. Pour in the coconut milk and bring quickly to a boil.
4   Process in a food processor until smooth. Season with salt and pour into a bain-marie, heating it to 140ºF (60ºC). Maintain at this temperature until serving.

For the mint oil
120 g mint leaves • 300 ml canola (rapeseed) oil

1   Blanch the mint leaves in boiling water for 5 seconds, then cool quickly in ice cold water.
2   Strain the leaves and squeeze them gently to extract the excess water.
3   Put the leaves and the canola oil in a Thermomix and process for 10 minutes at 160ºF (70ºC). Pass through a fine cloth and let cool.

To assemble
200 g nori seaweed • 200 ml soy sauce • 200 ml dendê oil • 200 ml mint oil

1   Cut the nori leaves into very fine julienne.
2   Gently pour some soy sauce, dendê oil, and mint oil into a deep plate.
3   Place the nori on one side. Finish with some liquid risotto.

BANANA ROYAL WITH COCONUT ICE CREAM AND COCOA CHIPS
Serves 12

For the brioche
1 kg wheat flour • 125 g egg yolk • 350 g unsalted butter • 20 g salt • 400 ml milk • 120 g sugar • 50 g yeast

1   Have all the ingredients at room temperature. In a stand mixer, beat the yolks with the flour and incorporate the butter gradually.
2   Dissolve the salt in the milk and add to the bread mixture.
3   Mix the sugar and the yeast and add to the mixture. Beat sufficiently to incorporate everything.
4   Divide the dough into 3 equal portions, place in silicone molds and let rise in the refrigerator for 24 hours.
5   Take out of the refrigerator and let stand at room temperature for 45 minutes.
6   Preheat the oven to 340ºF (170ºC).
7   Bake for 30 minutes. Cut into 2 (250-g) pieces.

For the banana royal
100 g egg yolk • 375 ml milk • 375 ml cream • ½ vanilla bean • 4 eggs • 350 g dried banana • 150 ml dark rum • unsalted butter, for greasing the pan • 150 g sugar

1   Mix the yolk with the milk, cream, seeds from the vanilla bean and eggs.
2   Blend the dried banana well with the dark rum.
3   Cut the crust off the brioche and slice the inside into 2-cm pieces.
4   Spread a (30 x 8-cm) sheet pan with butter and sugar.
5   Cover the bottom of the pan with a layer of brioche and then with a layer of dried banana. Follow up with another layer of brioche.
6   Finish the pan with a layer of the cream mixture.
7   Preheat the oven to 250ºF (140ºC).
8   Cover with aluminum foil and put it in the oven in a bain-marie for 25 minutes. Cool and refrigerate.

For the coconut ice cream
150 g fructose • 100 ml water • 1.2 liters coconut milk

1   Mix the fructose with the water over low heat until it forms a syrup.
2   Add the coconut milk, mix well and let cool. Immediately put it in a Pacojet.

For the cupuaçu syrup
300 g cupuaçu pulp • 125 ml water • 75 g sugar

Blend all the ingredients to a cream.

For the cocoa chips
125 ml glucose • 275 g sugar • 100 g Valrhona cocoa

1   Heat the glucose with the sugar to 260ºF (127ºC).
2   Remove from the heat and sift the cocoa into it. Mix quickly and put on a nonstick silicone baking mat to cool and harden.
3   Break into small pieces and process in a food processor until it has turned into a powder.
4   Preheat the oven to 320ºF (180ºC).
5   Cut shapes out of an acetate sheet to make a mold. Using the mold, sprinkle the cocoa powder to make a thin layer on the silicone nonstick baking mat. Bake for 4 minutes without ventilation.
6   Remove from the oven, cool and then carefully lift off the chips with a spatula. Keep in a dry place.

For the ganache
75 g sugar • 250 ml water • 250 g 50% bitter chocolate, chopped • 75 g creamy unsalted butter

1   Mix the sugar and water in a pan over low heat until the sugar dissolves.
2   When hot, gradually add the chocolate. Reduce for an hour, stirring constantly and not letting it boil.
3   Remove from the heat and incorporate the butter. Cool and set aside.

For the banana powder
100 g dried banana

Blend the dried banana to the consistency of powder. Sift and put aside.

To assemble
1   Place 3 pieces of banana royal on plate, separating each with a cocoa chip.
2   Put a line of cupuaçu syrup onto the plate.
3   With a pastry brush make a second line of chocolate ganache.
4   Put a little banana powder on the plate and a slice of dried banana on top.
5   Finish with a quenelle of coconut ice cream.

28

1
Sea scallops with coconut
milk, aromatic pepper, crispy
mango and Brazil nuts

2
Liquid coconut risotto with
dendê oil, mint, and nori

3
Banana royal with coconut
ice cream and cocoa chips

Alex Atala

I first met Jason when he came to work with me at Aubergine. He has had some fantastic experience and is one of the most open, committed and talented chefs I have come across. He is calm and incredibly focused, and his ability to pick out and put together flavors in a dish is remarkable. We made Jason executive chef at our restaurant Verre in Dubai, where he led the kitchen with great determination. He has totally revolutionized our approach to fine dining with his small portions—a kind of upmarket version of tapas or meze. As soon as we began discussing the plans for Maze, Jason mapped out a fresh new concept: a menu of French tapas with an Asian influence—suddenly he was coming up with some incredible, intense, dynamic flavors.

His menu changes daily with market specials, and many of the dishes are cooked on a charcoal robata grill, wood oven or on the plancha. He has also introduced line cooking, a method that is relatively unfamiliar in the UK, but favored in many top American kitchens.

My favorite dish at Maze has to be one of Jason's signature dishes, consisting of marinated beet, Sairass cheese, pinenuts and a Cabernet Sauvignon dressing. It's an elegant, subtle dish and beautiful to look at. Jason has become renowned for taking fairly simple and well-known dishes and turning them on their heads —for example, his peanut butter and cherry jam sandwich served with tonka bean cream and dehydrated cherries, a dish that has become a firm favorite with Maze guests.

Jason is incredibly innovative and is always developing different flavor combinations. On paper they perhaps shouldn't work together—but on the plate they are magical.

Gordon Ramsay

Jason Atherton was born in 1971 and began his career with stints under Pierre Koffmann and Nico Ladenis before working for Marco Pierre White at Harvey's and Restaurant Marco Pierre White. He followed this with an internship at elBulli, witnessing firsthand the dynamic, creative experience offered by Ferran Adrià. Atherton subsequently joined Gordon Ramsay at Aubergine, and quickly rose to executive chef. With the opening of Maze in 2005, Atherton gained more scope for experiment and creativity, establishing a changing menu of exquisite small French dishes with an Asian influence, which in 2006 won the restaurant a Michelin star. In 2008, Atherton and Gordon Ramsay launched Maze Grill, and in 2009 they opened the doors of Maze at the One&Only Cape Town in South Africa.

MENU

Jerusalem artichoke, braised wild duck, and cep brioche

~

Colchester crab, tartar of mackerel, marinated cucumber, and caviar

~

Marinated foie gras, Lincolnshire smoked eel, rhubarb, and ginger

~

Cornish red mullet, rabbit Bolognese, cuttlefish tagliatelle, squid paint, and asparagus

~

Roasted Anjou pigeon, 70% chocolate ganache, celery root textures, port, and blueberries

~

Buttermilk panna cotta, blood orange, and black olive caramel

~

Pliable chocolate, walnut ice cream, dehydrated lime curd, and spices

Jason Atherton

1
Jason Atherton at work

2
The dining room at Maze

3
In the open kitchen

Maze, London, UK

CORNISH RED MULLET, RABBIT BOLOGNESE, CUTTLEFISH TAGLIATELLE, SQUID PAINT, AND ASPARAGUS
Serves 4

For the rabbit sauce
6 rabbit shoulders • ½ large onion • 1 carrot, roughly chopped • 1 leek, roughly chopped • 1 celery stalk, roughly chopped • 2 cloves garlic, chopped • 1 sprig thyme • 1 tbsp tomato puree • 375 ml bottle white wine • 1 liter chicken stock

1 Preheat the oven to 400°F (200°C).
2 Roast the rabbit shoulders in a large pan in the oven until browned.
3 In another large pan, caramelize the onion, carrot, leek, celery, garlic, and thyme in oil.
4 Add the tomato puree and the white wine. Reduce over medium heat to make a glaze. Add the roasted rabbit shoulders and the chicken stock. Bring to a boil and let simmer for 20 minutes.
5 Strain though a fine sieve, then place the sauce back on medium heat to reduce by half. Set aside to use for the Bolognese.

For the rabbit Bolognese
300 g rabbit meat, minced • 1 large banana shallot, finely diced • 2 cloves garlic, finely diced • 1 tsp chopped rosemary • 1 tsp chopped thyme • 3 ripe plum tomatoes, seeded and chopped into 0.5 cm cubes • 2 tbsp tomato puree • 125 ml red wine • salt and pepper

1 In a large skillet, brown the rabbit. Strain off the fat and set the meat aside.

2 In a large pan, sweat the shallots, garlic, rosemary, and thyme in oil. Add the chopped tomatoes and let stew for about 5 minutes, mixing well. Add the tomato puree and wine and reduce to a glaze over medium heat. Add the rabbit and all of the rabbit sauce. Reduce further until thickened. Season.

For the garlic puree
cloves from 2 bulbs garlic, peeled • 200 ml whole milk • 200 ml heavy (double) cream

1 Blanch the garlic in boiling water and plunge immediately into ice water.
2 Bring the milk and cream to a boil, and add the garlic. Cook until the garlic is very soft.
3 With a slotted spoon strain out the garlic, reserving the liquid. Blend the garlic to a puree in a blender (liquifier). Add some of the cream-milk mixture to adjust the smoothness, and season.

For the red mullet
2 red mullet, filleted into 4 portions • olive oil, for drizzling and pan-frying • salt

Score each fillet several times with shallow parallel cuts on the skin side. Drizzle both sides with olive oil and salt. Pan-fry the fillets in olive oil for 3–4 minutes.

For the baby squid
4 baby squid, cleaned • olive oil, for frying

Fry the squid on a plancha in olive oil, and season.

1
Cornish red mullet, rabbit Bolognese, cuttlefish tagliatelle, squid paint, and asparagus

2
Roasted Anjou pigeon, 70% chocolate ganache, celery root textures, port, and blueberries

3
Buttermilk panna cotta, blood orange, and black olive caramel

For the cuttlefish
1 large cuttlefish body • 15 g butter • 75 ml fish stock

1 Cut the cuttlefish into 4 equal pieces lengthwise. Stack the pieces on top of each other and tightly wrap with plastic wrap. Freeze.
2 When frozen, slice thinly to make tagliatelle-like pieces.
3 In a pan, melt the butter and whisk in the fish stock. Add the cuttlefish tagliatelle and heat through. Season.

To serve
3 basil leaves, cut into thin strips and deep-fried • 3 stalks asparagus, blanched and cut into 2.5-cm pieces • olive oil, to drizzle • squid ink mixed with a little olive oil

1 Place some rabbit Bolognese in a bowl and put a red mullet fillet on top. Top with baby squid and asparagus.
2 Make a line of squid paint and place the cuttlefish tagliatelle at one end, with the deep-fried basil on top.
3 Finish with the garlic puree and drizzle with olive oil.

ROASTED ANJOU PIGEON, 70% CHOCOLATE GANACHE, CELERY ROOT TEXTURES, PORT, AND BLUEBERRIES
Serves 4

For the pigeon
2 pigeons, cleaned • vegetable oil, for melting butter • 50 g butter

1 Preheat the oven to 400°F (200°C).
2 Remove the pigeon legs, necks, and wings. Reserve for the sauce.
3 Place a frying pan over high heat and melt the butter with a drizzle of vegetable oil. When the butter is melted and foaming, place the pigeon in the pan and sear on all sides until evenly colored.
4 Place in the oven and roast until desired doneness, then remove and let rest in a warm place.

For the pigeon sauce
pigeon legs, necks, and wings • 2 shallots • 1 clove garlic • 2 sprigs thyme • 1 small bay leaf • 3 black peppercorns, crushed • salt and pepper • 2–3 tbsp sherry vinegar • 250 ml port • 400 ml chicken stock • 400 ml veal stock • 8 blueberries

1 Preheat the oven to 400°F (200°C).
2 Roast the pigeon legs, necks and wings in the oven.
3 In a large pan, caramelize the shallots, garlic, thyme, bay leaf, peppercorns and salt to taste.

Deglaze with the sherry vinegar.
4 Mix in the port and reduce to a glaze.
5 Add the legs, necks and wings and both the stocks. Bring to a boil and simmer for about 20 minutes until the legs are cooked through. Strain, and reduce the sauce until thickened. Season.
6 Just before serving, add the blueberries.

For the celery root puree and disks
1 head celery root (celeriac) • 475 ml heavy (double) cream • 475 ml whole milk • olive oil, for pan-frying • 100 ml Cabernet Sauvignon vinegar

1 Cut the celery root in half and cut 4 thin slices on a mandolin. Cut each slice into a circle about 5 cm in diameter. Set aside.
2 Roughly chop the rest of the celery root.
3 In a large pot bring the milk and cream to a boil. Add the celery root and cook until tender. Strain, and reserve the liquid.
4 Blend the celery root until smooth, adding some of the cooking liquid if necessary to adjust the consistency. Season.
5 For the disks, sear each one in a hot skillet with olive oil. Add the vinegar and reduce until the celery root is cooked through.

For the chocolate ganache
175 ml Banyuls vinegar • 50 g unsalted butter, cut into small cubes • 50 g bitter Valrhona chocolate, cut into small pieces

1 Reduce the vinegar to 50ml.
2 Pour into a double boiler and whisk in the butter one piece at a time.
3 Add the chocolate and mix well until incorporated.
4 Place over an ice bath and whisk occasionally while cooling.

To serve
micro herb sprigs • olive oil, to glaze

Place the pigeon in the dish with a serving of sauce and a dollop of celery root puree. Add a celery disk on top of the pigeon followed by a spoonful of the ganache. Drizzle with olive oil and sprinkle with micro herbs.

BUTTERMILK PANNA COTTA, BLOOD ORANGE, AND BLACK OLIVE CARAMEL
Serves 4–6

For the buttermilk panna cotta
¼ sheet leaf gelatin • ½ vanilla bean • 120 g heavy (double) cream • 150 g sugar • 360 g buttermilk • 15 ml lemon juice • 1 strip lemon zest • 120 g semi-whipped cream

1 Bloom the gelatin in a bowl of cold water until completely softened.
2 Place the vanilla bean on a chopping board and cut it in half. Using the back of a paring knife, carefully scrape the sticky seeds out. Reserve pod and seeds to one side.
3 Heat the heavy cream and add the sugar. Mix to dissolve over medium heat.
4 When the sugar is dissolved, reduce to low heat and whisk in the vanilla seeds, breaking them apart. Place the pod in to infuse. Let stand for 10 minutes over low heat then remove the pod.
5 Remove from heat and whisk in the gelatin until dissolved.
6 Pour in the buttermilk, lemon juice, and add the lemon zest, mixing well.
7 Pass through a fine sieve into a bowl set over an ice bath.
8 Once cool, fold in the semi-whipped cream.
9 Pour into chilled martini glasses and leave to set.

For the black olive caramel
100 g black olives, pitted • 15 g simple (stock) syrup • 100 g sugar • 40 g glucose • 10 ml water

1 Puree the olives until smooth and pass through a fine sieve over a medium bowl. Add the simple syrup.
2 In a pan, make a caramel with the sugar, glucose and the water. Cook until a deep caramel color.
3 Remove from the heat and whisk in the strained olive puree. Set aside to cool.
4 Adjust the consistency with more simple syrup if necessary.
5 Suck into mini pipettes for serving.

For the blood orange jelly
200 g blood orange juice • 1 leaf gelatin, bloomed in cold water

Heat about 50 g of the blood orange juice in a pan and dissolve the gelatin in it. Pass through a sieve into a bowl and add the remaining juice. Set aside.

For the puff pastry biscuit
60 g puff pastry dough

1 Preheat the oven to 350°F (180°C).
2 Roll the puff pastry into a rectangle about 0.25–0.5 cm in thickness. Cut into batons about 1 cm wide and 10 cm long.
3 Bake for about 3–5 minutes until puffed and golden brown. Let cool on a rack.

For the blood orange jam
75 g sugar • 5 g pectin • 37 ml water • 6 blood oranges, segmented

1 Mix the sugar and pectin together.
2 In a large pot, bring the orange segments and water to a boil. Whisk in the pectin and the sugar. Boil until jam stage, or 200°F (104°C). Remove from the heat and let cool and set in the refrigerator.
4 Using a hand blender, blitz slightly, keeping the jam slightly chunky.

For the blood orange granite
145 ml blood orange puree • 40 g simple (stock) syrup • 20 ml sparkling water

1 Whisk together the puree and the simple syrup. Place in the freezer and gradually whisk in the sparkling water. Let freeze, while whisking occasionally.
2 Scrape with a fork to break up.

To serve
lemon powder • orange powder • star anise powder • black olive powder • mini mint leaf

1 Pour a thin layer of orange jelly on top of the panna cotta.
2 Place the granite on top of the jelly layer.
3 Add a pinch of the powder garnishes and a mint leaf.
4 Spread a small amount of jam along top of the puff pastry. Place on a plate with martini glass.
5 Place a mini pipette opposite the puff pastry.

Jason Atherton

A local gourmand introduced Eneko Atxa to me as an ambitious young chef when I visited the Basque region of Spain recently. He recommended that I should definitely pay a visit to Azurmendi, even though the restaurant was outside the city center.

When I arrived, Eneko showed me to the restaurant's laboratory. He mentioned that he is currently interested in aromas, such as the scent of leaf mulch, or the sea, or hay. He extracts these aromas and adds them to his recipes to create stories on the plate for the visitors to enjoy. He was earnest but also humble as he talked about cooking.

It goes without saying that I dined at his restaurant after I was shown around the laboratory. The aroma of leaf mulch added to mushrooms, the aroma of the sea added to goose barnacles: These long-forgotten, tantalizing scents brought smiles all around the table! As I looked around, I noticed the gentle, relaxed murmur coming from the families that filled the restaurant, despite the fact that it was past two o'clock in the afternoon on a weekday. There were no businessmen rushing in for a frantic lunch. Everyone was passing time in a leisurely way, enjoying the innovative creations of the young chef. They were being reinvigorated. I felt I had witnessed the essence of the restaurant.

Yoshihiro Murata

Born in the Basque Country in 1977, Eneko Atxa grew up in a home that revolved around its kitchen, inspiring a lifelong devotion to his land and its products that continues to be a guiding principle. Atxa's early training took the form of stints at the highly respected restaurants Martín Berasategui and Mugaritz of San Sebastián, among others. He combines faultless technical cooking with a firm commitment to the Slow Food movement; his restaurant, Azurmendi, has a whole department concerned with sourcing seasonal and sustainable produce.

MENU

Free-range egg yolks
with truffle

~

Goose barnacles in two
services with natural sea
aromas

~

Lobster with refreshing
fried herbs and aromas
of smoked tea

~

The vegetable garden with
its natural aromas

~

Lightly roasted leeks in
a chickpea consommé and
chunks of fresh hazelnut

~

Iberian pork jowl with
sleeping flower

~

Glazed grouper in baby
cuttlefish oil with a pea
and cuttlefish *pil-pil* sauce

~

Squab on a chestnut
branch

~

In the vineyards

~

Strawberries and roses

~

Moss on the wall

Eneko Atxa

Azurmendi, Larrabetzu, Spain

1
The busy dining room
at Azurmendi

2
Beans growing in the garden

3
Eneko Atxa in his kitchen

GOOSE BARNACLES IN TWO SERVICES WITH NATURAL SEA AROMAS
Serves 4

Since 2008, we have been studying nature and its reactions and aromas in our restaurant, Azurmendi. We believe that the ability to "steal nature's soul" and offer it to our guests is a luxury. Through this dish we have tried to bring our diners closer to our coast, its scenery, and above all its aromas, because we believe that this is the best means we have of traveling to the past, the present, and future. We try to combine our ingredients with their natural sensations.

For the boiled goose barnacles
250 g goose barnacles • 1 liter water • 30 g salt

1 Boil the goose barnacles in the water with the salt for 1 minute.
2 Peel the goose barnacles, squeezing them one by one and extracting as much juice as possible.
3 Set aside the goose barnacle meat and the extracted stock.

For the sea gel
Goose barnacle shells • 80 g sea lettuce • 1 liter water • 1 g kuzu per liter

1 Make a reduced stock with the shells and the sea lettuce. When cool, add the jus obtained from the goose barnacles.
2 Add the kuzu to obtain the texture of a gel. Set aside.

For the sea broth
60 g sea lettuce • 80 g goose barnacle shells • 1 liter recently collected sea water

1 Put the sea lettuce, goose barnacle shells, and seawater from the Ogeia coves in a 500-ml glass. Keep it in its natural state, with its seaweed, sea creatures, and live particles (these are what give the water its special aroma; without them, this sea aroma would not be transmitted).
2 Apply energy to this mixture with an ultrasound machine for 40 minutes at a power level between 78% and 80%, cycle 7.
3 Strain and set aside.

For the mock seaweed
4 pieces of dehydrated witch's butter fungus • 1.2 liters concentrated cuttlefish stock

Blanch the witch's butter fungus in water and boil in the concentrated cuttlefish stock for 5 minutes. This makes the wild mushroom appear like seaweed, with iodized tones and what we think is a more pleasant texture.

To serve
sea stones • liquid nitrogen • samphire • 12 samphire shoots

1 Place some sea stones in a deep glass dish and pour some liquid nitrogen over them. (Liquid nitrogen should not be handled without training in how to use it safely.) Place a glass bowl on top of the ice (the stones should be seen through the bowl).
2 Put the sea gel into the bowl and add the goose barnacles, samphire shoots, and mock seaweed. Add the samphire at the end.
3 Meanwhile, boil the fresh goose barnacles and serve them warm on another plate.
4 Heat the sea broth.
5 When both dishes reach the diner, the broth will be poured into the dish with the dry ice, which will evaporate to create a kind of sea mist that will smell exactly like the sea.

IBERIAN PORK JOWL WITH SLEEPING FLOWER
Serves 8

For the pork jowl
500 g pork jowl (cheek) • salt and pepper • 4 cloves garlic • bay leaf • extra-virgin olive oil, 0.4% acidity

Season the pork jowl with salt and pepper and cook slowly, in olive oil, with the garlic and bay leaf over very low heat for approximately 3 hours. Once cooked, set aside to cool in its own fat.

For the chickpea broth
1.5 kg soaked chickpeas • 1.9 liters water • 1 carrot • 1 leek • 1 onion

Boil the chickpeas with the water and vegetables in a pressure cooker for 1 hour. Strain and set aside half the broth for the bread crumbs. Reduce the other further to use for finishing the dish.

For the bread crumbs
200 g fresh bread crumbs • finely chopped garlic • 3 eggs • extra-virgin olive oil, 0.4% acidity, for frying

Mix all the ingredients until the crumbs have a uniform consistency. Make into quenelle shapes and pan-fry in olive oil, but do not let them form a solid mass. Drain them and place in the chickpea broth. Let stand for at least 12 hours.

To serve
Szechuan shoot • Szechuan button

Sear the pork jowl in a very hot skillet with no fat, then dry on paper towels. Make a circle using the reduced chickpea broth on a dish. Place the pork jowl over it with a bread crumb ball next to it. Place a Szechuan shoot on top, together with a quartered Szechuan button.

SQUAB ON A CHESTNUT BRANCH
Serves 4

For the branch
1.4 kg manioc (cassava) • 500 g purple corn on the cob • 14 g volcanic salt • 500 g chestnut purée • 1 liter water • 45 g nuts (hazelnuts, almonds, and walnuts) • 5 g chestnut wood chips • 30 g sugar • 1 g white pepper

1 Peel the manioc twice, until you can see small crevices in its surface. Cut into 10-cm sticks, making as much use of the surface as possible.
2 Separate the purple corn kernels from the cob, setting aside the woody part. Mix the salt and chestnut purée with the water and bring to a boil.
3 Add the manioc and boil for approximately 45 minutes, until it is completely cooked. Let cool and reserve the stock.
4 Place everything in the stock in a container with the chestnut chips. Apply ultrasound for 25 minutes at 75%, cycle 7. This impregnates the manioc with the chestnut scent without altering its texture. Set aside.

For the chestnut leaf
feuille de brick pastry

Shape the brick pastry into a leaf and brush with the stock that the manioc was cooked in. Dry in the oven at 175°F (80°C).

For the sand
100 g butter • 100 g scalded chestnuts • 30 g reserved stock from boiling the manioc • 4 g salt

1 Mix all the ingredients to obtain a smooth paste. Wrap the mixture in paper or plastic wrap (clingfilm). Shape into a cylinder and freeze, then grate using a microplane grater.
2 Bake for 15 minutes at 265°F (130°C).

For the squab
2 squab

Sear the squab until the skin becomes crisp.

To serve
sliced chestnuts and nuts, for garnish

Brush the plate lightly with the stock. Scatter over a little sand. Arrange the manioc branch and the leaf to give volume. Place the squab on the branch. Finish by adding some sliced chestnuts and nuts.

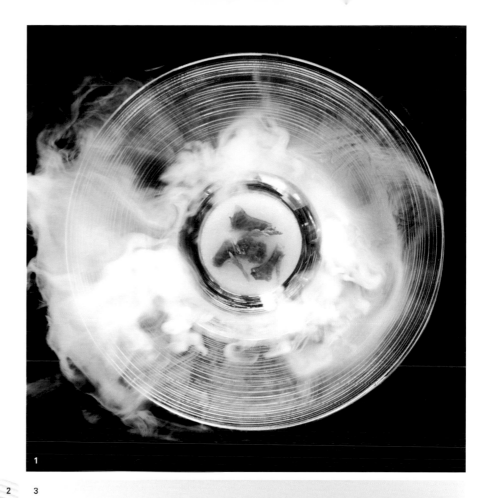

1
Goose barnacles
in two services
with natural sea aromas

2
Iberian pork jowl with
sleeping flower

3
Squab on a chestnut branch

Eneko Atxa

José was already an award-winning chef and international businessman when he chose to join us for a three-month stage at elBulli in 2007. I found it very interesting that an established Portuguese chef should decide to spend so much time with us. His eagerness to learn and desire to expand his already broad knowledge is highly impressive.

Since his time at elBulli, José has developed his own culinary language. His goal is to create a "techno-emotional" cuisine that is both Portuguese and modern. He chooses the very best ingredients and prepares them from traditional Portuguese recipes, but draws on cutting-edge techniques, learned during his travels and while at elBulli, that modernize his cuisine. Likewise Tavares Rico, the oldest restaurant in Lisbon (and at 225 years old it is surely one of the oldest in the world), is decorated with glass chandeliers and gilt-framed mirrors, which, juxtaposed with the stylish and modern presentation of his dishes, visually impart the same idea of mixing the old and the new. His Alentejo landscape is a case in point. The dish takes its inspiration from the topography of Portugal (the landscapes, the flowers, the sea, the sky, and the sun) and blends traditional Portuguese flavors with high-tech preparation techniques.

For José, the sensual experience of consuming his food is as important as the flavors themselves, and he mixes textures and contrasts temperatures accordingly. He demonstrates that a high level of creativity in cuisine can be found anywhere in the world. Together with other Portuguese chefs he aims to put his country on the world's gastronomic map. José's in my selection because only five years ago it was hard to imagine that Portugal would one day make an important contribution to the world of haute cuisine. José Avilez and his countrymen are still at the beginning of their journey, but the development of modern Portuguese cuisine is enormously significant to me.

Ferran Adrià

José Avillez was born in 1979 in Cascais, Portugal. He was encouraged to pursue a career in food by culinary writer Maria de Lourdes Modesto, and began with positions at the restaurants Fortaleza do Guincho and Quinta do Monte d'Oíro. During this time Avillez also trained under a number of the guiding lights of the culinary world, including Ferran Adrià, Alain Ducasse, Eric Frechon, and Claude Troisgros. In 2004, Avillez used his experience to open his own restaurant, 100 Maneiras, which met with widespread acclaim. In 2007 he started Life Style Cooking, a company offering a variety of services including take-away food, gourmet catering, and cooking lessons. He also joined Ferran Adrià at elBulli for three months, a pivotal experience, and later that year he accepted the post of executive chef at Tavares Rico.

MENU

Marine Transparency

~

Alentejo Landscape

~

Dogfish soup with fake grapes, coriander meringue, and crunchy bread toast

~

A bonfire at the beach: red mullet in a bed of sweet potato "embers" with charcoal flavors, edible branches, rosemary "smoke," and liver sauce

~

A dive in the sea: sea bass, sea water, bivalves, and seaweed

~

Roasted pigeon, a "Ferrero Rocher" of truffle and foie gras, sautéed chard, and a cinnamon-flavor sauce

~

Raspberry and wasabi sorbet

~

"Blinis and Caviar"

1

José Avillez

1
José Avillez with a chef
in the kitchen

2
Outside Tavares Rico
restaurant

3
In the dining room

4
José Avillez (center) working
at the stove

Tavares Rico, Lisbon, Portugal

ALENTEJO LANDSCAPE
Serves 4

Most of my inspiration comes from nature: the landscapes, the flowers, the sea, the sky, and the sun. Portuguese flavors and traditions are also crucial in the development of my work. This dish is the combination of these two sources of inspiration, and because of that it is one of the most representative of my culinary philosophy.

For the pig trotters
8 Iberian pigs' trotters • 56 g sea salt • 6 kg water • 120 g vinegar • 60 g salt • 2 onions • 1 clove • ½ carrot • ½ leek • 6 peppercorns • 2 cloves garlic

1 Split the trotters in half, singe the skin, remove all the hair, and rinse with running water.
2 Place the trotters on a large tray and sprinkle with salt (7 g of sea salt for each trotter), then put in the refrigerator for 24 hours. Rinse carefully.
3 Put all the ingredients in a large pan, and, when it reaches a boil, cook for 3½ hours.
4 Remove the trotters, reserve 2½ liters of stock and let cool. Bone the trotters.
5 Cut the trotters into 1-cm pieces of a similar shape.

For the trotter "sauté"
3 garlic cloves, green germ removed • 20 g sea salt • 50 g olive oil • 3 cilantro (coriander) sprigs • 90 ml red-wine vinegar

1 Mash the garlic and salt with a mortar and pestle to form a paste.
2 In a pan, sauté the garlic with olive oil. The garlic should cook but not turn brown. Add the trotters and cilantro sprigs and cover with approximately 1½ liters of the reserved stock. Add some vinegar and cook on low heat for at least 20 minutes.
3 Season with salt and vinegar if necessary. Remove the cilantro.

For the chlorophyll and cilantro gelatin
300 g spinach • 20 g cilantro (coriander) • 3 kg water • 6 g Citras • 6 g salt • 3.6 g agar agar • 3.4 g gellan

1 Cook the spinach and cilantro in boiling water for 5 seconds (remember to add 2 g of Citras for each liter of water). Cool in iced water and drain.
2 In a blender, mix the spinach and cilantro with 500 ml of water and 6 g of salt, strain through a Superbag. Chill.
3 For each 500 ml of liquid add 1.8g agar agar and 1.7 g gellan and stir.

Boil the liquid and pour it into trays, then chill in the refrigerator for at least 3 hours.

For the toasts
100 g bread • 400 g peanut oil

Cut the bread into thin slices and then into 1.5 x 3-cm rectangles. Preheat peanut oil at 340ºF (170ºC), then fry the bread until crunchy and golden.

For the scrambled egg foam
150 g eggs • 120 g egg yolks • 50 g butter, plus extra for cooking the eggs • 100 g cream • salt and pepper

1 Stir the eggs and yolks together. In a pan cook the eggs with a piece of butter. Season with salt and pepper.
2 Place the ingredients in a blender, add the butter and cream, and mix until it forms a puree.
3 Strain and insert the puree into a siphon. Add one cartridge and keep in the Roner at 130ºF (54ºC).

For the lemon meringue
400 g water • 2.5 g Metil • 8 gelatin leaves • 70 ml lemon juice • 6 g salt

1 For the lemon meringue, mix 100 g water with 2.5 g Metil and blend. Add it to the remaining water. Melt the gelatin leaves and add them.
2 Add the lemon juice and salt, and put aside at room temperature.

For the red-wine spherical raisins
2 g Gluco • 0.4 g Xanthan • 100 g red wine • 500 g water • 2.5 g alginate • 200 g sugar

1 Mix the Gluco, Xanthan, and wine in a blender.
2 Remove the air using a vacuum machine and set aside.
3 Place 200 g water in the food-processor and sprinkle 2.5 g alginate over it. Blend for 2 minutes and add the rest of the water. Place the alginate bath into a pan and make little spheres of the wine mixture by dropping spoonfuls into the alginate bath, to resemble raisins.
4 Remove from the alginate bath and put into the water. Strain them carefully and cover with sugar and leave for 35 minutes.
5 Remove the spheres from the sugar and wash them with wine.

For the pork sauce
40 g shallots • 60 g leeks • 2 garlic cloves • 50 ml olive oil, for sautéing • 200g Iberian pork meat • 40 g unsalted butter • 1 liter mineral water

1 Make a mirepoix with the shallots, leeks and garlic.
2 Caramelize the pork with the

olive oil. Add the mirepoix and let it caramelize.
3 Remove the excess oil and pork fat, add butter and cook for 2 minutes.
3 Add the water and let simmer for 20 minutes. Pass through a fine-mesh sieve (don't let the solids through, as it should remain thin). Let cool.

To serve
cilantro (coriander) sprouts • pork sauce • pepper • flowers • mixture of sprouts • sea salt • red-wine vinegar

1 Whisk the meringue until stiff.
2 Heat the pig trotters and season with salt and red-wine vinegar.
3 Heat the pork sauce and reduce it, add a piece of butter to the emulsion and season with red-wine vinegar, salt, and pepper.
4 Put the trotters in the center of the dish and cover with the chlorophyll and cilantro gelatin. Add the scrambled egg foam, meringue, toasts, sprouts and flowers, the spherical wine raisins, and the sauce.
Serve immediately.

ROASTED PIGEON, A "FERRERO ROCHER" OF TRUFFLE AND FOIE GRAS, SAUTÉED CHARD, AND A CINNAMON-FLAVOR SAUCE
Serves 4

This dish is inspired both by the commercial food industry and classic cuisine. A classic flavor combination is combined with a new concept of a salty "Ferrero Rocher."

For the pigeon
2 pigeons • salt, to taste • 8 black peppercorns • 1 branches of thyme • 2 bay leaves • 2 cinnamon sticks • 4 cloves of garlic • 50 ml Port wine • 1 branch of rosemary • 4 juniper berries

1 Tear the pigeon legs and breasts apart. Bone the legs and keep them aside for the sauce. Remove the excess fat from the breasts.
2 Season the pigeon legs with salt, half the thyme, bay, and cinnamon, and the garlic and Port, and marinate for 24 hours. Place them in a vacuum-pack bag and cook for 3 hours at 151ºF (66ºC).
3 Cool in a container with ice and water. Put aside in the refrigerator.
4 Season the breasts with salt, pepper, the remaining thyme, bay and cinnamon, and the rosemary and juniper berries, and marinate for 24 hours. Seal them in vacuum-pack bags and put aside in the refrigerator.

For the foie gras and truffle "Ferrero Rocher"
80 g foie gras • chicken stock, to cook the foie gras • 10 g cream • Port • 15 g unsalted butter • salt and pepper • 200 g Mycryo • 25 g Périgord truffle, finely chopped • liquid nitrogen

1 Cook the foie gras in chicken stock until it reaches 130ºF (54ºC) in the center. Cool it for 10 minutes.
2 In a blender, mix the foie gras with cream, Port, butter, salt, and pepper until it becomes homogeneous.
3 Heat the Mycryo in a small pan (maintaining the temperature).
4 Using a silicone mold, form small balls of the foie gras mixture, and roll them in the chopped truffle. With a needle, spear the foie gras truffles and plunge them in liquid nitrogen and then into Mycryo. Plunge again in liquid nitrogen and put aside in a refrigerator. (Liquid nitrogen should not be handled without training in how to use it safely.)

For the sauce
300 g pigeon bones • 50 g olive oil • 2 cloves garlic • 50 g shallots • 40 g leeks

1 Cut the bones in to pieces and caramelize with olive oil. Add the garlic, shallots, and leeks, and keep caramelizing.
2 Remove the excess fat, cover the ingredients with water, and boil slowly for 45 minutes. Strain through cheesecloth (muslin) and put aside.

For the Reineta apple puree
400 g Reineta apples • 2 cinnamon sticks • 40 g sugar • 20 g butter

1 Remove the cores and cook the apples in an oven preheated to 300ºF (150ºC) with cinnamon sticks, sugar, and butter for approximately 35 minutes.
2 Peel the apples and blend the pulp until it forms a puree. Put aside to cool down.

To serve
40 g chard • 20 g olive oil • 1 cinnamon stick • 40 g butter • 10 g hazelnut oil • 4 gold leaves • fleur de sel

1 Sauté the pigeon with the chard in the olive oil. Reheat the apple puree. Reduce the sauce and add the cinnamon stick. Finish with butter and hazelnut oil.
2 Cover the foie gras "Ferrero Rocher" with the gold leaf.
3 Place the ingredients as you wish on the plate and finish with the sauce and some fleur de sel.

1
Alentejo Landscape

2
Roasted pigeon, a "Ferrero Rocher" of truffle and foie gras, sautéed chard, and a cinnamon-flavor sauce

José Avillez

1 & 5
Selecting produce with
a supplier

2 & 4
Pascal Barbot in the kitchen

3
Flowers, for garnishing

Pascal Barbot

42

MENU

Marinated foie gras
with verjus and mushroom
galette

~

Nage of Norwegian
lobsters

~

Golden-brown cod,
new cabbage with papaya,
and green mango relish

~

Roast saddle of lamb
with miso eggplant

~

Endive with speculaas
butter and lime-flavored
banana

~

Jasmine eggnog

Pascal Barbot was born in 1972 in Vichy, France. After attending culinary school he gained an internship at Maxim's in Paris before moving on to Clavé restaurant, Clermont-Ferrand, in 1991. Later, Barbot moved to London as a commis chef at the Michelin-starred Les Saveurs, returning in 1993 to train at the Restaurant Troisgros, the three-Michelin-starred restaurant in Roanne, which gave him a crucial period cementing technical skills before he performed military service overseas. On his return, Barbot joined L'Arpège in Paris, spending four years working his way up the kitchen hierarchy and seeing the restaurant gain an extra Michelin star. After opening the lauded Ampersand in Sydney, Barbot worked at Lapérouse, Paris, and the Jacques Decoret restaurant in Vichy. In 2000 Barbot opened L'Astrance, his three-Michelin-starred restaurant in Paris.

In a bijou restaurant (with a pocket-sized kitchen), tucked away in the backstreets of Paris, Pascal Barbot is carrying out a quiet revolution. In the birthplace of haute cuisine and many traditions of gastronomy, Barbot is doing nothing less than reinventing French cooking.

The kitchen at L'Astrance is no more than fifteen meters square—the restaurant itself barely has room for twenty-five reservations—but this compressed space is the perfect setting for Pascal's minimalist cuisine. His stripped-down style requires a rigorous attention to detail and, unusually for a French chef, Pascal shuns the staples of Gallic cuisine such as butter and cream, preferring instead to achieve complex flavors using layers of meat and fresh produce.

In the relative quiet of the L'Astrance kitchen (the restaurant has a very small staff) Pascal is able to concentrate on refining his technique. There is very specific and measured intention in everything he does; he has a resolve and determination to achieve perfection in each dish. The chef has an undeniable preference for concision, clarity, and lightness, which brings a unique quality to his work.

Pascal is undoubtedly a meticulous craftsman, but he often refers to a dreamy imagination that carries him far away. He draws influence from all around the world: Australia, where he spent two years at Ampersand in Sydney, through Paris and Rome, to New Caledonia in Canada, where he served as personal chef to the Admiral of the Pacific. Asian influences are particularly visible in dishes such as his Eggplant Miso and Black Curry, and he often combines classic French dishes with Asian produce. Although passionate about his quest to discover fresh and original ideas and techniques, Pascal manages to remain loyal to his roots. As a child in his native Auvergne, he assisted his father in his vegetable garden and learned to prepare traditional cuisine through watching his parents in the kitchen.

Pascal's cuisine is in perfect harmony with the adventurous spirit of the times—even, perhaps, a little ahead of it.

Yoshihiro Murata

L'Astrance, Paris, France

NAGE OF NORWEGIAN LOBSTERS
Serves 6

For the nage
200 g shrimp (prawns) • 2 liters water • 1 bouquet garni • 20 g fresh ginger, sliced • 2 slices lemon • 1 carrot, cut into large cubes • 1 stick lemongrass

Make the nage first. Mix the shrimp with the water, add the bouquet garni, ginger, lemon, carrot and the stick of lemongrass. Simmer for 35 minutes and strain, reserving the liquid.

For the peanut butter
60 g fresh peanuts • 250 g butter • kaffir lime leaf, to taste • satay spices, to taste • 4 garlic cloves, marinated in vinegar then chopped • juice of ½ lime • 35 g ginger • 1 stick lemongrass (heart) • 1 tbsp peanut oil • 3 drops coconut essence • galangal, to taste

Toast the peanuts in the oven. Process the butter, toasted peanuts, kaffir lime leaf, satay spices, garlic, lime juice, ginger, lemongrass, peanut oil, coconut essence and galangal in a blender, and put aside.

For the Norwegian lobsters
12 good-sized live Norwegian lobsters (langoustines) • fruity green olive oil, for dressing

Partially cook the Norwegian lobsters by sautéing in the olive oil for 3–4 minutes, then peel.

To serve
2 small fennel bulbs, sliced thinly • 50 g parsley root (Hamburg parsley), julienned • 20 g ginger root, julienned • very white large mushrooms, cut into quarters • 4 leaves mint • 4 leaves cilantro (coriander) • 4 leaves Indonesian basil (kemangi) • olive oil

1 Finish cooking the Norwegian lobsters in the simmering nage for about 6–7 minutes, depending on their size.
2 Add the fennel, parsley root, ginger and mushrooms to the nage, cook for 1 minute, add the herbs, the Norwegian lobsters, the olive oil, and some shavings of peanut butter, and serve in deep plates or a large dish.

GOLDEN-BROWN COD, NEW CABBAGE WITH PAPAYA, AND GREEN MANGO RELISH
Serves 4

For the cod
4 (120-g) pieces of cod cut from the center of the fish • lightly salted butter

In a skillet, caramelize the pieces of fish, cook for 2 minutes on each side, season and glaze with the butter.

For the cabbage
1 new Duchy (or other "pointed") cabbage • butter, for cooking • fleur de sel • smoked pepper

Cut the tender inner leaves of the cabbage into 4 pieces and cook in a skillet with some butter. Keep them crisp and season with fleur de sel and smoked pepper.

For the mango and green papaya relish
green mango • yellow mango • green papaya • ripe papaya • kaffir lime leaf • lime juice • fruity green olive oil, to taste

Chop an equal quantity of all the fruits into a brunoise, add the finely chopped kaffir lime leaf (use the yellow mango to sweeten). Add lime juice if more acidity is needed, drain, and add the olive oil.

To serve
red curry paste • olive oil

Serve the fish with the cabbage, the papaya and green mango relish, and the curry paste, slightly diluted with olive oil.

ROAST SADDLE OF LAMB WITH MISO EGGPLANT
Serves 4

For the lamb
1 best-quality saddle of lamb • salt • pepper • salted butter

Brown the lamb in a broiler (grill), or in a skillet. Then season with salt, pepper, and salted butter and roast at 140°F (60°C) for about 1 hour. Alternatively, the lamb can be cooked sous-vide. Just before serving reheat and slice.

For the red pepper
1 red bell pepper • olive oil • thyme • rosemary • savory

For the red pepper, scorch it to peel it, then cut rounds about 4 cm in diameter and stew gently in olive oil for about 1 hour, with the thyme, rosemary, and savory. Drain and put aside.

For the eggplant
2 good-sized eggplants (aubergines)

Steam the eggplants whole in their skins for about 20 minutes, depending on size. Cut in 2 lengthwise and drain thoroughly.

For the miso mixture
35 g sake • 15 g Japanese mirin • 50 g sugar • 250 g miso (brown, good quality, not too salty) • 2 tsp peanut butter • 1 tbsp peanut oil • 1 egg yolk

1 Reduce the sake, mirin, and sugar until they form a fairly thin syrup. Add the thoroughly mixed miso.
2 Add all the peanut butter, oil and egg yolk to the mixture once it is cold (so that the egg yolk does not cook) and mix thoroughly.
3 Spread the miso mixture on the flesh side of each half eggplant to a depth of about 5 mm, and bake at 175°F (80°C) for 1 hour. Slice after cooking.

To serve
90 ml lamb jus

Serve the lamb with the baked eggplant, a piece of red pepper, and the lamb jus.

1

1
Nage of Norwegian lobsters

2
Golden brown cod and
new cabbage with papaya
and green mango relish

3
Roast saddle of lamb
with miso eggplant

2

3

Pascal Barbot

A region and its special chemistry—what we call a "terroir"—have their own lessons to teach you. Take Cédric's case. He was born in the Basque Country, and as a teenager he took his first professional steps at the restaurant of the Hôtel du Palais, Biarritz. He stayed there for eighteen months, and he was just twenty when he left. But the die was cast: He had fallen in love with the region and promised himself that he would return. He had decided where to put down his roots.

It must be said that the Basque Country has a strong personality, one that encourages such passions. Nestling between the Pyrenees and the Atlantic, it's a region unto itself, with its own language and culture—which was imprinted on Cédric's heart when he arrived in Paris.

After spending a few months at the Crillon, he began work as a commis chef at Alain Ducasse, on avenue Raymond Poincaré. Then I sent him to the Plaza Athénée, where he graduated as sous chef. He was so successful that I put him in charge of La Cour Jardin, the Plaza Athénée's summer restaurant. The three years he stayed there were a triumph. But he never forgot the promise he had made when he left Biarritz.

He took his time, sought advice, and set about learning his chosen "terroir." In March 2006, he bought the country inn of his dreams, a seventeenth-century building called "L'Auberge Basque."

Since April 2007, the Basque Country has had a new country inn that wonderfully demonstrates its traditions of hospitality and food culture. The setting is stunning, and inside it's comfortable and relaxed, but sophisticated at the same time. At table, you'll find all the flavors of the Basque Country: Banka trout and salmon from the River Adour, Ibaïona pork, chorizo, the famous "cheeks" of hake and salt cod (*kokotxas*), Espelette pepper, and white Navarre asparagus, not to mention fresh and mature sheep-milk cheese. Traditional recipes are revisited with intelligence and a light touch.

This "terroir" has given Cédric a lot, and he is returning it in full.

Alain Ducasse

Cédric Béchade was born in Limoges in 1976 and met Alain Ducasse when he was studying at the professional school in Souillac. After his national service, which he spent in the kitchens of the presidential Palais de l'Elysée, Béchade began his career in food in earnest at the Hôtel du Palais in Biarritz with Jean-Marie Gauthier in the late 1990s. A year and a half later, Béchade moved to Paris to work at the Hôtel de Crillon before joining Alain Ducasse to open his three-Michelin-star restaurant on the avenue Raymond Poincarré. Béchade collaborated with Ducasse for ten years before opening his own restaurant, L'Auberge Basque in April 2007. Béchade's self-proclaimed love for Basque food and culture is evident in his widely acclaimed menu, which reflects his search for inspiration in simplicity and elegance.

MENU

Petit-pois millefeuille with Ibaïona ventrèche, black radish vacherin and foie gras Mamia

~

Crisp lambs' sweetbreads with white Landes asparagus in cider vinegar

~

Salt cod with cocoa nibs, leek gratin with Guindilla peppers, and squid ink sauce

~

Mini spring rolls of pigeon from the Urruty farm with eggplant, tomatoes, and fava beans à la Navarraise

~

Le café

1
The dining room at L'Auberge Basque

2 & 3
Cédric Béchade in the kitchen

Cédric Béchade

L'Auberge Basque, Helbarron, France

CRISP LAMBS' SWEETBREADS WITH WHITE LANDES ASPARAGUS IN CIDER VINEGAR
Serves 6

For the white asparagus aïoli
200 g potatoes • coarse salt • 300 g white asparagus spears • butter and olive oil, for pan-frying • pinch of salt and a pinch of Espelette pepper • 150 ml light (single) cream • 1 clove garlic • 50 g orange juice, reduced • 50 ml olive oil

1 Preheat the oven to 350°F (180°C).
2 Bake the potatoes for 30 minutes on a bed of coarse salt, then mash them.
3 Trim the asparagus spears into 5-cm pieces, reserving the tips. Sweat the pieces in a casserole in a little butter and olive oil. Add salt and pepper to taste.
4 Pour in the cream and add the garlic. Cook for 20 minutes, then process in a blender, then pass through a conical strainer.
5 Mix the mashed potato with the asparagus puree and the orange juice, beat in the olive oil and check the seasoning. Pour into a siphon.

For the garnish
3 red onions • 250 ml cider vinegar • 4 blue Vitelotte potatoes • olive oil, for pan-frying • 1 egg yolk • zest of 1 orange

1 Peel the onions, cut them into 5-mm slices and cook in a vacuum-pack bag at 200°F (100°C) for 10 minutes, then remove.
2 Brown the slices of onion in a skillet, then deglaze with the cider vinegar until the onions are thoroughly coated and glazed.
3 Peel the potatoes, cut them into slices 1-mm thick using a mandolin, and fry in oil at 350°F (180°C).
4 Preheat the oven to 325°F (160°C).
5 Cook the egg yolk for 5 minutes in a steam oven at 200°F (100°C), let it cool, and put it through a strainer. Grate the orange zest on a microplane. Put the egg and the orange zest to dry in the oven until they have the consistency of bread crumbs.
6 Glaze the asparagus tips in reduced cider vinegar.

For the sweetbreads
600 g lambs' sweetbreads • 100 g cornstarch (cornflour) • clarified butter, for pan-frying

1 Blanch the sweetbreads in salted water, boil for 1 minute, drain, and chill.
2 Peel off the membranes.
3 Dip the sweetbreads in the cornstarch and fry in a skillet in clarified butter until crisp.

To serve
Arrange the sweetbreads, drops of asparagus aïoli, potatoes, onions, and asparagus tips in a row on the plate, one after the other. Crumble egg yolk on top of aïoli drops.

SALT COD WITH COCOA NIBS, LEEK GRATIN WITH GUINDILLA PEPPERS, AND SQUID INK SAUCE
Serves 6

For the squid ink sauce
200 g cod trimmings and bones • 1 leek • 1 carrot • 1 stick celery • 1 clove garlic • 500 ml white stock • 100 ml olive oil • 10 g squid ink • 10 g Espelette pepper puree

1 Soak the cod bones in water until they are fully de-salted, then mix the bones and the vegetable ingredients in a vacuum-pack bag, add the white stock and cook for 1 hour at 195°F (90°C) in a steam oven. Remove and drain, reserving the fish stock.
2 Put the olive oil into a pan, add the fish stock, boil for 20 minutes, bind with the squid ink, and season with the Espelette pepper puree.

For the leek gratin with Guindilla peppers
1 leek • white-wine vinegar, for washing the leek • olive oil, for frying • 1 clove garlic • 100 ml white wine • chicken stock • butter • 3 g agar agar • 12 Guindilla peppers • 50 g tempura batter • 10 g sparkling mineral water • 12 baby leeks • 2 Roseval or other firm salad potatoes • 10 g Espelette pepper puree

1 Separate the white and green parts of the leek, wash them in water mixed with a little white-wine vinegar, soak for 20 minutes and then rinse thoroughly.
2 Chop the green part of the leek and slice the white part into rounds.
3 In a covered pan, sweat the chopped green leek in a little olive oil with the garlic, deglaze with white wine, reduce by half, dilute with white chicken stock and simmer for 20 minutes.
4 Put the leek mixture through the blender, strain through a conical sieve to make a green puree, and chill.
5 Braise the slices of leek in a little olive oil and butter, then put aside.
6 When the green puree has chilled, stir in the agar agar and bring to the boil. Pour into a small silicon tart mold, arrange the rounds of leek on top, and place in a blast-chiller.
7 Cut the Guindilla peppers into rounds.
8 Mix together the tempura batter and mineral water, dip the baby leeks and deep-fry them at 350°F (180°C).
9 Preheat a fan oven to 260°F (130°C).
10 Cut the potatoes into 2-cm barrel-shapes, put them in a ceramic dish, and cover with the fish stock and Espelette puree.
11 Cook in the oven for 20 minutes.

For the cod with cocoa nibs, and final assembly
30 g ewe's milk cheese • 700 g salt cod • 100 g cocoa nibs • 1 bunch chives, chopped

1 Preheat the oven to 350°F (180°C).
2 Place shavings of the ewe's milk cheese over the leek gratins, and heat in the oven for 3 minutes.
3 Heat the rest of the leek puree and draw lines with it on the plate around the squid ink sauce.
4 Roll the cod in the cocoa nibs and chopped chives, broil (grill) for 2 minutes on each side and finish by baking in the oven for 3 minutes.
5 Put the cod on the plate, scatter the potatoes with their Espelette pepper puree around the cod along with the Guindilla peppers, the baby leeks, and the squid ink sauce. Finish with the baby leeks.

MINI SPRING ROLLS OF PIGEON FROM THE URRUTY FARM WITH EGGPLANT, TOMATOES, AND FAVA BEANS À LA NAVARRAISE
Serves 6

For the pigeons and sauce
6 pigeons • salt and pepper • olive oil and butter, for roasting • 2 shallots, coarsely chopped, plus 1 shallot, finely chopped • 2 sprigs thyme • 1½ cloves garlic, unpeeled and crushed with a knife blade • 1 liter white stock • white wine, to deglaze • Cognac, to deglaze

1 Trim and clean the pigeons inside and out, remove the breasts and wings, open them out and set them aside. Reserve the giblets.
2 Season the legs and cook them in a vacuum-pack bag at 160°F (72°C) for 2½ hours.
3 Break up the carcasses and roast them in a pan with a dash of olive oil. When roasted, add a piece of butter and continue to cook until they are caramelized.
4 Add the coarsely chopped shallots along with the thyme and 1 clove garlic.
5 When the carcasses are caramelized, remove the fat, pour in the white stock and cook for about 1 hour. Push through a conical strainer, boil the liquid to reduce by half, and set aside.
6 Clean the pigeon livers and hearts and sear them in a hot skillet. Season with salt and pepper, and once browned, add the finely chopped shallot and the remaining crushed garlic.
7 Deglaze the pan with the white wine, reduce by half, then deglaze with the Cognac, strain, and place in the blast-chiller.
8 Shred the flesh of the pigeon legs to mix with the stuffing.

For the stuffed tomatoes
12 cherry tomatoes • 50 g dried breadcrumbs • 1 sprig tarragon, chopped • 50 ml Cognac • 50 ml white wine • 1 sprig thyme, chopped • pigeon hearts and livers

1 Prepare the stuffing by mixing the Cognac, white wine, thyme, pigeon hearts and livers, and shredded pigeon legs.
2 Add the dried breadcrumbs and the tarragon.
3 Seed and core the tomatoes and stuff them with the mixture.
4 Bake in the oven for 5 minutes at 350°F (180°C).

For the tarragon relish
1 bunch tarragon • 30 g mustard • 10 ml sherry vinegar • 200 ml olive oil

1 Preheat the oven to 350°F (180°C).
2 Strip the tarragon leaves from the stalks and put the leaves in the bowl of a Pacojet container with the mustard, sherry vinegar, and olive oil. When thoroughly frozen, process in the Pacojet to obtain a thick oil.

For the spring rolls
2 eggplants (aubergines) • 1 sprig tarragon, chopped • 1 clove garlic, chopped • 150 g chorizo • 24 sheets rice paper

1 Cut the eggplants lengthwise, add the tarragon and garlic, and bake in the oven for 45 minutes.
2 Remove the pulp from the eggplant and chop it coarsely, then dice the chorizo and mix it with the pulp. Check the seasoning.
3 Dip the sheets of rice paper in cold water for 10 seconds, drain, roll each one round half a pigeon breast with the eggplant mixture, then fold and wrap up like a spring roll. Put aside.

For the fava bean puree
200 g fava (broad) beans • 1 white onion, finely chopped • olive oil and butter, for pan-frying • 1 clove garlic, crushed • 250 ml white stock

1 Brown the beans with the onion in a pan, in a mixture of olive oil and butter. Add the garlic.
2 Pour in the stock, boil for 10 minutes, process in a blender, and check the seasoning.

To assemble
80 g Sobrassada • clarified butter, for broiling • 50 g fava (broad) beans • 50 g dried tomato flakes, for garnish

1 Heat the fava bean puree.
2 To make the Navarraise sauce, bind the pigeon juices with the Sobrassada and pass through a conical strainer. Keep in a warm place.
3 Caramelize the spring rolls in clarified butter in a skillet, and while they are cooking fry the fava beans.
4 Place a spring roll and a tomato on the plate. Create a strip of the bean puree with the Navarraise sauce in the center, sprinkle the tomatoes with flakes of dried tomato, scatter the fried beans and add a few drops of the tarragon relish.

1
Crisp lambs' sweetbreads with white Landes asparagus in cider vinegar

2
Salt cod with cocoa nibs, leek gratin with Guindilla peppers, and squid ink sauce

3
Mini spring rolls of pigeon from the Urruty farm with eggplant, tomatoes, and fava beans à la Navarraise

49   **Cédric Béchade**

Martin's name is one that seems to have been bubbling away, just under the surface, for some years now. Working for such an acclaimed restaurateur as Tetsuya Wakuda, this is bound to happen. Recently, in talking to other Sydney chefs, Martin's name had moved to the forefront. And, with his restaurant Sepia now open, this is also being reflected in the media.

I had a wonderful meal at Tetsuya's four years ago. It is impossible to say what influence Martin had on this meal or on the dishes I particularly enjoyed, however I know how important it is for the owner of a restaurant who is also a chef to have someone he trusts at the helm of his kitchen. Now that Martin has his own restaurant and the opportunity to exert his style over a menu, it is wonderful to see how the influences in his career have combined to form a flavorsome, intelligent, and elegant identity of their own. Martin is able to combine three sometimes-incongruous elements—French technique, Japanese elegance, and Australian ingredients—in a way that seems effortless on the plate. Many chefs with less restraint, experience, and wisdom have struggled with this combination and ultimately end up cooking fusion food. This is absolutely not what Benn is about.

Martin has a light-handed approach in terms of his use of gentle cooking techniques such as slow poaching at low temperatures in olive oil and sous-vide cooking. His menu is strongly driven by seafood and whilst the basis of the preparation is French in nature, the accents and high notes are Japanese. Martin's obvious respect for ingredients, especially from the sea, and his demand for produce that is both high in quality and sustainable, helps to push the seafood industry forward, leading to better practices for all. A great example of this is his butter-poached blue-eye, which is served just cooked, resting on baby fennel with cuttlefish ribbons poached in rice wine and bacon floss.

Given that Sepia only opened in May 2009, I think there is much more to come from this rising star who has finally struck out on his own.

Shannon Bennett

Martin Benn was born in Hastings, UK, in 1974. He began his food career at the Oak Room in London, learning French gastronomy under Michel Lorrain. From there Benn moved to work at the Landmark and later the Criterion, where he came under the tutelage of Marco Pierre White. Moving to Australia, Benn spent a year at Sydney's Forty One Restaurant. He later gained a place at Tetsuya's, learning the fundamentals of Japanese cuisine from Tetsuya Wakuda and mastering them to become head chef at the age of 25. In August 2004, Benn moved to the Boathouse on Blackwattle Bay as executive chef, returning to Tetsuya's before a brief move to Hong Kong to undertake restaurant consultancy work. Back in Sydney, Benn opened Sepia restaurant in 2009, collaborating with George Costi to supply the restaurant with top-quality seafood.

MENU

Amuse bouche

~

**Confit of octopus
with mustard shortbread
shiro miso and green
apple salad**
Soave Classico

~

**BBQ Silver Lake eel set
on sushi rice with leek and
licorice powder**
Federspiel Grüner Veltliner

~

**Queensland spanner crab
and buckwheat risotto
with mustard butter and
shellfish essence**
New World Viognier

~

**Poached ocean trout,
braised shimeiji and
woodear mushrooms,
roasted buckwheat,
and bone marrow**
Grenache Rosé
or Pinot Noir

~

**Roasted squab salad,
confit potato, pickled beet,
and walnut vinaigrette**
Crianza Rioja

~

**Broiled Wagyu sirloin,
roasted baby carrots,
confit of shallot,
onion powder, and
roasted onion butter**
Syrah (Northern Rhône
or cool-climate Australia)

~

Pre-dessert

~

**Citrus marshmallows,
pineapple sorbet, mint
whip, and cilantro sprouts**
Botrytis Riesling

~

**Coffee, tea,
and petits fours**

Martin Benn

1–3
In the kitchen at Sepia

4
Martin Benn finishes broiled
Wagyu sirloin, roasted baby
carrots, confit of shallot,
onion powder, and roasted
onion butter

Sepia, Sydney, Australia

POACHED OCEAN TROUT, BRAISED SHIMEIJI AND WOODEAR MUSHROOMS, ROASTED BUCKWHEAT, AND BONE MARROW
Serves 1

This is a classic technique that I learned very early in my career; it has evolved utilizing Japanese philosophy and understanding umami.

For the trout
1 ocean trout fillet (small bones removed) • 10 g wakame (rinsed and hydrated) • zest of ¼ lemon • olive oil, to confit

1   Remove the gray and fatty areas from the skin side of the trout fillet.
2   Place the trout fillet on a cutting (chopping) board with the thickest end pointing away from you and the tail end closest to you. With the knife at a 20° angle, cut the fillet down the center line toward the back or loin side. Once you have the two halves, turn one of them around so that they are head to tail, so to speak.
3   Lay the wakame on top and sprinkle the lemon zest over the top.
4   Place the 2 fillets together on top of each other and shape into a cylinder.
5   Lay out some plastic wrap (clingfilm) on a counter and then place the stacked trout on top. Roll the parcel up tightly and let rest for 12 hours in the refrigerator.
6   Cut the trout into the size of portions required, then roll them in plastic wrap and return to the refrigerator.
7   Remove from the refrigerator 10 minutes before you are ready to cook them.
8   Heat a circulator bath to 110°F (43°C) and poach the trout for 10 minutes or until *mi-cuit*.
9   Remove the trout from the bath and remove the plastic wrap.
10 Place the trout into a small pot of olive oil at 110°F (43°C) and cook for 10 more minutes.

For the braised mushrooms
olive oil, for pan-frying and drizzling • 50 g shallots, finely chopped • 1 tsp garlic oil • 1 tsp chopped thyme leaves • 50 ml sake • 100 g shimeiji mushrooms, cleaned • 50 g woodear mushrooms• 100 ml dashi stock • 100 ml chicken stock • salt and pepper

1   In a heavy pan, heat a little olive oil over medium heat. Add the shallots and sweat gently until tender. Add the garlic oil and thyme and continue to cook for a few minutes.

2   Deglaze the pan with the sake and burn off the alcohol. Add the mushrooms and coat with the sake liquid. Pour in the dashi and chicken stocks and bring quickly to a simmer. Season with salt and pepper.
3   Skim the surface to remove any impurities, then remove from the heat and allow the mushrooms to cool at room temperature. Drizzle some olive oil over them and let stand for 30 minutes.

To finish and serve
bone marrow, soaked in ice water for 24 hours • wakame, washed • roasted buckwheat, blanched for 3 minutes in salted water • lemon zest • baby watercress • sea salt

1   Cut the bone marrow into 2-cm cylinders.
2   Cut the wakame into even strips and keep in the refrigerator until required.
3   In a small pan, heat the mushrooms with a little of the juice. Add the roasted buckwheat and warm through.
4   In another small pan, warm some of the mushroom juice. Add the bone marrow and warm through gently. Do not boil.
5   Add a little wakame to the mushrooms and warm through.
6   Spoon the mushrooms and wakame onto the plate.
7   Remove the trout from the olive oil and cut into 2 pieces.
8   Place the trout onto the mushrooms and wakame.
9   Spoon some of the warm mushroom, bone marrow, and buckwheat mixture around the trout.
10 Finish with a little lemon zest, baby watercress, and sea salt.

BROILED WAGYU SIRLOIN, ROASTED BABY CARROTS, CONFIT OF SHALLOT, ONION POWDER, AND ROASTED ONION BUTTER
Serves 1

The rich flavor of the Wagyu combined with the onion in three forms gives this dish an interesting take on a classic combination. The baby carrots add a little sweetness to the dish.

For the sirloin
200 g Wagyu sirloin, trimmed of excess fat • 10 g olive oil • pepper • 1 sprig of thyme • salt

1   Season the sirloin with pepper and then place in a vacuum-pack bag. Add the olive oil and thyme. Seal the bag on full vacuum and leave at room temperature for 30 minutes.
2   Heat an immersion circulator to 137°F (58°C) and then cook the meat in the bath for 10–12 minutes, depending on thickness. Remove from the bath and let rest.
3   Remove the meat from the bag, drain off the excess fat, season well, and then sear on the grill.
4   Remove, and let rest.

For the baby carrots
1 carrot • 5 Dutch carrots, turned • 20 g unsalted butter • 5 ml sherry vinegar • salt and pepper

1   Using a small Parisian melon baller, cut the carrot into 10 little pearls.
2   Blanch both the carrot pearls and turned Dutch carrots in boiling salted water, then refresh in very cold water.
3   Heat a sauté pan, add the butter, and once it begins to bubble, add the carrots. Season well, deglaze with the sherry vinegar, and drain before serving.

For the veal sauce
100 ml veal stock • 10 ml Port reduction • sherry vinegar, to taste • 10 g butter

Bring the veal stock to a boil, and add the Port and sherry vinegar. Whisk in the butter.

For the confit shallots
6 large shallots, finely chopped • ½ clove garlic, finely chopped • 100 ml olive oil

Place all the ingredients into a small pan and heat gently over low heat until tender.

For the onion butter sauce
olive oil, for pan-frying • 1 kg brown onions, chopped • 500 ml Madeira • 200 ml Port • 2 liters chicken stock • lecithin • butter

1   Heat a heavy pan on the stove and pour in some olive oil. Add the chopped onions, and sauté until golden brown and softened.
2   Deglaze the pan with the Madeira and Port, then reduce until all the liquid has evaporated. Add the chicken stock and reduce by half.
3   Pass the stock through a fine-mesh sieve, reserving the onions.
4   Pour the onion stock into a small pan, add the lecithin and let it dissolve. Add the butter and, using an immersion blender, blitz it to foam. Adjust the seasoning, and foam with the stick blender again.

For the roast onion powder
reserved onions from the stock • sea salt

1   Place the onions on a baking sheet and dehydrate in the oven overnight at 250° F (120°C) until crispy.
2   Place in a Thermomix and blend to a fine powder.
3   Add sea salt to taste and blend again.

To serve
1   Once the meat is well rested, cut it into 6 even strips and stack together on the plate.
2   Place the cooked glazed carrots around the meat and add a few spoons of confit shallots.
3   Sprinkle the roasted onion powder over the carrots.
4   Spoon the veal sauce over the meat to coat it, and around the plate.
5   Foam the onion butter sauce with the stick blender, and spoon it over the meat and carrots.

1
Poached ocean trout,
braised shimeji and woodear
mushrooms, roasted
buckwheat, and bone marrow

2
Broiled Wagyu sirloin, roasted
baby carrots, confit of shallot,
onion powder, and roasted
onion butter

Martin Benn

Mark Best

MENU

Apple pectin jelly
and kaffir lime sherbet

~

Fresh figs and goat curd
with milk vacherin

~

Southern rock lobster
with salted butter,
wakame, caramelized
yogurt, curry leaves,
and kombu

~

Hot chocolate ganache
with hazelnut croquant,
sweet onion, and rosemary

Mark Best was born in Australia in 1965, and began working as an electrician in a gold mine before starting his culinary career at age 25 with an apprenticeship at the Macleay Street Bistro, Potts Point. Five years later he opened his own Peninsula Bistro in Balmain, which developed a loyal following. Not content to rest on this success, Best developed an increasing desire to study French cuisine with its masters, and worked at Alain Passard's three-Michelin-starred L'Arpège and Raymond Blanc's Le Manoir Aux Quat' Saisons, developing an appreciation for the integrity, purity, and intelligence of French cuisine. His subsequent opening of Marque Restaurant in Sydney, in 1999, distilled the experience and inspiration of these ventures, maintaining an emphasis on evolving recipes that amplify their ingredients, working with the unique produce afforded by the restaurant's location to create dishes—such as sea urchin with sweetbreads and samphire—that have a quiet eye on cutting-edge culinary developments while remaining of their time and place.

1–3
Mark Best in the kitchen

4
The bar at Marque

5
In the dining room

Mark and I clicked straightaway—continuous conversation about suppliers and ingredients would always lead to how best to cook them. His restaurant is situated in Surry Hills in the inner suburbs of Sydney. Mark set up here when Surry Hills was not well known for great food, but with neighbors Kylie Kwong and Bill Granger he started to put the area on the map. Most people would suggest that this was a gutsy move for Mark and his wife Valerie. But knowing his background, his skill and his calm, calculated temperament it was, simply put, a smart move.

I have eaten Mark's food several times over the past eight years, and always found it progressive and thought-provoking. Well before we saw spherification and jellies in every restaurant Mark had perfected dishes that really made the diner think. A dish that sticks in my mind would have to be warm crab meat with almond and sweetcorn. Offering texture, luxury and artistic presentation, it basically consisted of all three components of the dish sitting in a beautiful luna bowl-plate, glistening and inviting one to eat and be ultimately satisfied and pleasured but at first challenged.

The unique aspect to Mark's cooking is the discipline involved. Many chefs forget the basics of cooking. Hygiene, clean glistening plates, well-informed waiters, wine matching—all of these principles are the footing for great food. Mark and his team get an "A" for all of them. Modern, forward-thinking techniques take over from here—freeze drying, slow cooking at accurate temperatures, cooking under pressure, infusing. The list is as great as the imagination….

The French repertoire is the basis for Mark's cuisine, and with it he marks a sort of revolution in Australia and in particular in New South Wales. Amazing native oysters, Japanese spiked iki-jime fish, bespoke herbs and vegetables and a new emphasis on secondary cuts of meat and the correct method of slow cooking using state-of-the-art equipment will make Mark a leader in the world of great French food.

Shannon Bennett

Marque Restaurant, Surry Hills, Australia

APPLE PECTIN JELLY AND KAFFIR LIME SHERBET
Makes 100 jellies

For the jelly
1.175 kg superfine (caster) sugar •
30 g powdered apple pectin • 1.07
liters apple juice • 8 g tartaric acid

1 Sift the sugar and pectin together into a heavy pan. Whisk in the apple juice and bring to a boil. Simmer until the temperature reaches exactly 224°F (107°C).
2 Mix the tartaric acid with a little hot water and add to the apple-sugar mixture. Whisk well and continue to simmer until the temperature reaches 233°F (112°C). Skim off any scum floating on the surface and let cool for 10 minutes.
3 Line a gastronorm tray with plastic and pour in the contents of the pan. Cool until set, preferably overnight.

For the sherbet
100 g Maltodextrin •
75 g confectioners' (icing) sugar •
5 g tartaric acid • 6 g kaffir limes

1 Sift the dry ingredients together.
2 Use a microplane to zest the limes and their essential oils over the top, reserving a little zest for serving. Rub together with clean dry hands and store in an airtight container until required.

To serve
1 Cut the jelly into 2-cm cubes and place on an appropriate-sized plate.
2 Put a teaspoon of sherbet onto each and a little fresh zest.

HOT CHOCOLATE GANACHE WITH HAZELNUT CROQUANT, SWEET ONION, AND ROSEMARY
Serves 10

For the ganache
275 g 70% chocolate couverture (Valrhona for preference) •
40 g Lescure salted butter •
110 ml pouring cream (35% fat)
• 3 eggs

1 Place the chocolate, butter and cream in a bowl over simmering water for 2–3 minutes on medium in a microwave. Melt evenly and stir to combine.
2 Lightly whisk the eggs and stir into the chocolate. Pour into a siphon and add two nitrogen canisters. Shake well and keep warm in a water bath at 114°F (45°C) until required.

For the hazelnut croquant
150 g hazelnuts • 150 g superfine (caster) sugar • 50 ml water •
300 g hazelnut paste • 150 g pailleté feuilletine

1 Preheat the oven to 320°F (160°C) and roast the hazelnuts until golden. Rub between 2 cloths to remove the outer skin.
2 Place the sugar in a heavy pan over medium heat with the water. Cook until just beginning to let off wisps of smoke. Add the hazelnuts and stir to combine. Pour onto a nonstick tray to cool.
3 Break into small pieces and place in a Thermomix. Blend at moderate speed (number 6) for 3–4 minutes until a "liquid praline" is produced.
4 Scrape into a mixing bowl and combine with the hazelnut paste and pailleté feuilletine. Keep at room temperature until required.

For the onions
500 g sweet white onions •
100 g turbinado (Demerara) sugar

1 Slice the onions finely. Place in a heavy pan and cover with a wax paper cartouche. Place over very low heat and cook until very soft and translucent, with no color. Pour off any excess water.
2 Spread the onion jam onto a nonstick silicone mat and dry for at least 24 hours in an evaporator until crisp and golden.
3 Place in a Thermomix and blend to a fine powder. Sieve and discard what is left behind. Blend the sieved onion with the sugar and store in an airtight container.

To serve
rosemary flowers

1 Place a spoon of hazelnut croquant onto each plate/bowl. Shake the siphon well and squirt the chocolate ganache over the top, keeping the tip (nozzle) still.
2 Garnish the ganache with rosemary flowers and the onion powder.

FRESH FIGS AND GOAT CURD WITH MILK VACHERIN
Serves 10

2 liters full cream milk (5% fat) •
200 g liquid glucose • Canola (rapeseed) oil, for greasing • fresh figs • fresh goat curd

1 Preheat the oven to 160°F (70°C).
2 Heat the milk and glucose to 194°F (90°C). Mix with a stick blender to make a fine mousse.
3 Place a nonstick silicone baking mat onto a baking sheet and grease with an aerosol of canola oil. Spoon blobs of the milk mousse onto the tray with even spaces in between. Cook for 4 hours, until crisp and dry.
4 Store the vacherins in an airtight container with silica moisture-absorption beads until required.
5 For the figs, the variety is not important; however, ripeness is essential. Choose figs close to bursting with nectar dripping from the base. Remove the stem and cut into quarters. The skin is delicious at this stage of ripeness.
6 We use very fresh goat curd, like a very fresh goat's ricotta. It should taste intensely of fresh milk with an acidic finish.

To serve
1 Place ¼ teaspoon of the curd into the middle of each plate to anchor the vacherin.
2 Place a vacherin on top and then a spoon of the curd.
3 Place a fig quarter on each. Repeat and finish with a vacherin, flat side up.

SOUTHERN ROCK LOBSTER WITH SALTED BUTTER, WAKAME, CARAMELIZED YOGURT, CURRY LEAVES, AND KOMBU
Serves 4

For the lobster
2 (600-g) southern rock lobsters •
4 (30-cm) sheets dried wakame •
160 g salted Lescure butter •
1 tsp white peppercorns

1 Place the live lobsters in the freezer for 30–40 minutes.
2 Quickly cut through the head of the lobster, piercing the brain with a sharp knife. Quickly blanch them in boiling water, then refresh in ice water. Use a small, sharp knife to cut the membrane between the head and body. Twist to separate the 2 parts. Reserve the head for another use. Twist the middle segment of the tail and pull carefully to remove the intestinal tract. Cut the tail in half with a sharp knife. Reserve until required.
3 Wash the wakame in cold water, then with hot water from the tap. Rinse again with cold.
4 Roast the peppercorns in a small pan until they begin to pop. Place in a coarse pepper grinder and use to season the lobster tails well.
5 Divide the butter into 4 slices and place a slice onto the flesh of each tail. Wrap each tail in a sheet of wakame. Seal each separately in a vacuum-pack bag on medium pressure. Cook sous-vide in a water bath at 130°F (52°C) for 8 minutes.

For the yogurt
3 tsp molasses • 200 g plain yogurt

1 Heat the molasses and mix with the yogurt. Pour into a vacuum-pack bag and seal with low pressure. Steam for 12 hours at 200°F (95°C). The yogurt will be caramelized, with a little milk fat split from the mass.
2 Pour into a Thermomix and blend at high speed to emulsify. Reserve until required.

For the kombu and curry leaves
50 g shio kombu • 12–16 curry leaves • 200 ml peanut oil • sea salt

1 Rinse the kombu in cold running water for 10 minutes. Pat dry, then place in an evaporator overnight till crisp.
2 Chop very finely with a heavy chef's knife and reserve.
3 Heat the peanut oil to 340°F (170°C). Fry until crisp, and drain on absorbent paper. Season with a little sea salt.

To serve
Place half a lobster tail on each plate and garnish with a teaspoon of yogurt, a sprinkle of kombu and 3–4 curry leaves per person.

1
Apple pectin jelly with kaffir lime sherbet

2
Hot chocolate ganache with hazelnut croquant, sweet onion, and rosemary

3
Fresh figs and goat curd with milk vacherin

4
Southern rock lobster with salted butter, wakame, caramelized yogurt, curry leaves, and kombu

1   2

3   4

57   **Mark Best**

April Bloomfield

Born in 1974, <u>April Bloomfield</u> attended culinary school in Birmingham, England, before taking a position at Kensington Place in London. After several other placements, including a stint at Bibendum, she joined the team at the River Café, working alongside Rose Gray and Ruth Rogers. This pivotal experience brought Bloomfield a new appreciation of simple foods and pure ingredients. From the River Café she went on to work at Chez Panisse in Berkeley, California, before she opened the Spotted Pig in New York City with partner Ken Friedman in 2004. The Spotted Pig serves an international cuisine with heart, with dishes hinting at Italian, French, and home-style American cooking. Filling a gap in the New York scene, the gastro-pub met with great success, receiving a Michelin star for four consecutive years. In 2008 Bloomfield opened her latest venture, the John Dory, also in New York, where she presides over the open kitchen, lending elegance to a broad menu of fish and seafood.

April Bloomfield constantly impresses me—when I eat her food, when I hear about her ideas, when I see her behind the line at her restaurants. She's one of the brightest culinary stars in the bunch. At only thirty-four April already has two über-successful and constantly packed hot-spot restaurants in New York City.

The Spotted Pig, April's first restaurant, is an ode to her mother country: England. Before the Spotted Pig, most New Yorkers didn't understand the term "gastro-pub"—but April soon changed that. Now the expression is widely known, and the one-star Pig will go down in history as the most casual of Michelin-reviewed restaurants to garner this honor. April's innovation and ability to spot the one or two gaps in New York cuisine and then turn that discovery into a huge success are backed by her skill, determination, creative vision and, of course, her amazingly intuitive palate.

More recently, she opened the John Dory, where I had the pleasure, once again, of seeing her turn a restaurant into a rousing success. An open kitchen can be the death of some chefs—the few who lack the ability to run an organized team and keep a clean work space. But to April, this open kitchen is a testament to her incredible organization and efficiency. We can all witness the care her team take over everything they make, from simple grilled octopus to complex seafood stew!

Respect for everyone and everything in the kitchen sets her aside and makes April successful. I'm proud to be associated with her cooking and can't wait for more.

Mario Batali

MENU

Beef tenderloin with
horseradish and
watercress roll

~

Corn soup with
chanterelles and chives

~

Roasted market
vegetables with goat
cheese and pumpkin seeds

~

Pork belly and cabbage
crepinette with crispy
pig's ears

~

Chocolate orange cake
with spiced cream

1
3

2
4

BEEF TENDERLOIN WITH HORSERADISH AND WATERCRESS ROLL
Serves 4

This dish makes a delicious appetizer or canapé.

350 g beef tenderloin • 3 tbsp olive oil • salt • freshly ground black pepper • 2 tbsp chopped thyme •1 tbsp balsamic vinegar • 15 tsp lemon juice • 25 g horseradish • 60 ml crème fraîche • 1 bunch watercress

1 Rub the beef with 1 tablespoon of the olive oil and season liberally with salt and black pepper.
2 Encrust the fillet with chopped thyme.
3 Sear on the grill over high heat for 2 minutes per side until a nice crust forms.
4 Remove from the pan and drizzle with 1 tablespoon of the olive oil, the balsamic vinegar, and 1 teaspoon of the lemon juice.
5 Place in the refrigerator to cool for 20 minutes.
6 While the meat is cooling, place the horseradish, crème fraîche, and the remaining lemon juice in a bowl and mix well. Season with salt and pepper to taste.
7 To assemble, slice the beef thinly and spread each slice with horseradish cream. Place sprigs of watercress in the center and roll up. Serve on a platter.

CORN SOUP WITH CHANTERELLES AND CHIVES
Serves 4

700 g corn kernels (sweet corn), cobs reserved • 120 g plus 3 tbsp unsalted butter • 15 shallots, thinly sliced • 60 ml milk • 60 ml heavy (double) cream • 225 g chanterelle mushrooms • salt • olive oil, for drizzling • 2 tbsp finely chopped chives • chili powder, optional

1 Place the cobs in a large pan and cover with cold water. Over high heat, bring the water to a rolling boil, then lower the heat and let simmer for 25 minutes.
2 Remove the cobs from the water. Reserve water for later use.
3 Melt 120 g butter in a sauté pan and sweat the shallots until soft, not allowing any color to develop.
4 Add the corn kernels and continue to cook until the corn is tender.
5 Add the milk, cream, and enough corn stock to just cover the corn. Bring to a boil and cook for 10 minutes. Season to taste.
6 Pour the pan contents into a blender and puree until smooth.

Strain through a fine-mesh sieve and season again to taste.
7 Melt the remaining 3 tablespoons butter in a separate sauté pan and sauté the chanterelles until soft. Season with salt to taste.
8 Pour the soup into a bowl, top with the chanterelles, and drizzle with olive oil. Garnish with chopped chives and a pinch of chili powder.

PORK BELLY AND CABBAGE CREPINETTE WITH CRISPY PIG'S EARS
Serves 4

For the pork belly
570 g pork belly • 2 pig's ears • 1 carrot • 1 celery stalk • ½ small onion • chicken stock, to cover

1 Preheat oven to 300°F (150°C).
2 Place the pork belly and pig's ears in a large braising pot with the carrot, celery stalk, and onion.
3 Add enough chicken stock to cover the meat. On the stove top, bring to a boil.
4 Cover the pot and continue to braise in the oven for 2–2½ hours until the pork is fork-tender.
5 Remove the pork belly from the pot and place on a baking sheet.
6 Remove the vegetables and set aside for later use in the cabbage stuffing.
7 Continue to braise the pig's ears in the oven for another hour, until you are able to push a finger through the cartilage.
8 Turn the oven up to 400°F (200°C).
9 Season the pork belly with salt and pepper and roast for 20 minutes. Once brown and crisp, remove from the oven and roughly chop the pork belly into 1–2 cm chunks.

For the cabbage crepinette
350 g Savoy cabbage • 120 g plus 2–3 tbsp unsalted butter • 1 small onion, thinly sliced • 2 cloves garlic, thinly sliced • 4 juniper berries, crushed • 120 g caul fat, in 1 large sheet

1 To prepare the cabbage, remove the tough outer layers and reserve 4 unblemished leaves.
2 Blanch the leaves, pat dry, and reserve on a flat baking sheet.
3 Slice the remaining cabbage into thin strips.
4 In a sauté pan, melt the butter until frothy and sweat the onion, garlic cloves, and juniper berries.
5 Add the cabbage and cook for 20 minutes until wilted and tender.
6 Chop the reserved carrot and celery from the braising pot and add to the cabbage.
7 Remove the pan from the heat

and add the chopped pork belly to cabbage. If necessary, add some cooking liquid from the braising pan to moisten the cabbage. Add salt to taste.
8 Form the stuffing into 4 equal-sized balls and place each ball on a blanched cabbage leaf. Wrap the cabbage, ensuring that there are no holes in the leaf.
9 Unravel the caul fat onto one large baking sheet and cut into 4 equal pieces.
10 Place a cabbage roll in the center of each square of caul fat. Wrap the cabbage once and fold the edges into the center. Roll one more time and fold the edges into the center again.
11 Preheat the oven to 350°F (180°C).
12 In a sauté pan melt the 2–3 tablespoons of butter, fry the crepinette, seam-side up, until golden brown. Finish in the oven for 10 minutes.

For the crispy pig's ears
oil for deep frying • Dijon mustard • salt and pepper

1 When the pig's ears are tender, remove them from the braising liquid and slice into 5-mm strips.
2 Fry the ears in a deep fryer with a splatter-proof top at 350°F (180°C) for 6–7 minutes.
3 When crisp, drain on a paper towel and season with salt. Keep warm.
4 To make the sauce, begin by skimming the fat from the braising liquid. Reduce the liquid over a low flame until slightly viscous. Add Dijon mustard and salt and pepper to taste. You should aim for a sharpness from the mustard, to cut through the fat.

To serve
Plate the crepinette on a warm plate, pour the sauce over lightly, drizzle with a little olive oil, and garnish with crispy pig's ears.

CHOCOLATE ORANGE CAKE WITH SPICED CREAM
Serves 4

For the chocolate orange cake
5 eggs • 350 g 70% bittersweet (plain) chocolate • 350 g unsalted butter • 200 g sugar • 125 ml bourbon whiskey • zest of 1½ oranges

1 Preheat the oven to 350°F (180°C).
2 Butter 4 (120-g) cake pans and line the bottoms with parchment paper.
3 Beat the eggs at high speed in a mixer with a whisk attachment until they triple in volume. Set aside.
4 In a double boiler, melt the chocolate and butter.
5 In a separate pan, bring the sugar, bourbon, and orange zest to a boil, then add to the melted chocolate.
6 Slowly pour the chocolate mixture into the eggs and mix thoroughly.
7 Pour the batter into the prepared cake pans and bake in a bain-marie for 20 minutes, or until the cake pulls cleanly from the side of the pan. Let cool in the bain-marie.

For the spiced cream
¾ tbsp grated nutmeg • seeds from 3 cardamom pods • 1 clove • 7 tsp ground cinnamon • 225 ml cream • 3 tbsp confectioners' (icing) sugar

1 Pound the nutmeg, cardamom seeds, clove, and cinnamon in a mortar and pestle until they have become a fine powder.
2 Place all the ingredients in a bowl and whisk until stiff peaks form.

To serve
Remove the cake from pan and transfer to a plate. Serve with a dollop of spiced cream.

1
Beef tenderloin
with horseradish and
watercress roll

2
Corn soup with chanterelles
and chives

3
Pork belly and cabbage
crepinette with crispy
pig's ears

4
Chocolate orange cake
with spiced cream

April Bloomfield

The first time I came across Robert Owen Brown he was cooking my food at the Manchester Food and Wine Festival in a huge teepee. It's always a little strange when someone cooks your food, but I was much heartened, if a little surprised, by Robert's decoration of the teepee with game birds, rabbits and hares that he had shot himself. He is a true hunter-gatherer, and not just on dry land—he will also go out on a fishing boat and catch the evening's menu.

I visited Robert at his pub, the Angel, in Manchester, which is very much a pub; not a glamorous gastro-pub, but a proper pub. I don't think Robert would take offense at this: between the two of us we thwarted the paltry collection of wine by marrying an Amorone with a Moulin à Vent to create our own blend. His knack for making an event out of dishes that are often sadly neglected is admirable. His Lancashire hotpot is the product of hours of braising all the unloved cuts of lamb, layering potatoes with just the right crust on them— and some fortunate person gets a mellow and delicious half-hour. He isn't afraid of a flourish either, serving his famed Eccles cakes with strawberries, whipped cream and a zingy butterscotch and ginger sauce.

Robert is quite a character and, despite cutting an imposing figure himself, did insist on calling me "Chef." He produces absolute wonders on two gas burners in a tiny kitchen, and told a fantastic story about roasting a turkey in a filing cabinet one happy Christmas. With this resourcefulness, and his "energetic" approach to sourcing great ingredients, Robert is a totally unique chef, making do and mending—but not so you would notice, when you sit down to glorious oxtail, or partridge shot by the man himself, followed up by a huge, creamy rice pudding. Robert offers proper food in a proper pub, made by a one-of-a-kind chef. Fantastic.

Fergus Henderson

Born in 1969 in Manchester, UK, Robert Owen Brown began his career at 18 at the city's Midland Hotel. The unique, uncompromising approach to cooking he revealed there has been his guiding principle ever since. After an apprenticeship at Chester's Grosvenor Hotel, Brown worked in Scotland, France, and Italy before returning home to some of Manchester's top restaurants, including stints at Brasserie St. Pierre, Reform, and Mr. Thomas' Chop-House. After moving on from the restaurant he opened in 2004, the Bridge, Brown founded the Angel pub. Located off the beaten track in Manchester's Rochdale Road area, it has enjoyed widespread acclaim since opening in 2008.

MENU

Black pudding potato cake with soft-poached egg and tangy tarragon sauce
Hakhamanesh English Organic Lager

~

Rack of Rossendale lamb, lamb stew, wild garlic, and duck-fat roasties
Yorkshire Black Sheep Ale

~

Eccles cakes served with a dollop of Dowson's clotted cream
J.W. Lees Harvest Ale, 2006

1
A delivery of British Limousin pork

2
A whole pig roasts on a spit for the Angel's St. George's Day feast

3
Robert Owen Brown with a plate of local black puddings

Robert Owen Brown

The Angel, Manchester, UK

BLACK PUDDING POTATO CAKE WITH SOFT-POACHED EGG AND TANGY TARRAGON SAUCE
Serves 4

170 g finely mashed potato •
1 tbsp chopped parsley • 1 tbsp
chopped chives • 170 g black
pudding, cut into 1-cm dice • 6 eggs
• 55 g all-purpose (plain) flour •
170 g fine bread crumbs • 140 ml
cream • 10 ml white-wine vinegar •
pinch of salt and pepper • 1 tbsp
chopped tarragon • oil, for deep
frying • 8 whole chives, to decorate

1 Mix together the potato, parsley,
chopped chives, black pudding,
and a little seasoning, and form
into a hockey puck shape.
2 Crack 2 eggs into a bowl and
beat them. Coat your potato cakes
first in flour, then egg, then bread
crumbs, and place on a tray in the
refrigerator.
3 In a heavy-bottomed pan,
reduce the cream by half, add
5 ml white-wine vinegar, and
season to taste. Add the tarragon
and let stand.
4 Preheat your deep-fat fryer to
350°F (180°C) and your oven to
400°F (200°C). Deep-fry the potato
cakes until they are golden, then
place on a baking tray in the oven
for 7 minutes.
5 Boil water in a pan, add the
remaining vinegar, turn down to
a simmer, and drop in the eggs.
By the time the eggs are poached,
your potato cakes should be ready.
6 To serve, top each cake with
a soft-poached egg, drizzle with
the tarragon sauce, and dress with
the whole chives.

RACK OF ROSSENDALE LAMB, LAMB STEW, WILD GARLIC, AND DUCK-FAT ROASTIES
Serves 4

For the rack
4 (3-bone) racks of lamb,
French-trimmed, with trimmings
retained for stew • 2 garlic cloves,
crushed • 4 tsp olive oil • salt and
pepper

1 Rub the racks with the garlic,
oil, and seasoning, then allow
to marinate for 4 hours.
2 Brown the lamb in a hot pan
and place in the oven preheated
to 500°F (260°C) for 10 minutes.
3 Remove from the oven and let
rest for 5 minutes, keeping warm.

For the stew
trimmings from the lamb racks,
diced • 1 tsp olive oil • 1 onion, finely
diced • 2 carrots, finely chopped •
1 tsp tomato paste • 225 ml lamb
stock • 125 ml good-quality red
wine • salt and pepper • 3 wild garlic
plants, roughly chopped

1 Brown the diced lamb in a hot
pan with the oil. Add the onion and
carrot, cooking gently until soft.
Add the tomato paste, stock, and
wine. Simmer gently for 1½ hours.
2 Season, and add the wild garlic
just before serving.

For the duck-fat roasties
1 kg Maris Piper potatoes • salt
• 125 g duck fat • 3 tsp flour

1 Peel and cut the potatoes into
even-sized pieces, place in large
pan, cover with water, and add salt.
Simmer vigorously for 3 minutes.
2 Place the duck fat into
a preheated roasting tray.
3 Drain the potatoes in a large
metal sieve or colander and shake
to roughen the surfaces.
Sprinkle with the flour and shake
to produce an even coating.
4 Carefully add the potatoes to the
sizzling fat and turn them so they
are evenly coated. Do not crowd
the pan.
5 Roast for about 45 minutes or
until crisp and golden, turning
during the process.

ECCLES CAKES SERVED WITH A DOLLOP OF DOWSON'S CLOTTED CREAM
Serves 12

40 g soft butter • 100 g superfine
(caster) sugar • 200 g currants •
pinch of nutmeg • 50 g candied
peel • pinch of ground ginger •
500 g puff pastry dough• clotted
cream, to serve

1 Combine the butter, sugar,
fruit, and spices.
2 Roll out the pastry to about
4 mm thick and cut into
10-cm circles.
3 Place a small spoonful of filling
into the center of each circle.
Draw the edges together over
the fruit and pinch to seal, then
turn over and press gently to
flatten the cakes.
4 Make a small slash in the top
of each cake and place on
a baking sheet.
5 Brush with a little water and
lightly dust with sugar before
baking for about 20 minutes at
425°F (220°C). Let cool and serve
with the cream.

1
Black pudding potato cake
with soft-poached egg and
tangy tarragon sauce

2
Rack of Rossendale lamb,
lamb stew, wild garlic,
and duck fat roasties

3
Eccles cakes served with
a dollop of Dowson's
clotted cream

I've known Mario since he was eighteen and first started to work in my kitchen at Babbo. I was excited and anxious for him to cook at Del Posto alongside Mark Ladner, but his inspiration comes from closer to home. He was influenced by his grandfather's kitchen as he experienced it while growing up in Queens, and he continues to be inspired by the people around him, including his family and his colleagues.

Mario's energy and ambition set him apart from day one. He's got strong opinions about food—what he likes, what needs improvement, how we can grow as a restaurant and as a team. Being able to express these opinions about food isn't a gimmick for him, it's his way of cooking. He truly wants to share his thoughts, experiences, and knowledge of Italian-American food. You don't see many chefs take that kind of initiative, and I've always respected Mario for that.

At Del Posto Mario worked directly under Mark as his right-hand man, and all the sous-chefs and cooks looked up to him for guidance and inspiration. And now that he's embarking on his new and already quite successful Aeronuovo in the Jet Blue terminal at JFK, we'll really begin to see how he shines.

The concept of the restaurant is perfectly aligned with Mario's vision as a chef—simple, fresh, affordable, seasonal Italian food that appeals to a large demographic. The policy of Aeronuovo is to use domestic products where possible and to present food that would be served in a traditional trattoria. This means that the menu is constantly changing to present the best of seasonal produce, and Mario continues to work hard to uphold the integrity of the food served in the airport. Constantly surrounded by travelers at JFK, Mario's lucky in that he gets to show people from all over the world what we do. He gets to show folks out there what authentic, seasonal Italian food is all about.

This role makes Mario not only a terrific chef with excellent abilities but also makes him an Italian-American ambassador of sorts. If he teaches just one person that real ricotta doesn't come from a Polly-O container then he's done a good job. I sense he will.

Mario Batali

Born in 1980, Mario Carbone was cooking fried calamari in the neighborhood restaurants of Queens, New York, by the age of 15. After formal training at the Culinary Institute of America, he began working for Mario Batali at Babbo. Impressing immediately with his tenacity and flair, he helped to open Lupa, Batali's Greenwich Village Roman osteria, under chef Mark Ladner, who would become a major influence. Carbone later witnessed precision French cuisine with Andrew Carmellini at Café Boulud, then working for Wylie Dufresne at WD-50. These formative experiences led to another post under his mentor Ladner, as executive sous chef at Del Posto, which gained two Michelin stars in 2007. Now chef of Aeronuova at New York's JFK Airport, Carbone has created a traditional trattoria with clean lines and local sourcing.

MENU

Roasted garlic zeppole

~

Mixed antipasti

~

Pork agnolotti with tomato marmellata and crisp pancetta

~

Tonno with Taggiasca olives, crispy rice, and arugula

~

"Manhattan Special" affogato

~

Strufoli

1
Mario Carbone
selecting olive oil

2–4
The chef in the kitchen at
Aeronuova

Mario Carbone

Aeronuova, Queens, NY, USA

ROASTED GARLIC ZEPPOLE
Makes 15 knots

The idea for this canapé or *assaggi* (taste) comes from my love for the pizzeria garlic knot. What better way to begin a fine Italian meal in Queens, New York City, than that?

For the confit garlic
2 heads garlic • 475 ml olive oil • 25 g thyme (whole sprigs)

1   Preheat the oven to 300ºF (150ºC).
2   Put the garlic in a small casserole with the olive oil and thyme. Bake for 45 minutes or until golden brown and tender.

For the batter, and to finish the zeppole
225 ml water • 85 g butter • 2 tsp salt • 175 g all-purpose (plain) flour • 4 eggs • 2 egg whites • 60 g Parmigiano Reggiano, grated • 85 g confit garlic • Maldon salt, to garnish

1   Preheat the oven to 325ºF (160ºC).
2   Boil the water with the butter and salt, then add the flour and stir until completely incorporated.
3   While the mixture is hot, begin adding the eggs and whites one at a time, allowing the batter to absorb each egg fully before adding another. Finish by adding the cheese and confit garlic and place in a disposable pastry (piping) bag without a tip (nozzle).
4   Pipe rosettes of the batter onto a baking sheet tray lined with parchment paper and bake for 25 minutes.
5   Brush the finished zeppole with some of the garlic oil and sprinkle with Maldon salt.

PORK AGNOLOTTI WITH TOMATO MARMELLATA AND CRISP PANCETTA
Serves 10

This dish was inspired by one of my best friends, Elizabeth Fraser, and her obsession for late-night BLT sandwiches. What could be better than those delicious flavors turned into a rich, savory pasta dish?

For the pasta dough
Makes 10 sheets
1 kg semolina flour • 20 egg yolks • semolina, for dusting

1   Combine the ingredients in a mixer with a dough hook and continue to mix on a low speed for 10 minutes. Remove the dough and let rest for 30 minutes.
2   Cut a 120-g piece off the dough ball and dust with semolina, then, starting on the widest setting, begin to pass it through your pasta machine. Reduce the number on your pasta attachment with every pass of the dough until you reach the smallest number on the roller. Dust with fresh semolina and reserve.

For the vegetable stock
4–5 liters water • 1 carrot • 1 stick celery • 1 onion • 1 fennel bulb

Simmer all the ingredients together for 3 hours, strain, cool and reserve.

For the filling
Makes 50 agnolotti
90 ml extra-virgin olive oil • about 5 kg pork shoulder, cut into 2.5-cm chunks • 5 white onions, sliced thickly • 120 g tomato paste • 225 g kosher salt • 12 black peppercorns • 4 bay leaves • 750 ml white wine • 750 ml vegetable stock

1   Put the olive oil in a large pan, heat, add the pork, and sear on all sides. Remove the pork, drain off any excess fat, and add the onions and tomato paste. Cook for 2 minutes, then season with the salt, peppercorns, and bay leaves.
2   Return the pork to the pan, add the wine and stock, and braise for 2½ hours or until tender.
3   To finish the filling, place the braised pork in a food processor and pulse quickly to create a smooth yet chunky consistency. Fill disposable pastry (piping) bags with the mixture and reserve.

For the tomato marmellata
90 ml extra-virgin olive oil • 2 cloves garlic, sliced • 275 g San Marzano canned tomatoes, strained • 1 tbsp salt • 25 g thyme leaves

1   In a wide-based pot heat the olive oil and add the garlic. Cook until the edges of the garlic start to brown but not burn.
2   Add the tomatoes, salt, and thyme. Cook for 10 minutes on medium heat, stirring constantly. As the water evaporates the sauce will thicken to a compote consistency. Remove from the heat and reserve.

For the pancetta
150 g pancetta, sliced very thinly

1   Preheat the oven to 325ºF (160ºC).
2   Place the pancetta slices on a metal rack set over a baking sheet. Bake for 15 minutes or until golden brown and crisp.

To assemble
2 eggs, beaten with 15 ml water • butter • thyme leaves • olive oil • cracked black pepper

1   Take 1 rolled pasta sheet and lay it flat on the counter. Pipe the pork filling out in 25-g piles, leaving space in between them.
2   With a brush, apply a very thin layer of egg wash around the piles of filling and then gently lay a second sheet of pasta on top. With your fingers, gently pinch the dough between each pile of filling to seal the agnolotti, then cut around them using a knife or pasta wheel.
3   Drop the agnolotti in boiling salted water until they float (about 3 minutes). For each serving, place 10 agnolotti in a pan with 2 tbsp butter, 2 sprigs of thyme, 2 tbsp water, and 1 tsp olive oil. Toss until fully emulsified, and spoon onto a plate.

To serve
Top the agnolotti with spots of the warm marmellata, fresh cracked black pepper, and the crisp pancetta.

"MANHATTAN SPECIAL" AFFOGATO
Serves 1

This dish is a playful New Yorker's take on a traditional trattoria classic. Instead of using hot espresso to pour over the gelato, I substitute coffee soda to produce an ice cream float, of sorts. This dish would make any New York Italian proud!

For the whipped cream
Makes 3 portions
225 ml heavy (double) cream • 85 g superfine (caster) sugar

Combine the ingredients in a stainless steel bowl and beat until the cream sticks to the whisk.

For the affogato
Makes 1 portion
85 g vanilla gelato (ice cream) • 60 ml coffee soda • 25 g whipped cream • 5 chocolate-covered espresso beans, chopped

Place a scoop of vanilla gelato in a chilled high-ball glass. Then pour the coffee soda over it and top the float with the whipped cream and crushed espresso beans.

1
Roasted garlic zeppole

2
Pork agnolotti with
tomato marmellata and
crisp pancetta

3
"Manhattan Special" affogato

Mario Carbone

Between 2002 and 2007 I officiated at the Haute Cuisine Premier Awards held by the Hong Kong Tourist Board. And in every one of those years Wai Man Chan has been the chef whose work has been consistently of gold medal standard. His creativity and his benign entrepreneurial spirit have left an extremely deep impression on me.

Chef Wai Man Chan is the embodiment of a traditional Chinese restaurant chef. With more than thirty years experience in the trade, he is unceasing in his pursuit of the creative spirit. The flavors he creates take the very best of the traditional, infused with original concepts and novel supplementary ingredients. He has created a brand of classic tastes which is both memorable and consistently praiseworthy. The first year he attended he presented a shining example of such taste sensations in his baked lobster with supreme sauce and fried vermicelli. He used chicken, golden Chinese ham, pork and shrimp simmered to a paste to make the sauce, then baked the lobster before pan-frying it in its juices in order to preserve the delicate flavor. It was then placed very carefully on the vermicelli. Apart from the delicious taste of the lobster itself, the vermicelli beneath soaked up its taste and character, creating a long-lasting taste sensation for those eating it.

His dishes stick closely in their delivery to the names he gives them. When they are not (entirely) Chinese, and the make-up of their flavors has been altered, the ingredients used in his side dishes invariably draw on traditional culinary techniques. His dishes all present a succession of flavors to customers who, like me, find themselves pleasantly surprised time after time. Wai Man Chan is content to be an ordinary man who enjoys his work—yet at the same time he is admired by specialist chefs.

Jacky Yu

Wai Man Chan was born in Hong Kong in 1958. The hard-work ethic instilled by his farm-based upbringing was rewarded when he ran his own kitchen by the age of 24. Although he left school at 12, he worked hard and was dedicated to his traditional apprenticeship, which was based on observation and extensive practice of the fundamentals of cuisine. Currently Master Chef of the Tai Woo Restaurant Group, Wai Man Chan has innovated constantly over his thirty years in the business, experimenting to create new dishes and to adapt traditional ones in line with modern ideas on healthy eating. Wai Man Chan has achieved numerous accolades in Hong Kong's culinary competitions, and he continues to develop his menu in response to the array of seasonal produce the city offers.

MENU

Crispy juicy stewed beef

~

Lobster with supreme sauce and fried rice vermicelli

~

Crispy soy mille feuilles and crispy rice in tomato consommé

~

Fried rice with fish julienne and ginger

Wai Man Chan

1
Wai Man Chan chooses
papaya at the market

2 & 5
Working at the stove

3
Selecting a lobster

4
Adding roe to a dish
before serving

Tai Woo Restaurant, Hong Kong, China

1
Crispy juicy stewed beef

2
Lobster with supreme sauce
and fried rice vermicelli

3
Crispy soy mille feuilles
and crispy rice
in tomato consommé

4
Fried rice with fish julienne
and ginger

CRISPY JUICY STEWED BEEF

Serves 4
The stewed meat will be velvety tender with a contrastingly crispy crust.

For the beef

3 tbsp chopped ginger • 3 tbsp chopped scallions (spring onion) • 175 ml Shaoxing wine • 1.2 kg beef brisket in one piece • 60 ml dark soy sauce • 125 ml light soy sauce • 60 g rock sugar • 1 sachet mixed spices (star anise, licorice, cinnamon bark, cardamom, bay leaves) • 3 cm galangal • 1 stalk lemongrass • 2.4 liters water

1 Mix together the ginger, scallions, and wine and rub this marinade into the brisket. Set aside for 2–3 hours.
2 Mix together the soy sauces, sugar, spices, galangal, lemongrass, and water in a stew pan.
3 Add the brisket, bring to a boil, then lower the heat, cover and stew for about 2 hours until tender.
4 Remove the brisket from the sauce and hang in a cool place to dry for about 2 hours.

For the spring roll crispies

2 spring roll wrappers • oil, for deep-frying • 2 tbsp golden syrup • 1 tsp white sesame seeds, fried

1 Cut the spring roll wrappers into 4-cm x 2-cm pieces. Cut a slit in the center, roll up the ends, push them through the cut, and secure into a bow shape.
2 Heat the oil to medium heat, and deep-fry the spring rolls until golden.
3 Remove from the oil and drain. Pour golden syrup over the crispies and dust with the sesame seeds before serving.

To serve

1 cucumber, sliced

1 Just before serving, deep-fry the whole piece of brisket in hot oil until the surface is crispy.
2 Cut into bite-size pieces, arrange on a plate, and pour a little spice sauce over the pieces.
3 Serve with cucumber slices and spring roll crispies.

LOBSTER WITH SUPREME SAUCE AND FRIED RICE VERMICELLI

Serves 4
This dish has a glittering golden color from the lobster and the sauce and the flavor is superb. Serve hot, or the rice vermicelli will become soggy.

250 g shrimp (prawns) in their shells • 2–2.5 liters water • 120 g dried rice vermicelli • 1 lobster (approximately 900 g–1 kg) • oil, for pan-frying • a little salt, sugar and pepper to taste • 2 tbsp cornstarch (cornflour) and 3 tbsp water to make a thickening paste

1 Blend the shrimp with their shells into a puree. Place the puree in a large pot, add the water, and simmer gently for 1½ hours until only 225 ml shrimp stock remains. Strain.
2 Soak the vermicelli in water for 45 minutes, then drain well. Shape into a square no thicker than 6 mm.
3 Chop the lobster into bite-size pieces, quick-fry in hot oil in a large skillet, then lower the heat and cook for a further 2–3 minutes. Remove from the skillet.
4 Pour off all but 2 tablespoons of the oil. Lower the rice vermicelli square into the oil and pan-fry until both sides are crispy. Remove, cut into small squares, and arrange on a plate.
5 Heat 1–2 tablespoons oil in the skillet, add the lobster pieces and the shrimp stock, season with a little salt, sugar and pepper, and cook for 1 minute. Stir in enough cornstarch paste to thicken the sauce. Cook until paste dissolves (10–15 seconds)
6 Pour the lobster and sauce over the crispy rice vermicelli. Serve hot.

CRISPY SOY MILLE FEUILLES AND CRISPY RICE IN TOMATO CONSOMMÉ

Serves 4 as a main course
This scrumptious vegetarian dish can be served as a snack too.

For the crispy soy mille feuilles

2 sheets soy • 150 g all-purpose (plain) flour • 1 tsp baking powder • ½ tsp salt • approximately 200 ml water • 1 tbsp oil, plus extra for deep-frying and pan-frying • a few stalks baby Shanghai bok choy, trimmed as flower buds • salt and sugar to taste • 1 tsp finely chopped red bell pepper • 2 tbsp chopped ginger • 50 g pine mushrooms, chopped • 2 tbsp chopped carrot • 2 tbsp chopped water chestnut • light soy sauce, to taste • cornstarch (cornflour) and water paste

1 Cut each soy sheet into 6 pieces, pile 10 small pieces together, and cut them again into 7 cm x 4 cm small stacks.
2 Whisk together the flour, baking powder, salt, water and 1 tablespoon oil to make a batter.
3 Coat each pile with batter, deep-fry in medium hot oil until golden and crispy, remove and drain well. Arrange on a plate.
4 Cook the bok choy in boiling water with a little salt and sugar, remove and drain. Arrange on the plate, and sprinkle with the bell pepper.
5 Heat 1 tablespoon oil in a skillet and sauté the ginger, mushrooms, carrot and water chestnut with a little light soy sauce, sugar and water, add enough cornstarch paste to thicken and cook for a few minutes. Pour over the crispy soy mille feuilles to serve.

For the crispy rice in tomato consommé

2–3 tomatoes • oil, for pan-frying and deep-frying • 2 tbsp tomato paste • 1 tbsp light (single) cream • 750 ml water • salt and pepper • 2 stalks leafy green vegetables • 200 g tofu • 1 tbsp chopped Chinese celery • 85 g cooked rice

1 Skin and de-seed the tomatoes and cut the flesh into dice. In a pan, heat 1 tablespoon oil and sauté the diced tomatoes. Add the tomato paste and water, bring to a boil, and simmer for 30 minutes. Add the cream and bring to a boil. Season to taste.
2 Slice the vegetable stalks and cut the tofu into dice. Add to the tomato consommé and cook for a while. Transfer to a tureen and sprinkle in the chopped Chinese celery.
3 Heat some oil in a wok, deep-fry cooked rice in hot oil until crispy. Drain excess oil on absorbent paper.
4 Add the crispy rice to the tomato consommé, and serve hot with the crispy soy mille feuilles.

FRIED RICE WITH FISH JULIENNE AND GINGER

Serves 4
The rice has a pleasant ginger fragrance and is great comfort food to serve in cold weather.

1 mandarin fish or other fish (approximately 600 g) • 1 egg white • ¼ tsp salt • a little pepper • ½ tsp cornstarch (cornflour) • 1 liter water • 180 g rice • oil, for pan-frying • 4 tbsp chopped ginger • 2 eggs, beaten • salt and sugar, to season • 2 tbsp chopped scallion (spring onion), plus extra for sprinkling • 2 tbsp chopped ginger • 2 tbsp shredded carrot • 2 tbsp cornstarch (cornflour) and 3 tbsp of water to make a thickening paste

1 Fillet the fish and cut the flesh into julienne strips, reserving the bones.
2 Mix together the egg white, salt, pepper, and cornstarch and set aside for 15 minutes.
3 Gently boil the fish bones in the water until it has reduced to 225 ml.
4 Cook the rice in the fish stock. When cooked, stir to loosen and leave to cool.
5 Heat 2 tablespoons oil, sauté 2 tablespoons of the chopped ginger until fragrant, then add the rice and beaten egg and a little salt and sugar to taste. Finally add the chopped scallion, toss together and remove to a plate.
6 Heat 240 ml oil, quick-fry the fish julienne until half-cooked, remove and drain.
7 Heat 1 tablespoon oil, sauté the remaining 2 tablespoons of chopped ginger until fragrant, add the shredded carrot and fish julienne, sprinkle a little salt and sugar to taste, then thicken with cornstarch and water paste for about 10–15 seconds. Add to the cooked rice and sprinkle with more chopped scallion.

When I step into David Chang's Momofuku Noodle Bar, which opened in New York City's East Village in 2003, the first thing I notice is the immediate connection between the cooks and the patrons. The same people who are sizzling pork belly and frying eggs behind the counter are the ones who hand you your finished bowl of noodles: perfect, simple noodles. In this egalitarian space, no reservations are taken and the prices are affordable. But beyond Momofuku's accessibility and liveliness, the simple truth is that the food is absolutely delicious.

David is a diligent, talented perfectionist: every bite of food reflects his incredible attention to detail and an intuitive, even brilliant, sense for taste combinations. What I like about David's cooking is that you can taste how he's been influenced by his family's Korean home cooking, by his years spent cooking in restaurants in Japan, and also by the freshest ingredients, purchased from local farmers. I wasn't at all surprised when I read that Henry David Thoreau's *Walden*, extolling nature and the simple life, is one of David's favorite books: the kitchen at Momofuku is run with care and attention to detail, and with respect for every task, no matter how small.

Not only does David source locally grown, sustainable ingredients, but as in Asian traditions, his dishes emphasize vegetables and grains—a prescient move to shift meat from main course to condiment. He cooks resourcefully, favoring variety meats and less well-known cuts of the whole animal. He pays his employees fairly. He understands that in order to cook and eat well, we have to know where our food comes from. I think that David's restaurants—Momofuku Noodle Bar, Ssäm Bar, and Ko—are the future of slow fast food.

Alice Waters

Born in 1977, David Chang trained at the French Culinary Institute in New York City and began his career under Jean-Georges Vongerichten at the Mercer Kitchen. He later worked for Tom Colicchio at Craft before moving to Japan, where he studied at kaiseki, izakaya, and ramen restaurants. On his return to New York, he opened his first restaurant, the Momofuku Noodle Bar, in 2004, serving handmade noodles and dim sum. In addition to his extensive studies and training, he draws inspiration from other chefs he respects, such as René Redzepi, Andoni Aduriz, Pascal Barbot, and Wylie Dufresne. He cites his extended family as his main influence, however, and it's important to him to make sure his restaurants are accessible to everyone. His food philosophy is simple: For Chang, getting it right means making his food as delicious as possible.

MENU

Raw scallop with
green apple and dashi

~

Roasted matsutake
mushroom with feta,
pine needle oil, and
pine nuts

~

Mackerel with kimchi
puree, oyster, and radish

~

Pork neck
with succotash

~

White peach sorbet with
streusel ganache and
milk crumbs

1
The bar at
Momofuku Ko

2
The dining room at
Momofuku Ssäm

3
David Chang
preparing a tomato salad

David Chang

Momofuku Ssäm Bar/Momofuku Noodle Bar/Momofuku Ko, New York, NY, USA

RAW SCALLOP WITH GREEN APPLE AND DASHI
Serves 4

4 diver or bay scallops, thinly sliced • poppy seeds, for sprinkling • sea salt, for seasoning • 250 ml dashi • 1 green apple, sliced horizontally, and into small thin wedges • 1 bunch scallions (spring onions), sliced to 2.5-cm in length, and sliced vertically as thinly as possible (then placed in ice water)

1 Place the sliced scallops in the center of the bowl.
2 Sprinkle the poppyseeds and sea salt on top of the scallops.
3 Pour the dashi into the bowl to cover half way.
4 Garnish with the apple, scallions, sea salt, and serve.

ROASTED MATSUTAKE MUSHROOM WITH FETA, PINE NEEDLE OIL, PINE NUTS
Serves 4

500 g matsutake mushrooms, cleaned • 125 g feta • 2 tbsp butter • 1 bunch chives • pine needle oil • salt • pine nuts, toasted • white pepper

1 Finely slice 400 g matsutake, as thinly as possible.
2 Bring the feta to room temperature, and mix until pliable.
3 In a pan, roast 100 g scored matsutake, adding the butter toward the end and basting.
4 Cut the chives into uneven lengths (ranging from 2.5 cm to 7.5 cm).
5 For serving, make a smear of feta on each plate. In a bowl, toss the chives with pine needle oil, salt, and white pepper and place over the feta. Add the grilled matsutake and pine nuts.

MACKEREL WITH KIMCHI PUREE, OYSTER, AND RADISH
Serves 4

100 g kimchi • grapeseed oil as needed • 50 g watermelon radish 50 g red ball radish • sea salt • sugar • 80 g Brussels sprouts, dark outer leaves discarded • 4 (110-g) Spanish mackerel fillets • oil, for searing • white pepper • 4 oysters, shucked • 1 g iwa nori • argan oil

1 Puree the kimchi in a blender or food processor. If thick, add a small amount of grapeseed oil.
2 Cut the watermelon radish into segments and toss with the pureed kimchi.
3 Slice the red ball radishes thinly and toss with a small pinch of salt and a large pinch of sugar to make a quick pickle.
4 Pull apart the Brussels sprouts, separating the leaves from the cores. Discard the cores. Prepare an ice water bath and put a large pot of water on to boil. Once it's at a rolling boil, salt the water very well and quickly blanch and then shock the Brussels sprouts leaves. Drain well and reserve.
5 Season the mackerel with salt and white pepper. Heat a puddle of oil on a plancha, flat-top, or wide skillet over high heat. After a minute, add the mackerel skin-side down and sear it until the skin is blistered. Remove from heat and set aside.

6 To serve, put a dollop of kimchi puree on each plate and smear it with the back of a spoon. Cut the seared mackerel in half and stack the pieces on top of one another. Arrange slices of red ball radish around the plate; nestle the shucked oyster up against the seared mackerel; arrange a few blanched Brussels sprouts leaves on the plate, scatter with the watermelon radish and iwa nori. Dot with argan oil and serve.

3 4 5

PORK NECK WITH SUCCOTASH
Serves 4

For the pork neck
300 g kosher salt • 270 g sugar
• 6 liters hot water • 2 bay leaves
• 25 g black peppercorns • 6 liters •
cold water • 10 g pink salt • 1 pork
neck

1 Mix the salt, sugar, hot water, bay leaves, and black peppercorns.
2 Mix the cold water with the pink salt.
3 Add the pork neck and confit 5 hours at 300°F (150°C) covered.
4 When tender, press between 2 sheet trays. Portion into serving size pieces.
5 Crisp on a griddle or pan to heat through.

For the succotash
100 g ground (minced) smoked, thick-cut pork belly • 12 g chanterelle mushrooms • 250 g lima (butter) beans • 175 g corn (sweetcorn) kernels • butter, for sautéing • 1 tbsp tarragon, chopped • 4 ml buttermilk • 120 g butter • 130 g arugula (rocket)

1 Sauté the pork belly, chanterelles, lima beans, and corn in pan.
2 Finish with a pinch of salt and pepper, chopped terragon, buttermilk, butter, and arugula.

WHITE PEACH SORBET WITH STREUSEL GANACHE AND MILK CRUMBS
Serves 4

For the white peach sorbet
70 g sugar • 35 g water • 400 g ripe white peaches • 2 g salt • citrus juice, to taste (this can be any combination of lemon, lime, yuzu, and so on)

1 Bring the sugar and water to a boil to dissolve the sugar. Strain and cool. You now have a sorbet syrup (see below).
2 Halve and pit the peaches. Puree them with their skins on. Pass the puree through a chinois.
3 Hand-blend the puree with the cooled sorbet syrup, salt and citrus juice. Taste and adjust the sugar, salt or citrus juice to taste as necessary. It should measure 20 Brix on a refractometer.
4 Freeze, and spin in a Pacojet or churn in an ice-cream maker.

For the streusel ganache
115 g butter • 115 g brown sugar • 3 g salt • 2 g ground cinnamon • 150 g flour • 75 g oats

1 Preheat the oven to 300°F (150°C).
2 In a mixer, beat together the butter and sugar. Combine all the dry ingredients, then add them to the butter and sugar mixture to produce a crumbly oat texture.
3 Spread on a parchment-lined baking sheet and bake for 25 minutes. Leave to cool.

To finish the streusel ganache
250 g milk • 50 g brown sugar • 6 g salt • 4 g ground cinnamon

Puree 400 g of the cooled streusel with all the finishing ingredients in a Vitaprep for 3–5 minutes until you have a thick puree. Pass through a fine-mesh sieve if necessary. Store in the refrigerator.

For the milk crumbs
75 g powdered milk • 90 g all-purpose (plain) flour • 25 g cornstarch (cornflour) • 40 g sugar • 4 g salt • 85 g unsalted butter, melted

1 Preheat the oven to 250°F (120°C).
2 Whisk all the ingredients (except the butter) together in a bowl.
3 Add the butter and mix until incorporated.
4 Spread on a parchment-lined sheet pan and bake for 10 minutes. Cool completely.

To finish and serve
75 g powdered milk • 225 g white chocolate, melted

1 In a clean bowl, fold together 300 g of the milk crumbs with the powdered milk and white chocolate. The result should be evenly coated white crumbs. Store in the refrigerator to keep crunchy.
2 To serve, smear 150 g of streusel ganache in each bowl. Take a large scoop of approximately 130 g of sorbet. Garnish with 150 g of milk crumbs. Serve immediately.

David Chang

1
Tomatoes roasted with garlic

2–5
Ricky Cheung in the kitchen
at Le Mieux

Ricky Cheung

MENU

Gazpacho aspic
with crabmeat

~

Scallop carpaccio with
tuna tartare, uni, and yuzu
vinaigrette

~

Seafood ravioli with
Norwegian lobster, wilted
arugula, and tomato salsa

~

Poché grillé of
young pigeon with
foie gras sauce

~

Mango feuilletés with
strawberry sorbet

Born in Hong Kong in 1961, Ricky Cheung began his culinary career in his uncle's restaurant at the age of 14. The apprenticeship lasted ten years and gave Cheung a solid grounding in all the basics of cooking, letting him approach a move to the French dining room of the New World Hotel with confidence. In 1989 he moved to the Renaissance Hotel to work under Paul de Ruyster of London's Michelin-starred Le Gavroche, gaining valuable knowledge of classical French cuisine. After spending six years assisting de Ruyster, Cheung took over his position as sous chef, before going on to open Le Mieux bistro in 2005. Here Cheung produces dishes with French accuracy and grace, blended with an Asian consciousness of spice and flavor. He serves guests with an honest and refined menu that is continually influenced by the variety and diversity of produce and cuisine found in Hong Kong.

Nationalistic pride quite understandably claims exclusive authorship and authority over national cuisines, and while the techniques can competently be mastered by outsiders, cultural roots count. However, in Ricky's French cooking it is easy to forget that boundaries exist; nor do they matter, because in his food one finds bountiful energy, great generosity of spirit, and intensity of depth, brilliantly capped by his quirky imagination. Clichéd as this may sound, one can almost grasp the soul in Ricky's creations.

In Hong Kong, where some of the biggest internationally acclaimed superstar chefs take center stage, the story of a local boy brought up on street food making good as a master chef in French cuisine is unlikely to be taken seriously. Such titles have to be awarded by the establishment and protocol dictates that status must be earned through strict formalities. In this scenario the enlightened, happy, creative chef, conjuring marvels of tastes, simply basking in the pleasure of his guests as they appreciate his food, is quite another breed.

In Ricky's food one finds a complexity in the layering of experiences, a sense of play and delight, visually teasing, challenging and provoking the taste buds to surprise and reward, to chart a journey of search and discovery, as spiritual and as impressionistic as is tangibly possible. But it is the greatness of heart in his creations that truly exemplifies the cultural similarities between the French and the Chinese. In this his food stands apart, and one sees the master at his art.

Jacky Yu

Le Mieux Bistro, Hong Kong, China

1

1
Gazpacho aspic with crabmeat

2
Scallop carpaccio with
tuna tartare, uni, and
yuzu vinaigrette

3
Seafood ravioli with
Norwegian lobster, wilted
arugula, and tomato salsa

4
Poché grillé of young pigeon
with foie gras sauce

5
Mango feuilletés with
strawberry sorbet

GAZPACHO ASPIC WITH CRABMEAT
Serves 15

For the gazpacho
10 g garlic • 325 g cucumber, peeled and seeded • 325 g tomato, sliced • 75 g red bell pepper, sliced • 30 g onion, sliced • 175 g tomato juice • 25 g sherry vinegar • 60 g olive oil • 5 g salt • 3 g basil leaves • 3 g lemon juice

1 Combine all the ingredients and leave to marinate for 8 hours.
2 Puree in a blender, then pass through a fine-mesh sieve.

For the gazpacho aspic
13 gelatin leaves, soaked in ice water

1 Remove the soaked gelatin leaves from the ice water, place them in a glass bowl, set over simmering water to melt, then whisk in the gazpacho.
2 Pour the mixture into small shot glasses and place them in the fridge for 4 hours, until set.

To assemble
50 g red bell pepper, brunoised • 50 g yellow bell pepper, brunoised • 50 g cucumber, brunoised • salt and pepper • 200 g crabmeat

1 Season the vegetable brunoise with salt and pepper to taste.
2 Spoon them onto the gazpacho aspic, and top with crabmeat.

SCALLOP CARPACCIO WITH TUNA TARTARE, UNI, AND YUZU VINAIGRETTE
Serves 1

For the yuzu vinaigrette
20 g yuzu vinegar • 20 g lemon juice • 2 g sugar • 50 g olive oil

Combine all the ingredients and whisk well.

For the tuna tartare
50 g tuna, diced • grated zest of ¼ orange • salt and pepper

1 Mix together the diced tuna and orange zest.
2 Season with salt and pepper, put the tuna tartare into a tian (small mold) and store in the refrigerator.

For serving
1 scallop • 10 g baby spinach • 20 g uni (sea urchin) • salt and pepper • olive oil

1 Slice the scallop, then arrange on the plate.
2 Toss the baby spinach with salt, pepper and olive oil, then place in the middle of the scallop.
3 Unmould the tuna tartare and sit it on the baby spinach.
4 Top with uni, and drizzle the yuzu vinaigrette around the dish.

SEAFOOD RAVIOLI WITH NORWEGIAN LOBSTER, WILTED ARUGULA, AND TOMATO SALSA
Serves 1

For the seafood ravioli
50 g sole fillet • 15 g shrimp (prawns) • 10 g sea scallop • 30 g egg white • 100 g cream • salt and pepper • 50 g fresh pasta dough

1 Put the sole, shrimp, scallop, and egg white in a food processor and work for 2 minutes. Gradually add in the cream and work until you have a smooth mousse. Season the seafood mousse with salt and pepper.
2 Roll out the pasta dough to a thin rectangle sheet. Spoon a dollop of seafood mousse on one side of the pasta sheet, then fold the other side to cover the mousse. Use a fluted pastry cutter to cut out round ravioli.
3 Poach the ravioli in simmering water for 4 minutes, then remove and keep warm.

For the tomato salsa
1 plum tomato, skinned, de-seeded, chopped • 1 shallot, chopped • 20 g olive oil • lemon juice, to taste • salt and pepper

Combine all the ingredients and season to taste.

For the wilted arugula and Norwegian lobster
20 g arugula (rocket) • salt and pepper • 1 Norwegian lobster (langoustine)

1 Sauté the arugula in a little olive oil, then season.
2 Poach the Norwegian lobster in boiling salted water for 45 seconds, then remove and keep warm.

To serve
Place the ravioli in the center of the plate, top with wilted arugula and poached Norwegian lobster, and spoon the tomato salsa around.

POCHÉ GRILLÉ OF YOUNG PIGEON WITH FOIE GRAS SAUCE
Serves 1

For the bouillon
700 g chinese yellow rice wine • 10 g dried mandarin skin • 10 star anise seeds • 5 cloves • 2 cinnamon sticks • 20 g five-spice powder • 200 g fresh ginger, sliced • 100 g scallions (spring onions) • 10 g Szechuan pepper • 6 liters water • 200 g salt

Combine all the ingredients in a stock pot. Bring to a boil, then lower the heat and simmer for 1 hour.

For the foie gras sauce
200 g chicken stock • 100 g cream • 100 g duck foie gras • salt and pepper

1 Place the chicken stock, cream, and foie gras in a pan, simmer for 10 minutes, then puree in a blender.
2 Pass the sauce through a fine-mesh sieve.
3 Season with salt and pepper.

For the pigeon
1 pigeon • bouillon, for pan frying • olive oil, for pan-frying

1 Poach the pigeon in the bouillon for 45 minutes at 130°F (60°C), remove and pat dry.
2 Heat a film of olive oil in a pan, and cook the pigeon till golden on all sides.
3 Cut the breasts and legs off the carcass, and keep in a warm place.

For the garnishes
50 g spinach • olive oil, for pan-frying • salt and pepper • 1 spear asparagus • ½ plum tomato

1 Preheat the oven to 350°F (180°C).
2 Sauté the spinach in olive oil, and season with salt and pepper.
3 Roast the asparagus and tomato in the oven for 3 minutes.

To assemble
1 Slice the pigeon breast and fan out on the plate.
2 Sit the leg on top of the spinach, place the tomato and asparagus next to the spinach, and spoon the foie gras sauce around.

MANGO FEUILLETÉS WITH STRAWBERRY SORBET
Serves 1

For the mango pastry cream
20 g egg yolk • 10 g sugar • 5 g all-purpose (plain) flour • 100 g milk • 100 g mango puree

1 Whisk the egg yolk and sugar in a bowl until pale, sift in the flour and mix well.
2 Combine the milk and mango puree in a pan and bring to a boil.
3 Pour the boiling mango milk onto the egg mixture, stirring well. Pour the mixture back into the pan and cook over gentle heat, stirring continuously. Boil for 2 minutes. Remove from the heat, cover with plastic wrap (clingfilm), and let cool.

For the puff pastry base and top
100 g puff pastry dough • oil for greasing baking sheet

1 Roll out the pastry to a thickness of about 2 mm, then cut out 2 pieces 5 x 10 cm.
2 Place the pastry on a greased baking sheet and let it rest in the refrigerator for 1 hour.
3 Preheat the oven to 300°F (150°C).
4 Place a smaller baking sheet on top of the pastry, then bake for 25 minutes. Remove from the oven and cool on a wire rack.

For the strawberry sorbet
500 g strawberry puree • 150 g sugar • 80 g glucose • 10 g lemon juice • 250 g water

1 Combine all the ingredients and whisk well.
2 Pour the mixture into an ice-cream maker and run for 10 minutes until frozen (or follow the manufacturer's instructions).

To serve
diced mangos, for serving • raspberries, for serving

1 Use a pastry (piping) bag to pipe some mango cream on to one piece of cooked pastry, then place another piece on top.
2 Garnish the pastry top with diced mango and fresh raspberries.
3 Serve with a scoop of strawberry sorbet.

Ricky Cheung

Ryan worked for me between 2002 and 2008. I first met him while having lunch at Raymond Capaldi's restaurant, Fenix. From the moment Ryan came out of the kitchen to speak to me about a position at Vue de Monde (with his boss's consent) I knew that he was unique. What's special about Ryan's cooking is his ability to make something out of nothing. The most memorable occasions when I have eaten his food were when he cooked the staff meal—everything from the softest homemade goat cheese gnocchi with tomato fondue to great Asian salads with salty, sweet, sour, and crunchy components. His technical discipline is also a great asset, as he will practice and repeat the same steps time and again until he has achieved the desired outcome. Ryan's energy, hunger for greater knowledge and technique, together with his personal love of classic food, combine to make him one of the best chefs ever to have come through the Vue de Monde kitchen.

Ryan first worked in Australia in 1999; first at Walter's Wine Bar and then at Fenix. Before that he was at the famous Mirabelle in London with Marco Pierre White and then spent time at Flacon de Sel. A lot of Ryan's training also came from books. He has a ferocious appetite for new ways of creating and combining flavours and textures very much in the elBulli style. He has also been heavily influenced by Andoni Aduriz from Mugaritz in San Sebastián, Spain, after Andoni paid an afternoon visit to us at Vue de Monde back in 2007.

Ryan uses Asian flavours ever so slightly in his cooking, giving it a real sense of individuality. Don't get me wrong; his food is very much in the Euro/Spanish/French mold—but he cleverly uses the pepperiness of Vietnamese mint in a garnish, for example, or will season with yuzu juice instead of lemon to give more depth to the flavor balance of a dish. The experimental, unconventional method of matching small bites of food with cocktails is Ryan's latest venture, and this is unique in the Singapore market where Ryan is currently working. His all-time favorite dish is black pepper crab, so expect a variation of this at the Tippling Club.

Shannon Bennett

Ryan Clift was born in 1977 and began dishwashing at the age of 14 in his hometown of Devizes in Wiltshire, U.K. Inspired by the pace and energy of the kitchen, he made his way to culinary college, progressing from there to a two-year stay at Claridge's in London. Since then, Clift has worked with the likes of Marco Pierre White, Peter Gordon, Emmanuel Renault, and Raymond Capaldi. In 1999 Clift moved to Vue de Monde in Melbourne, working under Shannon Bennett and gaining an appreciation of the business side of a restaurant. Clift's time as a chef at Vue de Monde prompted a wave of recognition for his stylish cuisine. In 2008 he launched The Tippling Club in Singapore as head chef and co-owner with the aim of taking modern food and cocktail matching to a new level of sophistication.

MENU

Amuse bouche
Pizza puffs with tomato, mozzarella balloon, and basil

~

Surf clam dashi with basil seed, cucumber, and dashi broth

~

Butternut soup with whipped goat cheese, bitter chocolate, and celery shoots

~

62°C egg with dried bacon, Parmesan, tomato, and garlic bread

~

Razor clam with shemeiji mushroom fricassee, and porcini

~

Foie gras orange with green tea paint, pistachios, and green shiso

~

Black pepper frog with onion puree, basil jelly, and crispy chicken skin

~

Lobster pea with paella stock, garden peas, and fried basil

~

Vegetable garden with porcini soil and baby borage

~

Pork belly scallops with braised walnuts, grapes, and spiced pumpkin

~

Pre dessert
Strawberry with fresh cream, ripped mint, and strawberry milk shake

~

Snowball with sudachi, white chocolate, and yuzu curd

~

Chocolate pineapple with whipped chocolate mousse, corn ice cream, and saffron bubbles

~

Passionfruit cloud with basil ice cream and basil crumble

~

Cucumber coconut with peanut powder, and chocolate twist

Ryan Clift

1
Ryan Clift finishes a dish

2
Herbs and petals drying

3
Dishes being served
in the restaurant

4
Sketches for a new dish

The Tippling Club, Singapore

1
Butternut soup with whipped
goat cheese, bitter chocolate, and
celery shoots

2
62°C egg with dried bacon,
Parmesan, tomato, and garlic bread

3
Vegetable garden with porcini soil
and baby borage

84

BUTTERNUT SOUP WITH WHIPPED GOAT CHEESE, BITTER CHOCOLATE, AND CELERY SHOOTS
Serves 6

For the soup base
1 butternut squash • 30 ml olive oil • 1 onion, chopped • 2 cloves garlic, chopped • 1 liter chicken stock • 500 ml milk • 100 ml concentrated chicken stock

1 Grate the squash.
2 Heat the olive oil and sweat the onion and garlic until soft.
3 Add the grated squash.
4 Sweat for 2 minutes and add the remaining ingredients.
5 Cook everything and blend to a smooth consistency in a Thermomix.

For the cocoa crunchy pearls
100 g unsweetened cocoa • 100 g maltodextrin • 200 g olive oil

1 Place the cocoa and Maltodextrin in a mixing bowl.
2 Slowly add the olive oil drop by drop until the cocoa and Maltodextrin emulsify. Stop adding olive oil once small pearl shapes form.
3 Heat a nonstick skillet on medium heat and sauté the pearls until dry and crunchy.

For the whipped goat cheese
100 g goat cheese • 500 ml milk • 500 ml chicken stock • 2 g salt • 6.5 g soy lecithin

1 Cut the goat cheese into small pieces.
2 Warm the milk, chicken stock, and goat cheese together to 154°F (62°C).
3 Remove from the heat and add salt and the soy lecithin.
4 Use a hand blender to blend everything together until smooth.

For the cocoa jelly
500 ml chicken stock • 120 ml sherry vinegar • 100 g sugar • 80 g unsweetened cocoa • 8 g Iota

1 Put all the ingredients into a Thermomix.
2 Heat to 190°F (80°C) and blend until smooth.
3 Remove from the Thermomix, pour into the desired container and chill.

To assemble
unsalted butter, 300 g per liter • xanthan gum • 500 ml liquid nitrogen • small pieces goat cheese, to garnish • micro green celery shoots, to garnish

1 Add 300 g unsalted butter to every liter of soup.
2 Warm the soup until the butter dissolves, then add 2 g xanthan gum.

3 Chill the soup to room temperature.
4 Pour 500 ml liquid nitrogen into a pot and freeze a small ladle in it until no bubbles come out from under the ladle. (Liquid nitrogen should not be handled without training in how to use it safely.)
5 Dip the bottom of the frozen ladle into the soup to form a frozen soup bowl.
6 Remove the ladle from the soup and rest for 1 minute.
7 Gently remove the frozen soup bowl from the ladle, using the tip of your thumb.
8 Fill the frozen soup bowl with whipped goat cheese and place on top of a small piece of goat cheese to balance the bowl on the tile.
9 Garnish with diced goat cheese, cocoa crunchy pearls, micro green celery shoots, and cocoa jelly on the opposite side of the tile.

62°C EGG WITH DRIED BACON, PARMESAN, TOMATO, AND GARLIC BREAD
Serves 6

For the eggs
10 fresh eggs

1 Heat a water bath to 190°F (62°C) and keep at a constant temperature.
2 Gently add the eggs.
3 Once the temperature returns to 190°F (62°C), cook for 24 minutes.

For the pancetta chips
500 g pancetta • parchment paper

1 Preheat the oven to 340°F (170°C).
2 Remove the skin from the pancetta and slice thinly.
3 Neatly place the sliced pancetta flat in between 2 sheets of parchment paper.
4 Bake for 15 minutes, until crisp.

For the bacon mayonnaise
15 rashers bacon • 1 liter chicken stock • 4 cloves garlic • 500 ml cream • 5 egg whites • 5 sprigs thyme • 1 onion • 0.9 g xanthan gum • 0.9 g guar gum

1 Slice the onion and crush the garlic.
2 Put all the ingredients, except the egg whites, xantham gum, and guar gum, into a large pan.
3 Bring to a simmer and cook for 25 minutes.
4 Strain and cool the bacon stock.
5 Add the egg whites, xanthan gum, and guar gum while blending the bacon stock in a Thermomix.
6 Transfer into a siphon and charge it twice.

For the garlic bread
1 loaf sourdough bread • 50 ml olive oil • 4 sprigs thyme • 4 cloves garlic

1 Trim off the sourdough crust.
2 Slice the bread into 1-cm cubes.
3 Heat the olive oil in a pan and add the sourdough. Pan-fry until golden brown.
4 Add the thyme and garlic and pan-fry for 1 minute.

For the Parmesan chips
500 g Parmesan cheese

1 Preheat the oven to 340°F (170°C).
2 Grate the Parmesan evenly over a nonstick baking sheet.
3 Bake for 10 minutes or until golden brown.

To assemble
tomato powder • deep-fried thyme

1 Place some garlic bread, Parmesan chips, and pancetta chips on the side of a bowl.
2 Crack 1 egg into a separate bowl.
3 Using a slotted spoon, carefully scoop the egg into the bowl containing the garnish.
4 Garnish with bacon mayonnaise, tomato powder and thyme.

VEGETABLE GARDEN WITH PORCINI SOIL AND BABY BORAGE
Serves 6

For the vegetables
1 baby carrot • 1 baby fennel • ½ baby leek • 1 baby turnip • 1 stalk Thai asparagus

1 Blanch all the vegetables until cooked.
2 Remove from the water and keep warm.

For the confit cherry tomato
1 cherry tomato

1 Slice off the eye of the cherry tomato and halve it.
2 Place the cherry tomato on a silicone nonstick baking mat.
3 Place in a dehydrator at 190°F (80°C) for 82 minutes.
4 Let cool and store in oil.

For the celery root paper
1 celery root (celeriac)

1 Trim off the celery root skin.
2 Use a Japanese wheel mandolin to obtain a long sheet of celery root.
3 Trim the celery root sheet to your required size and blanch for 20 seconds.
4 Refresh in ice water and pat dry.

For the asparagus puree
80 ml olive oil • 1 onion, diced • 500 g asparagus, chopped • 3 cloves garlic, crushed • 120 g butter • salt and pepper • 0.6 g xanthan gum • 0.6 g guar gum

1 Heat the olive oil in a skillet and sauté the onion, asparagus, and garlic.
2 Add the butter and seasoning when they are 80% cooked.
3 Place the mixture in a Thermomix and blend until smooth.

For the chicken juice emulsion
1 liter chicken stock • 100 g thyme • 20 g butter • 10 g truffle oil

1 Reduce the chicken stock with the thyme on low heat until one-third is left.
2 Let cool.
3 Just before serving, warm the chicken juice, add the butter and truffle oil, and emulsify.

For the porcini soil
300 g all-purpose (plain) flour • 80 g confectioners' (icing) sugar • 180 g porcini powder • 3 g salt • 400 g butter, softened

1 Sift the flour and mix all the dry ingredients together.
2 Add butter to form a dough.
3 Place 200 g of the porcini dough on plastic wrap (clingfilm) and roll into a cylindrical shape.
4 Place in the freezer, and when frozen, preheat the oven to 200°F (100°C).
5 Remove from the plastic wrap.
6 Grate the frozen porcini dough over a silicone nonstick baking mat and bake for 20 minutes.

For the pickled shimeiji mushroom
50 g shimeiji mushrooms • 100 g sherry vinegar • 100 ml olive oil • 1 clove garlic, crushed • salt and pepper, to taste

1 Mix all the ingredients together.
2 Marinate the mushrooms 30 minutes before service.

To assemble
sliced baby radishes, to serve • borage shoots, to serve

1 Put all the vegetables into a sous-vide bag with 20 g chicken emulsion.
2 Heat the asparagus puree and place 1 tablespoon in the center of the plate.
3 Remove all the vegetables from the sous-vide bag.
4 Arrange them neatly onto the asparagus puree together with some sliced baby red radish.
5 Place the celery root paper on the vegetables and cover with porcini soil to resemble a garden.
6 Garnish with the pickled mushroom and borage shoots.

Ryan Clift

1 & 4
Mauro Colagreco
plating dishes

2
Choosing produce at
a fish market

3
Buying tomatoes at the
vegetable stall

Mauro Colagreco

MENU

Salad of mixed beans with
trumpet zucchini, cherries,
and pistachio vinaigrette

~

Porcini carpaccio, quinoa,
and white caviar

~

Fava stew with peas,
mangetout, and
nasturtium flowers

~

Roasted white asparagus,
hazelnut mousseline,
absinthe, and wild
strawberries

~

Sea bass from the
Menton coast, celery root
mousseline puree, wild
sorrel, and smoked sauce

~

Milk leaf, light sage
mousse, chocolate bursts,
and burnt milk ice cream

Born to an Italian family in Buenos Aires in 1976, Mauro Colagreco studied cuisine after a move to Paris. He worked for Bernard Loiseau in 2002, which led to a position as sous-chef to Alain Passard the following year, whose high standards, absolute respect for the product, and sense of freedom impressed Colagreco and ensured that Passard would be a lifelong influence. Colagreco went on to work with Alain Ducasse at the Plaza Athénée, later becoming chef at Guy Martin's Le Grand Véfour in 2005. In 2006 he realized his dream of opening his own restaurant, Mirazur, in the small town of Menton on the French Riviera. Here Colagreco harnesses the possibilities inherent in the landscape, relying on what he can grow and gather to use in daring flavor combinations, resulting in recipes such as the delicately fresh and acidic tomato martini with saffron oil and wildflowers. His fresh, defined dishes won Mirazur its first Michelin star in 2007.

Mauro's restaurant Mirazur only opened in 2006, so, for lack of a better word, it is still an infant. However, when I ate there in 2007 it certainly felt like a young restaurant, but I would never have imagined that the place was only one year old. I was amazed to hear from Mauro that he and his front-of-house manager, Alain, had put all their dreams and money into this project. To embark on a venture of this kind without a financial backer takes a great deal of courage.

That courage is also something that you feel in Mauro's cooking. He is one of those chefs who relies on top-quality produce, and who therefore always seem to work with nature rather than against it. I was especially struck by the excellent fish and shellfish.

Mauro also has the courage to put a few top ingredients on a plate and let them take center stage. A good example is his famous sea bass, cooked to perfection and served with a lightly smoked sauce. When Mauro's brilliant mind is applied to this great produce the result is light, imaginative, and honest cuisine. Here, perhaps his mentor Alain Passard plays a part. Nevertheless, Mauro's gastronomic creations always demonstrate a very clear personal touch. He has already gained his first Michelin star, and been voted by Gault Millau one of the top chefs of tomorrow. In 2009 Mirazur entered the list of the world's 50 best restaurants, as published by the British magazine *Restaurant* at number 35. Mauro has really started to conquer the world.

René Redzepi

SALAD OF MIXED BEANS, TRUMPET ZUCCHINI, CHERRIES, AND PISTACHIO VINAIGRETTE
Serves 4

For the bean salad
200 g flat beans • 100 g lima beans (butter beans) • 100 g thin green beans • 100 g red and white cherries • 1 trumpet zucchini (courgette) • olive oil, for dressing the beans • white balsamic vinegar, for the vinaigrette • 50 g roasted pistachios • 1 shallot • 1 small piece of ginger • fleur de sel • 8 oxalis leaves, and 8 flowers common chickweed

1 Cook the beans in boiling salted water and refresh in ice water.
2 Pit the cherries and set aside in the refrigerator.
3 Thinly slice the zucchini with a mandolin.
4 Make a vinaigrette with the olive oil, white balsamic vinegar, and roasted pistachios. Finely dice the shallot and add to the vinaigrette.
5 Chop the ginger. Mix the beans with the chopped ginger, olive oil, and fleur de sel.
6 Arrange the beans in a plate to create volume, add the zucchini slices, cherries, oxalis leaves, flowers, and chickweed, and finish with the pistachio vinaigrette.

PORCINI CARPACCIO, QUINOA, AND WHITE CAVIAR
Serves 4

30 g heavy (double) cream • 100 g Parmesan cheese • 1 bunch flat-leaf parsley • 80 g butter • salt • 200 g quinoa • 8 medium porcini (ceps) • 20 arugula (rocket) leaves • 12 small sprigs of yarrow • 16 arugula (rocket) flowers • 12 g snail caviar • olive oil • fleur de sel

1 Make a Parmesan cream by heating the heavy cream to 150°F (70°C), pouring over the Parmesan and mixing in a blender.
2 Now make a green emulsion. Separate the parsley leaves from the stalks and wash the leaves. Bring 200 ml water and 50 g butter to a boil, pour over the parsley in a blender and whiz. Season with salt.
3 Heat the butter in a saucepan until it turns golden brown, add the quinoa and stir until the grains are transparent. Add the Parmesan cream, moisten with a small ladleful of water, cover with a circle of parchment paper and cook over low heat. Add water a little at a time until the quinoa is cooked. Set aside in a warm place.
4 Slice the porcini into thin shavings.
5 Place the quinoa in a dome in the center of the plate.
6 Cover with the porcini carpaccio, starting in the center of the plate to give the porcini volume.
7 Arrange the arugula, its flowers and the yarrow on the plate. Mix the snail caviar with a little olive oil and add to the plate.
8 Just before serving, season with fleur de sel and olive oil.
9 Emulsify the parsley mixture and place spoonful of foam around the carpaccio.

ROASTED WHITE ASPARAGUS, HAZELNUT MOUSSELINE, ABSINTHE, AND WILD STRAWBERRIES
Serves 4

120 g sugar • 100 ml Banyuls vinegar • 22 wild strawberries, • 100 g hazelnuts from Piedmont, roasted • 200 ml milk • 30 g black sesame seeds • 30 g hazelnuts • 5 g fleur de sel • 200 g unsalted butter • 5 g star anise • 5 g orange zest • 8 large white asparagus spears

• 12 small sprigs absinthe • 8 wild strawberries to dress the plate • 8 hazelnuts from Piedmont, roasted and halved, to dress the plate • strawberry flowers, to serve

1 To make a strawberry gastrique, heat the sugar in a pan until it turns to caramel, and deglaze with the Banyuls vinegar.
2 Add 22 wild strawberries. Cook for 10 minutes. Strain. Boil until the mixture is reduced to a thick syrup.
3 To make the hazelnut mousseline, crush the 100 g Piedmont hazelnuts and cook with the milk for 15 minutes.
4 Blend to form a thick, smooth cream.
5 To make a gomasio, roast the black sesame seeds and 30 g hazelnuts in a skillet over low heat.
6 Finely chop with a knife, and add the fleur de sel.
7 In a sauté pan, melt the butter with the star anise and orange zest. Cook the asparagus spears over low heat, letting them brown lightly.
8 To serve, draw stripes with the strawberry gastrique and a teardrop shape with the hazelnut cream. Sprinkle the asparagus with gomasio and place them in the center of the plate. Arrange the absinthe sprigs, wild strawberries, halved Piedmont hazelnuts, and strawberry flowers around the slate.

SEA BASS FROM THE MENTON COAST, CELERY ROOT MOUSSELINE PUREE, WILD SORREL, AND SMOKED SAUCE
Serves 4

1 kg dog cockles • 130 g butter • 200 g celery root (celeriac) • 500 ml whole milk • 4 sea bass fillets, each weighing about 80 g • olive oil, for pan-frying • 80 g wild sorrel • fleur de sel • small wild sorrel leaves

1 Put 325 ml water in a pan, add the dog cockles and bring to a boil, discarding any that fail to open. Save the cooking liquid (1 liter of liquid for 3 kilograms of cockles).
2 Add 30 g butter to the liquid and let it melt.
3 Place some sawdust in a flameproof dish and heat in the oven. When the sawdust is very hot, carefully light it with a match so that it burns out. Cover the dish with aluminum foil, piercing it to let the smoke through.
4 Place the dog cockles in their juice in the oven for 1 hour with the smoking sawdust. Taste and smoke for a little longer if necessary. Strain the smoked juices and emulsify with a hand blender just before serving.
5 Sweat the celery root with the remaining 100 g butter, add the milk and cook for 20 minutes. Blend to obtain a very smooth mousseline.
6 Cook the sea bass fillets in a sauté pan with a little olive oil.
7 Wilt the sorrel in olive oil over high heat for a few moments just before serving the dish.
8 To serve, place a quenelle of celery root mousseline in the bottom of a shallow bowl, add the sorrel, pour the smoked emulsified sauce onto it and top with the sea bass. Finish with fleur de sel and a few wild sorrel leaves.

MILK LEAF, LIGHT SAGE MOUSSE, CHOCOLATE BURSTS, AND BURNT MILK ICE CREAM
Serves 4

For the milk leaf
500 ml whole milk • 500 ml heavy (double) cream

1 Pour the milk and cream into a shallow dish and place this in a bain-marie.

2 Wait until a skin forms on the surface, then skim off this skin with a stick and spread it as thinly as possible on a silicone non-stick baking mat. Make three layers and dry the milk leaf in a dehydrator.

For the light sage mousse
150 ml cream • 50 g milk • sage from the garden, to taste • 50 g white chocolate • 1 gelatin leaf • 50 g white chocolate

1 Heat the cream with the milk and infuse the sage in this mixture for at least 15 minutes.
2 Strain through a fine-mesh sieve, warm the mixture again and incorporate the white chocolate, then the gelatin.

For the chocolate bursts
65 g butter • 35 g confectioners' (icing) sugar • 1 tsp instant coffee powder • 20 g unsweetened cocoa • 1 egg yolk • 100 g all-purpose (plain) flour, sifted

1 Preheat the oven to 340°F (170°C)
2 Rub together the butter and confectioners' sugar, then add the instant coffee powder and cocoa.
3 Add the egg yolk and sifted flour.
4 Shape this mixture into small balls and cook on the silicone non-stick baking mat for 8 minutes.

For the burnt milk ice cream
300 ml milk • 50 ml cream • 1 egg yolk • 30 g white sugar • 4 g stabilizer • 5 g glucose

1 Warm 200 ml of the milk, emulsify and burn the foam under the broiler (grill). Repeat this operation, transferring the burnt foam to a bowl each time.
2 Heat the remaining 100 ml milk with the cream, egg yolk, sugar, stabilizer, and glucose to 170°F (84°C). Incorporate the burnt milk, blend and strain. Transfer to an ice-cream maker.

For the caramel toffee
50 g white sugar • 35 g heavy (double) cream • 10 g butter • fleur de sel

1 Gently heat the sugar in a pan to make a dry caramel. Add the cream and bring to a boil.
2 Stir in the butter and finally add fleur de sel.

To serve
1 On a slate, draw stripes of caramel toffee all the way across.
2 Stack the milk leaves with the sage mousse like a mille feuille, making three layers of each.
3 Add a quenelle of ice cream and sprinkle chocolate bursts over the slate.

1
Salad of mixed beans, trumpet zucchini, cherries, and pistachio vinaigrette

2
Porcini carpaccio, quinoa, and white caviar

3
Roasted white asparagus, hazelnut mousseline, absinthe, and wild strawberries

4
Sea bass from the Menton coast, celery root mousseline puree, wild sorrel, and smoked sauce

5
Milk leaf, light sage mousse, chocolate bursts, and burnt milk ice cream

3

4

5

Mauro Colagreco

Do you know the Winnie-the-Pooh books? I'm suddenly reminded of the tiger character who exudes such enthusiasm and bounce. Chris Cosentino is the Tigger of the offal world.

I feel I have a kindred spirit in Chris; I don't think we so much met as naturally gravitated, giving a talk together once in New York. We're both known for offal (it's a strange thing to be known for), and a short while ago I happened to be in San Francisco for one of Chris's offal feasts at Incanto. A whole evening devoted to innards and extremities—what a happy gathering of like-minded folks it was. He puts me to shame; I may bang on a bit about nose-to-tail eating, but this gentleman lives the project. He even produced for us a dessert made with blood! At the same time as running his restaurant, he does nonstop cycling races, which seem to go on for days. You can't keep a good chef down; all this energy finds its way into his rigorous approach and fantastic menu.

Chris does a fabulous job of both branching out into new dishes (most recently experimenting with cured meats, such as lardo and coppa) and resurrecting ancient recipes, dusting them off, and giving them a new lease on life. People who come to my restaurant often say they'd like to bring their grandparents, which I take to be a compliment. If it was good 100 years ago, why shouldn't it—after a bit of tinkering—be good now? Chris is part of food's enduring tradition, a tradition that may be flexible, but doesn't change with every wind. Chris's cooking boils down to good eating, a project that makes more and more sense in an altered world. Eating all of the animal is simply polite, and can only have a happy effect on the planet.

Fergus Henderson

Chris Cosentino was born in 1973 in Newport, Rhode Island, and spent his childhood years clamming, involved in commercial fishing, and cranking the pasta machine in his great-grandmother's kitchen. Chris honed his skills in the kitchens of Rubicon and Chez Panisse, among others, and in 2002 took his first executive chef post at Incanto restaurant in San Francisco. A trusted group of suppliers has developed around the restaurant, in line with Cosentino's rigorous principles on the humane treatment of animals. The rustic Italian fare served at Incanto upholds culinary traditions as well as socially responsible practices. Cosentino continues to experiment and develop his menu, co-creating in 2007 Boccalone, an artisanal salumi line. His abiding passion for offal has led him to work on the definitive cookbook on the subject, distilling the years of experience that have made Incanto a shrine to nose-to-tail eating.

MENU

Crispy sweetbread and warm beef tendon with chiles and mint
Prosecco di Valdobbiadene Brut, Bortolomiol

~

Sicilian lamb spleen bruschetta, Caciocavallo, and salsa picante
Soave Classico Superiore La Rocca, Pieropan 2005

~

Chris' Last Meal: Boccalone sanguinaccio, duck egg, and warm oysters
Dolcetto d'Alba Pra di Pò, Germano Ettore 2006

~

Whole roasted spring lamb neck with sheep's milk polenta and gremolata
Barbera d'Asti Ca' di Pian, La Spinetta 2004

~

Candied cockscombs with cherries and vanilla rice pudding
Brachetto d'Acqui Rosa Regale, Banfi 2006

1
Chris Consentino with a friend

2–4
In the kitchen at Incanto

5
Chris with diners at the restaurant

Chris Cosentino

Incanto, San Francisco, CA, USA

1

2

1
Chris' Last Meal:
Boccalone sanguinaccio,
duck egg, and warm oysters

2
Whole roasted
spring lamb neck
with sheep's milk polenta
and gremolata

3
Candied cockscombs
with cherries and vanilla
rice pudding

3

CHRIS' LAST MEAL: BOCCALONE SANGUINACCIO, DUCK EGG, AND WARM OYSTERS

Serves 6

6 links of Boccalone sanguinaccio • butter, for frying • 500 ml rich pork stock • 24 oysters, shucked • 6 duck eggs • 2 tbsp finely chopped chives

1 Preheat oven to 350°F (180°C).
2 Start the blood sausages in a cold ovenproof pan with 2 tablespoon of butter, place over moderate heat and cook (very high heat will cause sausage casings to burst). Once there is color on one side, flip over and place in the oven.
3 While the sausages are cooking, fry the eggs sunny side up.
4 When they are ready, place 1 egg on each of 6 warm plates, then top with 1 sausage.
5 Deglaze the sausage pan with the pork stock, add the oysters, let simmer for 1 minute with 1 teaspoon of butter. Add the chives, then season to taste. Divide the oysters among the 6 plates.

WHOLE ROASTED SPRING LAMB NECK WITH SHEEP'S MILK POLENTA AND GREMOLATA

Serves 6

For the roasted lambs' necks
2 lemons • about 1 head's worth garlic cloves, plus 2 cloves, slivered, for sautéing the rapini • 2 bunches fennel fronds • 250 ml extra-virgin olive oil • salt • 1 tbsp coarsely ground black pepper • 6 (900-g) lambs' necks • 2 tablespoons olive oil • 2 bunches rapini

1 In a food processor fitted with a grinding or fine-chopping attachment, combine the lemons, garlic, and fennel fronds with the olive oil and black pepper, and grind together to make a marinade. Season the necks with salt and pepper, rub with the marinade, and let stand in the refrigerator overnight.
2 Preheat the oven to 200°F (100°C). Place the lamb necks in a roasting pan and bake for 6 hours, or until tender.
3 Heat the olive oil over medium heat. Add the rapini and 2 cloves garlic, and sauté until tender.

For the creamy polenta
150 g coarse-ground polenta • 1 liter water • 500 ml whole milk • 250 ml sheep's milk whey (if whey is unavailable, use sheep's milk) • 115 g unsalted butter • 120 g mascarpone cheese • 85 g pecorino Romano cheese, grated • 1 tbsp kosher salt • black pepper, to taste

1 Combine the polenta and water in a heavy-bottomed pot and bring to a simmer slowly over medium heat. Be sure to stir the polenta constantly so it doesn't stick to the pan.
2 Once the water has been absorbed, slowly add the milk, 120 ml at a time, until it is all absorbed. Cook for about 45 minutes, until the polenta gains a creamy consistency.
3 Add the butter and mascarpone and cook for 15 minutes more, constantly whisking, then add the pecorino. Remove from the heat.
4 Taste and adjust the seasoning to your liking. If the polenta gets too thick, add more milk to adjust the consistency.

For the gremolata
1 handful picked parsley • 1 handful picked mint • 1 handful picked chervil • 1 handful picked tarragon • zest of 2 lemons • 2 tbsp grated fresh horseradish (or more to taste) • salt • black pepper • extra-virgin olive oil, to coat

Mix the herbs, lemon zest, and horseradish. Season with salt and pepper, then add extra-virgin olive oil to coat.

To serve
Place a pool of polenta on each plate. Top with rapini and then one lamb's neck per plate. Garnish with gremolata

CANDIED COCKSCOMBS WITH CHERRIES AND VANILLA RICE PUDDING

Serves 6

For the cockscombs
12 cockscombs • 2 vanilla beans, including scrapings and pods • 1.8 kg sugar • 750 ml cherry puree • 2 lemons, juiced

1 Place the cockscombs with 2 liters of cold water and one vanilla bean in a heavy-bottomed stock pot and bring to a boil. Add half the sugar to the water and stir to dissolve. Cook the combs at a moderate simmer, skimming any scum off surface of water, until they are cooked through and soft, approximately 2 hours.
2 Meanwhile, prepare a simple syrup by combining the remaining sugar, vanilla bean, and 1 liter of water in a heavy stockpot over high heat, stirring until sugar is dissolved. Whisk the cherry puree into the syrup and adjust the flavor with some of the lemon juice. Remove from heat and set aside until the combs are cooked.

3 Carefully drain and rinse the combs of any residue. Heat the cherry syrup to just below a simmer and add the combs. Stir well and leave over a very gentle heat for 30–45 minutes, stirring occasionally.
4 Remove from the heat and store the combs in the cherry syrup. For best results, prepare the cockscombs a few hours before serving or the night before.

For the rice pudding
225 g short-grain Italian rice (arborio or carnaroli) • 1.44 liters whole milk • 1 vanilla bean, including scrapings and pod • 1 bay leaf • 55 g sugar • 250 ml cream

1 Place the rice, milk, vanilla bean, and bay leaf in a heavy-bottomed, nonreactive pot. Cover and bring to a boil, stirring occasionally. With the cover still on, turn the heat to low and cook, stirring every few minutes to ensure rice does not stick to the bottom, until rice has achieved the desired consistency, or for approximately 20–30 minutes. Remove from heat.
2 Remove the bay leaf and vanilla bean, and stir in the sugar. Pour into a container and cover with plastic wrap (clingfilm) directly on the surface. Refrigerate until set.
3 When ready to serve, slowly stir in the cream until the pudding is loose but will still hold some shape on a plate or in a bowl.

To serve
1 bunch Bing cherries • 1 bunch Rainier cherries

Place a few heaping spoonfuls of rice pudding in the center of a dessert plate. Take two warm cockscombs and arrange in a slight fan on top of the pudding. Garnish with a few halved and pitted cherries, and sauce with some reduced cooking liquid.

Note: Cherries maybe substituted by many varieties of fruit, such as strawberries, citrus fruits, or pomegranates, with equally good results.

Chris Cosentino

Restaurant Piazza Duomo lies in the heart of Piedmont, in the white truffle capital of the world, the city of Alba. It's right in the main square—surprisingly called Piazza Duomo!

I ate at Enrico's restaurant in 2006, and remember that I booked a table without really knowing anything about the chef, the restaurant, or the cuisine. I had just heard that it was a good restaurant in the region, with a fairly new chef, and I happened to be close by, attending the Slow Food convention in Turin. Since it was truffle season, I decided to book my table there and drive all the way from Turin to Alba.

Sometimes when you have no expectations you enter a given experience with a very open mind, and this was what happened to me and my friend that day in autumn 2006. We were completely overwhelmed by the place, the staff, and the energy we felt immediately on entering the restaurant. Furthermore, we were given several surprises throughout our four-hour Tour de Force of a lunch, with exceptional ingredients, outstanding preparations, beautiful platings, and fantastic tastes.

That day was one of the most memorable dining experiences of my life. What I found there was Italian cuisine made from the best, most flavorful Italian ingredients, transformed into light, innovative succulent dishes that for me reflected modern Italian cuisine but were still minimalistic.

Since then, I have found out that Enrico has spent a significant amount of time in Japan, studying the cuisine and working in the kitchens. Since I learned this, my experience at Piazza Duomo makes even more sense.

Enrico has the most positive energy surrounding him. He is always in a good mood. (Although I admit I'm saying this without interviewing his apprentices or a chef who overcooked the pasta on any given night.) He strikes me as a very open-minded person who has a gift for taking the best from his country's culinary world and combining it with his own brilliant mind and Japanese aesthetics, creating a cuisine where everything seems to come together.

René Redzepi

Enrico Crippa was born in Carate Brianza, Italy, in 1971. He began his career in food under Gualtiero Marchesi at his eponymous Milan restaurant, at the age of 16. He went on to train in some of the finest kitchens in Europe, working under Christian Willer at the Palme d'Or in Cannes, Gislaine Arabian at Ledoyen in Paris, Antoine Westermann at Buerehiesel in Strasbourg, Michel Bras at Laguiole, and Ferran Adrià at elBulli. The range and class of Crippa's experience lent him a sound knowledge of cutting-edge technique and expertise in classic cuisine. At 25, he left for Japan and spent three years as executive chef at Gualtiero Marchesi's Kobe restaurant and the Rihga Royal Hotel in Osaka. Returning to Italy with an appreciation of the purity and finesse of Japanese cooking, Crippa went on to establish the Ristorante Piazza Duomo, Alba, in 2003, where he serves classic Italian dishes reinterpreted with lightness and precision.

MENU

Salad 21, 31, 41

Royal sea bream with green apple sauce

~

Candied mackerel with thinly sliced white turnips, and Oriental cilantro

~

Nigiri rice pasta with tuna fish

~

Red jumbo shrimp from San Remo, accompanied by wine must

~

Potato purée from Alta Langa, quail egg, and Lapsang Souchong tea

~

Smoked herring and tuna consommé, quinoa, chestnuts, and foie gras

~

Potato gnocchi stuffed with Seirass cheese

~

Oriental rice with trout, miso, and vanilla

~

Fried scampi or fried fish

~

Sambucano loin of lamb roasted with fresh goat-cheese

~

Vanilla pain perdu

Enrico Crippa

1, 4 & 5
Enrico Crippa in the kitchen

2
A chef at the stove

3
Preparing chickens at
Piazza Duomo

Restaurant Piazza Duomo, Alba, Italy

1
Salad 21, 31, 41

2
Nigiri rice pasta
with tuna

3
Red jumbo shrimp from
San Remo, accompanied
by wine must

4
Potato gnocchi stuffed
with Seirass cheese

SALAD 21, 31, 41
Serves 4

For the wafers of fried cockscomb
200 g cockscomb seeds • 13 g bonito shavings • 1.2 liters water • Oil, for cooking

1 Cook the cockscomb seeds like a risotto in a pan with water and the bonito for 40 minutes, without salt.
2 Once cooked, leave to dry between 2 pieces of wax (greaseproof) paper. When they are dry, break into irregular pieces and fry them in cooking oil until crisp.

For the herb oil
500 g herbs, such as parsley or tarragon • 1 liter extra-virgin olive oil

Blanch the aromatic herbs in hot water for 10 seconds, drain well, and mix all together. Filter the oil through a sieve.

For the salad
160 g of mixed salad and herbs, such as: Gentilina, perilla, mâche, crespino, poppy, dandelion, primula, spinach, Treviso radicchio, trusset, red Swiss chard, beet leaves, tarragon, burnet, sorrel, savory, marjoram, red mizuna, green mizuna, mustard, chervil, chickweed, wild celery leaves, lovage, buon Enrico, green shiso, red shiso, dill, wild fennel, and nasturtium

Clean and wash salad and herbs well and toss together.

For the dressing
herb oil, to taste • Barolo vinegar, to taste • black and white sesame seeds, to taste • finely chopped seaweed, to taste • katsuobushi, to taste • candied ginger and juice of ginger, to taste

Combine the herb oil with the Barolo vinegar and add the remaining dressing ingredients.

To serve
Flowers, such as calendula, violets, primulas, borage, fiordaliso, chives and garlic

Season the salad with the dressing and place on a plate. Arrange the wafers on the salad. Place the flower petals on the salad.

NIGIRI RICE PASTA WITH TUNA
Serves 4

For the maccheroncini
32 maccheroncini pasta • 100 g carpione (a traditional Italian marinade for fish made with onion, carrots, celery, and vinegar) • 1.7 g Kappa

1 Cook the maccheroncini in boiling salted water for 10 minutes. Once cooked, drain and place on a large plate, then shape into a cylinder while it is still warm.
2 Bring the carpione to a boil and add the Kappa. Cover with plastic wrap (clingfilm) while still hot. When cold, slice into pieces the same size as the tuna. The carpione gives the pasta the right sweet-and-sour flavor and helps hold it all together.

For the tuna
About 200 g good-quality tuna

Cut the tuna into rectangular slices 3 mm thick, 7 cm long, and 4 cm wide.

To serve
black sesame seeds • marigold flowers • dried red shiso flowers • fresh green and red shiso flower • green herb oil • extra-virgin olive oil • Maldon salt

Place 2 pieces of pasta on each plate and half-cover with the tuna slices. Garnish with black sesame seeds, marigold and shiso flowers, herb oil, extra-virgin olive oil, and Maldon salt.

RED JUMBO SHRIMP FROM SAN REMO ACCOMPANIED BY WINE MUST
Serves 4

For the jumbo shrimp
4 fresh San Remo jumbo shrimp (prawns) • 12 grapes, cut in half • 1 tbsp tangerine (mandarin) juice • 1 tbsp oil • Maldon salt • dry shiso flowers, to taste

Wash and clean the shrimp, and place in a large dish with the grapes, mandarin juice, oil, salt, and dried shiso flowers, and marinate, refrigerated.

For the wine must
100 g sweet grapes • 1 pinch ascorbic acid

Blend together the sweet grapes, but only briefly, as the seeds will create a bitter taste. Pass the juice through a sieve and add the ascorbic acid. Keep refrigerated.

For the cream
1.5 g agar agar • 400 g grapes

Heat the agar agar to 195°F (90°C), chill in the refrigerator, then blend with the grapes. Keep refrigerated.

To serve
sprouted leaves of red and green shiso flowers • 1 large green shiso flower leaf • burnet leaves • dried yogurt powder • dried grape must powder • salt • extra-virgin olive oil • tangerine (mandarin) peel

Place a drop of wine must on a flat plate, then put a jumbo shrimp on top. Glaze the shrimp with wine must and decorate with the herbs, grapes and flowers.

POTATO GNOCCHI STUFFED WITH SEIRASS CHEESE
Serves 4

For the gnocchi
1 kg potatoes • 1 egg yolk • 300 g flour • 50 g Parmesan cheese • 15 g salt

1 Cook the potatoes (with skin on) in boiling water. Once cooked, peel the skin off and mash with a potato masher.
2 Add the egg yolk and slowly add the rest of the ingredients. Once mixed and kneaded together, let rest for 20 minutes.

For the stuffing
300 g Seirass cheese • milk, to taste • salt and pepper

1 Mix together the cheese with a little milk to make a stuffing. Season with salt and pepper.
2 Shape the gnocchi like ravioli, stuff it with the cheese stuffing, and seal it closed.

To serve
100 g porcini (cep) mushrooms, pan-fried • 4 tbsp meat jus or stock • olive oil

Cook the gnocchi (6 per person) in salted boiling water and serve with the meat jus, olive oil and porcini mushrooms.

Enrico Crippa

There are not many people I would trust to put a sticky dark round ball of something called "snus" under my top lip; in fact, Mathias Dahlgren may be the only person. (In case you were wondering, it turned out to be a strange, tarlike Swedish tobacco, so strong that it made my ears and toes tingle.) On our visit to his restaurant in Stockholm, Mathias welcomed us into his kitchen, and we cooked a lunch and a supper together. This struck me as remarkable, as kitchens are often apt to become slightly territorial places. To let other chefs run amok in one's kitchen—such charm is rarely seen.

To top it all, we were fed beautifully. The meal was delicious, Scandinavian in the best way, a product of Mathias' childhood and his feel for his national cuisine. Mathias presides over a traditional restaurant and a more relaxed dining hall next door where we sampled his cooking. The bar's menu has two sides, one offering only Swedish eatables and the other boasting tidbits picked from all over the world. Dishes arrive as small portions, intended for diners to order gradually, rather as you might buy rounds of drinks in a bar. The contrast between food turned out with beauty and exactitude, and easing up on the strict conventions for eating it, seems to encapsulate Mathias' very Scandinavian project. A happy combination of tradition and innovation defines this set-up, complemented by the thoughtfulness and precision that really come through in Mathias's menu. You can trace these qualities back to his kitchen, which boasts some beautiful handmade knives.

To me, anyone who thinks béchamel sauce is under-rated is a fine judge, and Mathias treated his perfectly—thick, but also silky and delicious. He is a chef with wise theories on everything, a true visionary.

Fergus Henderson

Mathias Dahlgren was born in 1969 near Umeå, Sweden, and trained at a traditional culinary school before opening the restaurant F12 with two friends. In 1996 he went on to open Bon Lloc, which won a Michelin star a year later. Serving a fusion of Catalan, Tuscan, Mexican, Oriental, Californian, and Swedish dishes, Dahlgren honed his technique and achieved widespread acclaim. In 2007 he opened his twin restaurants, Matbaren ("Food Bar") and Matsalen ("Dining Room"), in the Grand Hôtel, Stockholm. In 2009 they received a total of three Michelin stars, a testament to Dahlgren's loving and rigorous attention to sourcing the most seasonal, local ingredients possible. Dishes such as "Soup from theAtlantic," organic foie gras terrine with white mushrooms and summer truffles, or sorbet of plums on frozen flowers are served in a fine-dining setting in Matsalen, and informally to order in Matbaren, but always achieve perfection in taste and technique.

MENU

Tartare of beef and oyster

~

Swedish rye bread

~

Sorbets of sea buckthorn and Arctic angelica

~

Toast ice cream and Svezia cheese crème with thin sticks of Gotlandslimpa bread

~

Baked chocolate with toffee ice cream, caramelized nuts, caramel sauce, brown butter, and hung sour cream

1
Natural fats

2
Fresh herring

3
Mathias Dahlgren preparing ingredients in the "cold kitchen"

4
Working on a new dish

Mathias Dahlgren

1
2

3

4

Restaurant Mathias Dahlgren, Stockholm, Sweden

1
Swedish rye bread

2
Sorbets of sea buckthorn
and Arctic angelica

3
Toast ice cream and
Svezia cheese crème with thin
sticks of Gotlandslimpa bread

4
Baked chocolate with toffee ice
cream, caramelized nuts,
caramel sauce, brown butter,
and hung sour cream

SWEDISH RYE BREAD
Makes 10 (400-g) loaves

Day 1
1 kg water • 375 g crushed rye grains • 130 g coarse rye flour • 250 g sunflower seeds • 160 g linseeds • 54 g salt • 200 g rye sourdough starter

Mix all the ingredients together and let stand at room temperature until the next day.

Day 2
500 g water • 100 g yeast • 420 g molasses (dark treacle) • 400 g wheat flour • 150 g rye flour, sifted • 550 g rye flour, unsifted

1 Mix all the ingredients with yesterday's starter in a dough mixer for approximately 12 minutes at low speed.
2 Divide the dough into 10 (400-g) loaves. Let rise in a warm place for 45 minutes.
3 Preheat the oven to 425°F (220°C).
4 Bake with a little steam for the first few minutes. Lower the temperature to 365°F (185°C) and bake for 40 minutes more, opening the oven vent after the first 5 minutes.
5 Turn out the loaves immediately after baking and let them cool on a wire rack.

SORBETS OF SEA BUCKTHORN AND ARCTIC ANGELICA
Makes 15 taster portions

For the Arctic angelica sorbet
20 g fresh Arctic angelica • 10 g cilantro (coriander) • 10 g parsley • 10 g dill • 10 g mint • 100 g apple puree • 120 g sugar syrup • 150 g water • 35 g lemon juice • dried Arctic angelica, to serve

1 Combine all the ingredients except the dried angelica well in a mixer. Pour the mixture into Pacojet containers and freeze.
2 Sprinkle with dried angelica before serving.

For the sea buckthorn sorbet
200 g sea buckthorn juice • 125 g sugar syrup • 25 g glucose • 75 g apple puree

1 Combine all the ingredients well in a mixer. Pour the mixture into Pacojet containers and freeze.
2 Process the sorbet in the Pacojet.

TOAST ICE CREAM AND SVEZIA CHEESE CRÈME WITH THIN STICKS OF GOTLANDSLIMPA BREAD
Makes 20 taster portions

For the Svezia cheese crème
150 g Svezia cheese • 100 g milk • 300 g eggs • salt • ½ tbsp ground fennel seeds • cream, as necessary

1 Break down the cheese in a Thermomix. Add the milk and eggs. Use the "butterfly whisk" in the thermometer set at 175°F (80°C) and at speed 3.
2 When the crème has thickened, season it with salt and fennel. Add some cream to adjust the consistency.

For the toast ice cream
200 g white sourdough bread • 500 g milk

1 Slice the bread and toast it until brown. Put the toast in a bowl and pour in the milk.
2 Mix the bread and milk in a food processer and let stand and infuse for a few hours.
3 Strain the mixture and pour it into Pacojet containers along with half of the strained bread. Freeze.

For the thin sticks of Gotlandslimpa bread
200 g Gotlandslimpa bread

1 Cut the bread into millimeter-thin slices.
2 Preheat the oven to 300°F (150°C).
3 Cut the bread into strips and carefully lay on a baking sheet covered with wax (greaseproof) paper. Dry in the oven for about 15 minutes.

To serve
Spoon a small amount of Svezia cheese crème onto the plate. Place thin strips of bread on top of the plate branching out to form "rays" of bread. Finally, place a spoonful of ice cream on top.

BAKED CHOCOLATE WITH TOFFEE ICE CREAM, CARAMELIZED NUTS, CARAMEL SAUCE, BROWN BUTTER, AND HUNG SOUR CREAM

For the baked chocolate
Makes 10 individual 50-g cakes
100 g salted butter • 100 g semi-sweet (plain) chocolate • 110 g eggs • 20 g egg yolks • 80 g confectioners' (icing) sugar • 54 g all-purpose (plain) flour • 15 g unsweetened cocoa powder • caramelized cacao beans, chopped

1 Melt the butter in a pan on the stovetop. Remove the pan from the heat and add the chocolate, stirring until it has melted completely.
2 Whisk the eggs, egg yolks and sugar together in a bowl and fold in the chocolate mixture.
3 Sift the flour and cocoa into the mixture and whisk into a smooth batter. Pour into a pastry (piping) bag.
4 Preheat the oven to 400°F (200°C).
5 Grease 10 metal cooking rings with butter and dip them into the chopped caramelized cacao beans. Place the rings on a nonstick baking sheet. Fill them halfway with the chocolate batter and bake for 5–6 minutes. The chocolate should be creamy in the middle. Remove the steel rings immediately and serve.

For the toffee ice cream
Makes approximately 800 ml
200 g sugar • 200 g cream • 400 g milk • 1 vanilla bean • 98 g egg yolks • 2 g salt

1 Boil 120 g of the sugar with 120 g water in a saucepan until it forms a dark caramel. "Quench" the caramel by adding the cream and milk.
2 Bring the caramel mixture to a boil. Cut the vanilla bean lengthwise, scrape out the seeds and add both bean and seeds to the caramel.
3 Whisk the remaining sugar with the egg yolks and salt in a large bowl. Pour the boiling caramel mixture over the egg mixture and whisk together. Pour the mixture back into the saucepan and let simmer until it reaches 183°F (84°C).
4 Cool down immediately, strain the mixture and process it in an ice-cream maker.

For the caramelized nuts
Makes approximately 450 g
50 g salted butter • 100 g sugar • 150 g toasted almonds • 150 g toasted hazelnuts

1 Cook the butter and sugar in a pan until it forms a dark caramel. Fold in the almonds and hazelnuts.
2 Spread the mixture out on to a nonstick baking sheet and let cool. Chop roughly with a knife.

For the caramel sauce
Makes approximately 500 g
250 g sugar • 350 g water

1 Boil the sugar and 150 g of the water in a pan until it forms a dark caramel.
2 Stop the caramel by adding the remaining water. Let cool.

For the brown butter
200 g butter

Heat the butter in a pan until it turns golden brown and has a rich nutty aroma. Strain through a sieve.

For the hung sour cream
250 g sour cream

Hang the sour cream in a paper coffee filter for 24 hours.

To serve
Drizzle some caramel sauce around each plate followed by a drop of brown butter and hung sour cream. Place a disc of caramelized nuts on the plate then spoon the toffee ice cream on top. Finish by adding a baked chocolate cake.

Mathias Dahlgren

1 & 5
Kevin Davis with customers
at the Steelhead Diner

2–4
Produce and oysters
at the Pike Place Market

6
In the kitchen

Kevin Davis

5

6

Born in the American culinary mecca, world traveler and peripatetic flavor-monger Kevin Davis is on my radar right in my old backyard. Growing up in New Orleans with a Cajun background, it is almost impossible to remain indifferent to all the amazing food the area has to offer. But then traveling all over the world and around the United States from legendary New Orleans, through Napa valley, and now settled just above the flying fish fracas at the Pike Place Market in Seattle, Davis experienced all of his travels as culinary adventures.

As a chef he uses this knowledge and the repertoire of so many international regions and brings it into his dishes. Always curious and always learning, tasting, and trying, Davis's dishes are proof of this. His razor clam chowder is right next to a classic gumbo on the menu and both are perfect, personal, and pop with explosive flavor. My dad introduced me to the Steelhead Diner and it was love at first bite of the fried chicken spring rolls and the local Totten Inlet clams in a spicy "purgatory" remniscent of the best seafood dishes on the Amalfi coast south of Napoli.

Blending explosive Asian flavors with local produce and seafood is exciting. With so many ideas and aspirations in his canon, Davis is an exciting chef because he is always thinking about the next goal, the next dish, and seeking out extraordinary flavor combinations that simply make harmonious splendor. His dishes are interesting because they challenge the palate but also soothe the soul. Davis dabbles in modern technique but the flavors of Pike Place Market pack the joint night after night. Never boring, always thinking—this is what makes a great chef.

Mario Batali

MENU

Caviar pie
with traditional garniture
Argyle Extended Tirage,
Willamette, USA, 1997

~

Lobster mushrooms à la
Américaine with shaved
Washington truffles
and potato gnocchi

~

Kasu-marinated black cod
with kabocha squash, baby
bok choy, and carrot-
ginger salad
Dusky Goose Pinot Noir,
Willamette, USA, 2006

~

Coffee-crusted American
Waygu beef flat iron steak
with wild huckleberry
sauce Grand Veneur
and roasted farro risotto

~

Spiced stout pound cake
with poached pear, warm
pear puree, and sticky
Port syrup

Born in 1965 and a self-taught cook, Kevin Davis got his first restaurant job in 1984. He worked under Jacques Chibois at the Royal Grey in Grasse, southern France, and has since headed restaurants in Adelaide, Australia, New Orleans, and Seattle. In 2007 he and his wife, Terresa, opened the Steelhead Diner in Pike Place Market, Seattle. There he serves classic Southern American diner dishes using local ingredients from the Pacific Northwest, with an innovative Asian twist. His food draws on his many influences, including his own close-knit Cajun family and his time spent cooking in French, Italian, Creole, and seafood restaurants. To Davis, cooking is a primal rather than cerebral process, and he likes to keep things simple, guided by what's available in the market and drawing on his own rich culinary heritage.

1
Caviar pie with
traditional garniture

2
Kasu-marinated black
cod with kabocha
squash, baby bok choy,
and carrot-ginger salad

CAVIAR PIE WITH TRADITIONAL GARNITURE
Serves 12

For the caviar pie
1 white onion, finely chopped •
4 hard-cooked eggs, peeled and
finely chopped • 1 tbsp mayonnaise
• kosher salt and freshly ground
white pepper • 675 g cream cheese
• 75 ml sour cream • 60 g golden
whitefish caviar • 85 g truffled
whitefish caviar • 85 g beet and
saffron whitefish caviar • 60 g trout
caviar • 25 g American sturgeon
caviar

1 Remove the bottom from a
25-cm tart pan and wrap the round
sides with plastic wrap (clingfilm).
Set the bottom back in the pan.
2 Place the white onion in
a fine-mesh sieve and rinse under
cold running water, drain well, and
squeeze dry in a fine clean dish
cloth or paper towel.
3 Stir together the eggs and
mayonnaise in a small bowl,
season with salt and white pepper,
and refrigerate until needed.
4 Sprinkle the onion evenly over
the bottom of the tart pan and
smooth it out with a beveled cake
spatula to form an even layer.
Spoon the egg mixture over the
onion, then use the beveled cake
spatula to carefully spread the
egg mixture to form a second even
layer, smoothing the surface as
much as you can.
5 Combine the cream cheese and
sour cream in a food processor and
blend until very smooth. Spoon this
over the egg mixture and smooth
to the top of the tart pan evenly.
Cover the tart pan with plastic wrap
and refrigerate for at least 6 hours.
6 Decorate the top of the pie with
the different caviars in a bull's
eye pattern, beginning with the
outermost ring first and working
inward. Starting with the golden
whitefish caviar, form 1.5-cm
ring, followed by a 1.5-cm ring of
truffled whitefish caviar, followed
by a 1.5-cm ring of beet and saffron
whitefish caviar, followed by a
1.5-cm ring of trout caviar, followed
by a 5-cm-diameter circle of
American sturgeon caviar. Do your
best to not mix the caviars, keeping
the rings tidy.
7 Refrigerate for at least 1 hour,
or up to 24 hours, before serving.

To serve
140 g nonpareil capers •
120 g red onion, finely chopped •
4 hard-cooked eggs, yolk and white
finely chopped separately • 1 bunch
chives, finely chopped • toast points
(toasted sliced white bread, crusts
removed and cut into triangles)

When ready to serve, carefully
unmold the pie, lifting the base
up from the ring. Cut the pie into
wedges, and serve on chilled
plates, spooning the capers, red
onion, egg yolk, egg white, and
chives alongside. Pass the toast
points separately.

KASU-MARINATED BLACK COD WITH KABOCHA SQUASH, BABY BOK CHOY, AND CARROT-GINGER SALAD
Serves 4

For the kasu-marinated black cod
kosher salt • 4 (675-g) portions
black cod fillet, cleaned • 50 ml
water • 60 g sugar • 50 ml soy
sauce • 60 g kasu paste

1 Sprinkle a fine layer of kosher
salt evenly on the black cod fillets
as if to season before cooking
(approximately ¼–½ teaspoon
per side). Refrigerate, allowing it to
cure for 1 hour.
2 For the kasu marinade, place all
the ingredients except the cod in
a food processor or blender. Blend
until smooth. Refrigerate until
needed.
3 When the black cod fillets are
cured, coat with 250 ml kasu
marinade and allow to marinate
for 6–12 hours.
4 Just before you are ready to
cook, assemble the mise-en-place
for the stir-fry and ginger salad.
Assemble the ingredients for the
carrot-ginger salad.
5 Remove the fillets from the
marinade and remove any excess.
Place on a shallow nonreactive
baking pan. Place under
medium-high broiler (grill) and
cook for approximately 5 minutes,
or until golden brown.
6 Cook the filets into a 450°F
(230°C) oven.

For the carrot-ginger salad
120 g carrot, julienned finely •
25 g ginger root, julienned finely •
2 scallions (spring onions), whites
removed, julienned diagonally to
create long strips • ½ bunch cilantro
(coriander), rinsed, picked, and
stems removed • ½ tsp fish sauce
• 2 tbsp rice-wine vinegar • 1 tbsp
soy sauce • 1 tbsp lime juice • 1 tsp
prepared wasabi • 1 tsp lime zest,
finely chopped

1 Combine the vegetables and
herbs.
2 Combine the dressing ingredients
and toss with the salad.

For the vegetable stir-fry
75 ml blended oil (canola and
olive oil) • 1 small kabocha squash,
peeled and cut into medium dice
• 225 g chanterelle mushrooms,
cleaned and torn • 1 tbsp chopped
garlic • 1 tbsp ginger, grated • 500 ml
chicken stock • 2 bunches baby
bok choy ends, trimmed and cut in
quarters • 125 ml soy sauce

1 Heat 50 ml oil in a heavy-gauge
sauté pan or wok until smoking.
Add the kabocha squash and cook
until golden brown.
2 Transfer to a drip pan to remove
excess oil and add the remaining
oil to the pan. Return the pan to
high heat.
3 Add the chanterelle mushrooms
and sauté until browned.
4 Add the garlic and ginger and
sauté briefly, then remove any
excess oil from the pan.
5 Add the chicken stock and bring
it to a full boil.
6 Add the cooked squash followed
by the bok choy, bring to a boil, and
reduce by one quarter.
7 Finish with soy sauce and return
to a boil, then remove from the heat.

To serve
Divide the stir-fry between 4
warm bowls. Remove the black
cod from the oven and place on
top of the stir-fry. Garnish with the
carrot-ginger salad and serve.

Kevin Davis

Anthony Demetre trained under some of Britain's culinary greats: Marco Pierre White, Gary Rhodes, Gordon Ramsay, Bruno Loubet. These idols are knocked off their pedestals with a glance down at the menu at Arbutus or even its slightly upmarket sister, Wild Honey— a healthy showing of forgotten cuts (pig's head, trotters, lamb breast) gives a comforting twist to Demetre's creative and intelligent European dishes, a thrifty touch which seems more a product of Demetre's Midlands childhood than his culinary pedigree. And, what's more, it's affordable—Demetre and his business partner, Will Smith, were pioneers in 2006 when they opened Arbutus, offering every wine on the list by the carafe as well as the bottle.

Since then they have gone from strength to strength, with a Michelin star apiece for their restaurants, widespread recognition from critics and a strong base of returning customers. The reason for their sustained success is clear after a taste of Demetre's cooking; and this is where his training, instinct and experience reveal themselves, in dishes that are markedly sustainable and local, with perennial favorites like Welsh lamb breast with crushed potatoes (Arbutus) or gnocchi with anchovy, tomato and Cornish pollock (Wild Honey). Flavors often make their way across the Channel (salt cod brandade) or from as far as the Mediterranean (fresh ricotta, beetroot and apricot). Just before opening Arbutus, Demetre spent time working at a Parisian bakery, showing his continued thirst to develop and integrate new skills from throughout the culinary world.

Both Arbutus and Wild Honey maintain a gentle sense of occasion; bouillabaisse arrives in two halves, fish and boiled potatoes plated, and the heady broth in a copper pot, with aïoli, rouille and croutons, showing an attention to detail and assembly that brings just enough ceremony to a meal. The lasting impressions are balanced and delicious flavors, attentive service, and of course, the easy spirit that runs through a restaurant managed by such an impeccable team.

Shannon Bennett

Born in 1966 in England, Anthony Demetre began work as a commis chef in 1987, developing skills and techniques before moving on to Harveys under Marco Pierre White, and a taste of the pace and precision of a Michelin-starred kitchen. In 1990 Anthony moved to work for Gary Rhodes; then, after a brief stint with Pierre Koffman, he went to Bruno Loubet's Four Seasons Restaurant. He went on to work at Loubet's Bistrot Bruno and then L'Odeon, where he was head chef for three years. From here, Anthony became head chef at Putney Bridge Restaurant, which was awarded a Michelin star in 2000. In May 2006, Anthony opened Arbutus restaurant in Frith Street, Soho, with his business partner Will Smith. This was followed closely by a second restaurant, Wild Honey, in July 2007.

MENU

Dover sole terrine with Cornish shellfish

~

Squid and mackerel burger, parsley, and razor clams

~

Braised pigs' head, potato puree, ravioli of caramelized onions

~

Slow cooked breast of lamb, sweetbreads and golden sultanas

~

Vanilla cheesecake with Scottish raspberries

1
Dining room at Arbutus

2
Anthony Demetre

3–6
Chefs at work in the kitchen

Anthony Demetre

Arbutus/Wild Honey, London, UK

SQUID AND MACKEREL BURGER, PARSLEY AND RAZOR CLAMS
Serves 4

100 g razor clam meat • 1 glass white wine • 1 bunch flat-leaf parsley, picked • 1 handful sea purslane, plus more to serve • salt and pepper • 2 medium whole mackerel • 200 g squid, previously frozen to tenderize it • 1 tbsp chopped cilantro (coriander) • 1 tbsp grated ginger • 1 tbsp chopped garlic • 1 tsp grated lime zest • olive oil, for pan-frying

1 Cook the razor clams in their shells with a glass of white wine until they just open, then strain and reserve the juices.
2 For the parsley juice, blanch the parsley and a handful of sea purslane and liquidize them with a little of the cooking juices. Season with salt and pepper if necessary, then set aside.
3 Finely chop the mackerel and squid, and add all the remaining ingredients except the sea purslane, razor clams and parsley juice.
4 Let set in the refrigerator for a couple of hours.
5 Mold the mixture into 4 burgers. You can use plastic wrap (clingfilm) to hold their shape. Remove from the plastic wrap and pan-fry in olive oil.
6 Garnish with the cooked razor clams, sea purslane and parsley juice.

BRAISED PIGS' HEAD, POTATO PUREE, RAVIOLI OF CARAMELIZED ONIONS
Serves 4–6

2 pigs' heads, split in half • 300 ml red wine • 1 liter water • 4 tbsp chopped flat-leaf parsley • 5 shallots, chopped • salt and pepper • 6 onions, thinly sliced • 70 g butter • 50 g sugar • 100 ml red-wine vinegar • andouille sausage, for the ravioli • potato puree, to serve

1 Soak the pigs' heads in lightly salted water for 12 hours to remove the blood.
2 Singe the pigs' heads with a blowtorch to remove any hairs. Place them skin-side down into an ovenproof dish.
3 Add the red wine, shallots and the water to cover. Cover with a close-fitting lid and braise in the oven for 8 hours at 230°F (110°C). Remove from the liquid and set aside until cool enough to handle.
4 Skim the braising liquid and reduce it by half, or until it is syrupy.
5 Remove the bones, eyes and brain and discard them. Carefully remove the meat and set it aside. Remove the ears and thinly slice them.
6 Now combine the meat, ears and parsley in a bowl, season with salt and pepper, add the reduced braising liquid and pour into a terrine or loaf tin lined with plastic wrap (clingfilm) to help remove it more easily. Let set. Store for 2 days before eating.
7 To make the caramelized onion ravioli, cook the onions in the butter until golden brown, then add the sugar and caramelize. Add the vinegar and reduce until almost all the liquid has evaporated. Season and add a splash of water, then cook until the onions are soft and jammy.
8 Cook the andouille sausage and slice it thinly.
9 Just before serving, layer some caramelized onion between 2 slices of andouille sausage.
10 To serve, place a slice of pigs' head on the plate with the caramelized onion ravioli and some of the reduced braising liquid.

SLOW COOKED BREAST OF LAMB, SWEETBREADS AND GOLDEN SULTANAS
Serves 4–6

2 breasts of lamb, bones removed and reserved • 8 garlic cloves, pureed • 2 sprigs of rosemary, finely chopped • salt and pepper • 100 g butter • olive oil, for pan-frying • 2 onions, finely sliced • 1 tsp fennel seeds • 1 tsp herbes de Provence • 200 ml white wine • 200 g lamb's sweetbreads, blanched and peeled • 1 tsp honey • 1 tbsp balsamic vinegar • 1 handful golden raisins • vegetable puree, to serve

1 Ask the butcher to remove the bones from the lamb breast, but keep them to use for the cooking liquor.
2 Smear the flesh side of the breasts with the garlic, rosemary, salt and pepper. Roll the breasts, skin side outward, and tie them with kitchen string to resemble a jelly (Swiss) roll.
3 Take a pan big enough to hold them with a close-fitting lid and melt half the butter plus a splash of olive oil in it. Color the breasts until they are nicely golden all over (this could take 15 minutes or so, the slower the better). This helps render the fat needed for the next stage.
4 Take out the lamb and set aside. Now add the thinly sliced onions, fennel seeds and herbes de Provence and cook until very soft, about 15 minutes.
5 Place the breasts on top of the onions, add the wine, lamb bones, and enough water to half-cover the lamb. This is why the pan should not be too big—otherwise the braising stock won't have any flavor.
6 Lightly season the breasts, cover, tr ansfer to an oven preheated to 300°F (150°C) and cook for a minimum of 2 hours. The lamb should be tender to the touch. Lift the lamb out and keep warm until needed.
7 Reduce the braising stock until you have about 200 ml and strain through a fine-mesh sieve, pushing all the juices from the onions through. Set aside.
8 Heat the remaining butter with a little olive oil in a nonstick pan, increase the heat and sauté the seasoned lamb sweetbreads until golden. Add the honey and allow to caramelize a little, then add the vinegar, the golden raisins and 50 ml of the braising stock.
9 Toss the sweetbreads and golden raisins together, which will coat and glaze everything. Taste for seasoning and serve alongside the lamb. We serve a vegetable puree with this.

VANILLA CHEESECAKE WITH SCOTTISH RASPBERRIES
Serves 4–6

<u>For the base</u>
70 g flour • 70 g sugar • 70 g ground almonds • 7 g salt • 70 g butter

1 Mix together the flour, sugar, ground almonds, and salt.
2 Melt the butter and pour it over the dry ingredients. Work to a paste.
3 Press the paste into an ovenproof ring mold and bake at 325°F (160°C) until golden in color. Set aside and let cool.

<u>For the topping</u>
700 g cream cheese • 150 g mascarpone • 200 g sugar • 1 vanilla bean • 2 whole eggs • 8 egg yolks • fresh fruit, to serve

1 Combine all the ingredients and thoroughly whisk them together. Pour on top of your cooled biscuit base and bake at 225°F (110°C) until set.
2 Finish with a fresh fruit of your choice.

1
Squid and mackerel burger,
parsley and razor clams

2
Braised pigs' head,
potato puree, ravioli of
caramelized onions

3
Slow cooked breast of
lamb, sweetbreads and
golden sultanas

4
Vanilla cheesecake with
Scottish raspberries

Anthony Demetre

Sometimes—and this happens only rarely to me—just by talking to someone you can sense a passion for their trade, and you realize they are an unusual talent, possessing something indescribable that only a few people have. This is the impression I had of Kobe when I first met him.

I have actually never been to Kobe's restaurant, but I have met him several times at Noma, where we have served him as a guest. On top of this, I have seen him at culinary gatherings where he has presented the visions, ideas, and techniques behind his Flemish cuisine at his restaurant, In de Wulf.

Perhaps it is the fact that he was more or less born into gastronomy, as his mother ran In de Wulf before him. Back then, of course, it was a more humble eatery, and Kobe has now turned it into a hyper-modern, state-of-the-art restaurant that is always looking forward.

However, as Kobe himself says: "My technique is not just a gratuitous expression, a blind desire for innovation, but has the objective of creating an explosion of flavors, searching out top products and finding methods of preparation that more subtly bring out their flavor." He adds, "At In de Wulf, each dish has to have certain logic behind it."

It seems that Kobe's food is more intellectual than that of others. His food doesn't strike me as having an immediate burst of high flavor and satisfaction in your mouth. It is more subtle, working a lot with mouth feelings from textures and a strong idea behind it. When eating his food, it seems that you will actually have to make a decision whether you like it or not—or perhaps, said in a different way, whether you understand it or not.

René Redzepi

Born in 1980 in Dranouter, Belgium, Kobe Desramaults is heir to a long culinary heritage: his restaurant, In de Wulf, was run by his mother before him as a traditional Belgian brasserie. He began his career in food, however, at an Italian restaurant in the neighboring village of Westouter. This led to his defining experience —two years at the three-Michelin-starred Oud Sluis in the Netherlands, where Sergio Herman became an important mentor. From there, Desramaults spent ten months in Barcelona under Carles Abellan at Comerç 24, completing an important apprenticeship in the techniques of fine cuisine. Next Desramaults chose to return to his roots, taking over the kitchen of In de Wulf for his mother and revolutionizing it with his inventive treatment of local produce. Clean yet earthy dishes, such as razor shell with kohlrabi, duck liver, tapioca, and orange juice, or sorrel with angelica and apple, won In de Wulf well-deserved recognition, culminating in a Michelin star in 2005.

MENU

Appetizers
Potato chips with emulsion of cod caviar and egg yolk and shrimp

~

Pumpkin-Mimolette

~

"Royal" of duck liver and green herbs

~

Whelks, smoked herring, and green herbs

~

Smoked eel from Oosterschelde, celery root, and horseradish

Land & sea
Green apple and lobster, nasturtium, and borage

~

North Sea bass raw marinated, herbs and flowers from our garden

~

Millet, Zeeland mussels, cockles and razor-shell clams, shellfish broth, and algae powder

~

Norwegian lobster, artichoke, artichoke dressing, sunflower seeds "gomasio"

~

Ray, smoked egg yolk, fresh hazelnuts, and hazelnut butter

~

Sweetbread, smoked marrow, walnut, and porcini

~

Milk fungus and sponge fungus, emulsion of duck liver, pig's foot, and ham broth

~

Wild duck "Colvert," parsnip, parsley root, mustard, duck jus, St. Bernardus beer vinegar, and meadow cress

Sweet
St. Bernardus beer and chocolate

~

Fresh cheese, yogurt, and elderberries

~

Quince and star anise

Kobe Desramaults

1 & 3
Kobe Desramaults
plating dishes

2 & 4
Trimming meat in the
kitchen at In de Wulf

III

In de Wulf, Dranouter, Belgium

1	3
"Royal" of duck liver and green herbs	Green apple and lobster, nasturtium, and borage
2	4
Whelks, smoked herring, and green herbs	Millet, Zeeland mussels, cockles and razor-shell clams, shellfish broth, and algae powder

"ROYAL" OF DUCK LIVER AND GREEN HERBS
Serves 8

For the "royal" of duck liver
505 g milk • 375 g duck liver •
225 g whole egg • salt and pepper
• 3 g guar gum

Mix all the ingredients together, pass through a sieve, pour into bowls, cover with plastic wrap (clingfilm) and steam for 12 minutes at 185°F (85°C). Chill.

For the green herb jelly
20 g olives • 20 g flat-leaf parsley • 20 g chervil • 20 g tarragon • 20 g young spinach leaves • 400 g chicken stock •3 gelatin leaves • sourdough croutons, for garnish • wild herbs, for garnish

1 Mix all the ingredients together and pass through a sieve to make a chlorophyll juice.
2 Soak the gelatin leaves in water until soft. Bring the stock to a simmer and remove from the heat. Squeeze out the gelatin and add to the hot stock, stirring to dissolve. Let cool and mix in the chlorophyll
3 Let the herb mixture set on top of the chilled duck liver royal and top with sourdough croutons and wild herbs.

WHELKS, SMOKED HERRING, AND GREEN HERBS
Serves 8

For the smoked herring milk
250 g smoked herring • 500 g milk

Mix the ingredients together and pass through a sieve.

For the smoked leaves herring cream
3 sheets gelatin • 500 g smoked herring milk • 500 g whipped cream • salt and pepper

Dissolve the gelatin in the herring milk. Fold the herring milk into the whipped cream, season, then pour into a pastry (piping) bag.

For the rice crumble
100 g rice • sunflower oil, for frying • 14 g sea lettuce powder • 2 g Guérande salt • 2 g kombu algae powder

1 Deep-fry the rice at 410°F (210°C) in sunflower oil to puff it, then drain it on absorbent paper.
2 Mix the sea lettuce powder, the salt, and the algae powder with the puffed rice.

For the whelks
4 kg whelks, rinsed • 100 g celery, chopped • 100 g onion, chopped • 100 g carrot, chopped • 1 sprig of thyme • 6 bay leaves • 6 garlic cloves • 2 chicken legs • 20 black peppercorns

Cook all the ingredients gently in a pan for 1½ hours. Let cool in its own jus, remove the shells from the whelks, and clean them.

For the whelk dressing
50 g sunflower oil • 20 g canola (rapeseed) oil • 20 g Chardonnay vinegar • 40 g shallot, chopped

1 Mix the ingredients together and let stand for 12 hours, then pass through a sieve.
2 Cut the whelks in half and soak them in the marinade for 1 hour.

To serve
seasonal green herbs

Pipe some dots of herring cream onto a plate, then add the whelks and the rice crumble. Finish with the green herbs.

GREEN APPLE AND LOBSTER, NASTURTIUM, AND BORAGE
Serves 4

1 Granny Smith apple • 2 lobsters, approximately 450 g each • court bouillon, to poach the lobsters • 1 shallot, chopped • herbs • sour cream • salt and pepper • beurre monté, to serve

1 Slice the apple on a Japanese mandolin into 10-cm×5-cm ribbons.
2 Cook the lobster in the court bouillon for 2 minutes and chill in ice water immediately.
3 Remove the lobster claw meat and finely chop it. Mix with the shallot, herbs, sour cream, salt and pepper, and beurre monté, to make a tartare.

To serve
100 g butter • 200 ml lobster stock • 2 handfuls nasturtium leaves, plus extra to garnish • white-wine vinegar • salt • 200 g crushed ice • 1 g guar gum • borage leaves

1 Reheat the lobster tails in butter and lobster stock to a maximum of 140°F (60°C).
2 Mix the nasturtium leaves with vinegar, salt, crushed ice, and guar gum, and pass through a fine sieve to make a cress juice.
3 Roll up the apple slices with the lobster tartare to make rolls.
4 Place the lukewarm lobster tails next to them.
5 Finish with the cress juice, borage and more nasturtium leaves.

MILLET, ZEELAND MUSSELS, COCKLES AND RAZOR-SHELL CLAMS, SHELLFISH BROTH, AND ALGAE POWDER
Serves 4

For the broth
400 g mussels • 2 shallots, chopped • 3 sprigs of thyme • 3 bay leaves • 300 ml white wine • 5 g algae powder • 500 g sea lettuce • 200 ml water • 200 g kombu algae • 100 g shellfish, cooked • 3 g Sucro

1 Cook all the ingredients except the cooked shellfish and Sucro gently together for 10 minutes, then pass through a fine sieve, reserving the liquid.
2 Blend 200 g of the liquid with the cooked shellfish and Sucro to obtain a mousse juice, so that a foam is created on top.

For the millet
200 g millet • 200 g reserved mussel liquid

Cook for 20 minutes, adding water as necessary.

For the puffed millet
sunflower oil, for frying

Leave one quarter of the cooked millet to dry overnight between sheets of absorbent paper. Puff by deep-frying in sunflower oil at 410°F (210°C). Store in an airtight container.

For the millet puree
200 g cooked millet • 50 g reserved mussel liquid • 50 g cream • 20 g white-wine vinegar • 2 g algae powder • 500 g sea lettuce • salt and pepper

Cook all the ingredients together to obtain a risotto-like texture.

For the shellfish
10 razor-shell clams • 20 cockles • 20 mussels

Cook the shellfish until the shells open, remove the meat, collect the juice, and pass through a sieve.

To serve
algae powder, for serving • chickweed, for serving

Dress the plate with the millet puree and the puffed millet, warm the shellfish up to 140°F (60°C), cover them with the mussel foam, and finish with algae powder and chickweed.

Kobe Desramaults

1 & 2
Pascal Devalkeneer preparing
scallops and black truffle
on marrow

3
Oysters on the grill

4
Cherry tomatoes with basil
in olive oil

Pascal Devalkeneer

114

MENU

Size 5/0 Zeeland oyster grilled over a wood fire, buckwheat grains with mustard and nori
Louis Roederer,
Blanc de Blancs,
Champagne, France, 2003

~

Lightly cooked sea bass, tartare of Gillardeau oysters, oscietra caviar, and broccoli florets parmentier
Blanc Fumé de
Pouilly, Silex, Dagueneau,
Loire, France, 2005

~

Alternating scallops and black truffle on marrow bones
Chablis Grand Cru,
Les Preuses, Dauvissat,
Bourgogne, France, 2005

~

Cod loin fillet, roasted in its skin in salted butter, sliced cauliflower, hazelnuts, salad burnet with a speculaas biscuit base
Le Faîte, Côtes de St Mont,
Plaimont, France, 2006

~

Sautéed duck foie gras, tartare of heirloom tomatoes with lemon verbena and Banyuls, lime jelly
Condrieu,
Les Terrasses du Palat,
Villard Côtes du Rhône,
France, 2006

~

Pigeon breast grilled over a wood fire, carrot puree with almonds and nutmeg, roasted loquats, and lemon thyme
Le Pas de l'Escalette,
Le Grand Pas, Coteaux du
Languedoc, France, 2004

~

Chocolate medley, cocoa crunchy

Pascal Devalkeneer was born in 1965 in Belgium. After attending culinary school in Brussels, he spent two years as a commis chef at Surcouf, Chez Pierrot, and La Quintessence. In 1987 he became chef de partie at LaTruffe Noire, moving on after three years to Le Scholteshof. In 1992 he opened Le Bistrot du Mail and began to develop some of his classic signature dishes, such as alternating scallops and black truffle on marrow, which he took with him in 1999 when he opened Le Chalet de la Forêt. Citing the culinary influences of Michel Bras and Alain Ducasse, Devalkeneer captures Belgian flavors with a Mediterranean slant, using technically accomplished but simple dishes, and always maintaining a high regard for sustainable produce. Highlights such as hare roasted in its skin, with caramelized pears in red wine, continue the reputation of Le Chalet de la Forêt for capturing the tastes of the Belgian countryside with style and restraint.

This is Belgian cooking at its very best: serious, intellectual, honest, and well-executed. Pascal's food strikes a highly intelligent and thoughtful balance between the avant-garde and the traditional. I first met him, as with many fine chefs of his generation, at the Congreso lo Mejor de la Gastronomía in San Sebastian, and I have chosen him because he represents the thousands of chefs who understand the great importance of a high level of competence and a job well done.

Pascal is the perfect role model for young chefs in terms of professionalism and good manners, and it is this aspect that most interests me about his cuisine. The elegance of the working environment at Le Chalet de la Forêt in Brussels shows young stagers and trainees that a fine restaurant with a great reputation involves much more than a first-class kitchen. It is as much about atmosphere, perseverance, and hard work as it is about the menu.

Pascal has been known to compare his cuisine to fashion, noting that dishes come in and out of season much like produce. He also observes that trends, from the simple to the high-tech, are always infused with the mores of the time. A firm advocate of seasonal cookery, Pascal only uses ingredients that he himself would be happy eating. He chooses produce that is grown and raised naturally, a thoughtful policy that adds greatly to his cuisine. He also believes that cooking and eating should be a complete experience—a happy experience. The fact that he keeps all these things in mind when creating his menus ensures that his dishes appeal to all of the senses.

Ferran Adrià

1
Size 5/0 Zeeland oyster grilled over a wood fire, buckwheat grains with mustard and nori

2
Lightly cooked sea bass, tartare of Gillardeau oysters, oscietra caviar, and broccoli floret parmentier

3
Alternating scallops and black truffle on marrow bones

4
Cod loin fillet, roasted in its skin in salted butter, sliced cauliflower, hazelnuts, salad burnet with a speculaas biscuit base

5
Pigeon breast grilled over a wood fire, carrot puree with almonds and nutmeg, roasted loquats, and lemon thyme

SIZE 5/0 ZEELAND OYSTER GRILLED OVER A WOOD FIRE, BUCKWHEAT GRAINS WITH MUSTARD AND NORI
Serves 1

For the oyster (as an appetizer)
1 size 5/0 Zeeland flat oyster
100 g buckwheat • chicken stock, to cook the buckwheat

1 Open the oyster and reserve the liquid, remove it from its shell, and grill it very quickly without cooking it.
2 Roast the buckwheat for a few minutes in a hot oven and then cook it in the chicken stock.

For the oyster vinaigrette
reserved oyster liquid • lemon juice • 1 tsp mustard • canola (rapeseed) oil, to emulsify • salt and pepper • 1 sheet nori, finely chopped • chives or scallions (spring onions), thinly sliced

1 Take the liquid from the oyster and add a squeeze of lemon juice and the mustard, and emulsify the vinaigrette with canola oil. Season to taste.
2 Place the warm buckwheat in the oyster shells, with the warm grilled oyster, and coat with the vinaigrette. Add a finely chopped sheet of nori and the chives or scallions.

LIGHTLY COOKED SEA BASS, TARTARE OF GILLARDEAU OYSTERS, OSCIETRA CAVIAR AND BROCCOLI FLOWERS PARMENTIER
Serves 4

4 thick sea bass fillets, weighing 140 g • lemon juice • 1 tsp neutral-tasting oil • 8 size 3 special Gillardeau oysters, chopped • florets from 4 heads of broccoli • 25 g oscietra caviar • lemon zest, to finish • creamy mashed potatoes, to serve

1 Cut the sea bass into equal-sized strips and marinate in lemon juice and oil for 2 minutes. Place the strips on an 8-cm square cooking tray. Vacuum-pack and cook at 125°F (51°C) until lightly cooked through.
2 Mix the chopped oysters, the broccoli (which has been blanched for a very short time and refreshed), oscietra caviar, and oil.
3 Arrange the cooked sea bass with the chopped oysters on top.
4 Finish with a little lemon zest grated on a box grater.
5 Serve with creamy mashed potatoes made with lightly salted butter.

ALTERNATING SCALLOPS AND BLACK TRUFFLE ON MARROW BONES
Serves 4

Depending on the season, you can arrange the marrow bones on a mixture of fresh herbs, a salad of bulgur wheat or couscous, or a chicory or mixed green salad. Add a few sourdough croutons.

4½ marrow bones, cut lengthwise into 20-cm long pieces • 8 large live sea scallops, cut into 5 equal strips • salt and pepper • 40 strips of black truffle the same size as the scallops (about 2 (30-g) truffles – keep the truffle trimmings for the vinaigrette) • pepper • fleur de sel • shallots, to taste • port, sherry, balsamic and sherry vinegar, to taste • 1 spig thyme • 1 bay leaf • a few slices of ginger • veal stock, to taste

1 Soak the marrow bones for 2 days in cold salted water, then steam for as long as their size requires (approximately 20 minutes at 175°F (80°C)—the marrow should be thoroughly cooked and white).
2 To make the vinaigrette, chop the shallots and put them into a pan with the wines and vinegars, a little fleur de sel, thyme, bay leaf, and ginger. Bring to a boil and reduce by two-thirds.
3 Add the veal stock, bring to a boil, skim and reduce by one-third. Chop the truffle trimmings into 5-mm dice and add to the vinaigrette. Bring back to a boil and remove from the heat.
4 Beat in the olive oil and hazelnut oil, let cool, then add a generous amount of pepper. Let cool and reheat carefully when needed, without letting it boil.
5 Place the scallop strips on a buttered baking sheet, sprinkle with salt and pepper, and place a strip of truffle between each slice.
6 Warm the scallops for 3 minutes in a hot oven. They must remain translucent.
7 Alternate the scallops and truffles on the hot bone marrow and season with pepper and fleur de sel.

COD LOIN FILLET, ROASTED IN ITS SKIN IN SALTED BUTTER, SLICED CAULIFLOWER, HAZELNUTS, SALAD BURNET WITH A SPECULAAS BISCUIT BASE
Serves 4

1 small top-quality white cauliflower • hazelnut oil, to marinate, plus extra to serve • fleur de sel • 4 (200-g) thick cod fillets • olive oil, for cooking the cod • salted butter, for cooking the cod • 100 g speculaas biscuits • 50 g salted butter • 1 tbsp matured sherry vinegar, plus extra to serve • roasted hazelnuts, chopped, to serve • salad burnet, to serve

1 Using a mandolin, slice the cauliflower, keeping the slices as whole as possible, allowing 6 per person. Marinate the thinly sliced cauliflower for about 10 minutes on a baking sheet, in hazelnut oil and fleur de sel.
2 Fry the pieces of cod gently on the skin side. Sear them in pure olive oil, and finish with salted butter, basting frequently. The butter should be frothy and golden.
3 In blender, grind the crumbled speculaas with the salted butter into a smooth paste. Add the sherry vinegar.
4 To serve, arrange the marinated cauliflower in a fan shape. Place the cod on top of the speculaas paste with the chopped hazelnuts and salad burnet. Finish with a dash of hazelnut oil and sherry vinegar.

PIGEON BREAST GRILLED OVER A WOOD FIRE, CARROT PUREE WITH ALMONDS AND NUTMEG, ROASTED LOQUATS, AND LEMON THYME
Serves 4

For the pigeon
2 large pigeons weighing 550 g

1 If possible, grill the pigeon breasts very gently over a wood fire. If not, use a broiler (grill) to brown the skin and finish in the oven at 175°F (80°C) for 8–10 minutes.
2 Make a simple pigeon stock with the pigeon carcasses.

For the carrot puree
4 large carrots • ½ onion • oil, for browning • 50 g ground almonds • pinch of nutmeg • 25 g marzipan • 1 tbsp Amaretto

1 Cut the carrots into pieces and brown them in a small pan with the onion.
2 Puree them with the ground almonds, nutmeg, marzipan, and Amaretto.

For the loquats
4 fresh loquats, cut in half • salted butter

Fry the loquats gently in the salted butter and allow to caramelize.

To serve
lemon thyme, for garnish • almond oil, for garnish

Arrange the grilled breast, the carrot puree molded between two spoons or placed in a line, the loquats, and the lemon thyme on a plate. Finish with a dash of almond oil.

Pascal Devalkeneer

1
Ingredients at L'Autre Pied

2 & 3
Marcus Eaves in the
kitchen

4
Making sheets of pasta

Marcus Eaves

MENU

Open ravioli of Norwegian lobster, morel mushrooms, and spring truffle
Beaujolais Chardonnay, Terres Dorees, Jean-Paul Brun, Burgundy, France, 2007

~

Salad of young vegetables, pine nut and tarragon dressing
Pinot Gris, Mt. Difficulty, Central Otago, New Zealand, 2008

~

Seared foie gras, pickled violet artichokes, pineapple sorbet, and black pepper crisps
Vouvray Moelleux, Clos Baudoin, Prince Poniatowski, Loire Valley, France, 1997

~

Pan-fried cod, Jersey Royal potatoes, spring vegetable, and shellfish broth
Godello, Louro do Bolo, Rafael Palacios, Galicia, Spain, 2007

~

Best end of veal, white asparagus, steamed cornish clams, and horseradish cream
Valle d'Aoste, DOC, Fumin, Cave di Barro, Italy, 2004

~

Selection of French and British Farmhouse cheese
PN (Pinot Noir), VdT, Thierry Puzelat, Loire Valley, France

~

Baked Alaska, English rhubarb, and cardamom ice cream
Vermentino, V.T., Lughente, Cantina Giogantinu, Sardegna, Italy, 2005

~

"Tiramisu" coffee and dark chocolate, mascarpone ice cream, and espresso sorbet
Madeira, Malmsey, Colheita Blandy's, Portugal, 2001

Born in Leamington Spa, U.K., in 1981 as the son of a chef, Marcus Eaves began washing pots and pans in a small hotel at the age of 15. He moved on to culinary college, securing a position when he was sixteen at the two-Michelin-starred Simpsons Restaurant with Andreas Antona. Further training followed at Lettonie, Bath, under Martin Blunos. Eaves later worked with John Burton-Race at London's Landmark Hotel. In 2004 Eaves moved to cook for Claude Bosi at Hibiscus, later gaining a post at Pied à Terre. Here Shane Osborn was an important influence, becoming Eaves's partner in the opening of L'Autre Pied in 2007. After 14 months, L'Autre Pied was awarded a Michelin star, a testament to the skill and flair Eaves learned at the shoulders of some of the country's top chefs. His emphasis is on constant innovation and progress to create a fine yet informal dining experience.

I heard about Marcus through my friend Shane Osborn, but did not take much notice at first. I honestly felt that most young English chefs see cooking as a labor and not as an international phenomenon, and only focus in one direction. Look at Singapore, Thailand, or America—there are so many flavors, ingredients, and techniques, and they are all exciting. Michelin hasn't rated them, but that is insignificant—but most young Brits aren't trained like that.

Shane, being West Australian, had opened Marcus's eyes beyond the Michelin technical food of Britain, and I could see a real future star.

The most memorable meal I had at Marcus's restaurant was seafood-based, and I loved his delicate use of low-temperature cooking to bring out the natural texture of ingredients like trout and scallops. His presentation skills are unique and not overcomplicated. Marcus had worked as Shane's head chef and learned under difficult, cramped conditions, but in a well-organized kitchen, to become a leader.

Marcus's technique will always pay homage to his mentors, and with some mature planning and goal-setting, Marcus could become the next generation's leader, along with the likes of Sat Bains, taking great British ingredients through the "hangover period" the industry is currently facing. He also has the ability to cook great food at affordable prices, which is important for young chefs to take note of.

Marcus's signature dish—assiette of rabbit with pickled carrot—is a wonderful blend of technique, some slow-cooked leg meat rolled in herbed bread crumbs, liver and kidney cooked pink, the rack beautifully chimed with the rib bones' pearl-white, then balanced with a classic jus and a pickled carrot ribbon. However, the most important aspect to Marcus's cooking for me is using great British ingredients like Jersey Royal potatoes. His dish of baby petit pois and Jersey Royals, great butter emulsion, and beautifully cooked lobster was pure heaven!

Shannon Bennett

1

2

3

1
Open ravioli of Norwegian
lobster, morel mushrooms,
and spring truffle

2
Salad of young vegetables,
pine nut and
tarragon dressing

3
Seared foie gras, pickled
violet artichokes, pineapple
sorbet, and black pepper
crisps

OPEN RAVIOLI OF NORWEGIAN LOBSTER, MOREL MUSHROOMS, AND SPRING TRUFFLE
Serves 4

200 g basic pasta dough • 1 shallot, finely diced • 50 g white wine • 50 g water • 100 g unsalted butter, diced • 8 wild garlic leaves, roughly chopped • 20 g mixed soft herbs, finely chopped • 15 small morel mushrooms • 4 Norwegian lobster (langoustine) tails • spring truffle, for shaving

1 Roll out the pasta dough at the thinnest setting of the pasta machine. Roll through the machine several times to ensure it is all the same thickness.
2 Cut the pasta into circles using pastry cutters (70 mm would be ideal).
3 Blanch the pasta discs in salted water for around 45 seconds, then cool in cold water with a few ice cubes.
4 For the sauce, place the finely diced shallot into a small pan, cover with the white wine and heat. When the wine has reduced, add the water and bring to a boil. Once the liquid boils, slowly start adding the butter until the liquid forms a sauce consistency.
5 For the finishing touches, warm a medium-sized pan, add the butter sauce, then finish the sauce by adding wild garlic leaves, chopped herbs, and morel mushrooms.
6 Drop the Norwegian lobster tails into the sauce 30 seconds before serving and then serve.
7 Build the ravioli in separate layers using the pasta followed by the Norwegian lobster tails, and add some sauce and shaved truffle at the end.

SALAD OF YOUNG VEGETABLES, PINE NUT AND TARRAGON DRESSING
Serves 4

For the vegetables
12 orange baby carrots • 4 tbsp peas • 3 tbsp fava (broad) beans (shelled) • 2 baby zucchini (courgettes) • 6 mange-touts • 4 baby turnips • 12 spears English asparagus • 2 baby artichokes • 3 yellow carrots, sliced

1 Peel the orange baby carrots, pod the peas and fava beans, and cut the baby zucchini on the bias (angle) and the mange-touts into diamonds.
2 Peel the baby turnips using a small vegetable turning knife.

3 Take the asparagus and use a vegetable peeler to shave the thinnest amount off the skin possible, making sure the asparagus keeps its shape and is handled with care, as English asparagus can be very delicate.
4 Blanch all the prepared vegetables separately in boiling seasoned water and cook until tender, making sure the vegetables retain their bright, vibrant color.
5 Once all the vegetables are cooked, chill them in ice water again to retain their color, then drain off any excess water or ice.
6 Prepare the baby artichokes for pickling by taking off the excess leaves.
7 Pickle the artichokes using the same method shown in the foie gras recipe (right).

For the mayonnaise
2 egg yolks • 1 tsp Champagne vinegar • 1 tsp Pommery mustard • salt to taste • 100 ml vegetable oil • 100 ml extra virgin olive oil

1 Make the mayonnaise by whisking the egg yolks and vinegar together with the Pommery mustard and a touch of salt.
2 Next, slowly start adding the oils, making sure you whisk the egg yolk mixture continuously.
3 After a minute or two the mayonnaise will start to thicken. Continue this process for approximately 4 or 5 minutes, until all the oils have been incorporated.
4 Once the mayonnaise is finished it should all be the same consistency and will need a touch of seasoning.

For the dressing
1 heaping tbsp of toasted pine nuts • 1 tsp chopped tarragon

To finish the dressings, mix the tarragon, toasted pine nuts, and the mayonnaise together with a touch of lemon juice. This will form the base of the salad.

For the garnish
olive oil • squeeze of lemon juice • finely chopped herbs • 1 golden beet, sliced • 1 red beet, sliced

1 To serve, dress all the prepared and cooked vegetables in olive oil, salt, lemon juice, and a touch of finely chopped herbs.
2 Finally, arrange on the plate as shown in the photo, with the mayonnaise on the bottom and the vegetables on top, adding slices of different-colored raw beets to finish the dish.

SEARED FOIE GRAS, PICKLED VIOLET ARTICHOKES, PINEAPPLE SORBET, AND BLACK PEPPER CRISPS
Serves 4

For the foie gras
400 g good quality duck foie gras

1 Prepare the foie gras by cutting it into 100-g pieces using a hot knife.
2 Sear the foie gras in a hot nonstick pan until it has formed a nice caramelization.
3 Place the seared foie gras on a baking sheet in the oven at 355°F (180°C) for 2 minutes.

For the artichokes
4 baby violet artichokes • oil, for sweating • 1 tsp coriander seeds • 1 tsp white peppercorns • 50 ml white-wine vinegar • 100 ml good-quality sweet wine • 150 ml water • sea salt • 1 fresh bay leaf

1 Prepare the artichokes by breaking down the leaves and peeling off the outer skin.
2 Sweat them in a pan, cooking them without allowing them to take on any color.
3 Add the coriander seeds, bay leaf, white peppercorns, and white-wine vinegar, then reduce to a glaze.
4 Once the vinegar has almost disappeared, add the sweet wine and reduce again.
5 Next add the water, bring to the boil, and season using sea salt.
6 Simmer for 5 minutes.

For the sugar syrup, sorbet, and poached pineapple
400 g water • 200 g superfine (caster) sugar • 1 star anise • ½ cinnamon stick • 1 vanilla pod • 1 pineapple (½ diced and ½ roughly chopped)

1 Bring the water and sugar to the boil to form a sugar syrup, simmer with the spices and vanilla for approximately 5 minutes, then add the diced pineapple and infuse for a further 15 minutes.
2 Repeat the same process with the roughly chopped pineapple and this time, after the pineapple has infused, blend into a smooth puree and churn in an ice-cream machine.

For the black pepper crisps
300 g isomalt • 170 g glucose • 3 g cracked black pepper

1 Place the isomalt and glucose in a pan and heat to 315°F (158°C).
2 Once the sugar mix has reached

that temperature, take it off the heat and stir in the cracked black pepper.
3 Place the mixture onto a nonstick mat or tray and cool until the mixture becomes firm and brittle.
4 Once the mix has chilled, take a piece weighing around 30 g and warm it in the oven at moderate heat. The mix will then become soft and pliable.
5 Roll the pepper mix out on a piece of parchment paper and then place another sheet of paper on top. Roll the mix between the two sheets, making the crisp as thin as possible.
6 Once the crisp is rolled and chilled, store in a dry container in a cool place.

For garnish
50 g toasted hazelnuts, crushed • red amaranth • cilantro (coriander) micro-cress

1 When the foie gras is cooked, place on a cloth to drain excess fat, then onto the plate with the pineapple dice around.
2 Place the toasted hazelnuts on the plate using a teaspoon, then add the pineapple sorbet and a twist of cracked black pepper.
3 Finally, insert a piece of black pepper crisp into the pineapple sorbet, add the red amaranth and cilantro cress, and serve.

Marcus Eaves

I first met Didier in 1989, when he was a young medical student. I acknowledge that I contributed in a small way to diverting him from that respectable profession. However, his performance in the four years he spent at my restaurant at the Essex House in New York leads me to think that cooking has gained more than medicine has lost!

In 2005, Didier discovered the world of Champagne. The story obviously takes place in Rheims, the capital of that exceptional wine. The setting is the Château les Crayères, which has occupied a special place in fine cuisine for aeons. Didier arrived there with his unique style, which combines total technical mastery and a sensitive understanding of gastronomic history. After working in Monaco, Paris, and New York, Didier had discovered another world, and his first reaction was the right one: Go and learn all about it. Champagne is clearly of vital importance, but you still have to find a way of approaching this cultural monument.

Didier took the route of incorporating it into recipes. He does it subtly, taking care not to be weighed down by a rigid system: here in a delicate jelly that binds foie gras and Rheims ham together, there in a turbot stock accompanied by a paysanne of chopped vegetables. And then, working closely with his sommelier, Philippe Jamesse, he set up a very ingenious gourmet dialogue: he created a recipe to go with a particular Champagne. The exercise is planned down to the last detail: Every flavor has been thought through, the dish is constructed, the effects in the mouth are worked out according to the characteristics of a particular house or vintage. It takes all the cook's art and scientific know-how to carry off a challenge like that without slipping up.

If Didier succeeds triumphantly, it's because he uses much more than his technique and intelligence. Every one of these recipes is an ode to joy. When he's in the kitchen, this very sensible, organized, and demanding man always allows his heart to speak.

Alain Ducasse

Didier Elena was born in 1971 in Monaco. He attended culinary school in Paris, spending summers as a commis chef at Alain Ducasse's Louis XV three-Michelin-star restaurant in Monaco. On graduating, Elena joined the three-Michelin-star Restaurant Paul Bocuse before moving on to complete his National Service. After returning to Monaco, Elena worked at the Coupole restaurant, going back the same year for further training at Louis XV. In 1994 Elena moved to Roc Martin restaurant in Roquebrune Cap-Martin before opening Les Epicuriens in Nice as chef and co-owner. In 1997 he began to work as a consultant with Alain Ducasse, developing menus and cookbooks, before becoming head chef at Essex House in New York in 2000. In 2005 Elena returned to France and the Château les Crayères restaurant in Rheims, which has achieved two Michelin stars.

MENU

Nage of crayfish cardinal
with wild fennel
and chives

~

Roast and lacquered loin
of suckling pig,
with melt-in-the-mouth
pork belly

~

Calves' sweetbreads

~

Raspberry, fromage blanc,
lemon, and speculaas

1
Kitchen equipment

2 & 4
Mixing sauces at
Hôtel Château les Crayères

3
Plating dishes

5
Didier Elena finishing a dish

Didier Elena

122

Hôtel Château les Crayères, Rheims, France

1
Nage of crayfish cardinal with wild fennel and chives

2
Roast and lacquered loin of suckling pig, with melt-in-the-mouth pork belly

3
Calves' sweetbreads

4
Raspberry, fromage blanc, lemon, and speculaas

NAGE OF CRAYFISH CARDINAL WITH WILD FENNEL AND CHIVES
Serves 4–5

For the fennel stock
500 g fennel • 50 g onions • olive oil, for pan-frying • 10 g fennel seeds • 5 ml Ricard • 600 ml white stock

1 Finely slice the fennel and the onions, sweat in the olive oil in a sauté pan without letting them brown, and add the fennel seeds.
2 Deglaze the pan with the Ricard and reduce the liquid before moistening with the white stock.
3 Bring to a boil and simmer over gentle heat for 20 minutes.
4 Strain through cheesecloth (muslin) in a conical sieve.

For the fennel jelly
150 ml fennel stock • 3 g fennel seeds • 2 gelatin leaves

1 Heat the fennel stock with the seeds and let infuse, covered, for a few minutes.
2 Strain, add the gelatin, then keep at room temperature.

For the fennel bavarois
5 g fennel seeds • 200 g light (single) cream • 15 g heavy (double) cream • 200 g fennel stock • 1 gelatin leaf

1 Add the fennel seeds to the light cream, reduce by half, add the heavy cream with the fennel stock, and reduce until 500 g remains.
2 Stir in the gelatin, then pour onto a baking sheet with a 1.5 cm rim.
3 Set in the refrigerator, then cut into rounds with a pastry cutter.

For the coulis of crayfish
500 g crayfish shells • olive oil, for pan frying • ½ head garlic • ½ bay leaf • ½ sprig of thyme • ⅓ carrot • ⅓ onion • ⅓ stick celery • ½ leek • 10 g tomato concentrate • 130 ml Cognac • 3 tomatoes • 1 liter crayfish-cooking liquid • zest of 1 lemon • 150 ml light (single) cream

1 Brown the crayfish shells in the olive oil.
2 Chop the vegetables and herbs (except the tomatoes), then add them to the pan and sweat.
3 Pour in the tomato concentrate so that it covers the pieces, flambé with the Cognac, add the raw tomatoes and the crayfish cooking liquid, and simmer for 30 minutes.
4 Add the lemon zest 5 minutes before taking it off the heat.
5 Strain through a conical sieve, mix with the cream, and reduce until it has a smooth coating consistency.

ROAST AND LACQUERED LOIN OF SUCKLING PIG, WITH MELT-IN-THE MOUTH PORK BELLY
Serves 4–5

For the potato and black pudding layer
oil, for greasing • 45 strips of potato, cooked, 2-mm thick • 40 strips of black pudding, cooked, 2-mm thick

1 Take 5 stainless steel pastry rings, 8 cm long and 4 cm wide. Grease, then fill each one with 9 strips of potato and 8 strips of black pudding in alternate layers, starting and finishing with potato.
2 Cut in two, lengthwise, to serve.

For the pork belly
300 g belly pork • stock, for cooking

1 Cook the meat in the stock over a very low heat, then cool.
2 Cut into strips the same size as in the garnish above and brown over a gentle heat, basting regularly.

For the sausage cylinders
500 g pork • 150 g bacon • 100 g white bread, soaked in milk • 1 egg • 125 ml light (single) cream • 5 hollow potato tubes, cooked

1 Preheat the oven to 350°F (180°C).
2 Mince the pork with the bacon, then mix with the bread, egg, and cream. Shape into a cylinder and steam until cooked.
3 Carefully put the cylinders inside the potato tubes, and put them in the oven for a few minutes.

For the suckling pig
5 tenderloins of suckling pig • butter, to roast • garlic, to taste • thyme, to taste • salt and pepper, to taste

1 Preheat the oven to 350°F (180°C).
2 Roast the meat in foaming butter, then flavor with garlic and thyme.
3 Cut up the meat the same size as the other accompaniments, then plate up and season.

For the pork jus
1 kg pork trimmings • ½ onion • 1½ cloves garlic • 1 sprig thyme • 50 ml white wine • 500 ml white stock

1 Brown the pork trimmings over gentle heat. Cut up the onion and garlic and add them with the thyme. Sweat without browning.
2 Deglaze the pan with the wine, and reduce until all the liquid has evaporated.
3 Moisten with the white stock, then cook over gentle heat for 40 minutes. Strain.

CALVES' SWEETBREADS
Serves 4–5

For the calves' sweetbreads with celery root
200 g celery root (celeriac) puree • 50 g milk • 2.5 g agar agar • 500 g braised heart sweetbreads • truffle slices, for serving • celery root (celeriac) slices, for serving • beurre monté, for coating

1 Heat the celery root puree over gentle heat.
2 Heat the milk in a pan, pour in the agar agar in a stream, bring to a boil, and stir in the celery root puree. Keep at a warm working temperature.
3 Cut the sweetbreads into 4-mm slices. Put in the bottom of a rectangular stainless steel pastry cutter, pour a little celery root puree over them and let set in the refrigerator before cutting into bars.
4 To serve, decorate with thin slices of truffle and celery root, coated in beurre monté.

For the calves' sweetbreads
5 heart sweetbreads • 75 g black truffle • 100 ml veal jus

1 Blanch the sweetbreads in water for 5 minutes, cool, then trim and put in the refrigerator for 2 hours with a small weight on top.
2 Divide into portions and stud in 3 places with small sticks of black truffle. Roast on skewers for 20 minutes, brushing regularly with veal jus to glaze evenly.

For the truffled veal jus
250 ml reduced veal jus • 50 ml truffle jus • a little butter • 10 g chopped truffle

Dilute the veal jus with the truffle jus, add a piece of butter and end with the chopped truffle.

RASPBERRY, FROMAGE BLANC, LEMON, AND SPECULAAS
Serves 4–5

For the fromage blanc round
1 egg, beaten • 40 g superfine (caster) sugar • 150 g fromage blanc • 8 g all-purpose (plain) flour • 10 g light (single) cream

1 Preheat the oven to 320°F (160°C).
2 Mix the egg with the sugar, then add the fromage blanc, flour and cream. Pour the mixture into silicone muffin pans and bake in a bain-marie for 20 minutes. Turn out when cold.

For the lemon cream round
135 g egg, beaten • 135 g superfine (caster) sugar • 90 g lemon juice • 150 g butter, diced

1 Mix the egg, sugar, and lemon juice together, then cook in a bain-marie at 185°F (85°C) until the mixture becomes thick.
2 Stop the mixture from cooking further by removing from the heat, and add the butter.
3 Pour the mixture into silicone muffin pans the same size as the fromage blanc pans, but shallower. Place in the refrigerator, then turn out and place on top of the fromage blanc rounds.

For the lemon sorbet
75 g sugar • 65 g milk • 90 g water • 65 g golden syrup • 125 g lemon juice

1 Make a syrup by gently heating the sugar, milk, water, and golden syrup, until the sugar has dissolved, then add the lemon juice.
2 Churn in an ice-cream maker and put in the freezer.

For the raspberry sorbet
17 g sugar • 22 g glucose powder • 550 ml water • 125 g raspberry pulp • 100 ml raspberry liqueur

1 Make a syrup by gently heating the sugar, glucose powder, and water until the sugar has dissolved, then add the raspberry pulp and raspberry liqueur.
2 Churn in an ice-cream maker and put in the freezer.

For the speculaas cookies
30 g butter • 30 g brown sugar • 1 egg • 30 ml milk • 1.5 g ground cinnamon • 65 g flour • 1 g salt • fresh raspberries, to serve

1 Preheat the oven to 335°F (170°C).
2 Mix the butter with the sugar, then add the egg, milk, cinnamon, flour, and salt. Roll out the dough to 2 mm thick, then cut into strips. Roll, then bake for 7 minutes.

For the tapioca in lime milk
250 ml milk • zest of 2 limes • 15 g tapioca • 10 g sugar

Heat the milk with the lime zest and allow to infuse for 10 minutes. Strain, add the tapioca and sugar, then cook over gentle heat for 15 minutes. Serve cold.

Didier Elena

1–3
A chef works at the
wood-burning oven

4
The dining room at Franny's

5
Andrew Feinberg in
the kitchen

Andrew Feinberg

MENU

Dry-cured pancetta

~

Lettuces and herbs

~

Pork sausage with bell peppers

~

Clam and chilli pizza

~

Panna cotta

Andrew Feinberg was born in Boston, MA, in 1974, and studied at the French Culinary Institute in New York City. From there he went from strength to strength, training under Madeleine Kamman at the School for American Chefs in California and attending the International Wine Center in New York. Feinberg built on this experience, working at acclaimed restaurants such as Gramercy Tavern and Savoy, and finally opening Franny's In New York in 2004 with his wife and business partner, Francine Stephens, to wide acclaim from the city's food press. Franny's serves versatile and exquisite Italian dishes, insisting on sustainability and openness while maintaining a high standard of excellence. Always exploring new techniques and methods, including recently developing the restaurant's curing of meats, Feinberg works with a simple philosophy of serving each ingredient so that its unique flavor can be best appreciated, letting the excellence of Italian cuisine speak for itself.

Whenever I am in New York, I always stop by Franny's for the tomato and buffalo mozzarella pizzas after visiting the Brooklyn Museum or for a little late-night bite of pasta after catching the latest film.

Before they founded Franny's, its two owners, Francine Stephens and Andrew Feinberg, worked for restaurants and environmental nonprofit organizations. Together they have created something close to my ideal of a mom-and-pop restaurant: an unpretentious space that is inviting for adults and children alike and that serves food that is both subtle and vivacious. Andrew's cooking is inspired by his travels in Italy and his passion for the ritual of the shared meal. Every night, a glow radiates from the restaurant. You can feel it when you walk up to the front door.

Andrew's cooking philosophy is simple—as simple as his pizza topped only with extra-virgin olive oil and sea salt—and thoughtful. He and Francine are deeply committed to creating a business that is friendly to its employees, to its customers, and to the environment. Fruits and vegetables, dairy and eggs, and meat and fish are procured almost entirely from local and organic producers. The coffee is certified to be fair-trade and shade-grown. Andrew and his crew (young cooks and floor personnel, many of whom trained at the most celebrated established restaurants) make their own sausages, cure their own meats, and make a diverse and eclectic clientèle feel thoroughly at home. The restaurant is justifiably proud of its many other eco-friendly practices, which include converting its kitchen grease to biodiesel fuel and using recycled paper, biodegradable takeout containers, and environmentally correct cleaning products. That they manage to do all this without over-selling their own good intentions is a tribute to their culinary and managerial equilibrium.

Alice Waters

1
Dry-cured pancetta

2
Lettuces and herbs

3
Pork sausage with
bell peppers

4
Clam and chilli pizza

5
Panna cotta

128

DRY-CURED PANCETTA

pork belly • salt • curing salt

1 Buy pork belly with the skin on from a local farm. If the bones are intact remove them by sliding your boning knife under them and running it along until you have removed them. The belly must be flat and even. If any part of the belly is not flat, cut it off and reserve for another use. Now you are ready to cure it.
2 You will need a scale that measures grams for the salts and pounds to weigh your pork belly.
3 Having weighed the pork, calculate how much salt you need: you need 2.8% of the total weight of the meat (for example, 3 kg meat needs 84 g salt).
4 Calculate how much curing salt you need, which is 2.46 g per kg (for example, 3 kg meat needs 7.38 g curing salt). Check the instructions on the package, as each brand of curing salt is slightly different.
5 Measure out your salt and curing salt and combine them well. Place the meat in a roasting pan or baking sheet. Season on the flesh side only with half of the cure mixture, distributing it evenly. Let sit for 10–15 minutes. The salt will start to react with the meat and some sweating will happen. Season with the rest of the cure mixture. Cover the meat with plastic wrap (clingfilm) and place in the refrigerator.
6 After 24 hours, remove the meat from the refrigerator and pour off the liquid that has accumulated. Replace the plastic wrap on the meat and return it to the refrigerator for 10 days. Pour off any liquid that accumulates in the vessel.
7 After 10 days age the meat in a cool 52–58°F (12–14°C) room with a relative humidity of 70%. An old stone basement works well.
8 Age the pork belly for 6–8 weeks. It should feel dry and firm when pressed with a finger, and has now become pancetta.
9 Lightly scrub the pancetta to get rid of any mold that might have accumulated.
10 Trim the skin away from the flesh and slice the pancetta as thinly as possible.
11 Store the pancetta in the refrigerator.

LETTUCES AND HERBS

This salad is all about local ingredients and is the perfect way to begin a meal. Go to your favorite farmers' market or farmstand (farm shop) and purchase as many different types of lettuce as you can find. You want to look for lettuces with different textures and tastes: bitter, sweet, crunchy and soft.

escarole • bibb lettuce • puntarelle • radicchio • red dandelion • upland • cress • arugula (rocket) • parsley • mint • red onion • moscato vinegar • extra-virgin olive oil • salt and pepper

Wash and dry the lettuces separately, then mix together with the herbs in a bowl. Slice the onion thinly and add to the bowl. Dress the salad with the vinegar, oil, and salt and pepper.

PORK SAUSAGE WITH BELL PEPPERS

For the sausage
hog casings • 2 kg boneless • shoulder butt pork • 225 g pork belly • 148 g Parmesan cheese • 23 g garlic • 125 ml white wine • 39 g salt • 7 g black pepper • 5.6 g curing salt

1 First clean the hog casings. Rinse the salt off the exteriors and run cold water through the insides.
2 Cut the casings into 1-meter lengths.
3 Grind the meat through a 3/16 die (cutting plate). Mix the ingredients together very well until you have achieved a sticky texture. This will ensure that your sausage will not be crumbly.
4 Now you can stuff the sausage into casings. After stuffing you can either tie off individual sausages or you can twist them. Refrigerate the sausages for 6 hours.

For the peppers
red bell peppers • extra-virgin olive oil, for pan-frying • salt and pepper • red-wine vinegar

1 Slice the peppers in half and remove veins and seeds.
2 Warm some extra-virgin olive oil in a sauté pan. When the oil is beginning to smoke, add your peppers, then let them pan-fry undisturbed for a few minutes. They should develop a nice caramelized color. Add salt and pepper to taste and continue cooking until they are soft.
3 Remove the peppers to a shallow bowl. Sprinkle some red-wine vinegar over them and leave them to marinate for a few hours.

To finish
1 Preheat the oven to 350°F (180°C).
2 Warm a sauté pan with extra-virgin olive oil over medium heat. Slowly cook the sausage, maintaining medium heat and rolling the sausage around to achieve a golden brown color. When the sausage is browned, place it in the oven for 2–3 minutes. To serve, place the sausage on top of the peppers.

CLAM AND CHILLI PIZZA
Serves 6

Cook the pizza in a brick oven if you have access to one. If you are using a conventional oven at home, use a pizza stone.

For the clam sauce
extra-virgin olive oil, for pan frying • 1 onion, roughly chopped • 5 cloves garlic, smashed • 1 bay leaf • 350 ml white wine • 54 littleneck clams • about 225 ml cream

1 Heat the olive oil in a large deep pan and sweat the onion and garlic with the bay leaf.
2 When the vegetables are soft, add the white wine and cover.
3 Bring the liquid to a boil and place the clams in it. Cover and steam the clams over high heat. After about 5 minutes check to see if the clams have opened, and if so remove them from the pan and cool.
4 Strain the clam liquor and reduce it until the sauce starts to thicken. Add the cream and reduce further, then let the sauce cool.
5 Separate the clams from their shells. Reserve the meat and discard the shells.

For the pizza dough
12.25 g fresh yeast • 18.25 g salt • 475 ml ice-cold water • 700 g flour

1 In a large bowl, dissolve the yeast in the water. Add the salt and flour and mix until the dough starts to come together.
2 Turn the dough out onto a table and knead for about 10 minutes until smooth. Place the dough in a bowl, cover and refrigerate overnight.
3 Turn the dough out onto a table and cut into 6 (185-g) pieces. Roll each into a ball shape using the palm of your hand and rotate it in a clockwise motion. Cover the dough balls and let rest for 6–8 hours in the refrigerator.

To serve
chilli flakes • chopped parsley

1 Take the dough out of the refrigerator 1 hour before using it, and at the same time preheat the oven to 500°F (250°C). Alternatively, light a fire in a brick oven if you have access to one.
2 Stretch each dough ball into a pizza shape and spoon on just enough clam sauce to cover the dough — not too much, as it is very strong. Place 9 clams on top of the sauce and sprinkle with some chilli flakes. Repeat for the rest of the dough balls.
3 Bake until nice and browned. Finish each pizza with a little chopped parsley.

PANNA COTTA
Serves 6

¼ vanilla bean • 350 ml cream • 85 g sugar • 1 gelatin sheet • pinch salt • saba, for drizzling

1 Split the vanilla bean and scrape out the seeds into a pan. Add the cream and sugar and heat gently.
2 Place the gelatin sheet in a container and cover with cold water.
3 When the cream begins to boil, take it off the heat and strain the liquid into a bowl.
4 Remove the gelatin from the cold water and squeeze out any residual water clinging to it.
5 Add the gelatin to the hot cream and add the salt. Cool the cream over an ice bath.
6 When the cream is very cold, pour it into ramekins and cool for 6 hours in the refrigerator.
7 When you are ready to serve it, run a paring knife along the inside of each ramekin and turn out the panna cotta.
8 Drizzle with a teaspoon of saba to finish.

Andrew Feinberg

The chefs at our New York restaurant are constantly watching the competition in the city. They are my eyes and ears, and if I cannot be there myself they continuously keep me updated on New York's restaurant scene. It's rare that a chef captures the attention of a city, but one afternoon Josh Emmett, my head chef at Gordon Ramsay at the London, rang to tell me with great enthusiasm the details of a dinner he had at John Fraser's restaurant, Dovetail. Josh is one of the stars of my international team of chefs, and his praise and interest in John's cooking assured me he must be one to watch.

One of America's most exciting young chefs, John owes much of his classical training to his time at Thomas Keller's prestigious restaurant The French Laundry in California, where he spent two years in the kitchen. This training in European-style cooking is immediately evident in his menus at his Upper West Side restaurant, where he serves the highest-quality and freshest seasonal ingredients with absolute precision. His menu is focused and intelligently put together offering such dishes as Columbia river salmon with spring garlic, green gazpacho, almonds, quinoa, and gnocchi with pigs' trotters, cranberry beans, and truffles. John understands the paramount importance of seasonality and shops carefully for his produce, keeping his menu as local as possible.

He doesn't over-complicate dishes, but presents them cleanly and confidently with real finesse. His technique is both solid and accomplished, and in the last couple of years John has carved a name for himself and a reputation as one of New York's biggest talents. He is careful to move with the times as well, keeping his dishes modern by adding small, inventive twists along the way. Chefs like John Fraser don't come on to the restaurant scene often, and I am sure that he will be a dominant name for a long time to come.

Gordon Ramsay

Born in 1975, John Fraser began to cook between college semesters, with a stint learning how to prepare fish on Long Island, New York. Fraser proceeded to cook for two notable Los Angeles establishments, Cocco Pazzo and Raffles L'Ermitage Beverly Hills. From here, Fraser accepted a post at California's French Laundry as chef de partie to Thomas Keller, where he gained the confidence to explore food with playful creativity. Next Fraser moved to Paris, spending a year in positions at Taillevent and Maison Blanche, lending him crucial insight into global fine cuisine. Returning to the U.S., he opened Snack Taverna, an intimate Greek eatery, in New York City to learn more about the process of running a restaurant. After two years he became executive chef at Compass. In 2007, Fraser opened Dovetail 2007 in New York, where his menu has attracted notice for its focused purity and its energetic sourcing of artisanal ingredients and local produce.

MENU

Avocado, ramps, jicama, and hearts of palm

~

Poached egg with artichokes, Serrano ham, and herbes de Provence

~

Sautéed foie gras, graham crackers, and huckleberries

~

Baked sea scallop, sea urchin, and kumquats

~

Halibut confit, peas, scallions, and maitake mushrooms

~

Roasted sirloin with beef cheek lasagna, asparagus, and endive

~

Chocolate potato cake, Baileys, and honey crisps

John Fraser

1
Reviewing the day's menu

2
Checking produce deliveries

3
The restaurant dining room

AVOCADO, RAMPS, JICAMA AND HEARTS OF PALM
Serves 4

50 g ramp (wild leek) leaves •
1 bunch cilantro (coriander) • 350 ml
blended oil • salt • 1 eggplant
(aubergine) • all-purpose (plain)
flour, to coat • oil, for deep-frying •
salt • 2 avocados • 60 ml agrumato
(lemon extra-virgin olive oil) • black
pepper and fleur de sel, to taste •
20 thin slices hearts of palm •
24 sprig wild watercress • 24 jicama
sticks (batons) • 24 pickled ramp
sticks (batons) • extra-virgin olive oil

1   First make the ramp oil by
blending the first 4 ingredients
together in a blender.
2   For the eggplant chips, thinly
slice the eggplant, toss in flour
and deep-fry until crispy. Season
with salt.
3   To assemble the dish, for each
person carefully peel half an
avocado. Season with agrumato,
black pepper, and fleur de sel.
Drizzle ramp oil on top, then
place on top a salad of 5 slices of
hearts of palm, a quarter of the
watercress, 6 ramp sticks and
6 jicama sticks, seasoned with
olive oil and salt. Place 5 eggplant
chips on top of the salad.

POACHED EGG WITH ARTICHOKES, SERRANO HAM, AND HERBES DE PROVENCE
Serves 2

For the carrot puree
225 ml carrot juice • 150 g sliced,
peeled carrots • 1 tsp butter •
pinch cayenne pepper • salt, to taste

1   Combine all the ingredients in
a heavy pan and cook to reduce
until the juice has completely
evaporated.
2   While still hot, blend in a blender
until smooth. Pass through a
fine-mesh sieve to remove any
large pieces.

For the glazed onions
12 pearl onions • 1 tsp sugar
• 1 tsp butter • salt • red wine,
to taste • vinegar, to taste

1   Place the onions in a pan with
some water, the sugar, the butter,
and a pinch of salt. Cook until soft
and all the water has evaporated,
creating a glaze on the onion.
2   Season with a little red wine
and vinegar.

For the artichokes
1 onion • 2 cloves garlic, finely
chopped • 1 leek • 1 carrot •
60 ml olive oil • 125 ml white wine
• juice of 1 lemon • 2–3 artichokes •
6 whole artichokes • 225 ml chicken
stock • 1 bay leaf • 3-4 sprigs fresh
thyme • cracked black pepper •
kosher salt

1   Sweat the onion, garlic, leek, and
carrots in the olive oil until soft.
2   Add the white wine and lemon
juice, and reduce until evaporated.
3   Peel the artichokes, removing
the tough green skin and the
petals, and add along with the
chicken stock, the bay leaf, thyme,
pepper, and salt. Bring to a boil.
Skim the pot, and reduce to a low
simmer until artichokes are soft.
4   Cool the artichokes in the liquid.

For the eggs, and to finish
4 eggs • 475 ml heavy (double)
cream • 475 ml milk • 2 tbsp
butter • 4 tsp herbes de Provence •
12 pearl onions, glazed (see
above) • 12 artichokes, cooked
barigoule-style (see above) •
1 quantity carrot puree (see above) •
12 pieces Serrano ham, about 7.6 cm
long and 2.5 cm wide • 75 g day-old
bread • olive oil • 15 Picholine olives

1   Place the eggs in gently boiling
water for 5 minutes 25 seconds.
Immediately remove from the
water and cool until the shell can
be handled. Peel the egg, being
careful not to disturb the yolk, as
it will still be runny.
2   Heat the cream, milk, butter,
and herbes de Provence until
almost boiling, then remove from
the fire. Let rest for 10 minutes and
strain.
3   Heat the onions and artichokes
with a little of the artichoke
cooking liquid until warm.
Heat the carrot puree until warm.
4   Place some carrot puree in the
center of a bowl. Gently put 2 eggs
in the puree. Place 3 artichokes,
and onions around the eggs. Top
the artichokes with the Serrano
ham.
5   Use an immersion blender to
froth the herbes de Provence liquid.
Only plate the bubbles.
6   Season the bread with olive oil.
Pit the olives, and dry them in
a dehydrator them. Pulse together
in a food processor until the
texture of wet sand. Sprinkle on top
of the dish.

BAKED SEA SCALLOP, SEA URCHIN, AND KUMQUATS
Serves 4

For the scallop custard
1 clove garlic • ½ shallot, sliced
• 1 tsp butter • 200 g milk • 200 g
heavy (double) cream • 1 sea
scallop • 2 egg yolks and 1 egg
white • salt

1   Preheat the oven to 250ºF
(120ºC).
2   Sweat the garlic and shallot in
a pan with the butter. Add the milk,
cream, and sea scallop.
3   Lightly beat and add in the eggs,
and season with salt.
4   Place in ovenproof shot glasses
and bake in a water bath for
30 minutes or until set.

For the uni butter
25 g uni (sea urchin) • 50 g butter •
pinch Madras curry powder

Put all the ingredients in a food
processor and pulse until combined.

For the kumquat confit
6 kumquats • 200 g sugar • 225 ml
water • 2 cardamom pods

1   On a Japanese mandolin, slice
the kumquats about 1 mm thick.
2   Heat the sugar, water, and
cardamom over high heat until
a syrup forms. Pour it over the
kumquats and let cool at room
temperature.

To finish
4 uni (sea urchins) • 4 cilantro
(coriander) leaves • 1 tbsp wasabi
tobiko

1   Warm the custard in the oven
and top with uni, cilantro, and a few
confit kumquats.
2   Put uni butter on the scallop
and place under a salamander or
hot broiler (grill) until the butter
caramelizes, then top with wasabi
tobiko, evenly dispersed.

HALIBUT CONFIT, PEAS, SCALLIONS, AND MAITAKE MUSHROOMS
Serves 4

125 ml canola (rapeseed) oil
• 125ml extra-virgin olive oil •
3 sprigs thyme • 3 cloves garlic
• 4 (175-g) halibut steaks • salt and
pepper • 1 large scallion (spring
onion), cooked slowly in butter until
soft • 125 ml vegetable stock •
1 tbsp butter • Chardonnay vinegar,
to taste • 300 g peas, cooked until al
dente • 65 g spinach leaves • 10 mint
leaves, julienned • 85 g tomato
concasse • pinch grated nutmeg •
225 g maitake (hen of the woods)
mushrooms, sautéed

1   Heat the canola oil, olive oil,
thyme, and garlic in a heavy pan
to 150ºF (70ºC).
2   Season the halibut with salt
and white pepper. Place in oil for
8 minutes or until translucent.
3   Put the scallions, stock, and
butter in a pot. Season with
Chardonnay vinegar. Add the peas,
spinach, mint, and tomatoes.
Wait for 3 minutes and spoon into
a bowl.
4   Place the halibut on top of the
pea and onion ragôut, sprinkle
with nutmeg, and top with maitake
mushrooms.

1
Avocado, ramps, jicama,
and hearts of palm

2
Poached eggs with artichokes,
Serrano ham, and
herbes de Provence

3
Baked scallop, sea urchin,
and kumquats

4
Halibut confit, peas, scallions,
and maitake mushrooms

John Fraser

Some years ago I heard that there was a very young and interesting chef working in a restaurant called Tragabuches in Ronda, near Malaga in Andalusia. Now that he is head chef at the Calima Restaurant at the Gran Melia Don Pepe Hotel in Marbella, Dani García's cuisine continues to delight and fascinate.

The main characteristic of his cuisine is that it is avant-garde with an Andalusian spirit. Out of all the chefs I have ever known, Dani is the one who most successfully marries the avant-garde and the provincial. He has a unique ability to combine a feeling, in this case his attachment to his Andalusian roots, with highly technical elaboration and preparations, such as *las sopas frias* (his unique take on traditional cold soups) and *El tratamiento del mundo del mar* (a treatment of the world of the sea). His "*cocina*contra*dicion*," as the name suggests, is a cuisine full of traditional tastes and flavors, but conceptually and technically innovative and progressive.

Dani's food is provocative, witty, and exciting. Using the freshest seasonal ingredients, his preparation and presentation are never less than impeccable. He draws much of his influence from his environment: when you eat in his restaurant, the magic of Andalusia enters your body. Along with flavor and high technical excellence, Dani believes that memory is one of the most important aspects of his philosophy. A large part of his menu is based on his personal history, drawing on childhood memories such as the scents of the Andalusian coast and barbecues on Marbella's beaches. His experiments with classic dishes elevate traditional Andalusian cooking to new heights.

Constantly striving for perfection, as an emerging chef Dani has undeniably great potential. He has a long career in front of him, as well as exceptional honesty and passion. With the greatest of respect for all the other young chefs out there, I do believe he could become one of the best in the world.

Ferran Adrià

Born in 1975 in Marbella, Spain, Dani García followed stints at culinary school and the kitchen of Martín Berasategui Restaurant with a post at Málaga's Tragabuches restaurant. In 2000 he saw the restaurant gain a Michelin star. In 2005 he took on El Calima restaurant in Marbella, winning another Michelin star two years later, and he has since opened a second Calima in Tenerife. He was named Chef of the Year in 2009 by Spain's Royal Academy of Gastronomy. García's cuisine is always experimental, updating familiar flavors with a blast of modern technique: His oysters are served with "popcorn" made from a sherry, tomato, and olive oil mix frozen in liquid nitrogen to trigger taste memories. This familiar dish, rendered in an exciting new way, encapsulates García's balance of tradition and innovation.

MENU

The sea bed

~

Mock plum stuffed with slow-cooked foie gras in vanilla-mentholated stock

~

Lemon verbena yogurt with carrot planted in an Oreo cookie field

Dani García

1
Petits fours

2–4
In kitchen at El Calima

5
Dani García outside
the kitchen

El Calima, Marbella, Spain

THE SEA BED
Serves 4

The Andalusian coast features many underwater caves, coral, and canyons.

For the seafood and stock
500 ml water • 15 g kombu seaweed • ½ lemongrass stalk • 30 g dried bonito • 8 large clams • 16 cockles • agar agar (quantity will depend on amount of stock produced)

1 Heat the water with the kombu seaweed and lemongrass. Just before it boils, remove the kombu and add the dried bonito. It is important not to let the stock reach boiling point—simply cover and let stand for 40 minutes.
2 Strain and return to the heat. Blanch the clams and cockles in the same water.
3 Remove the clams and cockles when their shells start to open slightly, discarding any that fail to open. They must be half-cooked only. Shell and set aside.
4 Add 1 g agar agar for every liter of stock.
5 Place 2 cockles and 1 clam in each dish, and pour the stock over them to set. Refrigerate.

For the potatoes
6 violet potatoes • 1 shallot, finely chopped • olive oil, for dressing • salt • curry powder, to taste

1 Boil the violet potatoes in their skins for 15 minutes, then peel and press with a spider.
2 Cover the potatoes with double their depth in water and let stand for 12 hours, changing the water every 2 hours. They will gradually lose their violet color and turn blue-green, which will represent the sea bed.
3 When they are ready, add the shallot and a little olive oil, salt, and curry powder.

To serve
seaweed of different types • lemon zest

Add dressed blue potatoes to each dish in which the seafood and clam stock were allowed to set, and arrange seaweed on top. Finish with a little fresh lemon zest.

MOCK PLUM STUFFED WITH SLOW-COOKED FOIE GRAS IN VANILLA -MENTHOLATED STOCK
Serves 8

For the foie gras
1 liter milk • 1 liter water • 35 g salt • 1 fresh foie gras, about 500 g • oil, for pan-frying

1 Place the milk, water and salt in a bain-marie and heat to 90°F (30° C).
2 Meanwhile, separate the foie gras lobes, removing any visible veins with tweezers. Cut the foie gras into 60-g portions.
3 When the correct temperature is reached, put the foie gras in the bain-marie for 7 hours. During this time, pick up the foie gras portions one by one and gently rub them without removing them from the liquid so that they release most of their fat and blood.
4 Remove the foie gras and dry with clean cloths. Cover in plastic wrap (clingfilm) and freeze in a blast chiller.

For the plum broth and puree
1 kg plums • 4 liters water • 10 g salt • 100 g sugar • 30 g star anise • 1 vanilla bean • 20 g Szechuan pepper

1 Place all the ingredients in a vacuum-pack bag. Seal the bag and place it in a steam oven for 3 hours at 150°F (70°C).
2 Open the vacuum-pack bag and strain the liquid through cheesecloth (muslin), reserving the plums. Let the broth stand and skim any solids from the top. You will be left with a clear consommé without impurities.
3 Process the reserved plums in a Thermomix to make a puree. Strain through a fine-mesh chinois and set aside.

For the plum wafer
3 sheets obulato wafer • plum liqueur

Place the obulato on a nonstick silicone baking mat and brush with the plum liqueur. Place in a dehydrator at 110°F (42°C) until dried.

For finishing the foie gras
1 Preheat the oven to 275°F (135°C).
2 Heat some oil in a skillet to 350°F (180°C). Take the foie gras from the freezer and fry until it turns a golden color.
3 Remove the foie gras from the oil. Place on a baking sheet in the oven.
4 Remove the foie gras from the oven when the inside reaches 135°F (58°C). Use a spatula to coat it evenly with the plum puree.

For plating
salt flakes • samphire

Place the foie gras in the middle of the plate, put a piece of obulato on top and add the plum broth, soaking the foie gras so that the obulato is moistened. Add salt flakes and samphire.

LEMON VERBENA YOGURT WITH CARROT PLANTED IN AN OREO COOKIE FIELD
Serves 4

For the yogurt mousse
4 gelatin leaves • 500 ml heavy (double) cream • 500 g plain yogurt • 100 g sugar

1 Rehydrate the gelatin leaves in cold water. Half whip the cream. Heat a little yogurt and add the gelatin. Mix with the remaining yogurt and the sugar. Fold the cream into the yogurt. Keep in a pastry (piping bag) and refrigerate.
2 Stretch plastic wrap (clingfilm) over a counter and pipe a little of the mousse vertically onto the wrap. Enclose in the plastic wrap to give it an elongated shape. Freeze.

For the carrot gel (nitro gel)
750 g carrots • 30 g maltodextrin (vegetable gel)

1 Wash the carrots, blend them and pass the liquid through a fine-mesh chinois.
2 Heat 500 ml of the carrot liquid. Add the 30 g of gel and heat to 195°F (90°C) until it dissolves. Keep the carrot gel at 150°F (70°C).
3 Take the yogurt mousse from the freezer. Carefully remove the plastic wrap and prick with a needle. Prepare a polystyrene container with liquid nitrogen. (Liquid nitrogen should not be handled without training in how to use it safely.) Dip the mousse first in the liquid nitrogen, then the carrot gel, to obtain a fine carrot coating. Refrigerate.

For the lemon verbena mousse
300 g cream • 250 g milk • 10 g lemon verbena • 3 gelatin leaves • 50 g sugar • 30 g lemon juice • 25 g whipped heavy (double) cream

1 Put the cream, milk, and lemon verbena in a pan and let stand for 2 hours to infuse. Process through a fine-mesh sieve and set aside.
2 Rehydrate the gelatin in cold water. Heat a small quantity of the infusion and mix in the gelatin until fully dissolved.
3 Using a spatula, gradually add in the sugar, lemon juice, and yogurt infusion. Once mixed, gradually add the whipped cream, stirring constantly so that the mixture does not collapse. Refrigerate.

For the cocoa streusel
200 g butter • 100 g brown sugar • 200 g powdered almond • 180 g all-purpose (plain) flour • 20 g unsweetened cocoa powder • 3 g charcoal coloring • 70 g 70% couverture chocolate • 20 g cocoa nibs

1 Preheat the oven to 325°F (160°C).
2 Soften the butter by warming it slightly. Place in the bowl of a stand mixer all the ingredients except for the chocolate and the cocoa nibs. Mix well.
3 Meanwhile, melt the chocolate and gradually add the mixture to the other ingredients. Then add the cocoa nibs and finish mixing.
4 Make a cookie shape with the streusel and bake on a baking sheet for a few minutes. Take out and let cool.
5 Process until it acquires the consistency of sand, then refrigerate.

To assemble
diced carrot • marigold petals • bog stitchwort

1 Put the lemon verbena cream in the middle of the dish. Place a few pieces of diced carrot in the cream and cover with the "sand" to give the appearance of a field. Position the carrot in the sand as if it were planted.
2 Arrange a few marigold petals round about, and place a sprig of bog stitchwort in the carrot.

Dani García

1 & 2
Cruz Goler in the kitchen
at Lupa

3 & 4
Preserved herbs and
fruits in the kitchen

5
Rolling grissini

Cruz Goler

MENU

Pear and wild
watercress salad

~

Linguine with razor clams
and cardoons

~

Hanger steak with
parsnips, cauliflower and
salsa verde

~

Black pepper panna
cotta with figs

Cruz Goler was born in 1971 and began his career in food at Pittsburgh's Luma, absorbing Scott Bryan's comprehensive knowledge of Italian food and flavors at an early age. Later, in a post at Union Pacific under Rocco DiSpirito, Goler witnessed firsthand the pace and tenacity that make a chef; from there, he worked his way up to become chef de cuisine of Jean-George Vongerichten's Mercer Kitchen, exploring simple and clean flavors. In 2005, he opened Del Posto for the Batali–Bastianich group. He is currently head chef at New York's Lupa, a restaurant that knows the value of authenticity, featuring specialties from the Testaccio (meatpacking) neighborhood of Rome. Lupa lives up to its reputation, offering the experience of a Roman osteria in the heart of New York City.

I first ran into Cruz Goler at Jean-Georges mythic and tasty Mercer Kitchen in the early '90s. When the Batali-Bastianich team began to build Del Posto in 2005, we knew we had our most ambitious project to date and we needed a cerebral yet technically savvy and solid guy to help run the show. Having courted Cruz unsuccessfully in prior projects, finally getting him as executive sous chef was one of our smartest moves. His execution of the signature Vongerichten cuisine was clean, simple, and yet very complex. His mastery of Asian and Western technique and the ability to combine the two made for a formidable potential.

Already a successful chef in his own right, Cruz still took his time at Del Posto to learn about our very specific hybrid of Italian and geo-specific American products to create a food at once recognizable and challenging. He is extremely curious and always ready to learn more, particularly from our farmers and foragers. He honed his skills during his tenure at Del Posto and became a crucial player in the drive for Michelin recognition. We were awarded two Michelin stars in the second year. Cruz's cooking and management style had come to fruition.

As executive chef at Lupa, Cruz had some large shoes to fill, following Mark Ladner and, later, Steve Connaughton, but he made the transition and each item on the menu became at the same time his as well as truly Roman. He has maintained the integrity of every dish and added his own imprimatur and ideas without altering the consistency or the "Romanness" of the entire menu.

I see Cruz now in Lupa's small kitchen, expediting and running the show, and everything is well planned and executed.

We joke around that we like to call him "Cruz Control," but when you see him in the kitchen, it actually makes sense. He's got control over everything going on in the world of Italian cooking, and you can taste it in every delicious and simple bite of food.

Mario Batali

5

PEAR AND WILD WATERCRESS SALAD
Serves 2

1 pear, such as Bos or Bartlett Williams • salt • black pepper • juice of ¼ lemon • good-quality extra-virgin olive oil • 1 handful of wild watercress, locally harvested • aged sheep's milk pecorino cheese, such as Moliterno, to sprinkle on top

With a mandolin, shave the pear into thin slices and place in a mixing bowl. Season with salt, coarse black pepper, lemon juice, and finish with extra-virgin olive oil to taste. Add wild watercress to the bowl, lightly toss, and arrange on the plate. Crumble the pecorino on top of the salad and serve.

LINGUINE WITH RAZOR CLAMS AND CARDOONS
Serves 1

6 razor clams • olive oil, for pan-frying • ½ onion, diced • ½ bulb fennel, diced • 2 cloves garlic • 1 pinch dried red chili flakes • 250 ml dry white wine • 120 g linguine pasta • 1 stalk cardoon • ½ medium-hot long Italian pepper, sliced • salt and pepper • parsley, chopped, to taste • 1 lemon, for zest and juice • finishing-quality extra-virgin olive oil, to taste

1 Wash the razor clams. Place a medium pan on high heat. Add a tablespoon of olive oil and sweat the onions, fennel, garlic, and chili flakes. Deglaze the pan with white wine and reduce by half. Add the razor clams and cover the pan. As soon as clams begin to firm up, remove them from the pan and strain the remaining liquid through cheesecloth (muslin).
2 Clean the clams, discarding the stomachs. Slice the clams thinly against the grain and store in the strained cooking liquid.
3 Cook the pasta in salted boiling water for approximately 8 minutes, or until al dente.
4 While pasta is cooking, trim, peel, and slice the cardoon into 2.5-cm slices and sauté in a tablespoon of olive oil. Caramelize the cardoon until tender and golden.
5 Add the sliced Italian pepper to the pan. Just before the pasta is cooked, add the clams with their liquid to the pan. Drain the pasta and add to pan.
6 To serve, adjust the seasoning as needed with salt and black pepper. Add a pinch of chopped parsley, the zest of half a lemon, and a few drops of fresh lemon juice. Finish with a tablespoon of extra-virgin olive oil.

HANGER STEAK WITH PARSNIPS, CAULIFLOWER, AND SALSA VERDE
Serves 6

For the hanger steak
900 g hanger (skirt) steak, trimmed • olive oil, for marinating • 1 red onion, sliced • 1 sprig fresh rosemary • 1 head cauliflower • 6 cipollini onions

1 Marinate the hanger steak overnight in olive oil, red onion, and rosemary.
2 Season and gently sear the steak, then place in a low-temperature oven until it reaches 125°F (51°C) degrees. Allow to rest. Slice the steak and divide it into 6 portions.
3 Cut the cauliflower into small florets, season and toss with olive oil, and roast in a hot oven until tender and caramelized. Season the onions, toss with olive oil, and roast in a hot oven until tender, then remove the outer layer of skin.

For the parsnip puree
6 parsnips • 250 ml water • 1 tbsp butter • salt • black pepper

Peel and slice the parsnips into 1-cm pieces. Season and sweat in a covered pan with the water and butter. When tender, process in blender until smooth.

For the salsa verde
½ bunch basil, chopped • ½ bunch parsley, chopped • ½ bunch marjoram, chopped • 1 tbsp bread crumbs • 1 tsp red-wine vinegar • 3 tbsp finishing-quality extra-virgin olive oil • salt • black pepper

1 Combine all ingredients and season to taste. Set aside.

To serve
Place a small amount of parsnip puree on a plate, and place the slices of steak on top of puree. Garnish the steak with the roasted cauliflower and cipollini onions, and a small amount of salsa verde.

BLACK PEPPER PANNA COTTA WITH FIGS
Makes approximately 30 panna cottas

For the black pepper panna cotta
1.75 liters heavy (double) cream • 395 g sugar • 1 vanilla bean • 16 gelatin leaves • 4 tbsp freshly ground black pepper • 425 ml milk

1 Toast the black pepper in a pot. Add the cream, sugar, and vanilla bean and bring to a simmer.
2 While mixture is simmering, "bloom" the gelatin by soaking it in ice water until soft. Drain off the excess water and dissolve into the hot cream mixture. Once dissolved, remove from heat and add the milk. Place in an ice bath and cool until mixture is thick enough to suspend the black pepper and seeds from the vanilla bean.
3 Remove the vanilla bean and pour into 50-ml molds. Leave to set for 24 hours in the refrigerator.

For the fig compote
12 fresh figs • 1 liter Prosecco • 200 g sugar

Stem and quarter the figs and reserve. Bring the Prosecco and sugar to a boil in a pot to make a simple syrup. While still hot, pour the syrup over figs, steep for 10 minutes, then let cool.

To serve
Remove the panna cotta from molds and place onto a plate, putting the fig compote on top of it and around it.

1
Pear and wild
watercress salad

2
Linguine with razor clams
and cardoons

3
Hanger steak
with parsnips, cauliflower,
and salsa verde

4
Black pepper panna cotta
with figs

Cruz Goler

I have always fantasized about a restaurant in a garden, so Skye Gyngell's café-restaurant at Petersham Nurseries, just outside of London, is like a dream come true. Her guests are lucky enough to have an extraordinary view of the nurseries' greenhouses, topiary, and herb gardens and the remarkable landscape of Petersham Meadows.

Skye trained in Paris until 1985, when she moved to London and cooked at the French House, with Fergus Henderson and at the Dorchester, under Anton Mosimann. Since setting up the Petersham Nurseries café she has received a string of major awards and found time to write two cookbooks, *A Year in My Kitchen* and *My Favourite Ingredients.* She has also had a regular column in the *Independent* newspaper.

Skye cooks simple food, ethically sourced, as she puts it, "in respect of the seasons and in support of small, farmers and producers from the British Isles and further afield — products which capture the flavors of the people and places from which they originate." With Petersham Nurseries' resident forager and general manager, Wendy Fogarty, she seeks out the best available local products: pure sea salt from the Isle of Anglesey in Wales, cider made from rare Somerset cider apples, and heirloom varieties of vegetables from small family farmers and the nurseries' own kitchen gardens. By contributing to the local economy and respecting small artisans and farmers, the cookery that results from this collaboration celebrates good stewardship of the land and clean air and soil.

Skye's food is always fresh; she is most inspired by the kitchen garden at the nursery, whose herbs infuse the dishes with the most delightful flavor. I visited Petersham Nurseries in April a few years ago, and I vividly remember a delicious Dorset crab dish with white asparagus and a simple, but divine, combination of air-dried beef, sheep's-milk ricotta, and green tomatoes: food that reflected the setting's green pastures and cool mornings and tasted of a British spring.

Alice Waters

Skye Gyngell was born in Sydney, Australia, in 1963 and spent her youth there, undertaking various catering jobs before her departure for formal culinary study in Paris. She trained under Anne Willan at La Varenne, and in 1985, after a stint at the Dodin-Bouffant, moved to London to work at the French House with Fergus Henderson. A subsequent position in Anton Mosimann's team at the Dorchester in London saw Gyngell begin to hone her technique, which she put into practice over years of private catering for a host of illustrious clients. In 2004 she started to cook from a tiny kitchen at Petersham Nurseries in England, and has since taken the restaurant from strength to strength with a strictly seasonal cuisine of unfussy, charming dishes.

MENU

Quince Prosecco

~

Carpaccio of salt cod with preserved lemon, chile, capers, and mixed cress

~

Farro with porcini, aged Parmesan, and Barolo

~

Clementine sherbet

~

Robiola with chestnut honey and toasted hazelnuts

Skye Gyngell

Petersham Nurseries, London, UK

1
In the garden at
Petersham Nurseries

2
Skye Gyngell in the kitchen

3
Roasted quinces

4
Quince cordial

5
Toasted hazelnuts

CARPACCIO OF SALT COD WITH PRESERVED LEMON, CHILE, CAPERS, AND MIXED CRESS
Serves 2 (as an appetizer)

Salt cod is a personal favorite of mine. Whenever I put it on the menu at the restaurant, it walks very quickly out the door. Perhaps this is because in Britain, at least, it is not very often eaten at home. Here, we tend to think of it as complicated, and even a little scary. It's a hard, pungent-smelling, musty thing that resembles a piece of leather. What on earth are we meant to do with it? I realize that over-fishing makes cod a potential minefield, but I believe that the cultural value of salt cod makes it worth a risk. Its importance in the culinary traditions of the Basque Country cannot be underestimated. And it's very popular in Iceland, thanks to their sustainable fishing policies. The Marine Conservation Society recommends choosing line-caught cod from a sustainable stock. Talk to your fish supplier—ask if he stocks line-caught fish, and where it is from.

I have never found shop-bought salt cod satisfactory. Often it can be hard, sinewy, and massively over-salted. As a result, I became intrigued by curing the fish myself. The idea that you can take an ingredient in its purest form, and by respectfully manipulating it, turn it into something else, is incredibly gratifying.

Through trial and error I have achieved a cure that is gentle and succulent. In fact, the result is beautiful and delicate enough to serve raw and unrinsed. Sliced as finely as smoked salmon, drizzled with oil, lots of pepper and a squeeze of lemon juice, there's nothing like it.

How to cure your cod
Ask your fish supplier for a skinned cod fillet. Rinse it under cold water and gently pat it dry using a dish cloth. Lay the fish on a stainless steel rack which fits snugly inside a larger pan (that will later catch the drips while the cod is curing). Weigh the fish and season it all over with 1½ tablespoons of plain, good-quality sea salt per 500 g of fish. Go over the central section of the fish with a little more salt to ensure that this, the thickest part, also receives an even curing.

Loosely cover the whole pan with plastic wrap (clingfilm) to prevent the smell seeping into the rest of your refrigerator—home-curing cod is a very stinky business.

Refrigerate the pan and let cure for up to 7 days. Remove and rinse your bottom pan every day because, as the cod begins to firm, liquid will weep from its body. Your fillet will give off approximately 2 tablespoons of liquid per kg.

Often, depending on what I am intending to do with the end result, I only allow the fish to cure for 3 days. Rinsed and filleted into portions, this home-cured cod is gentle and delicate enough to serve simply grilled with a green sauce or roasted tomatoes and a really lemony aioli. If I serve it very finely sliced and raw, 3 days is also more than enough curing time.

For this dish, I suggest that you cure the salt cod for no more than 4 days. It does not need to be rinsed; the strong, clean flavors that accompany it more than counterbalance the slight salty flavor. You will need a really sharp knife to slice the cod into beautiful superfine sheets. You can buy preserved lemons, but it is so easy to do them yourself. Slice the fruits into quarters lengthwise, pack into a sterilized jar and sprinkle with sea salt. Seal tightly with a lid and leave at least 10 days before using—well kept, they will last for up to a year. The salt will transform their flavor from bitter to sour-sweet. Always remember to scrape away the bitter pulp and use only the zest.

1 salt cod fillet, weighing approximately 2½ kg, cured for 4 days • 1 red chile, very finely sliced • 1 tbsp capers (the ones packed in salt are so much tastier than the ones in vinegar), rinsed and dried • ½ preserved lemon (zest only), finely diced • 2 tbsp extra-virgin olive oil • juice of ½ lemon • small handful mixed cress

1 Using a sharp knife, slice the fish as finely as possible. Lay the fish in a single layer on a flat plate and sprinkle over it the chile, capers and diced lemon zest.
2 To serve, pour the olive oil over the fish, squeeze the lemon juice on top and scatter the cress over everything.

FARRO WITH PORCINI, AGED PARMESAN, AND BAROLO
Serves 6–8

I much prefer using legumes (pulses) and grains to potatoes. They have a sense of warmth and goodness to them and are a rich source of protein. The grain called farro is rarely seen or used in Britain, but has played a crucial part in the traditional cooking of central and southern Italy since Roman times. Farro has a delicate, nutty flavor and an almost ancient feel to it. It's both chewy and tender and is delicious served hot or cold. The great thing about farro is its ability to absorb the flavors with which it is cooked—so don't be too free with salt and vinegar.

I like to use wholegrain farro, usually labeled *perlato*, *semiperlato,* or *decorticato*. It cooks quickly and its flavor is refined. You can also get a type called farro *integrale* which has the whole outer, brown hull intact—it requires a few hours of soaking and a longer cooking time and retains a firmness similar to that of wild rice. Leftover farro keeps well covered in the refrigerator for a couple of days, and makes a lovely addition to risottos, soups, and bean and vegetable dishes.

2 tbsp extra-virgin olive oil • 1 yellow onion, peeled and finely chopped • 2 cloves garlic, peeled and chopped • 3 sage leaves, coarsely chopped • sea salt • 120 g dried porcini, soaked in 250 ml warm water • 300 g farro • 250 ml good-quality chicken stock • 250 ml Barolo or other full-bodied red wine • 75 g Parmesan, half grated and half shaved freshly • ground black pepper • hot bread, grilled quail, or grilled rabbit, for serving

1 Place the olive oil in a medium heavy saucepan over gentle heat. Add the chopped onion, garlic, sage and also a pinch of salt.
2 Remove half the porcini from the soaking water and chop roughly. Add to the pan and stir once or twice to combine. When the onion is soft (after 5 minutes or so), add the farro and mix well with the pan contents.
3 Add the chicken stock and wine and turn the heat up slightly. Cook for 20–30 minutes until nutty and tender. Stir and taste frequently.
4 Finish with the rest of the porcini and the greated Parmesan. Adjust the seasoning with a pinch or so of sea salt and a generous grinding of black pepper. Sprinkle with shaved Parmesan.
5 Serve hot with peasant-style bread. Alternatively, it's delicious with grilled quail or rabbit.

CLEMENTINE SHERBET
Serves 4

This icy-cold dessert is a very gentle way to finish a meal and is so light in flavor it's almost ethereal. The absence of eggs makes it refreshing rather than rich.

8 sweet, juicy clementines • 100 g superfine (caster) sugar • 200 ml heavy (double) cream • 1 vanilla bean, split lengthwise, seeds scraped out • 3 tbsp sherry (Lustau or Pedro Ximenez)

1 Slice the clementines in half and squeeze the juice. Strain and set aside.
2 Place the sugar, cream, vanilla seeds and pod in a small heavy pan over medium heat and bring to a boil. Reduce to a simmer and cook for about a minute—you simply want to infuse the cream with the flavor of vanilla and dissolve the sugar. Remove from the stove, and set aside to cool and continue to infuse.
3 Once the cream is cool, pour through a fine-mesh sieve onto the clementine juice. Stir well, add the sherry, pour into an ice-cream maker and follow the manufacturer's instructions.

1
Carpaccio of salt cod with
preserved lemon, chile,
capers, and mixed cress

2
Farro with porcini,
aged Parmesan,
and Barolo

3
Clementine sherbet

Skye Gyngell

Sure, making a sandwich seems simple enough to do—especially for a noted chef. But taking the sandwich to an art form and making a city demand it day after day takes true genius. Meet Tommy Habetz of Bunk Sandwiches. Thanks to Tommy, Oregonians can feast on one of the simplest but tastiest meals—the sandwich.

But before sandwiches and long before the West Coast stole him away forever, I first met Puff Daddy Habetz in my first New York kitchen at Po back in 1994. He was fresh off the line at Bobby Flay's delicious Mesa Grill and a little rough around the edges in the technical sense, but filled with passion and enthusiasm. I could see that he had a great ability to see what people wanted, and he delivered each time he was behind the line. Always with great input and interesting ideas as well as being quite eloquent and well read, he added to the value of the restaurant. Later on we opened Lupa together and I could count on his simple flair with pasta to be a technical score that I did not have to worry about. Having worked through the fun at high-end restaurants, Puff granted the wishes of those who love simple gustatory pleasures like a sandwich. Habetz's knack for understanding and creating food for everybody is a great achievement. When he was cooking at Ripe and at Meriweather, he sought to bring his impressive American and Italian cooking to a mainstream audience. He's always pushing the envelope and giving people a more unusual or creative version of the classic they crave. At Bunk Sandwiches he is now honing his craft in a most delicious direction.

Mario Batali

Born in 1972, Tommy Habetz was hired early in his career by Mario Batali to work at Po in New York. He sent Habetz to train under Paola di Mauro at her home and vineyard just outside Rome, an experience that developed Habetz's knowledge of classic Italian cuisine and assured him an integral role in opening Babbo in 1997 and Lupa in 1999. After working at Lucca in Boca Raton, FL, he moved in 2003 to Family Supper, the emerging Portland dining room run by the Ripe duo, also opening the Gotham Bldg. Tavern with them as executive chef. In 2006 he moved to Meriwether's Restaurant, since then choosing to concentrate on two new projects: Bunk Sandwiches, which opened in 2008 and boasts an inventive approach to sandwich-making, and Roman Candle, a traditional Roman trattoria due to open in Fall 2009.

MENU

Goat cheese, peperonata, and olive salad

~

Biscuits with rabbit gravy

~

Oxtail confit with celery and hot pepper relish

~

Salt cod with chorizo and black olives

Tommy Habetz

146

1–3
In the kitchen at Bunk
Sandwiches

4
Tommy Habetz buying
artichokes

Bunk Sandwiches, Portland, OR, USA

1
Goat cheese,
peperonata, and
olive salad.

2
Biscuits with
rabbit gravy

3
Oxtail confit
with celery and hot
pepper relish

GOAT CHEESE, PEPERONATA, AND OLIVE SALAD
Serves 4–6

These are some of my favorite flavors together on one sandwich. We use our own focaccia, but any good Italian bread will do. You could add a few anchovies to the peperonata, but you don't have to, if you want to keep it vegetarian.

For the olive salad
120 g green and Kalamata olives, pitted and coarsely chopped • 85 g carrots, coarsely chopped • 85 g celery, coarsely chopped • 2-3 cloves garlic, sliced thinly • 1 tsp thyme leaves • 1 tsp chopped parsley • 125 ml good extra-virgin olive oil • juice of 1 lemon • a good splash red-wine vinegar

Mix together all the olive salad ingredients, and let them marinate for at least a day.

For the peperonata
1 large red onion, sliced • 2 red bell peppers, cored and sliced • 2 yellow bell peppers, cored and sliced • 60 ml extra-virgin olive oil • 1 tsp tomato paste • a few cloves garlic, sliced thinly • 1 tsp thyme leaves • 2 tbsp red-wine vinegar or sherry vinegar

1   In a large sauté pan, over medium heat, cook the onions and peppers in the olive oil until they start to caramelize (about 10 minutes).
2   Add the tomato paste and cook until it starts to caramelize.
3   Take it off the heat, and stir in the garlic and thyme.
4   Add the vinegar. Season well.

For the goat cheese
About 225 g fromage blanc, or a good-quality, fresh goat cheese • about 60 ml milk

Thin out the goat cheese with a little bit of milk. Taste and season.

To assemble
focaccia or other bread

1   Lightly grill the focaccia.
2   Spread a good layer of the goat cheese on the bread. Add a little bit of the peperonata and olive salad. Squish it down and enjoy!

BISCUITS WITH RABBIT GRAVY
Serves 4–6

I would recommend either braising or confiting the rabbit in this recipe. If you have your own favorite biscuit (scone) recipe, then go ahead and use it. The one below is a straightforward buttermilk biscuit recipe. This dish is a bit of a cross between the Southern American dishes biscuits and gravy, and rabbit and dumplings. It is an open-faced sandwich and a bit messy, so should be served in a shallow bowl. Save any extra biscuits for another dish. They also make great fine bread crumbs.

For the braised rabbit
3–4 rabbit legs, well seasoned • a little bit of lard or olive oil • mirepoix for braising (carrots, celery, and onions, all roughly chopped, plus a split garlic bulb, and a couple of sprigs of fresh lavender or a pinch of dried lavender) • a few splashes of white wine • chicken broth, to cover

1   Preheat the oven to 350°F (180°C).
2   In a heavy pan, sear the rabbit legs in the lard or oil until brown.
3   Add the mirepoix, and cook for a few minutes more.
4   Add the wine and broth.
5   Cover tightly with parchment and foil and braise in the oven for 2½ hours, until the meat falls off the bone.

For the biscuits (scones)
About 450 g all-purpose (plain) flour • 2 tsp salt • 2 tsp baking powder • 2 tsp baking soda • about 175 g fat, half butter and half lard, or all butter—either way, cold and cut into little cubes • 475 ml buttermilk, plus more for brushing

1   Preheat the oven to 375°F (190°C).
2   Sift the dry ingredients together. Add the butter or lard and cut into the flour with a table knife until it looks like small pebbles.
3   Make a well, and add the buttermilk and mix until the dough comes together. Turn it out onto a floured surface and fold it over a few times. This will give it its layers.
4   Press it out to 4 cm thick. Cut the biscuits into rounds or squares or whatever shape you like.
5   Lay them onto an ungreased baking sheet (baking tray), brush them with a little more buttermilk and bake for 20–25 minutes until golden brown.

For the gravy
1 medium shallot, sliced • lard, for sautéing • 1 tbsp white wine vinegar • 1 garlic clove, crushed • about 2 tbsp Dijon mustard • about 125 ml broth (you can use the braising liquid, strained) • 225 ml cream • a few sprigs tarragon • salt and pepper

1   Season each stage as you go.
2   Sauté the shallot in the lard over medium heat until it starts to caramelize.
3   Add the vinegar and reduce until almost evaporated.
4   Add the garlic and mustard.
5   Add the broth and reduce until almost evaporated.
6   Add the cream and tarragon, and reduce by half.
7   Add the rabbit meat to warm through.

To serve
Split open a biscuit, pour a bit of the rabbit and gravy over it, and serve in a shallow bowl.

OXTAIL CONFIT WITH CELERY AND HOT PEPPER RELISH
Serves 4

This sandwich is influenced by the Roman dish *coda alla vaccinara*, a classic dish of slowly braised oxtail with tomatoes, celery, and pine nuts. I've added hot peppers to help cut through the richness of the oxtail. A good crusty bread is important to soak up all the fat and juices. Both relish and confit can be done a few days ahead and kept in the refrigerator.

For the oxtail confit
About 1.5 kg oxtail, cut into joints • 2 garlic cloves, crushed • a pinch of chili flakes • a dash of cinnamon • salt and pepper • fat, for the confit (preferably bacon fat or lard, enough to cover)

1   A few days before you want to cook the oxtail, rub it down with the garlic, chile, cinnamon, and salt and pepper. Place in the refrigerator to let the flavors develop.
2   To confit the oxtail, first preheat the oven to 250°F (120°C).
3   Place the pieces of meat in a heavy pan and cover with fat. Seal tightly with parchment paper and aluminum foil. Cook for 10–12 hours or overnight. The meat should then fall off the bone.
4   Scrape off excess fat and pick the meat off the bones.

For the hot pepper relish
4–5 stalks celery, sliced into 1-cm pieces • a few mixed bell peppers, seeded and chopped • a few tbsp olive oil • 1 tbsp tomato paste • a small handful of golden raisins • a small handful of pine nuts, toasted • a dash of unsweetened cocoa powder • a good splash of red-wine vinegar • a squeeze of lemon juice • a small handful of Italian parsley leaves

1   Sauté the celery and peppers in the olive oil over medium heat. Add a little bit of salt.
2   Once they have softened a bit, add the tomato paste and cook until it starts to caramelize.
3   Add the raisins, pine nuts, cocoa, vinegar, lemon juice, and parsley. Check the seasoning. This mixture will keep in the refrigerator.

To serve
Crusty bread, for serving

Heat a cast-iron pan over medium heat. Add the oxtail with a little bit of the confit fat and crisp it up a bit. Serve on crusty bread with a spoonful of the relish.

Tommy Habetz

1 & 2
Wassim Hallal in the kitchen

3
Tasting wines at Restaurant
Frederikshøj

4
Caviar, to accompany lemon
sorbet

Wassim Hallal

150

MENU

Caviar and lemon
Blancs de Blancs,
Champagne, France
~
Mosaic of tuna and caviar
Blancs de Blancs,
Champagne, France
~
**Shrimp, wild garlic, and
new potatoes**
Riesling Federspiel,
Wachau, Austria
~
**Lobster, Jerusalem
artichoke, and
sweetbreads**
Champagne (such as Krug),
France
~
Sole, truffle, and carrots
Grauburgunder, Baden,
Germany
~
**Foie gras terrine,
fig, and brioche**
Tokaji-Aszú, Hungary
~
**Tournedos Rossini
version WH**
Barolo, Piemonte, Italy
~
Rice and fruit
~
Strawberry and orange
·
**Cherry, licorice, and
chocolate**

Born in 1980, <u>Wassim Hallal</u> emigrated to Denmark with his family at the age of five from Beirut, Lebanon, where his father had owned a restaurant. Hallal began his own career in food in 2001 with an apprenticeship at Hotel Limfjorden in Thisted. He followed this with time at Hotel d'Angleterre and Formel B in Copenhagen, where head chef Nikolaj Kirkhe became an early role model in precision and drive. At the age of 19, Hallal took a position at the two-Michelin-starred Hotel Scoldeshoff in Belgium and had the chance to work with ingredients like caviar and truffles, which can be scarce in Denmark. In 2003 Hallal became head chef at Molskroen, moving to open his own Restaurant WH in Aarhus three years later. Situated in a Japanese garden outside Trige, it began as a brasserie and was developed into a fine-cuisine restaurant in 2008. Hallal's menu treats fresh ingredients with an intelligent twist to create playful, modern international cuisine with a touch of luxury.

Wassim is rightly considered to be one of the main figureheads of young Danish gastronomy. He had already been head chef at the famed Danish inn, Molskroen, before he opened his own restaurant in 2007, in the Aarhus area of Jutland. There he has started to explore his grand passion for fine French gastronomy. Although he also uses products from his surrounding *terroir* and more cutting-edge techniques freshly sourced from northern Spain, he is widely considered to be of the "classic school," using traditional gourmet products such as caviar, truffles, foie gras, tenderloin, and more, in signature dishes such as the famed Modernized Tournedos Rossini Anno 2008.

His Middle Eastern background does not seem to have had a great impact on his cuisine so far. Personally, I would love to see that in the dishes he creates, and I hope we will one day be able to taste a Tournedos Rossini with perhaps dates or harissa. His cuisine feels rounded like the person he is—very openhearted, honest, and generous, always seeking something true and original in his flavors. He also uses his talents in various culinary competitions: He has won the silver several times in competitions such as "Best Chef in Denmark" or the "Bocuse d'Or Qualifier," with many of his creations praised as the best of the year.

In many ways Wassim Hallal represents a different type of young talent than is usually seen in Denmark. First of all, he is not from the capital; secondly, he is an immigrant from Lebanon who came to Denmark as a young boy escaping from war; and finally, he has been raised in a Muslim environment. There is no doubt that it is more difficult to break through if you are not in the main city with all its natural advantages, such as PR, media, tourism, and guests. And of course he also has a different background from an average Danish blond "Mr. Jensen." Wassim Hallal is a fighter, as his success shows.

René Redzepi

Restaurant Frederikshøj, Aarhus, Denmark

1
Shrimp, wild garlic, and
new potatoes

2
Sole, truffle, and carrots

3
Tournedos Rossini
version WH

152

SHRIMP, WILD GARLIC, AND NEW POTATOES
Serves 4

In early spring there are not many greens to choose from at the vegetable store. But if you are lucky, you might find some wild garlic, also known as ramsons, in the woods. Pick the tender leaves first and later on the flowers, which come out after the leaves. In this dish I use quite big leaves, as they have a sharper taste than the smaller, tender leaves, which I use for decorating. They also contain more chlorophyll, which gives the puree a beautiful green color.

500 g small new potatoes •
2 shallots, chopped • 300 ml canola (rapeseed) oil • 325 ml white wine •
50 g wild garlic (ramson) leaves •
salt and pepper • 50 ml lemon juice • 20 g cooked shrimp (prawns), with shells • 250 g cooked shrimp (prawns), shelled • ½ bunch of dill, chopped • a few small wild garlic leaves and flowers for decoration

1 Scrub the potatoes carefully. Boil 20 of the smallest potatoes in lightly salted water until tender. Braise the rest of the potatoes and the shallots in a little oil and add the white wine. Cook them until tender and then add the wild garlic leaves. Blend the shallot and potato mixture to a smooth puree and add salt, pepper, and lemon juice to taste.
2 Deep-fry the shrimp with shells until crisp, and sprinkle with a little salt.
3 To serve, place the puree of potatoes on individual plates in a decorative way and distribute the shelled shrimp on top. Slice the boiled potatoes, toss them in a little dill, and place them and the crisp shrimp on the plates. Decorate with the tender leaves and flowers of the wild garlic.

SOLE, TRUFFLE, AND CARROTS
Serves 4

For the truffle sauce
2 tbsp honey • 2 tbsp dark balsamic vinegar • 1 bottle Madeira •
1 whole garlic, cut in half • 2 shallots, cut in half • 1 tbsp peppercorns •
2 liters brown veal stock • about 50 g butter • 25 g truffle • truffle oil, to taste • lemon juice, to taste • salt and pepper

Caramelize the honey in a pan, add the balsamic vinegar, and reduce. Add the Madeira and reduce again. Add garlic, shallots, peppercorns, and stock, and reduce by half. Sieve the sauce and boil down to the desired consistency with the butter, add the chopped truffle, and then add truffle oil, lemon juice, salt, and pepper to taste.

For the carrot puree
2 carrots • 20 ml orange juice
• 1 tablespoon honey

Boil the carrots in the orange juice and honey until tender. Remove the carrots and blend them to a puree. Save the juice for later use.

For the glazed carrots
8 small, thick carrots • butter, for glazing • salt • 1 tablespoon chopped dill

Blanch the carrots in boiling water for a few minutes until the skin loosens. Remove the skin. Just before serving, glaze the carrots in a small amount of the reserved orange juice and a little butter and season with a pinch of salt and the chopped dill.

For the carrot foam
1 shallot, finely chopped • 1 clove garlic, finely chopped • 1 carrot, finely diced • 100 ml white wine • orange juice • 300 ml chicken stock • salt and pepper • butter, for finishing

Sauté the finely chopped shallot and garlic and the diced carrot in a little oil. Add the white wine, the remaining orange juice, and the chicken stock. Boil together and season with salt, pepper, and a little butter. Blend to an airy foam with a hand mixer.

For the sole
4 large sole fillets • oil, for frying • salt and pepper

The sole fillets must be fried immediately before serving. Fry them over high heat in a little oil until golden on one side. Turn the fillets and fry them very briefly on the other side. Remove from the heat and season with a little salt and pepper.

To serve
20 g fresh truffle, grated just before serving • a few edible flowers for decorating, optional

Place the fish on the puree on individual plates and arrange the glazed carrots and the foam decoratively. Sprinkle with flakes of freshly grated truffle and a few edible flowers. Serve the truffle sauce separately.

TOURNEDOS ROSSINI VERSION WH
Serves 4

For the meat and ground meat
200 g foie gras • 500 g sirloin of beef • 10 g truffle, grated •
• 1 egg • 100 ml crème fraîche 100 g ordinary bread crumbs •
2 shallots, finely chopped • salt and pepper • flour, for rolling •
100 g egg whites • 100 g Chinese bread crumbs • canola (rapeseed) oil

1 Cut 4 neat slices of the foie gras and save the remainder for the stuffing. Cut the sirloin into a neat, uniform piece, approximately 7 cm in diameter. Grind (mince) the trimmings of meat and approximately 50 g of the foie gras and stir the ground meat with the grated truffle, egg, crème fraîche, ordinary bread crumbs, shallots, salt, and pepper. Mix well.
2 Roll out the ground meat on plastic wrap (clingfilm) and wrap the sirloin in the ground meat and the plastic wrap. Tie the wrap firmly and steam the meat parcel for approximately 10 minutes in a steam oven until the ground meat is cooked through, then refrigerate. If you don't have a steam oven, put the parcel in a saucepan with boiling water; remove the saucepan from the heat immediately, leave the meat in the saucepan for 10 minutes, then refrigerate until cold.
3 Unwrap the "meatloaf" and roll it in flour, egg whites, and the Chinese bread crumbs. Brown the meat on all sides in hot oil in a frying pan and then place it in a 325°F (160°C) oven for approximately 15 minutes. Take the meat out of the oven, but let it "relax" in a warm place covered by a dish towel before carving.

For the pea puree
50 g butter • 1 shallot, finely chopped • 100 ml white wine •
2 tbsp flour • 200 ml milk •
200 g frozen peas • salt and pepper

Melt the butter in a pan, add the chopped shallot and the white wine, and bring to a boil. Stir in the flour, add the milk, and boil until the mixture thickens. Add the peas and continue to boil until the peas are completely tender. Blend to a smooth puree and add salt and pepper to taste.

For the pearl onions
50 g fresh peas, shelled • 100 g pearl onions • butter, for glazing

Boil the peas in a little water. Place the onions in a pan with boiling water and remove the pan from the heat. Pop the onions out of their skins, glaze them in a little butter, and mix with the fresh peas when ready to serve.

For the truffle sauce
2 tbsp honey • 2 tbsp dark balsamic vinegar • 1 bottle Madeira • 1 whole garlic, cut in half • 4 shallots, roughly chopped • 1 tbsp peppercorns •
2 liters brown veal stock • 50 g butter •
25 g truffle, grated • 50 ml truffle oil, approximately • juice of ½ lemon
• salt and pepper

Caramelize the honey in a pan, add the balsamic vinegar, and reduce. Add the Madeira and reduce again. Add garlic, shallots, peppercorns, and stock and reduce by half. Sieve the sauce and boil down to desired consistency with the butter, add the truffle, and then add truffle oil, lemon juice, and salt and pepper to taste.

For serving
more grated truffle

Just before serving, fry the slices of foie gras briskly. Carve the sirloin in neat slices. Arrange the pea purée on 4 individual plates and place the glazed onions and peas on top. Then place the slices of meat with the foie gras on top, surrounded by the truffle sauce and a generous sprinkle of freshly grated truffle.

When Charlie Hallowell says, "I want to feed lots of people really good, simple, time-honored food that will sustain them in their lives," I cannot help but think of his North Oakland restaurant, Pizzaiolo. This is a place that's full of real food, music, and passionate young people. There is a garden out back where Charlie tends espaliered fruit trees and cultivates herbs in planters, and in the summertime he hosts open-air movie screenings and, memorably, Slow Food shrimp boils.

Charlie moved to the Bay Area twelve years ago to cook at Chez Panisse. Before that, he had travelled through China and Taiwan, studying Mandarin and eating his way through the regional cuisines. Although Charlie had never before cooked professionally, his generous spirit and sincerity, as well as his astonishing talent, endeared him at once to *la famille Panisse*. He forged deep relationships with many of the chefs at the restaurant, sharing friendship, wine, love, and, of course, food. At his own restaurant he serves the food that is closest to his heart: the robust, nourishing food of the Italian countryside.

When I eat at Charlie's, I am always delighted by the way he creates a dish, putting the ingredients together in a way that makes their textures and tastes shine. The physical space of Pizzaiolo reflects the gritty aesthetic of its North Oakland neighborhood, and it features the work of local artists and photographers on its walls. To eat there is to dive into Charlie's world (he lives upstairs with his two children). It's a world in which friends and family are inspirations and co-producers, and in which enthusiasm for life is reflected in every bite of ragù or nettle pizza.

Alice Waters

Charlie Hallowell was born in Minnesota in 1973. After a formative two years in China and Taiwan, Hallowell began work at Chez Panisse with Alice Waters and Cal Peternell. That restaurant's approach to sustainability, creativity, and passion in cooking permeates Hallowell's approach at his restaurant, Pizzaiolo, in California. He continues to serve the best in rustic Italian dishes that let the single and combined flavors of each day's produce speak. Hallowell's decision to focus on Italian cuisine is not random but predicated upon its honesty and authenticity; Italian cooking, he says, lets an artichoke remain an artichoke, and this ingredient-centric ideal dovetails perfectly with Hallowell's playful yet straightforward menu at Pizzaiolo.

1

MENU

Jerusalem artichoke, puntarella, and Treviso salad with anchovy, toasted walnuts, and Parmesan cheese

~

Monterey Bay sardines with Padrón peppers and marjoram and gypsy pepper salsa

~

Spaghetti with Monterey Bay squid, basil, peperoncini, and bread crumbs

~

Margherita pizza

Charlie Hallowell

1
Aging meat at Pizzaiolo

2
Jars of homemade grissini

3
Charlie Hallowell placing pizza
in the wood-fired oven

4
The bar at Pizzaiolo

5
Tossing pizza dough

Pizzaiolo, Oakland, CA, USA

1
Jerusalem artichoke, puntarella, and Treviso salad with anchovy, toasted walnuts, and Parmesan cheese

2
Monterey Bay sardines with Padrón peppers, and marjoram, and gypsy pepper salsa

3
Spaghetti with Monterey Bay squid, basil, peperoncini, and bread crumbs

JERUSALEM ARTICHOKE, PUNTARELLA, AND TREVISO SALAD WITH ANCHOVY, TOASTED WALNUTS AND PARMESAN CHEESE
Serves 4ish hungry people

This is perhaps the best salad in the world. It is classic Rome in the fall (autumn) and winter. The puntarella is so wonderful and astringent, the Jerusalem artichokes have a sweet, crunchy, nutty goodness that rounds it out, and the Treviso seems to stand perfectly between the two, adding texture, color, and the flavor of cool weather that only chicories can hold. Add the savory anchovy, the fat and tang of the Parmesan, and the earthiness of the walnuts and you have near perfection!

For the vinaigrette
approximately 12 anchovy fillets • extra-virgin olive oil, to taste • juice of 1–2 lemons • 1 tbsp red-wine vinegar • sea salt and pepper, to taste

Take 3 anchovy fillets and melt them in the oil over the pilot of your stove or a really low flame. Don't cook them, just melt them. This will give the vinaigrette a deeper, more interesting flavor. Then pound the rest of the anchovies to a chunky paste in a mortar and pestle. Mix the melted anchovy, the pounded anchovy, lemon juice, and the red-wine vinegar with about 250 ml of delicious extra-virgin olive oil. Taste it. It should have a good amount of acid, and quite a strong anchovy flavor. It should be delicious, and strong enough to stand up to the bitterness of the chicories. If not, it probably needs more anchovy or lemon.

For the salad
2 heads Treviso (red radicchio), sliced across the head in 1-cm thick slices (like ribs), rinsed and dried • approximately 500 g Jerusalem artichoke, cleaned, thinly sliced and left in water so it doesn't oxidize • 2 mature heads puntarella, greens removed, sliced into the thinnest possible strips and stored in ice-cold water to keep it crispy and help it curl up • salt and pepper • 120 g walnuts, toasted and with the skins rubbed off, rough chopped and tossed with extra-virgin olive oil • Parmesan cheese, to shave over the salad at the end

Take the Treviso and toss it with the Jerusalem artichokes, the puntarella and some of the vinaigrette. There should be about the same amount of each ingredient. The vinaigrette should coat the salad well, but not too much. Add salt and pepper to taste. Lay the salad out flat on four plates, as if it just kind of fell down from the heavens. Lightly sprinkle some of the walnuts on each plate and shave some Parmesan over the top with a vegetable peeler. Gobble up.

MONTEREY BAY SARDINES WITH PADRÓN PEPPERS, AND MARJORAM, AND GYPSY PEPPER SALSA
Serves 4

This is one of my favorite summer dishes, combining great elemental flavors: the oily, fishy quality of the sardines, the sweetness of the gypsy peppers, the earthiness of the marjoram, and the subtle heat and smokiness of the Padróns. This is a classic wood-oven dish, but if you don't have a wood oven you can definitely use a grill. This is a very fast-cooking dish; the fish take just a few minutes.

8 whole sardines (or Sierra Mackerel or other oily fish), gutted and scaled, treated with love and respect • sea salt, for seasoning • olive oil, for grilling • 60 g chopped flat-leaf Italian parsley and marjoram, in about equal proportions • 3 gypsy peppers of different colors, finely diced • really good olive oil, for soaking the salsa, and tossing with Padrón peppers • 3 large shallots, finely diced and macerated in red-wine vinegar • 10 pickled Calabrian peppers, seeded and sliced very finely • salt, to taste • 225 g Padrón peppers

After purchasing, keep the sardines cold, and eat them fresh, like right now. Dress the fish with a good amount of sea salt and some olive oil and either put it in the oven or on a hot clean grill. In the oven it can be cooked in a cast-iron pan, or on a baking sheet. On the grill you will need to turn it after about 2 minutes. While the fish is cooking, mix up your salsa. You want the salsa to be about equal amounts herb and pepper. Mix up the herbs, the gypsy peppers, and the olive oil first. Soak the salsa with olive oil, but don't drown it. Add your shallots and Calabrian peppers next, and some salt, but do it thoughtfully, tasting as you go. This salsa should err on the acidic side to balance the fat of the fish.

Once the salsa is done, check your fish. If you touch the flesh of the fish with your finger and it seems like you could just push it right off the body, it's done. If it's still holding firm, give it another minute.

Right at the end throw the Padróns, either in the oven in another cast-iron pan, or on the grill. Toss them with some salt and olive oil first and let them cook until they start to wrinkle and color.

To serve
Lay out 2 fish on each plate, sprinkle some salsa over the fish and place the Padróns around the plate so it looks beautiful. Eat!

SPAGHETTI WITH MONTEREY BAY SQUID, BASIL, PEPERONCINI, AND BREAD CRUMBS
Serves 4–6

This is one of my favorite pasta dishes. It is oily and spicy and crunchy, and brings the aroma of the field and the ocean together as well as any dish I've ever cooked. I think you should only cook it if you can get great fresh squid. If not, my suggestion would be to cook a different pasta. If basil isn't available, marjoram can work well, as can parsley. A word on cooking pasta: To do it well is very, very difficult. I know world-class cooks who can't make a decent pasta. Chris Boswell and Cal Peternel are the masters, and the more I watch them the more I realize the importance of the entire process.

From the very beginning you are building layers of flavor, layers that are only really seen at the end when you bring it together. Try to get as much color in your pan as you can without burning the onions or the squid, and really pay attention in that last minute as the pasta cooks in the sauce. If it seems dry or too oily, splash a bit more pasta water in there. If it seems just soupy and not alive, turn up the heat and really let the liquid cook hard. Mostly, be present, pay attention to what you are doing. Pasta is like a young child, so simple and yet so totally profound; very needy, but if given the right attention capable of true greatness.

450 g good dry spaghetti (I like the thicker varieties for this pasta) • salt • oil, for frying • 900 g fresh squid, cleaned and sliced into rings • 1 red onion, about 150 g the amount of squid, sliced thinly • 60 g fresh basil leaves • peperoncini flakes, to taste • very good olive oil, for drizzling • 70 g bread crumbs from yesterday's leftover bread, preferably toasted sourdough

Bring the water for the pasta up to a boil in a large pan. You can't really have too much water. When it's up to a boil add salt until it tastes about as salty as the ocean. Add your pasta.

Put a 20-cm sauté pan on the stove and get it hot, very hot. Add some oil to the pan and immediately add the squid and the red onion. Add some salt. The squid will quickly release its liquid and for a second the pan will seem stewy. Let it cook hard and develop some color. Toss it every once in a while, but don't fuss with it. Let the squid and the onions cook through and brown, to develop a base for the sauce. When the onions are completely cooked and a fond (highly flavored liquid) has developed, add the basil and wilt it into the squid. You might want to add some good oil at this point and a few pinches of peperoncini, but don't add the pepper flakes too early or they will burn in the hot oil.

When the spaghetti is still very al dente, about two-thirds cooked, pull it out of the water. Add as much of it to the pan as will fit, but still allowing you to toss the pasta without destroying your kitchen. Add about a cup of the pasta water and a good douse of very good extra-virgin olive oil. The water will deglaze the pan, and then as you bring it up to a boil it will emulsify with the oil to make a delicious thick squid sauce.

Finish cooking the spaghetti in this sauce. When it has reduced to a thickness that coats the pasta, is a little juicy but not at all soupy, add a few more pinches of peperoncini, taste and plate on 4 pasta plates. Sprinkle bread crumbs over the top and serve.

In true fairy-tale fashion, Anna Hansen started as dish-washer at the French House Dining Room and ended up as our head chef there. She cites her Danish grandmother as an early mentor, which is in keeping with the fairy-tale slant of her restaurant, the Modern Pantry, a place decorated with a certain Danish restraint. This Scandinavian influence brings a delicacy tempered with warmth to the feel of Anna's menu, and filters through as the precision that keeps its flavors tasty and unusual.

There's a sort of cheeky pixie quality to Anna's cooking. She has gone down the fusion route, allowing a broad collection of influences to come together in many smaller combinations, which automatically appeal to the nibbler in me. Cod and saffron paté with hijiki toast made an appearance, and krupuk quail eggs with chile and lime dipping sauce. We had cassava chips with tomato chile jam and crème fraîche, and black fried squid, which came with a fantastic slaw of fennel, jicama and spiced cashews. Anna puts together innovative combinations with confidence and charm: Fusion food is normally a bit racy for me, but her menu captures everything that is appealing about it.

But Anna's cooking isn't just playful crunchiness and dressing—she knows exactly what she's doing with slow-cooking (whether ox-cheek or octopus). The charming conjunction of experimentation with this crucially firm foundation comes to light in the way the Modern Pantry is set up: soothing restaurant upstairs, bustling café downstairs—friendly and flexible and modern. The day I visited, the tasty appetizer assortment was followed by Anna's signature dish, a sweet-cured shrimp omelet, which originally came about when she was attempting to make her own dried shrimp. The accidental genius that conjured this omelet shows something of the flair a good chef should have for making use of happy mistakes. There's something refreshingly honest about it—after all, food misbehaves, just as humans do.

Fergus Henderson

Born in 1970 in Montreal, Anna Hansen grew up in Auckland, New Zealand. Moving to London at the age of 22, she found a job as a dishwasher at the recently opened French House Dining Room, headed by chefs Fergus Henderson and Margot Clayton (now Henderson). Both became important mentors, instilling Hansen with the open-minded spirit of nose-to-tail eating. In 1994, Hansen moved to a post at Green Street under another important culinary influence, Peter Gordon, later working with him at the Sugar Club in Soho. After a two-year stint here, Hansen set up her own catering company, the Cooker, in 1999, running this project alongside the Providores and Tapa Room, which she and Gordon opened in 2001 to widespread acclaim. In 2008 she launched her solo venture, the Modern Pantry in Clerkenwell, where she serves subtle, playful fusion dishes and has received a "Bib Gourmand" from the Michelin Guide.

MENU

Krupuk quail eggs with chile lime dipping sauce

~

Tea-smoked foie gras terrine, pomegranate molasses, roast grapes, umeshu jelly, and sumac lavosh

~

Sugar-cured shrimp omelet, with green chiles, scallions, cilantro, and smoked chile sambal

~

Chermoula baked line-caught sea bass with quinoa, tomatillo and preserved lemon salad, and spiced toasted seeds

~

Earl Grey panna cotta, Maury jelly, Manuka honey, and sesame seed wafer

Anna Hansen

1
Anna Hansen

2 & 5
In the dining room

3
The kitchen

4
Outside the Modern Pantry

The Modern Pantry, London, UK

1

3

2

4

1
Krupuk quail eggs with
chile lime dipping sauce

2
Sugar-cured shrimp omelet
with green chiles, scallions,
cilantro, and smoked
chilli sambal

3
Chermoula-baked
line-caught sea bass with
quinoa, tomatillo and
preserved lemon salad, and
spiced toasted seeds

4
Earl Grey panna cotta,
Maury jelly, Manuka honey,

KRUPUK QUAIL EGGS WITH CHILE LIME DIPPING SAUCE
Serves 6

For the chile lime dipping sauce
1 lime • 300 ml white wine • 250 ml water • 150 g palm sugar • 1 red chile, split lengthwise • 3 star anise • 2 pieces of asam

1 Cut the lime in half and juice it.
2 Put all the juice, half the squeezed lime, and the remaining ingredients in a pot and gently simmer until syrupy. Discard the lime half before serving.

For the quail eggs
1 dozen quail eggs, soft-boiled and peeled • 500 g raw krupuk crackers, blitzed to a coarse crumb (we make these ourselves using boiled rice and dried scallop roe powder, but you can buy very good-quality ones in most Chinese supermarkets)

Double coat the eggs in the krupuk crumbs, then refrigerate.

To serve
1 Deep fry the quail eggs until golden.
2 Serve immediately with the chile lime dipping sauce.

SUGAR-CURED SHRIMP OMELET WITH GREEN CHILES, SCALLIONS, CILANTRO, AND SMOKED CHILE SAMBAL
Serves 6

For the sugar-cured shrimp
18 large shrimp (prawns), peeled, split lengthways and de-veined • 1 lemon grass stalk, bashed gently with a rolling pin or other suitable implement and chopped into 4 pieces • 30 g ginger, peeled and sliced • 3 lime leaves, shredded • 1 tsp chipotle chili flakes • 1 tbsp soy sauce • 1 tbsp fish sauce • 100 g sugar • 15 g Maldon salt

1 Mix all the ingredients thoroughly and leave to marinate for 24 hours, then rinse and pat dry.
2 Refrigerate in an airtight container until ready to use.

For the smoked chile sambal
2.5 liters canola (rapeseed) oil, for frying • 250 g red bell peppers, sliced • 250 g white onions, sliced • 250 g whole ripe cherry tomatoes • 80 g garlic, sliced • 80 g ginger, peeled and julienned • 25 g dried shrimp, ground in a spice grinder • 1 large dried chipotle chile, stalk removed, and soaked until soft in hot water • 125 ml tamarind paste • 40 ml fish sauce

1 Heat the oil in a pan to 325° F (180° C), then deep-fry the bell peppers, onions and cherry tomatoes separately in small batches until they are a rich golden brown—almost burnt-looking—draining them on paper towels and tipping them into a large bowl as you go.
2 Fry the garlic and ginger, in separate batches also, until just golden brown.
3 In a small skillet, pan-fry the ground shrimp in a little of the oil until aromatic, then add to the bowl along with the remaining ingredients and mix thoroughly.
4 Blitz the sambal in batches in a food processor until almost smooth, emptying it out into another bowl as you go. Mix the processed sambal together thoroughly and let cool. Place in an airtight container and refrigerate until needed.

For the omelet
12 eggs • salt • butter, for cooking • 1 green chile, sliced into very thin rounds • 1 bunch scallions (spring onions), finely sliced

1 Whisk 2 eggs together in a small bowl with ½ tsp of sambal and a small pinch of salt.
2 Heat some butter in an omelet pan over moderate heat, and when it begins to sizzle add 6 shrimp halves. Toss these in the pan until almost cooked, then pour in the seasoned eggs. Swirl the pan once or twice, then reduce the heat.
3 Sprinkle over 3 chile slices and a small handful of scallions.
4 When the eggs look almost cooked, use a flat heatproof rubber spatula to fold the omelet in half. Slide onto a plate and keep in a warm place while you repeat the process for the rest of the omelets.

To serve
1 bunch cilantro (coriander), picked

Garnish each omelet with cilantro and a spoon of the sambal.

CHERMOULA BAKED LINE-CAUGHT SEA BASS WITH QUINOA, TOMATILLO, AND PRESERVED LEMON SALAD, AND SPICED TOASTED SEEDS
Serves 6

For the chermoula
1 tbsp cumin seeds, toasted and ground • 1 tsp coriander seeds, toasted and ground • 1½ tsp sweet smoked paprika • ½ tsp dried chili flakes • 1 tbsp fresh ginger, finely chopped • 1 tbsp fresh turmeric, finely chopped • 2 cloves garlic, crushed • 2 shallots, finely chopped • zest and juice of 2 lemons • ½ bunch chopped flat-leaf parsley • 1 bunch cilantro (coriander) leaves, chopped • 1 tsp Maldon salt • 100 ml extra-virgin olive oil • 1.2 kg line-caught sea bass, cut into 6 portions

1 Mix all the chermoula ingredients together.
2 Marinate the sea bass in the chermoula for half an hour before you plan to eat.

For the spiced toasted seeds
100 ml olive oil • 1 handful fresh curry leaves • 2 tsp fennel seeds • 2 tsp poppy seeds • 1 tsp kaloonji (black onion) seeds • 1 tsp black mustard seeds • 200 g sunflower seeds • 200 g pumpkin seeds • 1 tbsp amchur • 1 rounded tsp Maldon salt

1 Heat the oil over moderate heat in a heavy skillet.
2 Add the curry leaves and pan-fry until aromatic, then add the fennel, poppy, kaloonji and mustard seeds.
3 Reduce the heat a little and continue to pan-fry, shaking the pan until they begin to pop, then add the sunflower and pumpkin seeds.
4 Keep shaking and tossing the seeds in the skillet regularly to ensure even toasting.
5 Once golden, remove from the heat and add the salt and amchur.

For the quinoa, tomatillo, and preserved lemon salad
50 ml olive oil • 1 large red onion, sliced • ¼ tsp sweet smoked paprika • 50 ml sherry vinegar • 400 g cooked quinoa • 3 medium tomatillos, diced • 2 tsp finely diced preserved lemon • 1 handful chopped cilantro (coriander) plus some leaves • 1 small handful chopped mint • juice of 1 lime

1 Heat the oil and caramelize the onion in it, then add the smoked paprika and sherry vinegar and continue to cook until the vinegar has evaporated.
2 To make the salad, toss together the remaining ingredients along with a couple of handfuls of the spiced seeds.

To finish
extra-virgin olive oil • 50 g mustard leaves • lime wedges

1 Preheat the oven to 425° F (220°C).
2 Heat some oil in a pan and add the sea bass skin-side down. Cook for a minute or so until the skin caramelizes, then transfer to the oven. Bake until just cooked.
3 Spoon some quinoa salad onto a plate and scatter a few mustard leaves around.
4 Place the sea bass skin-side up and sprinkle with toasted seeds.
5 Finally squeeze over the fish a wedge of lime and add a dash of extra-virgin olive oil.

EARL GREY PANNA COTTA, MAURY JELLY, MANUKA HONEY, AND SESAME SEED WAFER
Serves 6

For the Maury jelly
2 gelatin leaves • 500 ml Maury wine • 40 g granulated sugar

1 Soak the gelatin leaves in cold water for a minute or so to soften.
2 Bring 150 ml of the Maury to a boil and, after squeezing out as much water as possible from the gelatine, whisk it in.
3 Divide the jelly between 6 (200-ml) molds and refrigerate to set. While the jelly is setting, make the panna cotta.

For the Earl Grey panna cotta
150 ml milk • 300 ml cream • 65 g sugar • 4 gelatin leaves • ½ tsp Maldon salt • 1 tsp Earl Grey tea leaves

1 Bring the milk, cream and sugar to the boil in a pan.
2 Soak the gelatin leaves in cold water for a minute or two to soften.
3 Add the Earl Grey to the milk and cream mixture, whisk in the gelatin, remove from the heat and let infuse for 30 minutes.
4 Strain through a fine-mesh sieve and let cool.
5 Once the jelly has set, fill the molds with the panna cotta.
6 Cover and refrigerate for 2–3 hours or until set.

For the sesame and Manuka honey wafer
75 g butter, softened • 120 g superfine (caster) sugar • 60 g all-purpose (plain) flour • ¼ tsp ground ginger • 1 egg white • 3 tbsp Manuka honey • 1 tbsp black sesame seeds

1 Preheat the oven to 325° F (180°C).
2 Cream the butter and sugar.
3 Add the remaining ingredients and beat until smooth.
4 Spread the mixture as thinly as possible onto a parchment-lined baking sheet and bake for 9 minutes until a deep golden color.

To finish
1 Hold the molds under the hot water tap for several seconds.
2 Place each mold upside-down on a plate and gently shake until the panna cotta slips out.
3 Serve with a shard of wafer.

Anna Hansen

My relationship with Alberto dates back many years to when he first visited the kitchens at elBulli. Since that visit I have followed with growing interest his preoccupation with creating a Spanish cuisine that is both traditional and contemporary, with dishes that succeed at being both classically Spanish and wildly inventive. A typical example is his Strawberries stuffed with asadillo, a dish of roast peppers from his homeland, Castilla La Mancha. He is, without a doubt, the best chef currently creating cutting-edge versions of time-honored Spanish recipes, using Spanish philosophy and the very best Spanish products.

Alberto is a great lover of rice, and a great scholar of the ingredient and its preparation. His restaurant's website has coined the term "rice-olution," which is exactly what he is starting. For his paella, he goes back to the basic construction of the dish: for each recipe the rice is cooked in a specific stock with the aim of "creating a perfect balance of textures and identifiable, distinct flavors from the very first grain of rice you taste." He then only has to select from a small range of ingredients, such as lobster, snails, or ham, to create new and distinct versions of this age-old dish—a far cry from the overcooked, tourist-pleasing cliché that paella had become. He has done the same for tapas, which he serves at the table rather than at the bar, as is the practice in Castilla La Mancha. Now in France, he still serves bite-size dishes but they are creative, stylish, and include everything from gazpacho to puddings. The menu at Fogón changes every month and his only rule is that the table must never be empty.

It is very difficult to define Albert's style because of its unorthodox nature, but tradition is at its heart. He is the fourth generation of chefs in his family, which shows in his dedication to classic national dishes and ingredients. His food is as elegant and visually pleasurable as it is technically masterful. Alberto's creativity has paved the way for other chefs, and his cuisine will become a touchstone in the future for any discussion of the bridge between modernity and tradition in Spanish cuisine.

Ferran Adrià

Alberto Herráiz was born in Castilla La Mancha, Spain, in 1962, into a family of four generations of restaurateurs. He began his career in the family's restaurant, Mesón Nelia in Cuenca, gaining a sound, hands-on background in traditional Spanish cuisine and visiting the restaurants of family friends. By 1984 he was head chef at Mesón Nelia, and in 1987 he opened the restaurant Neli to provide a platform for his fine cuisine. Herráiz moved to Paris in 1997 to open Fogón, a little piece of Spain in Paris, where he specializes in rice dishes, and particularly simple, refined paellas with distinctive flavors and textures. In 2005 Herráiz moved Fogón to a larger location, winning his first Michelin star in 2009.

MENU

Cauliflower and sesame gazpacho with cauliflower couscous

~

Squid with coconut sauce

~

Asparagus, young beet tops, and popcorn salad

~

Radishes with *grelos* (turnip top) sauce

~

Strawberries stuffed with *asadillo*

~

Rice with Iberian ham

~

Strawberries in sherry vinegar

Alberto Herráiz

1
Outside Restaurant
Fogón, Paris

2
Cooking paella

3
Alberto Herráiz

Fogón, Paris, France

1
Center: Cauliflower and
sesame gazpacho with
cauliflower couscous.
Clockwise from the top:
Squid with coconut sauce;
asparagus, young beet tops,
and popcorn salad; radishes
with *Grelos* (turnip top)
sauce; sugar-glazed radishes,
dried tuna and hazelnut;
strawberries stuffed
with *asadillo*

2
Rice with Iberian Ham

3
Strawberries in sherry vinegar

CAULIFLOWER AND SESAME GAZPACHO WITH CAULIFLOWER COUSCOUS
Makes 2 liters

For the gazpacho
1 kg cauliflower • 200 ml whole milk • 50 g white bread • 100 ml sherry vinegar • salt • 200 ml olive oil • 100 ml sesame oil • pepper • ground ginger to taste • 700 ml water

1 Cut the cauliflower into florets and cook it gently in enough milk to cover in a pan sealed with plastic wrap (clingfilm). Reserve the milk for use later.
2 Soak the bread in the vinegar. Mix it with the cauliflower, a little salt, and the olive oil and marinate for 12 hours in a sealed box in the refrigerator.
3 Blend this mixture with the sesame oil, more salt, pepper, and a pinch of ground ginger.
4 Add water and milk until the texture becomes creamy. Strain and keep cold until ready to serve.

For the cauliflower couscous
200 g blanched cauliflower (it must remain really firm), cooled and grated to resemble couscous • 3 chives, chopped thinly • 30 g carrots, diced • 1 spring onion, diced • 1 prune, diced • 5 g black sesame seeds • toasted bread ring (optional)

Mix everything together and arrange in a toasted bread ring or put in small bowls to serve with the gazpacho.

SQUID WITH COCONUT SAUCE
Serves 8

For the coconut sauce
4 sprigs rosemary • 1 onion, chopped • 30 g butter • 30 g all-purpose (plain) flour • 100 ml white wine • 2 cans coconut milk

1 Pan-fry the rosemary and onion in the butter.
2 When cooked, add the flour and stir to make a roux.
3 Deglaze the pan with the wine, then add the coconut milk.
4 Let rest, then blend in a blender and strain.

For the squid, and to finish
8 cleaned squid, cut into tubes 3 cm long • peas, boiled in water • artichoke, cut into strips, dredged with flour, and fried • squid heads, dredged with flour and fried

1 Just before serving, cook the squid on a griddle pan and shape them into tubes. Reheat the peas in the coconut sauce.
2 Fill the tubes with the peas.
3 Top with coconut sauce, and add 2 strips of artichoke and 1 squid head.

ASPARAGUS, YOUNG BEET TOPS, AND POPCORN SALAD
Serves 6

300 g asparagus, thinly sliced • salt and pepper • 100 g mustard leaves • 100 g young beet tops • 100 g mizuna greens • 40 g popcorn • 50 g salted almonds, roasted • 50 g sweet corn, fried and broken up very finely • 100 ml vinaigrette, made with sherry vinegar and mustard, thoroughly emulsified

1 Marinate the strips of asparagus in salt for 15 minutes, then rinse in iced water.
2 Mix all the ingredients in a large bowl, season, and serve in 6 large glasses.

RADISHES WITH GRELOS (TURNIP TOP) SAUCE
Serves 8

500 g turnip tops • 300 ml olive oil • salt, pepper, and ground ginger to taste • radishes

1 Blanch the turnip tops, let cool and blend in a blender with a little water to obtain a thick paste.
2 Season and make an emulsion with the olive oil and strain.

To serve
Make a swirl of grelos sauce on a plate and top with a few radishes.

STRAWBERRIES STUFFED WITH ASADILLO
Serves 8

For the asadillo
50 g onions • 50 g shallot • oil, for cooking • 4 cloves garlic, cut in half • bay leaves • 1 sprig thyme • 500 g tomatoes • 200 ml fresh tomato juice • 380 g can piquillo peppers • 10 ml soy sauce • 10 ml vinegar • 20 g brown sugar • 2 punnets strawberries

1 Thinly slice the onions and shallots, then poach them in a little oil, the garlic cloves, a few bay leaves and thyme.
2 Blend the tomato flesh in a blender and strain. When the onions are cooked, add the tomatoes and tomato juice and let it reduce slowly.

3 Wash and dice the peppers. Add them once the tomato juice is well reduced, then add the soy sauce, vinegar, and brown sugar.
4 Cook all together slowly for 1 hour, then cool quickly.

To finish
24 strawberries • 3 scallions (spring onions), cut into thin strips • 24 capers with stems • 24 olives stuffed with anchovies

Make an opening in each strawberry using a melon baller and stuff with the asadillo. Top with 2 slices of scallion and a caper, put an olive alongside.

RICE WITH IBERIAN HAM
Serves 1

40 g carrots • 40 g scallions (spring onions) • 40 g asparagus • 40 g cauliflower • 40 g zucchini (courgettes) • 25 g turnips • 15 g ham oil, or olive oil •3 hazelnuts • pink ham fat, to cook the rice • salt, to taste • 85 g rice • 125 g tomato sauce • pimienton (bittersweet paprika), to taste • 150 g ham stock • 35 g Iberian ham, cut into thin strips • 0.2 ml liquid saffron

1 Julienne the carrots and asparagus and cut the rest of the vegetables into pieces. Fry them in a paella pan with the oil. Add the ham fat, and when it has colored, season and add the rice. Cook until it becomes translucent, then add the tomato sauce.
2 Add the pimienton, mix well, then add the ham stock and the liquid saffron. Spread out the paella evenly in the pan and allow 17 minutes from the moment it comes to the boil.
3 Preheat the oven to 300°F (150°C).
4 After 12 minutes, remove the ham fat and stir the rice to release it from the sides and bottom of the pan, then put it in the oven. Sprinkle fine strips of ham over the paella before serving.

STRAWBERRIES IN SHERRY VINEGAR
Serves 10

For the strawberries
1 kg strawberries • 100 g beet (beetroot), diced • 1 bunch mint, finely chopped • Szechuan pepper, to taste

Cut the strawberries into quarters, then add the beet, mint and pepper.

For the strawberry syrup
300 g strawberries • 100 g sugar • 1 lemon

Gently heat all the ingredients until the sugar has dissolved, then blend in a blender.

For the sherry mousse
500 g sugar • 200 ml sherry vinegar • 200 ml water • 1 liter heavy (double) cream for every 400 g syrup made from the above 3 ingredients

Gently heat all the ingredients to make a syrup. Cook to the long thread stage, then let cool. Whip the cream with the cooled syrup.

To serve
Mix the strawberries, the mint, pepper, and beet in a bowl. Then add the strawberry syrup and mix. Serve in a glass and cover with the sherry mousse.

Alberto Herráiz

1 & 2
Making garganelli

3 & 4
In the kitchen

5
Terrace of the restaurant

Benjamin Hirst

MENU

**Zucchini flower and
mussel fritters**
For England, Spumante
Metodo Classico,
Blanc de Noir-Giuseppe
Contratto, 2000

~

**Baby artichokes
alla Romana with a goat
cheese fondant**

~

**Zucchini flowers filled
with sheep's ricotta with
Pachino tomatoes,
pine nuts, and basil**
Frascati Superiore, Fontana
Candida-Lazio, Italy, 2007

~

**Yellow pumpkin soup
with porcini mushrooms,
borlotti beans, and toasted
bread with rosemary**

~

**Garganelle with
guinea fowl breast,
wild asparagus, and
Chiodini mushrooms**
Ribolla Gialla, Volpe Pasini,
Friuli Venezia Giulia,
Italy, 2008

~

**Cod cooked in the oven,
artichoke alla Giudea and
black-olive salsa**

~

**Veal sweetbreads
wrapped in Parma ham
with a "Vignarola" of
fava beans, peas, and
cos lettuce**
Balciana, Verdicchio,
Sartarelli, Marche,
Italy, 2006

~

**Pineapple tarte tatin
and sorbet**
Mueggen, Passito di
Pantelleria, Salvatore
Murana, Sicilia,
Italy, 2006

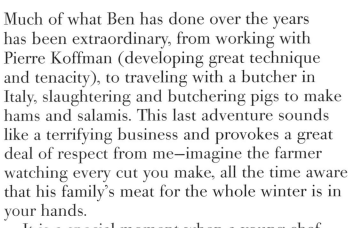

Ben Hirst was born in England in 1966, and after early artistic training, launched into energetic pursuit of a career in food. He worked in a variety of acclaimed restaurants in Italy and France, and completed stints in England with Pierre Koffmann and Fergus Henderson as mentors. After traveling widely to become proficient with Italian cooking technique and absorbing a wealth of local food tradition, he opened his own restaurant, Necci, in Rome in 2007. Ben encourages Necci's profile as a community hub and somewhere to taste the best in Italian cooking with a constantly changing array of simple but perfect dishes that unlock the impact of the freshest ingredients. Ben's focus remains on Central Italian food, and he recreates its dishes with a touch of British steadiness and an eye to sustainability. He absorbed early on Fergus Henderson's philosophy of nose-to-tail eating and the ideas of the Slow Food movement, and insists that Necci makes almost everything in-house, from sausages to marmalade. His rigorous and curious approach keeps the restaurant branching out into all the fascinating possibilities of Italian food, and his most recent plans for Necci include attached pastry and ice cream shops.

Much of what Ben has done over the years has been extraordinary, from working with Pierre Koffman (developing great technique and tenacity), to traveling with a butcher in Italy, slaughtering and butchering pigs to make hams and salamis. This last adventure sounds like a terrifying business and provokes a great deal of respect from me—imagine the farmer watching every cut you make, all the time aware that his family's meat for the whole winter is in your hands.

It is a special moment when a young chef does something extraordinary, such as opening a restaurant in Rome, cooking Roman food for Romans. This was an act of true independence, which Ben has seen through some serious setbacks. His restaurant hums with a happy buzz and feels Italian, but with a cast of something different—Italy, seen with a fresh eye. This kind of exchange and interchange of culture through food is one of the most exciting things to see, especially when it's pulled off with such style and dedication.

The dinner I had there was a joy! I believe it's called a stage dive, when you hurl yourself off the stage in the hope that your fans will catch and carry you. Ben carried us through his wonderful courses with great capability—the problem is that the occasion was so festive (grappa is a delicious drink) that many of the finer gastronomic points have blurred into one marvelous evening. Though the memory is foggy, I can remember handmade ochietta pasta, and bitter *puntarella* chicory may have reared its head. Ben is a chef with great range—he may be able to competently butcher a cow, but the signature dish he treated us to (zucchini flowers filled with sheep's ricotta, with Pachino tomatoes, basil, and pine nuts) is delicate and lovely. And I know there was something delicious for pudding.

Fergus Henderson

BABY ARTICHOKES ALLA ROMANA WITH A GOAT CHEESE FONDANT
Serves 4

16 baby artichokes • juice of 1½ lemons • extra-virgin olive oil, as needed • 30 g mint, chopped • 30 g parsley, chopped • zest of ½ lemon • 4 cloves garlic • coarse salt • 400 g fresh goat cheese • 150 g milk • cracked red pepper, for garnish • mint, thyme, parsley, or marjoram, for garnish

1 Trim the artichokes: Remove the tough outer leaves and dark part of the underside, and cut across the top, removing the tougher tips of the central leaves. Rub the artichoke with lemon, then place into cold water into which the juice of 1 lemon has been squeezed.
2 To cook, drain the artichokes, place in a pan, and cover with half water, half extra-virgin olive oil. Add the mint, parsley, zest of ½ lemon, garlic, and some coarse salt. Bring to a boil and then simmer until al dente. Leave to cool in the cooking liquid.
3 For the goat cheese fondant, remove the rind from the goat cheese and place in a bowl over boiling water to soften with the milk. Blend the cheese and milk together until you have a nice creamy consistency. Chill the mixture.
4 To serve, remove the cheese fondant from the fridge at least 40 minutes before serving so it has time to soften slightly.
5 Cut the base of the artichokes so they sit nicely on the plate and place a quenelle of goat cheese alongside it. Garnish the artichokes with cracked red pepper and garnish the goat cheese with different herbs: mint, thyme, parsley, or marjoram.

GARGANELLE WITH GUINEA FOWL BREAST, WILD ASPARAGUS, AND CHIODINI MUSHROOMS
Serves at least 12

For the garganelle pasta
40 egg yolks • 1 kg 00 flour

1 Mix the egg yolks into the flour and work the pasta until you have a smooth dough. Cover the dough in plastic wrap (clingfilm) and let rest for 1 hour.
2 Roll out the pasta as thinly as possible and leave to dry slightly. Be careful it does not dry out too much and become brittle.
3 Cut the pasta into 4-cm squares using a pasta wheel and then take one square of pasta at a time and place it on a *tavoletta* at an angle, with one of the points of the square pointing at you (a tavoletta is a ridged wooden board used for making garganelle).
4 Place the wooden rod at the tip of the point and then roll the pasta around the rod, pushing it down the *tavoletta* to give the pasta a ridged texture. The end result is a penne-shaped pasta with a serrated surface running around the pasta, as opposed to along the pasta in the classic penne. (If the pasta is too wet then the garganelle lose their cylindrical form.)
5 Let the pasta dry.

For the sauce
1 breast of guinea fowl, cut into small dice • 250 g wild asparagus • extra-virgin olive oil • 1 clove garlic • 150 g chiodini mushrooms • 250 ml guinea fowl stock • 40 g grated pecorino cheese • freshly ground black pepper • zest of ½ lemon

1 Trim the guinea fowl and cut it into small cubes.
2 Wash the asparagus and cut it into 3-cm lengths, discarding the tough parts. Blanch the asparagus for 30 seconds in boiling water and then refresh. (The flavor can be too strong, especially as the asparagus season comes to an end.)
3 Place a little extra-virgin olive oil in a pan with garlic and warm the oil. When hot, add the guinea fowl and season with salt. Fry for about 20 seconds before adding the chiodini mushrooms, and cook for another 30 seconds. Add the asparagus spears and remove the clove of garlic, then add the warm guinea fowl stock. Let this reduce by half.

4 Cook the pasta until it is al dente in plenty of boiling salted water. Drain the pasta, add to the pan, and toss in the stock until the pasta is nicely coated.
5 Mix the grated pecorino cheese into the pasta. Season with freshly ground black pepper, garnish with zest, and serve immediately.

VEAL SWEETBREADS WRAPPED IN PARMA HAM WITH A "VIGNAROLA" OF FAVA BEANS, PEAS, AND COS LETTUCE
Serves 4

600 g sweetbreads • court bouillon, to cook the sweetbreads • 8 slices Parma ham • 1 pig's caul • 500 g fava (broad) beans • 200 g peas • 1 cos lettuce • 1 new-season onion • oil, for frying • extra-virgin olive oil, for roasting • 1 clove garlic • 1 sprig thyme • chicken stock • salt and pepper • 1 tbsp pesto

1 Place the sweetbreads in container under running water for about 2 hours, or until the water runs clear.
2 Trim the sweetbreads, then poach in court bouillon for 10 minutes. Let cool in the court bouillon. When cold, remove the stock, trim off any more membranes, and cut into 150-g portions.
3 Lay out 2 slices of Parma ham next to each other and wrap the sweetbreads in the ham, then in the pig's caul.
4 Pod the beans and blanch in boiling water for 10 seconds. Drain them and refresh in iced water. Remove the skin of the beans. Pod the peas. Wash and chop the cos lettuce. Slice the onion finely.
5 Heat some oil in a frying pan and sear the sweetbreads on all sides. Spoon the oil over the sweetbreads so it becomes uniformly colored and crisp as it cooks. Finish cooking in the oven at 400°F (200°C) for 10 minutes.
6 While in the oven, cook the onion in extra-virgin olive oil until translucent. Add a clove of garlic, a sprig of thyme, and the peas. Cook for a minute before adding a ladle of chicken stock. Reduce the stock by half before adding the fava beans and cos lettuce. Season with salt and pepper.
7 To serve, mix a spoonful of pesto into the "vignarola" and place in a line along the plate. Cut the sweetbreads in half on an angle and place on top of the vegetables.

PINEAPPLE TARTE TATIN AND SORBET
Serves 6

For pineapple sorbet
1 liter unsweetened pineapple juice • 300 ml sugar syrup • glucose • juice of 1 lemon • 100 g stem ginger • 3 tsp ground ginger • 500 ml milk

Mix the pineapple juice with the syrup, glucose, ground ginger and lemon juice. Add the stem ginger, chopped very finely, then churn in an ice-cream machine. After 5 minutes, add the milk and churn until set.

For the tarte tatin
400 g superfine (caster) sugar • 1 pineapple, skin and core removed, cut into 2-cm-thick wedges • puff pastry dough • 50 g butter • candied fruit, for garnish

1 Make a caramel with the sugar and pour some of the caramel into the bottom of 6 small tart pans to cover the bottom. Return the pan with the remaining caramel to the heat and caramelize the pineapple segments. Place the segments on a rack to drain off some of the liquid (reserving the liquid), then place in the tart pans on top of caramel.
2 Roll out the pastry to about 5 mm thick, cut into circles, and cover the tart pans. Bake at 400°F (200°C) for 20–25 minutes. Remove from the oven and carefully turn out the tarts.
3 Glaze the tarts with the reserved liquid from the pineapple.

To serve
Place the tarte tatin in the middle of the plate and place a ball of pineapple sorbet on top. Garnish with candied fruit.

1
Baby artichokes alla Romana
with a goat cheese fondant

2
Garganelle with guinea fowl
breast, wild asparagus, and
Chiodini mushrooms

3
Veal sweetbreads wrapped
in Parma ham with a
"Vignarola" of fava beans,
peas, and cos lettuce

4
Pineapple tarte tatin
and sorbet

Benjamin Hirst

1 & 2
Jing-long Huang

3 & 4
The exterior and dining
room at Long Lai

Jing-long Huang

MENU

**Baked duck with
sliced vegetables and
sesame sauce**

~

Pickled bitter gourd

~

**Stir-fried pork with
dried tofu**

~

**High-grade
Shaoxing wine chicken**

<u>Jing-long Huang</u> was born in Taiwan in 1976. After studying at the National Kaohsiung Hospitality College for Chinese Culinary Arts, he spent more than twenty years working at his family's restaurant, Long Lai. He was influenced profoundly by the culinary experience of his parents, perfecting the signature dishes of the restaurant through long practice while remaining open to the other possibilities offered by the fusion of cuisines in Taiwan. He aims to present Taiwanese cuisine in an innovative way, using tasty and healthy ingredients, and making the most of the agricultural and maritime produce of the island. Jing-long travels overseas frequently to acquire new inspiration from the local foods and flavors of other cultures.

2

When I recently chaired the Taiwan Haute Cuisine Summit in Taipei, I immediately recognized Jing-long Huang. But while he is extremely well-established as one of the top hundred in Hong Kong and other places, in Taiwan, Jing-long Huang is still seen as a new young chef. This is surprising, since he has won lots of awards, published many cookery collections, been both guest and producer for several TV cooking shows, and worked as researcher and creative consultant for various cookbooks and products.

On top of this busy schedule, he took over his father's creative work. His father operated his restaurant Long Lai for twenty years, and Jing-long has now taken it over.

His speciality is practically styled seafood and creative Chinese–Western fusion dishes. His dishes have an intense Taiwanese taste, and he has added personal twists to create his very own Taiwanese flavors, such as flying fish stir-fried rice—after frying specially processed Taiwanese flying fish in oil, he adds salmon flakes and egg-fried rice, and then spreads this on a serving plate that holds the roasted flying fish and pine nuts, giving the dish a pleasantly sweet flavor. Jing-long Huang controls the cooking heat very carefully so that every grain of fried rice has a consistent infusion of flavors. Another of his signature dishes is Blanched Chopped Chicken Thighs — Jing-long bones, then parboils the thighs to maintain the fresh and sweet flavor of the chicken. When the dish is put on the table, it is drenched in the fragrant chicken stock.

Apart from building on his father's handicraft, Jing-long has also created new and improved cooking methods for Taiwanese dishes to suit the tastes of the modern food connoisseur, adding his masterly experience and leaving this new generation's lasting legacy on the world of food and drink in Taiwan.

Jacky Yu

BAKED DUCK WITH SLICED VEGETABLES AND SESAME SAUCE

Serves 10 (as an appetizer)

200 g baked duck breast (you can substitute smoked chicken or poached chicken breast) • 50 g celery • 1 chile • 120 g radishes • 40 g carrots • 40 g leeks • 50 ml liquid seasoning • 2 tbsp sesame sauce • 1 g sugar • 1 tbsp sesame oil • white sesame seeds, to serve

1 Slice the baked duck breast.
2 Slice the vegetables and mix with the duck.
3 Mix the rest of the ingredients to make the dressing. Toss.
4 Serve with white sesame seeds.

PICKLED BITTER GOURD

Serves 10

This is a traditional cold appetizer in Taiwan, especially in the summer. The melon is thought to reduce the body's temperature.

1 bitter gourd or bitter melon, approximately 600 g • 80 ml plum cordial • 4 cloves garlic, sliced • 2 chiles, sliced • 50 ml liquid seasoning • 2 tbsp sugar • 100 ml mirin • 150 g fresh pineapple, sliced

1 Cut the bitter gourd in half, and remove the white part of the bitter melon, which can make it less bitter, and slice it. Also slice the pineapple.
2 Put the bitter gourd into freshly boiled water to soften it, then into cold water to reduce the temperature.
3 Mix the plum cordial, garlic, and chiles with the bitter gourd, then mix in the liquid seasoning, sugar, and mirin. Keep in the refrigerator for 1 day.
4 Serve the dish with some fresh sliced pineapple.

STIR-FRIED PORK WITH DRIED TOFU

Serves 6

120 g bean curd (dried tofu), sliced • 1 leek • 1 chile • 50 g celery • 300 g pork butt (shoulder) • 10 g salty black beans • 30 g dried daikon (mooli) • 2 tbsp liquid seasoning • 1 tsp sugar • ½ tsp white pepper • 3 tbsp water • 30 ml Shaoxing rice wine

1 Cut the tofu, leek, chile, and celery into 4-cm pieces.
2 Fry the pork butt until the fat comes out, then fry the tofu in the fat until golden brown.
3 Place all the ingredients in a pan, and reduce the liquid to a saucelike consistency.

HIGH-GRADE SHAOXING WINE CHICKEN

Serves 6

600 g chopped chicken leg or wing • 30 ml plus 3 tbsp liquid seasoning • 50 g ginger, sliced • 50 ml thick soy sauce • 2 tbsp sugar • 200 ml water • 4 asparagus stalks, sliced • 80 g mushrooms, sliced • 80 g carrots, sliced • 150 ml high-grade Shaoxing wine

1 Marinate the chicken with 3 tsp liquid seasoning and fry until golden brown.
2 Stir-fry the ginger and add the thick soy sauce, sugar, and water, then reduce the liquid to a sauce consistency.
3 Add all the vegetables to the pan, cook for 5 minutes, and add the high-grade Shaoxing wine.
4 Before serving, add some liquid seasoning to enhance the flavor.

1
Baked duck with sliced
vegetables and sesame sauce

2
Pickled bitter gourd

3
High-grade Shaoxing wine
chicken

4
Stir-fried pork with dried tofu

Jing-long Huang

The technical hitch of a certain amount of wine accompanying a memorable meal can often make the term "memorable" something of a misnomer, but there are still moments when you know something magical has happened.

For my first Sunday lunch at the Anchor and Hope, Jonathon produced a great plate of cured ham. Or was it a terrine. Ah, yes, I remember it well. But then came the main course, a cast-iron pot of joy served to each table: chicken cooked with cream, peas, and morels. Fantastic, with a judicious use of cream; not a cream sauce, just a happy slither. The act of placing such an excellent object as that chicken pot at the center of the meal captures something of the nice, simple ritual of English food. Jonathon produces excellent and honest cooking, while making just the right nod to the ceremony of eating. I can say, with a certain haziness, that dessert included prunes soaked in Armagnac. You should start to get the picture.

Jonathon cooks proper bourgeois food, by which I mean food that you might find in the mythical, ideal neighborhood restaurant; food to be relied upon, that isn't trying to fool you. Jonathon cooks with a healthy leaning toward France (not a bad place to lean toward), but his feet are planted firmly in Britain: monk's cheeks, clams, and bacon; deviled kidneys and potato cake; tripe and chips. All the good bits of meat are here, kept company by all the beet-y watercress-ness of the best English vegetables.

When the Anchor and Hope opened it lifted the benchmark for gastro-pubs, and took Jonathan's cooking to new culinary heights. They don't take reservations, so one has to turn up off-the-cuff to enjoy his exquisitely turned-out dishes, which matches Jonathon's nature nicely. He's a joy to watch at work, looming over his food with masterful command, not giving the ingredient a chance to misbehave.

Fergus Henderson

Jonathon Jones was born in Edinburgh in 1971. On leaving school at 16, Jones began an apprenticeship at Edinburgh's Caledonian Hotel, before training unpaid in two restaurants in Burgundy, each with three Michelin stars and a large dose of kitchen aggression. These were happily followed by a job at Le Mimosa, Bridget Pugh's restaurant outside Montpellier. Here Jones learned the possibilities to be found in cooking whatever the market offers each morning. He later returned to London and positions with an array of respected chefs, including Dan Evans at Fire Station, Adam Robinson at The Brackenbury, and Fergus Henderson at St. John, each of whom lent Jones a different type of knowledge or inspiration, creating a unique alchemy that has sustained his career ever since. In 2003 Jones opened the Anchor and Hope in Waterloo, London, where he serves a menu of thoughtful and hearty British dishes.

MENU

Winter vegetables with warm anchovy dressing

~

A Toast to Burns: Haggis with mashed potatoes and rutabaga

~

Roast teal with Seville orange, chestnuts, and poached quince

~

Selection of cheeses

~

Monbazillac caramel custard

1–3
Workings for the new menu amongst fresh produce

4
Jonathon Jones (second from the right) with kitchen staff at the Anchor and Hope

5
Fresh cheeses

Jonathon Jones

Anchor and Hope, London, UK

1
Winter vegetables with
warm anchovy dressing

2
A Toast to Burns: Haggis with
mashed potatoes and rutabaga

3
Roast teal with Seville orange,
chestnuts, and poached quince

WINTER VEGETABLES WITH WARM ANCHOVY DRESSING
Serves 8

This is our take on the classic dish, bagna cauda, from Piedmont in Italy. We serve variations throughout the year, changing the vegetables to suit the season. The dressing is incredibly robust and savory. I'm a bit addicted, and pair it with many plainly broiled (grilled) or poached meats, sea bass or mullet, or even over a poached egg on toast.

For the dressing
200 g unsalted butter • 40 anchovy fillets in olive oil • 12 cloves garlic, finely chopped • 1 red chile, split • 1 healthy sprig of rosemary • 400 ml dry white wine • 1 liter heavy (double) cream • pepper

1 Melt the butter with the oil from the anchovies over moderate heat in a heavy pan. Add the garlic and sizzle for 30 seconds without allowing it to take on any color.
2 Add the anchovies, chile, and rosemary and stir with a whisk, until the anchovies have broken up and melted.
3 Add the wine, turn up the heat, and cook off the alcohol, then add the cream, bring slowly to a boil, whisking occasionally, and reduce to a good coating consistency. Discard the rosemary and chile, and season with a few turns of the pepper mill.

For the vegetables
2 large heads fennel, trimmed, quartered, and lightly steamed • 8 stems salsify, peeled, cut into 5-cm lengths, and boiled until tender with the juice of a lemon • 1 medium cauliflower, cut into florets and lightly steamed • 4 carrots, peeled, steamed whole until tender, and quartered lengthwise • 4 medium beets (beetroot), boiled with a splash of vinegar, peeled, and quartered • 1 small bunch Swiss chard, separated into leaves and steamed until tender • 1 bunch sea kale, lightly steamed • half a head of puntarelle or other chicory, cut into 10-cm lengths and soaked for an hour in iced water

Arrange all the vegetables in separate piles on a large plate. Put warm dressing into a small heated pitcher (jug) and let people help themselves.

A TOAST TO BURNS: HAGGIS WITH MASHED POTATOES AND RUTABAGA
Serves 8

All of these recipes were served for lunch at the Anchor and Hope on Sunday, 25 January, the birthday of Robbie Burns, Scotland's much-loved, long-dead, national poet. Haggis is made by mincing the mixed pluck (liver, lungs, and heart) of a sheep with its suet. It is softened with oatmeal and spiced with pepper, encased in the sheep's stomach and boiled. It sounds medieval and probably is, but I promise you it tastes delicious.

1.5 kg rutabaga (swede), boiled and mashed with a piece of butter • 1.5 kg floury potatoes, boiled and mashed with a piece of butter • 1 bottle of your favorite whisky (we like Ardbeg) • 1 lb 3 oz haggis (haggis makers have no use for kilograms), boiled until piping hot • 1 Scotsman, Ideally with knowledge of Burns

1 Have the rutabaga and potatoes already on the table. Fortify your Scotsman with a large glass of whisky and send him to table with the haggis and a large knife.
2 Pour everyone a whisky, have slightly inebriated Scotsman recite Burns's "Ode to a Haggis" and viciously split open the pudding, clash glasses, drink, and eat.

ROAST TEAL WITH SEVILLE ORANGE, CHESTNUTS, AND POACHED QUINCE
Serves 8

Teal is the smallest of the wild ducks that cross Britain in deep winter and is an affordable seasonal treat. Its rich, gamey flesh marries well with the bitter juice of Seville oranges, whose very short season happily overlaps with that of teal.

The foie gras or butter tucked in the cavity serves as a rough gauge of doneness for the teal — for me, half melted, and it's about medium rare — and keeps the bird moist as it rests. Add any juices collected to the pan juices.

For the poached quince
4 large quinces, peeled, quartered, and cored • 250 g sugar • 150 ml white wine • 1 star anise • 1 cinnamon stick • 1 sprig of rosemary • 2 bay leaves • 1 red chile, split • 1 lemon, sliced

1 Put all the ingredients in a stainless steel pan, add cold water to just cover, and bring gently to a boil, stirring now and again to ensure the sugar dissolves.
2 Cover, turn down to a gentle simmer, and poach until the quinces are tender (½ hour to 1 hour).
3 Let cool before packing in a very clean preserving jar. Keeps for weeks in the refrigerator.

For the roast teal
8 sage leaves • 8 walnut-size chunks of cold foie gras terrine or butter • 8 oven-ready teal, at room temperature, seasoned inside and out • 230 ml whisky • juice of 3 Seville oranges • 32 boiled and peeled chestnuts (I buy them ready-prepared) • 230 ml game stock, chicken stock, or water • salt and peppr to taste • watercress

1 Set a cast-iron frying pan on moderate heat.
2 Put the sage leaves and foie gras or butter inside the birds and carefully brown them all over in the duck fat.
3 Roast in a hot oven until medium rare — only about 7 minutes — then pour out most of the fat from the pan, pour the whisky over the birds and flambé, douse in the orange juice, and turn the teal over in pan juices.
4 Remove the birds and rest in a warm place upside down for 7 minutes.

5 Meanwhile, add the chestnuts and stock or water to pan and boil. Taste your juice for seasoning and reduce if necessary.
6 Put a bouquet of watercress in the cavity of each bird and put on a plate with a pile of chestnuts and a chunk of poached quince. Anoint with the pan juices, which, as Fergus Henderson might say, should be less a sauce, more a morning mist.

Jonathon Jones

A restaurant can take a town by storm. Jacob Kenedy's Bocca di Lupo is just such a restaurant. Coming from a stint at Moorish restaurant Moro, he was ready to pounce—and pounced he has. I first sampled Jacob's cooking when Bocca di Lupo had just opened, and there was hardly a soul to be seen—now, you can barely get a table.

Bocca di Lupo has responded with considered perfection to the extraordinary hunger of the English for Italian food (in spite of a certain difficulty we have with growing red bell peppers and the like). Jacob has achieved tremendous success, with a menu that displays style and flair: a list of less prevalent Italian delicacies, labeled with their regions of origin, rather like a wine list—this seems to suggest that Jacob wants not just to produce wonderful food, but to re-create the secret back alleys of Italian cooking with faithful accuracy. These joyous little dishes hit the nail on the head: rabbit tunato, a bitter chicory risotto, lamb and ham with fresh broad beans, a wealth of lovely cured meats, and so on. In fact, sausages are made in-house, showing Jacob's attention to the important details. He's not afraid of a challenge, either, with sanguinaccio (a sweet paté of pig's blood and chocolate, from Abruzzo) making an appearance on the pudding menu.

Bocca di Lupo has an open kitchen and a big bar to sit at, from which a kind of chef-theater can be observed. The menu, meanwhile, allows each dish to be ordered in different sizes, and is oriented towards sharing a few dishes rather than ordering one solo. These traits show Jacob's modern flexibility; he has captured something about the way people increasingly like to eat, as well as making food that is just delicious.

Fergus Henderson

Born in 1980, Jacob Kenedy completed a long apprenticeship at Moro, the London restaurant specialising in Moorish cuisine. Rising to become head chef, he learned the basics over a fruitful ten-year association with the restaurant's owners, Sam and Sam Clark, collaborating with them on three cookbooks. He followed this with time at Boulevard in San Francisco, where Nancy Oakes became an important mentor. When he opened Konstam in London as head chef for Oliver Rowe, Kenedy managed his own kitchen, gaining the assurance that led him to open Bocca di Lupo in Soho in 2009, at the age of just twenty-eight. The restaurant specializes in Italian cuisines, explored with a contemporary eye and executed with style and authority.

MENU

Tuna tartare
with capers, orange,
and pine nuts

~

Blood orange salad

~

Trofie with pesto

~

Squab stuffed
with squash and
chestnuts

~

Cassata Siciliana

1
Jacob Kenedy in the kitchen

2
The bar and open kitchen
at Bocca di Lupo

3–5
Jacob preparing ingredients

Jacob Kenedy

Bocca di Lupo, London, UK

1
Tuna tartare with capers,
orange, and pine nuts

2
Squab stuffed with
squash and chestnuts

3
Cassata Siciliana

TUNA TARTARE WITH CAPERS, ORANGE, AND PINE NUTS
Serves 4

This dish is very simple, so the quality of the ingredients is of utmost importance. The tuna must be ruby-red and bright. It is best cut from the eye of the loin—any other parts will be fiddly to dice, with wastage in the sinewy bits. The capers should be fat and ripe, packed in salt, the olive oil fruity, and preferably from Sicily, and the pine nuts Italian or Spanish (these are longer than their Chinese counterparts, and much more flavorsome). This dish also makes a good canapé, with the tuna either on toast or on lightly salted discs of cucumber.

For the tuna
bread, preferably ciabatta or similar • 40 g pine nuts • oil, for frying • 360 g prime tuna loin • 50 g salted capers • grated zest of ½ orange • 3 tbsp extra-virgin olive oil • black pepper • 1 tbsp chopped parsley

1 Preheat the oven to 325°F (160°C).
2 Cut the bread into incredibly thin (2-mm) slices, and toast in the oven until pale gold.
3 Toast the pine nuts to the same color—it is better to fry them in a little oil, then drain them, but they can be toasted in the oven at the same time as the bread.
4 Dice the tuna into even 5-mm cubes. A little practice and a sharp knife help.
5 Soak the capers for a few hours in cold water until tolerably salty, then drain and squeeze dry.
6 Chop coarsely, then stir in the olive oil and orange zest along with a pinch of black pepper.
7 When you are about ready to eat, stir together the tuna, caper dressing, pine nuts, and parsley. Taste for seasoning. Serve with the toast on the side.

SQUAB STUFFED WITH SQUASH AND CHESTNUTS
Serves 4

1 small butternut squash • 45 ml extra-virgin olive oil • salt and pepper • 200 g cooked chestnuts • 100 g butter • 6 sprigs thyme • 4 whole squab pigeons • 1 head radicchio Castelfranco, leaves torn • ½ head Treviso tardivo, leaves picked • the best balsamic vinegar you can afford — preferably at least 20 years barrel age

1 Preheat the oven to 425°F (220°C).
2 Peel the squash and cut into sections about 8 cm long by 2 cm wide. Toss with 30 ml of the oil, salt and pepper, and roast until tender and slightly browned.
3 For ease, I use precooked chestnuts which come in a vacuum pack. Separate the chestnuts, and put in a small ovenproof dish with 50 g of the butter, 4 sprigs of the thyme, salt, pepper and a splash of water. Cover tightly and bake until tender—about 30 minutes. Leave the oven on.
4 Meanwhile, prepare the squab. This is the only difficult part of the dish, and the aim is to remove the carcass bones, leaving the skin of the birds intact, with only the leg and first wing bones remaining.
5 First sever the wings at the first joint (elbow).
6 Now use a small knife to cut between the breast and the wishbone on both sides. Extend the cut down to separate the wingbone from the carcass. Make a small, horizontal cut to separate the skin from the top of the wishbone.
7 Put down the knife—hands only from now on.
8 Use your thumbs to separate the breast from the breastbone, then work around to separate the muscles, skin and tendons from the carcass. Always apply inward pressure—pressing into the bone will help remove all the muscle, and help prevent tears in the skin.
9 Dislocate the legs at the hip joint, and, using your thumbs and fingers, work your way from the breast around to the backbone.
10 Finally, when you near the parson's nose, or the fleshy lump near the neck, just pull the skeleton out from the flesh.

11 Stuff each bird with a couple of pieces of squash, 3–4 chestnuts, and a few thyme leaves. If you've done a good job of boning them, a single toothpick will close up the hole at the wing end of the bird.
12 Season the birds with plenty of salt and a little pepper, then brown them in the remaining butter carefully on all sides.
13 Roast them in the oven for about 10 minutes, then let rest for another 5–10 minutes in a warm place. The flesh needs to be medium-rare, and the stuffing just warm.
14 Toss the salad greens with the remaining oil, salt, and pepper. Arrange on a plate, and nest the birds on top (toothpicks removed). Drizzle with the balsamic vinegar—perhaps 2 tbsp for the 4 birds, and serve.

CASSATA SICILIANA
Serves 12–16

This cake is equally good at breakfast, lunch, and dinner. I have a great appetite for it, and so have never had the opportunity to find out exactly how long it keeps in the refrigerator but suffice it to say long enough.

500 g best-quality marzipan (high nut content, not too much sugar) • 2 tsp pistachio paste, or a few drops green food coloring • enough sponge cake to line your pan, either homemade or bought • a little sweet Marsala • 600 g cow-milk ricotta • 150 g sugar • 500 g sheep-milk ricotta (or cow, if sheep is hard to find) • 40 g chocolate, chopped finely • 400 g confectioners' (icing) sugar • juice of 1 lemon • 120 ml water • 2 quarters of candied orange peel • 1 good wedge of candied citron (cedro)

1 Line a cake pan with plastic wrap (clingfilm). For the classic shape, use a tatin pan—about 24 cm wide, 4 cm high, with gently tapering sides.
2 Take a walnut-size lump of marzipan and work together with the pistachio paste to make a nice green color.
3 Roll into a thin sausage, press flat to make a ribbon, and cut lengths to press against the sides of the pan to make vertical stripes.
4 Roll the remaining marzipan 3 mm thick, and line the pan. Press into the corners and against the sides, so the green bands stick to it.
5 Cut the cake into 5-mm sheets, and line the bottom and sides of the pan with it (this will make a layer within the marzipan). Sprinkle with Marsala to moisten.
6 Finely puree the cow-milk ricotta and sugar (either a food processor or a whisk will do), then turn into a bowl and stir in the sheep-milk ricotta and chocolate. Use this mixture to fill the cake.
7 Cover with another layer of sponge, again moisten with Marsala, and refrigerate under a weight to set the cake.
8 Turn out onto a plate and remove the plastic wrap. It is best if the plate is a few mm smaller than the cake, so the excess frosting (icing) can drip off.
9 Mix together the confectioner's sugar, lemon juice and water and frost (ice) the cake. Cut the candied peel into strips and decorate it. Refrigerate until ready to serve.

It is said that Tom swears in French in his own kitchen. I love this idea. This is a delightful sign that he has learned something from his long stays in the restaurants of our fine country. But I am certain of something else: because of this experience with Pierre Koffmann, Guy Savoy, and in my restaurant, Louis XV in Monaco, Tom has forged exceptional technical skills.

And that's not the end of the story. Tom's passion gives him an extra dimension. Equipped with his solid technical skills, Tom arrived in Edinburgh and literally reinvented Scottish cooking. To do this, he started by exploring all the region's resources, and in doing so, he discovered all its wealth. He haunts the port of Anstruther for its Dublin Bay prawns and visits Orkney for its wonderful scallops. He finds his pork in Dumfriesshire, his lamb in Perthshire, and his mallard ducks in Kilmarnock. He has his chanterelle pickers, his raspberry supplier in Blairgowrie, and his grouse, partridge, and woodcock hunters. A masterly demonstration: Every region has its treasures, and everything begins with the land.

Then Tom reread the Scottish culinary repertoire in the light of his experience in contemporary cooking. No, there is no reason to limit yourself to porridge and smoked salmon, and neither is there any reason for haggis to remain an unchanging monument that no one wants to visit anymore. This work of "revisiting," of constructing a culinary identity, is essential. It has universal importance. Cooking always expresses the truth of a region: that is, an encounter with nature and culture. You always need to discover it and immerse yourself in it. Then cast free of it to bring it alive, changing it into cooking for today.

Tom is traveling this road, and he is doing it with panache and energy, as if he has kept in his heart a little of the Mediterranean that he got to know in Monaco.

Alain Ducasse

Born in Scotland in 1977, Tom Kitchin began washing dishes at 13 years old. After attending cooking college in Perth, he moved to London at 19 to a position under Pierre Koffmann at La Tante Claire, with its three Michelin stars. His five years there provided a rigorous grounding in the fundamentals of French cuisine, which Kitchin augmented with a year at Restaurant Guy Savoy in Paris. Next he moved to Monaco and spent two years at Alain Ducasse's Louis XV. After a position as a private chef, Kitchin returned to Scotland in 2006 with his wife, Michaela, to open the Kitchin. At this sleek, modern space in the Leith area of Edinburgh, he presides over a menu that combines proficient French technique with the best Scottish produce, including shellfish that Kitchin receives alive, straight from the boat. His reinventions of Scottish flavors with a French delicacy won the Kitchin its first Michelin star in 2007.

1
Tom Kitchin at work

2
Opening sea scallops at the Kitchin

3 & 5
Out diving for wild scallops

4
Foraging for fresh herbs in the woods

6
Choosing asparagus

MENU

Carpaccio of sea scallops from Orkney, hand-dived by Robert and served with apple sorbet, radish, apple, dried cranberry, and a citrus dressing

~

Razor clams from Arisaig cooked to order and served with diced vegetables, squid, chorizo, and lemon confit, garnished with wild herbs

~

Roasted tail of Norwegian lobster from Anstruther, served with boned and rolled pig's head and a crispy ear salad

~

Poached wild North Sea halibut, served with spring vegetables in a seafood consommé

~

Rump of lamb from Dornoch, served with kidney, crispy belly, and a compote of red onions cooked with Szechuan pepper and apricot

~

Highland crowdie cheesecake mousse served on a rhubarb tartan with Scottish berries, jelly, and almond shortbread

Tom Kitchin

The Kitchin, Edinburgh, UK

1

Razor clams from Arisaig
cooked to order and served
with diced vegetables, squid,
chorizo, and lemon confit,
garnished with wild herbs

2

Roasted tail of Norwegian
lobster from Anstruther,
served with boned and rolled
pig's head and a crispy
ear salad

3

Highland crowdie cheesecake
mousse on a rhubarb tartan
served with Scottish berries,
jelly, and almond shortbread

RAZOR CLAMS FROM ARISAIG COOKED TO ORDER AND SERVED WITH DICED VEGETABLES, SQUID, CHORIZO, AND LEMON CONFIT, GARNISHED WITH WILD HERBS

Serves 4

For the vegetables
1 carrot • 1 zucchini (courgette) • 100 ml vegetable oil • 100 g fava (broad) beans, podded weight • 1 lemon

1   Peel the carrot and cut into 5-mm dice. Peel the zucchini then dice the white part.
2   Gently sauté the carrot and zucchini in 1 tsp vegetable oil for 3–4 minutes, then set aside.
3   Remove the tough outer skin from the fava beans.
4   Zest the lemon and squeeze the juice and set aside for later.

For the razor clams
8 razor clams (spoots) • 2 shallots, peeled and finely chopped • 100 ml white wine

1   Wash the razor clams well in cold running water, making sure to rinse away any sand and grit. Discard any that are open.
2   Take a pan large enough to hold all the clams and place it on high heat. Add the clams, shallots, and white wine, and immediately cover the pan with a tight-fitting lid so that the clams steam.
3   After 1–2 minutes all the clams should be cooked. Discard any that remain unopened.
4   Remove the clams from the shells, reserving the shells.
5   Slice the clam meat thinly at an angle around the brown intestine. Set aside.

For the squid and chorizo
30 g chorizo • 100 ml heavy (double) cream • 50 g chopped chives or parsley • 20 g unsalted butter • salt and pepper • 100 g squid

1   Reduce the clam cooking liquor by half.
2   Add the chorizo, cream, and chopped vegetables, herbs, and fava beans while the liquid is simmering, stirring constantly.
3   Once the cream has thickened slightly, add the sliced clams, lemon juice and zest, and finish with a piece of butter.
4   Cut the squid into triangles and cook quickly in a hot pan.

To serve
1 bunch of chives, chopped • 4 sprigs of dill • 1 bunch of fresh amaranth leaves, chopped • 2 sprigs of chervil • 10 g wild flowers

1   Place 2 shells on each plate, and pile the razor clams, vegetables, and chorizo in creamy juices into them.
2   Put the squid on top, and garnish with the herbs and flowers.

ROASTED TAIL OF NORWEGIAN LOBSTER FROM ANSTRUTHER, SERVED WITH BONED AND ROLLED PIG'S HEAD AND A CRISPY EAR SALAD

Serves 6

For the pig's head sausage
1 pig's head (de-boned and tied, with the ears removed) • 2 additional pig's ears • 2 carrots, roughly • chopped • 1 stick celery, roughly • chopped • 1 white onion • 2 bay leaves • 1 sprig of thyme • 1 tsp herbes de Provence • 1 tsp ground cumin •1 tsp fennel seeds • salt and pepper • olive oil, for frying

1   Carefully burn the ears and pig's head with a blow torch to remove all hairs.
2   Wrap all 4 ears in muslin and place with the head, carrots, celery, onion, bay leaves, and thyme into a very large stock pot. Cover with water, bring to boil, and cook for 3½ hours. Take pot off heat and leave pig's head to cool.
3   Remove the cheeks from the pig's head and separate the fat from the skin. Discard fat. Lay a piece of plastic wrap (clingfilm) on a chopping board and put the skin, hair side down, on the plastic wrap.
4   Shred the meat from the pig's cheeks, and mix with the herbs and spices, and a pinch of salt and pepper.
5   Lay a line of the cheek meat mix in middle of skin and roll it into a sausage about 6 cm in diameter. Wrap tightly in plastic wrap and leave in fridge to set for 12 hours. To serve, cut sausage into slices 3-cm thick and fry in a little olive oil until cooked through.

For crispy pig's ears
olive oil, for frying

1   Remove the cooked pig's ears from the muslin and trim off the muscles. Wrap the ears in plastic wrap and put in the refrigerator under a heavy weight for 24 hours.
2   Shred the ears very finely with a sharp knife. Heat a dash of olive oil in pan and add small piles of the shredded ears. Fry for a minute or two, then flip and fry the other side until crisp. Remove and drain on kitchen paper, then keep warm.

For the Norwegian lobsters
salt • 6 Norwegian lobsters (langoustine) tails

Bring a large pan of water to a boil and add 2 tablespoons salt. Separate the tails of the Norwegian lobsters from the body and drop the tails into the boiling water for 10 seconds. Remove and refresh in bowl of iced water. Peel the tails by pressing the shells together gently and peeling off to leave only the meat. (Be careful not to cut yourself on the sharp shells.)

For serving
salad leaves, for garnish

On each plate, put a slice of pig's head sausage with some salad leaves. Top with some pig's ears and add 1 Norwegian lobster tail.

HIGHLAND CROWDIE CHEESECAKE MOUSSE SERVED ON A RHUBARB TARTAN WITH SCOTTISH BERRIES, JELLY, AND ALMOND SHORTBREAD

Serves 6

For the cheesecake mousse
450 g crowdie cheese • 125 g sugar • 1½ tbsp all-purpose (plain) flour • 1 tbsp vanilla extract • zest of 1 lemon • 1 egg • 1 egg yolk • 140 ml buttermilk

1   Preheat the oven to 340°F (170°C).
2   Put the cheese, sugar, flour, vanilla, and lemon zest in a blender and mix until smooth.
3   In separate pitcher (jug), stir the egg and egg yolk into the buttermilk, then pour into the blender with the cheese mixture and blend again until smooth.
4   Pour into a 23-cm baking dish, cover with aluminum foil, and bake for 35–40 minutes until set.
5   Let cool, then transfer the mixture to a blender and blitz until smooth. Leave to set in the refrigerator for at least 1 hour before serving.

For the shortbread
150 g all-purpose (plain) flour • 25 g confectioners' (icing) sugar • 120 g butter • 75 g almonds (with their skins)

1   Sieve the flour and the confectioners' sugar together into a bowl. Add the butter and knead by hand until the mixture is light and forms a dough.
2   Add the almonds and continue to knead, then shape the mixture into a rectangular log. Wrap in plastic wrap (clingfilm) and chill in the refrigerator for at least 2 hours, or until very firm.
3   Preheat the oven to 375°F (190°C) and line a baking sheet with parchment.
4   Cut the dough into 1-cm slices and lay out on the baking sheet. Bake for 12–14 minutes until golden brown, then let cool for 5–10 minutes on the baking sheet to set firm before removing to a wire rack.

For the rhubarb
3 stalks rhubarb • 400 g sugar • juice and zest of 1 lemon • 600 ml water

1   Cut 2 of the stalks of rhubarb into pieces about 10 cm long. Using a mandolin or a very sharp knife, slice these pieces into 3-mm strips and set aside.
2   Place the sugar, lemon zest, and lemon juice in a pan with the water and bring to a boil, then remove from the heat.
3   Put the rhubarb strips in a bowl, pour the hot syrup over them, and let cook for 5 minutes, until just soft.
4   Remove the rhubarb and put in the refrigerator to cool. Keep the syrup for later.

For the jelly
2 gelatin leaves or 4 g powdered gelatin

1   Bring 200 ml of the reserved poaching syrup to a boil, then take it off the heat.
2   Soak the gelatin in a bowl of cold water for 5 minutes, squeeze out excess moisture and add to the poaching liquid.
3   Mix well, pour into a mold, and let set in the refrigerator.

For the strawberry crisps
100 g sugar • 100 g water • 15 strawberries

1   Boil the sugar and water together to make sugar syrup.
2   Slice the strawberries thinly, dip into the syrup, then dry for 3-4 hours until crisp at 176°F (80°C).

To serve
100 g strawberries • 100 g raspberries • lemon thyme

1   Overlap 10 rhubarb strips to form a tartan pattern. Place the shortbread on top of the rhubarb.
2   Place a scoop of cheesecake mousse on top of the shortbread. Add some strawberries and raspberries, and slices of rhubarb jelly beside the mousse.
3   Garnish the cheesecake mousse with strawberry crisps, lemon thyme, and poaching syrup.

I first met Anatoly when he presented a culinary demonstration at the Congreso lo Mejor de la Gastronomía in San Sebastian in 2007. His cooking brings to mind the historic cuisine of the tsars and reminded me that Russia was once a world power in gastronomy. I saw that Anatoly heralded a new vision of the culinary world with Russian gastronomy playing a key role. I think he feels this way too, and is very interested in bringing Russian food to the forefront of European cuisine.

What I find particularly interesting is the fact that Anatoly has opened the world's eyes to the culinary language of his country. Russian cuisine is generally pigeonholed in the West by its stereotypes—primarily caviar, vodka, and borscht. However, in Anatoly's hand these clichéd dishes take on their own gastronomic language. Borscht remains on the menu as his signature dish which he presents using the newest techniques of contemporary cooking; but it can be eaten alongside ice fish served with eggplant paper, radish emulsion, and vegetable mousse or chicken with salsify, beet foam, and microvegetables. Anatoly serves elegant and inspired dishes that could come from no other place than Moscow.

His menus range between nine and fourteen courses, which leaves him a lot of room to be creative. It is his aim to ensure that each lengthy menu works as an entity. Menus of this size also enable him to present a vast array of ingredients, which showcase crops and gastronomic influences from throughout the Russian territories. In short, he wants to remind the diner that Russia is more than ballet and snow, and I have chosen Anatoly because I think we should look to Russia for the future of gastronomy.

Ferran Adrià

1

Anatoly Komm was born in 1967 in Moscow. After a career as a fashion importer, he took a job in 1990 in a restaurant named Palazzo di Spaghetti, augmenting the training and skills he gained there with periods of working travel, which took him everywhere from Hong Kong to Antigua. This grounding in culinary knowledge and technique allowed Komm to open his own restaurant, Green.It, in 2001. He set out to develop Russia's international reputation for organic agriculture—springing from the possibilities inherent in its varied climate zones—and gastronomy, sourcing all his ingredients from within his vast home country. He is presently executive chef of the restaurants Varvary, Kupol, Kommpartiya, and Green. It, all in Moscow.

MENU

Crayfish tail with
vegetable paste

~

Beet salad with herring
and sprats ice cream

~

Far East Trubach with dill

~

Far East oyster with
lemon foam

~

Kholodets (jellied ground
meat) with carrots and
beet macaroni

~

Cod liver snow and
bread cigar

~

Mackerel and potato
with sunflower oil

~

Pea soup

~

Pike-perch with smoked
homemade cheese

~

Borscht with truffle

Anatoly Komm

1
Market fish stall

2 & 3
Anatoly Komm in the kitchen

4
The restaurant dining room

BEET SALAD WITH HERRING AND SPRATS ICE CREAM
Serves 13

For the beet jelly
1 kg celery root • 1 kg celery stem • 300 g tomatoes • 200 g beet (beetroot) juice • 7 g gelatin

1   Prepare a celery broth by combining celery root, celery stem, and tomatoes in 3 liters of water and cooking for 1 hour.
2   Mix the beet juice with 200 g celery broth. Melt the gelatin into this mixture. Refrigerate, then cut into dice.

For the herring
215 g preserved herring fillet • 150 g milk • 100 g cream (33% fat)

Chop the herring fillet and mix with milk and cream. Freeze. Process twice with a Pacojet when frozen.

For the sprats
200 g preserved sprats • 50 g milk • 100 g cream (33% fat) • 0.5 g grated nutmeg • 1 g salt

Chop the sprats, mix them with milk and cream, season with nutmeg and salt, then freeze. Process twice with a Pacojet when frozen.

For the paste cones
125 g butter • 190 g sugar • 63 g flour • 0.5 g salt • 90 g orange juice • 5 g cuttlefish ink

Whip the butter and sugar in a mixer, gradually adding the flour (mixed with the salt), orange juice, and cuttlefish ink. Roll out the paste to a thickness of 2 mm on a nonstick silicone mat. Make circles of 10cm in diameter and then halve them. Bake for 5–7 minutes at 350°F (180°C). Form cones from the semi-circles while hot.

For the vegetables
100 g boiled potatoes • 100 g boiled carrots • 30 g pickled cucumber • 50 g canned green peas

Chop all of the vegetables and mix them together.

For the pickled cucumber foam
pickled cucumber

Squeeze the pickled cucumbers. Blend the juice until it becomes foam.

For the vegetable sorbet
150 g boiled beet (beetroot) • 100 g boiled potatoes • 100 g boiled carrots • 100 g pickled cucumbers • 80 g vegetable oil • 4 g sugar syrup • 1.5 g salt • 0.5 g black pepper

Chop all the vegetables and mix with remaining ingredients. Put into a Pacojet container, freeze. Process with Pacojet several times when frozen.

For serving
Put a portion of the beet jelly and the vegetables into a martini glass. Put the vegetable sorbet on top of it. Pour the foam around. Serve with paste cones filled with herring and sprats.

COD LIVER SNOW AND BREAD CIGAR
Serves 20

For the cod liver snow
130 g canned cod liver • 5 g cod liver oil • 0.5 g salt • 200 g milk • 10 g gelatin

Put the cod liver into Pacojet containers, add the cod liver oil, salt, and milk. Freeze. Process twice when frozen. Melt in a water bath and add the melted gelatin. Put the mixture into a siphon and charge it.

For the sunny cream
100 g carrot, peeled and boiled • 100 g processed cheese • 55 g mayonnaise • 1.5 g garlic • 1 g garlic oil • 10 g milk • 2.5 g gelatin

Cut the carrot, put it into Pacojet containers, add the cheese, mayonnaise, garlic, garlic oil, and milk. Freeze. Process with Pacojet twice when frozen. Melt the mixture in a water bath, strain it, and add the melted gelatin. Put the mixture into a siphon and charge it.

For the poached egg
1 egg yolk

Wrap the egg yolk in oiled plastic wrap (clingfilm) like a packet. Boil for 3 minutes.

For the bread cigar
50 g rye bread • liquid nitrogen

Cut the rye bread into bricks, pour liquid nitrogen over them. (Liquid nitrogen should not be handled without training in how to use it safely.)

For serving
salad leaves

1   Put a little frozen piece of bread on the plate. Place the egg near it and cover with the sunny cream.
2   Dispense the cod liver snow from the siphon, freeze it with liquid nitrogen, then crush it with a pestle and add to the plate.
3   Decorate with salad leaves.

MACKEREL AND POTATO WITH SUNFLOWER OIL
Serves 13

For the coated potato
30 g lactose • 30 g kaolin • 3 g cuttlefish ink • 50 g water • 200 g boiled cherry potatoes

Blend the ingredients except potatoes until smooth, then use the mixture to coat the potatoes.

For the isomalt capsules
100 g isomalt • 50 g water • vegetable oil

Melt the isomalt in the water, boil for 10 minutes. With resulting caramel create small capsules and fill each one with 2 g vegetable oil.

For the dill stone
50 g maltose • 130 g dill oil

Blend the maltose and oil. Shape the mixture into a stone and roast it with a blowtorch.

For the mackerel
160 g cold-smoked mackerel fillet

Remove the skin and bones from the fillet of mackerel. Cut into portions.

For finishing
rings of leek • black and white salt

Heat the coated potatoes in the oven for about 2 minutes at 350°F (180°C). Put on a plate. Add a portion of mackerel, the dill stone, rings of leek, and the capsules filled with vegetable oil, then decorate with black and white salt.

BORSCHT WITH TRUFFLE
For 100 portions

For the borscht sorbet
340 g fresh beet (beetroot) • 60 g olive oil • 30 g fresh carrot • 50 g fresh cabbage • 12 g parsley • 5 g garlic • 10 g dried tomato • 40 g lemon juice • 12 g sugar • 1 g salt • 1 g cumin • 0.01 g chili oil • 35 g water

1   Peel and grate the beet, and brown it in olive oil. Cook the carrot and cabbage in boiling water, chop them and mix with parsley, garlic, and dried tomatoes. Add the remaining ingredients.
2   Put the mixture into the Pacojet container and freeze in a blast-chiller.
3   Process in a Pacojet twice when frozen.

For the beet paper
12 g Metil • 300 g fresh beet (beetroot) juice

Melt the Metil in the beet juice. Beat with a blender. Spread the mixture over a flat sheet tray. Freeze for about 24 hours, then dry at room temperature for about 2 hours.

For the dried porcini broth
1 kg dried porcini • 1½ liters water

Cook the porcini and water to make 100 g concentrated broth.

For the truffle foam
225 g cream (33% fat) • 225 g milk • 30 g butter • 100 g white truffle • 0.5 g salt • 10 g sugar

Mix the cream, milk, butter, and porcini broth. Bring to a boil. Chop the white truffle and add to the mixture, along with some salt and sugar. Whip the mixture.

To serve
Put some broth on the bottom of a plate. Cover with the truffle foam. Wrap the borscht sorbet up in the beet paper and put it in the middle of a plate. Put a slice of truffle near it.

1
Beet salad with
herring and sprats
ice cream

2
Cod liver snow
and bread cigar

3
Mackerel and potato
with sunflower oil

4
Borscht with truffle

Anatoly Komm

1

2

3

Filip Langhoff

MENU

This menu represents the Fall and is inspired by the Finnish forests and the cold Norwegian Sea.

Salmon confit 108°F (42°C) with pickled beet, Swedish caviar, and horseradish cream

~

Cream of foie gras soup with roasted cashew nuts and apple sorbet

~

Barley "risotto" in lobster stock with Norwegian shellfish, carrots, and sea buckthorn

~

Chicken bouillon "dashi" with seaweed, mussels, and sautéed halibut

~

Pigeon with onions, porcini mushrooms, and flavors of the forest

~

Finnish blue cheese, Norwegian spruce shoot jelly, and blue berries

~

October cloudberries with chocolate ganache, cloudberry sorbet, and fallen leaves

Born in Helsinki, Finland, in 1980, Filip Langhoff began his culinary life tasting herbs as a child in his grandmother's garden. His curiosity piqued, as an adult he went on to three years of formal culinary training. In 2000 Langhoff moved to Oslo, Norway, gaining experience in various restaurants before a brief time at Edsbacka Krog in Stockholm, Sweden. Witnessing the rigorous standards that resulted in the restaurant's two Michelin stars opened Langhoff's eyes to the possibilities of fine cuisine. After spending time at elBulli in Spain, Langhoff returned to Oslo in 2005 and is now chef at Michelin-starred Spisestedet Feinschmecker.

Originally hailing from Finland, Filip Langhoff now finds himself in Norway as head chef at Feinschmecker in Oslo. The restaurant is owned by the legendary Norwegian chef Bent Stiansen, the first Scandinavian ever to win the Bocuse d'Or. The biennial contest, held in Lyon, France, is widely recognized as the unofficial world championship for chefs. Since then, Stiansen has run his famous restaurant in the center of Oslo to incredibly high standards, and has had a Michelin star for years.

I first met Filip some years ago when he worked with us for a month in the kitchen at Noma. Even then he struck me as a very gifted chef. His work ethic, palate, and organizational skills were all outstanding. A few years later Filip chose to follow in his mentor Stiansen's footsteps and take part in the Bocuse d'Or. I was a judge in the final and he did extremely well considering his youth and his relative lack of competitive experience. Filip did not end up on the podium that year, but maybe he should have.

What I found most surprising about Filip was that you could really see and taste in his food that he was a chef with personality and a strong opinion. In Lyon he knew what he wanted, and there was a very distinct style once you peeled away the layers of pretentiousness that are often found in dishes created for such events. His cooking was heavily oriented towards his home country. For instance, he used fresh spruce shoots and beech in his dishes, which created a strong link to the landscape of Finland. Furthermore, his food exhibited a subtlety and calmness that is quite unusual in such a young chef. If this is how he has developed in just a few years, perhaps one day Filip will indeed find himself on the Bocuse d'Or podium claiming the first prize.

René Redzepi

1
Pigeon with onions,
porcini mushrooms, and
flavors of the forest

2
October cloudberries
with chocolate ganache,
cloudberry sorbet and
fallen leaves

Filip Langhoff

PIGEON WITH ONIONS, PORCINI MUSHROOMS, AND FLAVORS OF THE FOREST
Serves 10

In this dish, the combination of sweet onions and acidic cranberries and spices brings out the flavor of the pigeon in an amazing way. The hazelnuts and porcini mushrooms accentuate the lovely aromas of the forest.

For the pigeon
5 pigeons • salt • pepper • 100 g butter • 5 cloves garlic • 5 thyme sprigs • 5 g juniper twigs • 10 juniper berries • clarified butter, for pan-frying

1 Pluck the pigeons and remove the legs and thighs, leaving only the 2 breast fillets on the carcass. Rub the insides of the carcasses with salt and pepper.
2 Put the butter, garlic, thyme, juniper twigs, and berries under the carcass and vacuum-pack each carcass separately in a vacuum bag. Poach in a water bath with an immersion circulator at 140°F (60°C) for around 45 minutes, until the internal temperature reaches 135°F (58°C).
3 Brown the breasts in a pan in the clarified butter, skin side down. Let the meat rest for 2–3 minutes before carving from the carcass.
4 Season with salt and pepper.

For the onion puree
300 g onions • 150 ml water • 150 g butter • 1 rosemary sprig • 1 garlic clove • 2 juniper berries • 10 g salt • pepper

1 Combine all the ingredients in a pan, cover and cook until the onion is tender. Uncover and reduce over high heat until most of the liquid has evaporated.
2 Drain off the fat, remove the herbs and puree with an immersion blender until smooth. Season with salt and pepper.

For the onion chips
4 shallots • crumiel (honey powder)

1 Preheat the oven to 250°F (120°C).
2 Cut the shallots lengthwise 1 mm thick with a mandolin and place on a baking sheet. Sift crumiel over the shallot slices. Dry in the oven for around 20 minutes.

For the pickled onions
15 tiny onions • 50 ml water • 50 g sugar • 25 ml shallot vinegar • 1 heather twig

1 Peel and halve the onions. Bring the water, sugar and vinegar to a boil. Vacuum-pack all the ingredients in a vacuum bag. Poach at 185°F (85°C) for 35 minutes.

2 Cut the onions in half and sauté, cut-side down, to caramelize.

For the porcini mushrooms
10 small porcini (cep) mushrooms • 50 g butter • salt and pepper

1 Clean and trim the mushrooms, reserving the trimmings. Halve and sauté in butter.
2 Season with salt and pepper.

For the forest crumble
100 g hazelnuts in their shells • 4 juniper berries • 10 g juniper needles • 30 g dried cranberries • 10 ml gin • 10 ml hazelnut oil

1 Preheat the oven to 300°F (150°C). Toast the nuts for around 4 minutes, then shell them.
2 Process the juniper berries and needles in a blender. Press through a fine sieve to make a fine powder.
3 Place the nuts in a food processor and process until coarsely chopped. Add the cranberries, juniper powder, gin and hazelnut oil. Pulse 4 times.

For the cranberry jelly
100 ml cranberry juice • 1 g Gellan

1 Combine the juice and Gellan in a small pan and heat to 200°F (95°C), stirring constantly.
2 Transfer the pan to an ice bath and whisk until cold. Press the gel through a fine-mesh sieve, and store in a pastry (piping) bag.

For the porcini reduction
100 g porcini (cep) mushroom trimmings • 100 g shallots • 2 juniper berries • 30 ml oil • 100 ml port • 200 ml veal stock

1 Peel and chop the shallots.
2 Heat the oil in a skillet and sauté the mushrooms and shallots with the juniper berries.
3 Deglaze the pan with the port. Add the stock and reduce over low heat until half the original quantity remains. Pass through a fine-mesh sieve. The mixture should have an intense porcini flavor.

To serve
heather flowers

1 For each person, trail a drop of onion puree across the plate and make a smaller drop with the cranberry jelly.
2 Cut a pigeon breast in half and place the halves on either side of the puree.
3 Add the rest of the ingredients, leaving space in between.
4 Glaze the meat with the reduction.
5 Sprinkle forest crumble over the top. Garnish with heather flowers.

OCTOBER CLOUDBERRIES WITH CHOCOLATE GANACHE, CLOUDBERRY SORBET, AND FALLEN LEAVES
Serves 10

Inspiration for this dish came from the October forests and their wonderful colors. And that is when cloudberries taste best.

For the cloudberry sorbet
500 g cloudberries • 350 g sugar • 60 g glucose • 450 ml water • 2 g gelatin • 2 tbsp lime juice

1 Process the berries with an immersion blender.
2 Bring the sugar, glucose and water to a boil, add to the berries, blend and strain.
3 Soak the gelatin in cold water to soften. Stir into the cloudberry mixture until dissolved.
4 Stir in the lime juice.
5 Freeze in an ice-cream maker, then store in an airtight container in the freezer.

For the caramel ice cream
150 g sugar • 1.5 liters plus 150 ml whole milk • 200 ml evaporated milk • 2 g gelatin • 40 g glucose • 150 ml whole milk

1 Caramelize the sugar in a heavy-based pan.
2 Bring 1.5 liters milk and evaporated milk to a boil. Reduce over low heat until around half the original amount remains.
3 Soak the gelatin in cold water to soften. Add the hot milk mixture with the remaining ingredients and let cool.
4 Freeze in an ice-cream maker, then store in an airtight container in the freezer.

For the cloudberry coulis
450 ml cloudberry juice (available frozen) • 50 ml 50% sugar syrup • 5.5 g agar agar • 50 ml lime juice

1 Combine 300 ml of the cloudberry juice with the sugar syrup and agar agar in a pan and boil for 2 minutes.
2 Strain, then refrigerate.
3 When cold, add the lime juice and remaining cloudberry juice and mix in a blender.
4 Strain, spoon into a pastry (piping) bag and refrigerate.

For the ganache
360 ml whipping cream • 240 g semisweet (dark) chocolate • 210 g milk chocolate • 30 g butter • 30 ml cloudberry juice

1 Bring the cream to a boil. Chop the chocolate into pieces and melt in the hot cream. Beat in the butter. Stir in the cloudberry juice.

2 Pour a 2-cm-thick layer into a tray or terrine, encase in plastic wrap (clingfilm) and freeze.
3 When frozen, cut into pieces 7 cm long and 2 cm wide. Freeze again for later use.

For the lime sugar
4 limes, washed • 50 g sugar • 25 g popping candy

1 Grate the lime zest on a microplane. Combine with the sugar and store in an airtight container.
2 Mix with popping candy just before use.

For the pickled cloudberries
100 g sugar • 50 ml vodka • 20 ml lime juice • 1 vanilla bean • 20 g Norwegian spruce syrup • 400 g fresh cloudberries

1 Dissolve the sugar in the vodka in a small pan on low heat. Add the lime juice, the seeds from the vanilla bean and the spruce syrup.
2 Vacuum-pack the berries in the liquid.
3 Poach in a water bath with an immersion circulator at 125°F (60°C) for 2 hours.

For the chocolate crumbs
100 g sugar • 2 g rosemary needles • 100 g finely ground almonds • 60 g all-purpose (plain) flour • 25 g unsweetened cocoa • 85 g butter, melted • 8 g salt

1 Blend the sugar with the rosemary until it resembles fine crumbs. Add the remaining ingredients. Roll the frozen crumb mixture in a log shape in plastic wrap (clingfilm), then freeze.
2 Preheat the oven to 250°F (120°C).
3 Grate the frozen crumb mixture on a fine grater and semi-dry in the oven. Store in an airtight container.

To serve
flowers • green herbs • oil, for deep-frying

1 Deep-fry half the flowers and herbs at 300°F (150°C). Drain on paper towels.
2 Fold the ice cream into the sorbet to obtain a marbled effect.
3 Arrange pickled berries in the middle of each plate and place some of the ganache at the side. Set aside to come up to room temperature. Top the berries with chocolate crumbs and sorbet. Arrange the coulis and deep-fried flowers and herbs around the berries. Sprinkle with lime sugar.

1
Placed orders in the kitchen

2
Ka Lun Lau in the kitchen

3–5
Razorshells, clams, and crabs

6
Freshly prepared sauces

Ka Lun Lau

MENU

Sweet and sour
pickled radish

~

Gourmet seafood soup

~

Stir-fried grouper fillet

~

Lobster in dried scallop
sauce on crispy noodles

~

Mantis shrimp in sesame
teriyaki sauce

~

Deep-fried battered
oysters

~

Deep-fried crispy chicken

~

Blanched leafy greens in
local oyster sauce

~

Mud crab in black pepper
and durian cheese sauce

~

Fried rice, à la chef-god

~

Red bean sweet soup

Ka Lun Lau was born in Hong Kong in 1984 in the idyllic fishing village of Liufushan. Food is in his genes: Both his grandfathers were prominent seafood suppliers, while his mother opened the restaurant where he went from apprentice to executive chef in three short years. Lau began his formal training at the Happy Seafood Restaurant at the age of 13; by 16 he was bringing his own touch to the restaurant's specialities and buying all the produce. Lau recognizes the critical importance of produce in creating flavor, particularly in seafood dishes. With an eye on sustainability, he partially owns seafood farms in Australia, the Philippines, Myanmar, and Thailand, ensuring steady supplies and avoiding damaging fishing practices. His dishes showcase the best seafood, highlighted with the flavors of his local cuisine.

On Hong Kong's food and drink scene, and throughout the local media (to which he is no stranger), Ka Lun Lau is seen as a culinary virtuoso. Many people know him by the appellation "Young Legendary Chef B," although everyone calls him familiarly "Young B."

Both his paternal and maternal grandfathers were famous local seafood wholesalers, and his mother set up the well-known Happy Seafood Restaurant at Liufushan. Young B was already cooking in the family kitchen at the age of eight, and became assistant chef at the age of fourteen. By eighteen he was already being hailed as the "Oyster King of Liufushan" by the media. At the age of twenty-three, when many future chefs have barely started out in the business, he had already won a special commendation from the Cordon Bleu Culinary Arts Institute in France as well as being named a grand master of international haute cuisine by the international committee of the Les Amis d'Escoffier society.

When I first ate at his restaurant several years ago the food left a very deep impression on me: he was barely twenty, just out of adolescence, yet I saw him deal with the people around him as a man of the world. The flavors were those of a past-master, not of a novice. As well as his signature oyster dishes his cuisine includes sensational stir-fries of meat, mushrooms and seafood. In addition there are dishes such as shellfish boiled in bitter alcohol, which uses a wine called Red Rose Dew, accompanied by curry paste, peanut paste, iced candies, dried onion, rice with shrimp, and other fried or boiled condiments. My favorite is his peppered and salted Lainiao prawns: with its fresh-in-the-mouth fragrance succeeded by a pungent kick, this is a post-aperitif seafood dish of which one cannot have enough.

Young B's industry reflects his age. He is full of a verve and vigor which is beginning to mature into a wisdom beyond his years, and I truly believe that when that day of fulfillment is reached he will become even more famous.

Jacky Yu

Happy Seafood Restaurant, Hong Kong, China

STIR-FRIED GROUPER FILLET
Serves 4

380 g freshly prepared grouper fillet • 225 g celery • oil, for stir frying • ginger, sliced • garlic, freshly chopped • shallot, freshly chopped • yellow chives, cut into short lengths • salt • sugar • ½ egg white • caltrop starch • ground white pepper • sesame oil, to serve

1 Cut the grouper fillet into rectangular pieces weighing about 20 g each.
2 Cut the celery into thick strips and set aside.
3 In a wok, heat some oil to 340°F (170°C). Put in the grouper pieces and toss briefly until medium-well done. Drain.
4 Heat another wok, add some oil, and stir-fry the celery, garlic, shallot, and chives until cooked. Put in the grouper pieces and the salt and sugar. Stir in the egg white, starch, a little water, and pepper to make a thickened glaze, and drizzle with some sesame oil. Toss and serve.

LOBSTER IN DRIED SCALLOP SAUCE ON CRISPY NOODLES
Serves 4

I consider local lobsters the best in terms of flavours and texture. However, they are not always in steady supply. That's why I turned to lobsters from southern and western Australia for similar results. When you cook crustaceans such as lobsters and mantis shrimp, never rinse them after you have cut them into pieces. Otherwise, their flavorful juice will be washed off.

For the dried scallop sauce
80 g dried scallops • 110 ml water • 75 ml oil • shallot, sliced • onion, diced • Chinese celery, sliced • red chiles, finely shredded

1 Soak the dried scallops in the water for 45 minutes.
2 Heat a wok and add the oil. Stir-fry the shallot, onion, Chinese celery, and red chiles until fragrant. Add the dried scallops together with the soaking water. Stir well and cook until done.

For the lobster
1 Australian lobster, weighing about 1.2 kg • 240 g raw thin egg noodles • oil, for cooking • 40 g XO sauce • 20 g spicy bean sauce • Shaoxing rice wine

1 Rinse and prepare the lobster. Chop into chunks.
2 Briefly blanch the raw noodles in boiling water. Drain. Fry in a wok with some oil until crispy. Arrange on a serving plate.
3 Toss the lobster pieces in warm oil until half cooked. Drain.
4 Heat a wok and add some oil. Put in the dried scallop sauce, the XO sauce, and the spicy bean sauce. Put in the lobster and mix well.
5 Add the wine, sizzle and cover with a lid. Cook for about 4 minutes, until the lobster is cooked. Pour the lobster and sauce over the bed of fried noodles on the serving plate.

MANTIS SHRIMP IN SESAME TERIYAKI SAUCE
Serves 4

I go for giant mantis shrimp weighing about 400 g each. When eating them, remember that the shells are prickly and it's not a good idea to bite them. To shell mantis shrimp, do so segment by segment from the tail towards the head. Then pull out the whole chunk of flesh.

2 fresh giant mantis shrimp (prawns), weighing about 400 g each • oil, for deep-frying and stir-frying • 20 g onion, diced • 20 g shallot, sliced • 200 g Chinese celery, cut into short lengths • red chile, shredded • scallions (spring onions), diced • 20 g garlic • sesame oil, for seasoning and for drizzling over finished dish • 4 tbsp light soy sauce • 1 tsp sugar • liquid seasoning • 1 tbsp Japanese teriyaki sauce • black and white sesame seeds

1 Make an incision along the belly of the mantis shrimp without cutting all the way through. Cut each shrimp into 3 pieces.
2 Deep-fry the mantis shrimp in hot oil until they float. They should be slightly undercooked at this point. Drain and set aside.
3 Heat a wok and stir-fry the onion, shallot, Chinese celery, red chile, scallion, and garlic until fragrant. Add the sesame oil, soy sauce, sugar, seasoning, and teriyaki sauce, and cook to a syrup-like glaze.
4 Put the mantis shrimp back in and toss them in the sauce. Stir until the sauce reduces.
5 Sprinkle black and white sesame seeds over the shrimp, and, if you like, dribble with a few drops of sesame oil (take care not to overpower the delicate flavor of the shrimp). Transfer to a serving plate.

DEEP-FRIED BATTERED OYSTERS
Serves 4

For the oysters
12 live oysters, shucked, about 120 g each after shucking • salt, to rub the oysters • caltrop starch, to rub the oysters

Rub the oysters with some salt and caltrop starch. Rinse well. Poach the oysters in gently simmering water until cooked. Wipe them dry with a paper towel.

For the marinade
ground white pepper • salt • sugar caltrop starch

Mix together the marinade ingredients, then mix well with the poached oysters. Leave for 20 minutes.

For the deep-frying batter
600 g all-purpose (plain) flour • 80 g wheat starch • 40 g caltrop starch • 60 g baking powder • 600 ml water • oil, for deep-frying

Beat together the batter ingredients. Heat a wok and half-fill it with oil. Dip the oysters into the batter, then drop them into the hot oil one at a time, and deep-fry until golden. Drain and serve.

MUD CRAB IN BLACK PEPPER AND DURIAN CHEESE SAUCE
Serves 1

1 male mud crab, weighing about 720 g • oil, for stir-frying • shallot, sliced • garlic, finely chopped • ground black pepper • 3 slices Cheddar cheese • salt • sugar • 3 large chunks durian flesh, pitted

1 Prepare the crab and chop into pieces. Toss them in hot oil until half cooked. Drain.
2 Stir-fry the shallot, garlic, and black pepper in a little oil until fragrant. Put in the crab pieces and toss well.
3 Add a little water, salt, and sugar. Stir until the water reduces.
4 Arrange the cheese and durian flesh over the crab. Cover with a lid and turn off the heat. Leave for 3 minutes before serving.

FRIED RICE, À LA CHEF-GOD
Serves 2

A chef's skill is indispensable to a great dish, but the quality of the ingredients is not to be overlooked either. It even applies to a simple dish like this—I found the Golden Phoenix brand of rice has the most appropriate stickiness. For the best presentation use eggs with deep yellow yolks, so that the rice looks gilded.

For the marinade
salt • sugar • caltrop starch • ½ egg white

Combine all the ingredients.

For the rice
40 g scallops, diced • 40 g squid, diced • 40 g ostrich, diced • oil, for cooking • 4 eggs, beaten • 380 g steamed rice, cooled and preferably day-old • 20 g shiitake mushrooms, diced • 80 g sugar snap peas, diced • scallion (spring onion), finely chopped • 1 tsp liquid seasoning • 80 g tobiko (flying fish roe)

1 Add the marinade ingredients to the diced scallops, squid, and ostrich. Mix well and leave for 20 minutes.
2 Put some oil in a wok. Heat to 300°F (150°C), and toss the scallops, squid, and ostrich briefly. Drain.
3 Heat a wok and add some oil. Stir-fry the eggs and rice to coat each rice grain thinly in egg. Add the mushrooms, sugar snap peas, scallion, and seasoning, and mix well. Transfer to a serving plate and garnish with tobiko.

1
Stir-fried grouper fillet

2
Lobster in dried scallop
sauce on crispy noodles

3
Mantis shrimp in sesame
teriyaki sauce

4
Deep-fried battered oysters

5
Mud crab in black pepper
and durian cheese sauce

6
Fried rice, à la chef-god

Ka Lun Lau

I met Alvin Leung at the Congreso lo Mejor de la gastronomía in San Sebastian. With his blue hair and tattoos Alvin certainly looks like the *enfant terrible* of the culinary world, but to me, he embodies the excitement and drive of thousands of young Chinese chefs who are currently developing their visions of a new national cuisine. This culinary revolution may take years to come to fruition, but when it does it will be a defining moment in the history of Chinese cooking.

Alvin's cuisine could be defined as primarily Chinese, but it has a lot of Western influences. Since he is of Chinese origin, but born in England and raised in Toronto, he has experienced first hand the culinary practices of both East and West. His dishes bring together the many different approaches and tastes of Chinese cuisine (such as Cantonese, Shanghainese, and Chiu Chow amongst others), and match them with an array of Western styles of cooking (French, Italian, English and so on). With such wide combinations, Alvin is able to continue creating what he terms "X-treme Chinese" dishes indefinitely. I believe that his creativity will in time evolve more toward China than to the West.

Alvin never apprenticed as a chef, but this lack of training frees him from the r estraints of formal approaches in the kitchen and allows him room to experiment with his food. He embraces a global sphere of influence, learning from books and television as well as seeking advice from other chefs, and as a result his ideas are limitless and unconstrained. Eating is not solely about nourishment in his restaurant. Alvin regards eating as an experience for all the senses, and through activating the senses he aims also to activate the minds of his diners. He desires to take them outside their comfort zone, presenting completely new variations of taste and texture that push the boundaries of their expectations.

I have chosen Alvin because of what he represents. He is, quite simply, a symbol of a culinary revolution.

Ferran Adrià

Born in London in 1961, Alvin Leung was raised in a family with Chinese ethnic origins, and began to cook at the age of 10. With an environmental science degree and a background as an acoustic engineer, Leung has no formal training as a chef. However, through extensive study and travel including visits to elBulli, the Fat Duck, and Joël Robuchon's restaurant, he has engaged energetically in charting a new direction for Chinese food. At his restaurant, Bo Innovation in Hong Kong, opened in 2004, Leung reinterprets regional Chinese dishes through cutting-edge Western technique. The result is a menu of fresh and surprising dishes, updated for a modern palate but with strong roots in the local specialties of Shanghai and Canton, which won Leung his second Michelin star in 2008.

1
Alvin Leung with his kitchen knife

2
Staff take a break at Bo Innovation

3
Dining room at the restaurant

4
Staff prepare dishes at the tableside

5
Leung (right) working in the kitchen

6
Fish drying in the sun, on Lantau island

MENU

1000 year-old egg: crispy pickled ginger cone

~

Oyster: green onion, lime, and ginger snow

~

Caviar: smoked quail egg, crispy taro, and crust

~

Uni: "dan dan" noodles, grilled salmon roe, and mixed herbs

~

Toro: foie gras powder, freeze-dried raspberry, and mustard herb

~

Molecular: xiao long bao

~

Scallop: Szechuan jolo, woba, and peas

~

Cod: fermented black beans, organic honey, pickled bok choy, and ginger shoot

~

Wagyu: M9+, black truffle soy, cheung fun

~

Black sesame soda

~

Chocolate sticky rice dumpling

Alvin Leung

Bo Innovation, Hong Kong, China

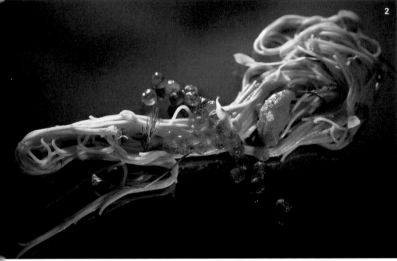

1
Oyster: green onion,
lime, and ginger snow

2
Uni: "dan dan" noodles,
grilled salmon roe, and mixed
herbs

3
Molecular: xiao long bao

4
Scallop: Szechuan jolo,
woba, and peas

5
Cod: fermented black beans,
organic honey, pickled bok
choi, and ginger shoot

6
Black sesame soda

OYSTER:
GREEN ONION, LIME, AND GINGER SNOW
Serves 4

For the green onion lime sauce
100 g green (spring) onions • 100 ml ordinary olive oil • 30 g fresh cilantro (coriander) • lime juice, to taste • salt • sugar

1 Remove the white of the green onions, keeping only the green. Place them under hot running tap water for 1 minute. Refresh them in an ice bath. Do the same for the cilantro.
2 Blend the cilantro, green onion, and olive oil at high speed until liquefied.
3 Strain the mixture through cheesecloth (muslin), and season with lime juice, salt, and sugar to taste.

For the ginger snow
300 g fresh ginger, peeled • 1 tbsp lemon juice • sugar

1 Put the ginger through a juicer, then strain. Add the lemon juice and sugar, then freeze.
2 Make the ginger snow by scraping the surface with a spoon.

For the oysters
12 freshly shucked oysters

To serve, place ½ teaspoon green onion sauce on each oyster and add the ginger snow immediately before serving.

UNI:
"DAN DAN" NOODLES, GRILLED SALMON ROE, AND MIXED HERBS
Serves 4

100 g red bell pepper • 20 g red chile • 50 g olive oil • 30 g pine nuts • salt • 200 g spaghettini • 30 g fresh uni (sea urchin) • 30 g salmon roe, grilled • mixed herbs, chopped

1 Char-grill the red bell pepper and red chile, and remove the skin and seeds.
2 Blend the pepper and chile with the olive oil and pine nuts until liquefied.
3 Strain and season them with salt.
4 Cook the spaghettini until al dente, mix it with the pepper sauce and decorate with uni, grilled salmon roe, and mixed herbs.

MOLECULAR:
XIAO LONG BAO
Serves 4

For the xiao long bao
500 g minced pork • 30 g ginger, peeled and oiled • 20 g shallots, chopped • 30 g green (spring) onions, chopped • 20 g Chinese Shao Hsing Hua Tiao Chiew (rice wine) • sesame oil, to taste • dark soy sauce, to taste • sugar, to taste • salt, to taste

1 Mix all the xiao long bao ingredients in a metal tray and cover with plastic wrap (clingfilm). Steam for 1 hour.
2 Strain, reserving the liquid.

For the spherification
distilled water • Algin • Xantana • Gluco • oil

1 Mix 5 g Algin into 1 liter distilled water.
2 Add 7 g Xantana and 30 g Gluco for each liter of xiao long bao liquid.
3 Carefully submerge approximately 1 tablespoon xiao long bao liquid into the Algin mixture. Remove the xiao long bao spheres after 2 minutes and rinse in distilled water.
4 Heat the xiao long bao spheres slowly in oil at approximately 115°F (45°C) until ready to serve. Remove them from the oil, rinse in hot water, and serve.

SCALLOP:
SZECHUAN JOLO, WOBA, AND PEAS
Serves 4

For the Szechuan jolo sauce
50 g jolo (Chinese pickle sauce) • 20 g Chinese vinegar • 20 ml Chinese Shao Hsing Hua Tiao Chiew (rice wine) • 3 g chile powder • 3 g paprika powder • 30 g butter • oil, for frying

Mix all the ingredients and emulsify with the butter.

For the scallops
4 scallops

Pan-fry the scallops.

For the garnish
80 g fresh peas • 100 g Chinese woba (rice ball) • oil, for frying

1 Pan-fry the fresh peas lightly and add approximately 5 teaspoons jolo sauce. Pour the mixture over the pan-fried scallops.
2 Decorate with a broken-up woba.

COD:
FERMENTED BLACK BEANS, ORGANIC HONEY, PICKLED BOK CHOY, AND GINGER SHOOT
Serves 4

For the fermented black bean marinade
100 g fermented Chinese black beans • 50 g honey • 3 cloves garlic

1 Soak the fermented black beans in water for 10 minutes. Drain and blend them with honey and garlic.
2 Pass the mixture through a fine-mesh sieve.

For the black cod
500 g black cod

Marinate the cod with the black bean mixture for 2 days. Scrape mixture off the cod and broil (grill) until cooked.

To serve
pickled bok choy and ginger shoots

Serve garnished with pickled bok choy and ginger shoots.

BLACK SESAME SODA
Serves 4

100g black sesame seeds • 100g white sesame seeds • 500ml water • 80g sugar

1 Roast the black and white sesame seeds in a pan at 400°F (200°C) for 8 minutes.
2 Transfer seeds to a saucepan, and add the water and sugar until desired sweetness is attained.
3 Bring the mixture to a boil and then simmer for 20 minutes.
4 Remove from heat. Blend and put through a fine-mesh sieve, reserving only the liquid. Cool.
5 Strain again, put into a siphon, and apply a CO_2 cartridge.
6 Fill four glasses from the siphon and serve.

1 & 4
Jereme Leung in the kitchen

2 & 3
Meat and pulses at the market

Jereme Leung

MENU

Chilled drunken chicken
topped with Shaoxing
wine shaved ice

~

Quail egg with
glutinous wine brine and
flying fish roe

~

Double-boiled Japanese
kurobuta pork soup
scented with
Shaoxing wine

~

Paper-wrapped chicken
with an assortment of
nutritional Chinese herbs

~

Deep-fried jumbo shrimp
coated with a wasabi
dressing and crisp
shrimp flakes

~

Three-colored Shanghai
salted pork with rice

~

Duo of dark and
white chocolate,
fresh fruit praline

Jereme Leung was born in 1971 and began to cook at thirteen years old in the restaurants of Hong Kong. A long apprenticeship rendered him dazzlingly competent in the four main disciplines of Chinese cookery: dim sum, barbecue, wok, and knife work. He went on to become executive chef to the Mandarin Oriental Hotels, managing kitchens from Jakarta to Hong Kong and assisting with the opening of hotels in Surabaya and Kuala Lumpur. In 2000 he moved on to become executive chef at the six-star Four Seasons Hotel in Singapore. He has received many awards and accolades, but continues to grow and develop, making regular pilgrimages to China's regions to seek out fresh inspiration since moving to the country in 2003. He has also launched the Whampoa Club at locations in Shanghai and Beijing. Each restaurant reinterprets Leung's contemporary take on Chinese food, dubbed "New Chinese Cuisine," with menus informed by the local produce.

The first time I noticed Jereme Leung was when I bought his cookbook. I was very impressed by his extremely creative ideas and exquisite recipes.

His dishes are very pleasing to the eye and overbrimming with invention, remarkably artistic and yet still full of flavor.

His intensely Chinese-flavored southern milk, onion ice cream, and Iced Chicken with Yellow Rice Wine all made a deep impression on me. In this last dish the chicken was placed in a sturdy wineglass and submerged in an alcoholic ice cream before it was placed on my table. The iced chicken meat warms in the mouth, and the taste of the alcohol diffuses slowly, giving a new twist to the extremely traditional Shanghai tipsy chicken dish.

The traditions and history of Chinese cuisine are vastly important to Jereme. In a recent interview he said that "cooking Chinese dishes well is not only dependent upon having a fundamental understanding of the techniques involved, but also upon a great knowledge of the entirety of Chinese culture."

Jereme Leung is a brilliant all-rounder in the sphere of Chinese cuisine, and it would be difficult to overestimate his talents. International tourists and local customers fall in love with his Shanghai style and enjoy, as I did, his varied classical feasts, typical of this coastal culture.

Jacky Yu

Jereme Leung Concepts Limited, Hong Kong, China

1
Chilled drunken chicken
topped with Shaoxing wine
shaved ice

2
Quail egg with glutinous
wine, brine and flying fish roe

3
Double-boiled Japanese
kurobuta pork soup scented
with Shaoxing wine

4
Deep-fried jumbo shrimp
coated with a wasabi dressing
and crisp shrimp flakes

5
Duo of dark and white
chocolate, fresh fruit praline

CHILLED DRUNKEN CHICKEN TOPPED WITH SHAOXING WINE SHAVED ICE
Serves 4

For the marinade
5 scallions (spring onions) • 5 slices ginger • 1 tbsp sugar • 2 star anise seeds • 4 bay leaves • 4 tbsp salt • 300 ml Shaoxing rice wine • 1 tbsp Chinese white rice wine

Bring 1 liter water to a boil and add the scallions, ginger slices, sugar, star anise seeds, bay leaves, and salt. Simmer for 3 minutes, then turn off the heat. Allow the mixture to cool before adding the Shaoxing wine and white rice wine. Strain and keep half the liquid aside for the chicken, and place other half in the freezer to freeze it hard.

For the chicken
5 scallions (spring onions) • 5 slices ginger • 5 tbsp Shaoxing rice wine • 1.4 kg chicken • 2 cinnamon sticks

1   Bring 1.5 liters of water to a boil and add the scallions, ginger slices, and Shaoxing wine. Turn to low heat and simmer the chicken until cooked.
2   Immediately soak the poached chicken in ice water to cool it down. Debone the chicken, place in the reserved marinade, and leave for at least 24 hours in the refrigerator.
3   Cut up the chicken and place it in serving dishes. Shave ice from the frozen marinade with a spoon and put it on top of the chicken. Serve immediately.

QUAIL EGG WITH GLUTINOUS WINE BRINE AND FLYING FISH ROE
Serves 3–6

30 quail eggs • 30 g scallions (spring onions) • 30 g ginger • 10 g sugar • 15 g Shaoxing rice wine • 15 gelatin leaves • 750 cl water • 50 g flying fish roe •

1   Boil the quail eggs, peel them and cut them in two, then put aside for later.
2   To make the glutinous rice wine brine, add the scallions, ginger, sugar, Shaoxing wine, and gelatin leaves to the fresh boiling water, then stir to an even consistency.
3   When the glutinous rice wine reaches an even consistency, drench the sliced quail eggs by immersing them in it, then place them in the refrigerator to chill until they are ready to serve.
4   Cut the remaining glutinous rice wine into squares.
5   To finish, place a small amount of flying fish roe on each square as decoration.

DOUBLE-BOILED JAPANESE KUROBUTA PORK SOUP SCENTED WITH SHAOXING WINE
Serves 1–2

130 g minced *kurobuta* pork • 10 g water chestnuts • 10 g black mushrooms • 5 g cilantro (coriander) root, chopped • 5 g ginger • 200 ml basic Chinese stock • salt, to taste • 1 tsp cooking oil • ground white pepper • 100 ml Shaoxing wine

1   Hand-mince the *kurobuta* pork finely, paying attention not to overmince. Place it in the refrigerator until it feels cold in the center, but not freezing.
2   Finely chop the other ingredients. In a deep pot, add the minced meat and stir constantly in one direction until it starts to form a lump.
3   Add the other ingredients and slowly add enough ice water and Shaoxing wine until meat is the correct consistency.
4   Season the basic stock and pour the stock into a No 3 steaming vessel. Steam over high heat for 3 hours.
5   Sprinkle the cilantro root onto the mixture, add some Shaoxing wine, and serve immediately.
6   Evenly portion it into soup bowls.

DEEP-FRIED JUMBO SHRIMP COATED WITH A WASABI DRESSING AND CRISP SHRIMP FLAKES
Serves 3

For the wasabi dressing
Makes 30 portions

300 g wasabi powder • hot water, to dissolve the wasabi powder • 6 lemons • 4 (300-ml) cans condensed milk • 2 (3-kg) tubs mayonnaise

1   Stir the wasabi powder into hot water to dissolve, mix evenly, and set aside. Juice the lemons and set aside.
2   Take the wasabi mixture and blend until fine, then add condensed milk and the mayonnaise and blend slowly, adding the lemon juice a little at a time. Once blended, keep in a cool place until needed.

For the deep-fried jumbo shrimp
approximately 300 g jumbo shrimp (king prawn) meat (from 6 shrimp) • 3 g salt • 15 g sugar • 7.5 g potato starch • 1 tbsp semi-powdered egg white • 1 tbsp corn oil • 3 fresh tiger shrimp (prawns) • 300 g vegetable oil • black sesame seeds, to serve

1   Rigorously wash the shrimp meat in fresh, clean water, then dry thoroughly. Remove the intestines, using paper towel to soak up any remaining moisture, and set aside for later.
2   Mix the salt, sugar, potato starch, and semi-powdered egg white along with some corn oil and stir to even consistency. Add the shrimp and marinate.
3   After soaking the fresh shrimp in water and removing shells and antennae, shred and place in hot oil to fry until golden brown, then remove, drain, and put aside.
4   Pulverise the well-marinated shrimp meat.
5   Heat the vegetable oil to 175°F (80°C), then place the shrimp meat in oil and deep-fry until crisp. Drain. Decorate the dish with 200 g evenly mixed wasabi dressing and top with a few fried shrimp and some black sesame seeds as decoration.

DUO OF DARK AND WHITE CHOCOLATE, FRESH FRUIT PRALINE
Serves 3–4

4 seedless green grapes • 4 longan (dragon's eyes) • 100 g semisweet (dark) chocolate • 100 g white chocolate • 40 g chili powder

1   Take the grapes and longan, wash and dry thoroughly, peel and core the longan, and put them aside for use later.
2   In separate pans set over hot water at about 140°F (60°C), melt the white and dark chocolate. Take off the heat and leave to cool.
3   Dip half of the grapes into cooled dark chocolate, then let dry at room temperature.
4   Dip whole longan into the white chocolate and when dry, sprinkle a little chili powder over them to decorate.

When people ask this man from Toulouse why his restaurant is in Marseille, his answer sounds as if he is stating the obvious: "But I couldn't cook anywhere else!" To top it all, Une Table au Sud is in the Vieux Port, the city's most legendary spot. This approach is intriguing: It wasn't merely a practical opportunity, it is the result of a deep-seated phenomenon that, I think, happened in two phases.

You learn to cook with intelligence and tenacity. It is a hard profession, particularly in the early years, when you have to keep repeating the same actions to acquire the basic reflexes. Gradually, once you have mastered the fundamentals, cooking becomes a question of organizing your work, sharing tasks, and paying close attention to detail. Like every chef, Lionel followed this grueling course, from Toulouse to Paris. But practicing scales still does not make you a musician.

Invention comes from the memory and from the heart. Lionel was lucky enough to have plenty of memories and a big heart. As always, his family had played their part. His maternal grandmother from Toulouse passed on the secrets of the cassoulet, and his paternal grandmother helped him discover the flavor of *dafina*, a stew that is emblematic of Jewish cooking in Morocco. Une Table au Sud has the taste of his childhood memories. He is steeped in them, and it is to them that he wishes to dedicate himself. Which made Marseille the obvious choice: It is one of the most beautiful cities on the western Mediterranean, a melting pot of flavors and accents.

There is one thing that Lionel has completely understood and heartily practices. Cooking at Le Sud is all about sharing and celebration, and this forms his special creative approach. This is not a question of technical virtuosity but of returning food to its rightful place at the heart of daily life. The flavors are always impassioned and sometimes daring, the range of flavors eclectic: Cumin, dates, and honey rub shoulders with game, fish, and vegetables in season. Generosity is an infinite source of creativity.

Alain Ducasse

Lionel Lévy was born in 1974 in Paris, later attending culinary school in Toulouse. After working at Le Pastel under Gérard Garrigues, he moved on to complete his military service. Following this, Lévy returned to his home city and a year at Eric Fréchon's La Verrière. In 1996 he joined Restaurant Alain Ducasse, training there for two years as a commis chef and absorbing new methods of flavor combination while sharpening his technical skills. After further experience at La Grande Cascade and Spoon, Food & Wine, in 1999 Lévy opened his own restaurant, Une Table au Sud in Marseille. The restaurant experiments with the Mediterranean flavors that were Lévy's training ground, serving dishes that might recall the cuisine of Rome, Morocco, or Madrid. These use carefully selected ingredients such as Corsican citron, crapaudine beet, purple carrots, or striped red mullet, combined with innovation and flair, creating a menu that won Une Table au Sud a Michelin star in 2005.

MENU

A sort of anchoïade

~

Asparagus, chicken wings, and abalones fried in brown butter

~

Norwegian lobster fricassee

~

Bouillabaisse milk shake with marinated sardines on toast

~

A new look at strawberry tart

~

Chocolate mousse with chocolate nibs

Lionel Lévy

1
Lionel Lévy at
Une Table au Sud

2
In the restaurant dining room

3
Plating dishes in the kitchen

Une Table au Sud, Marseille, France

A SORT OF ANCHOÏADE
Serves 8

For the anchovies
300 g anchovies in salt • 6 cloves garlic • 20 ml sherry vinegar • 50 ml olive oil • salt • Espelette pepper, to taste • 2 tbsp squid ink • 1 liter cream

1 Blend the anchovies in a blender with the garlic, vinegar, olive oil, salt, Espelette pepper, and squid ink. Bring to a boil with the cream, and strain.
2 Put in a siphon, charge with 2 cartridges and keep cool.

For the vegetable accompaniments
2 yellow zucchini (courgettes) • 2 green zucchini (courgettes) • olive oil, for pan-frying • 1 head garlic • thyme, to taste • bay leaf, to taste • salt • Espelette pepper • 4 red bell peppers • 2 green bell peppers • 2 onions • 30 ml Pastis

1 Preheat the oven to 250°F (120°C).
2 Dice the zucchini finely, and pan-fry in olive oil with the garlic, thyme, bay leaf, salt, and Espelette pepper. Cool and set aside.
3 Bake the bell peppers in the oven for 30 minutes.
4 Slice the onions and sweat in a skillet with some olive oil, then deglaze with Pastis, reduce, and cook for 20 minutes.
5 Peel the bell peppers, and slice into rings.

For the fennel panisses
1.5 kg fennel • 250 g chickpea flour • 20 g butter • 1 ladle olive oil, plus a little extra for pan-frying • salt

1 Put the fennel through a juicer.
2 Bring the juice to a boil, then sift in the chickpea flour and add the butter.
3 Add the olive oil and the salt, and cook for 5 minutes.
4 Spread the panisse mixture onto a plate to a depth of 3 cm, then leave to cool in the refrigerator.
5 Cut the panisses into circles and pan-fry in a little olive oil.

To serve
Serve the anchoïade with the vegetables and the fennel panisses.

ASPARAGUS, CHICKEN WINGS, AND ABALONES FRIED IN BROWN BUTTER
Serves 4

8 chicken wings • salt • Cubeb pepper, to taste • 80 g butter • 50 ml olive oil • 30 ml sherry vinegar • 4 large white asparagus spears • 2 mild Cévennes onions • salt • sugar, to taste • 160 g peas • 1 ladle chicken stock • 12 small abalones, shelled • 1 clove garlic, chopped • 1 tbsp finely chopped parsley • a little lemon juice

1 Bone the chicken wings, season with salt and Cubeb pepper, and pan-fry in the olive oil for 12 minutes over gentle heat, adding the butter when they start to brown. Deglaze with vinegar. Set aside and keep warm.
2 Peel the asparagus twice and cook in a large quantity of salted boiling water.
3 Slice the onions and sweat in a pan with a little of the butter, some salt and a little sugar. Once the onions have softened, add the peas. Sprinkle lightly with salt and sugar. Finish the cooking with a little chicken stock.
4 Heat a piece of butter gently until it browns, then cook the abalones for 1 minute. Add the garlic, parsley, and asparagus. Deglaze with a squeeze of lemon juice.

To serve
Arrange the chicken wings and abalones attractively on a rectangular plate with the vegetables.

NORWEGIAN LOBSTER FRICASSEE
Serves 4

8 Norwegian lobsters (langoustines) • 1 red bell pepper, chopped • 2 beef tomatoes, chopped • 150 ml olive oil • 1 onion, chopped • 2 cloves garlic, chopped finely • thyme • 1 bay leaf • chicken stock • 100 ml white wine • a little sherry vinegar • 8 pieces edible orchid, for garnish

1 Clean the Norwegian lobsters, cut them in half, and gut them. Set aside.
2 Pan-fry the bell pepper and tomatoes in a little oil with the onions, garlic, thyme, and bay leaf. When the vegetables have softened, add the white wine. Cook for a few minutes, add the stock and cook.
3 Fry the Norwegian lobsters in a little oil in a nonstick skillet for 2–3 minutes, and deglaze with sherry vinegar.

To serve
Serve in a soup plate garnished with edible orchid or orange zest.

BOUILLABAISSE MILK SHAKE WITH MARINATED SARDINES ON TOAST
Serves 8

For the marinated sardines
500 g sardines • 150 g green beans • salt • juice of 1 lemon • sweet almond oil, to taste • 3 scallions (spring onions), finely chopped • bread sticks, toasted

1 Remove the skin and bones from the sardines and cut them into small dice.
2 Cook the beans in boiling salted water, and cut to the same size as the sardines.
3 Season the sardines with lemon juice, almond oil, and scallions. Pile onto the toasted bread.

For the egg cappuccino
10 eggs • 125 g mascarpone cheese • 20 g butter • 50 g olive oil • salt, to taste • Espelette pepper • 2 saffron threads

Place all the ingredients in the Thermomix and process at setting 7 for 8 minutes.

For the fish soup
2 kg fish • 2 sticks celery • 2 carrots • 1 onion • 2 fennel bulbs • 1 leek • 1 orange • 20 g soya lecithin • saffron, to taste • Pastis, to taste

1 Make your favorite fish soup recipe with the ingredients listed above.
2 Put the fish soup mixture into a siphon and insert 2 gas cartridges.
3 Dispense the whipped fish soup mixture into a milkshake glass and top with the egg cappucino. Insert a straw. Drink with the sardine toasts.

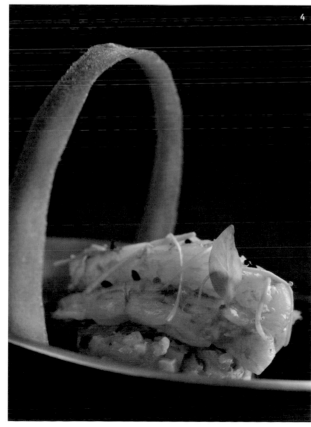

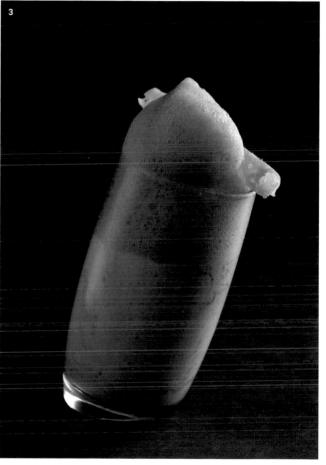

1
A sort of anchoïade

2
Asparagus, chicken wings,
and abalones friend in
brown butter

3
Bouillabaisse milk shake with
marinated sardines on toast

4
Norwegian lobster fricassee

Lionel Lévy

Spending seven years studying architecture, as I did, you learn to interrogate the whys and wherefores as you build something permanent. Even though it's not so permanent, cooking deserves the same level of attention. Edwin Lewis is a structurally sound chap, with nothing of baroque surface decoration or skin-deep plastering about his work—philosophically, a chef after my own heart.

All parties attending lunch at the Bank House Brasserie were converging on King's Lynn from different locations, which added a certain quality to the occasion. Everything became beautifully smooth again, however, when my choice arrived—a splendid, soothing, but uplifting rabbit pie. To soothe and uplift at the same time is one of the hardest gastronomic moments to bring about.

Much wine was consumed that day, and, as Pepys might say, all was very merry. Ed's food is firm and superb in its Britishness, down to his fantastic joyous mound of ham, egg, and chips. He gets certain things effortlessly and exactly right—his steak sandwich stands on its own two feet. Yet, crucially, Ed knows how to keep things interesting, combining good English flavors with style (barley broth with haddock and dumplings), and occasionally giving his guests a little surprise—salmon fishcakes with French fries and tomato sauce comes not with ketchup, but with an actual, creamy tomato sauce. And it works.

Ed was my first head chef, appointed when my Parkinson's got too much in the kitchen. A truly good egg and a wonderfully calm teacher, he accompanied me on my first book tour to North America, proving the perfect person to have around in that blur and bustle. His cooking is the perfect example of fantastic English dishes being created without fuss, and it is just as quietly passed on to those who have the chance to work for him. He shows a rare understanding of restraint; here is a chef for whom time is not a dirty word, which contradicts splendidly the popular misconception that there is no time.

Fergus Henderson

Born in 1970 in England, Edwin Lewis launched his career with stints at a number of renowned restaurants, including Soho's Groucho Club, the Brackenbury Restaurant, and Alastair Little in London, where he developed a discerning appreciation of modern British cuisine. He interspersed his early career with two years of travel in Australia and Southeast Asia, returning with a new enthusiasm for cooking fish. Lewis moved from Alastair Little to assist Fergus Henderson at St. John Restaurant, where he spent a period of intensive, happy learning, developing his own style of tasty, homely food characterized by an insistence on the slow-growing and slow-cooking of locally sourced ingredients. He has great respect for historic methods of food preparation, integrating these with his own ideas to produce dishes that provide an antidote to frenetic modern existence. He now serves up these dishes as head chef at the Bank House Brasserie in King's Lynn, Norfolk.

MENU

Brown shrimp, white cabbage, and fennel salad with chervil and lemon olive oil

~

Norfolk rabbit pie with mash and greens

~

Rhubarb fool

Ed Lewis

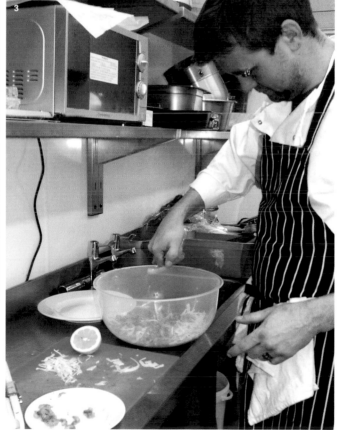

1
Ed Lewis in the dining room
at the Bank House

2
Ingredients for rhubarb fool

3
Ed Lewis in the kitchen

BROWN SHRIMP, WHITE CABBAGE, AND FENNEL SALAD WITH CHERVIL AND LEMON OLIVE OIL
Serves 6

This dish uses locally caught brown shrimps and is based loosely on coleslaw, but with a saline twist. A Japanese mandolin will help with shredding the vegetables, but if you don't have one just use a very sharp, large chopping knife.

150 g small brown shrimp (prawns), peeled • ½ small white cabbage • 2 bulbs of fennel, cores removed and finely shredded • 1 bunch chervil with very little stalk, picked and roughly chopped • salt and freshly ground pepper • juice of 2 lemons • 100–150 ml extra-virgin olive oil

1 Combine the shrimp, white cabbage, fennel and chervil. The mixture should look white, but be heavily flecked with pink and green.
2 Season with salt and pepper.
3 Whisk the lemon juice and oil to make the dressing.
4 Toss with the dressing to give a healthy sheen, plate and serve.

NORFOLK RABBIT PIE WITH MASH AND GREENS
Serves 6

A two-day job, but the results are most worthwhile. I would say this is my signature dish, combining as it does locally produced quality ingredients, in season, in a simple and traditional way. The dish has a stunning quality of flavor as well as being immensely comforting and warming to eat.

Day 1

1 jointed rabbit (2 legs, 2 shoulders and 1 saddle). Your butcher should be able to help with this—you don't want the ribcage area • 2 large white onions, shredded • 4 carrots, chopped fingernail size • 4 sticks celery, chopped as the carrots • 1 large twig sage • 2 garlic cloves, smashed • white wine, to cover • 225 g all-purpose (plain) flour • pinch salt • 120 g butter • about 2–3 tbsp water

1 Place the rabbit pieces in a container and add the onion, carrot, celery, sage, and garlic.
2 Barely cover the rabbit in white wine and place in the refrigerator to marinate.
3 Now make your pastry. Sieve the flour and salt into a bowl. Rub in the butter until you have a sandy texture. Make a well in the center and add sufficient water to make a fairly firm paste. Handle as little and as lightly as possible. Wrap the pastry in plastic wrap (clingfilm) and place in the refrigerator with the rabbit.

Day 2

salt and pepper • oil, for pan-frying • 2 heaped tsp English mustard powder • all-purpose (plain) flour, for dusting • milk, for brushing the pastry rim • potatoes, to serve • green vegetables, to serve

1 Preheat the oven to 350°F (180°C).
2 Take the rabbit from the refrigerator (the pastry gets a lie in).
3 Extract the flesh from the other marinade matter and then separate the vegetables from the juice.
4 In a roasting pan, sweat the vegetables until soft but not colored. Season with salt and pepper and put to one side.

5 Now brown the rabbit in oil in a hot skillet and season with salt and pepper.
6 When brown, add the rabbit to the vegetables and place the roasting pan back on medium heat.
7 Liberally dust the pan with the mustard powder and flour. Combine well to distribute evenly.
8 Now pour in the white wine from the marinade and stir, still on medium heat, until a silky sauce coats all.
9 Cover with aluminum foil and cook in the oven until the flesh comes away from the bones. The shoulder will be the toughest. If it bends at the joint, it's done.
10 Lift the flesh from the pan and allow the broth to cool; meanwhile, take the pastry from the refrigerator.
11 When the rabbit flesh is cool enough to handle, remove the meat from the bones and add back to the vegetables and sauce. This is the filling.
12 Now roll out two-thirds of the pastry to line a 25-cm greased pie plate (dish).
13 Heap your filling into the pie, reserving most of the sauce for use as gravy.
14 Roll out your lid to larger than your pie plate. Brush the rim of the base with milk and place the lid on top. Crimp the edges with a fork and trim off the excess pastry.
15 Make a small hole in the middle of the pie and chill for 30 minutes.
16 Preheat the oven to 400°F (200°C).
17 Peel some potatoes, boil them, and prepare your green vegetables.
18 Bake the pie for 40–50 minutes until golden brown.
19 In the meantime make the mashed potatoes, reheat the gravy and cook the green vegetables. Dinner is now ready!

RHUBARB FOOL
Serves 6

Rhubarb is grown all around us in Norfolk. Forced, indoor-grown champagne rhubarb is available from mid-December to mid-April; outdoor maincrop rhubarb from mid-March to the end of June. Both are good, but late rhubarb can be bitter and may require additional sugar and extra cooking.

1 kg English forced champagne rhubarb (outdoor if unavailable) • 120 g superfine (caster) sugar • juice of 1 orange, plus a few strips of zest • a walnut-size piece of ginger, squashed • 600 ml heavy (double) cream • shortbread cookies (biscuits) for serving

1 Stages 1–5 can be done the previous day, if you wish. Cut the top and bottom ends off the rhubarb, then wash and chop into 1-cm lengths.
2 Add the chopped rhubarb to the sugar, orange juice, zest and ginger in a pan so that it covers the bottom to a depth of a few cm.
3 Stir well, then put the pan onto medium heat, stirring all the time to help break down the rhubarb.
4 Remove from the heat while there are still some resistant lumps. Most of the rhubarb pieces will have broken down, making the mix juicy and compote-like.
5 Chill this mixture in the refrigerator.
6 To serve, spoon some rhubarb compote into the base of a glass.
7 Whip the cream until thick but still smooth and silky.
8 Stir some rhubarb into the cream, keeping back 6 teaspoons to garnish the top.
9 Now dollop your creamy compote on top of the fruit, garnish, and serve with shortbread cookies (biscuits).

1
Brown shrimp,
white cabbage, and
fennel salad with chervil
and lemon olive oil

2 & 3
Norfolk rabbit pie
with mash and greens

4
Rhubarb fool

Ed Lewis

I feel slightly guilty about including Josh in this list, as it doesn't include some other very talented chefs, who also work for me. But that said, I am very proud of Josh. For young chefs, the formula for success is easy: "Stick at it." I always told Josh that the bad days make the good days, and Josh takes this philosophy to new heights.

His main goal while working for me at Vue de Monde was to get hands-on experience and learn as much technique as possible. He embraced what I see as the cornerstone of a good restaurant—make everything yourself, including puff pastry, breads, rolls and stocks. As an employer, when you see this attitude you develop trust. Our fine-dining restaurant is a first for Muscat, a pioneering endeavor that will set Josh up to take on the world.

Josh's passion for the sea is evident in his food. Muscat is the perfect setting for spearfishing and foraging for crayfish and squid, caught that morning, then on the menu for lunch. Produce from the garden, combined with Josh's embracing of local spices, has helped Vue become a central part of the Muscat dining scene.

One of Josh's recent creations, baby squid with almond gazpacho, Omani cucumber, and black olive powder, really sums up how much Josh is influenced by his surroundings and how he soaks up nature and puts it on the plate. This dish combines the influence of his time at Mugaritz, both in its presentation and its Spanish ingredients, with his discovery of Oman and its locally caught seafood and Omani cucumbers. The color palette of this dish also has a certain cool earthiness to it that reminds me of the Middle East.

Fresh ingredients, sometimes served raw, lifted with reductions and dressings extracted from shells and bone of the same ingredient, give Josh's food its signature. Combine that with great desserts and an understanding of budgets and customer needs, plus a love of cooking that is only surpassed by a love of eating delicious food, and you have the formula for a great success story: Josh Lewis.

Shannon Bennett

Josh Lewis was born in Australia in 1985. He attended culinary school from the age of sixteen, later moving to Melbourne to work under Shannon Bennett at Vue de Monde. This four-year stint was crucial for Lewis, who worked his way up to become head pastry chef. In 2008 Lewis gained a scholarship and traveled to the Spanish Basque country, working at the restaurant Mugaritz and witnessing firsthand the running of a kitchen garden. Lewis is currently head chef at Bennett's restaurant in the Al Bustan Palace Intercontinental Hotel in Muscat, Oman. Since 2008 he has combined his knowledge with the local produce of the region, maintaining good relationships with suppliers including Mola, a local fisherman who brings baby squid to the restaurant each day, so fresh that their skins change color as the chef pays for them. Lewis has also set up a garden to bring unusual ingredients to Vue's dishes, rendering his menu truly unique in the city.

MENU

Fried whitebait in yuzu salt with baked potato consommé
Dom Pérignon, France, Champagne, 1999

~

Baby squid with white cucumbers, almond gazpacho, and black olive
Tateyama Shuzo, Junmai Daiginjō-Shu, Tateyama Ginrei Amaharashi, Toyama, Japan

~

Foie gras and gingerbread sandwich with preserved lemon noodle
Château Pierre-Bise, Quart de Chaume, Chenin Blanc, Loire Valley, France, 2005

~

Sultan Ibrahim wrapped in carrot on piccalilli spread and leaves
Kumeu River, Mate's Vineyard, Chardonnay, Auckland, New Zealand, 2004

~

Lemon verbena lemonade

~

Rabbit vitello tonnato
Gran Reserva, Viña Bosconia, Tempranillo Blend, Rioja Alta, Spain, 1981

~

Bread puffs filled with whipped Brie de Nangis on nut soil and sweet wine golden raisins
Cossart Gordon, Sercial 5 Years, Madeira, Portugal

~

Blood orange lollipop dipped in sangria jelly with lemon sherbet

~

Red grape and vanilla cloud with nitrogen berries
Nigl, Eiswein, Grüner Veltliner, Kremstal, Austria, 2006

~

My Black Forest
Chambers, Grand Muscat, Victoria, Australia

Josh Lewis

Vue, Muscat, Oman

1
Baby squid with white
cucumbers, almond gazpacho,
and black olive

2
Sultan Ibrahim wrapped
in carrot on piccalilli spread
and leaves

BABY SQUID WITH WHITE CUCUMBERS, ALMOND GAZPACHO, AND BLACK OLIVE
Serves 6

For the cleaned baby squid
4 baby squid

Start by cutting the squid in between the tentacles and the eyes, separating the tentacles from the tube, and remove the beak by pressing gently. Set the tentacles aside for this recipe and reserve the tube for another use.

For the white cucumbers
2 Omani cucumbers

Peel away the outer skin, as it can be bitter. Take a small paring knife and make a small incision in the cucumber, not cutting all the way through. Then angle the knife back toward you and pull rather than cut. The finished cucumber pieces should appear to have been broken.

For the almond gazpacho
100 g fresh shelled almonds • 25 g fresh white sourdough bread, crusts removed, soaked in water, and squeezed dry • ½ garlic clove, peeled • ½ white onion, peeled and diced • 150 g Sultana grapes, washed and picked • 25 ml sherry vinegar • 50 ml extra-virgin olive oil • sea salt

Place the almonds, sourdough bread, garlic, onion, and grapes into a blender and blitz on high speed until smooth. Once smooth, keep the blender on its lowest speed, add half the vinegar, and slowly drizzle in the oil. Taste and adjust seasoning with remaining vinegar and salt. Place in the refrigerator and rest for 6 hours before serving.

For the black olive powder and fenugreek leaves
250 g black olives, pitted • small bunch of fenugreek leaves

1   Place the olives in a dehydrator and allow to dry completely. Once dry, use a knife to finely chop olives into a powder. Do not blend the olives, or you will release the oils and make a paste. Store in an airtight container.
2   For the fenugreek leaves, use scissors to trim the younger leaves growing at tip of the plant. Use only the younger leaves and discard the rest of the bunch. Wash the leaves and store in airtight containers.

To serve
oil, for greasing • salt and pepper • butter, for frying

Use the broken cucumbers to make a short line through the center of the plate. Lightly oil and season the baby squid tentacles and sauté quickly on high heat. Add small knob of butter and continue to sauté until butter takes on the nutty characteristics of beurre noisette. Remove from pan immediately. To plate, stand the baby squid tentacles up in between the cucumbers. Dot the almond gazpacho and black olive powder around. Finish with the fenugreek leaves.

SULTAN IBRAHIM WRAPPED IN CARROT ON PICCALILLI SPREAD AND LEAVES
Serves 6

For the Sultan Ibrahim
6 (150-g) Sultan Ibrahims (red snappers) • vegetable oil, for deep frying • 5 large carrots, peeled • 100 g olive oil infused with 2 cloves crushed garlic • juice of ½ lemon • sea salt

1   Remove the scales and clean inside the fish, being careful not to damage the flesh. Place the cleaned fish on a board and with a sharp filleting knife, cut behind the pectoral fin all the way to the backbone. Then angle the knife down toward tail to remove top fillet, stopping approximately 1.5 cm before the end of the tail so the fillet is still connected to the fish.
2   Turn the fish over and repeat the process carefully. This should leave you with two fillets that are still connected at the tail, with the carcass in the middle.
3   With a pair of scissors, cut the bone as low to the tail as possible, removing the carcass. There should still be a piece of bone left (around 5 mm)—this is essential for keeping the fillets attached at the tail.
4   To wrap the fish in carrot, preheat a deep fryer with clean vegetable oil to 350°F (180°C). Cut each carrot into 6–7-cm sections. Place a piece of carrot on a Japanese mandolin to make spaghetti-like strands and turn, applying constant pressure and speed to ensure the strands are as long as possible. Repeat with the remaining pieces of carrot. Blanch the carrot strands in the fryer for 2–3 seconds, to make them more pliable.
5   To wrap the fish, take 2 strands of carrot and, with your fingers, pinch the tops together. Then run your fingers down the length of the carrot strands to straighten them out and stick them together.
6   Holding the carrot at the top, pick up fish and start to wrap the carrot around, working your way from the head to the tail, keeping it straight and together, with no gaps. Leave tail exposed and, if necessary, tuck or cut the remaining carrot so the joins cannot be seen.
7   Preheat an oven to 350°F (180°C). Place the wrapped fish on square of wax (greaseproof) paper and drizzle with a little garlic-infused olive oil and freshly squeezed lemon juice, and season with sea salt. Keep warm until serving.

For the piccalilli spread
¼ cauliflower • 5 baby onions, peeled • 1 large Spanish onion, peeled • 5 g salt • ½ cucumber • 150 ml white-wine vinegar • 75 g malt vinegar • 1 g dried chile, chopped • 95 g superfine (caster) sugar • 15 g English mustard powder • 5 g ground turmeric • 8 g cornstarch (cornflour) • salt and pepper

1   Cut the cauliflower into small florets, the baby onions in half, and the Spanish onion into 1-cm dice. Place the cauliflower and onions into a bowl and sprinkle with the salt. Let stand for 24 hours. After 24 hours, rinse in cold water, then dry.
2   Peel and seed the cucumber and cut into 1-cm dice. Sprinkle with a little salt and leave to stand for 10–15 minutes. Rinse in cold water, then dry. Add the cucumber to the cauliflower and onions.
3   Boil the 2 vinegars together with the chile, let cool for 30 minutes, then pass the liquid through a sieve, discarding the chile.
4   Mix together the sugar and remaining dry ingredients in bowl. Once the vinegar has cooled, mix a little of it into the dry ingredients. Bring the bulk of the vinegar back to a boil, pour into the sugar mixture, and whisk until blended. Bring the mixture back to a boil and cook for 3 minutes.
5   Pour the mixture over the vegetables, mix well and leave aside to cool. Once cool, blend on high speed until the piccalilli is completely smooth.

For the picked local leaves
local red and green spinach • purple basil leaves • tips of baby fennel

1   Gently wash the leaves and store in an airtight container.
2   To assemble, start by using a small palette or other wide, flat knife to smooth the piccalilli spread over the center of the plate. Lay the fish over the piccalilli on a slight angle. Arrange the local leaves around the larger end of the fish.

Josh Lewis

1–3
Kelly Liken buying produce at
the Vail Farmers' Market

4 & 5
In the kitchen

Kelly Liken

MENU

Tomato consommé,
homegrown cherry
tomatoes

~

Elk carpaccio,
bulgur tabbouleh salad,
mustard aioli

~

Potato-crusted trout fillets
with shallot-studded
haricots verts,
cherry tomato,
lemon beurre blanc,
and pea tendrils

~

Colorado wildflower
honey–glazed duck breast
cornmeal crepes,
herb salad, confit of duck

~

Salt-crusted Colorado rack
of lamb, Colorado pea and
green onion sauté,
pea tendril salad, and
minted pea emulsion

~

Fresh fruit "bruschetta"
with toasted orange-
flower water pound cake,
macerated seasonal fruit,
and edible flowers

Born in 1976, Kelly Liken studied physics before beginning to concentrate on food. In 2002 she graduated first in her class from The Culinary Institute of America in New York, having already spent time at the Inn at Little Washington, where chef Patrick O'Connell introduced her to the techniques of refined cooking. Liken went on to work at Splendido at the Château in Beaver Creek, Colorado, bolstering her practical experience. In 2004 Liken opened Restaurant Kelly Liken, featuring her own take on a progressive American cuisine. Kelly's menu harnesses the abundant produce of her local area, using ingredients such as bison, elk, and wild porcini mushrooms from the surrounding hillsides. In summer 2008, Liken opened Rick and Kelly's American Bistro in Edwards, Colorado, giving more room for her mixture of the honesty of home cooking and the technique and care of fine cuisine.

Every time I've been out in Colorado for the past four years, it's not even a question: I always visit Kelly at her namesake restaurant. The food there is pure, seasonal, fresh as can be, and always so perfect in every way. When Kelly first came on the scene and I met her and tried her sensational cooking, I knew right away she'd be a star. And a star she became! Just a short time later Kelly was the toast of the town, and her restaurant the "it" place to go, especially for us chefs and foodies during June, when we all head to the Rockies to take in the Aspen Food & Wine Classic festival.

In many ways, Kelly has raised the bar for good seasonal food out in the Rockies, and she still serves what people crave. She uses vegetables to inspire her creativity more than proteins. She almost always builds a dish around a vegetable instead of following the traditional focus on meat, and she never buys it if she can't find it grown locally. Sourcing food can sometimes be tough in the winter, especially in the mountains, but Kelly's menus are always interesting and always delicious. My children dream of her potato-crusted trout and the sticky bun sundae, and I share those dreams too!

But food aside, what makes Kelly really outstanding and sets her apart from her contemporaries is her determination and her obvious passion. She's unwilling to forego quality and won't settle for anything less than perfect, and that makes her an excellent chef in my eyes and one whose work I will emulate and taste as often as I can.

Mario Batali

Restaurant Kelly Liken, Vail, CO, USA

POTATO-CRUSTED TROUT FILLETS WITH SHALLOT-STUDDED HARICOTS VERTS, CHERRY TOMATO, LEMON BEURRE BLANC, AND PEA TENDRILS
Serves 4

For the potato-crusted trout fillets
8 rainbow trout fillets, skinned • 5 eggs, beaten • 10 fingerling potatoes, sliced into paper-thin disks • 110 g all-purpose (plain) flour • 225 g haricots verts (French beans), blanched • butter and olive oil, for sautéing • salt and pepper • 1 pint heirloom (or other) cherry tomatoes

1   Dust the skin side of the fillets in flour and then dip in the beaten eggs. Lay the fillets, egg side up, on a sheet pan (baking tray). Place potato slices on the fillets to resemble scales on a fish.
2   Warm the haricots verts in a sauté pan in a little butter or olive oil and season with salt and pepper. Add the tomatoes to the hot pan until skin starts to blister. Keep warm while you sauté the fish.
3   Cover the bottom of a large sauté pan with olive oil. Heat until just smoking, and season the fish with salt and pepper. Place the fish carefully, potato side down, in the pan and cook until potatoes are golden brown and crispy, about 3 minutes. Flip over and remove the pan from the heat while you place the haricots verts and tomatoes on the plates.
4   Top the vegetables with the fish.

For the lemon beurre blanc sauce
250 ml dry white wine • 2 shallots, chopped • 1 sprig fresh thyme • 10 black peppercorns • 1 bay leaf • 450 g cold unsalted butter, cut into cubes • juice of 1 lemon • salt and pepper

1   Put everything except the butter and lemon juice in a saucepan, bring to a simmer, and reduce until syrupy.
2   Whisk in the butter, 1 piece at a time, off the heat, until it is all melted and incorporated.
3   Stir in the lemon juice and season to taste with salt and pepper.
4   Keep in a warm place, off direct heat. The sauce can be made up to 1 hour in advance, and kept warm.

SALT-CRUSTED COLORADO RACK OF LAMB, COLORADO PEA AND GREEN ONION SAUTÉ, PEA TENDRIL SALAD, AND MINTED PEA EMULSION
Serves 10

For the salt-crusted lamb
handful of parsley, finely chopped • handful of thyme, finely chopped • 2 tbsp garlic, chopped • salt and pepper • 1 (8-bone rack) Colorado lamb, French-trimmed

Mix together the parsley, thyme, garlic, salt, and pepper and rub the lamb. Wrap the bones with foil. Grill on medium heat, fat-side down, for about 6–8 minutes. Finish coloring to the desired doneness, and let rest for at least 3 minutes before slicing.

For the sauce
60 g lamb trimmings • 120 g onions, chopped • 90 g carrots, chopped • 70 g celery, chopped • 1 tomato, chopped • 4 cloves garlic, chopped • 1 bouquet garni • 120 ml red wine • 1 liter veal stock

1   Brown the lamb trimmings, onions, carrots, and celery in a pot on medium-high heat.
2   Once browned, add the tomato, half the chopped garlic, bouquet garni, and red wine to the pot.
3   Add the veal stock, reduce by half or until the desired flavor is reached. Strain and reserve for later.

For the spring pea sauté
110 g fava (broad) beans, blanched and refreshed • 100 g English peas, blanched and refreshed • 40 g green (spring) onions, chopped • 1 tbsp unsalted butter • 3 tbsp mint, chopped • 30 g pea tendrils, picked • 1 tbsp olive oil • 2 tsp salt •1 tsp black pepper, freshly ground • 175 ml whole milk

1   In a sauté pan on medium heat, combine the fava beans, three-quarters of the English peas, green onions, and butter. Sauté for about 2 minutes or until heated through and add half the mint.
2   For the mint-scented froth, bring the milk to a boil and add the remaining English peas and mint. Process in blender until smooth.

To assemble
2 cups pea tendrils, picked • 1 tbsp olive oil • 2 tsp salt • 1 tsp black pepper, freshly ground

1   Lightly coat the pea tendrils with olive oil, salt, and pepper. Set out 4 plates. First place seasoned pea tendrils on each, then top with the warm spring pea sauté. Next, pour 50 ml sauce around plate.
2   Remove the foil from the Colorado lamb, cut into 4 portions and plate. Finally, process the English pea-milk mixture with an immersion blender to incorporate air and create froth. Garnish the lamb with froth, and enjoy.

FRESH FRUIT "BRUSCHETTA" WITH TOASTED ORANGE-FLOWER WATER POUND CAKE, MACERATED SEASONAL FRUIT, AND EDIBLE FLOWERS
Serves 8

For the orange-flower water pound cake
450 g butter • 225 g sugar • 2 tbsp orange-flower water • 6 eggs, separated • 220 g flour

1   Butter a loaf pan, then shake with sugar to coat the insides. Preheat the oven to 180°C (350°F).
2   Cream the butter and orange-flower water for approximately 5 minutes. Add three-quarters of the sugar and cream for another 5 minutes until smooth, fluffy, and no longer gritty.
3   Add 6 egg yolks, one at a time, to the butter and sugar mixture, and beat just until combined. Transfer to a large bowl.
4   In a dry mixing bowl, whisk the egg whites until stiff peaks form. Add the remaining sugar and whisk for approximately 2 minutes until whites become shiny and glossy.
5   Add half the egg whites to the butter mixture in large bowl and fold it in. Add the remaining egg whites. Fold in the flour with a spatula until any lumps have disappeared.
6   Spoon the batter into the prepared loaf pan, three-quarters full, and bake in the still oven for 50 minutes.

For the fruit macerated in floral syrup
450 g sugar • 500 ml water • 2 tbsp lime zest, plus more for garnish • juice of 3 blood oranges • 1 tbsp orange-flower water • handful of grapes • 2 oranges • 225 g strawberries • fresh edible flowers, for garnish

1   Bring the sugar, water, and lime zest to a boil. Add the blood orange juice and orange-flower water, and simmer for 10 minutes.
2   Cut bite-size pieces of oranges, grapes, and strawberries, and add to the cooled syrup.
3   To serve, slice the pound cake and toast in the oven until golden brown on top. Spoon a generous amount of fruit on each slice, then drizzle floral syrup on the toasted pound cake so it soaks up the juices. Grate fresh lime zest on top, and garnish with fresh edible flowers.

1
Potato-crusted trout fillets with
shallot-studded haricots verts,
cherry tomato, lemon beurre
blanc, and pea tendrils

2
Salt-crusted Colorado
rack of lamb,
Colorado pea and green
onion sauté, pea tendril salad,
and minted pea emulsion

3
Fresh fruit "bruschetta" with
toasted orange-flower water
pound cake, macerated
seasonal fruit, and edible
flowers

Kelly Liken

Tung-Yuan Lin

MENU

Caffè taro

~

Pomodoro

~

Caffè lychee

~

Spaghetti with
mushrooms and
coffee cream

~

Roman Empire

~

Caffè batata

Tung-Yuan Lin was born in 1973 and has been working in the coffee industry for twelve years. He cofounded the Italian-style GaBee. in Taiwan in 2004. There he serves innovative beverages and foods showcasing coffee, with specialities such as caffè batata, a rich, balanced coffee infused with the flavor of sweet potato, an important regional ingredient in Taiwan. Winner of the first and third Taiwan Barista Championships, he represented Taiwan in 2007 at the World Barista Competition. Since then he has been instructing in professional coffee-making, judging barista competitions, and demonstrating his skills all over Asia. Tung-Yuan Lin is renowned for the delicacy and finesse of his coffee, and his pioneering work in promoting excellent coffee-making all over Asia.

I met Tung-Yuan Lin four years ago on the Taiwan *Haute Cuisine Food and Drink* program. His GaBee. café, had been open for just over a year, but it was already Taipei's most fashionable coffee house and Lin Tung Yuan was being hailed by the people of Taipei as their "coffee king."

In his coffee paradise, he is able to use the foam on the top of the coffee to create skillful and magical patterns, dazzling and beautiful in form, in the shape of flowers, leaves, feathers, butterflies, geese, seashells, and so forth, impressing and entertaining his coffee-drinking customers.

His incorporation of local flavors is inspired: ranging from yellow gourd juice coffee, strong Eastern tea iced coffee, and plum wine coffee, to rich Taiwanese iced white gourd coffee, longan coffee, and peanut coffee. He even spices drinks with sesame and orange peel, leaving you with a deep impression of two elements to every cup of coffee. Another example of this: eggplant is skinned then flaked and frozen, and finally immersed in boiling coffee; when the coffee has brewed and the eggplant cooled, brown sugar is added to taste. The eggplant flavor is both clean and distinct, winning over the taste buds.

Another creation is the "coffee mash," where boiled potato is mixed with a lotus mash made from cream, milk, confectioner's sugar, and brown sugar, which is in turn mixed with the coffee. Just before it is served, a layer of caramelized sugar is spread over the cup, and the scent of the roasted beans is both delicious and appealing. Tung-Yuan Lin's coffee is truly superb and worthy of high praise.

Tung-Yuan Lin's name is now unparalleled within the coffee business, yet despite winning many international awards and rosettes for technical skill on the exhibition circuit, he remains modest about his success and continues as conscientiously as ever to promote his business ethic in the coffee world both at home and abroad.

Jacky Yu

1–3
Tung-Yuan Lin at work
at GaBee.

4 & 5
Latte art

1
Caffè taro

2
Pomodoro

3
Caffè lychee

4
Spaghetti with mushrooms
and coffee cream

5
Roman Empire

6
Caffè batata

CAFFÈ TARO
Serves 1

1 taro • 20 ml whipped cream •
10 g brown sugar, plus extra to
serve • 120 ml Americano coffee
• 20 ml nondairy creamer •
1 coffee bean

1 Steam and peel the taro,
reserving the skin.
2 Mash the taro, adding the cream
and sugar.
3 Using an ice cream scoop, scoop
a ball of mashed taro and place it
in a coffee cup.
4 Brew the Americano coffee using
a French press. Pour into the cup.
5 Pour the nondairy creamer
slowly into the cup.
6 Slice the taro skin into thin strips.
7 Garnish the coffee with the taro
strips, coffee bean, and brown sugar.

POMODORO
Serves 1

3 Balconi Yellow tomatoes •
1 tomato • 60 ml espresso • a few
ice cubes • 30 ml sugar syrup •
brown sugar, to coat • 1 kumquat •
1 sprig mint

1 Place 1 yellow and 1 red tomato
in boiling water.
2 Peel the red tomato and scoop
out the seeds.
3 Wrap the red tomato in plastic
wrap (clingfilm) and place in the
freezer.
4 Slice 2 Balconi Yellow tomatoes
and peel the one that has been
cooked.
5 Brew a shot of espresso. Add the
espresso, ice, and sugar syrup to
a cocktail shaker and shake.
6 Place the sliced Balconi Yellow
tomatoes and the frozen tomato
into the cup.
7 Pour the coffee into the hole of
the frozen tomato.
8 Stick the peeled Balconi Yellow
tomato onto a fork and coat with
brown sugar.
9 Squeeze the juice of the
kumquat into the coffee and
garnish with mint leaves and the
sugar-coated tomato.

CAFFÈ LYCHEE
Serves 1

5 lychees • 30 ml espresso • a few
ice cubes • 15 ml nondairy creamer
• 20 ml sugar syrup • 100 ml milk

1 Choose a perfect lychee to be
used as garnish. Leaving the stem
on, cut it in half from the bottom,
but do not cut all the way through.
Remove the seed and peel the
skin back.
2 Remove and finely chop the
flesh of another lychee.
3 Remove the flesh of the
remaining 3 lychees and juice
them. Add the flesh of the minced
lychee to the juice.
4 Brew a shot of espresso and put
the espresso and ice into a cocktail
shaker.
5 Add the nondairy creamer and
sugar syrup to the espresso and
shake.
6 Use a milk frother to froth
the milk.
7 Put the lychee juice and pulp
into the cup and add the coffee.
8 Spoon the froth onto the coffee
and garnish with the lychee
prepared in step 1.

SPAGHETTI WITH MUSHROOMS AND COFFEE CREAM
Serves 2

30 g onion • 60 g mushrooms •
30 g butter • 150 ml white sauce
• 180 g spaghetti, cooked •
10 g Parmesan cheese, grated,
plus extra to serve • 15 ml cream
• 30 ml espresso • 2 red cherry
tomatoes • 3 Balconi Yellow
tomatoes • 4 leaves bird's nest
fern, cooked • 10 g coffee beans

1 Stir-fry the onion and mushrooms
for 5 minutes with the butter.
2 Add the white sauce and simmer
for 2 minutes.
3 Add the precooked spaghetti
and continue simmering for a
further 3 minutes.
4 Add the Parmesan cheese
and cream, and stir for about
30 seconds.
5 Transfer the spaghetti onto
the serving plate using spaghetti
tongs, leaving as much sauce in
the pan as possible.
6 Add the espresso to the sauce
and stir, then pour the sauce over
the spaghetti.
7 Place the sliced fresh tomatoes
and boiled bird's nest fern on either
side of the dish.
8 Garnish with the coffee beans
and grated Parmesan.

ROMAN EMPIRE
Serves 1

1 slice lemon • 5 ml grappa •
30 ml espresso • 10 g beet sugar
• 3 g coffee sugar

1 Remove the seeds from the
lemon slice.
2 Pour the grappa into a shot glass.
3 Brew the espresso and pour into
the glass.
4 Place the lemon slice on top of
the glass.
5 Heap the sugars onto the lemon.

CAFFÈ BATATA
Serves 1

1 sweet potato • 10 ml whipping
cream • 200 ml milk • 10 g rock
sugar • 11 g brown sugar • 30 ml
espresso • a few ice cubes • 1 dollop
whipped cream • 1 coffee bean

1 Wash and steam the potato.
2 Peel and slice a 5-mm-thick
finger of potato to make a length
slightly wider than the diameter
of the glass, to be used as garnish.
Keep the skin for later use.
3 Put the rest of the potato in a
blender. Add the whipping cream,
100 ml milk, the rock sugar, and
10 g brown sugar and blend.
4 Pour the blended potato mix
into a martini glass, filling it to
about halfway.
5 Brew an espresso shot and pour
it into a small pitcher (jug) filled
with ice to cool. Holding the glass
at an angle, pour the espresso
slowly onto the side of the martini
glass, creating a layer over the
blended potato.
6 Froth the remaining milk with
a milk frother. Carefully spoon
the froth into the martini glass,
creating the third layer.
7 To prepare the garnish, heat
and dry the potato skin in
the microwave, then cut it into
thin slices.
8 Sprinkle a little brown sugar
on the potato finger. Using a
blowtorch, heat the brown sugar
until it caramelizes.
9 Put a dollop of cream onto the
center of the potato finger and
place a coffee bean on top.
10 Sprinkle a few pieces of the dried
potato skin on top of the cream.

Tung-Yuan Lin

Donald Link grew up in Cajun country, sharing family meals with his grandparents and savoring food his grandfather had hunted, fished, or farmed. The young Donald grew up hunting for frogs in the rice fields, killing and dressing farm chicken for his family's mighty fifty-person Tuesday night suppers, and making thousands of pounds of traditional Cajun sausages. These days, Donald is rediscovering the food of his Louisiana childhood in all its diversity and simplicity—and it is this rich cultural, culinary, and family history that draws me straight to Cochon when I come to New Orleans.

Earlier in Donald's professional career he attended cooking school and worked at a diverse selection of restaurants in San Francisco. When he returned to New Orleans for good in 2000 he opened Herbsaint, a small and stylish restaurant that he still owns. But in 2006 he was able to open Cochon, fulfilling his lifelong dream, and serve the food he grew up eating.

Cochon is a vibrant community restaurant—my favorite kind of place to eat. When I am there I might sample a beautiful gumbo or pickled greens from one of his rustic, joyful menus. The portions are always generous, but with a certain restraint, achieving a balance that is rare in most New Orleans restaurants. And I adore his Southern hospitality.

Although Donald's charcuterie, made from scratch from heritage breeds of pork, is to my mind among the best in the world, I also love his way with organic vegetables and salads. The family feeling in the food is so strong that it comes as no surprise to learn that Donald's sister-in-law grows the backyard lettuces and arugula. I am confident that his inclination to serve overlooked Southern vegetables and plants that once were common will help reconnect New Orleans to its bountiful horticultural and agricultural past, a gastronomic history unlike any other in the United States, with European and African roots and intertwining traditions, both tropical and temperate.

Alice Waters

Donald Link was born in 1969 in southern Louisiana and began his culinary career washing dishes at the age of fifteen. He progressed to cooking in various Louisiana restaurants and a stint at culinary school in San Francisco. He returned to New Orleans in 2000 to open his own restaurant, Herbsaint, where an uncompromising approach to quality melded with Link's preparations of Southern staples, like shrimp and grits, quickly won a loyal following. Though set back by the floods, Link opened the doors of his second restaurant, Cochon, in 2006. Link sets great store in tradition and authenticity, fitting Cochon out with a huge wood-burning oven, an approach he extends to sourcing food as well as cooking it: He regularly gathers wild produce and assists in butchering animals. This connection to the processes at work in his cuisine have led Link to set up the Cochon butcher's shop, which is due to open soon.

MENU

Duck and andouille gumbo
Marcel Lapierre Morgon, 2007

Catfish court bouillon
Huet Vouvray Le Mont, 2004

Rabbit with drop dumpling biscuits
Domaine de l'Arlot Cote de Nuits Villages "Clos Du Chapeau," 2005

Lemon blackberry tartlet with sweet mascarpone
Alois Kracher Trockenbeeren Auslese #7, 2001

Donald Link

Herbsaint Restaurant/Cochon Restaurant, New Orleans, LA, USA

1
Catfish court bouillon

2
Rabbit with drop
dumpling biscuits

3
Lemon blackberry
tartlet with
sweet mascarpone

CATFISH COURT BOUILLON
Serves 4

Any type of seafood stock will work for this dish, so don't get too concerned with following recipes for stocks. Make them taste good by using all the scraps from what you are working with. I recently made this recipe with a crayfish stock, because I just so happened to have some on hand. Traditionally court bouillon is made with fish stock, but shrimp (prawn) stock, or virtually any shellfish stock, or even chicken stock, will work just fine. Do not, however, make this with water, because it won't be worth the effort, flavor-wise. At the very least, take two whole, small fish and chop them up to make a quick fish stock with the scraps from your prepared vegetables.

1 tbsp butter • ½ medium onion, finely chopped • 1 stalk celery, finely chopped • ½ bell pepper, finely chopped • 1 medium tomato, diced • 1 jalapeno or serrano pepper, finely chopped • 4 cloves garlic, finely chopped • ½ tsp dried thyme • 1 tsp salt • ¼ tsp each white pepper, black pepper, paprika • 125 ml dry white wine • 350 ml fish or shrimp stock (see above) • 450 g (3–4) catfish fillets, cut into 10-cm pieces • salt and pepper • 60 g flour • 60 g cornmeal, preferably white and finely ground • 2 tbsp vegetable oil or bacon fat • 15 g parsley, coarsely chopped • 20 g scallions (spring onions), chopped • juice of 1 lemon • 5 basil leaves, coarsely torn • hot steamed rice, for serving

1 Melt the butter in a large skillet over medium heat. Add the onion, celery, pepper, tomato, jalapeno, garlic, thyme, salt, white pepper, black pepper, and paprika and cook, stirring, until softened, for about 5 minutes. Add the white wine, bring to a boil and simmer until it has almost completely evaporated, about 10 minutes, then add the stock and simmer for 10 minutes more. Remove the skillet from the heat and cover to keep warm.
2 Season the catfish with salt and pepper. On a plate or in a pie pan, whisk together the flour and cornmeal. Heat the oil in a cast iron skillet over medium-high heat. Dredge the filets in flour and cornmeal mix, shaking to remove any excess, and transfer to the skillet.
3 Sauté the fish for 3 minutes on the rounder, fuller side, then flip the fish and add the sauce (using a spatula to scrape it into the skillet, then let simmer for 5–8 minutes, until the fish is just cooked through. Stir in the parsley, scallions, lemon juice and fresh, torn basil.
4 To serve, gently remove the catfish with a slotted spatula and set over rice, then spoon a generous amount of sauce over the catfish.

RABBIT WITH DROP DUMPLING BISCUITS
Serves 8–10

For the dumplings
120 g all-purpose (plain) flour • 2 tsp baking powder • 1 tsp dried oregano, crumbled • ¼ tsp cayenne pepper • scant 1 tsp black pepper • scant 1 tsp salt • 1 large egg, lightly beaten • ½ small onion, finely chopped • 2 tbsp melted butter • 125 ml whole milk

1 In a medium bowl, whisk together the flour, baking powder, and seasonings.
2 In a small bowl, whisk together the egg, onion, butter, and milk.
3 Using a fork, stir the wet ingredients into the blended dry ingredients. Do not overmix. You should be able to scoop up a spoonful of batter, turn the spoon on its side, and watch the batter fall slowly off the spoon. If it runs off the spoon, it's too liquid, so you need to add a few more tablespoons of flour.
4 You can use the batter immediately, but I prefer to chill it for at least 30 minutes. Meanwhile, make the rabbit stew.

For the rabbit stew
2 (1.2–1.5-kg) rabbits • salt and ground black pepper • all-purpose (plain) flour, for dusting • 2 tbsp vegetable shortening (fat) • 4 slices thick bacon, sliced into lardons • vegetable oil • 1 small onion, coarsely chopped • 2 stalks celery, coarsely chopped • 1 small carrot, sliced into 2.5-cm rounds • 2 cloves garlic, smashed • 225 ml wine • ½ bunch fresh sage • ½ bunch fresh thyme • 1.5 liters chicken stock

1 Season the rabbits generously with salt and pepper. Dust with flour and remove any excess (this will be easier if they are cut up, but they don't have to be).
2 Heat a large cast iron skillet over medium heat. Add the shortening and bacon and pan-fry, stirring, until the shortening has melted and the bacon has cooked halfway and rendered much of its fat. Drain the bacon fat from the skillet and set aside.
3 Meanwhile, heat the vegetable oil over medium-high heat in a large cast iron Dutch oven (casserole dish). When the oil is very hot, add the rabbit pieces (or whole rabbits) and cook until evenly browned, using tongs to turn the rabbit as necessary.
4 Add the onion, celery, carrot, and garlic and cook, stirring, until the vegetables are coated with fat, then add the wine. Bring the mixture to a boil, reduce the heat and simmer until reduced by half. Add the sage, thyme, and chicken stock, return to a boil, reduce the heat, cover, and simmer until the meat pulls easily away from the bone (turning the rabbit once or twice for even cooking). This will take about 45–60 minutes.
5 When the rabbit is cooked, use tongs to transfer it to a baking dish. Strain the vegetables, reserving just the broth. Use your fingers to separate the rabbit from the bones, feeling carefully for any small bones, and set aside.

For the vegetables
1 medium onion, finely chopped • 2 parsnips, medium diced • 1 poblano chile, finely chopped • 2 carrots, medium diced • 2 stalks celery, finely chopped • 5 cloves garlic, finely chopped • 1 tbsp dried oregano • 5 bay leaves • 2 tsp salt • ½ tsp ground black pepper • 4 tbsp all-purpose (plain) flour • 3 tbsp whole grain mustard • 125 ml dry white wine

1 Heat about 2 tablespoons of the reserved bacon fat in the Dutch oven over medium heat. Add the onions, parsnips, poblano chile, carrots, celery, garlic, oregano, bay leaves, salt, pepper, and the reserved bacon and cook, stirring, for about 5–7 minutes until softened.
2 Dust the pan contents with the 4 tablespoons of flour, add the mustard and wine and cook, stirring, until the pan is deglazed and most of the wine has evaporated.
3 Add the reserved stock, scraping up any browned bits. Simmer for about 10 minutes, then add the reserved rabbit meat and simmer for an additional 20 minutes.
4 To finish the dish, preheat the oven to 450ºF (230ºC). Drop spoonfuls of the dumpling batter on top of the stew about 1–2 cm apart and bake until the tops turn a golden brown.

LEMON BLACKBERRY TARTLET WITH SWEET MASCARPONE
Makes 12

For the tartlet shells
400 g butter • 200 g superfine (caster) sugar • ¼ tsp salt • 1 egg plus 1 egg yolk • 1 tsp vanilla extract • 700 g all-purpose (plain) flour

1 Preheat the oven to 325ºF (160ºC).
2 Cream together the butter, sugar, and salt.
3 Add the eggs and vanilla, and mix until incorporated, scraping the side of the bowl.
4 Add the flour, and mix until just combined. Roll it out, and using a cookie cutter, divide into approximately 12 pieces and use it to line the tartlet pans.

For the filling
450 g butter • 450 g confectioners' (icing) sugar • zest of 4 lemons • 6 eggs • 75 g all-purpose (plain) flour • 2 baskets fresh blackberries • ½ tsp salt • ½ tsp vanilla extract • 700 g mascarpone cheese, sweetened to taste • confectioners' (icing) sugar, to garnish • mint, to garnish

1 Preheat the oven to 325ºF (160ºC).
2 Cream together the butter, sugar, and lemon zest until light and fluffy.
3 Beat in the eggs slowly, one at a time, scraping the sides of the bowl between each egg.
4 Thoroughly incorporate the flour and salt, and stir in the vanilla.
5 Divide the blackberries among the tartlet shells and top with 1½–2 tablespoons of the lemon zest mixture, taking care not to overfill. Bake for 11–15 minutes, or until golden brown. Let cool slightly before carefully turning out of the tart pans.
6 Serve with sweetened mascarpone. Dust with confectioners' sugar and add a sprig of mint to garnish.

Donald Link

Paolo Lopriore

MENU

Salad of seaweeds,
aromatic herbs, and roots

~

Elicoidali, black pepper,
and pecorino Romano
cheese

~

Risotto "marinara style"

~

Porcini mushrooms
and samphire

~

Anchovy aspic "a scapece"

~

Entrecôte of veal, celery,
and tuna fish

~

Ewe's milk curds and wild
shoots

~

Parfait of smoked sugar

~

Carrots, hazelnuts, lemon,
and vanilla

Born in 1973 in Italy, Paolo Lopriore began his career in food at the age of eighteen, soon becoming a commis chef at the Restaurant Gualtiero Marchesi in Milan. There head chef Gualtiero Marchesi fostered in Lopriore what has become a lifelong penchant for culinary renewal, through digging deeply into a gastronomic culture without ever betraying it. The next seven years took Lopriore on a whirlwind tour through a range of top restaurants in Italy and France, ending at the Restaurant Troisgros in Roanne, with its three Michelin stars. This wealth of experience instilled Lopriore with a respect for rigorous standards. He returned from his travels to Italy in 2002 to settle at the Restaurant Il Canto in Siena, where he continues to apply his unstinting curiosity and extensive expertise to a lauded menu of studied yet creative Italian cuisine, creating subtle and atmospheric dishes.

1
Paolo Lopriore in the
kitchen at Il Canto

2
Preparing fresh herbs

3
Plated starters

4
Mussels, rice,
and saffron

My friend, the photographer Bob Noto, took me to Il Canto once and I was deeply moved by the art of Paolo Lopriore. He really puts a part of himself into each and every dish he composes, striving to give his guests a fleeting sensation of being, if only for a few minutes, adrift at sea, or lying in a field of grass. I know that he would love to be rid of the restrictions of tables and chairs and feed his guests in the freedom of a wood or a cornfield.

Paolo's cuisine is simultaneously traditional Italian and thoroughly modern. He is open to any influence, but maintains a very deep Italian feeling. One might say that he is one of the few chefs whose work can be compared to poetry. You can be a good chef, even a great chef, but some chefs have a special sensibility that really marks them out. This is the exceptional quality that distinguishes Paolo—he is a poet who uses his cuisine as his language.

He is deeply influenced by observation—observation of the chefs he has trained under, and a quiet study of his environment. As well as drawing on lessons learned from Gualtiero Marchesi (the influential Italian chef who constantly renews his cuisine by digging deeply into his gastronomic culture), he colors his palate with details of Siena, from its inhabitants and its ancient city walls to the luxuriant nature that surrounds it. His salad of seaweed, aromatic herbs, and roots encapsulates the artistry of his cuisine, a harmony of chaos that savors the purity of each and every ingredient.

In Italy I have a lot of good friends who are chefs and are already very well known. Paolo is not yet recognized outside his native country, but I have every confidence that his star will soon rise, since in my opinion he is one of the true greats.

Ferran Adrià

1
Salad of seaweeds, aromatic
herbs, and roots

2
Elicoidali, black pepper, and
pecorino Romano cheese

3
Risotto "marinara style"

4
Entrecôte of veal,
celery, and tuna fish

5
Carrots, hazelnuts,
lemon, and vanilla

SALAD OF SEAWEEDS, AROMATIC HERBS, AND ROOTS
Serves 4

1 head of curly endive • 4 sorrel leaves • 4 leaves Good King Henry • 4 leaves French watercress • 4 rue tips • 4 leaves Chinese mustard • 16 chervil tips • 1 sheet nori • 4 g wasabi paste • 12 g sweet-and-sour ginger • 4 radishes, sliced • 4 leaves absinthium • 4 leaves sea fennel • mixed edible flowers

1 Clean the endive, separating the green part from the yellow and removing the core. Wash the aromatic herbs carefully and dry them delicately. Cut the nori in julienne strips.
2 On 4 individual plates, put 2 dabs of wasabi, lay the endive on top, and garnish with the aromatic herbs, ginger, sliced radishes, nori, sea fennel, and lastly, a few flower petals.

ELICOIDALI, BLACK PEPPER, AND PECORINO ROMANO CHEESE
Serves 4

300 g water • 30 g fresh black peppercorns • 5 g agar agar • salt and pepper • 5 g oil • 40 pieces of elicoidali pasta • 40 g pecorino Romano cheese, grated

1 Put the water in a large casserole with half the pepper, bring everything to a boil, remove from the heat, and let stand for about 30 minutes. Adjust for salt and strain, reserving the water.
2 Put the water mixture back on the heat, bring it to a boil for the second time, add the agar agar, and after bringing it to a boil again on a high heat, chill it while stirring constantly with a whisk.
3 Once cooled, add 3 tablespoons oil and whisk the mixture as if making a mayonnaise. Remove the remaining peppercorns from the stalk, add them to the mixture, and put in the mixer on high speed for 5 minutes. Let stand in the refrigerator overnight.
4 Separately, in plenty of salted water, cook the elicoidali, drain them, dress them lightly with the remaining 2 tablespoons oil, and, using a pastry (piping) bag, stuff 24 of them with the black pepper and agar agar preparation. Leave the rest of them empty.
5 Heat the elicoidali in the microwave for a few minutes and arrange them on 4 individual plates covered with pecorino Romano.

RISOTTO "MARINARA STYLE"
Serves 4

4 medium oysters • 30 g seawater (from reducing 2 tsp parsley chlorophyll with 200 g seawater) • 30 g crustacean coulis, made by roasting 2 kg shrimp (prawn) shells with olive oil, tomato, and pepper, then pounding and straining • 30 g squid ink • 280 g Carnaroli rice • 30 g butter • 120 g white wine

1 Shuck the oysters, put them in a bowl with their own juices, and mix all together with an immersion blender. Filter through a strainer and put the liquid in the refrigerator.
2 Put the seawater, the crustacean coulis, and the squid ink diluted with a little water in 3 separate vaporizers.
3 Toast the rice with the butter in a big pan, add the white wine, then let boil with enough lightly salted water to make a risotto. Take the pan off the heat and thicken the risotto with the oyster mixture.
4 Serve on 4 individual plates and spray the 3 different vaporizers over the top.

ENTRECÔTE OF VEAL, CELERY, AND TUNA FISH
Serves 4

30 g dried tuna (katsuobushi), thinly sliced • 25 g vegetable oil • 2 (140-g) veal sirloin pieces • salt • 1 bay leaf • extra-virgin olive oil • 12 Serragghia capers • 12 celery leaves • pepper, to taste

1 Vacuum-pack the dried tuna with the vegetable oil in a bag and cook in a double-boiler at 140°F (60°C) for about 7 hours.
2 Line a baking pan with wax (greaseproof) paper. Open the bag, reserving the oil, and arrange the tuna with the slices well apart in the pan. Let the tuna air-dry.
3 In a large pan, put water, salt, and a bay leaf, cover with plenty of oil, and bring to a boil, dip in the veal sirloin, turn off the heat, and let them cook for about 6-10 minutes.
4 After letting the meat rest, cut each sirloin into 4 pieces, arrange them on a plate, and add the capers, reserved oil, celery leaves, salt, pepper, and tuna slices.

CARROTS, HAZELNUTS, LEMON, AND VANILLA
Serves 4

400 g carrot juice • 200 g butter • 150 g hazelnut paste • rock salt, to taste • zest of 1 lemon • 1 vanilla bean • 4 carrot sprout leaves

1 Use an ice-cream maker to prepare a carrot sorbet from the carrot juice, and let stand in the freezer at 10.5°F (-12°C) for approximately 4 hours.
2 In a large bowl, cream the butter, add the hazelnut cream and a few crystals of rock salt, homogenize the mixture, and transfer to a rectangular container in the refrigerator until it solidifies.
3 Grate the lemon zest and scrape out the seeds from the vanilla bean.
4 On 4 individual plates, place the carrot leaves, a twirl of nut butter, the lemon zest, the vanilla seeds, and a quenelle of carrot sorbet.

Paolo Lopriore

Locally born, Willin Low is typical of Singaporean tradition in adhering closely to convention. His early life evolved in textbook fashion: after military service he went to university, and after graduation he went to the United Kingdom where he studied law as expected. After returning home, he took up the vocation to which everyone considered him the most suited—that of a lawyer.

After eight distinguished years in the legal profession, he decided to move to his true vocation. As a foreign student in the United Kingdom he had found British food hard to digest, so he had begun to experiment in the kitchen and honed his culinary skills.

And now his true desire was to be a chef. He used what he had earned as a lawyer to set up a restaurant where he fuses elements of Western cuisine with traditional Singaporean dishes, changing their form rather than their essence and so finding something fresh and new. If I have to pick out one of his dishes, then Lasha Italian rice is one which has been extremely successful. He combines the typical Singaporean delicacy of lasha, thick soup, with a salted Italian rice preparation but uses rice lightly fried in the Western tradition, turning what was originally a highly flavored Italian dish into one strongly infused with a southern Asian flavor. He also makes use of classic sesame envelopes to accompany Western desserts such as ice cream.

Willin's phenomenally creative style has been instrumental in both preserving and anchoring the traditional culture of food and drink in Singapore as well as greatly profiting the world of haute cuisine through the explosion onto the scene of a unique and outstandingly inventive mind.

Jacky Yu

Willin Low was born in Singapore in 1972. Studying law in England left him homesick for familiar food, but difficulty in finding ingredients meant he often cooked pastas combined with the flavors of Singapore, cementing a flexible approach to experimentation that still governs his menu. After returning to Singapore to work as a lawyer for eight years, Low decided to pursue his true passion: food. After offering an informal private catering service at weekends, he persuaded the executive chef at Garibaldi, a fine-dining Italian restaurant, to hire him as a kitchen hand. Following a six-month stint there he opened his own restaurant, Wild Rocket, in 2005. There he captures traditional Singaporean recipes in new, globally inspired interpretations, with dishes like slow-braised dark-soy pork rigatoni. Wild Rocket was closely followed by a bar, Wild Oats, which opened next door to the restaurant in 2006, and Relish, a gourmet burger and beer restaurant, in 2007.

MENU

Onsen-styled quail egg with Malossol caviar and homemade aioli

~

Slow-braised dark soy pork rigatoni

~

Crustacean oil spaghetti with Alaskan king crab

~

Roast Chilean sea bass with kecap manis garlic

~

Duck leg confit with Mom's yam cake and plum mustard

~

Yam paste Orh Nee mille feuille with coconut ice cream

1

Willin Low

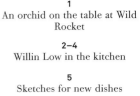

1
An orchid on the table at Wild Rocket

2–4
Willin Low in the kitchen

5
Sketches for new dishes

1. Chinese Spooned Cod Cakes with Spicy Malay Relish
   - chervil
   - ayam masak merah sauce
   - cod cake

2. White Truffled Cream Mixed Wild Mushroom in Peranakan Pastry Cups
   - spring onion
   - mixed mushroom
   - kueh pie ti shell

3. Tiger Prawns with Lemon Mayo, Chives & Avruga Caviar
   - chive
   - caviar
   - fancy toothpick
   - lemon mayo
   - boiled tiger prawn
   - shot glass

4. Aioli Blue Swimmer Crab Tartlets with Salmon Roe
   - salmon roe
   - crab w̄ aioli
   - tartlet shell

5. Thai Basil Coconut Chicken Mince on Teriyaki Rice Crackers
   - spring onion
   - chili padi
   - chicken mince
   - rice cracker

6. Mini Baked Potatoes with Sour Cream Scallion Bacon
   - bacon bits
   - spring onion
   - sour cream
   - baby potato

Relish/Wild Rocket, Singapore

1
Onsen-styled quail egg
with Malossol caviar and
homemade aioli

2
Slow-braised dark soy
pork rigatoni

3
Crustacean oil spaghetti
with Alaskan king crab

4
Roast Chilean seabass
with kecap manis garlic

5
Duck leg confit with Mom's yam
cake and plum mustard

6
Yam paste Orh Nee
mille feuille with
coconut ice cream

ONSEN-STYLED QUAIL EGG WITH MALOSSOL CAVIAR AND HOMEMADE AIOLI
Serves 4

For the aioli
2 cloves garlic, chopped • 1 tsp salt • 2 egg yolks • 475 ml extra-virgin olive oil • 2 tbsp water • 2 tbsp lemon juice

1 For the aioli, process the garlic, salt, and egg yolks in a food processor until well combined.
2 Slowly add the oil, processing to form a thick mayonnaise.
3 Transfer to a bowl. Stir in the water and lemon juice. Cover with plastic wrap (clingfilm) and refrigerate until required.

For the quail eggs
4 quail eggs • 2 tsp Malossol caviar • 1 small stalk scallion (spring onion), chopped • 4 chive stalks for garnish

1 Prepare a pan of boiling water and gently place the eggs into it. After 1 minute scoop up the eggs and gently remove the shells. The whites should be cooked but the yolk will still be runny when the whites are broken.
2 Take 4 small dishes, spoon in some homemade aioli, followed by the caviar, and place an egg on top of the caviar. Sprinkle with scallions and garnish with a chive stalk.

SLOW-BRAISED DARK SOY PORK RIGATONI
Serves 4

100 g pork collar • 60 ml good-quality dark soy sauce • 1 tbsp light soy sauce • 1 tbsp kecap manis (sweet Indonesian soy sauce) • 1 cinnamon stick • 1 star anise • 1 tsp white peppercorns • 100 g rigatoni pasta • 60 ml chicken stock • grated Parmesan, for serving • cream, for serving

1 Put all the ingredients, except the rigatoni and chicken stock, in a large pan and add enough water to cover the pork.
2 Bring to a boil and let simmer, adding more water whenever the liquid level falls below the top of the pork.
3 Once the meat is very tender, remove it from the sauce and reduce the sauce by at least half until syrupy in consistency.
4 With a fork, shred the meat finely. Pour the reduced sauce over the meat and keep refrigerated overnight.
5 Cook the rigatoni as per the package instructions, or until al dente. Spoon the meat mixture and sauce into a skillet, add a little chicken stock and toss in the rigatoni. Add some grated Parmesan cheese and a dash of cream.

CRUSTACEAN OIL SPAGHETTI WITH ALASKAN KING CRAB
Serves 4

1 lobster carcass • 1 crayfish carcass • 1 liter canola (rapeseed) oil • 1 sprig rosemary • 1 sprig tarragon • 100 g spaghettini pasta • 1 clove garlic, sliced • 1 tsp dried chili flakes • 60 ml fish stock • salt • 2 Alaskan king crab legs, boiled and shelled • 1 tsp dried seaweed flakes • 1 tsp dried bonito flakes • 1 tsp chopped English (curly) parsley

1 To make the crustacean oil, coarsely crush the lobster and crayfish carcasses in a mortar and pestle, then sauté with 125 ml canola oil and the rosemary and tarragon sprigs over moderate heat until very brightly colored.
2 Add the remaining canola oil and simmer for 40 minutes. Strain through a fine mesh sieve lined with cheesecloth (muslin).
3 Cook the spaghetti until al dente, then set aside.
4 Sauté the garlic and dried chili flakes in some crustacean oil until the garlic is golden brown.
5 Add a little fish stock, toss in the pasta, add some salt to taste and then add the crab legs and some more crustacean oil and toss well.
6 Divide among 4 plates and sprinkle generously with the seaweed, bonito and parsley.

ROAST CHILEAN SEA BASS WITH KECAP MANIS GARLIC
Serves 4

4 (80-g) Chilean sea bass fillets • salt and pepper • 2 tbsp olive oil • 20 stalks baby asparagus • 4 cloves garlic, sliced • 2 tbsp kecap manis (Indonesian sweet soy sauce) • dash of red wine

1 Preheat the oven to 500°F (250°C).
2 Season the sea bass fillets with salt and pepper, then brown them in olive oil in a nonstick skillet over high heat.
3 Blanch the baby asparagus.
4 Roast the fillets in the oven for 4–5 minutes.
5 In the meantime, sauté the garlic until golden brown, then add the kecap manis and red wine. Let it simmer for a while.
6 Place the asparagus on the plates with the fillets on top, then pour the kecap manis mixture over it.

DUCK LEG CONFIT WITH MOM'S YAM CAKE AND PLUM MUSTARD
Serves 4

For the duck leg confit
1 tsp salt • 1 tsp pepper • 2 duck legs • 2 cloves garlic, crushed • 1 bay leaf • 2 sprigs thyme • 900 g duck fat

1 Rub the salt and pepper evenly over the duck legs and place in a shallow dish.
2 Place 1 clove garlic, the bay leaf, and 1 sprig of thyme over the legs, cover with plastic wrap (clingfilm) and refrigerate overnight.
3 Next day, preheat the oven to 200°F (100°C).
4 Melt the duck fat in a small pan.
5 Brush the salt and seasonings off the duck and arrange in a single snug layer in a high-sided baking dish or ovenproof pan.
6 Pour enough melted fat over the duck to cover it and place the confit in the oven. Cook for 2–3 hours at a very slow simmer—just an occasional bubble—until the duck is tender and can be easily pulled from the bone.
7 Remove the confit from the oven. Cool, and store the duck in the fat.

For the yam cake
400 g rice flour • 1.2 litres warm water • 50 g dried shrimp (prawns) • 1 tbsp shallot oil • 10 g salt • 10 g sugar • 150 g yam, peeled and cut into 2-cm cubes

1 Mix the flour with some water to form a dough.
2 Place in a large pot and add all the other ingredients, stirring constantly over low heat until the mixture is a thick paste.
3 Pour the paste onto a baking sheet, spread it evenly and steam for 45 minutes.
4 Remove to cool, then cut the steamed cake into the desired size and shape.

To assemble
1 tbsp wholegrain mustard • 1 tbsp Chinese plum sauce

1 Preheat the oven to 500°F (250°C).
2 Mix the mustard and the plum sauce well.
3 Sear the duck leg, skin down, until the skin is crispy.
4 Put the leg on a baking sheet and heat in the oven for 5 minutes.
5 Remove the skin, cut into small pieces, and set aside.
6 Shred the duck and remove the bone.
7 Take 4 plates and put a piece of yam cake on each, then spoon some duck meat over and top with the crispy skin. Drizzle the plum mustard over and serve.

YAM PASTE ORH NEE MILLE FEUILLE WITH COCONUT ICE CREAM
Serves 4

200 g yam, peeled • salt • 1 tbsp sugar • 2 tbsp shallot oil • 8 gingko nuts, peeled and cooked • 1 sheet frozen filo pastry (approximately 21 cm x 30 cm) • butter for brushing • homemade coconut ice cream, to serve

1 Cut the peeled yam into large pieces and place in a pan with enough water to cover. Add a pinch of salt and the sugar.
2 Cook until tender, then mash the yam with a fork, adding shallot oil to round out the taste and some of the boiling water to obtain a smooth consistency like peanut butter.
3 Add the gingko nuts and mix well.
4 Preheat oven to 425°F (220°C).
5 Cut the filo pastry into 8 equal pieces, brush with some butter and bake for 5 minutes until golden brown.
6 To serve, take 4 dishes and spoon some yam paste into each. Place a pastry sheet over the top, and repeat with yam paste and pastry sheet and then yam paste again. Top with a scoop of coconut ice cream.

Willin Low

On a trip to Sydney in 2008, I was fortunate enough to be able to have a meal at The Icebergs Dining Room and Bar on Bondi Beach and was blown away by the place. The design was cutting-edge, the ambience was buzzy and relaxed, and the views were stunning, but most of all I had a meal that still stood out in my mind months later.

Robert Marchetti's menu is light, healthy, and packed full of flavor. His philosophy is simple — good honest, healthy food cooked well. There is still a common misconception that healthy food is often dull and tasteless, but Marchetti has overthrown this by serving an exciting, refreshing, yet nourishing and wholesome menu. Wherever he can, he will cut back on adding unnecessary fats in his cooking, often opting for dairy-free dishes.

His menus are governed by the seasons and dominated by fish and seafood, due to the restaurant's incredible location right on the ocean. Each day, depending on what has been brought in by the catch in the morning, the restaurant will serve an array of whole fish and fillets. The freshness of the fish speaks for itself, and it is served simply with a choice of fine-cut Mediterranean vegetables, lightly pickled, or a roasted tomato sauce. Other dishes that really stand out on the menu include an incredible ocean trout tartare with a little chile, shallot, lemon, and orange dressing, and hand-dived Coffin Bay half-shell scallops served with a tomato, chile, garlic, and radish salad.

One of Marchetti's aims at The Icebergs is for diners leaving the restaurant to feel great about themselves. He doesn't necessarily push boundaries in terms of inventive combinations or new techniques, but instead takes fantastic produce and showcases it at its best, in fun, light, fresh, and flavorful dishes.

Gordon Ramsay

Born in Australia in 1974, Robert Marchetti began his career cooking alongside his brother in the family's Melbourne restaurants, Café Maximus, Marchetti's Latin, and Marchetti's Tuscan Grill. After working at other eateries in the city and posts in Japan and Malaysia, Marchetti returned to the family business as executive chef at Marchetti's at Reef House in Palm Cove, Cairns, repeatinghis success at Marchetti's Latinand Marchetti's Tuscan Grill. In 2002 he began to collaborate on the idyllic beach house project that was to become The Icebergs Dining Room and Bar on Bondi Beach in Sydney. Marchetti's menu there reveals a Mediterranean influence born out of his father's Italian origins that is echoed more strongly just up the beach at his other venue, North Bondi Italian Food. Marchetti's cuisine is light and fresh, appealing to all tastes in its healthiness and punchy flavor.

MENU

Burrata, artichoke salad; My Salumi on wooden boards: Ossocollo, Coulatello, Cacciatore, warm Piadina; "Gambaretti" lightly dusted local shrimp, lemon, aioli
Terredora Falanghina, Campagnia, Italy, 2007

~

Crab, soft polenta, chile, garlic, and lemon
Tenuta Sant' Antonio Monte Ceriani Soave Superiore, Verona, Italy, 2006

Hervey Bay half-shell scallops, tomato, green chile, garlic and radish salad, peas, basil, lemon, and feta salad
Audrey Wilkinson Reserve Chardonnay, Hunter Valley, Australia, 2006

~

Raspberry tart with rosewater syrup, and chocolate pearls
Braida Brachetto d'Acqui, Piemonte, Italy, 2007

Robert Marchetti

1
Robert Marchetti with fresh
produce suppliers

2
Menus at North Bondi

3
The dining room at Icebergs

Icebergs Dining Room & Bar, North Bondi Italian Food, Giuseppe Arnaldo & Sons, Sydney, Australia

1
Burrata and artichoke
salad (bottom left)

2
Crab, soft polenta,
chile, garlic, and
lemon (top left)

3
Hervey Bay half shell
scallops, tomato,
green chile, garlic,
radish salad
(bottom left)

4
Raspberry tart with
rosewater syrup and
chocolate pearls
(bottom right)

BURRATA, ARTICHOKE SALAD
Serves 2

For the lemon vinaigrette
40 ml lemon juice, freshly squeezed • 40 ml red-wine vinegar • 2 cloves garlic, crushed • 3 tbsp Dijon mustard • ½ tbsp salt • 160 ml extra-virgin olive oil

Combine the lemon juice, vinegar, crushed garlic, mustard, and salt in a bowl. Whisk to combine. While still whisking, slowly add the oil. This dressing is also used for the scallop salad.

For the burrata and artichoke salad
2 globe artichokes • lemon juice, to taste • ½ bunch scallions (spring onions), thinly sliced • 10 mint leaves, torn • ½ bunch parsley, picked • 2 pieces burrata, or buffalo mozzarella if not available • 4 chives • virgin olive oil, to taste • pepper

1 Take off the first few layers of the artichoke leaves until the inside leaves take on a yellow-white color and become slightly tender. Discard the outside leaves. Rub the exposed flesh with a small amount of lemon juice to prevent the artichoke turning black.
2 Cut the stem about 10 cm from the base of the flower and peel with a vegetable peeler or small knife until it becomes white and tender. Again, rub the flesh with lemon juice. Cut the artichoke in half lengthwise and, with a teaspoon, remove the fibrous inner section. Once again rub with lemon juice.
3 With a sharp knife, cut across the artichoke as finely as possible. Working quickly to prevent the artichoke from discoloring, dress it with about 20 ml of the lemon vinaigrette. Add the scallions, mint, and parsley. Toss well. Arrange the salad on 2 plates and place the burrata on top. Tie 1 or 2 chives around the top of each piece of burrata, grind a small amount of pepper over the top, and drizzle with the olive oil.

CRAB, SOFT POLENTA, CHILE, GARLIC, AND LEMON
Serves 2

200 ml chicken stock • 1 tbsp butter • salt • 50 g instant polenta • 50 ml extra-virgin olive oil • ½ tsp red chile, chopped • ½ tsp garlic, chopped • 150 g crabmeat, picked • 1 tbsp parsley, chopped • juice of ¼ lemon • salt and pepper

1 Place the chicken stock, butter, and a pinch of salt in a heavy-based pot. Bring to a boil and whisk in the polenta, adding it in a slow, steady stream while whisking continuously so that no lumps form. Turn the heat down to low and cook for a further 4–5 minutes, stirring occasionally.
2 In a small frying pan, heat the oil, chile, and garlic. Cook on medium heat until the garlic becomes translucent and fragrant. Add the crabmeat and warm through. When warmed, add the parsley, lemon, and a little salt and pepper.
3 Place 3–4 tablespoons polenta in the center of a plate. The polenta should have the consistency of thickened cream—if too thick, add a little more stock or warm water. Spoon the crab into the middle of the polenta and serve immediately.

HERVEY BAY HALF-SHELL SCALLOPS, TOMATO, GREEN CHILE, GARLIC, RADISH SALAD
Serves 2

12 wild sea scallops, in the shell • 1 large green chile, seeded and thinly sliced • 2 cloves garlic, finely chopped • 2 tbsp extra-virgin olive oil • 4 cherry tomatoes, sliced 4 mm thick • salt and pepper • 3 medium radishes • 1 bunch watercress, picked • 90 ml lemon vinaigrette (see Burrata, Artichoke Salad recipe)

1 Preheat the oven to 400°F (200°C).
2 Clean the scallops by removing the small muscle on the outside of the white flesh. If it has roe on it, leave this on. Place back into the shell and store in the refrigerator.
3 In a bowl, mix together the sliced chile, garlic, and olive oil. Spoon a generous amount onto the scallops, place 2 slices of tomato on each scallop, season with salt and pepper, and then place the scallops on an ovenproof tray.
4 Bake in the oven for 5–6 minutes or until just cooked.
5 Slice the radishes so they resemble matchsticks. Combine with watercress and dressing.
6 Once the scallops are cooked, remove from the oven and quickly place an even amount of the salad on top of each scallop in its shell, spoon a little dressing over the salad.
7 Place a little watercress on the plate underneath the shells (to stop the shells sliding) and serve immediately.

RASPBERRY TART WITH ROSEWATER SYRUP AND CHOCOLATE PEARLS
Serves 2

For the sweet pastry
200 g unsalted butter • 180 g confectioners' (icing) sugar • 1 vanilla bean • 2 eggs • 330 g all-purpose (plain) flour • 150 g ground almonds

1 Grease 2 (10-cm) tart pans.
2 Cream the butter, sugar, and vanilla. Add the eggs one at a time. When this is combined, fold in the dry ingredients. Mix until well combined. Wrap in plastic wrap (clingfilm) and allow to rest in the refrigerator for 1 hour.
3 Remove from the refrigerator and cut into small pieces, about 50 g each. Roll the pastry as thinly as possible. Gently place into the tart pans, ensuring that it is pressed firmly into all corners. Using a knife, trim off the excess pastry. Place in the freezer for about 30 minutes.
4 Preheat the oven to 325°F (160°C).
5 Remove the pans from the freezer and line with baking paper. Fill each tart with rice and bake for 8–10 minutes, or until the pastry turns golden brown. Remove the rice and let cool.

For the mascarpone cream
180 ml milk • ¼ vanilla bean • 2 egg yolks • 40 g plus 2 tbsp sugar • 15 g all-purpose (plain) flour • 2 egg whites • 330 ml cream • 330 g mascarpone

1 Combine the milk and vanilla in a heavy-based pot and bring to a boil. In the meantime, combine the yolks and 40 g sugar and whisk until smooth. Whisk in the flour.
2 When milk has boiled, pour a small amount onto the eggs and whisk to combine. Add the egg mixture to the rest of the milk and place over medium heat. Cook for about 5 minutes until the mixture thickens. Stir continuously with a wooden spoon.
3 Remove from the pot and set aside to cool.
4 Whisk the egg whites and 2 tablespoons sugar until stiff peaks form. In a separate bowl, whisk three-quarters of the cream until it is the same consistency as the egg whites. Mix the remaining cream and mascarpone together until smooth. In a large bowl, combine all the components and gently fold together.

For the raspberry and rose water syrup
500 g frozen raspberries • 100 g sugar • pinch of salt • 1 tbsp lemon juice • rose water, to taste • grappa, to taste

Combine the raspberries, sugar, and salt in a bowl and cover with plastic wrap. Leave in a warm place for at least 1 hour. Strain the mixture and discard the raspberries. Add the lemon juice, rose water, and grappa to taste.

To assemble
1 punnet fresh raspberries • chocolate pearls (optional)

Fill the tart shells with the mascarpone cream until about three-quarters full. Arrange raspberries on top so they are all facing same direction. Scatter about 6–8 chocolate pearls on the top. Serve the raspberry and rose water syrup in a small pitcher (jug) so it can be poured at the table.

Robert Marchetti

Mediterranean cuisine is dear to my heart for hundreds of reasons. One—and not the least—is its great diversity. The *"riz en bouillon"* (rice cooked in stock) of Latium is not the same as Sicilian risotto, which in turn is very different from the rice they cook in Valencia. And just look at the many types of flour: spelt in Provence, sweet chestnut flour in Corsica, navy bean flour in Catalonia, potato here, wheat there. Or the infinite methods (national, local, or "the way your granny does it") of making couscous throughout North Africa. In this way, sharing the same foundations, the generous use of olive oil in particular, Mediterranean cuisine encompasses a wonderful regional variety.

So yes, you could say that Christophe does Mediterranean cuisine. He attended an excellent school to study it, then spent four years at the Louis XV, my restaurant in Monaco. Starting as a third commis chef, in only three years he became sous chef to Franck Cerutti, the chef de cuisine. Then I asked him to take charge of the restaurant at Hôtel L'Andana, at Tenuta La Badiola, in Tuscany. From Provence to Tuscany: still the Mediterranean, of course, but a totally different cuisine.

If you want to describe it, you have to talk about the place itself. We're in the Maremma, to be precise, which was once a marshy region, beside the Tyrrhenian sea. A huge Tuscan estate, with a country house that once belonged to the Dukes of Tuscany, form parameters that define Christophe's cooking. From the vines and olive trees of the estate, L'Andana makes its own wine and olive oil. But the region used to be poor and salt was expensive: there was none in the local bread. This tradition has been kept up, too, and all the cooking is adapted to the food culture of the Maremma, both elegant and rustic: delicate *crostini di fegatini* (chicken-liver toasts) tasty *salsa capperi e alici* (rabbit-liver toasts with fennel, celery root, tapenade and scallions), creamy *stracciatella di bufala* (a soup of fava beans, ricotta and buffalo milk cream). The dukes would certainly have made Christophe an honorary citizen of Tuscany.

Alain Ducasse

Born in 1974 in Rennes, France, Christophe Martin began his career in food at the age of fifteen, taking a variety of jobs in the prestigious restaurants of the region. He went on to join L'Auberge Bretonne at La Roche-Bernard for two years, before continuing his training at L'Auberge de L'Ill for two years. At the age of 26, Martin became a third commis chef at Alain Ducasse's restaurant Louis XV in Monaco. After three years of learning and craft, bringing finesse to his technical skills and working his way up the kitchen hierarchy, Martin became assistant to Franck Cerutti. In 2004, Alain Ducasse appointed him head chef at L'Andana, in Tenuta la Badiola in Tuscany, where Martin prepares his unique and classic cuisine with the best products of the region.

Christophe Martin

1, 2 & 4
Chefs at work in the kitchen
at L'Andana, Tenuta la Badiola

3
Christophe Martin in
the kitchen

1
Tripe salad with an
herb pistou,
pine kernels, and wild
salad greens

2
Salt cod in an
herb crust, with
white navy beans

3
Zuppa Inglese

TRIPE SALAD WITH AN HERB PISTOU, PINE KERNELS, AND WILD SALAD GREENS
Serves 4

For the tripe
400 g blanched tripe • 50 g celery • 1 scallion (spring onion) • olive oil • coarse-ground pepper • 100 ml white wine • 100 ml chicken stock • 80 ml olive oil

1   Cut the tripe into 5-mm strips and set aside.
2   Wash and trim the celery and cut diagonally into 5-mm pieces.
3   Peel and finely chop the white part of the scallion (keep the green part for the salad).
4   Sweat the celery and scallion in a pan with a dash of olive oil and a pinch of coarse pepper. Add the tripe, mix it in, and let it soften.
5   Pour in half the white wine and reduce until dry. Pour in the rest of the wine and reduce by half.
6   Pour in the chicken stock and cook for 15 minutes until the juices are syrupy.
7   Let the tripe cool, then add the olive oil. Mix thoroughly, then put in a cool place.

For the herb pistou
30 g pine nuts • 1 bunch arugula (rocket)• 3 sprigs parsley • 3 sprigs dill • 3 sprigs marjoram • 3 sprigs basil • salt • 100 ml olive oil

1   Toast the pine nuts in a dry skillet. Pour them out onto a piece of absorbent paper. Keep half for garnish.
2   Wash, dry, and trim the arugula, and crush it.
3   Wash, dry, and strip from the stem the leaves of parsley, dill, marjoram, and basil.
4   In a mortar, pound half the pine nuts until they form a puree. Add salt.
5   Gradually add arugula and herbs, continuing to pound until the mixture forms a paste. Then stir in olive oil, little by little, mixing it in with a pestle.

For the croutons
100 g French baguette • wine vinegar, for coating the baguette • olive oil, for frying

1   Cut the baguette into 3-mm slices. Spread the slices out on a baking sheet and moisten with vinegar.
2   Heat a dribble of olive oil in a skillet and fry the croutons until golden. Set them aside.

For the wild salad greens
100 g bitter salad greens • olive oil • salt

Sort, wash, and thoroughly dry the bitter salad greens. Finely chop the green part of the scallion you set aside. Put the greens and scallion together in a bowl. Season with a dribble of olive oil and a pinch of salt.

For garnish
balsamic vinegar • pepper

To serve, reheat the tripe and check the seasoning. Divide it onto plates. Add a good quantity of salad and sprinkle vinegar, croutons and reserved pine nuts on top. Add a good dash of pepper. Serve with pasta.

SALT COD IN AN HERB CRUST, WITH WHITE NAVY BEANS
Serves 4

For the navy beans
200 g fresh white navy (haricot) beans, shelled • 1 clove garlic • 1 sprig thyme • salt • 1 scallion (spring onion)

1   Put the beans in a pan. Add the garlic, crushed with the blade of a knife, and the sprig of thyme. Cover with plenty of water. Do not add salt. Simmer for 25–30 minutes until very soft. Add salt right at the end.
2   Let the beans cool, then set aside in their juice. Peel the scallion, chop, and set aside.

For the salt cod
1 (500-g) thick salt cod fillet, de-salted • 80 g unblanched almonds • 1 sprig rosemary • 1 sprig thyme • olive oil, for frying • 10 g butter • 1 preserved lemon

1   Cut 4 rectangles measuring 10 x 4 cm from the center of fillet. Bone them carefully.
2   Using a knife, chop the almonds (with their skin). Chop the rosemary. Put them both into a mixing bowl and add the thyme, stripping the leaves off the stem. Mix thoroughly.
3   Put a dribble of olive oil into a skillet and fry the pieces of cod until golden on all 4 sides.
4   Pour the contents of the mixing bowl into a skillet. Fry the mixture while basting the fish, until the almonds are slightly golden. Then add the butter and a drop of olive oil. Dice the skin of the preserved lemon and add it. Baste again.

To finish
olive oil • 2 tbsp pistou • 4 cloves preserved garlic • olive oil • pepper

1   Cover the surface of the pieces of cod with a crust of herbs.
2   Heat a dribble of olive oil in a pan. Sweat the chopped scallion for 1 minute without allowing it to brown.
3   Drain the beans and pour them into a pan. Reheat gently. Add the pistou, mixing it thoroughly, then add the preserved garlic.
4   To serve, place a piece of cod on each plate and place the beans beside it. Pour on a dribble of olive oil and add a good dash of pepper.

ZUPPA INGLESE
Serves 10

For the ladyfingers
6 eggs • 150 g sugar • 60 g superfine flour • 60 g potato flour

1   Preheat the oven to 340°F (170°C). Separate the eggs. Beat the yolks with 100 g of the sugar until the mixture becomes white. Beat the whites with the rest of the sugar.
2   Carefully mix the beaten egg whites into the yolk and sugar mixture. Sift flour and potato flour together, add them, and mix carefully.
3   Spread the mixture onto a baking sheet measuring 40 x 60 cm so that it is 2-mm thick. Bake for 12 minutes.

For the cream
500 g milk • 5 egg yolks • 70 g sugar • 30 g cornstarch (cornflour) • 1 vanilla bean • 50 g butter • 50 g rum

1   Boil the milk. Beat the yolks with sugar until the mixture becomes white. Add the cornstarch. Pour in the milk, add vanilla pod, and bring to a boil, cooking for 4 minutes. Take off the heat and add butter.
2   Leave to cool, then add the rum. Mix thoroughly. Put in a cool place.

For the Alchermes punch
250 g water • 75 g sugar • 1 liter Alchermes liqueur

Boil the water and sugar. Allow the mixture to cool, then add the Alchermes liqueur. Put in a cool place.

For the Italian meringue
100 g egg white • 135 g sugar • 10 g glucose • 45 g water

1   Using an electric whisk, start gently beating the egg whites with 35g sugar. Boil the rest of sugar, the glucose, and water to 250°F (121°C).
2   Pour this hot sugar over the whites while beating at high speed. Reduce the speed and continue to beat until the whites are warm. Pour them out and keep in a cool place.

To finish
confectioners' (icing) sugar

1   To make the zuppas, cut the ladyfinger biscuit mixture into 30 rounds measuring 10 cm in diameter.
2   Using a brush, soak both sides generously with Alchermes punch until they are colored all the way through.
3   Put the cream in a pastry (piping) bag with a 12-mm tip (nozzle).
4   Put a 1-cm layer of cream into 10-cm-diameter molds. Place a biscuit on top and cover with a layer of cream. Add another biscuit and another layer of cream. Add a third biscuit and finish with a thin layer of cream.
5   Smooth it out well, cover the molds with plastic wrap (clingfilm), and put them in the refrigerator.
6   To serve, using a spatula, cover the whole surface of each zuppa with Italian meringue. Sprinkle with confectioners' sugar. Put them under a broiler (grill) for 30 seconds, until the meringue is slightly golden. Arrange on plates.

Christophe Martin

Andrew McConnell

MENU

Bluefin tuna sashimi,
shaved calamari,
pickled cucumber,
and wasabi snow

~

Scallops, artichoke soup,
migas, and almond milk

~

Wood-grilled quail, foie
gras parfait, celery root,
and golden raisins

~

Steamed pear and suet
pudding, licorice ice
cream, and confit lemon

1 & 4
Andrew McConnell at work

2, 3 & 5
In the kitchen at Cutler and
Co.

6
Cured sausages hanging in the
wine store

Andrew McConnell was born in 1969 in Melbourne, Australia. He trained at some of the finest restaurants in the city, including Marchetti's Latin, Tansy's, and O'Connell's Hotel. His apprenticeship continued with three years at M on the Fringe, Michelle Garnaut's Hong Kong restaurant, while planning the opening of her Shanghai restaurant, M on the Bund. In 2001 he opened his first restaurant, Dining Room 211, with his brother Matthew as co-chef; a year later, the brothers shared the Young Chef of the Year Award. McConnell went on to open Three, One, Two and then, in 2008, Cumulus Inc., both equally lauded. In 2009, he opened Cutler and Co., where he continues his project of providing thoughtful fine cuisine while encouraging sustainability and a sense of participation in eating; his pheasant baked in hay and a salt crust is brought to the table, cracked, and then removed for carving, involving guests in the cooking process.

Andrew McConnell has been on the Melbourne dining scene for some time now. I first met Andrew when he opened his first restaurant with his brother in 2001. I admired his approach to food: simple, honest flavors that combine well. It reflected the man himself, as there was a tremendous amount of honesty about him—no pretend smiles and compliments, just an honest, dedicated chef.

There have been many memorable dining moments with Andrew. He opens on Sunday, my only day off, which has enabled me to watch and eat his food and track its evolution. I have found the food at his more casual eatery, Cumulus, to be most memorable, particularly the simple serving of great delicacies such as the Moonlight oysters. Then there is his combination of fresh goat's curd, smoked mackerel, and beautiful textures and colors of raw beet. Also his rework of one of my favorite classic dishes, the rum baba. A little touch of modern technique with a vanilla *espuma*, a large rum baba presoaked in beautiful syrup, then a rum bottle plonked on the table—no explanation needed!

Andrew developed into a very good chef through the guidance of Michelle Garnaut at her restaurants in Hong Kong and Shanghai. Appreciation of Chinese technique and use of such a broad array of ingredients gave Andrew a large repertoire and also the mental ability that comes from working in such a busy, foreign environment, managing a large brigade.

I feel Andrew uses his experience in China with a well-chosen restraint and pace, that doesn't try to show you everything he can do in one sitting. His food has a simplicity that would be beyond a lot of chefs.

Andrew's next exciting evolution is the introduction of his new restaurant, Cutler and Co, and the use of his delicate char grill. He takes his inspiration from Spain's famous Etxebarri, where food is grilled with delicacy and precision—not just thrown on like an old-fashioned barbecue!

Shannon Bennett

Cutler & Co./Cumulus Inc., Melbourne, Australia

BLUEFIN TUNA SASHIMI, SHAVED CALAMARI, PICKLED CUCUMBER, AND WASABI SNOW
Serves 4

For the bluefin tuna
50 g sashimi grade bluefin tuna per person

Trim and slice the tuna and keep chilled.

For the pickled cucumber
200 g sugar • 200 ml water • 2 small Lebanese cucumbers

1 Gently warm the sugar and water. When the sugar has dissolved, put mixture aside to cool.
2 Peel the cucumber, de-seed it, and cut into 1-cm pieces. Place in a vacuum-pack bag with just enough liquid to cover the cucumber. Vacuum on full strength and leave to pickle for 1 hour.

For the dill oil
1 bunch dill, blanched and squeezed out • 100 ml sunflower oil

Chop the blanched dill and blend with oil to a fine puree. Hang the puree in fine cheesecloth (muslin), and let hang until the oil is released.

For the wasabi snow
45 ml milk, plus 1 tbsp • 45 ml cream • 6 g cornstarch (cornflour) • 250 ml buttermilk • 45 ml horseradish juice • salt, to taste

Bring 45 ml milk and cream to a simmer; add 1 tablespoon cold milk to the cornstarch to make a thin paste. Whisk the cornstarch paste into the simmering milk, continue to whisk, and cook for 2 minutes until thick and glossy. Remove from the heat and gradually add the buttermilk, whisking all the while. Finally add the horseradish juice, strain, season with salt, and freeze in a Pacojet canister for 24 hours.

For the shaved calamari
1 tube fresh, cleaned calamari • 2 tbsp sunflower oil

Open the calamari by slicing along one edge, making 1 large, flat piece. Place in a vacuum-pack bag with 2 tablespoons sunflower oil. Seal the bag and cook in a hot-water bath at 150ºF (65ºC) for 30 minutes, then refresh in iced water. Remove the calamari and clean with paper towels. Lay the calamari flat and shave finely, horizontally, with a knife.

To assemble
seaweed lettuce salt • salt

Chill the plate for serving the dish. Arrange the tuna on a chilled plate and season with sea lettuce salt. Drain the pickled cucumber and toss with the calamari shavings and 1 tablespoon pickling liquid. Season with salt. Arrange the cucumber and calamari on and around the tuna, drizzle with dill oil. Puree the wasabi snow in a Pacojet and add 1 tablespoon of the fine powder to each plate.

WOOD-GRILLED QUAIL, FOIE GRAS PARFAIT, CELERY ROOT, AND GOLDEN RAISINS
Serves 4

For the quail
4 quail • 500 ml water • 2 tbsp salt • 2½ tbsp sugar • 4 juniper berries • 4 black peppercorns • 1 strip lemon zest • 1 thyme sprig • ½ clove garlic

1 Debone the quail, removing the fillets and legs separately. Remove the thigh bone from each leg, and trim any excess skin. Make a saltwater brine by bringing the water, salt, sugar, and spices to a simmer, then immediately place in the refrigerator to cool.
2 Submerge the quail in the brine for 20 minutes. Remove the quail, pat dry with paper towel, and reserve for later use.

For the golden raisin puree
100 g golden raisins

Place the raisins in a pot of boiling water. Blanch for 1 minute, strain, and puree.

For the spice mix
30 g hazelnuts, lightly roasted and peeled • 1 tsp ground allspice • 1 tsp juniper berries • ½ tsp white pepper • pinch salt • ½ tsp orange powder • 1 tbsp soft brown sugar

Blend the nuts and spices in a spice grinder, add the orange powder and sugar. Blend well, until a fine powder.

For the foie gras cigar
1 sheet homemade filo pastry or Tunisian brik pastry • 3 tbsp clarified butter

Cut the pastry into 4 x 9-cm sheets. Brush each sheet with clarified butter, wrap pastry around a 1-cm diameter steel baking rod, and cook at 325ºF (170ºC) for 8 minutes or until golden brown. Remove the pastry cigars from steel rods while still warm. Store in an airtight container.

To assemble
8 celery root (celeriac) sticks (batons) • duck fat • 18 roasted hazelnuts, peeled and halved • 4 grilled scallions (spring onions) • 12 dehydrated Brussels sprout leaves • 120 g foie gras parfait

1 Grill the quail over hot coals.
2 Meanwhile, roast the celery root in duck fat in a moderate oven, basting and turning regularly to obtain an even golden color.
3 Spread 1 tablespoon raisin puree on the base of plate; place the grilled quail and celery root on the raisin puree.
4 Scatter the hazelnuts, scallions, and Brussels sprout leaves judiciously over the quail.
5 Finally, pipe the foie gras into the cigars, arrange between the quail pieces, dust the quail with the spice mix.

STEAMED PEAR AND SUET PUDDING, LICORICE ICE CREAM, AND CONFIT LEMON
Serves 8

For the pear and suet paste
700 g whole pears, peeled and grated • zest and juice of 1 lemon • 10 pieces candied ginger, chopped • 120 g turbinado (Demerara) sugar • 8 dried pear halves, chopped • 30 g dried bread crumbs • pinch cinnamon • 100 g clean suet, grated

Mix all the ingredients well. Refrigerate for 1 hour before use.

For the pudding mixture
175 g all-purpose (plain) flour • 1½ tsp ground ginger • ½ tsp ground allspice • ½ tsp quatre-épices • 90 g almond meal • 25 g baking powder • pinch salt • 175 g suet • 90 g fresh bread crumbs • 2 eggs beaten • 100 g crystallized ginger • 3 tbsp grated fresh pear • 180 g golden syrup • 150 ml milk • butter, for greasing

1 Sift flour, spices, almond meal, baking powder, and salt into a bowl. Make a well in the center of flour mixture, add the remaining ingredients, vigorously mix by hand to incorporate.
2 Line a buttered pudding mold with parchment paper. Add 1½ tablespoons of the pudding mixture to each mold, spread out evenly. Layer the pudding mixture with 1½ tablespoons of the pear and suet paste, spread evenly. Finally, top with another 1½ tablespoons of the pudding mixture. Seal with aluminum foil and steam for 1½ hours.

For the licorice ice cream
800 ml milk • 400 ml cream • 350 g organic soft licorice • 12 egg yolks • 200 g sugar • 50 g glucose

1 Warm the milk, cream, and licorice, bring to a simmer, stirring to dissolve the licorice. Whisk together the egg yolk and sugar, pour hot licorice liquid over the egg yolk, and whisk to incorporate.
2 Return the ice cream base to stove, adding glucose, and cook until thickened. Strain and freeze in Pacojet canisters for 24 hours.

For the milk gelatin
100 ml milk • ¼ vanilla bean, split • 10 g sugar • 1 strip lemon zest • 1 leaf gelatin

Bring the milk to a simmer with the vanilla bean, sugar, and lemon zest. Add the gelatin and stir to dissolve. Leave the liquid to cool to room temperature, strain, and set in the refrigerator.

For the hazelnut powder
2 tbsp hazelnuts • 1 tbsp hazelnut oil • pinch salt • pinch sugar • 4 tbsp tapioca • 4 tbsp maltodextrin

In a food processor, blend the ingredients together to form a fine powder.

For the lemon syrup
60 ml lemon juice • 60 g soft brown sugar

Bring the lemon juice and brown sugar to a simmer, then cool to room temperature.

To assemble
In a bowl, sprinkle 1 tablespoon hazelnut powder, dice the set milk gelatin, and arrange on the hazelnut. Turn the pudding from its mold onto a bowl, and drizzle with a little lemon syrup. Serve with a quenelle of the licorice ice cream.

248

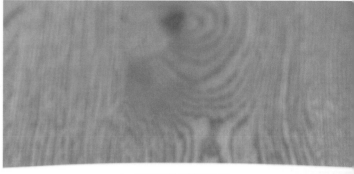

1
Bluefin tuna sashimi, shaved
calamari, pickled cucumber,
and wasabi snow

2
Wood-grilled quail, foie gras
parfait, celery root, and
golden raisins

3
Steamed pear and suet
pudding, licorice ice cream,
and confit lemon

Andrew McConnell

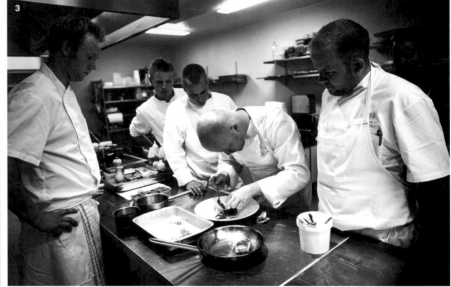

Jakob Mielcke

MENU

Scallops, hibiscus, granny smith, and ice salad
Grüner Veltliner, Hochrein, Rudi Pichler, Wachau, Austria, 2005

~

Foie gras, ao-nori, ponzu, and bull kelp
Côteaux du Loir, Domaine de Bellivière, France, 2005

~

Red mullet, celery root, miso, and fennel
Puligny-Montrachet, Les Combettes, Domaine Leflaive, France, 2002

~

Lamb, corn, rhubarb, and kelp
Blaufränkisch, Tannenberg, Hans Nittnaus, Burgenland, Austria, 2007

~

Duck, beet, apricot, and ginger
Cornas, Granit 60, Vincent Paris, France, 2006

~

Chocolate, apple, lychee, and almond
Maury, Domaine de Blanes, France, 2006

~

Carrot licorice, pineapple, coconut, and rum
Monbazillac, Cuvé de Monstres, Châteaux les Cailloux, France, 2001

~

Licorice, sea buckthorn, malt, and licorice root
Côteaux du Layon St. Lambert, René Mosse, 2007

Born in Aarhus, Denmark, in 1977, Jakob Mielcke began his career as a chef at the Restaurant Under Klippen, Holstebro, before moving a year later to Paris as head chef at La Petite Sirène. Next he moved to Pierre Gagnaire, which won its third Michelin star in 1998. There he learned the importance of the way a chef interacts with his team. In 2002 Mielcke headed to London and the Michelin-starred Sketch, before returning to Denmark as head chef at Jan Hurtigkarl & Co in Ålsgårde. In 2007 he became executive chef and co-owner of Mielcke & Hurtigkarl, a Copenhagen institution, where he supervises a monthly overhaul of the menu. Closing the restaurant completely from January until March and traveling around the globe to gain fresh inspiration, he returns every year with a fresh round of delights such as scallops with hibiscus and Jerusalem artichokes.

Jakob Mielcke is considered one of the biggest talents in Copenhagen, and perhaps even in Scandinavia, right now. His restaurant, Mielcke & Hurtigkarl, is situated in one of the most beautiful parks in Copenhagen, Frederiksberg garden. The restaurant, which Jakob runs in partnership with Jan Hurtigkarl, is an old classic in Copenhagen. Hurtigkarl's legendary father used to be the chef owner of the premises. After the father's death, Jan and Jakob took over the restaurant. After a wall-to-wall renovation working with some of the city's youngest, most modern artists, they have given this legendary restaurant a new life. Since then, Jakob's unusual talent and very "different" cuisine (for Copenhagen, that is), has already made its mark on the dining scene.

He is a chef who has traveled the world, and worked with great masters such as Pierre Gagnaire, both in his restaurants in London and in the infamous three-Michelin-starred one, in Paris. Gagnaire also seems to have had a big impact upon the style of Jakob's cuisine. A world-traveling cuisine with roots in the local *terroir*, it uses specialties from his discoveries around the globe: curry from Madras, black Indian salt, green rice from Vietnam, fresh sansho berries from Kyoto or dates from Lebanon. Everything is married together with local products—asparagus from the north of Copenhagen, vegetables from southern Denmark or wild flowers from the surrounding forests, or perhaps the best shellfish and fish from the North Sea. In music, a great mix like this could be called "world music"; Jakob's cuisine is an enthusiastic "world cuisine" without boundaries. Always playful, inventive, curious and full of life, his cuisine never stands still, and is always taking new strides into the modern.

René Redzepi

1
Scallops, hibiscus, granny smith, and ice salad

2
Foie gras, ao-nori, ponzu, and bull kelp

3
Red mullet, celery root, miso, and fennel

4
Chocolate, apple, lychee, and almond

SCALLOPS, HIBISCUS, GRANNY SMITH, AND ICE SALAD
Serves 1

For the scallops
1 scallop per person • 3 g hibiscus, powdered • 3 g salt • 4 g sugar • 1 g white pepper • 5 bunches chives • 500 ml vegetable oil

1 Remove all the intestines from the scallop. Put the intestines aside and keep cold.
2 Make a rub by combining the hibiscus, salt, sugar, and pepper in a bowl.
3 Roll the sides of the scallops in the rub and marinate for 3 hours in the refrigerator, turning halfway through.
4 Wash off the rub and dry the scallops. Cut them and place them on a plate.
5 Wash the chives and blitz them in a blender with the vegetable oil until it gets warm enough to smoke a little. Strain the oil through a cheesecloth (muslin).

For the hazelnut crumble
220 g butter • 300 g toasted hazelnuts • 300 g almond flour • 40 g all-purpose (plain) flour • 16 g salt

Melt the butter and mix with the other ingredients. Vacuum-pack the dough and put in the freezer. Cut it and bake at 275°F (140°C) on a nonstick silicone baking mat.

For the salad
ficoide glaciale • edible flowers • melon • pomegranate • applewood-smoked dulse seaweed from Maine

Make a salad from *ficoide glaciale*, edible flowers from your garden, melon, pomegranate, and dulse seaweed.

For the rosewater gelatin
1 liter rosewater extract (mild) • 100 g vanilla sugar • 5 g Gellan

Boil the rosewater extract with other the ingredients while mixing. Spread it out on a plastic sheet and cut it into a circle once set.

For the scallop ice cream
nonsweet ice cream stabilizer that works with your ice cream machine

Make a light stock with the reserved scallop intestines. Cool it and mix it with the ice cream stabilizer.

For the apple gel
200 ml green apple juice • 5 chives • corn stabilizer

Mix the juice of green apples and chives with corn stabilizer until a gel-like consistency is obtained.

To serve
In the middle of a plate, place the apple gel, covered by rosewater gelatin. Cut the scallop in half horizontally and put the 2 pieces around the gel. Garnish with the ice cream, salad, and hazelnut crumble.

FOIE GRAS, AO-NORI, PONZU, AND BULL KELP
Serves 20

For the foie gras
1.5 kg foie gras • 22 g salt • 4 g white salt • 225 ml birch alcohol • ao-nori sheets

1 Remove the veins from the foie gras. Marinate the foie gras in salt and birch alcohol overnight. Roll up in finger-thick rolls and steam at 50°F (120°C) for 20 minutes.
2 When cool, cut them into chunks and roll in the nori sheets.

For the ponzu gel
2 liters yuzu juice • 1.08 liters dark soy sauce • 1.08 liters light soy sauce • 900 ml sake • 900 ml mirin • 200 g kombu seaweed • 300 g katsuo flakes, freshly shredded • 5 g agar agar • 10 gelatin leaves

1 Heat the liquids and put in the seaweed. Cook for 10 minutes, strain, and cook with katsuo flakes. Strain again and reduce until it tastes perfect.
2 Thicken the liquid with agar agar and gelatin, let cool, and blend until it's a shiny, creamy consistency.

For the garnish
oil, for deep frying • bull kelp from Vancouver Island • raw chanterelles • fresh hazelnuts • wild raspberries • chamomile • anise • hyssop flowers

Deep-fry the bull kelp. Dress a plate with raw chanterelles, fresh hazelnuts, wild raspberries, chamomile, anise, and hyssop flowers. Place a foie gras nori roll on the plate with a small amount of ponzu gel.

RED MULLET, CELERY ROOT, MISO, AND FENNEL
Serves 1

For the dashi
5 liters water • kombu • 600 g katsuo • white Kyoto miso, as needed • 125 g butter

1 Bring the water to a boil, add the kombu and cook for 10 minutes, then strain and cook again with the katsuo for another 10 minutes. Strain again.
2 Just before serving, take 500 ml dashi and add the white Kyoto miso to taste. Add the butter, heat it, and foam with a blender.

For the mullet
100 g red mullet • dashi (recipe below)

1 Cut fillets of red mullet from the bone and make a classic tomato sauce from the bones and head of the fish.
2 Poach the red mullet fillets in the dashi just before serving.

For the celery root and artichoke
1 celery root (celeriac), the size of a fist • milk, as needed • dashi, as needed • salt, as needed • cream, for the celery root puree • sourdough bread, to serve • oil, to fry the bread • garlic, to taste • mini fennel, to serve • mini artichokes, to serve

1 Cut the celery root into cubes and cook it, covered, in milk and dashi with salt. Cut out parchment paper to make a lid for the casserole.
2 When the celery root is cooked, strain it to remove all liquid. Blitz with some of the cooking liquid and a little reduced cream.
3 Cut thin slices of sourdough bread and fry them in oil with a little garlic.
4 Blanch the mini fennel and glaze it before serving.
5 Peel the mini artichoke and cut in two. Prepare it in a classic barigoule style.

For the salad
shiso leaves • edible flowers • fresh seaweed from coast of Ireland

Mix the shiso leaves, edible flowers, and fresh seaweed.

To serve
Place the red mullet on a plate and garnish with the foamed dashi, sourdough slices, fennel, artichoke, and salad.

CHOCOLATE, APPLE, LYCHEE, AND ALMOND
Serves 30

For the chocolate ganache
600 g chocolate • 260 g butter • 240 g cream • 32 g Jägermeister

Make a ganache by combining the ingredients and heating gradually in a double boiler. Cool it in the shape of small balls.

For the dough
100 g water • 25 g white wine • 50 g egg • 40 g sugar • 120 g flour • 25 g butter • pinch salt • 50 g cocoa powder • 1 liter vegetable oil

1 Mix all the ingredients except the oil and keep cool.
2 Heat the oil to approximately 325°F (160°C). Take a ball of ganache, roll it in the dough and then fry it.

For the almonds
100 g fresh almonds • 150 ml fresh almond oil • 1 liter Malto

Grate the fresh almonds directly onto a plate. Mix the almond oil and Malto in a food processor. Fry for a minute then mix again.

For the apple-chives
20 g Gluco • confectioners' (icing) sugar, as needed • 300 ml juice of Granny Smith apples and 20 chives • 1 liter water • 5 g Algin

1 Mix the Gluco, confectioners' sugar, and juice, and leave in the refrigerator. Mix the water and Algin, then leave in the refrigerator to chill.
2 Once the ingredients are fully chilled, shape small spheres of apple-chives and put in them in the Algin until the gel is strong enough to hold sphere shape. Store the spheres in a little apple syrup.

For the Metil-lychee foam
200 g water • 3.5 g Metil • 100 g water • 100 g sugar • 140 g lychee juice • 5 gelatin leaves

1 Mix water and Metil and leave in the refrigerator for 12 hours at 40°F (4°C).
2 Make a syrup from 100 g water and 100 g sugar, then let cool.
3 Mix 175 g of the Metil mixture with 20 g lychee juice in a food processor and add syrup.
4 Heat 120 g lychee juice and melt the hydrated gelatin sheets. Cool to below 105°F (40°C) and add them to the food processor while whisking at full speed. Whisk until it has a cloudy, firm consistency.

To serve
flowers • Korean seaweed, for garnish

To serve, dress with flowers that remind you of the sea, and Korean seaweed with its vinegary taste.

I have known Russell Moore as both colleague and friend for nearly twenty-five years. There are few people in this world who can cook over an open fire as passionately as he does, with the creativity and confidence of someone who is both a talented chef and an expert bodysurfer. The food at his restaurant, Camino, is some of the most delicious and uncompromising that I know of.

Russell came to Chez Panisse when he was twenty-two and began working in the kitchens of both the downstairs restaurant and the café upstairs. When he eventually worked his way up to the position of café chef, his menus were simultaneously robust and sophisticated, and our customers loved his charcuterie. His influences include his Korean-American upbringing in Los Angeles, and he often cooks with peppers and pickles, but he feels most at home cooking over the glowing embers of an outdoor grill or an open hearth. I remember one occasion in 2006, when we cooked in Vienna for Peter Sellars's New Crowned Hope festival celebrating Mozart's 250th birthday. Russell was responsible for cooking a full menu in the 18th-century kitchen of an old castle without such modern conveniences as gas or electricity, and with only the illumination provided by candles and candelabras.

Camino is a stunning restaurant space. Customers eat family-style on long beautiful tables fashioned from storm-felled redwoods from Mendocino County in Northern California (or at private tables if they prefer). With its big iron chandeliers, heavy beams, and massive walk-in fireplace at one end of the room, Camino is rather like the warm and welcoming refectory of an order of particularly well-fed and jovial monks. The menu is short but satisfying, and everything tastes like what it is. Nearly every dish is cooked in the wood-burning oven or over the coals in the fireplace—the beating heart of the restaurant. Needless to say, Russell pays scrupulous attention to his ingredients. His sources are impeccable, and he honors them by cooking with a good-natured and almost radical simplicity.

Alice Waters

Russell Moore was born in 1963 and spent his childhood in Los Angeles, where he encountered a bewildering variety of ethnic cuisines that piqued his interest in food. In 1985 he began work with Alice Waters at Chez Panisse, cooking for both the café and the restaurant. In 1996 he started to collaborate with suppliers to create the daily lunch and dinner menus for the café, acting as a spokesperson for Chez Panisse's stance on sustainable food sourcing. In 2008 Moore opened his own restaurant, Camino, in Oakland, CA, where the daily specials are cooked on the restaurant's large, open fireplace. Moore's menu explores the boundaries of this method and his produce purchasing policy to create hearty yet sensitive dishes. Offerings such as a zingy eggplant gratin served with egg and polenta, a wood-oven-roasted sea bass with cherry tomatoes, cucumber, and yogurt, or a perfect cherry tart make Camino's menu both approachable and flawless.

MENU

Mosel gin cocktails

~

Sardines roasted in
fig leaves with cucumbers
and roasted pimientos

~

Artichokes cooked in the
coals with sheep-milk
ricotta and herb salad

~

Lamb leg à la ficelle with
braised and grilled ribs,
Merguez sausage, and
fresh shell beans

~

Roasted, stuffed figs

1
Vegetables and herbs

2
The restaurant dining room

3–6
In the kitchen at Camino

Russell Moore

255   Camino, Oakland, CA, USA

1
Sardines roasted in fig leaves with cucumbers and roasted pimientos

2
Lamb leg à la ficelle with braised and grilled ribs, merguez sausage, and fresh shell beans

3
Roasted, stuffed figs

SARDINES ROASTED IN FIG LEAVES WITH CUCUMBERS AND ROASTED PIMIENTOS
Serves 4

Sardines benefit greatly from being cooked on the bone (as most things do). They have an extremely short shelf life, so only choose to cook this dish if the sardines look pristine. The fig leaf will scent the sardines with a pleasant coconut fragrance. The fig leaves should not be eaten (they are not poisonous, just not that great to eat). At Camino we roast these in a very hot wood-burning oven. At home they can be roasted in a 500°F (260°C) oven for similar effect.

4 roasted and peeled pimientos (or red bell peppers) • 3 tbsp olive oil • salt and pepper • red-wine vinegar, homemade if possible • 4 fresh sardines • 4 fig leaves or grape leaves • 6 lemon cucumbers (or equivalent amount of best available cucumbers), thinly sliced • juice of 1 lime or lemon • a few tbsp picked marjoram leaves

1 Preheat the oven to 500°F (260°C).
2 Season and marinate the pimientos with 1 tablespoon olive oil, salt, pepper, and red-wine vinegar (at Camino we use our own vinegar for everything.) Leave for an hour or two, then roast in the oven.
3 Scale, gut, and remove the gills from the sardines, leaving the fish on the bone with the head intact. Drizzle some olive oil over them and season all over with salt and pepper.
4 Wipe the fig leaves clean with a damp cloth. Place the sardines on the fig leaves (shiny side up) and into an ovenproof baking dish or cazuela. The fig leaves will curl around the fish as they bake. The sardines are done when they are tender at the bone, about 5–8 minutes.
5 While the sardines are roasting, season the cucumbers with lime juice, 2 tablespoons olive oil, salt, and marjoram leaves.
6 When the sardines are done, place them on a plate, still on the fig leaf. Place the roasted pimientos next to them and scatter the cucumbers over everything.

LAMB LEG À LA FICELLE WITH BRAISED AND GRILLED RIBS, MERGUEZ SAUSAGE, AND FRESH SHELL BEANS
Serves 6

For the lamb à la ficelle
Cooking lamb à la ficelle requires a large fireplace or outdoor cooking area. The lamb leg also needs room to be hung by its shank with the other end of the leg 5–7.5 cm from the surface of the hearth. An alternative is to simply roast the leg in a baking dish at 400°F (200°C), turning it over every 20 minutes or so.

1 lamb leg, aitchbone removed and trimmed of excess fat • salt and pepper • 4 cloves of garlic • 60 g of mint leaves • olive oil, for the marinade

1 Liberally season the leg with salt and pepper.
2 Using a mortar and pestle, pound the garlic and mint to a paste. Stir in some olive oil and smear the mixture all over the leg. Truss the lamb with butcher's twine. The lamb should be marinated for at least 2 hours before cooking and this can be done the night before. It is important the lamb sit at room temperature for 2 hours before cooking.
3 Build a large fire half an hour before cooking the lamb. Using heavy fireplace tools, move the fire about 5 cm back from where the lamb will be hanging. Tie a length of butcher's twine to the shank of the leg and hang the leg in front of the fire. Give the lamb a good spin and let it unwind in front of the fire. The leg will unwind and wind up by itself for a few minutes and will need another good spin from time to time. Place a shallow dish of the cooked shell beans below the lamb to catch the drippings.
The secret to this method is to adjust the fire to focus its heat on the thickest part of the lamb and to make the fire hot enough to brown the leg nicely. Depending on the distance from the fire, the size of the fire, and the temperature of the lamb, roasting the leg should take from 50 minutes to 1½ hours. The leg is done when the internal meat next to the bone is about 115°F (46°C). Because of the high cooking temperature, the internal temperature of the lamb will continue to rise for a few minutes while resting.
4 Allow at least 20 minutes for the lamb leg to rest before carving.

For the braised and grilled lamb ribs
1 rack of lamb ribs, with belly attached • salt and pepper • aromatic vegetables, such as onions, celery, carrots and fennel, sautéed • white wine, for braising • about 700 ml chicken or lamb stock

1 The day before cooking, season the ribs and attached belly with salt and pepper.
2 Fold the belly over the ribs and secure with butcher's twine. Place the ribs on top of a bed of the sautéed aromatic vegetables. Pour some white wine over the ribs and add the chicken or lamb stock.
3 Put the ribs in a 400°F (200°C) oven without covering. Turn the ribs over every 20 minutes or so until they are tender at the bone. At Camino, all this happens in the morning, with just the residual heat from the night before.
4 To serve, cut chunks of the meat with the bone attached and grill over a medium fire until brown and crispy on the outside.

For the merguez sausage
900 g boneless lamb shoulder • 2 tsp cumin • 1 tsp caraway seeds • 4 or 5 medium spicy chiles (New Mexico, ancho, mulato, or some combination) • black peppercorns • 4 garlic cloves • 1 tbsp sea salt • 1 tbsp olive oil • lamb casings

1 Trim the lamb shoulder of any oxidized external fat, while leaving as much creamy-colored fat as possible.
2 Cut the lamb into 2.5-cm cubes and refrigerate while getting the spice mixture together.
3 Toast the cumin and caraway in a medium hot skillet until just beginning to smoke. Break open the chiles and knock out the seeds. Using an electric spice grinder or mortar and pestle, grind the chiles with the toasted cumin and caraway and some whole black peppercorns.
4 Peel the garlic cloves and pound to a paste with a mortar and pestle.
5 Mix the lamb cubes with the spice mixture, salt, and olive oil. Grind (mince) the meat through the medium plate of a meat grinder (mincer). Mix the meat with your hands and fry up a small patty to check for seasoning. The mixture should have slightly more seasoning than you want at this point.
6 Stuff the mixture into lamb casings and twist into links. Prick the sausages with a sharp skewer.
7 Grill the sausages over a hot fire. The sausages can remain slightly pink in the middle (there is no pork in these sausages).

For the shell beans cooked in the fire
A terracotta bean pot (olla) from Central America, Mexico, or Spain works particularly well for cooking in a fire if it has been previously soaked.

600 g fresh shelled beans, such as flageolet, cannellini, or cranberry beans • few sprigs summer savory (can substitute winter savory, thyme, or rosemary) • 2 bay leaves • 4 cloves garlic, lightly smashed • 125 ml fruity olive oil • sea salt, to taste

1 Put all the ingredients in a pot that will fit them comfortably. Add enough water to cover the beans by 1 cm. Place the pot directly on burning coals (it's fine to lean the pot against a piece of burning wood).
2 Once the water has come to a boil, adjust the position of the pot to bring the water down to a simmer. The trick is to taste frequently to gauge when the beans will be done and to correct the level of salt.
3 The beans should be cooked 15–30 minutes after the liquid comes to a boil.

ROASTED, STUFFED FIGS
Serves 5–6

175 g unsalted butter • 2 tbsp sugar, plus extra for sprinkling • 2 egg yolks • 1 tbsp all-purpose (plain) flour • pinch of salt • 130 g toasted, ground almonds • 130 g ground amaretti cookies • 1 tsp grated orange zest • 10–12 figs • fruity red wine, for drizzling • orange juice, to cover • cold cream, slightly sweetened, to serve

1 Cream the butter and sugar. Add yolks and stir to combine. Mix in all the other ingredients, except the figs, red wine, orange juice and cream.
2 Cut the tips of the figs in an X pattern, about one-third of the way down. Fill each fig with about a teaspoon of stuffing. Place the figs in an ovenproof dish, sprinkle with sugar, and drizzle with red wine and enough fresh orange juice to cover the bottom of the dish. Bake at 400°F (200°C) until puffed and browned.
3 Serve warm with slightly sweetened cold cream.

I have known Marcos's father, Pedro, for many years, and over the last four or five years Marcos has developed a great talent for cooking. In the family restaurant his father controls the managerial side while Marcos, with Pedro's support, now runs the culinary side.

The Asturias region in northwest Spain marks the starting point for this young chef. The restaurant, Casa Gerardo, has been in existence since 1882, and local Basque influences have always featured strongly in the dishes. Marcos not only wants to continue this tradition, but also to celebrate it. He still uses his grandmother's recipes, and works hard to ensure that the restaurant remains true to its roots and does not become pretentious.

In the Basque manner, Marco's main aim is to draw out and enhance the natural flavor of his ingredients. As a result, he uses only the freshest produce. Ingredients from the coast and surrounding countryside are without a doubt among the best in the world, and it is particularly pleasing to see Marcos bringing Cantabrian cooking to the level of avant-garde cuisine, and at the same time creating his own personal style.

Marcos puts a lot of passion and patience into nurturing Casa Gerardo, and ensuring its continued success. The century and more of history resting on his shoulders is a heavy responsibility, but one which, with his flair and commitment, Marcos will no doubt fulfill admirably.

Ferran Adrià

Marcos Morán was born in 1979 in Prendes, Spain, and began his career in food as a waiter at the restaurant founded by his ancestors in 1882. After attending culinary school in Gijón, Morán completed training at an array of the best restaurants in Spain, including Ca l'Isidre in Barcelona; Arzak, Fagollaga, and Zuberoa in San Sebastián; elBulli and Celler de Can Roca in Girona; Las Rejas in Cuenca; and El Poblet in Alicante, always returning to Casa Gerardo to put this varied training into practice. By 2005, Morán had worked his way up to become the restaurant's head chef. He places great emphasis on his rich culinary heritage: his grandmother's recipes and the glimpse they provide of traditional Asturias gastronomy, which his father developed with an eye on the new Basque cuisine. Morán has since brought his own influence to bear on the menu at Casa Gerardo, with a greater focus on seasonality and local sourcing.

MENU

Apple cocktail

~

Crunchy Asturias
cheese sandwich

~

Croquettes of compango

~

Anchovy with oiled cheese

~

"Muddy" oyster

~

Razor clam in almond fat

~

White argan with turnip,
asparagus, and resin
on the plate

~

Tiny peas in juice

~

Mullet liver in the sea

~

Spider-crab, head, and leg

~

Egg in consommé of
squid and eucalyptus

~

Mackerel in green moss
and crust

~

Mullet, essences,
and potato

~

Cod, Joselito dewlap
and strawberries

~

Prendes fabada
(traditonal stew of beans
and pork)

~

Apple 100%

~

Pears, wine, and walnuts

~

Creamy rice pudding

Marcos Morán

1
Marcos Morán at work

2
Joselito ham

3
The kitchen at Casa Gerardo

Casa Gerardo, Asturias, Spain

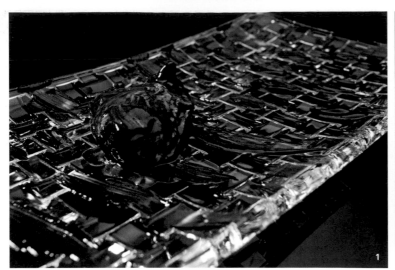

"MUDDY" OYSTER
Serves 1

For the oyster
1 Girardeau oyster
2 g pine nut oil

Vacuum-pack the oyster with the pine nut oil.

For the "mud"
30 g pine nut fat (pine nuts and pine nut oil crushed to a paste) •
1 g water • 5 g pine nut oil • salt •
5 g Macallan whisky • 15 g coffee
• 10 g brown caramel

1 Mix all the liquid ingredients and make an emulsion with the fats which resembles black mud.
2 Cook the oyster at 145°F (62°C) for 3 minutes and rest in a bowl painted with mud. Paint the oyster with mud too.

WHITE ARGAN WITH TURNIP, ASPARAGUS, AND RESIN ON THE PLATE
Serves 2

500 g turnip • 200 g argan oil • 25 g white wine • 2 g salt • 20 g Glice •
12 white asparagus spears • raw turnip, sliced, to serve • preserved lime, cut into pieces, to serve • macadamias, toasted • coprinus mushrooms, to serve • white truffle oil, to serve • onion sprouts, to serve

1 Cut the turnip into very thin slices and soak in iced water for 24 hours. Next, squeeze out the water and coat with the argan oil and wine.
2 Warm the argan oil to 140°F (60°C) and dissolve the Glice in it. Reserve.
3 Cook half the asparagus until it has a smooth texture and the other half until it cooks down and becomes a mush.
4 To serve, put the carpaccio of turnip with argan oil on a crystal plate, top with the raw turnip, pieces of lime, toasted macadamias, asparagus, coprinus, 3 drops of truffle oil, and the sprouts.

SPIDER-CRAB, HEAD, AND LEG
Serves 2

For the spider-crab
1 live spider-crab

1 Open the live spider-crab, detaching the head. Discard the water and put the head, corals, and other edible parts in a Thermomix.
2 Heat the mixture to 140°F (60°C), to facilitate the soft protein coagulation of the spider-crab for 15 minutes. Strain the juice and keep cool.
3 Remove the spider-crab legs and cook them to 175°F (80°C) for 3 minutes. Peel and reserve the meat.

For the apple
1 cider apple • sweet cider (L'Alquitara del Obispo)

1 Slice the apple and place in a vacuum-pack bag with the sweet cider. Let marinate.
2 To serve, put the legs and apple slices in a bowl and serve them with a pitcher (jug) of the natural spider-crab juice.

MACKEREL IN GREEN MOSS AND CRUST
Serves 2

For the mackerel
1 mackerel fillet, in 30-g pieces
• salt • 2 g green pistachio oil

Vacuum-pack the pieces of mackerel with a little salt and the pistachio oil.

For the green moss
1 large zucchini (courgette)
• 200 g codium seaweed

1 Boil the zucchini for 3 minutes. Peel the zucchini and take only the flesh, throwing away the skin and seeds.
2 Liquidize the codium seaweed and mix the zucchini flesh with the codium juice. Cook at 140°F (60°C) for 24 hours. The result is a green mixture with the taste of the sea and the look of moss.

For the crust
1 sea lettuce

1 Grill the sea lettuce to make a green crust.
2 To serve, cook the mackerel sous-vide at 140°F (60°C) for 3 minutes. On a dish, put a line of moss, the mackerel, and the sea-lettuce crust.

1
"Muddy" oyster

2
White argan with turnip, asparagus, and resin on the plate

3
Spider-crab, head and leg

4
Mackerel in green moss and crust

4

Marcos Morán

Hisato Nakahigashi

MENU

Gingko nuts
dressed with miso

~

Mackerel sushi

~

"Pregnant" sweetfish in
yuzu miso sauce prepared
on Japanese cedar

~

Simmered matsutake
mushrooms and eel
served in a wan bowl

~

Mixed mushrooms and
beef belly in nabe hot pot

Born in Kyoto, Japan in 1969, <u>Hisato Nakahigashi</u> is the son of Yoshitsugu Nakahigashi, a respected chef and proponent of *tsumikusa* cuisine, a unique style of cooking that uses Japanese herbs. His son Hisato has mixed this heritage with an inquiring openness to the cuisine of other cultures. He trained at culinary college in France before spending time as a waiter at a range of three-Michelin-starred restaurants throughout France. In 1993 Nakahigashi returned to Japan to train in traditional Japanese cuisine, eventually taking over the family restaurant, Miyamaso in Hanase, Kyoto, in 1995. His menu is inspired by the local culture of Hanase—the cuisine retains the flavors of the Heian period, but is updated and revitalized by the personal technique of Nakahigashi, acquired over his varied career. He continues to develop the Miyamaso brand, alongside other culinary consultation projects.

I've known Hisato Nakahigashi from the day he was born. This is because it is customary in my hometown of Kyoto for cooks to be close family friends over many generations. His father, Yoshitsugu Nakahigashi, was an outstanding chef and an expert in the field of Japanese cuisine. My respect for him continues to grow to this day. When his father suddenly passed away, Hisato was still being trained in Kanazawa—he took over the restaurant without ever having had the chance to work next to and be taught by his legendary father. It was the beginning of Hisato's struggles. Whatever he did, people would bring up his father and voice dissatisfaction. There were times when he shunned the "*tsumikusa* cuisine" that his father conceived, focusing on handpicked wild herbs and plants—though it later became synonymous with his restaurant, Miyamaso—and instead tried his hand at a more artful and urbane cuisine. He visited chefs who had known his father personally (I was one of them) and eagerly sought to be taught by them, listening to the words that could not be passed on to him by his father.

Despite its designation as "*tsumikusa* cuisine," the food that is served at Miyamaso today is not what was conceived by Yoshitsugu Nakahigashi (Hisato's father). It is the work of Hisato Nakahigashi. Miyamaso serves the abundant produce of the mountains in highly refined dishes prepared with the utmost care. Hisato has succeeded in introducing a witty, light touch to the refinement attained by his father.

Yoshihiro Murata

1
Hisato Nakahigashi
picking mushrooms

2
Various mushrooms

3–5
Preparing mackerel for sushi

6
Gingko nuts

Miyamaso, Kyoto, Japan

1
Gingko nuts dressed with miso

2
Mackerel sushi

3
"Pregnant" sweetfish in yuzu
miso sauce prepared on
Japanese cedar

4
Simmered matsutake
mushrooms and eel served
in a wan bowl

5
Mixed mushrooms and beef
belly in nabe hot pot

GINGKO NUTS DRESSED WITH MISO
Serves 15

30 g dried shiitake mushrooms • 100 g ginger • 60 g salad oil • 1 kg red miso • 50 g sugar • 200 g gingko nuts • hoba leaf (Japanese large-leaf magnolia), dried

1 Soak the dried shiitake in water to rehydrate, then chop finely.
2 Grate the ginger.
3 Put the oil into a pan and fry the shiitake and ginger. Add the red miso and sugar, and keep mixing at low heat until the color changes.
4 Peel off the hard shell of the gingko nuts. Boil them and remove the thin skin.
5 Light a small coal stove, place a dried hoba leaf on top, and heat the boiled gingko nuts and miso mixture on it.

MACKEREL SUSHI
Serves 4

For the pickled ginger
50 g young fresh ginger • salt • 100 ml vinegar • 50 ml water • 50 g sugar

Slice the young ginger and boil it lightly. Drain it in a colander, lightly salt, and remove the excess water. Make a sweet vinegar (amazu) by mixing the vinegar, water, and sugar and immerse the ginger in it.

For the mackerel
1 mackerel • salt (10% of weight of mackerel)

Cut the mackerel into fillets, sprinkle with salt, and let it stand in the refrigerator for half a day.

For the pickling vinegar (tzukezu)
200 g rice vinegar • 100 g sugar

Mix the vinegar and sugar. Thoroughly remove all excess water from the salted mackerel and immerse in the tsukezu for about 2 hours. Take the mackerel out of the tsukezu and set aside for about 2 hours.

For the sushi rice
200 ml water • 20 g vinegar • 4 g salt • 16 g sugar • 200 g sushi rice, cooked • 10 g white sesame seeds, roasted and finely chopped (kirigoma) • 50 leaves kinome (young leaves of Japanese pepper or sansho), for garnish

1 Make the dressing for sushi rice by mixing the water, vinegar, salt, and sugar.
2 Cool down the rice immediately after it has been cooked by fanning it while cutting the vinegar dressing and kirigoma into it, trying not to break the rice grains.
3 Peel the thin outer skin off the mackerel, cut it into 15-mm wide slices, and make a cut in the middle of each slice.
4 Lightly form a round shape with about 6 g sushi rice, insert it into the mackerel, and garnish with kinome.

"PREGNANT" SWEETFISH IN YUZU MISO SAUCE PREPARED ON JAPANESE CEDAR
Serves 10

10 "pregnant" sweetfish (komochi ayu) • salt, for marinating • 300 ml sake • 150 ml mirin • 100 ml soy sauce • 200 g tsubu-miso • sudachi juice • 1 yuzu, sliced • 20 Japanese cedar (sugi) boards • bamboo strings, as appropriate • 2 sudachi

1 Cut the head and tail off the "pregnant" sweetfish and marinate it for 2 hours in water with 3% of its weight in salt added. Drain in a sieve and remove the excess water.
2 Mix the sake, mirin, soy sauce, and tsubu-miso. Squeeze the sudachi juice into it and add the yuzu slices. Immerse the sweetfish into the miso mixture and leave for 3 days.
3 Remove the miso thoroughly from the sweetfish and char-grill it. Sandwich it between Japanese cedar boards, bind with bamboo strings, and cook it for 10 minutes in an oven preheated to 350°F (180°C) to transfer the aroma of the Japanese cedar to the fish.
4 Place the sweetfish on a plate and garnish with the sudachi.

SIMMERED MATSUTAKE MUSHROOMS AND EEL SERVED IN A WAN BOWL
Serves 1

130 ml first-brewed (ichiban) dashi • yuzu rind • 25 g eel • salt • 50 g matsutake (pine mushrooms) • pale ½ tsp light soy sauce • sake, to taste • yellow chrysanthemum petals, to serve

1 Make the dashi with dried kelp and dried bonito shavings.
2 Cut the yuzu rind into small pine leaf shapes.
3 Cut the eel open, slice the bones and meat (honegiri technique, leaving the skin intact), and sprinkle with salt.
4 Char-grill the eel and matsutake until crisp. Tear the matsutake in half with your hands.
5 Put the dashi into a pan, season with salt, light soy sauce, and sake to make a soup base.
6 Place the matsutake, eel, and yuzu rind in a bowl, pour the soup base into it, and sprinkle with chrysanthemum petals.

MIXED MUSHROOMS AND BEEF BELLY IN NABE HOT POT
Serves 5

1 kg beef belly • 1.5 liters water • 1 liter sake, plus 100 ml • 160 ml soy sauce • 100 g sugar • 2 broiled (grilled) leeks • 30 g ginger • 1 star anise • 200 g maitake mushrooms • 200 g shimeiji mushrooms • 200 g nametake mushrooms • 100 g daikon • dashi, made with bonito and kombu • salt • light soy sauce, to season • mirin, to season • 1 leek, julienned • kuzu, to thicken

1 Truss the beef belly with cooking string and brown it in a pan.
2 Put the beef belly into a pressure cooker with the water and sake and cook for around 90 minutes.
3 Cool the beef down and remove the fat that floats on the surface. Transfer the meat into a sieve and pour hot water over it.
4 Put 700 ml of the beef cooking liquid from which the fat has been removed, the soy sauce, sugar, 100 ml sake, the leeks, ginger, star anise, and the prepared beef belly into a pan and braise for 3 hours at 250°F (120°C).
5 Boil the mushrooms lightly and drain.
6 Cut the daikon into fairly large chunks and cook in a second-brewed dashi (niban dashi) seasoned with salt, light soy sauce, and mirin.
7 Cut the leeks into julienne strips.
8 Put the prepared mushrooms and daikon with the soup into a nabe pot. Slowly add the sauce from the braised beef to adjust the flavor. Once the flavor is correct, add the kuzu to thicken, then add the beef to reheat it. Garnish with the julienned leek.

Hisato Nakahigashi

I "rediscovered" Motokazu about three years ago. Of course, I knew about his restaurant Nakamura, an establishment that opened its doors 200 years ago, but I had not visited it for a long while. I did not think that it offered anything in particular that made a visit imperative at the time.

It was the French chef Pascal Barbot who made me aware that the cuisine served at Nakamura was indeed exceptional. I was astonished! I used to think Pascal's cuisine and that of Nakamura as being diametrically opposed. Frankly, I did not think that there was any originality in Nakamura's cuisine.

The food prepared by Motokazu is not by any means unfamiliar at first sight. The sake-marinated broiled tilefish and the white miso zoni soup prepared generation after generation have not changed in appearance. They do, however, taste superbly good and new.

Motokazu seeks ingredients of the highest quality and makes the most of the characteristics of each through simple cooking techniques. It is common practice to prepare the white miso zoni soup by mixing white miso into dashi and adding seasoning. Motokazu, however, does not use dashi. He cooks the miso with water for hours. He does not even add seasoning. Despite that, the result is stunningly exquisite.

Yoshihiro Murata

Born in Kyoto in 1962, Motokazu Nakamura was a novice when he underwent *unsui* training at Tenryu-ji, the head temple of the Rinzai school. The mindful approach to cuisine imparted in that early teaching remains strong today; Nakamura still bases his avoidance of waste and respectful relationship with suppliers on the tenets he learned at Tenryu-ji. After further training at the Soden Kyo no Aji restaurant, he became owner of Nakamura restaurant, Kyoto, in 2006. Nakamura aims to uphold the tradition of *isshi soden*, the handing down of recipes to successive generations. Bringing the best from ingredients, while respecting the increase in global consciousness of healthy eating, dovetails perfectly with Nakamura's instinct for restrained presentation— guests are encouraged to eat the meat of the marinated tilefish before dousing it with dashi to create a broth, a considerate way of eating that was popular when Kyoto was the capital of Japan.

MENU

Gazami crab
and salmon roe dressed
in grated daikon

~

White miso mustard
zoni soup

~

Seared tilefish and
pike eel, matsutake
mushrooms, with mixed
seasonal vegetables
in vinegar

~

Kumo-nishiki plate
with mackerel sushi,
pickled young ginger,
candied Tanba chestnut,
Kurama-style "pregnant"
sweetfish, lemon pot
with fermented squid and
sweetfish, abalone and
turnip skewer, and
miso-pickled sea bream
and shrimp skewer

~

Conger eel and turnip
surinagashi soup

~

Sake-marinated broiled
sweetfish, warm sake,
kelp dashi

~

Steamed sticky rice with
mullet roe in sauce

~

Daishiro persimmon with
tea jelly and lemon scent

Motokazu Nakamura

1
Outside Nakamura restaurant

2–4
Motokazu Nakamura in the kitchen

5
Fish on the grill

267   **Nakamura, Kyoto, Japan**

1
Gazami crab and salmon roe
dressed in grated daikon

2
Mackerel sushi

3
Conger eel and turnip
surinagashi soup

4
Steamed sticky rice with
mullet roe in sauce

GAZAMI CRAB AND SALMON ROE DRESSED IN GRATED DAIKON

1 gazami crab (Japanese blue crab) • 2 tbsp salmon roe pickled in soy sauce • 1 piece daikon (mooli), 5-cm long • citrus vinegars, to taste • Japanese wild parsley (*mitsuba*), for garnish • vinegar • soy sauce

1   Select a fresh crab and steam it over high heat for 15 minutes with the belly side down and for 10 minutes with the shell side down.
2   Select high quality salmon roe (*ikura*) pickled in soy sauce (the skin of each egg should be tight but soft and the contents are glutinous).
3   Grate the daikon, rinse it and mix it with several types of citrus vinegars.
4   Place the meat of the crab and the salmon roe onto a plate, cover with grated daikon and finely chopped Japanese wild parsley (*mitsuba*). Pour in vinegar mixed with the same amount of soy sauce (*nibaizu*).

MACKEREL SUSHI

1 fatty mackerel • salt, to cover • vinegar, to cover • 150 g uncooked rice • 2 tbsp rice vinegar • sake, to taste • ¾ tbsp sugar• salt, to taste • pickled ginger, for garnish

1   Rinse the mackerel with water, slit open along the back, cover with a generous amount of salt and let it stand for a day.
2   Cut the mackerel in half and remove all the bones.
3   Immerse the mackerel in vinegar with the skin side down for 10 minutes, turn it over and let it stand for 5 more minutes.
4   Place the mackerel on an inclined cutting (chopping) board to drain the vinegar (about 30 minutes).
5   Meanwhile, cook 150 g rice and allow it to stand for about 15 minutes.
6   To make seasoned rice vinegar, put the rice vinegar, sake, sugar, and salt into a pan and mix over low heat to dissolve all ingredients.
7   Put the rice into a wooden barrel, making a mountain shape. Pour the rice vinegar over it and swiftly and thoroughly cut the vinegar into the rice with a rice paddle. Cover the rice with a wet cloth and let stand for 15 minutes. Change the cloth and let stand until the rice cools down.
8   Make bar shapes with the rice, the same shape as the mackerel pieces.
9   Rip the thin skin off the mackerel.
10 Place it onto a wet cloth with the skin side down and make a rectangular shape.
11 Place the pickled ginger and the sushi rice over the mackerel, wrap up with a wet cloth and shape the sushi with a bamboo-woven mat.
12 Cut it into slices and serve on a dish.

CONGER EEL AND TURNIP SURINAGASHI SOUP

1 fatty conger eel • tamari soy sauce • prepared wheat gluten (*awafu*) • mirin • Japanese broth (*suimono*) • turnip • turnip leaves• dried wood-ear mushrooms • kuzu, to thicken • sea urchin roe, to garnish • wasabi, to garnish

1   Select a live, fresh and fatty conger eel. Pin it down, open it up, glaze with tamari soy sauce and broil (grill).
2   Deep-fry the *awafu*. Add mirin to the (*suimono*) base and bring to a boil.
3   Peel away the thick layers off the turnip's surface, grate using a fine grater and remove excess water by placing the grated turnip on paper towels to drain.
4   Boil the turnip leaf and puree with a food processor.
5   Reconstitute the wood-ear mushrooms in water and finely chop them.
6   Place the broiled (grilled) conger eel, *awafu*, and wood-ear mushrooms in a steam cooker and steam.
7   Cook the grated turnip and pureed turnip leaves in the *suimono* in separate saucepans and thicken with kuzu.
8   Put the broiled eel, *awafu*, and mushrooms into a bowl, pour in the grated turnip followed by the pureed turnip leaves. Garnish with sea urchin roe and wasabi.

STEAMED STICKY RICE WITH MULLET ROE IN SAUCE

Sticky rice • mullet roe • tea • dashi seasoned with pale soy sauce and salt • kuzu, to thicken • turnip leaves • dried wood-ear mushrooms • sudachi juice • koro-yuzu zest

1   Soak the sticky rice in water for an hour, then cook it.
2   Slice the mullet roe into 1-mm slices.
3   Toast tea in a pan until fragrant to make *hoji-cha* (roasted tea).
4   Make some dashi, season it with pale soy sauce and salt, put the roasted tea into it, let infuse, then strain the contents.
5   Add the kuzu to the dashi mixture to thicken and squeeze the sudachi juice into it.
6   Put the sticky rice into a bowl, place mullet roe over it and pour the thickened sauce over it. Sprinkle with a little koro-yuzu zest.

Motokazu Nakamura

I first tasted Akhtar's cooking at Craft in New York City. Having worked under the tutelage of great chefs like Loretta Keller in San Francisco and Tom Colicchio in New York, Akhtar's cooking was brilliant and focused—his dishes really shone. Craft gave him the perfect platform to work with an extensive menu and really show people the depth of his studies in flavor.

Akhtar first learned about the subtleties of spices from his mother, who also gave him an appreciation for rustic and home cooking. Now at Elettaria he has exceeded all expectations and opened up what will be the first of many great restaurants on the block. And since it is just steps away from my home I have the privilege of tasting his dishes all the time. He never fails to thrill me with his use of Indian flavors and his unusual, but always excellent, twist on classic dishes. Akhtar is proud of his heritage and it shows. The crab resala is the signature dish at Elettaria and it perfectly exemplifies the ideology of the restaurant. The dish is based on a typical stew from northern India, which is usually made with lamb or chicken. Akhtar uses rich crab meat rather than lamb and warms the meat in a beurre blanc sauce that has been given the Nawab touch by adding onion puree and turmeric to the sauce. The flavors work as a whole, and emphasize the rustic elements of Indian cuisine that Akhtar finds fascinating, updated with Western flourishes.

He welcomes the opportunity to show his customers the nuances and flavors that they may have never heard of (and might be resistant to try just based on the name). His lamb is enhanced by kalonji, a spice often used in naan bread, and he presents gnocchi with mushrooms and bacon spiced with fenugreek. These examples illustrate the genius of his cooking—adding innovative flavor to dishes we are comfortable with. Akhtar's never-tiring mind and spare use of white noise makes his food a must-eat on my list of favorite haunts.

Mario Batali

Born in 1972 in Louisville, Kentucky, Akhtar Nawab says his earliest food experiences were the traditional Indian meals cooked by his mother. These sparked an interest in food that led him to the California Culinary Academy. From there he moved to San Francisco restaurant Bizou, where he worked under Loretta Keller. This proved an important foundation in technique and allowed Nawab to develop his own style. He later pursued further training at Jardinière and La Folie, moving to New York in 1998 to work for Tom Colicchio at Gramercy Tavern. In 2001 he assisted Colicchio in opening the much-lauded Craft, spending a year as sous-chef there. Next he moved to Craftbar, where he was chef de cuisine and later executive chef. In February 2008, Akhtar opened his own restaurant, Elettaria, in Manhattan's West Village, where his dishes seek pairings between pure ingredients and the spices that complement their flavor. The result? Innovative palettes of tastes in which salsify is matched with fenugreek, or *kuri* squash with sumac.

MENU

**Crab resala,
Parisian gnocchi,
basil seeds, and turmeric
and onion soubise**
Nicolas Ulacia e Hijos,
Txakolina, Basque,
Spain, 2007

~

**Day boat scallops,
pork belly, soybeans,
and radish salad**
Domaine Labbé,
Vin de Savoie Mondeuse,
France, 2005

~

**Berkshire pork ribs,
garam masala,
cucumbers, and yogurt**
Anima Negra, AN/2,
Mallorca, Spain, 2005

~

**Halibut, tapioca, and
pea leaves**
Dr Konstantin Frank,
Rkatsiteli, Finger Lakes,
New York, USA, 2006

~

**Bavette, chanterelles,
salsify, and bacon**
D'Arenberg, Laughing
Magpie, McLaren Vale,
Australia, 2005

~

**Guinea hen, truffled
ricotta agnolotti, and
parsnips**
Sandro Fay, Sforzato,
Lombardy, Italy, 2005

Akhtar Nawab

1
Akhtar Nawab at the
farmers' market

2
Elettaria dining room and
open kitchen

3
Nawab finishing a dish

1
Crab resala, Parisian gnocchi,
basil seeds, and turmeric and
onion soubise

2
Day boat scallops, pork belly,
soybeans, and radish salad

3
Bavette, chanterelles, salsify,
and bacon

CRAB RESALA, PARISIAN GNOCCHI, BASIL SEEDS, AND TURMERIC AND ONION SOUBISE
Serves 4

For the crab
1 (450-g) peekytoe crab, picked through for bits of shell • salt

Boil the crab in salted water.

For the beurre blanc
2 shallots, finely chopped • 125 ml vinegar • 125 ml white wine • 60 g butter, diced

1 Put the shallots, vinegar, and wine in a pan. Bring to a boil and simmer until reduced by 90%.
2 Whisk in the butter, a piece at a time, to achieve a smooth sauce. Strain.
3 Add the cooked crabmeat to the beurre blanc and warm gently.
4 Using a slotted spoon, remove the crabmeat, draining most of the butter.

For the Parisian gnocchi
175 ml water • 85 g butter • 150 g all-purpose (plain) flour • 3 eggs, beaten • 2 tbsp basil seeds

1 Put the water and butter in a pan. When the butter has melted, add all the flour and stir vigorously. Cook for at least 10 minutes on low heat, stirring often.
2 When the flour smells cooked, take the pan off the heat. Stir in the eggs, one at a time. When fully incorporated, add the basil seeds.
3 Let the dough cool for 20 minutes.
4 Put the dough into a pastry (piping) bag. Over a large pot of boiling salted water, cut the gnocchi from the pastry bag. Cook until they float to the surface. Transfer the gnocchi to an ice bath to cool.
5 Remove from the water and dry on paper towels.
6 Place in a medium pan and roast until well caramelized.

For the onion soubise
120 g butter • ½ tsp ground coriander • 1 tbsp turmeric • 1 onion, julienned • ½ tsp arborio rice • 1 tbsp whole yogurt • fried herbs

1 Heat the butter in a large pan and when foaming add the coriander and the turmeric, then the onions and the rice. Sweat, covered, until soft.
2 Add the yogurt and cook for 10 minutes more.
3 Pour the onion mixture into a blender and puree until smooth. Pass through a chinois.

For serving
1 Pour a small amount of the soubise into a bowl, sufficient to cover the bottom of the bowl.
2 Spoon crabmeat and gnocchi into the bowl and garnish with fried herbs.

DAY BOAT SCALLOPS, PORK BELLY, SOYBEANS, AND RADISH SALAD
Serves 4

For the scallops
450 g large day boat scallops • salt and pepper • 2 tbsp olive oil • 2 tbsp butter

1 Season the scallops with salt and pepper.
2 In a medium cast-iron pan add 2 tablespoons olive oil then add the scallops.
3 Caramelize over medium to high heat until scallops are evenly brown.
4 Add the butter and as it melts, baste the scallops until cooked medium.
5 Reserve the cooked butter for the radish salad.

For the pork
475 ml water • 200 g sugar • 120 g salt • 4 sprigs thyme • 1 tbsp peppercorns • 1 chile • 1 fresh pork belly • oil or butter, for caramelizing • 1 carrot, cut into pieces • 1 stick celery, cut into pieces • 1 onion, cut into pieces • 1 liter chicken stock

1 Put the water, sugar, salt, thyme, peppercorns, and chile in a large pan and bring to a boil. Cool, then add the pork. Let sit in the brine for 3 hours.
2 Preheat the oven to 275°F (140°C).
3 In another large pan, caramelize the carrot, celery, and onion. Add the chicken stock and bring to a boil. Add the pork, cover, and braise until tender. It will take about 4 hours.
4 Remove and cool. Peel off the skin and portion the meat.

For the soybean puree
2 shallots, chopped • 4 tbsp olive oil • 1 tbsp butter • 225 ml chicken stock • 225 g fresh soybeans, peeled

1 Sweat the shallots with the olive oil and butter in a medium pan. Add the chicken stock and simmer. When reduced by half, add the soybeans. Simmer until tender. Cool the mixture.
2 When completely cool, transfer to a blender and puree.

For the radish salad
2 radishes, sliced thin on a mandolin • 1 tbsp sherry vinegar • 1 tbsp finely chopped chives • 2 sprigs chervil, picked • 4 tbsp fresh boiled soybeans • 2–5 cm piece of horseradish

1 Put the butter reserved from the scallops, radishes, vinegar, chives, chervil, and boiled soybeans into a bowl and gently toss all ingredients.
2 Grate horseradish over the salad.

For serving
Place 2 scallops on a plate accompanied by 2 tablespoons of soybean puree, some of the pork belly, and the radish salad.

BAVETTE, CHANTERELLES, SALSIFY, AND BACON
Serves 6

For the bavette steak
700 g bavette (skirt or flank) steak, trimmed • salt and pepper • 60 ml olive oil • 4 sprigs thyme • 120 g butter

1 Season the meat with salt and pepper.
2 Heat the oil in a heavy pan until medium hot. Add the beef and caramelize on all sides, then add the thyme and the butter.
3 Lower the heat and cook gently, basting often, until the meat is just warmed all the way through. Use a cake tester to check for doneness.
4 When cooked, remove from the pan and let rest.

For the salsify
10 stalks salsify, peeled • 225 ml white wine • 4 sprigs thyme • 120 ml olive oil • 120 g butter • 2 tbsp ground fenugreek • juice of 3 lemons

1 Put the salsify in a large pan with the wine, thyme, half the olive oil, and enough water to cover. Bring to a simmer slowly and cook until tender. Remove and cool.
2 When cool enough to handle, slice the stalks in half lengthwise and again lengthwise, to produce 4 quarters.
3 Remove 2.5 cm from each end of the salsify and reserve.
4 Slice the rest into 5-cm sticks (batons). Put the remaining oil in a skillet and add the sticks, fenugreek, and lemon juice. Let caramelize, taking care not to move the sticks too early. When browned, add the butter, and when it is foaming and brown stir the sticks. With a slotted spoon, lift out and drain away the butter.

For the salsify puree
225 ml milk • 1 bay leaf • 2 cloves garlic • 2 tbsp olive oil

1 Put the reserved salsify ends in a large pan. Add the milk, bay leaf, and garlic. Simmer until tender.
2 Transfer to a blender and puree. While the blender is running, add the olive oil to make a smooth emulsion.

For the chanterelles
60 g butter • 275 g chanterelle mushrooms, cleaned

1 Heat the butter in a skillet and when foaming, add the mushrooms.
2 Cook until slightly crisp and deeply caramelized.

For serving
Place the bavette steak on a plate, on top of a bed of salsify puree, salsify sticks, and chanterelles.

Akhtar Nawab

Davide Oldani

MENU

Caramelized onion with
hot and cold Parmesan

~

Bread, black pepper,
Marsala wine, and
fluffy rice

~

Ox tongue and tomatoes
"pizzaiola"

~

Curdled milk, D'O caviar,
and asparagus

~

Fruit and beet ravioli
with mascarpone, and
green tea ice cream

~

D'O coffee

4

1–3
Davide Oldani in the kitchen

4
Laying place settings at D'O

Born near Milan in 1967, Davide Oldani attended hotel college, and was hired right after graduation by Gualtiero Marchesi. Oldani later worked under Albert Roux at Le Gavroche in London and Alain Ducasse at Louis XV in Monte Carlo, emerging with a technical and intuitive understanding of fine cuisine. He went on to develop his experience through food and beverage consultation work for various multinational companies, raising the international profile of Italian food. In 2003 Oldani returned to Italy to open his own restaurant, D'O, which quickly received its first Michelin star. Oldani aspires to make excellent Italian cooking accessible to all by using ingredients that are in season, which also guarantees the best flavor. Oldani has created a menu that evokes surprise and delight by celebrating contrasting flavors, limiting the use of fat, and teasing the best from basic ingredients to create a fine dining experience for everyone.

With an unquestionable knack for a telling turn of phrase, Davide often says that he does "pop food." But behind the expression there is an exciting reality. To start with, history seems to be repeating itself. After working for a time with the great Italian chef Gualtiero Marchesi, Davide traveled the world for many years. He discovered many different types of cooking and acquired solid skills. Then, one fine day, he felt the need to return to Italy. He went back to Marchesi, this time as sous chef, and eventually decided to set up his own restaurant in Cornaredo, the little town where he was born, near Milan.

So he was back where he had come from. But without any nostalgia. On the contrary, he had the firm intention of using his great skill to develop a new approach. He is convinced that good cooking is not a question of money: You must be able to cook the humble onion with as much talent as you can the illustrious lobster. In other words, good cooking must be accessible to as many people as possible—popular, or "pop," as he likes to say. If this approach was only about economics, it would hardly be of interest to a chef like me. In fact, it has led him to explore new, completely original pathways.

Above all, Davide has brought back into favor meats and fish that are rarely seen in high-class restaurants. Cod, sardines, and anchovies are welcomed, and veal tongue is prepared with skill. Kidneys, tripe, and lamb's fries are given pride of place.

Davide's cooking provides a lesson to ponder. Top-class cooking and family cooking are generally perceived as being poles apart, but in fact they have to interact. They have much to say to each other on techniques and ingredients. Using the most sophisticated techniques with the humblest ingredients allows new flavors to be discovered, providing gourmets with the utmost pleasure every day.

Alain Ducasse

D'O, Milan, Italy

1
Caramelized onion with hot
and cold Parmesan

2
Bread, black pepper, Marsala
wine, and fluffy rice

3
Ox tongue and tomatoes
"pizzaiola"

CARAMELIZED ONION WITH HOT AND COLD PARMESAN
Serves 4

For the onions
2 onions, approximately 10 cm in diameter

Cut the onions in half and cook them in a steam oven. Dry thoroughly when cool.

For the quick puff pastry dough
50 g '00' all-purpose (plain) flour • 50 g unsalted butter • 2 g salt • 10 ml cold water

1 Mix together all the ingredients.
2 Roll out on a floured board, fold the pastry over itself, then turn through 90°, roll it out again, and repeat a total of 6 times. After the second and fourth turns put the dough in the refrigerator, covered with plastic wrap (clingfilm), for 30 minutes.
3 Roll out the pastry to a thickness of 2 mm, cut it into 8-cm squares and pierce them with a cutting wheel. Keep refrigerated.

For the crystallized sugar
125 g superfine (caster) sugar • 60 g unsalted butter

1 Cook the sugar with the butter over low heat for 5 minutes.
2 Let it cool, then pour off the excess whey.

For the hot and cold Parmesan cream
500 ml milk • 5 g salt • 15 g superfine (caster) sugar • 150 g Parmesan cheese, grated • 5 g cornstarch (cornflour), mixed in a little cold water

1 Bring the milk, salt, and sugar to a boil. Remove from the heat, and add the Parmesan. Blend at top speed for 4 minutes, then strain and let cool.
2 Work half the sauce into a thick cream in an ice cream maker and thicken the rest to a creamy consistency in a pan over gentle heat with the cornstarch. Keep warm.

To finish
Maldon salt

1 Preheat the oven to 350°F (180°C).
2 Place 18 g crystallized sugar in each individual mold and top with an onion half, cut side downwards.
3 Cover with pastry and bake for approximately 35 minutes.
4 Turn onto plates, sprinkle with a pinch of Maldon salt, and cover with some of the hot sauce and a spoonful of the thick chilled Parmesan cream.

BREAD, BLACK PEPPER, MARSALA WINE, AND FLUFFY RICE
Serves 4

For the rice
320 g Carnaroli risotto rice • 2 liters hot salted water • 160 g unsalted butter • 80 g Parmesan cheese, grated • 10 ml white-wine vinegar • 1 g salt

1 Lightly toast the rice in a heavy pan, then cook it on low heat for about 30 minutes by ladling the salted water over it little by little, stirring constantly.
2 Off the heat, add the butter, Parmesan, and white-wine vinegar. Add salt to taste and keep it fluffy.

For the bread
30 g unsalted butter • 150 g fresh bread crumbs • 20 g Parmesan cheese, grated • 1 g salt

1 Melt the butter in a skillet, add the bread crumbs and let them brown.
2 Off the heat, mix in the Parmesan. Add salt if necessary.

For the sauce
50 g Marsala wine syrup, reduced from 400 ml Marsala wine • 2 g cornstarch (cornflour), mixed in a little cold water • 80 g unsalted butter

Heat the reduced Marsala wine, mix with the cornstarch paste and whisk in the butter.

To serve
1 g freshly ground black pepper

Place the rice in bowls and top with a twist of ground black pepper, a spoonful of the bread crumbs, and the Marsala sauce.

OX TONGUE AND TOMATOES "PIZZAIOLA"
Serves 4

For the tongue
1 kg ox tongue • 1.5 liters water, for boiling • 50 g onion, chopped • 50 g carrot, diced • 50 g celery, chopped • salt • sunflower oil, for pan-frying

1 Boil the tongue with the vegetables in the water for about 3 hours.
2 Drain the tongue, peel it, sprinkle it with salt, then roll it in plastic wrap (clingfilm) to make a cylinder shape.
3 Cool in a rapid-cooling unit, then cut it into slices 3 cm thick.
4 Heat a little sunflower oil in a large skillet and brown the slices on both sides.

For the tomatoes
5 tomatoes (300 g), skinned and seeded • 1 g salt • 10 g extra-virgin Ligurian Taggiasca olive oil • 20 g baby capers in salt, rinsed • 8 g fresh oregano leaves

Chop the tomatoes into irregular, medium-size pieces and dress with the salt, the olive oil, the capers, and the oregano

For the sauce
180 g reduced veal stock • 5 g cornstarch (cornflour), mixed in a little cold water • 20 g unsalted butter • 60 g sweet-and-sour syrup, made by reducing 100 g white-wine vinegar with 50 g sugar • salt, to taste

In a pan over medium-low heat, blend the veal stock with the cornstarch and the butter, add the sweet-and-sour syrup, and season with salt to taste.

To serve
Arrange the slices of tongue in the center of a plate, top them with the dressed tomatoes, and pour the sauce over the top.

Davide Oldani

Gustav Otterberg

MENU

Mackerel and raw shrimp
from Captain Mikeal on
the ship *Kennedy*
of Björkö

~

Clams and oysters
from Vilsund

~

Perch from Ängsö Island

~

Entrecôte from
an Uppland farm

~

Rhubarb from Gotland

1 & 2
Gustav Otterberg
at work

3
Fresh ingredients
at Leijontornet

Gustav Otterberg was born in Växjö, Sweden, in 1982. Through early training and inspiration from chefs such as Noma's René Redzepi, Otterberg has risen to become head chef at Leijontornet in Stockholm, bringing the restaurant to increased prominence and gaining a Michelin star in 2008. Traditional skills play a great part in Otterberg's aim to contribute to a modern Nordic cuisine. Creating a meal in January purely from locally sourced produce takes patience and flair, with no opportunity to fall back on typical staples (tomatoes, for instance, are banned). Otterberg regularly consults his nonagenarian grandmother to revive traditional culinary techniques, varying the menu with foraged foods and perfecting his preservation of summer fruits to tide him over the winter. Often the charm of Otterberg's cuisine lies in pleasures that are simple and unexpected, such as his home-churned butter.

Gustav Otterberg is the up-and-coming comet on the Swedish dining scene. Still in his twenties, and already having a Michelin star, his Swedish interpretation of the Nordic cuisine is something to look out for. Add to this, the fact that he is also a father to a daughter, and he has already achieved more than most people dream of.

Gustav is half forager, half chef—or perhaps half beast, half man. Every day before work he stops in a local forest or park to see what nature has come up with during the last twenty-four hours. Have the ramson onions started to flower? Have the wild pea shoots started to sprout? What other wild plants, roots, and berries will he have to marry with his homemade blood sausage, the terrine of eel, the bleekroe, the white asparagus, the potatoes dug up the same morning—or will it all be served with the cooked pigs head?

As it has been said many times before that chefs and restaurants cook whatever is in season. Here, at Gustav's restaurant Leijontornet, this is taken to the extreme. For him and his staff in the kitchen, a carrot is not just a carrot. A carrot has an early season, a mid season, and a late harvest season where it shows its different qualities and textures—and reveals its true nature. And the kitchen uses all these different phases to express just that.

Gustav's restaurant, like Noma, relies almost solely on the small farmers and producers from the local region, because he has restricted himself to only using products from this area. Therefore, his close relationship with farmers, gatherers, fishermen, etc. is essential for his cuisine. When you have this type of relationship with your producers you can only allow yourself to do so much with their products. When you know how much they put into their work, you can never manipulate it too much. This is something you really feel in Gustav's cuisine: respect, purity, humbleness, and a very strong link to its roots. If Gustav can continue his path for the many years to come, he will be one of the men to define the Swedish cuisine of the future.

René Redzepi

MACKEREL AND RAW SHRIMP FROM CAPTAIN MIKEAL ON THE SHIP *KENNEDY OF BJÖRKÖ*
Serves 4

For the mackerel
4 mackerel fillets from the back of the fish • salt • 100 ml vinegar • 2 ml sugar • 100 ml water • 1 yellow onion, finely chopped • 1 carrot, finely chopped • 2 tbsp dill seeds

1 Cut each mackerel fillet into 5 and gently salt them. Leave for an hour.
2 Mix together the remaining ingredients, heat them in a pan, and maintain at 108°F (42°C).
3 Add the mackerel and let it reach the same temperature at its core. Cool, and leave for 24 hours.

For the raw shrimp
3 cooked shrimp (prawns) • 100 g coarse salt • 16 large raw shrimp (prawns)

1 Preheat the oven to 480°F (250°C).
2 Roast the cooked shrimp for 10 minutes, then blend with the coarse salt to make a shrimp salt.
3 Dry at 195°F (90°C) until it feels dry enough to mix again.
4 Peel the raw shrimps and let them reach room temperature, then season with the shrimp salt.

For the gooseberry crème
200 g gooseberries • 50 g sugar • 2–3 tbsp instant thickener • salt

1 Put the gooseberries and sugar in a pan and add enough water to cover the fruit. Bring to a boil, then remove from the stove.
2 Leave for 10 minutes, pour off the water, and mix the fruit to a puree. Add the instant thickener and season to taste with a little salt.

For the emulsion of horseradish and butter
25 ml butter • 4 eggs, boiled for 4 minutes • 25 ml horseradish juice • lemon juice • salt

1 Heat the butter in a skillet until it browns, without letting it burn.
2 Mix the eggs with the horseradish juice.
3 Pour in the butter, a little at a time, and season to taste with lemon juice and salt.

For the cucumber in dill water
100 g dill • 200 ml water • salt • 1 cucumber, finely diced

Mix together the dill, water, and salt. Strain, then add the cucumber.

To serve
sea pea buds and flowers • dill • common wood sorrel

The shrimp should be at room temperature. Disperse the ingredients on a plate so that each element is visible. Sprinkle the peas, dill, and wood sorrel over everything.

CLAMS AND OYSTERS FROM VILSUND
Serves 4

For the mussels
40 large blue mussels • butter • 6 sprigs thyme • salt

1 Blanch the mussels in boiling water until they open.
2 Remove the mussel meat and pan-fry quickly in a hot skillet with the butter, thyme, and salt.

For the oyster emulsion
150 g oysters, shucked • 50 g dark ale (Nils Oscar Imperial Stout) • 50 g rye bread • 40 g parsley • 300 ml colza oil • vinegar • salt

1 Put all the ingredients except the oil, vinegar, and salt in a blender.
2 Blitz until smooth, then carefully mix in the oil and season to taste with vinegar and salt. Finish by passing through a fine mesh sieve.

For the salmon roe
40 g salmon roe • 2 oysters • 2 tbsp finely chopped chives • 2 tbsp finely chopped scallions (spring onions) • 10 g cold smoked salmon, finely chopped • lemon juice

Mix all the ingredients together, and season to taste with lemon juice (it should be quite tart).

For the zwieback sticks
24 thin sticks zwieback bread • butter, for pan-frying • salt

1 Preheat the oven to 300°F (150°C).
2 Put the butter in an ovenproof skillet and heat until it browns, without letting it burn. Distribute the bread sticks evenly in the skillet and heat in the oven for 10 minutes.

To serve
16 seakale flowers

Place 5 spoonfuls of oyster emulsion over the mussels. Dot the plate with salmon roe, then top with foam from the sauce. Sprinkle the seakale flowers over everything. Garnish with zwieback.

ENTRECÔTE FROM AN UPPLAND FARM
Serves 4

We choose to serve only the outer section of the entrecôte because it is so tender.

For the entrecôte
600 g entrecote steak • salt • black pepper • butter, to finish

1 Preheat the oven to 400°F (200°C).
2 Cut the meat into 4 rectangular pieces, season with salt and pepper, and sear in a hot skillet. Finish with a little butter, and baste the meat.
3 Put it in the oven until it reaches a core temperature of 110°F (44°C). Then remove the meat from the oven and let it rest until it reaches 130°F (55°C) at the core. Cut into thin slices to serve.

For the onion puree
8 yellow onions, coarsely chopped • oil, for frying • sugar, to taste • salt • 100 g butter

1 Pan-fry the onions in a little bit of oil until golden, then season with salt and sugar. Add the butter and let it melt.
2 Pour on enough water to cover the onions. Boil until soft, then strain off the liquid.
3 Blitz the onions in a blender, and season to taste with salt and sugar (we always mix in a little food thickener in our purees for a smoother result).

For the pickled fresh onion
8 small onions • 600 ml water, plus more for soaking • salt • 200 ml vinegar • 40 g sugar • butter, to finish

1 Soak the onions in salted water for 2 minutes.
2 Combine the vinegar, sugar, and water in a pan to make a brine, and bring to a boil. Season to taste with salt.
3 Add the onion, and boil it until soft. Leave in the brine for 48 hours before serving.
4 When serving, reheat the onion in some of the brine with a dash of butter.

For the fiddlehead ferns
100 ml vinegar • 300 ml water • salt • 20 stems fiddlehead ferns

1 Bring the vinegar and water to a boil and season to taste with salt.
2 Add the ferns and put the whole thing in the refrigerator. Leave for at least 3 days before serving.

To serve
fried ramson leaves (wild garlic) • chive flowers

First place the onion puree onto the dish, then pile the entrecote on top, followed by the onions and fiddleheads.

1
Mackerel and raw shrimp
from Captain Mikeal on
the ship *Kennedy of Björkö*

2
Clams and oysters
from Vilsund

3
Entrecôte from an
Uppland farm

Gustav Otterberg

For the past twenty years Scott Peacock has been one of the reigning experts on the cuisine of the American South. In Georgia, he has cooked over the open hearth of the Atlanta History Center and in the kitchen of the Governor's mansion, where he was chef for four years. He knows that the authenticity of Southern cooking depends on fresh seasonal ingredients prepared simply and artfully. In the spring and summer, that might mean scallions stewed in butter and fresh field peas in cream; in the fall and winter, corn pudding and slow-cooked oxtails.

I was not surprised to learn that Scott's first love was music and that his musical compositions preceded his kitchen compositions. He loves opera, and such Southern art as the famous quilts of Gee's Bend, Arkansas. Scott is also a gifted writer and speaker; his articles have appeared in major periodicals and anthologies.

Scott's home-style cooking is simply irresistible. When I land in Atlanta, I head straight for Watershed, his beautiful restaurant in Decatur. Watershed is at once sophisticated, welcoming, and cozy. Dining with Scott is a particular pleasure because of his soft voice and his witty, erudite conversation. No matter what else is on the menu, I eagerly await that first biscuit, made with home-rendered lard and served with a generous pat of butter, country ham, and homemade blackberry preserves.

Scott brought these very biscuits to Slow Food Nation. During the two hottest days of our San Francisco summer, he baked thousands of tiny, perfect buttermilk biscuits for festival-goers. Each day of the festival, I would emerge into the bright sunlight outside City Hall from hours of intense roundtable discussions about the future of the American food system and head straight to Scott's booth for a bite of biscuit and a snippet of conversation. Then I would retreat to the shade and contentedly finish my biscuit topped with the Virginia ham and preserves he had brought along.

Alice Waters

Scott Peacock was born in 1962 in Georgia in the U.S. He was a private chef to two governors of Georgia before moving on to open Atlanta's Horseradish Grill in 1994. His recently published cookbook, *The Gift of Southern Cooking*, features his recipes and ideas alongside those of his mentor, Edna Lewis. This matriarch of Southern cuisine has been influential in the development of Peacock's cooking. Lewis milked her own cows and could tell when a cake was ready by "listening" to it; this instinctive, personal approach to food finds its way onto Scott Peacock's menu. The Southern cuisine that he serves at the Watershed Restaurant in Decatur, Georgia, emphasizes fresh, seasonal, regionally grown ingredients of the highest quality, prepared with simplicity and restraint. In May 2007, Scott received the James Beard Foundation's award for Best Chef in the Southeast.

MENU

Deviled eggs, pimento cheese and celery, and cucumbers dressed with vinegar and sugar

~

Southern vegetable plate: sliced tomato, yellow squash and vidalia onion, field peas simmered in rich pork stock, gingered beets, spicy collard greens, fried okra, and cornbread muffin

~

Banana pudding

1–2
Scott Peacock grating cheese and sorting beans at Watershed Restaurant

Scott Peacock

Watershed Restaurant, Decatur, GA, USA

1
Deviled eggs, pimento
cheese and celery,
and cucumbers dressed
with vinegar and sugar

2
Banana pudding

DEVILED EGGS, PIMENTO CHEESE AND CELERY, AND CUCUMBERS DRESSED WITH VINEGAR AND SUGAR
Serves 12

For the mayonnaise
1 tbsp cider vinegar • 1 tbsp freshly squeezed lemon juice • 1 tsp sea salt • 1 tsp dry mustard • 2 egg yolks • 350 ml vegetable oil or light olive oil, or a combination • 1 tbsp hot water

1   Put the vinegar, lemon juice, salt, and mustard into a bowl, and whisk or stir until the salt and mustard are dissolved.
2   Add the egg yolks, and beat until smooth.
3   Add the oil drop by drop at first, and then in a slow, steady stream, whisking or stirring constantly until all the oil has been incorporated and you have a very thick emulsion. Stir in the hot water until smooth. Refrigerated, homemade mayonnaise will keep for up to 1 week.

For the pimento cheese
275 g extra-sharp (mature) Cheddar cheese, grated • 7 tsp cayenne pepper, or to taste • salt to taste, if needed • 5– 6 grinds black pepper • 3 tbsp finely chopped roasted red bell pepper or pimento • 12 stalks celery

1   Stir together all the ingredients, except the celery, with 180 g of the homemade mayonnaise in a mixing bowl until well mixed and creamy. Taste carefully for seasoning, and adjust as needed.
2   Cover and store, refrigerated, until ready to use.
3   Cut off and discard the bottoms of the celery stalks. Reserve the stalks until ready to serve.

For the sliced cucumbers
225 ml cider vinegar • 100 g granulated sugar • ½ tsp salt • ½ tsp freshly ground black pepper • 4 kirby cucumbers, peeled if waxed and thinly sliced

1   Put the vinegar, sugar, salt, and pepper in a nonreactive mixing bowl, and stir until the sugar is dissolved. Add the cucumber slices, and toss well to mix.
2   Cover, and chill for 1 hour.
3   Taste, and adjust the seasoning if needed. Serve very cold.

For the deviled eggs
12 large eggs • 1 tbsp kosher salt • 1½ tbsp cider vinegar • ½ tsp sea salt, or more to taste • 1 tsp granulated sugar • 2 tbsp heavy (double) cream • 2 tbsp finely chopped chives, chervil, or tarragon, or a mixture of 2 or more (optional)

1   Put the eggs in a large pan and pour in enough water to cover them by 5 cm. Add the kosher salt and 1 tablespoon of the vinegar. Bring to a hard boil over light heat. Immediately remove from the heat and cover.
2   Let the eggs sit, covered, for exactly 10 minutes. Then drain, and immediately run cool tap water over the eggs to stop the cooking. Shake the pan as you do so, to crack the eggshells all over.
3   When cool enough to handle, carefully peel the eggs. Then slice the top third of each egg off crosswise, and with a spoon remove the yolks to leave the whites as "cups."
4   Using a wooden spoon or spatula, rub the yolks through a fine sieve into a mixing bowl. Blend in the remaining vinegar, sea salt, sugar, and 120 g homemade mayonnaise until the mixture is very smooth. Blend in the heavy cream. Taste carefully for seasoning, adding sea salt, vinegar, or sugar if needed. If the filling mixture is too dry, you may add a bit more mayonnaise or heavy cream.
5   Use a teaspoon or pastry (piping) bag to fill the "eggcups". Arrange the filled eggs on a plate, and sprinkle, if desired, with the finely chopped herbs on top.

For serving
Place the deviled eggs and sliced cucmbers on a plate. Spread some pimento cheese along the stalks of celery and arrange on the plate.

BANANA PUDDING
Serves 8

For the angel food cake
120 g cake (plain) flour, sifted • 275 g granulated sugar • 12 egg whites, at room temperature • ½ tsp cream of tartar • ¼ tsp salt • 1 tbsp water • 1½ tsp vanilla extract

1   Preheat the oven to 375°F (190°C).
2   Sift the flour and half the sugar together twice onto wax (greaseproof) paper or a plate, and set aside.
3   Put the egg whites into a large, clean mixing bowl, and beat them on low speed until frothy. Add the cream of tartar, salt, water, and vanilla, and gradually increase the beating speed until the egg whites begin to mound softly. Sprinkle the remaining sugar over the whites a third at a time, beating only until each addition is incorporated. Don't overbeat. The egg whites should be very moist and glossy, and just firm enough to form soft peaks.

4   Sift a quarter of the reserved flour and sugar over the beaten whites and gently fold in. Repeat 3 times, folding in each successive addition only until all of it has been incorporated.
5   Carefully and evenly spoon the batter into an ungreased 25-cm tube pan. With a long spatula or butter knife draw a line through the center of the batter along the entire circumference of the pan (this will release any large pockets of air, which if left could result in large tunnels or holes in the finished cake).
6   Bake for 35–40 minutes, until the cake is golden brown and springs back to the touch. Remove from the oven, and invert the cake to cool completely in the pan. Then use a long, straight-edged spatula to loosen the cake from the sides of the pan and turn out. Store tightly covered.

For the custard
475 ml whole milk • 475 ml heavy (double) cream • 1 vanilla bean • 12 egg yolks • 160 g granulated sugar • 30 g all-purpose (plain) flour • pinch of salt • 3 tsp vanilla extract

1   Put the milk, half the cream, and the vanilla bean into a nonreactive pan. (Don't split the vanilla bean, just twist and bend a bit to bruise it and release its oils.) Heat slowly until just below a simmer, then cover, remove from the heat, and let steep for 20 minutes.
2   Meanwhile, put the egg yolks in a bowl and whisk in the sugar, followed by the flour and the salt, mixing until completely smooth and lump-free.
3   Remove the vanilla bean from the steeped milk and cream, and slowly whisk the milk and cream into the egg yolks. Return the mixture to the pan and cook, whisking constantly, over moderate heat until the custard thickens and begins to bubble. Be sure to whisk all over the bottom of the pan as well as along the bottom edges. Cook for 1 minute after the custard begins to boil, then remove from the heat. At this point, it should be very thick.
4   Strain through a fine-meshed sieve into a mixing bowl, and immediately whisk in the remaining cream and the vanilla extract.

For assembly stage 1: the cake and bananas
6 thick slices angel food cake cut into 2.5-cm cubes and lightly toasted, or about 400 g vanilla wafers • 4 large ripe bananas, peeled and sliced 1-cm thick

1   Preheat the oven to 400°F (200°C).
2   Spoon a thin layer of the custard into a large ovenproof baking dish. Top with a layer of cubed angel food cake and sliced banana. Spoon more custard over and continue layering, ending with custard.

For assembly stage 2: the meringue
8 egg whites, at room temperature • ½ tsp vanilla extract • 85 g plus 2 tbsp granulated sugar

1   Put the egg whites into a spotlessly clean bowl and beat slowly until frothy. Add the vanilla, and continue beating until the egg whites are just beginning to form soft mounds.
2   While still beating, begin sprinkling the sugar a third at a time, beating only until each addition is incorporated before proceeding to the next. When all the sugar is incorporated, beat the egg whites until they are moist and very glossy and hold peaks that are firm but still bend when lifted on the end of a whisk.
3   Immediately spoon the beaten egg whites over the assembled pudding and, using a spoon or spatula, spread them to the edge to get a good seal between the meringue and the sides of the baking dish. Work quickly to make decorative swirls and patterns in the meringue.
4   Put the dish immediately into the oven to bake for about 5 minutes, until golden brown. (Check after 2 minutes to see how the meringue is browning, and turn the dish from time to time, if needed, to ensure even browning.)
5   Serve the banana pudding warm or at room temperature.

The culinary flair of Tom Pemberton reminds me very much of a particular scene in *Star Wars*. Luke Skywalker is zooming along on his way to blow up the Imperial Death Star when he hears the voice of Obi-Wan Kenobi, who tells him to 'use the force'. The result is an inspired display of technical prowess. Like exploding Death Stars, the cooking of sweetbreads demands considerable Jedi powers.

Tom's restaurant is Hereford Road in west London, and he doesn't seem to have left its very open kitchen since he set up there, serving British food with the wholehearted approach to meat-eating that I like; here you can eat cow's curd done to perfection, or a perfect braised oxtail that arrives on a dish for sharing. Tom gives a platform to superior British ingredients (samphire, lovage) and lets them speak for themselves. He knows what people want in a pudding, with lots of meringuey, fruity English goodness in evidence at the foot of his menu. Hereford Road is a place with a sort of neighborhood feel and, like all the best restaurants, slots nicely into the fabric of the city.

I must admit that I'm no stranger to Tom's cooking. But his force was strong the day I ate at Hereford Road (and, by all accounts, is very much in evidence every day). I had the sweetbreads as a starter, and when I came to the main course I had to have them again. Too often sweetbreads get treated too roughly, almost seared in the pan, resulting in a sort of sad smear of brown. Tom's, though, were cooked with measured patience, allowing the time for a crust of gorgeous nutty brown to form. Tom both knows and feels timing, giving all his food a special savor. I hope he realizes what a Jedi knight he is.

Fergus Henderson

Tom Pemberton was born in 1969 in London. After studying history and the law, he found his true vocation in food. He acquired technical prowess by learning in the kitchens of some of the country's best chefs. After working under Dan Evans at the Anglesea Arms, the London gastro-pub, he moved to cook for Fergus Henderson. This training, which culminated in Pemberton's position as head chef at St. John Bread & Wine, helped the young chef to develop his own approach to nose-to-tail eating. In 2007, Pemberton realized his dream of opening his own restaurant—Hereford Road, in Notting Hill, an approachable, local restaurant that serves thoughtful and hearty British dishes. His simple, generous menu showcases the lesser-used cuts of meat, featuring ingredients from an array of small British suppliers, which he aspires to supplement through intelligent foraging. In 2009 Pemberton received a Bib Gourmand from the *Michelin Guide*, a testament to his instinct and flair.

MENU

Lamb's tongue and sweetbreads, pearl barley, parsley, and mint

~

Lemon sole with curly kale, sea beet, and brown shrimp

~

Whole braised oxtail and carrots

~

Orange and sloe sorbet

~

Selection of British cheeses (Strathdon Blue, Ragstone, Ardrahan)

Tom Pemberton

1–3
Tom Pemberton, and the
kitchen at Hereford Road

4 & 5
Straight from the oven

Hereford Road, London, UK

LAMB'S TONGUE AND SWEETBREADS, PEARL BARLEY, PARSLEY, AND MINT
Serves 4

6 brined lambs' tongues • 4 large carrots, half sliced, half chopped • 1 head celery, half sliced, half chopped • 2 brown onions, half sliced, half chopped • 1 bunch thyme • salt, for boiling plus seasoning • 4 leeks • 1 bay leaf • juice of ½ a lemon • 12 large lambs' sweetbreads • 200 g pearl barley • 300 ml olive oil, plus additional for pan-frying • 1 bunch flat-leaf parsley • 1 bunch mint • 2 round shallots, peeled • a few capers • 1 clove garlic • pepper • butter, for pan-frying • sherry vinegar, for deglazing

1 Take the lambs' tongues out of their brine and soak them in cold water for a couple of hours. Then cook them without boiling, in plenty of water with a little of the carrot, celery, onion, and thyme. They will be ready when the skin begins to peel off one of the tongues easily. Remove from the pot and peel all the tongues while still warm. Return to the cooled cooking liquid.
2 Fill a roomy pan with cold, salted water, and add some sliced onion, leek, celery, and the bay leaf. Bring to a boil, add a little of the lemon juice and blanch the sweatbreads for 4–5 minutes until firm. Peel off the fat and membrane while still warm.
3 Wash the pearl barley and cook in boiling water with a rough dice of onion, celery, leek and thyme until tender. Drain, discard the vegetables and dress the pearl barley in a little olive oil.
4 When the pearl barley is cool, briefly toast it in a medium–hot oven.
5 Pick and wash the parsley and mint, and roughly chop it. Slice the shallots and place in a mixing bowl with the herbs, capers, and pearl barley.
6 Make a dressing with the remaining olive oil, lemon juice, and garlic. Finely slice the round shallots.
7 Season the sweetbreads with salt and pepper.

8 Heat a large skillet until very hot, then turn down the heat to medium and pan-fry the seasoned sweetbreads in some oil and butter. The aim is for the sweetbreads to be golden brown all over. When they are nearly finished, slice the lambs' tongues in half down their length and add to the pan. Turn the tongues, allowing them to caramelize on each side. Add a splash of sherry vinegar to the pan to deglaze.
9 Add the hot tongues and sweetbreads to the mixing bowl, dress with the olive oil and lemon dressing and check the seasoning. Divide among 4 plates.

LEMON SOLE WITH CURLY KALE, SEA BEET, AND BROWN SHRIMP
Serves 1

1 lemon sole • 60 g butter • a good handful each of curly kale and sea beet • 120 g peeled brown shrimp (prawns) • 1 lemon • extra-virgin olive oil, for dressing • salt and pepper • pinch of grated nutmeg

1 Trim and season the lemon sole. Place dark-skin side up, with a dab of butter on top, under an overhead broiler (grill). When it is nicely golden and the skin has crisped, turn. Return to the broiler with another dab of butter and cook briefly until light golden.
2 Blanch the curly kale and sea beet in boiling water for 1 minute until tender. Toss together with a handful of shrimp. Dress with the juice from half the lemon, and 3 times this amount of extra-virgin olive oil.
3 Season with salt, pepper, and nutmeg, and serve accompanied by the remaining half lemon.

WHOLE BRAISED OXTAIL AND CARROTS
Serves 2

1 whole oxtail • salt and freshly ground pepper, to season • oil, for browning • 15 shallots, peeled and left whole • splash of balsamic vinegar • ½ bottle of red wine • 1 bunch organic carrots • bouquet garni of rosemary, thyme, and bay leaf • ½ head of garlic (ideally cut horizontally from a whole head) • 1.5 liters stock (made the previous day from oxtail and beef bones)

1 Preheat the oven to 425ºF (220ºC).
2 Trim any excess fat from the base of the oxtail, but leave some on for flavor and moistness in the finished dish. Season the oxtail with salt and pepper.
3 In order to cook the oxtail whole you will need a large fish poacher or long roasting pan to accommodate its length. Brown the oxtail on top of the stove, then place in the oven to brown further for 5 minutes. Remove from the oven and turn the temperature down to 350ºF (180ºC) ready for braising.
4 Brown the shallots in a skillet to give a good color. Toward the end, add the balsamic vinegar and red wine and simmer to reduce. When the liquid has nearly all gone, add the shallots and their juices to the oxtail.
5 Trim the carrots. Add them to the oxtail and shallots together with the bouquet garni, garlic, and stock.
6 Cover the poacher or roasting pan with a lid or aluminum foil and braise for 3½ hours. Take off the lid and brown in the oven for 20 minutes. Check for seasoning before serving.

ORANGE AND SLOE SORBET
Serves 8–10

2 liters freshly squeezed orange juice • 500 g superfine (caster) sugar • 700 g glucose • 750 ml still mineral water • 100 ml sloe gin

1 Warm the orange juice, then dissolve the sugar and glucose in it. Take off the heat.
2 Add the water and cool quickly to room temperature.
3 Add the sloe gin. Churn in an ice-cream maker.

1
Lamb's tongue and
sweetbreads, pearl barley,
parsley, and mint

2
Lemon sole with curly kale,
sea beet, and brown shrimp

3
Whole braised oxtail and
carrots

4
Orange and sloe sorbet

Tom Pemberton

When I first encountered Ricardo's cuisine, I was not in particularly good shape for dinner. I had been eating at Pierre Gagnaire's restaurant in Paris six hours earlier, and was afraid I would not be able to finish the dishes at his restaurant in Bilbao. Luckily that wasn't the case!

The most prominent characteristic of Ricardo's cuisine is that it "tastes good." It is food that has carefully been prepared with local ingredients and with those who will be eating the dishes in mind. This may sound rather unexceptional, but it is in fact extremely difficult to find such cuisine nowadays. His cooking may not be at the forefront of fashion, but it cannot be simply reduced to traditional local cuisine: It lives in the present.

He is also extremely gifted in the sophisticated balancing of acidic flavors, not just on one plate, but also throughout the courses. The soup made with local specialty baby squids that I had the chance to try that day was superb.

Ricardo never seeks to be eccentric. He prepares delicious food that is made for people to genuinely enjoy. He mentions that his credo could be summed up as *"producto, tradición e innovación."* Three words that Japanese cuisine, or indeed cuisine across the world, should take to heart.

Yoshihiro Murata

Born in 1970, Ricardo Perez grew up in Trespaderne, Spain, in a family of Basque origin and surrounded by the agricultural heritage that informs his restaurant today. He attended a culinary school before taking up a post at the Basque Centre in Gran Canaria and cooking at restaurants from Bilbao to Madrid. He worked under Martín Berasategui in Lasarte, whom Pérez credits for early lessons in skill, discipline, and respect for raw ingredients. He ended at Café de Paris in Biarritz, moving from there to work with Ferran Adrià at elBulli. After a spell at the Hotel NH Villa de Bilbao, where he developed his professional technique and capacity for management, he founded his own restaurant, Yandiola, close to the Guggenheim in Bilbao. Here he is engaged in a constant dialogue with the traditional cuisine of Bilbao, mixing flavors with creativity and style.

MENU

Cod slices, black olives, and anchovies
Tilenus Crianza, D.O. Bierzo, Bodegas Estefanía, Spain, 2005

~

Tomato aspic and black-face Carranzana sheep cheese with smoked fish
Pago Santa Cruz, D.O. Ribera del Duero, Bodegas Hermanos Sastre, Spain, 2004

~

Poached eggs and charcoal-grilled Euskal Txerria *lukainka*
Luberri Cepas Viejas, D.O. Rioja, Bodegas Luberri Monje Amestoy, Spain, 2004

~

Euskal oiloa capon cooked three ways, with seasoned vegetables
NEO, D.O. Ribera del Duero, Bodegas Conde-Neo, Spain, 2005

~

***Mungiako taloak* (flat corn cakes)**
Urezti Itsasmendi Bizkaiko Txakolina, Bodegas Itsasmendi, Spain

Ricardo Perez

1 & 2
Ricardo Perez in the kitchen
at Yandiola

3
Drying vegetables

4
Fish fillets on a grill

Yandiola, Bilbao, Spain

1
Cod slices, black olives,
and anchovies

2
Tomato aspic and black-face
Carranzana sheep cheese
with smoked fish

3
Poached eggs and charcoal-
grilled Euskal Txerria
Lukainka

4
Euskal *oiloa* capon cooked
three ways, with seasoned
vegetables

5
Mungiako Taloak

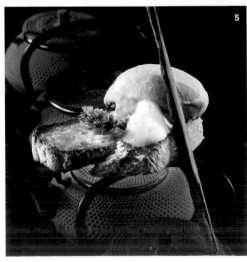

COD SLICES, BLACK OLIVES, AND ANCHOVIES
Serves 4

For the cod slices
Meat from the back of 1 cod's neck, sliced thinly

Cook the fish in salted water at 165°F (75°C) for 3–4 minutes.

For the smoked anchovy foam
400 g anchovies • 600 ml milk • smoked salt • cream

Infuse the anchovies in the milk with smoked salt, add the cream, and chill. Put the liquid in a siphon, and let cool for several hours.

For the potato tiles
700 g potato • 500 g butter • 1 tbsp Aragón black olive paste

1 Make a potato puree by boiling the potatoes until cooked, then blend with the butter and olive paste.
2 Make the potato tiles in a nonstick skillet by browning a small amount of puree and creating a thin potato slice.

For the tomato soup
15 tomatoes on the vine • extra-virgin olive oil • salt

Create an emulsion by blending the tomatoes, olive oil, and salt.

To serve
olive paste • salt • chervil leaves

1 Place the olive paste in an 8-cm diameter mold, then the cod slices, the potato tiles, and finally the smoked anchovy foam.
2 Pour a small amount of tomato soup around the fish next to the fresh chervil leaves. Season to taste.

TOMATO ASPIC AND BLACK-FACE CARRANZANA SHEEP CHEESE WITH SMOKED FISH
Serves 4

8–10 tomatoes, enough to make 300 ml tomato juice (see method) • salt • 6 gelatin leaves, rehydrated in cold water • 200 g fresh black-face Carranzana sheep cheese, chopped, plus 150 g for grating • fresh dill, chopped, to taste • smoked fish, such as salmon, bluefish, sardine, or anchovy • virgin olive oil from the Olivos Milenarios of the Maestrat • chervil, chopped, to serve • chives, chopped, to serve • 1 round loaf of bread, sliced very thinly

1 Chop the tomatoes with a little salt, pass it through a strainer, and finally strain it through cheesecloth (muslin) without pressing on it, leaving the juice to drain out for several hours.
2 Heat 300 ml of the tomato juice and dissolve the hydrated gelatin in it, then let it set in the refrigerator in a square container, with small squares of fresh chopped cheese and the dill.
3 To serve, place a rectangular piece of aspic on the plate over some smoked fish slices. Add the grated cheese, a small amount of olive oil, and the rest of the aromatic herbs. To introduce a crunchy element, add an extremely thin slice of bread.

POACHED EGGS AND CHARCOAL-GRILLED EUSKAL TXERRIA LUKAINKA
Serves 4

4 eggs from a Basque chicken • 75 g *lukainka* (Basque pork) • 4 potatoes with skins • extra-virgin olive oil • thyme, to taste • 100 ml milk • 100 g fresh butter • salt • concentrated jus from a roast suckling pig (reduced stock made from the bones and head) • toasted spelt bread sticks

1 Poach the country eggs, covered in plastic wrap (clingfilm) in water at 195°F (90°C) for 3 minutes, then place them in ice water.
2 Barbecue the *lukainka* over a charcoal fire.
3 To make mashed potatoes, slice the potato and put in the oven, with oil and fresh thyme, at 350°F (180°C) for 30 minutes, then peel and mash it with butter and pass it through a fine strainer.
4 To serve, use the potatoes as the base, then the sliced *lukainka*, and the poached egg on top. Serve with the suckling pig jus and the toasted bread sticks.

EUSKAL OILOA CAPON COOKED THREE WAYS, WITH SEASONED VEGETABLES
Serves 4

1 clove garlic, finely chopped • 5 onions, chopped • 6 carrots, chopped • 6 leeks, chopped • 6 ripe tomatoes, chopped • 2 liters red wine • 1 Euskal oiloa capon, removing the carcass (and setting aside), and separating the legs, wings, and breasts • 20 black peppercorns • 3 bay leaves • cornstarch (cornflour), to thicken • salt • oil, for frying

1 Preheat the oven to 400°F (200°C). Roast the garlic, onions, carrots, leeks, and tomatoes in a pan for 30 minutes.
2 On the stove, in a large pan, reduce the red wine by half, then add the roasted vegetables and carcass bones. Add the peppercorns and bay leaves and cover with water. Simmer slowly for 3 hours.
3 After it has simmered for 3 hours strain the liquid that's left in the pan and transfer to a smaller pan. Let it reduce by half. Thicken with the cornstarch, strain it, and add salt, to taste.
4 Gently cook the capon legs sous-vide in a vacuum-pack bag at low temperature for 8 hours with the reduced sauce. Meanwhile, fry the wings in oil until they become crunchy and brown.
5 Cook the breast over a charcoal fire for a short time.
6 Serve the capon with seasoned vegetables and the thickened sauce.

MUNGIAKO TALOAK (FLAT CORN CAKES)
Serves 4

1.5 liters milk • 175 g sugar • 1 cinnamon stick • orange and lemon zest • 50 ml Cointreau • 1 loaf of bread made with Talo de Mungía flour, or toasted corn flour • salt, less than a pinch • 50 g sugar • 50 ml water • 15 g butter • cane sugar, to caramelize • Talo ice cream (ice cream made of Talo flour or corn flour), to serve • fresh mint leaves, to serve

1 Blend the milk with 175 g sugar, cinnamon, orange and lemon zest, and Cointreau. Cut the bread into rectangles of 3 x 3 x 8 cm, and soak them in the milk mixture with a tiny amount of salt.
2 Caramelize 50 g sugar and when it starts to brown, add the butter, a bit of the milk mixture, and then, when it is well diluted, add the bread. Glaze it until it is hot, then finish by caramelizing it with cane sugar and a blowtorch.
3 Serve with more of the cold milk infusion, Talo ice cream, and mint leaves.

Ricardo Perez

One day a young man hardly twenty years old came to see me, recommended by a fellow chef. The first thing that struck me was his expression. It was the fierce expression of someone who has ambitions, is ambitious to learn, face difficulties, swallow the world in one gulp. In short, I liked his expression.

Jean-François worked for twelve years with me, at the Louis XV in Monaco, and the Plaza Athénée in Paris, where he was head chef for a year or two. In 2004, I sensed that the young man with the fierce expression wasn't satisfied. The time had come to open a new chapter, and that is how Jean-François started work at Les Ambassadeurs.

Jean-François's culinary knowledge is impressive. He is never slow to point out that in a recipe where everyone thinks you should use a white stock, historical documents show that in fact a brown stock is needed. In some people, such extensive knowledge would lead only to a repetitive style. Jean-François's is exactly the opposite: He uses his knowledge to be continually inventive, without making the mistake of some less diligent chefs—risky deconstructions, irritating clashing flavors, for example.

How does Jean-François Piège successfully achieve this happy combination of tradition and inventiveness? First, because he balances ingredients and technique. Today everything can be emulsified, frozen, dried, liquidized, or crafted as one wishes. In a world that is perpetually searching for surprises, technology means that you don't have to think: You only have to let the machines do the work to give the impression that you are making something new. But novelty is not creativity. When anything is possible, you need a very good compass to find your way. Though Jean-François does not lack daring or humor, it is the ingredient that shows north, giving him a very effective reference point. Ultimately, however, if Jean-François Piège has made a success of combining tradition and inventiveness, it is because he has talent.

Alain Ducasse

Born in 1970, Jean-François Piège originally wanted to become a gardener, but soon his love and knowledge of food led him into the kitchen. He started his career at Chabichou in Courchevel, followed by time at the Château Eza. Here, Bruno Cirino encouraged him to join the Hôtel de Crillon in Paris to work alongside Christian Constant. After spending his national service year in the kitchens of the presidential Palais de l'Elysée, Piège joined Bruno Cirino again, this time at the restaurant Élysées du Vernet. He later worked alongside Alain Ducasse at the Louis XV, where he perfected his culinary technique. Piège's passion for the best products and his love of perfection led Ducasse to appoint him head chef at the Plaza Athénée. Since February 2004, Piège has been head chef at Les Ambassadeurs in Paris, where he continues to innovate and create timeless, classic dishes.

MENU

Norwegian lobster caviar

~

Line-caught sea bass
with crisp rice and morels

~

Wild turbot with a jus
and Crécy garnish

~

Lebanese-style marinated
chicken breasts
in pita bread

~

Strawberry charlotte

Jean-François Piège

1–3
Jean-François Piège plating
an intricate dish

4
In the kitchen at
Les Ambassadeurs

Les Ambassadeurs, Paris, France

1
Line-caught sea bass with
crisp rice and morels

2
Wild turbot with a jus and
Crécy garnish

3
Lebanese-style marinated
chicken breasts in pita bread

1

3

2

LINE-CAUGHT SEA BASS WITH CRISP RICE AND MORELS
Serves 4

For the line-caught sea bass
4 thickly cut pieces of sea bass • 2 tbsp olive oil • salt and pepper

1 Lightly coat the pieces of fish with the olive oil, starting with the flesh side, and brown them in a skillet.
2 Season with salt and pepper after cooking them.

For the crisp rice
300 g basmati rice • 30 g butter • 450 ml water • salt • 300 g young Comté or Gruyère cheese, grated

1 Preheat the oven to 375°F (190°C).
2 Cook the rice in the butter in a shallow pan for a couple of minutes, then add the water.
3 Add salt, then bake, covered, for 13 minutes.
4 When cooked, let it stand for 5 minutes with the lid still on, then add the grated cheese.
5 Mix the rice and cheese together and check the seasoning, then press between 2 baking sheets.
6 When it has cooled, cut the rice into fingers and pan-fry, dry, in a nonstick skillet.

For the stewed morels
200 g morel mushrooms • unsalted butter • salt • chicken stock, to cover • 50 ml Jura vin jaune or medium-dry sherry • whipped cream, to finish

1 Sweat the morels in a pan in butter heated until it foams, add salt to taste, barely cover with chicken stock, place a lid on top and boil for 15 minutes.
2 Add a dash of vin jaune or sherry to finish, and marble with a spoonful of whipped cream.

WILD TURBOT WITH A JUS AND CRÉCY GARNISH
Serves 4

For the Créances carrots
14 carrots with their tops • olive oil • fleur de sel • 4 cloves garlic, unpeeled • 1 piece ginger • 1 bouquet garni (with parsley stalks) • 750 ml light (single) cream

1 Grade the carrots for size, then peel, keeping them whole, and wash them in a bowl of cold water. Reserve the tops.
2 Cut the carrots into sticks (batons), cutting the ends diagonally.
3 Preheat the oven to 400°F (200°C).

4 Sweat the carrots in olive oil in a cast-iron pan, season with fleur de sel and add the cloves of garlic, ginger, and bouquet garni.
5 Cover with the cream and bake, covered, until very tender.

For the emulsion of carrot, parsley, and ginger
700 ml carrot juice • 300 ml orange juice • 1 (3-cm) long piece ginger, peeled • the cream in which the carrots were cooked • 1 bunch parsley

1 Make a carrot-orange juice by blending the carrot and orange juices with two-thirds of the ginger, then straining.
2 Take three-quarters of the cream in which the carrots were cooked, dilute it with carrot-orange juice and strain through a conical sieve.
3 Add the parsley leaves and remaining ginger, put them through the blender and strain again.
4 Emulsify at the last moment using a hand-held blender.

For the carrot tops and julienne of fried carrots
1 sand carrot (from the Landes) • 1 liter grapeseed oil • the carrot tops

1 Cut the sand carrot into fine julienne strips and pan-fry in the oil.
2 Deep-fry the carrot tops in grapeseed oil, between 2 skimmers.
3 Drain everything on paper towels.

For the dried orange zest
1 orange

1 Preheat the oven to 175°F (80°C).
2 Remove the zests from the orange with a zester, chop into a fine brunoise, then dry in the oven.

For the parsley-flavored jus perlé
2 bunches parsley • salt • 2–3 cloves garlic • olive oil

1 Strip the parsley leaves from the stalks, and wash them. Fill a pan with salted water and bring it to the boil. Blanch the parsley leaves for 5 seconds, drain them through a skimmer and chill immediately in a bowl of ice cubes.
2 Drain, keeping a small quantity of the water.
3 Put the parsley through a juicer with the garlic and the reserved water.
4 Add a dash of olive oil.

For the carrot and mustard relish
50 g carrots • 20 g butter • 10 g mustard from Meaux • freshly ground black pepper

1 Make a fine brunoise of carrot and sweat it in the butter. Deglaze with a dash of carrot-orange emulsion and cook, covered.
2 Reduce gently, bind with the mustard, and add black pepper to taste.

For the wild turbot
1 x 5 kg turbot • fleur de sel • 50 g butter • 1 clove garlic, unpeeled • lemon juice

1 Remove the head and tail of the turbot, fillet it and remove the skin from both sides.
2 Cut each fillet along its length into pieces 14-cm long and weighing about 80 g. Allow 2 pieces per person. Season with fleur de sel.
3 Pan-fry the pieces of turbot in foaming butter without browning and add the garlic.
4 Deglaze with the carrot-orange emulsion as the turbot cooks, letting it caramelize. When cooked, put it on a wire rack.
5 To make the jus to accompany the fish, continue to deglaze with the carrot-orange emulsion until it has the correct consistency.
6 Acidify with a drop of lemon juice, filter through a small fine strainer, pour into a small pitcher (jug) and add a spoonful of the emulsion.

To serve
400 ml veal stock

1 Arrange the carrots on the plate, place the turbot on top, and add a dash of veal stock.
2 Coat with the emulsion, and sprinkle with the julienne, fried carrot tops, and dried orange zest.
3 Draw 2 lines, one with the parsley jus perlé and the other with the carrot and mustard relish.
4 Serve the rest of the veal stock separately, in a sauceboat.

LEBANESE-STYLE MARINATED CHICKEN BREASTS IN PITA BREAD
Serves 4

For the marinade and chicken
½ bunch flat-leaf parsley • 1 red onion • 2 vine-ripened tomatoes • 4 chicken breasts • mixture of Lebanese spices and flavorings to make 10 g: cumin seeds, fennel seeds, star anise, sumac, powdered Espelette pepper, crushed thyme flowers, fresh grated coconut, toasted white sesame seeds • 1 lemon • 3 tbsp olive oil

1 Chop the parsley and thinly slice the red onion.
2 Cut the tomatoes into quarters, remove the seeds and cut into strips.
3 Cut the chicken breasts into small escalopes 5-mm thick.
4 Sprinkle the bottom of a dish with a third of the spice mixture.
5 Lay the escalopes flat, sprinkle with half the onion, the tomatoes, the parsley, and another third of the spice mixture.
6 Repeat with the remaining marinade ingredients, moisten with the juice of the lemon and the olive oil, cover with plastic wrap (clingfilm) and put in a cool place for at least 12 hours.

For filling the pitas
salt and pepper • 50 g tomato concentrate • 1 clove garlic, chopped • 4 pita breads (Lebanese bread)

1 Take the chicken escalopes out of the marinade, removing the scraps of spice and vegetable but reserving these and the liquid.
2 Sprinkle the chicken with salt and sear rapidly on both sides on a griddle or in a very hot skillet, without using fat.
3 Preheat the oven to 400°F (200°C).
4 Drain the marinade liquid, reserving the solids. Add salt and freshly ground black pepper to the liquid and put both aside.
5 Mix together the tomato concentrate and chopped garlic. Open the pita breads and coat the inside with this mixture.
6 Roll the cooked escalopes in the garnish from the marinade and push them into the pitas.
7 Put the pitas on a baking sheet or ovenproof dish and bake for 4–5 minutes.

To serve
pureed chickpeas, to serve • parsley sprigs, to serve • tomato quarters, to serve

1 Shape the pureed chickpeas into a quenelle and arrange on a flat plate with a sprig of parsley on top, 3 tomato quarters, and a ring of marinade round the edge.
2 When the pitas are crisp, cut them in half diagonally and arrange them on the plate in a cross shape.

Jean-François Piège

Glynn Purnell

MENU

Poached egg yolk, smoked
haddock milk foam,
cornflakes, and curry oil

~

Royal of goat cheese and
pineapple on sticks with
deep-fried watercress

~

Monkfish masala, Indian
lentils, coconut, coriander,
and pickled carrots

~

Duck rolled in licorice
charcoal, Japanese black
rice, tamarind, licorice
puree, salsify, and green
beans

~

Egg surprise, marinated
strawberries, strawberry
sorbet, black pepper
honeycomb, and tarragon

Born in Birmingham, England, in 1975, Glynn Purnell began to wash dishes at the Hilton Metropole at the age of 14. He soon moved on to the Michelin-starred Simpsons under Andreas Antona, who supported Purnell through spells working under Gary Rhodes at The Greenhouse, Gordon Ramsay at Aubergine, and the eponymous Alistair Little at Frith Street, all in London. Antona also saw him undertake training periods in Birmingham's twinned town of Lyons, at the Michelin-starred Zaldiaran in Northern Spain, and at the three-starred Le Jardin des Sens in Montpellier. Purnell moved on from Simpsons to work for Claude Bosi at the two-Michelin-starred Hibiscus in London before joining Jessica's in Birmingham as head chef, where he won the city its first Michelin star in 2005. Purnell opened his own restaurant, Purnell's, in 2007, and has since received a Michelin star for a cuisine that experiments with flavor, reflecting Birmingham's ethnic mix in dishes such as masala-spiced monkfish with red lentils, pickled carrots, and coconut.

Glynn Purnell completed a stage with me at Aubergine in the 1990's and shone through as a talented young chef even during this short stint. At the time he was working for Andreas Antona at Simpsons, an exceptional Michelin-starred restaurant in Birmingham, and was learning from one of the best. During his time at Simpsons with Andreas, Glynn not only worked for me at Aubergine but also had the chance to travel more widely, working stages in Montpellier, Lyon, and in the Basque region of Northern Spain. After leaving Simpsons he worked for a short stint at Claude Bosi's Hibiscus before being appointed to the position of head chef at Jessica's in Birmingham, a restaurant where his delicate, inventive yet minimalist cooking came into its own.

Glynn didn't have everything handed to him on a silver plate growing up. He was brought up on an estate and learned to cook through having to help look after his family. When he was in his teens he ended up pot washing and sweeping the floors in the kitchens of the Birmingham Hilton Metropole but his sheer determination and focus meant that soon he was allowed to switch from floor to food, even if it was the usual hotel fare. Move forward fifteen years and he was running a full brigade in a Michelin-starred kitchen.

I firmly believe that Glynn's absolute determination in life is a dominant factor in what he has achieved so far, but he also has an incredible natural talent. His ability to take everyday ingredients and turn them on their head, while still turning out delicious dishes, captures the imagination of every guest. Flavors from the food of his childhood often form the basic idea behind a dish and the execution on the plate is normally very simple but it is made in such a way as to combine a complex array of tastes and textures. His raspberry parfait "jelly and ice cream," and poached egg yolk, smoked haddock, milk foam, cornflakes, and curry oil are two such dishes.

Glynn's cooking pushes boundaries, but it is presented in such a light, simple manner that the diner is not intimidated but delighted.

Gordon Ramsay

Purnell's, Birmingham, UK

ROYAL OF GOAT CHEESE AND PINEAPPLE ON STICKS WITH DEEP-FRIED WATERCRESS
Serves 4–6

For the royal of goat cheese
300 ml heavy (double) cream • 115 g goat cheese, crumbled • salt and freshly ground black pepper • 3 free-range eggs, beaten • small handful of Parmesan or Cheddar cheese, finely grated (for the top)

1 Preheat the oven to 425°F (220°C).
2 Pour the cream into a small pan and bring to a boil over high heat. Add the goat cheese and season with salt and pepper.
3 Pour into a bowl, add the beaten eggs, whisk, and pass through a sieve into an ovenware dish. Sprinkle the top with cheese.
4 Place the dish in a baking pan, and fill with boiling water to halfway up the sides of the dish to make a bain-marie. Cook in the oven for 25–30 minutes.

For the gelatin
200 ml fresh pineapple juice • 1 gelatin leaf

1 Heat the pineapple juice in a small pan over medium heat.
2 Place the gelatin leaf in a small bowl, cover with cold water, and leave until softened. Drain off the water, squeeze out the excess, and add the soaked gelatin leaf to the pan containing the hot pineapple juice.
3 Remove the pan from the heat and let the gelatin dissolve for 1–2 minutes. Stir well, then pour into a square container to set.
4 Once set, cut into 2.5-cm squares.

For the pineapple
½ large pineapple, peeled • 250 g butter, melted

1 Reduce the oven temperature to 250°F (120°C). Submerge the pineapple in melted butter in a small baking pan and gently cook in the oven, turning frequently, for 10 minutes or until tender.
2 Cut into 2.5-cm squares.

For the syrup
500 ml fresh pineapple juice

Pour the pineapple juice into a nonreactive pan and simmer over medium heat for 5 minutes or until reduced to a syrup. This should make around 200 ml of syrup.

For the garnish
300 ml vegetable oil, for deep-frying • small handful fresh watercress
1 Pour the vegetable oil into a large pan or deep-fryer and heat

to 350°F (180°C) or until a small cube of bread turns golden in 30 seconds.
2 Carefully drop the watercress into the hot oil and deep-fry for 1 minute or until crisp. Remove with a slotted spoon and drain on paper towels.

To serve
1 Cut the goat cheese royal into pieces the same size as the pineapple squares, and place the goat cheese on top of the pineapple. Place the gelatin squares on top of the cheese, and push a cocktail stick through the middle to secure.
2 Place 2 goat cheese royals onto each of 4–6 plates, pour the pineapple syrup over the top and garnish with deep-fried watercress.

MONKFISH MASALA, INDIAN LENTILS, COCONUT, CORIANDER, AND PICKLED CARROTS
Serves 4

For the pickled carrots
3 carrots, peeled and sliced • 1 tbsp fenugreek seeds • 1 tsp ajwain seeds • 1 tsp mustard seeds • ½ tsp onion seeds • 1 tsp cumin seeds • 3 tsp chili flakes • 1 tsp salt • vegetable oil, to cover carrots

1 Preheat the oven to 120°F (50°C).
2 Dry out the carrot slices in the warm oven overnight, then place in a sterilized jar.
3 Mix the spices and salt with the oil, pour over the carrots in the jar, and leave for a couple of weeks (longer if you can).

For the masala spice mix
¼ cinnamon stick • 2 tsp fenugreek seeds • ½ tsp fennel seeds • 1½ tsp black mustard seeds • 5 cloves • 1 tsp coriander seeds • 1½ tsp cumin seeds

Place all the spice mix ingredients in a mini-food processor and blend to a powder.

For the monkfish
4–5 tbsp salt • 4 (100-g) monkfish fillets • 25 g butter

1 Sprinkle the salt over the fish and leave for 5–6 minutes to draw out excess moisture. Wash the salt off thoroughly under cold running water.
2 Wrap the washed monkfish in a clean dish towel and leave overnight in the refrigerator.

3 Seal each piece of fish in a separate vacuum-pack bag and cook for 11 minutes in a water bath at 145°F (63°C).
4 Melt the butter in a frying pan until foaming. Remove the fish from the bags, then sear on both sides for 2–3 minutes or until golden brown and crisp all over.

For the red lentils
½ onion, chopped • a little vegetable oil • 1 tbsp mild curry powder • 225 g red lentils • 500 ml chicken stock • ½ red chile, finely chopped • 2 heaping tbsp chopped fresh cilantro (coriander) • salt, to taste

1 Sweat the chopped onion in a drizzle of oil for 4–5 minutes, or until softened. Stir in the curry powder. Add the red lentils, stir well, then cover with chicken stock and simmer for 10–15 minutes or until the lentils are tender.
2 When cooked, stir in the chile and cilantro and season with salt. Set aside.

For the garnish
1 (400-ml) can coconut milk • salt • ½ fresh coconut, flesh only, thinly sliced into strips on a mandolin

1 Pour the coconut milk into a pan and add a pinch of salt. Simmer for 15–20 minutes, or until reduced by half.
2 Heat a skillet and toast the coconut strips until golden brown and fragrant.

To serve
fresh cilantro (coriander) shoots (sprouted seeds)

1 Scatter the powdered spice mixture onto a plate and roll the monkfish pieces in it.
2 Spoon the lentils onto a serving plate and place the monkfish on top.
3 Drizzle over the top a little of the reduced coconut milk, then garnish with the toasted sliced coconut, pickled carrots, and fresh cilantro shoots.

DUCK ROLLED IN LICORICE CHARCOAL, JAPANESE BLACK RICE, TAMARIND, LICORICE PUREE, SALSIFY, AND GREEN BEANS
Serves 4

For the duck
4 (175-g) duck fillets, trimmed • 25 licorice roots, roasted until blackened, then blended into a powder

1 Roll the duck in the licorice powder and seal in plastic using a vacuum-packing machine.
2 Pour hot water into a large pan, heat to 144°F (62°C), add the vacuum-packed duck and boil for 16 minutes.
3 Remove from the water and rest for 5 minutes.

For the tamarind jam
15 tamarind fruit, pods removed • juice of ½ lime

1 Place the tamarind fruit into a medium nonreactive pan, add the lime juice and enough water to cover the tamarinds, and cook until softened.
2 Drain, pass through a fine-mesh sieve to remove the pits and stones, and then blend with a hand blender until smooth. Set aside and keep warm.

For the licorice puree
20 pieces black licorice

1 Place the licorice in a small pan with a little water and melt over low heat.
2 Blend with an immersion blender until smooth, pass through a fine-mesh sieve, and keep warm.

For the black rice
55 g butter • 175 g Japanese glutinous black rice • 600 ml strong beef stock • ground ginger • rock salt and freshly ground black pepper

1 Melt half the butter in a pan, add the rice, and stir to coat the grains.
2 Add the beef stock and simmer over medium heat, stirring frequently, until the rice is tender.
3 Drain off the stock and reserve.
4 Season the rice to taste with the ginger and salt.
5 Reduce the reserved stock, whisk in a piece of butter, and season with salt and pepper.

For the beans and arugula
150 g green (French) beans • 25 g butter • 150 g wild green or red arugula (rocket), picked through • salt and freshly ground black pepper

1 Drop the beans into a large pan of salted water and blanch for 2–3 minutes. Drain, refresh in iced water, and chop finely.

2 Melt the butter in a pan, add the chopped beans and the arugula and stir until the arugula has wilted. Season with salt and pepper.

For the salsify
2 salsify roots, peeled and cut into logs • 25 g butter • salt and freshly ground black pepper • 300 ml vegetable oil, for deep-frying

1 Place half the salsify logs in a pan of boiling salted water and blanch for 2–3 minutes. Drain and dry well.

2 Melt the butter in a small pan, add the blanched salsify, and gently fry until softened and turning golden brown. Season well with salt and pepper.

3 Finely slice the rest of the salsify on a mandolin.

4 Pour the vegetable oil into a medium pan and heat until a small cube of bread turns golden in 30 seconds. Carefully place the salsify slices in the hot oil and deep-fry until golden brown.

5 Remove from the oil with a slotted spoon and dry on paper towels. Season with salt and pepper.

To finish and serve
rock salt • ground ginger • beef gravy

1 Remove the duck from the plastic, dry off with paper towels and caramelize the outside of the duck with a mini blowtorch to give it a charcoal-cooked flavor.

2 Season the duck with rock salt and ground ginger, and slice.

3 Dress 4 plates with the tamarind jam and licorice puree.

4 Place a line of rice and some pan-fried and deep-fried salsify on each plate.

5 Top with the sliced duck, and garnish with the cooked arugula and green beans.

6 Drizzle a little beef gravy over the top, and serve.

1
Royal of goat cheese and pineapple on sticks with deep-fried watercress

2
Monkfish masala, Indian lentils, coconut, coriander, and pickled carrots

3
Duck rolled in licorice charcoal, Japanese black rice, tamarind, licorice puree, salsify, and green beans

Glynn Purnell

Theo Randall

MENU

Pan-fried squid
with borlotti beans,
chile, anchovy, parsley,
and chopped arugula

~

Risotto di peperoni

~

Monkfish with prosciutto,
artichokes, capers, parsley,
and Charlotte potatoes

~

Pigeon marinated in
Marsala and roasted on
bruschetta with arugula
and chanterelles

~

Ricotta cheesecake

Born in 1970 in Surrey, UK, Theo Randall developed a passion for food during family trips to the Italian countryside. He began his professional food career at the age of 18 with Max Magarian at Chez Max in Surbiton. In 1989 he joined the newly opened River Café in London; Randall went on to spend two years there, putting to use his relationships with small artisan suppliers. In 1991, Randall moved to Chez Panisse in California and the team of Alice Waters and Paul Bertolli. There Randall developed his technique and learned the importance of provenance and sourcing ingredients. Returning to the River Café as head chef and partner, Randall saw the restaurant win its first Michelin star. In 2006 Randall opened his own restaurant, Theo Randall at the InterContinental on Park Lane in London, where he serves a lively, flavorful menu of Italian dishes, ranging from hearty Bolognese dishes in the winter to fresh Ligurian dishes in the summer.

Theo has a background that the majority of chefs would die for. He led the kitchen of the acclaimed River Café for fifteen years, under the directorship of Rose Gray and Ruth Rogers. Earlier in his career he completed stints with some of the world's most renowned chefs, including Alice Waters of Chez Panisse, Paul Bertolli, and Max Magarian.

Theo's training says a lot about his cooking— he showcases the very best produce, cooked simply. It's not that he necessarily creates anything particularly groundbreaking or revolutionary, but he shows off ingredients to their best.

His philosophy is to create a seasonal, uncomplicated menu that is absolutely packed with flavor. He serves the type of food that people really love to eat. This philosophy is epitomized at his London restaurant. His starters include a beautiful fresh Devon crab salad and a stunning buffalo mozzarella salad with green tomatoes and olives. A particular dish that stands out is wood-roasted Cornish monkfish, which he serves with rosemary, Roseval potatoes, artichokes, and pancetta. Monkfish has a fantastic meaty texture but can taste slightly bland, and the strong, salty flavor of the pancetta gives it a real kick.

What is even more interesting about Theo is that he draws inspiration for his menu from the different regions of Italy, choosing to cook more robust, hearty dishes from the Piemonte region in the winter months, lighter dishes from Rome and the surrounding countryside in the spring, and vibrant dishes full of flavor from Puglia and Campagna during the summer months.

The full process is incredibly important to Theo, not just the method of cooking, but going from field to fork. The provenance of his ingredients is key, from how the cattle are raised and killed, to how the vegetables are grown, to how the olives are processed.

Gordon Ramsay

5

1–5
Theo Randall
preparing meat, fish,
and parsley at the
InterContinental

PAN-FRIED SQUID WITH BORLOTTI BEANS, CHILE, ANCHOVY, PARSLEY, AND CHOPPED ARUGULA
Serves 4

For the beans
300 g borlotti beans • 1 sprig sage • 1 red chile, pricked with a knife • 1 garlic clove, cut into quarters • 2 tomatoes • salt and freshly ground black pepper • 3 tbsp olive oil • 1 tsp red-wine vinegar

1 Soak the borlotti beans overnight in plenty of clean cold water. Drain and transfer to a large pan with 3 times their volume of water.
2 Add the sage, chile, garlic, and tomatoes. Bring to a boil, then reduce the heat to a simmer. Simmer gently for 1 hour or until the beans are tender (the time may vary depending on the age of the beans).
3 Drain off three-quarters of the cooking liquid, then transfer the beans and the remaining cooking liquid into a bowl. Remove and discard the chile and sage. Remove the garlic, mash with a fork, then return to the beans and stir through.
4 Season with salt and black pepper, and stir in the olive oil and vinegar.

For the squid
6 whole fresh squid • salt and freshly ground black pepper • extra-virgin olive oil, to drizzle • 1 red chile, seeded and finely chopped • 3 anchovy fillets, chopped • 2 tbsp chopped flat-leaf parsley • juice of ½ lemon

1 Peel off the squid wings and outer membrane and remove the head and intestines. Cut in half lengthwise and scrape out the inside with a knife. Wash thoroughly with cold water and pat dry.
2 Lay the squid pieces flat, skin-side down, and score with a sharp knife in a crisscross pattern.
3 Season the squid with salt and freshly ground black pepper and rub a little olive oil into the skin.
4 Place a nonstick pan over medium heat. When hot, add the squid, scored side down. Cook for 1 minute until golden brown, then turn over.
5 Add the chile, anchovy fillets, parsley, and lemon juice to the pan.
6 Remove the squid and quickly slice into bite-sized pieces. Return immediately to the pan and toss briefly through the other ingredients.

To serve
handful chopped arugula (rocket), dressed with olive oil and lemon juice

Place a spoon of the borlotti bean mixture in the center of a plate. Place a small amount of arugula on top and then the chopped squid.

RISOTTO DI PEPERONI
Serves 4

2 red bell peppers • 2 yellow bell peppers • 1 red onion, chopped • 3 sticks celery, chopped • olive oil, for pan-frying • 300 g risotto rice • ½ glass white wine • 2 liters chicken stock • 4 ripe plum tomatoes, skinned, seeded, and finely chopped • 150 g Parmesan, grated • handful of fresh basil, ripped • 75 g unsalted butter • salt and pepper

1 Char-grill the peppers until black, place in a bowl, and cover with plastic wrap (clingfilm). Peel off the black skin and wash off the seeds, chop finely, and set aside.
2 In a large pan, soften the onion and celery in the olive oil, add rice, cook for 5 minutes, add the white wine, then stock, and stir continuously until the rice has absorbed all the stock.
3 When the rice is almost ready, add the chopped peeled peppers, tomatoes, Parmesan, basil, and butter, and stir vigorously to obtain a lovely, creamy consistency.
4 Season with salt and pepper, then serve.

MONKFISH WITH PROSCIUTTO, ARTICHOKES, CAPERS, PARSLEY, AND CHARLOTTE POTATOES
Serves 2

4 Roman artichokes • 75 ml olive oil, plus extra for frying • 1 clove garlic • 2 tsp chopped parsley • ½ glass white wine • 2 (160-g) fillets monkfish • oil, for searing • 300 g Charlotte potatoes, boiled and sliced • 1 tbsp small capers • 100 g sliced prosciutto • 1 lemon

1 Trim the outer leaves off the artichokes, cut tops off, and scoop out the choke. With a potato peeler, peel down the stem as far as the tender center.
2 Place in a pan, heads down, with the olive oil, ½ clove of garlic, and 1 teaspoon chopped parsley.
3 Add the white wine and cook with a lid on for 25 minutes or until tender.
4 Cool and slice lengthwise.

5 In a large, heavy skillet, sear the monkfish on one side in a little bit of oil, turn it over, and take it out of the pan.
6 Add the potatoes and cook for 1 minute until they are a light golden color, then turn over.
7 Place the monkfish back in the pan on top of the potatoes with the sliced artichokes, capers, parsley, and chopped garlic (½ clove), and cover with prosciutto.
8 Bake at 400°F (200°C) for 6–8 minutes.
9 Squeeze half a lemon into the pan and add a dash of olive oil.
10 Serve the monkfish on top of the potatoes, with the artichokes and prosciutto on top.

PIGEON MARINATED IN MARSALA AND ROASTED ON BRUSCHETTA WITH ARUGULA AND CHANTERELLES
Serves 12

For the pigeons
12 squab pigeons • 3 glasses Marsala • 3 cloves garlic, thinly sliced • ½ bunch thyme • olive oil, for frying • 12 slices bruschetta • 24 slices pancetta

1 Using a sharp small knife, make an incision along the back of the pigeon. Insert the knife under the skin and, starting with the leg, being careful not to rip the skin, work around the carcass, pulling the whole bird off and leaving no bones except the legs.
2 Marinate the pigeons with Marsala wine, garlic, and thyme, and leave for 1 hour.
3 In a heavy skillet, heat a little olive oil and sear the skin on both sides for 1 minute. Add the bruschetta and pancetta, and place in the oven at 375°F (190°C) for 4 minutes.
4 Remove from oven and place the pigeon on the bruschetta, skin side up, and cook for a further 3 minutes.

For the chanterelles
1 clove garlic • 1 kg fresh chanterelle mushrooms

Clean the chanterelles. Fry a clove of garlic in the same olive oil used for the pigeon, then add the chanterelles and cook for 3–4 minutes.

For the arugula, and to serve
300 g wild arugula (rocket) • olive oil • 1 lemon

1 Dress the arugula with olive oil and lemon juice.
2 On a cutting (chopping) board, cut through the pigeon at an angle so you have 2 legs on one half and the breast on the other.
3 Smear the cooked chanterelles on the bruschetta, put the arugula on the serving plate with the bruschetta and pigeon, and place the pancetta on the top.

RICOTTA CHEESECAKE
Serves 8

For the sweet pastry
100 g unsalted butter • 1 egg yolk • 150 g all-purpose (plain) flour • 50 g confectioners' (icing) sugar

1 Preheat the oven to 325°F (160°C). Blend all the ingredients until they form a dough and chill for 30 minutes.
2 Roll out and cut to size of a tart pan with a removable base.
3 Bake for 20 minutes. Let cool.

For cheesecake mix
80 g raisins • 3 tbsp sweet Marsala • 100 g superfine (caster) sugar • 1 tbsp all-purpose (plain) flour • 450 g sheep ricotta • 3 eggs, separated • 60 ml heavy (double) cream • 60 ml crème fraîche • 1 vanilla bean • ¼ tsp salt

1 Soak the raisins in the Marsala.
2 Add the sugar and flour to the ricotta and beat until smooth.
3 Add the egg yolks, creams, Marsala, raisins, and vanilla bean.
4 Beat the egg whites with salt.
5 Fold in the ricotta mixture and pour into the tart pan with the cooked sweet pastry on the base.
6 Bake for about 50 minutes at 325°F (160°C).

1
Pan-fried squid with borlotti
beans, chile, anchovy, parsley,
and chopped arugula

2
Risotto di peperoni

3
Monkfish with prosciutto,
artichokes, capers, parsley, and
Charlotte potatoes

4
Pigeon marinated in Marsala
and roasted on bruschetta
with arugula and chanterelles

5
Ricotta cheesecake

1

2

3   4

5

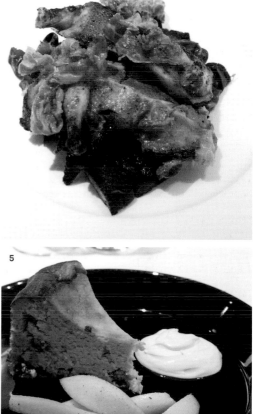

Theo Randall

David Rathgeber

MENU

Quenelles of fish in Nantua sauce

~

Young wild partridge with buttered cabbage

~

Farmhouse chicken in a vinegar fricassee

~

Scallops with Champagne

David Rathgeber was born in 1973 in the Auvergne region of France. He began his career in food with extensive training in classic French cuisine, with apprenticeships under Philippe Groult at Amphycles, Guy Legay at the Paris Ritz, and Gérard Vié at the Trois Marches. He went on to be hired by Alain Ducasse, occupying almost every possible role in his kitchens. Rathgeber began at the Plaza Athénée, passing through Aux Lyonnais and ending as head chef at Chez Benoît. Rathgeber gained a Michelin star for the restaurant in 2006, and became involved in a range of Ducasse's projects, from writing cookbooks to developing Benoît in New York and Tokyo. In September 2008, Rathgeber took over his own Paris restaurant, L'Assiette, where he serves traditional French dishes with a subtle modern touch, from white tuna steak with spinach, lemon, capers, and croutons to crème caramel with salted butter.

1
In the kitchen

2
Interior of L'Assiette

2

If David were a kitchen utensil, he'd be a casserole. Indeed, from an early age his roots in the Auvergne instilled in him a liking for dishes that cook gently for hours in the oven, such as stuffed cabbage, or potée, an old-fashioned, slow-cooked dish of meat and vegetables. He has a special relationship with casseroles of every size, and couldn't do without them. He's even written a cookbook on the subject.

David's professional career has reinforced the preferences he developed as a child. Bistro cooking holds no secrets for him. He headed the kitchen staff at my Paris "inn," Aux Lyonnais, and then was head chef at Benoit, another of my bistros. After working with me for twelve years, he set up on his own and bought L'Assiette, an old Paris bistro (naturally) with a great reputation. So David's a great lover of bistro cooking.

It's easy to understand: This type of restaurant has a charm like no other. It's where you come to find the city's soul: Walls with a patina of age, regular customers who always sit at the same table, colorful owners who like to scold their clientele. They're a focus for their local neighborhood and a benchmark for the type of cuisine people call "traditional bourgeois cooking."

The food is in keeping with this slightly cheeky conviviality. The recipes are quite unusual, because they're directly descended from home cooking—you eat there "as if you were at home." Nowadays, of course, the chefs' technique has moved on, and the traditional *hareng pomme à l'huile* (potato salad with pickled herring) or the hearty hare *à la royale* that David serves are modern professional interpretations of very old recipes. But happily, in adapting them for current tastes, he has preserved all their lively spirit.

The vitality of bistro cooking makes me hopeful. It's a very clear sign of the good health of cooking in general. And, let's say it, I believe it testifies to the fact that people today are still in search of pleasure. And that's very reassuring.

Alain Ducasse

1
Quenelles of fish
in Nantua sauce

2
Young wild partridge with
buttered cabbage

3
Farmhouse chicken
in a vinegar fricassee

QUENELLES OF FISH IN NANTUA SAUCE
Serves 6

For the quenelles
These can be prepared the day before serving.

1 (1.5-kg) zander (pike-perch) or pike fillet • 700 ml light (single) cream • 300 g butter, softened • 3 eggs, plus 3 egg yolks • salt and pepper • 2 pinches of Espelette pepper

1   Bone the pike fillets. Using the fine plate, process the fish through a grinder (mincer). Strain the fish to remove any excess liquid and place it in a large bowl.
2   Add the cream and mix, adding the eggs, egg yolks, and butter. Beat until smooth, adding the salt, pepper, and Espelette pepper. Adjust the seasoning if necessary.
3   Cover the bowl with plastic wrap (clingfilm) and rest in a cool place for 12 hours.
4   Bring a large pan of water to a boil, add some salt, then reduce the heat to 175°F (80°C).
5   Shape the fish mixture into quenelles between 2 large spoons and place them in the water to cook for about 20 minutes.
6   Carefully remove the quenelles from the pan, drain, and store in a cool place.

For the crayfish
30 crayfish • olive oil, for frying • 4 cloves of garlic, crushed • sprigs of parsley • 400 ml Cognac

1   Remove the intestines from the crayfish, also removing the heads and tails to use separately.
2   Heat the oil in a pan and sear the tails with the garlic and parsley.
3   Remove from the heat, deglaze with the Cognac, cover and rest for 5 minutes.
4   Remove the tails and peel them, leaving the last ring of shell attached, and set aside.
5   Strain through a conical sieve, retaining the cooking liquid.

For the sauce
olive oil, for frying • 2 onions, cut into 3-mm cubes • 1 celery stalk, cut into 3-mm cubes • 8 cloves garlic, crushed • sprigs of parsley, chopped • 50 g butter • 200 ml Cognac • 300 ml white wine • 5 ripe tomatoes, quartered • 1 stalk of fennel, chopped and dried on paper towels • salt • white pepper • pepper

1   Heat the oil and add the crayfish heads. Cook for 5 minutes until brown.
2   Add the onions, celery, garlic, parsley, and butter, and sweat the vegetables for 5 minutes.
3   Deglaze with the Cognac and the white wine, then flambé the pan.
4   Add the tomatoes and fennel, and cook for 1 hour over gentle heat, adjusting the seasoning if necessary.

To finish the dish
500 ml light (single) cream pepper

1   Preheat the oven to 285°F (140°C).
2   Arrange the quenelles in an ovenproof dish and add half the crayfish cooking liquid, so that the quenelles are half-covered. Bake for 20 minutes, until slightly risen and glazed with sauce.
3   In a pan, gently heat the remaining cooking liquid, with the cream, adding the crayfish tails to it.
4   Remove the quenelles from the oven and pour the cream sauce and crayfish tails over them, adding a few twists of black pepper.

YOUNG WILD PARTRIDGE WITH BUTTERED CABBAGE
Serves 10

For the partridge
10 young wild partridges • olive oil • 300 ml duck fat • salt and pepper • 14 g garlic, crushed • 300 g white grapes • 400 ml Cognac • 270 g cooked free-range pork belly • 400 ml young partridge jus • 40 black olives

1   The day before, pluck, singe, and thoroughly clean the partridges. Remove the wishbones.
2   Separate the legs from the breasts and pack the breasts in vacuum bags.
3   Chop the livers and hearts of the partridges and keep in a bowl, covered by a film of olive oil.
4   Cook the breasts sous-vide at 140°F (60°C), reaching a core temperature of 130°F (54°C). Alternatively you can roast the partridges whole, with legs attached, for 10 minutes at 350°F (180°C).
5   When the partridges are cooked, place them overnight in a bowl of cold water containing ice cubes.
6   Cook the partridge legs in a pan, in duck fat, at 140°F (60°C), season, and add garlic.
7   When cooked, cool them in a rapid-cooling unit or refrigerator. (When ready to serve, let the legs return to room temperature in duck fat.)
8   The next day, peel and seed the grapes, then put them in a bowl covered by a little Cognac in the refrigerator.
9   Cut the pork belly into 2.5-cm squares and put in the refrigerator, covered.
10   Reheat the partridge breasts sous-vide, in vacuum packs, at 127°F (53°C) for about 20 minutes. Take them out of the vacuum packs and wipe gently. Keep the breasts warm in partridge jus and add the grapes.
11   When ready to serve, brown the breasts and legs in a pan in olive oil.
12   Add the partridge jus and black olives, and stir with a strong circular motion.
13   Brown the pork belly in olive oil in a pan and keep warm on a griddle.

For the giblet roast
300 g small farmhouse loaf of bread • reserved partridge livers and hearts • 300 g preserved foie gras • Cognac, to taste

1   For the giblet roast, cut the farmhouse bread into slices just under 1 cm thick and toast on both sides under a broiler (grill).
2   In a large bowl, mix the livers with cubes of preserved foie gras. Season well and add a dash of Cognac.
3   Spread the toasted bread with the giblet roast.
4   When ready to serve, bake the giblet roast at 338°F (170°C).

For the buttered cabbage
1.3 kg buttered cabbage • 110 g butter • 15 g salt • 3 g freshly ground black pepper

1   Remove the tough outer leaves of the cabbage and discard. Cut the cabbage into fine shreds.
2   In a saucepan combine the cabbage and butter over medium heat and cook for a few minutes. Season with salt and freshly ground black pepper.

To serve
10 slices roast bacon • 2 g coarse-ground pepper

1   Place a serving of buttered cabbage in the center of a plate.
2   Add a slice of roast bacon, and a serving of partridge breast, legs, and pork belly.
3   Put the giblet roast on the plate and add a ring of partridge jus, with some grapes. Sprinkle with coarse-ground pepper.

FARMHOUSE CHICKEN IN A VINEGAR FRICASSEE
Serves 10

350 g onions • 1.3 kg tomatoes • 1.2 liters white stock • 3 kg chicken legs • olive oil • 100 g butter • 60 g garlic • 250 ml aged wine vinegar • 50 ml balsamic vinegar • 100 ml white wine • 1.2 liters white stock • 30 g chicken stock powder • 1 bouquet garni • 10 g salt • 3 g pepper • ¼ bunch tarragon • sherry vinegar, to taste • 2 g coarse-ground pepper • 2 g fleur de sel

1   Peel and wash the onions and cut into 1-cm thick slices.
2   Skin the tomatoes, cut in two horizontally, and remove the pulp and seeds.
3   Strain the pulp and seeds though a conical sieve to obtain the juice.
4   Heat the white stock.
5   Singe the chicken legs and cut in two at the joint.
6   Season the legs and cook in a skillet with olive oil, frothy butter, garlic, and slices of onion until the legs are golden brown, then remove.
7   Sweat the slices of onion for a few minutes and deglaze the skillet with the vinegars.
8   Reduce the vinegar completely, then add the white wine. Boil the white wine and reduce it for about 4 minutes.
9   Add the tomato juice, white stock, chicken stock powder, and bouquet garni. Bring to a boil again and skim.
10   Cover the chicken fricassee and cook on very low heat for about 25 minutes.
11   When the fricassee is cooked, remove the meat and put it in a bowl covered with a damp cloth so it does not dry out.
12   Remove the garlic cloves, peel and crush them, then put them back in the cooking liquid. Reduce the cooking liquid until it has the desired consistency.
13   Cool the cooking liquid in a cooling unit or refrigerator.
14   Pack individual portions of fricassee in plastic food boxes. Add 150 g of cooking liquid to each portion and keep in the refrigerator.
15   When ready to serve, heat up portions in a pan. Add a piece of butter. Cover and simmer gently.
16   Season with salt and pepper and sprinkle with chopped tarragon, then add a dash of sherry vinegar, a twist of coarse-ground pepper, and fleur de sel, and serve.

David Rathgeber

I met Albert Raurich for the first time in 1997, when he came to elBulli as a young stager. He quickly distinguished himself in the kitchen and became part of the permanent staff as chef de partie the following year. In 2001 he became chef de cuisine in the elBulli kitchen, a position he held until 2007 when he decided to branch out on his own and open a restaurant in Barcelona—the Asian-inspired tapas bar Dos Palillos at the Casa Camper hotel.

Alberto is one of the most "*bullinianos*" cooks I have ever known. He spent almost ten years with us and his cuisine, which follows the Asian tradition in its form, skillfully blends Asian influences with the knowledge and experience he gained at elBulli, giving it a unique soul and personality.

What I find particularly interesting about Albert's cuisine is his ability and vision in combining avant-garde gastronomy with traditional Asian styles, while still managing to maintain a great respect for Asian cuisine. He takes a purist approach to Asian techniques, valuing the raw materials highly and choosing the finest seasonal ingredients.

Albert has said, "Eating tapas is not only a way of eating, but rather a philosophy of life." Along with sommelier Tamae Imachi, (who was also at elBulli from 2002 to 2004) and head chef Takeshi Somekawa, at Dos Palillos Albert explores how the principles of tapas—assorted foods and flavors eaten in small portions as snacks, using toothpicks—have existed in Asian cuisine for many years. The concept at Dos Palillos is to unify the philosophy behind the Spanish tapas with the "tapas" of Asian gastronomy. With this kind of cuisine Albert, together with other chefs who are working in the same direction, is forging an exciting, innovative path between the new ideas of the West and the ancient traditions of the East.

Ferran Adrià

Albert Raurich was born in 1970 in Barcelona. He followed culinary school with a year at the city's Los Inmortales, an Italian restaurant where he gained confidence and a solid knowledge of pasta-making. After a year in military service, cooking game shot by the officers, he returned to a position at Els Pescadors under Joseph Maulini, gaining a thorough grounding in the handling and preparation of fish. From here, Raurich went on to become chef de cuisine at Barcelona's Café de L' Academia. In 1997 he had the good fortune to be hired by Ferran Adrià at elBulli, where he stayed for the next eleven years, the final seven as chef de cuisine. Raurich honed his technique to the highest standard during this time, taking part in every facet of the creative life of elBulli. With the support of Adrià, he opened Dos Palillos in 2008, where he combines the Spanish tapas tradition with Asian cuisine.

MENU

Curry chicken crisp

~

Vietnamese fresh spring rolls

~

Ankimo: Japanese-style monkfish liver

~

Bonito and sea urchin chawanmushi

~

Chanquete tempura with green shiso

~

Toro temaki

~

Stir-fried baby vegetables

Albert Raurich

1
Making elBulli Chinese tarts

2
Fruits and vegetables
at the market

3
Albert Raurich planning
a new menu

4
Peeling shrimp

5 & 6
The crowded bar
at Dos Palillos

CURRY CHICKEN CRISP
Serves 10

Eat at room temperature, with your fingers, all year round.

1 kg chicken skin • potato starch, for dusting • sunflower oil, for pan-frying • salt • Madras curry powder

1 With a sharp knife, remove any excess fat from inside the chicken skin, together with any feathers or hairs. Clean in plenty of cold water.
2 Blanch the chicken skin in boiling water for 30 seconds.
3 Drain the skin, spread it out on a baking sheet lined with parchment paper, and freeze.
4 Once frozen, cut the skin into strips 2.5 cm wide and as long as possible.
5 Dust the strips with potato starch, covering them well. Shake off any excess starch.
6 Pan-fry in sunflower oil at 335°F (170°C).
7 When crisp, drain and dry on paper towels.
8 Season with salt and curry powder.

BONITO AND SEA URCHIN CHAWANMUSHI
Serves 10

Eat hot, with a small spoon, between December and April. Try to eat a little chawanmushi and sea urchin with each spoonful.

For the bonito and kombu dashi
1 liter mineral water • 10 g kombu seaweed • 30 g *katsuobushi* (dried bonito)

1 Put the mineral water and kombu seaweed in a large pan and hydrate for 2 hours.
2 Place the pan on medium heat, and lower the heat just before the water boils. Remove the kombu seaweed and add the katsuobushi.
3 Immediately remove from the heat. Cover the pan and let infuse for 10 minutes.
4 Strain through a fine-mesh sieve without applying any pressure.

For the chawanmushi
250 g free-range egg • 2 tbsp mirin • 2 tbsp sake • 3 g salt

1 Beat the egg, mixing in the dashi, mirin, sake, and salt.
2 Pour 35 ml of the mixture into each of 10 ceramic bowls.
3 Cover and steam for 12 minutes at 200°F (100°C).
4 Remove from the steam and let cool, uncovered. Once cool, cover again and set aside until you are ready to finish and present the dish.

For the sea urchin roe
10 live sea urchins

1 Scald the sea urchins in boiling water for 10 seconds.
2 Carefully cut along the bottom of the sea urchins with scissors.
3 Strain the liquid through cheesecloth (muslin). One by one remove the roe from the sea urchins and place in the liquid. Set aside until you are ready to finish and serve.

To finish and serve
1 Heat the chawanmushi at 160°F (70°C) for 3 minutes.
2 Arrange the sea urchin roe on top of the chawanmushi. Cover and heat for another minute before serving.

CHANQUETE TEMPURA WITH GREEN SHISO
Serves 10

Eat hot, with chopsticks, in a single mouthful, in March, April or May.

For the chanquete parcels
10 green shiso leaves • 250 g *chanquetes* (Spanish whitebait)

1 Cut the shiso leaves into 4 strips of 2 x 6 cm.
2 Place 6 g whitebait on top of each shiso strip.
3 Roll to make 40 parcels, and set aside.

For the rice tempura batter
130 g rice flour • 200 ml mineral water

Mix the rice flour with the mineral water and let stand for at least 30 minutes.

To finish and serve
335 ml sunflower oil • salt

1 Heat the sunflower oil to 350°F (180°C).
2 Coat the parcels in the tempura batter and drain the excess. Fry in the hot oil until crisp.
3 Drain any excess oil. Gently dry over paper towels, salt lightly, and serve.

STIR-FRIED BABY VEGETABLES
Serves 10

Eat hot, with chopsticks, at any time of year, substituting seasonal vegetables as appropriate. When eating, alternate the vegetables.

For the baby vegetables
100 g baby carrots • salt • 200 g baby corn • 200 g snow peas (mangetout) • 300 g pak choi hearts (about 10 pieces) • 100 g dried Judas ear mushroom • 150 g *suan cai* (pickled cabbage)

1 Peel the baby carrots and cut them in 4 lengthwise.
2 Wash the baby corn in mineral water and cut in half diagonally. Blanch in boiling salted water for 15 seconds, then chill in iced and salted water.
3 Clean the snow peas. Remove the string from the side and cut in half diagonally.
4 Cut the outer parts of the pak choi diagonally into pieces the same size as the snow peas. Cut the hearts in half.
5 Rehydrate the Judas ear mushroom in warm water.
6 Peel the *suan cai* and cut diagonally into 6 x 0.2-cm pieces.

For the sauce
85 ml oyster sauce • 55 ml soy sauce • 22 ml Shaoxing wine • 85 ml reduced chicken stock • 11 g potato starch

1 Pour the oyster sauce, soy sauce, Shaoxing wine, and chicken stock into a bowl and dissolve the potato starch in the mixture.
2 Put the sauce into a squeezy bottle and set aside for finishing and presentation.

For the stir-fry base
10 g dried garlic • 10 g fresh ginger • 2 tbsp sunflower oil

1 Peel the garlic and ginger and chop finely.
2 Heat a wok. Add the oil and brown the garlic and ginger in it.
3 Remove and set aside for finishing and presentation.

To finish and serve
sunflower oil, for pan-frying • salt • black pepper • sesame oil • cilantro (coriander) shoots • white begonia flowers • red begonia flowers • elderflowers

1 Heat a wok and add plenty of sunflower oil, covering the sides well. Drain, leaving approximately 1 tablespoon oil in the wok.
2 Lightly stir-fry the baby vegetables.
3 Add the garlic and ginger, taking care not to burn them.
4 Immediately add the sauce and reduce until it sticks to the vegetables. Lightly season with salt, black pepper, and sesame oil.
5 Arrange the vegetables on a plate and scatter the shoots and flowers over them.

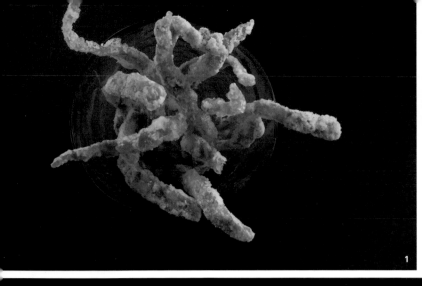

1
Curry chicken crisp

2
Bonito and sea urchin
chawanmushi

3
Stir-fried baby vegetables

4
Chanquete tempura
with green shiso

Albert Raurich

I met Lyndy after a mistake in the kitchen years ago. When I was at Aubergine we served a chocolate fondant dessert that had a clear paper lining. Lyndy had ordered one but when it arrived at her table the waiter had left the paper on. I went out into the dining room to apologize, and that's where it started.

Lyndy isn't just professional and capable, but enthusiastic, charming and extremely hard-working. She and the fantastic, young, dynamic team she has built are dedicated to making a complete success of every event they run. Absolute Taste was originally focused on providing catering and hospitality for VIP guests of large companies such as Vodafone, McLaren, and Mercedes, and the company has now grown to become the leader in its field.

A couple of years ago, when we were planning a tasting menu for the Hampton Court Music festival, we decided that a few changes were needed. Rather than waiting until our next meeting, Lyndy ran through all the changes there and then. I didn't find out for another couple of days that she had missed a flight in order to make those changes. That's dedication.

Lyndy has the patience of a saint and huge tolerance. I have to cook for fifty or sixty diners whereas she has to cook for hundreds in one sitting—yet every one of her dishes arrives in front of the guest looking impeccable and tasting sensational. It's incredible to watch her running one of the larger events. She is calm, composed, and utterly focused, watching each and every dish coming out of the kitchen, occasionally tasting to check that it's up to her high standards. No mistakes ever manage to slip by Lyndy—no wonder Absolute Taste has a worldwide reputation.

Gordon Ramsay

Lyndy Redding was born in Scarborough, U.K., moving to London as a teenager to attend Tante Marie culinary school. As a nervous new graduate, Redding set up her catering and event-designing company, Absolute Taste, and the company has since gone from strength to strength. Redding provides unflappable Michelin-standard outdoor catering for hundreds of guests at a time, working for clients like Formula 1 teams or David Beckham. Faced with each new catering location, Redding remains flexible and works with her team of chefs to tailor each menu to its event, building up a dizzying recipe repertoire of cuisines and flavors. She cites culinary influences including Thomas Keller, of the French Laundry, and Gordon Ramsay, with whom she recently purchased the culinary school where she trained. At Tante Marie she aims to improve standards in food education through a more dynamic apprenticeship scheme, and also provides cooking courses through Absolute Taste.

Canapés

Salt-and-pepper-crusted beef tenderloin skewers with horseradish cream

~

Tuna tataki with radish, apple, and mustard served on chopsticks

~

Pea and mint tartlets with feta and fresh mint

~

Parmesan haddock goujons with a caper aioli

~

Parmesan shortbread with buffalo mozzarella topped with slow-roasted cherry tomato and homemade pesto

~

Extra-long cheese straws

Bowl food

Green Thai chicken curry with basmati rice

~

Salad of five-year-old Iberico ham, aged Manchego cheese, white peach, tashkin mint, and arugula with a Jerez sherry dressing

~

Baby sausage and mash: Cumberland sausages, with a cream pomme puree topped with onion gravy and crispy shallot

Three-course dinner

Wild mushroom tartlet with English asparagus served with an herb hollandaise

~

Seared sea bass fillet with a warm tomato and basil dressing, with roasted new potatoes and spinach topped with deep-fried stuffed zucchini flowers and a lemon beurre blanc

~

Vanilla panna cotta with rhubarb jelly topped with strawberry and rhubarb compôte and served with homemade shortbread

Lyndy Redding

1 & 3
Lyndy Redding preparing
for an event

2
Redding in the kitchen

Absolute Taste, London, UK

1
Salt-and-pepper-crusted
beef tenderloin skewers with
horseradish cream

2
Tuna tataki with radish, apple,
and mustard served
on chopsticks

3
Parmesan haddock goujons
with a caper aioli

4
Pea and mint tartlets with
feta and fresh mint

5
Extra-long cheese straws

SALT-AND-PEPPER-CRUSTED BEEF TENDERLOIN SKEWERS WITH HORSERADISH CREAM
Makes 12

Prepare these ahead of time. They're for cooking on the barbecue, but keep an eye on them as they'll be ready in a matter of minutes.

200 g beef tenderloin • 1 handful fresh rosemary and thyme leaves, chopped • 1 clove garlic, crushed • sea salt and freshly ground black pepper • 1 tbsp horseradish mixed with 280 ml crème fraîche

1 Soak 12 wooden skewers in cold water for at least 20 minutes. This helps to prevent burning during cooking.
2 Meanwhile, slice the meat into 12 equal-size pieces and heat a broiler (grill) or lightly oiled chargrill pan until smoking.
3 Mix together the herbs and the garlic.
4 Skewer a piece of beef onto each wooden stick and season well with salt and pepper. Sprinkle with the chopped herbs and crushed garlic mixture, pressing gently so that it sticks to the meat.
5 Char-grill for 2 minutes on each side, making sure they are still slightly rare.
6 Serve immediately with a pot of horseradish crème fraîche for dipping.

TUNA TATAKI WITH RADISH, APPLE, AND MUSTARD SERVED ON CHOPSTICKS
Makes 10 canapés

200 g sashimi-grade tuna fillet, cut into a cylinder shape, from the head end • 2 tsp sesame oil • 25 ml light soy sauce • 1 Granny smith apple • 4 radishes • 1 tsp wholegrain mustard • 1 tbsp mirin • small bunch micro-cress or baby greens

1 Rub the tuna with the sesame oil and just a splash of soy sauce to season.
2 Heat a heavy nonstick pan till it begins to smoke, then take it off the heat and sear the tuna for just 5–10 seconds all over.
3 Remove from the pan, put on a plate, and dress with the rest of the soy and sesame oil. Chill for at least 30 minutes.
4 Grate the apple and radish into a small bowl and dress with the mustard and mirin.
5 Slice the tuna as thinly as possible, and place a pinch of the apple and radish mix onto the center of it. Place a few sprigs of micro-cress on top and wrap the tuna into a small bundle.

PEA AND MINT TARTLETS WITH FETA AND FRESH MINT
Makes about 30

400 g frozen peas • 2 shallots • 50 g butter • 1 handful mint • 1 tsp white-wine vinegar • salt and pepper, to taste • 3 eggs, separated • 100 ml crème fraîche • 115 ml heavy (double) cream • 100 g feta cheese • 30 mini tartlet shells (either homemade or good-quality bought)

1 Preheat the oven to 325°F (160°C).
2 Defrost the peas by leaving them out for an hour on a baking sheet or by running cold water over them for 10 minutes.
3 Roughly chop the shallots into small dice, and sweat in a skillet for 10 minutes on low heat with the butter.
4 Once the shallots are transparent and soft, transfer to a blender and pulse for 30 seconds.
5 Add the peas and most of the mint (reserving a little to garnish) and keep blending (you may need to add a splash of water to get them going). Stop occasionally to scrape down the sides of the blender, and continue to blend until you have a smooth puree.
6 Season with the wine vinegar and the salt and pepper.
7 Whisk the egg yolks with the crème fraîche and most of the cream, season, and stir into the pea puree.
8 Beat the feta with the remaining cream and put into a pastry (piping) bag.
9 Fill each tartlet shell with the pea puree to the rim, but be careful not to overfill. Bake for 5–10 minutes until just set. Remove from the oven and let cool.
10 To serve, pipe a little creamed feta on top of the tartlets, and shred the rest of the mint and sprinkle on top to garnish.

PARMESAN HADDOCK GOUJONS WITH A CAPER AIOLI
Makes 10 canapés

2 cloves garlic, unpeeled • 150 ml mayonnaise • 2 tbsp capers • zest and juice of ½ lemon • 200 g haddock fillet • salt and pepper • 50 g all-purpose (plain) flour • 1 egg • splash of milk • 100 g panko (Japanese crunchy) breadcrumbs, or similar • vegetable oil, for frying

1 Preheat the oven to 400°F (200°C).
2 Roast the garlic cloves in the oven for about 20 minutes until bursting out of their skins. Once cool, skin and mash with a fork or the back of a spoon. Put into a bowl and mix in the mayonnaise, the capers, the lemon zest and most of the juice.
3 Slice the haddock into finger-size goujons, then season with salt and pepper, and dredge with the flour.
4 Whisk the egg and milk together and toss the goujons in this mixture.
5 Roll the goujons in the breadcrumbs until well covered.
6 Deep-fry in hot oil until golden brown and crispy.
7 Season well with salt and a squeeze of lemon, and serve with the caper aioli.

EXTRA-LONG CHEESE STRAWS
Makes about 50

100 g Dijon mustard • 50 g wholegrain mustard • 500 g frozen puff pastry dough (all-butter if possible), thawed • 200 g Parmesan cheese, finely grated • 20 g paprika

1 Preheat the oven to 340°F (170°C).
2 Mix together the mustards and spread thinly and evenly over the pastry.
3 Mix together the Parmesan and paprika, sprinkle over the pastry, and then slice into 1-cm strips.
4 Hold one end of a pastry strip and use the palm of your hand to roll it into a twist, pressing gently to incorporate the Parmesan into the pastry. Repeat for the remaining strips.
5 Bake on a baking sheet for 8–10 minutes, taking care not to let them get too brown, but still making sure they are fully cooked (otherwise they will bend).
6 Remove from the oven and let them cool and firm up before moving them.

Lyndy Redding

I have known Mads Refslund for years, ever since he was an apprentice at Noma, my restaurant in Copenhagen. Already back then it was obvious that he had rare talent. He was curious, open-minded, patient, and ambitious. Since then his will and his ambition have grown stronger. Mads's kitchen at MR is more defined and pure than ever; it has transformed from good regional cuisine to a deeply personal and intelligent, almost artistic way of thinking about food: "Everything flows, I try to always be in a state of flow, which keeps my ideas and hands working and exploring. My quest is to explore the origin of the elements behind every dish I produce, and then focus on the food source's freshness. The hardest task is not to pollute pure taste with excessive preparation and cooking. This is the philosophy around which my cuisine is built."

International contemporary restaurants around the world today are becoming increasingly similar. When dining at one of these restaurants I rarely have a sense of time and place. Most of the products are imported from around the world and the menu always offers the obvious luxury items such as caviar and foie gras, prepared in comparable ways. Eating at MR is different, though. There, I always have a sense of time and place. You taste what time of the year it is, and get the feeling that this particular meal could only exist here, at this restaurant.

René Redzepi

Mads Refslund was born in 1977 in Copenhagen, where he has carved out an illustrious career in food that began with training at culinary school and positions at the restaurants Formel and Coquus, among others. He moved on to become head chef at major Copenhagen restaurants The Paul, Noma, and Kokkeriet before opening his own restaurant, MR, in 2005. He cites the natural environment of his country as a major inspiration in cooking, as well as a concern with the fleeting quality of experience and a desire to preserve taste and resist overpreparation. The results of this philosophy are dishes that are perfectly at home, with just a dash of poignancy: "Burning Fields," for instance, is a starter of roots and truffles with smoke that recalls the practice of the farmers on the small island of Samsø, who burn their fields each year to make way for fresh seeds. Refslund's whimsical yet formidable cuisine won MR its first Michelin star in 2005.

MENU

Mackerel and coconut with porcini and almond dust

~

Raw foie gras and Norwegian lobster with walnuts and wood sorrel

~

Burning Fields: aroma and textures of burning fields

~

Roasted sea scallops with pumpkin, carrots, and sea buckthorn

~

Hazelnuts with Jerusalem artichoke, vanilla, and sea salt

~

Forest: aromas from the woods

Mads Refslund

1 & 2
Mads Refslund in the
kitchen at MR

3
Foraging for mushrooms
in the woods

MR, Copenhagen, Denmark

MACKEREL AND COCONUT WITH PORCINI AND ALMOND DUST
Serves 4

Sea and forest meet. Mackerel, representing the richness of the sea, is the perfect match for the nutty flavor of raw porcini.

Dried woodruff, to taste • coconut flour, to taste • salt • 4 mackerel fillets • lemon juice, for marinating • fresh porcini (ceps), to make the lasagne • fresh coconut, to make the lasagne • dried porcini, for grating • almonds

1 For the woodruff powder, roast the coconut flour in a dry pan until golden, then crush in a mortar along with the woodruff and some salt.
2 Rub the mackerel fillets in salt about 1 hour before serving. Cut each fillet into three and squeeze some lemon juice over them.
3 Cut the fresh porcini and fresh coconut into thin slices, and arrange one by one in layers. Grate the dried porcini and almonds over this "lasagne" of porcini and coconut so that it looks like ash.

RAW FOIE GRAS AND NORWEGIAN LOBSTER WITH WALNUTS AND WOOD SORREL
Serves 4

Usually foie gras is cooked, but when served in its natural state its has a much purer flavor. The foie gras and raw Norwegian lobster melt together like oil and butter. Balance is achieved by the sharpness of lime, wood sorrel, and salt.

200 g foie gras, cleaned • 120 g Norwegian lobster (langoustine) tails, cleaned • 12 fresh walnuts in their shells • milk, for boiling the walnuts • wood sorrel, cleaned • juice of 1 lemon • 4 tbsp walnut oil • salt

1 Freeze the foie gras and Norwegian lobster tails 24 hours before serving.
2 Shell the walnuts and give them a short boil in milk, then quickly place them in ice water, and thinly slice them.
3 Cut the frozen foie gras and Norwegian lobster tails into paper-thin slices. Now you should have flakelike components for the dish.
4 Arrange the slices of foie gras and Norwegian lobster tails in 4 little squares, then scatter the walnuts, wood sorrel, lemon juice, walnut oil, and salt over the squares.

BURNING FIELDS: AROMA AND TEXTURES OF BURNING FIELDS
Serves 4

In late summer and early fall (autumn), farmers burn their fields to prepare the soil for new crops. This dish consists of what has escaped the heat by growing underground — beets, truffles, carrots, other roots. An entire biosphere of life is to be found beneath the ashes.

For the potato and mushroom powder
170 g potatoes • 1 tsp salt • 250 g dried shiitake mushrooms • 2 tsp muscovado sugar • 170 g honey-roasted peanuts

Slice the potatoes very thinly on a mandolin and poach in salted water. Refresh in ice water, then dry until crisp. Blend all the ingredients together in a blender.

For the peanut vinagrette
juice of 1 lime • 1 tbsp honey • 200 ml peanut oil

Squeeze the lime juice into the honey, and blend in oil with a hand blender.

For the smoked potatoes
12 small red potatoes, boiled • salt • peanut oil, for rubbing • sawdust and hay, for smoking

Rub the cooked potatoes with a little salt and peanut oil and put them on a rack to fit a half-size gourmet tray. Line the tray with aluminum foil and sprinkle it with sawdust and hay. Place the tray under a broiler (grill) until the hay starts to burn. Set the rack with the potatoes over the tray, transfer to a burner, cover with aluminum foil so that the fire is stifled and the potatoes smoke.

For the truffle puree
1½ shallots, cut into small dice • 1½ cloves garlic, finely sliced • 30 g white button mushrooms • 50 ml sherry • 100 ml mushroom bouillon • 100 g truffle from Gotland • 15 g parsley root (Hamburg parsley), cooked • 1 tbsp black truffle oil • salt • squid ink, to color

Roast the shallots, garlic, and mushrooms, add the sherry and reduce until the sherry is completely evaporated. Add the mushroom bouillon and reduce by half. Blend the mixture with the truffles, parsley root, truffle oil, and salt to taste. Color with squid ink.

For the roasted peanut mayonnaise
1 lemon • 25 g butter • 50 g Jerusalem artichokes, peeled • 2 soft-boiled eggs (4 minutes) • 100 ml peanut oil • salt

Halve the lemon and roast on a broiler (grill) pan. Caramelize the Jerusalem artichoke in butter in a heavy pan, then deglaze the pan with water. Let cool. Blend the Jerusalem artichoke with the soft-boiled eggs, then slowly incorporate the peanut oil, while stirring, to create a mayonnaise. Add the juice from the roasted lemon, and salt to taste.

For the butter emulsion for cooking vegetables
4 heads of Romaine lettuce • 4 small carrots • 4 bonbon beets • 4 yellow beets • 4 small fennel bulbs • 4 small red onions • 4 green onions • 4 small Jerusalem artichokes • 12 wild onions • 200 g butter • 200 g water

1 Blanch all the vegetables in separate pans until almost cooked.
2 To create a butter emulsion, bring the water and butter to a boil and blend.
3 Bring the emulsion almost to a boil and add the blanched vegetables to finish cooking. Marinate in the peanut vinaigrette before serving.

For the raw marinated vegetables
4 radishes with tops • 4 slices truffle • 4 thin slices candy beets • 4 thin slices Jerusalem artichoke • 4 thin slices carrots • 20 roasted peanuts

To serve
Put 3 dots of truffle puree and roasted peanut mayonnaise on the plate randomly. Scatter all the vegetables around the plate, then sprinkle with potato and mushroom powder.

FOREST: AROMAS FROM THE WOODS
Serves 4

This dessert is a walk in the forest, and every element is found in the forest surroundings. All the senses are awakened with this dish: the taste is delicate, the colors are natural, and the imagination is stimulated to explore the aromas of the trees in the forest.

For the oak cream
500 ml whipping cream • 90 g sugar cane • 30 g oak bark • 6 egg yolks

1 Bring the cream and sugar to a boil with the bark and let it rest for 30 minutes.
2 Preheat the oven to 225°F (110°C).
3 Strain the cream through a sieve and whip in the egg yolks. Transfer to an ovenproof dish. Bake for 55 minutes in a bain-marie, then cool and pass through a sieve.

For the hazelnut paste
300 g hazelnuts, skinned and roasted • 300 g milk • 10 ml condensed milk, boiled

1 Place all ingredients in a Pacojet container and freeze.
2 When frozen, blend it twice.

For the pine needle oil
65 g neutral oil, such as canola (rapeseed) • 50 g fresh pine needles

1 Heat the oil to 150°F (70°C), add the pine needles and let it rest for 50 minutes.
2 Strain the oil and discard the pine needles.

For the airy pine needle chocolate
500 g chocolate • 65 g pine needle oil

Melt the chocolate in a bain-marie and blend it with the pine oil until airy and smooth. Fill a siphon with the mixture, add 3 gas cartridges, shake really well and then dispense into a half-gourmet tray. Quickly, to trap the air bubbles, put the tray in a vacuum-pack bag, then vacuum the tray, but stop the vacuum machine before it creates a complete vacuum. Cool down.

For the chestnut cake
270 g butter • 260 g sugar • 2 eggs • 1 egg white • 360 g flour • 10 g baking powder • 140 ml milk • 400 g chestnut puree

1 Preheat the oven to 350°F (180°C).

2 Beat the butter and sugar, add the whole eggs one by one, then the egg white, beating all the time. Fold in the flour and baking powder, then stir in the milk and the chestnut puree. Rest in the fridge for 1 hour, then bake for 35 minutes.

3 When cooked, crumble into pieces and dry in the Hold-o-mat overnight.

For the birch ice cream
350 ml milk • 150 ml cream • 100 g birch bark • 2 egg yolks • 200 g sugar • 1 tbsp food thickener

1 Boil the milk and cream with the birch bark, then let infuse for 30 minutes.

2 Whip together the egg yolks and sugar, strain the birch bark infusion into the mixture, and add the food thickener. Freeze.

To assemble and serve
8 fresh hazelnuts, for garnish • 8 fresh walnuts, for garnish • 12 pieces wood sorrel, for garnish

Spread the hazelnut paste on the plate with a brush, sprinkle some chestnut cake randomly, add a few pieces of pine needle chocolate, the nuts, and the wood sorrel. Place 3 mounds of the oak cream around the hazelnut paste. Finish with a quenelle of the ice cream.

1
Mackerel and coconut with porcini and almond dust

2
Burning Fields: aroma and textures of burning fields

3
Raw foie gras and Norwegian lobster with walnuts and wood sorrel

4
Forest: aromas from the woods

Mads Refslund

1, 2 & 4
At Tsukiji fish market

3
The dining room
at Sushi Saito

5
Koji Saito preparing sushi

Koji Saito

MENU

White shrimp

~

Octopus simmered
in mirin and soy sauce

~

Steamed abalone

~

Scallops on a skewer

~

Small rice bowl with
sea urchin roe

~

Soy sauce-marinated
salmon roe

~

Fatty tuna belly

~

Mildly fatty tuna belly

~

Lean part of tuna

~

Japanese flounder

~

Arch shell

~

Japanese horse mackerel

~

Conger eel

~

Thick Japanese omelet
with shrimp

Koji Saito was born in Chiba prefecture, Japan, in 1972. He began his culinary career at the age of 18 with stints in restaurants in Chiba and Ginza. During this time Saito encountered his lifelong mentor, Masatsugu Kanesaka, whom he assisted, at the age of 27, in his newly opened restaurant, Ginza Kanesaka. The restaurant went on to receive an overwhelming critical reception, including two Michelin stars. In 2002, Saito became head chef at Kanesaka's branch restaurant, Akasaka Kanesaka, following this success with the 2005 opening of Akasaka Saito to great acclaim, quickly winning the restaurant a Michelin star. Since then, Saito has opened his own restaurant, Sushi Saito, in Tokyo. He regards the finesse and technical mastery needed to create sushi as being akin to theater, with the restaurant acting as a stage for the chef's skill, spirit, taste, and service, a method of preserving ancient techniques through their enactment.

An editor who I have known for ten years and who I trust more than any guidebook when it comes to restaurants in Tokyo once asked me me, "There's a sushi restaurant that I think is the best in Tokyo. Would you like to join me for a meal there?"

To put it simply, Saito's sushi is exemplary in the outstanding *anbai* (level of quality) of everything in his cuisine. The size is first of all optimal. I deem it highly important that sushi should be made into a size that allows the flavor to be enjoyed most thoroughly but it usually comes either too large or too small. Encountering sushi of the perfect size is regrettably rarer than seeing a shooting star.

Moreover, Saito's sushi presents a perfect balance between *shari* (rice) and *neta* (the topping), both in terms of size and flavor. It would be impossible to list all the aspects, such as changing the rice periodically to keep the right temperature or slicing the fish in different ways according to the type of the fish (slicing white meat fish and blue-backed fish relatively thickly and thinly, respectively, for example), in which Saito's careful work can be discerned. The fact that the sushi is packed to a consistency of my personal liking is, too, a major factor in my love for Saito's work. It is delightful to perceive Saito's young energy in each and every one of the sushi that have been made with the utmost care in producing the perfect *anbai*.

Yoshihiro Murata

1
White shrimp (left), octopus simmered in mirin and soy sauce (center), and scallops on a skewer (far right)

2
Soy sauce-marinated salmon roe (bottom right)

3
Thick Japanese omelet with shrimp (bottom right)

4
Koji Saito preparing sushi

WHITE SHRIMP
Serves 3–4

200 g white shrimp (prawns) • kelp (kombu)

1   Remove the shells of the shrimp and soak in salt water for 2–3 minutes.
2   Drain all excess water and sandwich between two sheets of kelp for 1–2 hours.
3   Remove the shrimp and serve.

OCTOPUS SIMMERED IN MIRIN AND SOY SAUCE
Serves 3–4

1 octopus • 1 daikon • soy sauce, to taste • mirin, to taste • sugar, to taste • kelp (kombu)

1   Rub the octopus with salt to remove sliminess.
2   Sever the tentacles from the body.
3   Beat the tentacles with the daikon to make them tender.
4   Simmer the tentacles in water, soy sauce, mirin, sugar, and kelp for ½–1 hour, then serve.

SCALLOPS ON A SKEWER
Serves 1

3 scallops, white meat only • salt

1   Wash the scallops thoroughly with salt water.
2   Place the scallops on a skewer and let dry in the shade.
3   Sprinkle with a little salt, grill over high flame, and serve.

SOY SAUCE-MARINATED SALMON ROE
Serves 3–4

1 skein salmon roe (*sujiko*) • salt • kelp dashi (seaweed soup stock) • mirin, to taste • soy sauce, to taste

1   Wash 1 skein of salmon roe with salt water and carefully remove the skein.
2   Soak in salt water for 1 minute.
3   Drain in a colander and remove all excess water.
4   Immerse in kelp dashi seasoned with mirin and soy sauce, and let stand for 5–10 minutes, then serve.

THICK JAPANESE OMELET WITH SHRIMP
Serves 30

700 g Japanese gray shrimp (prawns) • 180 ml water • mirin, to taste • salt, to taste • sugar, to taste • 13 eggs

1   Remove the shrimp shells.
2   Boil the shrimp in water, then mince them when cooked.
3   Add mirin, salt, and sugar to the shrimp, then mix in the eggs.
4   Pour into a yakiban pan and heat from above with charcoal for 1 hour, then serve.

Koji Saito

1–3
Chris Salans in the kitchen
at Mozaic

4
The restaurant's dining garden

Chris Salans

MENU

Mozaic teaser

~

Mozaic's "Caesar" salad,
polenta-crusted soft-shell
crab, romaine lettuce,
garlic croûton,
and Parmesan crisp

~

Confit Tasmanian
salmon, Pernod-infused
bouillabaisse emulsion,
Balinese saffron risotto,
and local "Keladi" rhubarb
in a Pinot Noir reduction

~

Crispy seared foie gras
in a trio of mango puree,
candy, and chip

~

Crispy seared duck
breast, vanilla-coriander
braised fresh Belgian
endives, sautéed black
trumpet mushrooms, and
Guinness beer emulsion
in a jasmine balsamic
reduction

~

Fresh A.O.C. Pont l'Evêque
cheese, orange marjoram
agar agar, and
olive sauce

~

Valrhona Jivara milk
chocolate mousse,
cinnamon gelée,
candied kumquats, and
caramelized almonds in
a Spanish saffron syrup

~

Petits fours

Chris Salans was born in Washington, DC, in 1970, though he grew up in France, where the regional cuisine of his mother's native Sologne made game and mushrooms an early culinary influence. Salans's energy and drive are evident in the variety of his career: He moved from the Cordon Bleu cooking school in France to a position under David Bouley at Bouley's Bakery in the US, and then to Bali. Mozaic, his restaurant there, has won a flurry of accolades for the thought and flair that Salans lends to the blending of authentic Indonesian cooking with Western culinary techniques. He applies rigorous standards of quality to a changing menu that is governed by his wanderings through the wildernesses or night markets of Bali, meaning that his constant dialogue with the freshest Indonesian flavors is expressed each evening on the restaurant plate.

I first heard about Chris while reading the *Grandes Tables du Monde* guidebook, flicking through and seeing all the usual great restaurants in Paris and London, and then I came across Mozaic in Bali. I was intrigued. A year later I happened to be invited to the West Australian Truffle Festival, and who happened to be there? Chris Salans. He had read about it and was very eager to come and meet, taste, and talk. Five years later, this determination has not flagged.

It took me a few years to finally get to Bali and enjoy dinner at Mozaic, but after eating there I came to the realization that it's too hard to judge restaurants in a ranking. Put in Paris or Melbourne, Mozaic's decor would be nothing special, but in the beautiful small village of Ubud, set among the low-lying mountain region of rice paddies and jungle, it is remarkable. I found the best of Chris's cuisine combines local flavors with classic technique, like his seafood salad combining baby squid and a langoustine-style shrimp with tamarind and a hint of saffron sauce. This, in a tropical setting, with my beautiful wife and a great bottle of Hugel Vendange Tardive Gewürtztraminer—I have had no better meal.

Chris talked a lot about the influence of working under Alain Senderens at Louis Carton for a number of years. A hugely disciplined and gifted chef, Senderens was famous for matching food with wine. You can see this influence in Chris's wine list and his classical approach to the menu.

Chris recharges his enthusiasm by reading as many books as possible as well as working in the kitchens of colleagues and even making the odd phone call to ask about technique. I would have to imagine that after tasting suckling pig joint, called *babi guling* in Ubud, that pork is his favorite ingredient. Combined with local herbs and palm hearts, this emphasizes what Chris will become well known for. The discovery is just beginning.

Shannon Bennett

1
Crispy seared duck breast,
vanilla-coriander braised
fresh Belgian endives, sautéed
black trumpet mushrooms and
Guinness beer emulsion in
a jasmine balsamic reduction

2
Valrhona Jivara milk chocolate
mousse, cinnamon gelée, candied
kumquats, and caramelized almonds
in a Spanish saffron syrup

CRISPY SEARED DUCK BREAST, VANILLA-CORIANDER BRAISED FRESH BELGIAN ENDIVES, SAUTÉED BLACK TRUMPET MUSHROOMS, AND GUINNESS BEER EMULSION IN A JASMINE BALSAMIC REDUCTION
Serves 4

For the seared duck breast
2 (200–250 g) duck breasts

Pan-sear a duck breast on the skin side only until all the fat has rendered. Flip the breast onto its other side and remove the pan from the heat. Allow the duck to rest to room temperature in the pan. The duck will be perfectly cooked, tender, and moist.

For the endives
300 g endives • ½ tsp coriander seeds • 4 vanilla beans • pinch of salt and pepper • 65 g butter • ¼ tsp confectioners' (icing) sugar

1 Take the endive leaves off and discard the stalks.
2 Toast the coriander seeds and crush them.
3 Split the vanilla beans and remove the seeds.
4 Cook the endives sous-vide with all the other ingredients in a sealed vacuum-pack bag and steam in the oven at 195°F (90°C) for about 45 minutes or until cooked.

For the sautéed black trumpet mushrooms
100 g black trumpet mushrooms • olive oil, for sautéing • 1 tbsp butter • 1 tbsp shallots, chopped • 1 tsp thyme, picked • salt and pepper to taste • 1 tsp chopped chives

Sauté mushrooms in hot oil on a pan. Add the butter, chopped shallots, and thyme leaves. Season with salt and pepper to taste. Finish with chopped chives.

For the Guinness emulsion
650 ml Guinness • 30 g dried prunes • 30 g sugar • 200 ml light beer • salt and pepper to taste

1 Simmer the Guinness with the prunes and sugar until reduced by half. Allow to cool and refrigerate for 24 hours.
2 Bring the Guinness base to a boil and blend until smooth. Strain. Add the light beer and season with salt and pepper to taste. Aerate with a hand blender to create a foam.

For the jasmine balsamic reduction
350 ml balsamic vinegar • 300 g black grapes • 200 g glucose • 8 drops jasmine aroma

Simmer the grapes, glucose, and balsamic vinegar and reduce by three-quarters. Strain and reduce to the desired consistency. Add the jasmine aroma when the mixture is cold.

To serve
sprig of fresh herbs, to garnish, such as marjoram

On a dinner plate make a circle of jasmine balsamic reduction. Caramelize the endives in a hot pan and place them in the center of the reduction. Top with slices of the duck magret, then the sautéed mushrooms and a few spoons of the Guinness emulsion. Garnish with a sprig of fresh herb.

VALRHONA JIVARA MILK CHOCOLATE MOUSSE, CINNAMON GELÉE, CANDIED KUMQUATS, AND CARAMELIZED ALMONDS IN A SPANISH SAFFRON SYRUP
Serves 20

For the cinnamon gelée
50 g cinnamon • 50 g water • 500 ml milk • 2 egg yolks • 10 g sugar • 300 g milk chocolate Jivara (40%) • 1½ (1.5-g) gelatin leaves

1 Boil the cinnamon sticks in water until infused, then strain to obtain cinnamon water. Bring the cinnamon water and milk to a boil. Remove from stove.
2 Make a sabayon with the egg yolk and sugar over a bain marie. Add to the milk–cinnamon mixture. Add the chopped chocolate into the sabayon mixture until fully melted.
3 Soak the gelatin in cold water. Add to the sabayon mixture and stir until well dissolved. Fill a 0.5-cm diameter, 1-cm long plastic tube. Freeze. When ready to serve, remove the gelée from the tube, twist the tube until gelée comes out. Cut in half.

For the chocolate ladyfingers
15 egg whites • 200 g sugar • 15 g egg yolk (approximately 1 yolk) • 150 g strong flour • 50 g unsweetened cocoa

1 Whip the egg whites and sugar into a meringue in a mixer. Remove from machine. Fold the egg yolks into the meringue.

2 Sift the flour and unsweetened cocoa together. Fold into the mixture.
3 Spread with a spatula on a nonstick silicone baking mat over a baking tray. Bake at 325°F (160°C) for approximately 15 minutes. Remove from the oven. Set aside. Stamp out with a 3-cm ring cutter.

For the chocolate mousse
5 egg yolks • 35 g sugar • 330 ml milk • 100 g semisweet (dark) chocolate (Araguani 72%) • 230 g milk chocolate (Jivara 40%) • 3 (1.5 g) gelatin leaves • 330 ml heavy (double) cream

1 Make a sabayon by cooking the egg yolks and sugar over a bain marie until the sugar is dissolved and the mixture slightly thickens, or reaches 180°F (82°C).
2 Boil the milk, then set aside. Pour the sabayon into the hot milk and combine. Add both chocolates to the hot sabayon and stir gently to incorporate.
3 Soak the gelatin leaves in cold water, then squeeze out any excess water. Add to the warm chocolate sabayon mixture. Set aside to cool.
4 Semi-whip the cream. Fold the whipped cream into the sabayon mixture.
5 In metal rings lined with thick, clear plastic, place 1 ladyfinger at the bottom of each ring. Place 1 piece of frozen cinnamon gelée in the center of each ring. Fill in the ring with the chocolate mousse, and blast-chill immediately. When set, spray each mousse with chocolate.

For the poached kumquat and saffron syrup
1 kg kumquats • 600 g glucose • 200 g sugar • 300 ml water • 1 g Balinese saffron

1 Bring all the ingredients except the saffron to a boil until the liquid is reduced and the kumquats have a shiny glaze. This will take about 1½–2 hours.
2 Remove the kumquats and add the saffron. Simmer for a little longer. Return the kumquats to the syrup and refrigerate.

For the caramelized almonds
300 g almond flakes • 100 g sugar • 50 g brown sugar • 4 cinnamon sticks • 10 ml water • 75 g egg white (approximately 2 whites)

Mix all the ingredients together. Place on a nonstick silicone baking mat on a baking tray.

Bake at 300°F (150°C) for approximately 20 minutes or until crispy. Let cool to room temperature. Break into the desired size and store in an airtight container.

For the cinnamon emulsion
2.5 liters water • 50 g cinnamon sticks • ½ piece orange peel • 1 vanilla bean • 75 g sugar

Bring all the ingredients to a boil and reduce by half. Set aside to cool. To serve, warm the emulsion and aerate with a hand blender to create a foam.

For the chocolate orange tuile
70 g orange peel • 60 g sugar • 200 g steamed rice • 20 g sticky rice flour • 10 g unsweetened cocoa

1 Blanch the orange peel 3 times, until the bitterness is gone, then remove from the water.
2 Blend all ingredients to a smooth puree and pass through a fine sieve. Spread into the desired shape on a nonstick silicone baking mat and bake at 200°F (100°C).

To serve
whipped cream, for serving • sprig of herbs, to garnish, such as lemon balm

Place a chocolate mousse in the center of each plate. Make patterns of chocolate mousse and saffron–kumquat syrup on the plate, then add 2 pieces of poached kumquat. Top the mousse with whipped cream, caramelized almonds, cinnamon emulsion, and 1 chocolate orange tuile. Garnish with a sprig of fresh herbs.

Chris Salans

I met Thorsten Schmidt at Noma at the beginning of 2004. The restaurant had recently opened, and Thorsten was a guest. I remember we served him terrine of eel and potatoes with horseradish, amongst a lot of other dishes we haven't cooked in a while. The second time I met him was as a guest in my kitchen—he was inspired and wanted to see more. Thorsten liked eel. Since then our relationship has grown into a friendship, a friendship where we try to inspire each other, across the country, with new ideas, produce, recipes, or anything gastronomical that's worth sharing.

In fact, our two restaurants are closely related. Not literally speaking, but in a more spiritual way. Like Noma, Thorsten's restaurant is one of the pioneers within Nordic regional cuisine. Perhaps that definition is the only certain thing you can say about his style of cuisine. The spiritual part of it is set, but everything else is left to Thorsten's mental gastronomical playground, and it's a place where anything can happen. Rules are broken, textures are invented, concepts are improved, and produce adapted—in a good way, that is. He's constantly searching for new ways or methods to get his spiritual cuisine into the spotlight.

Through the years he has produced creations such as "At Norwegian scout camp" (that actually won the prize at the Omnivore Food Festival 2008 as the most whimsical-sounding name for a dish) or "The dome", as well as more normal-sounding dishes such as ice cream made from oak bark, and sunchokes transformed into sinful cakes. And all this happens with the biggest respect for nature and seasonality.

The chef Juan Mari Arzak once told me that in order to be creative, you must think like a young child. Now that I have a child of my own, I finally understand what he meant. A child is without prejudice, ready to learn new ways, always driven by a natural curiosity. This is the best way I can describe Thorsten.

René Redzepi

Thorsten Schmidt was born in 1976 and studied cooking in Bremen, Germany. After a position at the city's Michelin-starred Bistro Grasshoff, Schmidt moved on to cook at Sallingsund Færgekro in the north of Denmark. Schmidt also worked at Molskroen in Aarhus, rising to become deputy chef and later pursuing stints at various restaurants in France. In 2005 Schmidt opened Aarhus's Malling & Schmidt, swiftly gaining widespread acclaim for his experimental Nordic cuisine. A proponent of multi-sensory gastronomy, Schmidt displays a fascination for challenging the way diners interact with food, through surprises such as nitrogen-frozen gems of horseradish, and unorthodox flavor combinations, combining corn and licorice powder as a pre-meal snack.

MENU

Champagne
Agrapart, Cuvée Venus, 2002

~

Snacks:
Juniper-smoked potato chips
and chive emulsion
Salty bonbons on cold-pressed canola oil
Dehydrated pumpkin
Corn with licorice powder
Vegetable flakes and
kipper emulsion
Herbs and raw vegetables
Warm smoked-cheese crème

~

Relaxing aroma

~

Appetizers:
French toast and mustard
Thin-sliced heavy bacon
Icelandic "corals" with
seaweed emulsion

~

The Danish beach: sea grass
"seafood" and salted herbs
Dog Point, Section 94
Sauvignon Blanc, Marlborough,
New Zealand, 2006

Swedish caviar and blinis,
sweet cicely and "rich"
koldskål made from
sheep's milk
Soleil de Chine, Domaine St.
Nicolas, Brem, France, 2005

At Norwegian scout
camp: baked potato, foil,
and baked twist bread
Diel de Noir, Schlossgut
Diel, Nahe, Germany, 2005

~

The ecological garden in
three servings: fragrance,
bouillon, and sorbet

~

Young veal, whey, and
green "grass," grain,
and sauce à la rustic
manor house
Vina El Pison, Artadi, Rioja,
Spain, 2004

~

Unripened grain tops and
wild flowers with
ice-cold "moss" on
wheatgrass
La Rosa Selvatica Moscato
D'Asti, Piemonte, Italy, 2007

~

Wood-shaved oak tree:
ice cream with salted
wood shavings
TBA Grüner Veltliner, Nigl,
Kremstal, Austria, 2006

~

"Separating ice cream"
and berries with
ground almonds,
sunflower marzipan, and
root crop "coconut"

~

Coffee and tea

~

Fresh herbal sorbet and
potted peach

~

Ice-cold "buffet" popcorn
Warm sago porridge with
compote

~

Fruit bacon

~

Potato chips in aromatic
chocolate

~

Grandmother's unbaked
cookies

~

Herb chocolate and
biscuit cake

~

Airy chocolate with
"warm" spices

Thorsten Schmidt

THE DANISH BEACH: SEA GRASS "SEAFOOD" AND SALTED HERBS
Serves 4

The dish is inspired by my early youth at the beach, standing in the water, keeping the diving goggles on the surface, looking at the seabed with its seaweed, crayfish, and small stones. This dish captures that unique moment, one that many Danish boys had at the beach.

For the oyster crème
100 g junket, lightly drained • 20 g cream • 50 g oyster water • 2 salt • 5 g lemon juice

Mix all the ingredients and add salt and lemon juice to taste.

For the seaweed mayonnaise
2 pasteurized egg yolks • 35 g baby spinach • 3 g salt • 1 tbsp seaweed vinegar • 30 ml seaweed oil • sour wild apple juice, to taste

1   Blend the egg yolks, spinach and salt until the liquid is green. Add the vinegar and then add the oil gradually to make a thick mayonnaise.
2   Season with salt and add the sour apple juice to taste.

For the seaweed dust
dried seaweed, to taste

Grind the dried seaweed in a coffee mill or spice grinder until it has turned to fine dust. Add salt to taste.

For the vacuum-pickled cucumber
200 g cucumbers, peeled • 500 g 15% sugar pickling mix • 20 g seaweed vinegar

1   Vacuum-pack the cucumbers with the pickling mix and vinegar and leave to pickle for 45 minutes until the cucumber turns lightly transparent.
2   Unpack the cucumbers and cut them into pieces. Add salt just before serving.

For the oysters
4 large cleaned Lime Fiord oysters, shucked and liquid reserved • 50 g oyster water

Steam the oysters for 20 seconds, and put them back into the cold oyster water. Set aside to cool.

For the scallops
4 large scallops • 4 g salt • 4 g sugar • zest of ½ a lemon

Mix the the scallops, salt, sugar and lemon zest well and set aside to cool for 24 hours. Then they are ready to be served.

For the vinaigrette
50 g organic cold-pressed rapeseed oil • 15 g 3-year-old apple balsamic vinegar • 15 g shallots, finely chopped • 2 g Swedish maple syrup • 2 g salt • long pepper, to taste

Mix all the ingredients together and season with salt and pepper.

For the ice-cold horseradish
1 liter whole milk • 100 g horseradish, grated • 5 g Aquavit gold • 3 g salt • 50 g lecithin

1   Mix all the ingredients and put them in a vacuum-pack bag for 1 hour.
2   Drain the milk mixture and pour it into a siphon, then charge with 2 cartridges.
3   "Cook" the milk mixture in liquid nitrogen until it becomes crisp and frozen. (Liquid nitrogen should not be handled without training in how to use it safely.)
4   Crush the frozen horseradish milk into small, abstract pieces and serve immediately.

To serve
100 g fresh Norwegian seaweed, rinsed and ready to use • 100 g cottage cheese • watercress, to garnish • fresh horseradish, finely shredded • glasswort, to garnish

1   Marinate the cucumbers, oysters, and scallops in the vinaigrette. Serve the dish on top of a plastic bag filled with water to create the feeling of being on the beach.
2   Place a little sand from the beach on a flat plate, and add small mussel shells.
3   Place the plastic bag on top of the sand and serve the seaweed, mayonnaise and cottage cheese on top of the bag.
4   Add the other components and decorate with watercress and fresh shredded horseradish. The frozen horseradish is served directly to the guest. It is important that the dish is only eaten from a spoon.

AT NORWEGIAN SCOUT CAMP: BAKED POTATO, FOIL, AND BAKED TWISTBREAD
Serves 4

The idea of this dish is to take you back to nature around the bonfire. We serve this dish with a small fire and Scout-style cutlery that diners have to unwrap. It is designed to create the feeling of being at Scout camp, with all the good memories that turned it into a magic moment.

For the Norwegian salmon prepared over a bonfire
600 g Norwegian salmon fillet, boned and trimmed • 20 g juniper berries, chopped • 10 g allspice berries, chopped • 20 g verbena, chopped • 50 g salt • 20 g sugar

1   Place the salmon in a tray. Spread the juniper berries, allspice, verbena, salt and sugar evenly on the salmon and leave it for 24 hours.
2   Rinse the spices off the salmon and dry it with a cloth.
3   Cut the salmon in pieces 7 mm thick and smoke them with the baked potatoes for 10 minutes (see below).

For the Nordic hollandaise
12 g salt • 42 g lemon juice • 20 g mustard • 580 g clarified butter • 105 g plums • 195 g eggs

1   Blend all ingredients except the butter.
2   Heat the butter to 150°F (65°C) and process in a blender until it has a thick texture. Add the rest of the ingredients.
3   Pour into a siphon and charge with 2 cartridges. Keep the siphon at 135°F (56.7°C).

For the spruce salt
100 g spruce needles from a Norwegian spruce • 100 g sea salt

1   Grind the spruce needles in a coffee grinder for 2 minutes.
2   After 2 minutes, chop them further with a knife.
3   Grind the chopped spruce needles together with the salt in the coffee grinder for another 2 minutes.

For the bonfire-smoked baked potato puree
300 g baked potatoes, skinned and mashed • a piece of wood • 50 g whole milk

1   Carefully set fire to the wood over a gas flame until there is a heavy smoke.
2   Using tongs, carefully put the smoking wood in a box together with the mashed potatoes and place a lid on the box.
3   Leave the wood and the mashed potatoes in the box for approximately 4 minutes.

4   Heat the milk in a pot and add the spruce salt.
5   Add the smoked mashed potatoes and mix it together. The temperature must remain lower than 150°F (65°C). Add the Nordic hollandaise from the siphon to a ratio of 1:1.
6   Mix the potato until it reaches a homogeneous mass with a creamy, thick texture.
7   Add spruce salt to taste.

For the malt croutons
225 g egg white • 30 g glucose • 4 g baking powder • 80 g flour • 20 g malt flour • 3 g salt • 10 g seaweed powder • 10 g blackberry powder

1   Blend all the ingredients in a Thermomix at 99°F (37°C) for 5 minutes at maximum speed.
2   Pour the mixture into a siphon and charge with 3 cartridges.
3   Dispense the mixture into a plastic container with small holes.
4   Cook the mixture in the microwave for approximately 1.5 minutes at 450 W.
5   Dry the mixture in the oven at 212°F (100°C) and break it into small pieces.

For the vegetable ashes
2 whole leeks, washed and cut in half • salt, to taste • sugar, to taste

1   Tear the leek into pieces and dry them in the oven at 340°F (170°C) for 35 minutes, until they have turned black.
2   Grind the leek in the coffee grinder with a little salt and sugar until they turn to a fine powder.

For the white ashes
100 g maltodextrin • 40 g bonfire-smoked and clarified butter (smoked in the same way as the potato puree) • 2 g salt • 1 g vegetable ashes • 1 g sugar • 2 g silver dust

Whisk all the ingredients together and add salt to taste.

For the "embers"
100 g dried chopped cranberries • 4 silver leaves

Mix together the cranberries and the silver leaves with a fork so they appear like small embers.

For the twistbread
25 g yeast • 500 ml lukewarm water • 900 g flour • 1 tsp salt • 1 tsp sugar • 50 ml oil

1   Dissolve the yeast in the water, then add half of the flour so it turns into a thin paste.

2   Add the salt, sugar, and oil. Mix the ingredients thoroughly and add the rest of the flour.
3   Knead the dough thoroughly for several minutes and put aside to rise.
4   Shape the dough, then bake the twistbread over the bonfire.

For the twistbread sauce
1 liter whole milk • 1 twig of red spruce, about 100 g • 35 g butter • 2 g lecithin • 2 g red spruce salt • extra whole milk, if necessary • sugar, to taste • apple juice, to taste • cold-pressed linseed oil, to serve

1   Vacuum-pack the whole milk and twistbread and cook it in a bain-marie at 175°F (80°C) for 1 hour.
2   Drain the milk from the twistbread and then mix 300 g of the milk with butter and red spruce, salt, lecithin and, if necessary, a little extra milk until right consistency is reached.
3   Heat the sauce to 140–160°F (60–70°C) and blend to an airy consistency before serving.
4   Drain it and add sugar and apple juice to taste.
5   Serve with the vegetables cut up into small pieces and cold-pressed linseed oil in an insulated glass bowl.

To serve
1   Serve with the potato puree at the bottom of the dish, covered with a fine layer of vegetable ashes. Place the crispy malt croutons on top and spread around the chopped cranberries.
2   Fry the smoked salmon briefly in a hot pan for 30 seconds and serve it immediately. Blend the twistbread sauce immediately before serving and add to the dish.
3   Garnish the dish with silver leaves.
4   To accompany the dish, carefully place a piece of smoking coal using tongs in a small box to add the scent of a bonfire.

1
The Danish beach: sea grass "seafood" and salted herbs

2
At Norwegian scout camp: baked potato, foil, and baked twist bread

Thorsten Schmidt

Every Saturday I drive across the Bay to the Ferry Plaza Farmers Market on the Embarcadero in San Francisco, where I visit my farmer friends and shop for the best produce on the planet. Before I head home, the place to stop is Boulettes Larder, where I can eat a late breakfast at a little table outdoors on the rear plaza of the Ferry Building. Amaryll cooks the best eggs I have ever eaten: absolutely fresh, indescribably divine. With Amaryll's eggs on my plate and an herb salad, with the span of the Bay Bridge and the hills of Berkeley and Oakland in the background, and with the stalls of my favorite market in the middle distance, I feel utterly at home.

Amaryll has a culinary and artistic aesthetic unlike any other I have encountered, in this country or abroad. She has been influenced by her personal history—she grew up eating her Hungarian grandmother's refined and hearty Central European meals—and by her artistic and musical passions, which range from the photographs of Anselm Kiefer to the compositions of Chopin, Liszt, and Keith Jarrett. She is also an integral part of a network of local farmers, artists, family, and colleagues that includes the Buddhist community at Green Gulch Farm in Muir Beach, who have supplied her restaurants with pristine produce for over twenty-five years.

At Boulettes, Amaryll and her partner, Lori Regis, have created a business that is a restaurant and retail counter by day and a private venue for dinner parties by night. The food includes dishes from North Africa, Turkey, and Greece, as well as the more familiar Mediterranean cuisines. An open kitchen and dining room invite you to watch the chefs as they work. Daily changing menus feature artfully restrained dishes that are guided by Amaryll's discretion; she cooks with innate knowledge both of the ingredients' origins and how they should best be prepared. Whether it is those delightful eggs or another thoughtfully composed dish, it will be beautifully arranged on the plate and a model of clarity. Amaryll's cooking is pure artistry: inspiration, knowledge, and care magically come together.

Alice Waters

Amaryll Schwertner was born in Budapest, Hungary, in 1955. Her family emigrated to the United States In 1956 as refugees. Through a hardworking career, including time at Greens and Chez Panisse, Schwertner became chef du cuisine and executive chef at Sol y Luna, Stars, and Premier Cru in San Francisco. Schwertner sees her cooking as the ultimate subtle expression of crucial philosophical and political concerns, framed within a creative process, and influenced by her partner and collaborator, Lori Regis. Schwertner waits for a spark of inspiration to trigger the development of each dish for Boulettes Larder, her current venture. She developed an interest in foraging under the tutelage of Michel Bras and Cesare Giaccone, among others, grounding an instinctive concern for the environment within the ideas of the international Slow Food movement. She takes the seasonal ingredients supplied by growers as her point of departure for creating beautiful and intelligent dishes using her special blend of alchemy and technical prowess.

MENU

Eastern Mediterranean salad with purslane, mint, cilantro, dill, mâche, za'tar, pomegranate seeds, persimmon, cucumber, and barrel-aged feta
Bruno Gicosa Roero Arneis, Piemonte, Italy, 2007

~

Balkan pasta pillows filled with a compôte of wild and cultivated herbs
Marisa Cuomo "Costa d'Amalfi Italy," Campania, Italy, 2008

~

Hungarian cabbage leaves stuffed with Kurobuta pork shoulder, sauerkraut with quince, and smoky pork belly
Batic Cabernet Franc Riserve, Vipava, Slovenia, 2006

~

Rice cake with roasted sour cherries and yogurt ice cream
Kiralyudvar Tokaji Cuvee "Ilona", Tarcal, Hungary, 2002

~

Mignardise

Amaryll Schwertner

1–3
Amaryll Schwertner making
pasta pillows, grinding spices,
and mixing greens

4
The dining room at Boulettes
Larder

5
Schwertner with Lori Regis at
the farmer's market

Boulettes Larder, San Francisco, CA, USA

1
Eastern Mediterranean
salad with purslane, mint,
cilantro, dill, mâche,
za'tar, pomegranate seeds,
persimmon, cucumber, and
barrel-aged feta

2
Dressing for salad

3
Balkan pasta pillows filled
with a compôte of wild
and cultivated herbs

4
Hungarian cabbage leaves
stuffed with Kurobuta pork
shoulder, sauerkraut with
quince, and smoky pork belly

5
Rice cake with roasted sour
cherries and yogurt ice cream

EASTERN MEDITERRANEAN SALAD WITH PURSLANE, MINT, CILANTRO, DILL, MÂCHE, ZA'TAR, POMEGRANATE SEEDS, PERSIMMON, CUCUMBER, AND BARREL-AGED FETA
Serves 4

For the vinaigrette
2 gray shallots, diced into a fine brunoise • 6 tbsp 9% acidity red-wine vinegar • sea salt • juice of 1 pomegranate, reduced to 4 tbsp • 350 ml extra-virgin olive oil • cracked black pepper

1 Macerate the shallots in the red-wine vinegar with a pinch of salt.
2 Let sit for 15 minutes, add the pomegranate juice, and then whisk in the olive oil. Season with pepper.

For the salad
550 g cleaned purslane, picked into small clusters (or mâche, mizuna, chervil, young dandelion, minutina, agretti, or mixed herbs) • 2 each picked mint, cilantro (coriander), and dill leaves • 1 Fuyu persimmon, peeled and thinly sliced • 2 tbsp fresh pomegranate seeds (or dried Persian barberries) • 25 g shaved citron peel • 70 g bronte pistachios, toasted • 2 tbsp za'tar • 1 Armenian or Mediterranean cucumber, diced into a fine brunoise

To serve
60 g barrel-aged feta cheese, crumbled

1 Toss the purslane together with the mint leaves, persimmon, pomegranate seeds or Persian barberries, citron peel, pistachios, za'tar, and cucumber.
2 Dress with the vinaigrette, and season with salt and pepper to taste.
3 Garnish with feta.

BALKAN PASTA PILLOWS FILLED WITH A COMPÔTE OF WILD AND CULTIVATED HERBS
Serves 4–6

For the herb compote filling
1 tbsp caraway seeds • 1 tbsp cumin seeds • sea salt, to taste • 4 cloves garlic, minced • 3 bunches scallions (spring onions), sliced • 475 ml olive oil • 3 tbsp Aleppo pepper • ½ preserved lemon, rinsed, pith removed, zest sliced very thinly • leaves, picked from their stems, of 2 bunches cilantro (coriander) • leaves of 3 stems lovage •

leaves of 3 stems mint • leaves of 3 stalks dill • leaves of 2 bunches large flat parsley • leaves of 1 bunch fenugreek • 1 bunch dandelion greens, chopped • 1 bunch mustard greens, chopped • 1 bunch chard or erbette chard, chopped • 1 bunch cavolo nero, chopped • tops and bottoms of 1 bunch radishes • tops of ½ bunch carrots • 1 fennel bulb • a 15-cm piece of fresh ginger, peeled and minced very finely

1 In a dry sauté pan, toast the caraway seeds and cumin seeds until just warm. Crush together in a mortar and pestle with a little sea salt.
2 Wilt the garlic and onions in the olive oil. When translucent, add the Aleppo pepper, the preserved lemon, and all the herbs and vegetables. Add the ground caraway and cumin. Wilt over low heat, covered with baking parchment, to a very soft consistency. Stir occasionally to stew the greens, not fry them. The mass should be heavy, soft, and aromatic, nearly marmalade-like in texture. This can take 1–2 hours of braising on very low heat.
3 Cool and drain, reserving the cooking juices. Chop the greens to a fine texture, adding back cooking liquid as needed to moisten them.

For the pasta dough
500 g all-purpose (plain) flour • 2 tsp salt • 3 eggs, beaten • 250 ml sour cream

1 Mix the flour and salt on a wooden board.
2 Make a well in the flour and add the eggs and sour cream. Stir together, and then knead into a soft but firm dough.
3 Rest the dough for an hour under a clean floured dish towel.

To finish
toasted hazelnuts • melted butter

1 Roll out the rested dough thinly on a floured board and cut 5-cm rounds with a floured cutter. Spoon the herb compote onto the center of each, fold over to make a crescent shape, and crimp the edges. Chill the crescents for 30 minutes.
2 To cook the pasta, briskly simmer in salted water for 5–10 minutes until they float. Garnish with the toasted hazelnuts and melted butter.

HUNGARIAN CABBAGE LEAVES STUFFED WITH KUROBUTA PORK SHOULDER, SAUERKRAUT WITH QUINCE, AND SMOKY PORK BELLY
Yields 20 stuffed cabbages

For the seasoned sauerkraut
500 g sauerkraut, homemade if possible • 1 quince, peeled, cored, and poached • 225 ml white wine • 1 tbsp caraway seeds • 2–3 bay leaves

Braise all the ingredients in a skillet for several hours.

For the stuffed cabbage
1 liter rich pork stock • crème fraîche, to bind • 5 Kurobuta "black pig" pork shoulders, coarsely ground (minced) • 175 g parcooked long-grain rice • 250 g diced onions, caramelized in lard • sea salt • 6 tbsp Sarawak peppercorns, ground in a mortar and pestle • 2 tbsp sweet Hungarian paprika • 20 leaves from Savoy cabbage or cavolo nero, blanched and patted dry

1 Combine all the ingredients except the cabbage leaves in a mixing bowl and set over an ice bath for 1 hour. Sauté a small amount, taste, and adjust the seasoning as needed.
2 Fill the cabbage leaves with the pork mixture, and fold each one over to cover the pork without compressing the roll.

To assemble and finish the dish
225 g thick-cut smoked pork belly, cooked in the oven at 350°F (180°C) for 10 minutes, then drained • rich pork stock • 1 tbsp crème fraîche, optional

1 Preheat the oven to 375°F (190°C).
2 Place half the braised sauerkraut in a heavy casserole with a lid. Tuck the smoked pork belly into the sauerkraut and place the cabbage rolls on top. Cover with the remaining sauerkraut. Pour enough rich pork stock over the cabbage rolls to cover by three-quarters of the height of the cabbage.
3 Cook, covered, in the oven for 35–45 minutes, until the rolls are soft and the pork is cooked through.
4 Garnish individual servings with crème fraîche.

RICE CAKE WITH ROASTED SOUR CHERRIES AND YOGURT ICE CREAM
Serves 8

This is a recipe from Sarah Ellsworth, pastry chef at Boulettes Larder.

For the cake
200 g Bomba paella rice • pinch of salt • kernels of 20 cherry pits (stones), cracked and steeped in 1 liter half and half (half milk and half cream) • 60 g butter, plus more for greasing • 120 g sugar • zest of 1 lemon • 1 vanilla bean • 3 eggs, separated • 50 g sour cherries, pitted (stoned)

1 Preheat the oven to 350°F (180°C).
2 Boil the rice in water for 5 minutes.
3 Drain, and boil again with 250 ml water, salt, and cherry kernels steeped in half and half.
4 Add the butter, sugar, lemon zest, and vanilla bean.
5 When well cooked, remove the vanilla bean. Spread the rice onto a baking sheet and cool.
6 Add the egg yolks to the cooled rice.
7 Whip the egg whites to soft peak stage and fold into the rice.
8 Fold in the cherries.
9 Butter and line a 22-cm cake pan with parchment, and pour in the mixture.
10 Bake for 1 hour and 15 minutes.

For the ice cream
450 g yogurt • 60 g sugar • 85 g glucose • 1 tsp lemon juice

1 Warm the yogurt, sugar, and glucose. Let cool.
2 Add the lemon juice and freeze in an ice cream maker.

For the roasted sour cherries
175 g pitted (stoned) sour cherries • 50 g sugar

1 Preheat the oven to 400°F (200°C).
2 Toss the cherries with the sugar. Cook in the oven until the juices are released and begin to concentrate.

To serve
Place a portion of cake on a plate. Top the cake with a spoonful of ice cream and drizzle roasted sour cherries around the edge of the plate.

Amaryll Schwertner

Ben Shewry was first announced to Melbourne as a force to be reckoned with when he was named "Best New Talent" by Australian *Gourmet Traveller* magazine in 2008. That night I met Ben and found him very shy and humble, with a tremendous energy about him. I soon made time to eat his food, with great expectations—and I really enjoyed the youthful fun and experimental nature of his dishes.

Ben often presents flavors that may not appear to work together; however, trust pays off and allows you to enjoy such unexpected combinations as cauliflower cheese with blood plum and clove oil, and smoked trout broth with crackling, basil seeds, and fresh smoke.

Ben's food is also memorable for its setting. Imagine a leafy inner-city suburb of Melbourne with a middle- to high-income population (sometimes the most challenging group to attract to a local restaurant) with a simple shop front and bar. There, in the tiniest of kitchens, you will find Ben.

No one dish stood out as my all-time favorite in that first meal—it was more the overall theater of each dish. Smoked trout with a glass cover that when removed makes a huge puff of smoke appear, brushes of reductions, unique crockery, all set in lovely but modest surroundings. This is what makes Melbourne's restaurant scene so great.

What is unique about Ben's approach to his menu is that he looks beyond his limitations. Each morning he walks along the shore near his Bellarine Peninsula home (nearly two hours from the restaurant), picking sea lettuces and indigenous herbs that he uses to bring alive, both visually and flavorwise, his modern French/Australian menu.

Ben has embraced the methods of forward-thinking chefs like Heston Blumenthal—smokers, vacuum cooking, slow poaching—and used them as an inspiration for adaptation. I'm sure Ben will one day inspire others with techniques he develops himself.

Shannon Bennett

Ben Shewry was born in New Zealand in 1977. He completed early training at the Roxborough, before moving to gain experience at restaurants in Australia and America. As a young chef, he undertook a stint under David Thompson at Nahm in London, prompting a visit to Thailand to study Thai cuisine, developing his understanding of palate and seasoning. Shewry's innovative and exploratory approach is enshrined at Attica in Melbourne, where he has been head chef since 2005, gaining widespread recognition. This continuing acclaim is due partly to Ben's constant drive to find and perfect new ideas—a drive that has become part of Attica's weekly routine, in the form of a Tuesday "chef's table" night, which features untested and experimental recipes.

MENU

Snow crab
Chandon ZD Blanc de Blancs, Yarra Valley, Victoria, Australia, 2005

~

Smoked trout broth, crackling, basil seeds, and fresh smoke
Romate Palo Cortado sherry, Jerez, Spain

~

Washington marron tail, cured beef, and wild sea flora
Salomon Undhof Hochterrassen Grüner Veltliner, Kremstal, Austria

~

Potato baked in the earth it was grown in, saltbush, and mojama
Eric Bordelet Poiré Granit cider, Normandy, France

~

Kingfish, chorizo, almond, and squid
Ocean Eight Chardonnay, Mornington Peninsula, Victoria, 2007

~

Glenloth pigeon, celery, borage, and bitter onion
Shobbrook Shiraz, Seppeltsfield, South Australia, 2007

~

Terroir
Champalou Vouvray Demi Sec, Loire Valley, France, 2006

~

Violet crumble
La Morandina Moscato d'Asti, Piedmont, Italy, 2007

Ben Shewry

1
The dining room at Attica

2 & 3
In the kitchen

4
Ben Shewry finishing plates

5 & 6
Gathering herbs on the coast

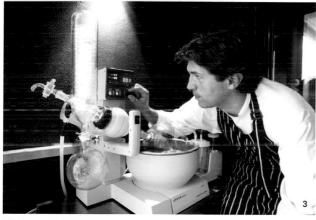

Attica, Melbourne, Australia

SMOKED TROUT BROTH, CRACKLING, BASIL SEEDS, AND FRESH SMOKE
Serves 8

For the trout broth
1 small onion • 1 stem celery • 1 small head of fennel • 150 g bacon scraps • 150 ml white wine • 1 piece galangal • ½ tsp white peppercorns • ½ bunch scallions (spring onions) • 1 piece kombu • 1 kg smoked trout • pinch citric acid • 12 egg whites • 500 ml water

1   In large pan, sweat the onion, celery, fennel, and bacon for 5 minutes over medium heat.
2   Add the wine and simmer until reduced by half.
3   Add the galangal, white peppercorns, scallions, kombu and smoked trout. Cover with water and cook at 175°F (80°C) for 2 hours. Pass through a cheesecloth (muslin) and place in the refrigerator to cool.
4   Once cold, check the seasoning and add citric acid. Thoroughly whisk in the egg whites, pour into a medium pan, and bring to a simmer over medium heat, stirring regularly, until the whites start to cook and rise to the surface. Simmer for 4 minutes, then gently pass the broth through a cheesecloth.
5   Check seasoning and add 500 ml water to refresh the broth.

For the sorrel oil
2 bunches sorrel • 60 g spinach leaves • 225 ml grapeseed oil • 1 pinch citric acid • 25 g Maltodextrin

1   Place the sorrel, spinach, and grapeseed oil in a blender and blend until smooth. Season with the citric acid. Pass through a fine-mesh sieve lined with cheesecloth (muslin). Set aside for 10 minutes to allow the oil and water to separate.
2   Using a ladle, gently skim the oil, leaving the water behind. Place the Maltodextrin in a bowl and add the sorrel oil until it is the texture of bread crumbs.

For the garnish
500 g Woodbridge smoked ocean trout (or similar), cut into 2-cm cubes • 1 packet pork crackling, cut into 1-cm cubes • 1 punnet chive shoots, snipped • 1 punnet red radish shoots, snipped • 20 g basil seeds, reconstituted in warm water, then drained

1   Place 1 teaspoon sorrel oil powder in warm bowl. On top, place 5 pieces of trout, and on top of the trout, a few pieces of crackling, shoots and seeds.
2   Heat the broth to a gentle simmer and pour into individual pitchers (jugs).
3   Fill an electric pipe with 100 g fine smoking chips, such as hickory or applewood, and light it. Fill 8 Riedel "O" series chardonnay glasses with smoke from the pipe and invert the glasses over garnishes. Place in front of your guests, then remove all the glasses at once.
4   Pour the broth into bowls.

TERROIR
Serves 8

For the beet cake
100 g sugar • 385 g freshly ground almond • 500 g flour, sifted • 24 g baking powder, sifted • 1 g salt • 1 liter egg whites, at room temperature • 550 g butter, cooked until nut-brown and cooled to room temperature • 4 large beets (beetroots), finely grated on a microplane

1   Place the sugar, almonds, flour, 15 g baking powder, and salt in a stand mixer and whisk. Add the egg whites and whisk for 30 seconds, add the butter and whisk until smooth. Keep in refrigerator until ready to use.
2   Preheat the oven to 300°F (150°C). Line a 30-cm baking pan with wax (greaseproof) paper.
3   Mix the grated beets and cake batter together with 9 g baking powder until smooth.
4   Pour the batter into a cake pan and bake for 35–40 minutes or until the cake is well cooked. Remove from the oven and cool on a wire rack.
5   Once the cake has cooled to room temperature, grate with the coarse side of a box grater. Place in an airtight container until needed.

For the fromage blanc sorbet
350 ml milk • 150 g sugar • 100 g liquid glucose • 500 g fromage blanc • juice of 1 lemon

1   In a medium-sized pan, bring the milk, sugar, and glucose to simmer. Remove from the heat and let cool.
2   Place the fromage blanc into bowl and whisk in the lemon juice. Whisk the cooled milk mixture into the fromage blanc until smooth.
3   Freeze and churn in a Pacojet or churn in an ice-cream maker according to the manufacturer's instructions. Place in a freezer until needed.

For the sorrel ice
500 ml water • 115 g sugar • 2 bunches sorrel

In a blender, blend the water, sugar, and sorrel together for 2 minutes. Pass through a fine-mesh sieve, discarding the solids. Pour the sorrel water into a small steel tray and place in the freezer. Allow to freeze for 5–6 hours, breaking up the ice crystals with a fork as they form.

To finish
150 g dehydrated beetroot, made by drying grated beetroot in a oven at 122°F (50°C) or in a dehydrator • 75 g freeze-dried raspberries • 95 g dried cranberries, finely chopped • ½ tsp toasted barley, ground • 75 g freeze-dried blackberries • 95 g traditionally dried raspberries, finely chopped • ¼ tsp quatre épices • pinch of Murray River salt to taste

Place the grated beetroot cake in a large bowl and add the dried beetroot, raspberries, cranberries, barley, and blackberries, and quatre épices. Toss together and season to taste with salt.

To serve
1 golden kiwifruit (cut into 1-cm dice and dressed with few drops of lime) • 16 borage flowers • 1 container sorrel shoots, leaves trimmed

Place 1 teaspoon of the seasoned beetroot mixture in the middle of 8 bowls. Place 3 pieces of kiwifruit in each bowl. Scoop a medium-sized scoop of fromage blanc sorbet into each bowl. Cover the sorbet with the rest of beetroot crumb mixture to make little mounds. Scatter the flowers and sorrel shoots over the top and then scatter 1 tablespoon sorrel ice over each and serve.

1 & 2
Smoked trout broth, crackling,
basil seeds, and fresh smoke
(lifting glass and pouring broth)

3
Terroir

Ben Shewry

1
Hideki Shimoguchi tasting
dishes

2
Outside Chikurin

3
The restaurant dining room

Hideki Shimoguchi

342

MENU

Matcha tofu

~

Assortment of
seasonal appetizers

~

Seared pike conger and
blanched pike conger sashimi

~

Japanese mugwort tofu in
rikyu-style soup or dobin-mushi
(seasonal ingredients steamed
in a Japanese teapot)

~

Sweetfish broiled with salt

~

Bean curd skin and Amela
tomato soup

~

Conger eel steamed in green tea

~

White asparagus and clams with
green-tea vinegar dressing

~

Matcha noodles with blue
swimmer crab

~

Green tea jelly with shiratama
dumplings

Hideki Shimoguchi was born in 1970 in Uji, Japan, where watching his father cook at the family's restaurant planted in him a seed of curiosity about food. After attending a Kyoto culinary college, he worked for seven years under Yoshihiro Murata at his restaurant, Kikunoi. This training helped Shimoguchi rapidly develop his cooking techniques, such as knife skills, and his understanding of flavors and ingredients. In 1997 Shimoguchi moved to work with his father, Toshiharu, at Chikurin, where he learned to specialize in Kyoto cuisine and sushi. In 2003 Shimoguchi became head chef and owner of Chikurin. He offers an original take on traditional Kyoto *kaiseki* cuisine, featuring the abundant local seafood and preparing dishes with green tea, a specialty of the region. Guests travel for miles for menu favorites such as white asparagus and clams with new green tea, which show Shimoguchi's wit and skill in action.

As I was preparing for a hiring interview about fifteen years ago, I was contacted by a culinary school. "There will be a student called Shimoguchi amongst your interviewees. I suggest you not hire him. He's a roughneck who was beyond our control." Hideki was indeed involved in countless fights after he started working at my restaurant. He was unforgiving toward what he deemed unreasonable carelessness. He would always fight against his seniors. He may have fought, but for ten years he also worked more than anyone else. In time he acquired skills that no one could fail to acknowledge: unwavering mastery in seasoning, accurate knife skills, and the ability to compose his dishes.

It is possible to learn the essence of cooking, of what makes food taste good, by eating his dishes. Cooking is not about toying with ideas and presentation. It is, instead, about a highly trained cook discerning the best in ingredients, to reveal the blessings of nature with refined skill. Neither the cook nor the ones eating the food he or she prepared should fail to retain a sense of gratitude toward nature. There is a firm distinction between cooking, and entertainments such as dramatic performances.

Hideki opened his own restaurant in his hometown of Uji five years ago. He has been committed to the development of dishes with green tea, Uji's local specialty, and has made the restaurant into the most well-known in the region, relying purely on word of mouth.

Yoshihiro Murata

Chikurin, Uji, Japan

JAPANESE MUGWORT TOFU IN RIKYU-STYLE SOUP OR DOBIN-MUSHI
Serves 4

The powerful aromas of the Japanese mugwort tofu and the miso-sesame soup are an ideal combination. Moreover, the verdant cooling sensation of the mugwort tofu makes the miso-sesame dashi lighter. White miso soups are a familiar dish in Japanese cuisine, but the lack of a sesame soup led me to invent one. The name comes from the fact that sesame-flavored dishes are often denoted as "rikyu-style" in Japanese cuisine.

50 g Japanese mugwort paste • 35 g sesame paste • 100 g kudzu starch • 1.6 liters dashi • salt • light soy sauce, to season • mirin, to taste and to cook • sake, to taste and to cook • 4 Kuruma shrimp (prawns) • 2 bamboo shoots • 100 g white miso

1   For the mugwort tofu, stir the mugwort paste, 25 g sesame paste, and kudzu into 900 ml of the dashi.
2   Heat this mixture, and season with salt and soy sauce once it has thickened. Pour into a gelatin mold (nagashi-kan) and let cool.
3   Make some happoji sauce by seasoning a little dashi with some mirin, sake, soy sauce, and salt.
4   Remove the heads from the shrimp and set aside, then simmer the shrimp meat in more sake, light soy sauce, and mirin.
5   Boil the bamboo shoots in water left over from washing rice, if available. Clean, and simmer in the happoji sauce.
6   Simmer the shrimp heads in the remaining 700 ml dashi to make a broth, add the remaining sesame paste, white miso, and sake, and season with light soy sauce. Strain.
7   Cut the mugwort tofu, the shrimp and the bamboo shoots into bite-size pieces, place in a bowl and pour the dashi broth over the top.

CONGER EEL STEAMED IN GREEN TEA
Serves 8

This recipe involves the introduction of a technique to extract theanine, the main component of the umami taste in green tea, into the dashi. In Japan, tea leaves are not just used to produce tea but are themselves eaten. The inspiration for this recipe is drawn from chazuke, a traditional Japanese dish made by pouring green tea over cooked rice, usually with savory toppings.

For preparing the conger eel
4 conger eels • 900 ml sake • 900 ml water • sugar, to taste • 200 ml soy sauce

Slit open, slice and trim the conger eel and simmer in the sake, water, sugar, and soy sauce for 15 minutes.

For cooking the dish
10 g green tea leaves • 300 ml dashi • 150 g glutinous rice powder (domyoji) • 150 g millet (awa) • sake, to simmer the tea leaves • pale soy sauce, to simmer the tea leaves • mirin, to simmer the tea leaves • small amount of lily bulb, chopped • 4 gingko nuts, chopped • small amount of Judas' ear fungus • salt, to taste

1   Soak the green tea leaves for 60 minutes in dashi kept at 86°F (30°C). Strain to separate the green-tea dashi and the leaves, keeping both.
2   Mix the glutinous rice powder, the awa, and the green-tea dashi, place in a mold, and steam in a steam convection oven for 15 minutes.
3   Simmer the reserved tea leaves in sake, soy sauce, and mirin.
4   Unmold the steamed rice powder mixture, and cut into bite-size pieces. Add the simmered tea leaves, the lily bulb and the gingko nuts to make dumplings.
5   Wrap the prepared conger eel around the dumplings and arrange on a plate.

For the gin-an (silver) sauce
900 ml dashi • salt, to taste • pale soy sauce, to taste • kudzu starch, to thicken

Heat the dashi, seasoning it with salt and pale soy sauce, and adding enough kudzu starch to thicken. Pour over the eel and dumplings.

WHITE ASPARAGUS AND CLAMS WITH GREEN-TEA VINEGAR DRESSING
Serves 4

The verdant flavor of green tea is reminiscent of seaweed, and together with the clams conjures up the aroma of the sea. The clams and green tea play complementary roles, while the sweetness of the gyokuro green tea (a fine, expensive type of green tea whose name translates as "jade dew", a reference to the pale green color of the infusion) matches that of the white asparagus.

For the tosazu sauce
450 ml dashi • 150 ml vinegar • 30 ml pale soy sauce • sugar, to taste • kelp, to taste • dried bonito shavings

1   Heat the dashi with the vinegar, pale soy sauce, sugar, and kelp.
2   Once boiling, add the dried bonito shavings.

For the sweet vinegar (amazu) sauce
vinegar • water • sugar • kelp

Bring the vinegar, water, sugar, and kelp to a boil and then let cool.

For the asparagus and clams
4 large Japanese cockles (torigai) • 1 geoduck clam • 10 g green tea leaves (gyokuro) • 2 shoots myoga ginger, sliced • 8 spears white asparagus • rock salt • perilla flower buds, to serve • dried sea cucumber ovaries (hoshi-konoko)

1   Blanch the cockles and clam in very hot water and immediately immerse in icy water.
2   Soak the green tea leaves for 2 hours in the tosazu sauce, at 86°F (30°C) to make the green-tea vinegar.
3   Blanch the ginger, and pickle it in the amazu sauce overnight.
4   Peel the asparagus, steam in a steam convection oven for 6 minutes, and sprinkle with rock salt.
5   Cut the cockles and clam, ginger, and asparagus into bite-size pieces, arrange on a plate, and pour the green-tea vinegar over it. Garnish with perilla flower buds and dried sea cucumber ovaries.

1
Japanese mugwort tofu
in rikyu-style soup
or dobin-mushi

2
Conger eel steamed
in green tea

3
White asparagus and
clams with green-tea
vinegar dressing

345   **Hideki Shimoguchi**

1–3
Clare Smyth in the kitchen

Clare Smyth

MENU

Tomato consommé
with spring vegetables,
poached Norwegian
lobster, and caviar

~

Pressed foie gras
with peppered Madeira
jelly, smoked duck,
and peach and almond
crumble

~

Pan-fried sea scallops
from the Isle of Skye
with peas, crispy bacon,
quail eggs, and
baby gem lettuce

~

Butter-poached
Scottish lobster tail
with English asparagus,
morels, wild garlic,
spring truffles, and herb
farfalle

~

Oven-roasted pigeon
from Bresse
with grilled polenta,
smoked ventrèche,
braised shallots,
and baby beets

~

Summer fruit pudding
with black pepper
fromage frais sorbet

~

Bitter-chocolate cylinder
with coffee mousse,
milk ice cream,
honeycomb, and
Irish whiskey

Clare Smyth was born in Northern Ireland in 1978, leaving for England at the age of 16 to attend culinary college. She moved on to a position as sous-chef at Bibendum in London, and from there to the St. Enedoc Hotel in Cornwall, spending vacations gaining further experience under Michael Caines and Heston Blumenthal. She joined Restaurant Gordon Ramsay in 2002 as a sous-chef, applying herself to the role with tenacity and vigor. In 2005 she left for France, working for three months as a private chef before negotiating a placement at Louis XV, Alain Ducasse's traditional and revered restaurant in Monaco, after just four weeks of intensive French instruction. She returned to the three-Michelin-starred Restaurant Gordon Ramsay in 2007, a head chef at the age of just 29 and the only woman to hold this position at a restaurant with this accolade. Smyth serves an intelligent, perfectly executed menu of French cuisine, her varied and intense culinary experience permeating each dish.

A chef like Clare Smyth comes through the kitchen maybe once every ten years. The last time I spotted someone like her was when Angela Hartnett joined Aubergine back in 1995. She has a self-determined level of focus and a tunnel vision for perfection that is incredibly rare. Some might find her intimidating, she has such a level of composure, but she leads the kitchen with a controlled elegance. Clare is absolutely unflappable and cannot be fazed. Whatever ingredients you put in front of her, whatever dish you ask her to create, you can be guaranteed that she will take it to a different level.

She gained some fantastic experience while training, working with Michael Caines and Heston Blumenthal in the UK and traveling as far as Sydney to gain further experience. She joined us in 2002 at Restaurant Gordon Ramsay as a sous chef, and was quick to impress. She took leave in 2005 to work as a private chef in France and to spend a couple of years at Louis XV Alain Ducasse.

We were thrilled to be able to welcome Clare back to the restaurant in 2007 as head chef. She's retained three Michelin stars at the restaurant for the last two years and is still the only female chef in the UK to run a restaurant with this accolade, and she's not even turned thirty. She has excelled beyond any expectations in a male-dominated environment.

Clare serves beautifully simple, subtle French cuisine with real finesse. She exudes creative flair and dresses each and every dish impeccably. Butter-poached Scottish lobster tail with English asparagus, morels, wild garlic, spring truffles, and herb farfalle, and pressed foie gras with peppered Madeira jelly, smoked duck, and peach and almond crumble have become firm favorites with guests.

Gordon Ramsay

Restaurant Gordon Ramsay, London, UK

1
Pan-fried sea scallops
from the Isle of Skye
with peas, crispy bacon,
quail eggs, and
baby gem lettuce

2
Oven-roasted pigeon
from Bresse
with grilled polenta,
smoked ventrèche,
braised shallots and
baby beets

PAN-FRIED SEA SCALLOPS FROM THE ISLE OF SKYE WITH PEAS, CRISPY BACON, QUAIL EGGS, AND BABY GEM LETTUCE
Serves 4

For the pancetta crisp
500 g pancetta, trimmed (trimmings reserved)

Slice the pancetta into very thin pieces. Place on a tray lined with a nonstick silicone baking mat and cover with another. Put another tray on top to weight it. Bake at 350°F (180°C) for about 9 minutes. Remove from the oven and trim. Bake for an additional 4 minutes until crisp.

For the pea velouté
reserved pancetta trimmings • 8 sea scallops, cleaned and trimmed, corals removed • 1 clove of garlic • 2 sprigs of thyme • 4 pea shells, finely shredded • 500 ml chicken stock • 500 g fresh peas, shelled • salt

First make a scallop stock by sweating the pancetta trimmings and scallops until they release their juices. Add the garlic, thyme, and pea shells and cook over low heat, about 5 minutes. Pour in the chicken stock and bring to a boil, reduce the heat and simmer, for about 20 minutes. Pass through a fine mesh sieve into a pot. Bring back to a boil, and add the fresh peas to make the velouté. Cook until tender, about 2 minutes. Puree and pass through a fine mesh sieve into a bowl set over an ice bath. Season to taste.

For the peas, bacon, and girolles
100 g bacon lardons • 40 g girolle mushrooms • olive oil, for pan-frying • 500 g peas • salt

Fry the lardons and girolles in a small pan with some olive oil. Reduce the heat and mix in the peas. Season with salt.

For the sea scallops
8 sea scallops, about 250 g each, in the shell

Sear the scallops until golden brown, about 1 minute each side, with a teaspoon of butter to baste.

To serve
12 baby gem leaves, drizzled with vinaigrette • 4 quail eggs, fried

Place a serving of pea velouté on a plate, with 2 scallops on top. Gently place a quail egg on top of the scallops, followed by the dressed lettuce leaves.

OVEN-ROASTED PIGEON FROM BRESSE WITH GRILLED POLENTA, SMOKED VENTRÈCHE, BRAISED SHALLOTS, AND BABY BEETS
Serves 4

For the ventrèche
500 g smoked pork belly • 10 sprigs of thyme • 1 bay leaf • 5 white peppercorns • 2 onions, halved • 1 carrot, halved • 4 celery stalks, chopped • 5 garlic cloves

Soak the pork belly overnight in water in the refrigerator. Remove from the water and rinse. Place the belly in a large pot with the thyme, bay leaf, and peppercorns. Add enough water to cover and bring to a boil. Reduce the heat and add the onions, carrot, celery, and garlic. Simmer until cooked, about 3 hours. Allow the pork to cool slightly in the liquid. Remove and place between 2 trays with a weight on top. Chill. When cold, cut into cubes and fry on all sides in a hot pan.

For the pigeon
2 whole pigeons (500–600 g each) • Butter, for basting

Brown the pigeon in a pan until colored on all sides. Baste with butter and cook until the desired doneness is reached. When rested, remove the breasts from the crown and trim off the excess fat and cartilage. Wrap in aluminum foil and place in oven to reheat.

For the polenta
240 g water • 20 g butter • salt • 50 g polenta • 20 g Parmesan, grated • 3–4 tbsp mascarpone

Combine the water, 10 g butter, and salt to taste in a pan. Bring to a boil. Add the polenta and whisk until smooth, cover and cook over low heat until soft, about 40 minutes. Mix in the remaining butter, Parmesan, and season to taste. Spread on a tray lined with plastic wrap (clingfilm) and chill. Portion the polenta, spread the mascarpone on top, and sprinkle with Parmesan. Place under the broiler (grill), and brown until golden.

For the confit of pigeon
4 pigeon legs • 2 sprigs of thyme • 2 cloves of garlic • 1 bay leaf • 150 g duck fat

Prepare the pigeon legs by removing the thigh bone and rolling the drumsticks in plastic wrap to form ballotines. Poach for 2 minutes, and let cool. Remove the plastic wrap. Confit the legs by placing them into a small pan with the thyme, garlic, bay leaf, and duck fat. Cook slowly over low heat for about 30 minutes.

For the pigeon sauce
5 pigeon carcasses and wings, chopped • 1 shallot, chopped • 2 cloves garlic, chopped • 2 sprigs thyme • 1 bay leaf • 5 white peppercorns • sherry vinegar, to deglaze • 250 ml port • 500 ml chicken stock • 500 ml veal stock

Brown the pigeon carcasses and wings in a pan. Remove and reserve the bones, and sweat out the shallot and garlic. Add the thyme, bay leaf, and peppercorns, and cook for about 2–3 minutes. Deglaze the pan with the sherry vinegar and add the port. Reduce until thickened, and then pour in the chicken and veal stock and return the bones. Bring to a boil, then reduce heat and let simmer for about 40 minutes. Strain through a fine mesh sieve.

To finish
4 shallots • vegetable oil, for braising • 4 baby beets • 4 baby carrots • stock, for reheating • 1 tbsp butter • 4 dates, peeled • 4 pieces of foie gras, sliced and sautéed

Braise the shallots in a little vegetable oil. Boil the beets and carrots until cooked. Remove from water and reheat with a little stock and butter. Reheat the pigeon confit with dates and a small amount of pigeon sauce. Arrange the pigeon, foie gras, vegetables, and polenta on a plate. Drizzle with pigeon sauce and serve.

Clare Smyth

1–3
Yosuke Suga in the kitchen

4
Preserved vegetables

5
Serving soup at L'Atelier de
Joël Robuchon

Yosuke Suga

MENU

Sea urchin in a tender jelly, under a blanket of cauliflower cream
Bruno Paillard "Brut Millésimé," Champagne, France, 1996

~

Norwegian lobster carpaccio with toasted poppy seeds
Grüner Veltliner "Federspiel," Weingut J. Donabaum, Austria, 2006

~

Caramelized eel layered with smoked foie gras
Riesling Grand Cru Schlossberg, Domaine P. Blanck, Alsace, France, 2004

~

Turnip velouté and crab ravioli with yuzu
Greco Di Tufo, Vinosia, Campania, Italy, 2006

~

Day boat scallop in the shell with Cancale seaweed butter
Chardonnay, Kumou River, New Zealand, 2005

~

Sautéed amadai in a yuzu broth with lily bulbs
Chenin Blanc/Viognier, Miles Mossop "Saskia," South Africa, 2006

~

Free-range caramelized quail stuffed with foie gras, with potato puree
Châteauneuf-du-Pape, Château de Beaucastel, France, Rhône, 1990

~

Grapefruit segments, grape wine gelée, and mint sorbet
Muskat "Galileus" Tilia, Slovenia, 2006

~

Golden sugar sphere, vanilla ice cream, and saffron mousse
Bruno Paillard Rosé, Champagne, France

~

Espresso coffee served with salted caramel chocolate

Yosuke Suga was born in 1976 in Japan, and was introduced to French cuisine through his father's restaurant in Nagoya, Chez Kobe. After graduating from high school, Suga traveled to Lyon for six months to learn French, returning to Japan and stints at various restaurants and hotels, before he took over the family restaurant from his father at the age of 19. There, Suga was introduced to Joël Robuchon, going on to work alongside the master chef following his retirement from the restaurant kitchen in 1996, when he began to travel as a consultant, producing small, private dinners. In 2003 Suga opened L'Atelier de Joël Robuchon in Tokyo as its successful executive chef. In 2006, after an eleven-year association with Robuchon, Suga became executive chef of his restaurant at the Four Seasons Hotel in New York, moving on in 2009 to open L'Atelier de Joël Robuchon in Taipei. The classic, unique French cuisine that he produces has won the organization a range of industry accolades.

When I think of Yosuke Suga, people such as baseball player Ichiro Suzuki or soccer player Hidetoshi Nakata come to mind: lone geniuses who are free from the spell of nationality.

There is an elderly gourmand who is so well-known that anyone involved with Japanese cuisine knows his name. He is even on good terms with the legendary Joël Robuchon. Yosuke was introduced to me by this gourmand as a "diamond" about ten years ago. He was then a young, somewhat boyish chef who worked in the laboratory set up by Robuchon, who had by then retired. Yosuke began to visit my kitchen every time he came back to explore the world of Japanese cuisine with the young chefs working alongside me.

In 2003, Yosuke was appointed executive chef of the Robuchon restaurant that opened in Tokyo. While people reveled in Robuchon's meticulously accurate cuisine, most people visited the restaurant to enjoy dishes that called France to mind, rather than for Yosuke's interpretation of the menu.

In 2006 he made a fresh start in New York. Yosuke's cuisine has gained in luster, and the playfulness typical of his cooking has now been matched with careful attention to detail and exceptional skill.

Yosuke, now in Taipei, prepares food that boasts a certain lightness, as he relies not on cream or butter but the use of diverse citrus fruits and Japanese herbs such as shiso (perilla). It's the birth of a cuisine that has elegantly leaped beyond the confines of nationality: the "Suga Cuisine."

Yoshihiro Murata

1
Caramelized eel layered
with smoked foie gras

2
Day boat scallop in
the shell with Cancale
seaweed butter

3
Sautéed amadai
in yuzu broth with lily bulbs

CARAMELIZED EEL LAYERED WITH SMOKED FOIE GRAS
Serves 8

For the piment d'Espelette cream
500 g heavy (double) cream • 6 g piment d'Espelette • salt and pepper

Whisk the cream until soft peaks form. Season with piment d'Espelette, salt, and pepper.

For the smoked foie gras
550 g foie gras

Smoke the foie gras for 15 minutes. Season and place in a convection oven at 175°F (90°C) and cook for 30 minutes. Slice with a meat slicer into 7-mm thick slices.

For the eel mille-feuille
2 pieces Japanese eel • 50 g veal jus • black pepper • brown sugar, to garnish • chopped chives, to garnish

1　Lay out slices of smoked foie gras on parchment paper. Caramelize the eel under the salamander or hot broiler (grill).
2　To assemble, line a terrine mold with the parchment paper. Place the trimmed foie gras on the bottom of the mold as the first layer. Lightly brush veal jus on the foie gras and season well with black pepper. Repeat the foie gras layer and then make an eel layer. Place parchment paper on top of the mold to cover and press. Let set overnight in the refrigerator.
3　To unmold, remove the paper top and slice into 8 portions.
4　To serve, sprinkle brown sugar on top of each portion and caramelize with a blowtorch. Spoon the cream onto the plate. Garnish with chopped chives.

DAY BOAT SCALLOP IN THE SHELL WITH CANCALE SEAWEED BUTTER
Serves 4

Grapeseed oil, for searing • 4 live diver scallops • salt, to taste • 4 scallop shells, boiled and scrubbed clean • 16 g Bordier seaweed butter • coarse salt, for plating • seaweed, to garnish • lime slices, to garnish

1　In a hot sauté pan, add some grapeseed oil and sauté the scallops, lightly salted, on one side until golden brown.
2　Remove the scallops and place each one in a clean shell, seared side up. Slice the butter into 4 (4-g) slices and place one on top of each scallop. Place the scallops under the broiler (grill) until the butter is sizzling and is beginning to brown along the edges.
3　Make a small pile of salt on each plate and place a shell on top of the salt. Press down to secure. Garnish the plate with a bit of seaweed and a lime slice.

SAUTÉED AMADAI IN A YUZU BROTH WITH LILY BULBS
Serves 4

For the amadai broth
1 kg tilefish (*amadai*) bones and head • grapeseed oil, for sautéing • 4 liters water • 50 g shallots, thinly sliced • 30 g garlic, thinly sliced

1　Chop the tilefish bones and head into 7.5-cm pieces and soak in water for a few hours to remove all impurities. Dry the bones well.
2　Sauté the bones in a hot pan with grapeseed oil until golden in color. Deglaze the pan with water.
3　Transfer the bones and deglazing liquid to a roasting pan and continue to roast in a 350°F (180°C) oven until a very deep golden brown.
4　Bring the water to a boil and add the roasted amadai bones, shallots and garlic. Simmer for 30 minutes.
5　Remove from heat and infuse for 15 minutes. Strain through a fine-mesh sieve and cool.

For the amadai and garnish
1 leek, white part only • oil, for deep-frying • salt • 240 g tilefish (*amadai*) fillets (4 pieces in total) • 2 lily bulbs • 12 pieces micro-leek • 8 pearl onions • 10 ml yuzu • 10 g kuzu • 10 ml Vermouth • 4 pieces hanaho flower • 4 pieces sancho leaf • bergamot oil, to serve • piment d'Espelette, to taste

1　Finely julienne the white part of one leek. Deep-fry the leeks at 275°F (140°C) until light golden brown. Remove onto a paper towel and season with salt. Set aside for later use.
2　Separate the petals of the lily bulb and clean off any brown spots. Blanch in boiling salted water until cooked through. Refresh in an ice bath and set aside.
3　Peel the pearl onions and slice into thin rings. Separate each ring, discarding the centers. Blanch in boiling salted water until cooked through. Refresh in an ice bath and set aside.

4　For the tilefish, heat 400 ml *amadai* broth and season with the piment d'Espelette, Vermouth, kuzu, and yuzu juice. Add the micro-leeks, blanched lily bulbs and blanched pearl onions and heat through. Season with salt and pepper.
5　Saute the tilefish fillets in a sauté pan with grapeseed oil, skin-side down first, until the skin is crispy and golden brown. Flip over and cook until the fish is cooked through.

To serve
1　Place one piece of cooked tilefish in a bowl, add approximately 100 ml of tilefish broth, half a lily bulb, 3 pieces of micro-leek and 2 pearl onions.
2　Top the tilefish with a fried crispy leeks, one piece of hanaho flower, one sancho leaf and a few drops of bergamot oil.

A few years ago a journalist asked me to recommend an "interesting chef in his thirties who differed from the conventional image of Kyoto cuisine." I came up with some names, but the journalist was not happy with them, feeling that there was no great difference between them and the chefs of a generation ago. Seeking help from my juniors, I came across the name of Takuji Takahashi, a chef with a thorough knowledge of wines who actively includes international ingredients such as Jinhua ham, foie gras, or truffles in the preparation of Japanese cuisine.

It is said that food reflects the person who has cooked it, and this is exactly the case with Takahashi: willful and delicate, luxurious but rational.

The dish he prepared using sweet corn for a cooking study group stunned me. Wanting to use the shape of the corn kernel but deeming the texture of the skin unnecessary, he proceeded to peel each kernel with a knife and to remove the germs by hand because of the bitterness that they added. This meticulous approach was juxtaposed with a *kinton* (a traditional Japanese sweet served after a meal) made with lavish amounts of truffles. This unexpected, unique, and extravagant dish won the hearts of the visitors. Takahashi is not an egoistical attention-seeker. He might be young, but he is also quite wise.

Yoshihiro Murata

Takuji Takahashi was born in Japan in 1968. He trained at Kitchou under Teiichi Yuki, one of the most prominent figures in twentieth-century Japanese cuisine. From there he moved on to Kinobu in Kyoto, where he has remained for the past ten years, rising to become its proprietor and head chef. Takahashi has collaborated with top French chefs, including Jean-François Piège, Jacques Pourcel, and Thierry Marx, even studying to become a master sommelier; however, he balances these forays into European gastronomy with extensive knowledge of sake and applies his varied methods to a menu grounded in Japanese tradition. The arresting taste combinations of dishes such as gazami crab with caviar, chestnut, and egg-and-rice-vinegar dressing are rooted in Takahashi's high regard for precision, even to the level of examining the chemical components of food. Coupled with the natural, exuberant execution of his dishes, Takahashi's menu presents what is intentional as unintentional.

MENU

Gazami crab with caviar

~

Autumnal hassun plate

~

Thinly sliced raw sea bream and Japanese lobster

~

Scallop eye dumpling soup

~

Raw sea urchin roe and abalone in jelly

~

Hagi-style deep-fried Kuruma shrimp

~

Shark fin and sesame tofu in nabe pot

~

Rice with matsutake

~

Japanese persimmon mousse, kyoho grape, and pear jelly

Takuji Takahashi

1
Writing the day's menu

2
In the kitchen at Kinobu

3
Takuji Takahashi
choosing turnips

4
The dining area

5
Fresh fish at the market

Kinobu, Kyoto, Japan

1
Gazami crab with caviar

2
Autumnal hassun plate

3
Scallop eye dumpling soup

4
Raw sea urchin roe
and abalone in jelly

5
Shark fin and sesame tofu
in nabe pot

GAZAMI CRAB WITH CAVIAR
Serves 4

5 egg yolks • 10 g sugar •
50 ml rice vinegar • 4 chestnuts, steamed and pureed • 4 okra •
1 wheat gluten sheet (shonai fu) • dashi, to cook the shonai fu •
2 shoots myoga ginger •
amazu sweet vinegar (made with 100 ml water, 75 ml rice vinegar, and 100 g sugar) •
1 Japanese blue (gazami) crab •
salt • 40 g caviar • raw chestnut, finely chopped, for garnish

1   Put the egg yolk, sugar, rice vinegar, and chestnuts into hot water and cook slowly.
2   Cook the okra in boiling water, then finely chop it.
3   Roast the wheat gluten sheet, then boil it in the dashi.
4   Boil the myoga ginger, slice it, then place it in the amazu sweet vinegar to pickle it.
5   Wash the crab in water, season with salt, and steam it for 17 minutes. Extract and reserve the meat once it has cooled down.
6   Place portions of each component on a plate and garnish with raw chestnut and caviar.

AUTUMNAL HASSUN PLATE
Serves 4

For the miso-marinated broiled silver pomfret
4 fillets of silver pomfret • 200 g miso • 20 ml sake • 20 ml mirin •
10 g sugar

1   Marinate the silver pomfret in a mixture of the miso, sake, mirin, and sugar for 3 days.
2   Skewer the fish and grill it over a charcoal fire.

For the glazed Kuruma shrimp
4 Kuruma shrimp (prawns) •
100 ml dashi • 30 ml mirin • 5 ml pale soy sauce • salt to taste

Boil the shrimp, then cook them briefly in the dashi with the mirin, pale soy sauce, and salt.

For the lily bulb Oribe-style
500 ml water • 100 g sugar •
1 lily bulb

Prepare a sugar syrup with the water and sugar. Clean the lily bulb and cook it in the syrup.

For the chestnuts stewed in soy sauce and sugar
4 chestnuts in their skins •
1–2 liters liquid left over after washing rice (togijiru) •
10 g baking soda • 270 ml water • 90 ml sake • 50 g sugar •
50 g crystal sugar (zarame)

1   Immerse the chestnuts in the liquid left over after washing rice with baking soda and let them stand for 17 hours, and remove the fibers and skins while soaking in the water.
2   Cook the chestnuts in boiling water until tender.
3   Remove the excess water, steam for 30 minutes in a steam cooker, then cook them with water, sake, sugar, and crystal sugar for 30 minutes.

For the deep-fried gingko nuts
8 gingko nuts • oil, for deep-frying • salt, to taste

Shell the gingko nuts and deep-fry them in oil heated to 320°F (160°C), then sprinkle with salt.

For the broiled shimeiji mushrooms and chrysanthemum greens dressed with white tofu sauce
1 block of silken tofu (kinugoshi-dofu) • 10 ml pale soy sauce • 15 g white miso
• salt to taste • 5 g sugar •
1 bunch chrysanthemum greens (kikuna) • 80 g wild shimeiji mushrooms

1   Place a weight over the tofu to drain the water. Put it into a food processor with the soy sauce, white miso, salt, and sugar and mix until smooth.
2   Cook the chrysanthemum greens and broil (grill) the shimeiji mushrooms.
3   Mix together the chrysanthemum greens and shimeiji mushrooms and serve on a plate with the white tofu sauce.

SCALLOP EYE DUMPLING SOUP
Serves 4

300 g scallops • salt • 6 g gluten-free flour (ukiko) • 30 ml dashi •
1 turnip • 4 Japanese mustard spinach (komatsuna) stalks •
1 Japanese red carrot (kintoki) •
4 shiitake mushrooms • broth (made with 720 ml dashi, 5 ml pale soy sauce, 3 g salt) •
1 yuzu, sliced

1   Cut 100 g of the scallops into quarters and lightly sprinkle them with salt.
2   Put the remaining scallops into a food processor, add the gluten-free flour and dashi, and mix thoroughly.
3   Mix the ingredients from steps 1 and 2, make round shapes, and immerse them in the boiling broth to cook.
4   Slice the turnip and cook in boiling water.
5   Cook the Japanese mustard spinach, carrot, and shiitake mushrooms in boiling water, and let them stand in the dashi.
6   Place the scallops in a bowl, followed by the vegetables. Pour in the broth and garnish with yuzu.

RAW SEA URCHIN ROE AND ABALONE IN JELLY
Serves 4

1 abalone • 20 g kombu • 70 ml pale soy sauce • 120 ml mirin
• 150 ml sake • 4 Awaji sea urchins • 10 perilla flowering seed pods, for garnish • 1 piece ginger, julienned, for garnish

1   Clean the abalone and cook it in a pressure cooker for 1 hour.
2   Strain the stock from the cooked abalone and pour it into a pan. Add the abalone, kombu, pale soy sauce, mirin, and sake and cook for 20 minutes. Let it cool down, then put it into the refrigerator to stand overnight.
3   Cover the sea urchin with abalone and the jellied broth.
4   Garnish with perilla pods and julienned ginger.

SHARK FIN AND SESAME TOFU IN NABE POT
Serves 10

For the broth
1 chicken • 10 g kombu • 25 g Jinhua ham • broth made with 5:1 ratio of water to sake, for cooking the chicken • 1 liter water • 500 ml sake • 35 ml pale soy sauce • 35 ml mirin • rock salt, to taste

1   Put the chicken, kelp, Jinhua ham, water, and sake into a pan and bring to a boil. Once boiling, carefully skim to remove all the scum.
2   Lower the heat and continue to boil until it is reduced to about a third. Strain and reserve the broth.
3   Add the water, sake, pale soy sauce, mirin, and rock salt to the broth and bring to a boil. Once boiling, skim to remove all the scum, lower the heat, and simmer until the desired consistency is achieved.

For the shark fins
4 shark fins • 1 white leek
• 50 g ginger • 200 ml sake
• 2 liters water

1   Put the shark fins, leek, ginger, sake, and water into a steam cooker and cook for about 2 hours.
2   Soak the shark fin mixture in the water to rid it of leek and ginger aroma, then drain off all the water. Cook for 2 hours in the prepared broth.

For the sesame tofu
100 g kuzu • 150 g sesame paste • 100 ml sake • kuzu root starch, as needed • ginger juice squeezed from 1 piece of ginger
• 1 Kujo leek

1   Dissolve the kuzu and sesame paste into water to make a paste. Add the sake.
2   Cook over high heat, stirring constantly, adding kuzu root starch if needed. Once the right consistency is achieved, pour it into a chilled container. Place the container over iced water to cool it down.
3   Cut the tofu into appropriate-sized chunks once it has cooled down.
4   Warm the tofu thoroughly and put it in a nabe pot with broth and shark fins.
5   Add the ginger juice to taste, and garnish with chopped Kujo leeks rounded into a nice shape.

Takuji Takahashi

Mona Talbott is the chef and director of the Rome Sustainable Food Project, a collaborative dining program that nourishes scholarship and conviviality at the American Academy in Rome. Guided by the indomitable spirit of the Roman table, the Project reconstructs a model for sustainable dining in an institution.

As head of this project, Mona is re-establishing ancient connections between agriculture and culture. Her vision of the marriage of art and scholarship with food is profoundly beautiful. Since Mona founded the Project, scholars and fellows are no longer embarrassed to invite visiting dignitaries, family, and friends to eat at the Academy cafeteria instead of one of Rome's many fine *trattorie* and restaurants.

When Mona arrived in Rome in August 2006, Giovanni Bernabei of San Giovanni Incarico, the organic farmer from whom she was hoping to source many of her ingredients, interviewed *her* to see if she would use his vegetables in the right way. She passed the test. Today Giovanni and his wife, Assunta, are the presiding guardian spirits of the Project. Giovanni's portrait hangs on the kitchen wall, and his framed manifesto is displayed above the bar. Together Giovanni and Mona have delved into Roman food history and *la cucina povera*, reviving historical dishes such as *zuppa di fave e cicoria*, a dried fava bean and chicory soup that is delicious, nutrient-rich, and, according to folkloric tradition, the favorite food of Hercules.

At the Academy, Mona's guiding tenet is *rus in urbe:* in the heart of the city, the fertile countryside. Not only is food grown there, it is used economically. Foraging, recycling, and composting are all incorporated into the daily routine. Cooks pick olives from nearby trees and press them into the oil that is poured over dishes in their kitchen; day-old bread is turned into croutons in the fireplace; and visiting scholars, fellows, and their guests all engage in food preparation.

At the heart of Mona's cooking is an almost mystical synthesis of food with time, place, and memory. Naturally, the dining table at the Academy is now one of my favorite places to eat in the world.

Alice Waters

Born in 1963, Mona Talbott first encountered cooking with her grandmother, a lover of Quebecois food who encouraged Talbott's culinary flair. After five seasons as a cook in the reforestation camps of northern British Columbia, Talbott earned an arts degree then attended culinary school. She progressed from a brief internship at Chez Panisse to working there full-time, training in all departments. Talbott's apprenticeship under Alice Waters cemented her cooking style and led to an enduring professional association. She followed her time at Chez Panisse with a spell of travel in France, cooking at various fish restaurants as long as her work visa lasted. Since then Talbott has undertaken a range of roles, from private chef to the Clintons, to developing products for delicatessen company EAT, to implementing a range of not-for-profit projects based on sustainability and Slow Food. She currently lives and works at the American Academy in Rome.

MENU

Dried fava bean and
chicory soup

~

Farro pasta with pounded
walnut, pecorino Romano
and marjoram

~

Shaved celery and radish
salad with anchovy

~

Chestnut flour cake with
raisins and pine nuts

~

Sheep milk ricotta

Mona Talbott

358

1
Mona Talbott in the kitchen

2
Long dining table within
the colonnade

3
Lunch at the
American Academy

Rome Sustainable Food Project at The American Academy, Rome, Italy

DRIED FAVA BEAN AND CHICORY SOUP
Serves 6 generously

This dish is delicious brain food. Academy scholars have commented that their concentration and focus improves after eating this soup.

1 onion • 1 carrot • 60 ml extra-virgin olive oil • 1 dried chile • 500 g dried fava (broad) beans without skins • 2 liters cold water • 1 bay leaf • salt • 300 g wild dandelion (*cicoria di campo*) • 2 cloves garlic, peeled and crushed • grated Pecorino Romano and olive oil, for drizzling • freshly ground dried chiles, for garnish

1   Dice the onion and carrot and sauté in olive oil in a medium saucepan. Add the chile and fava beans and cover with 2 liters of cold water. Bring to a boil and reduce the heat to a simmer. Add the bay leaf, season with salt to taste. Cook for approximately 45 minutes or until the beans are very tender and falling apart and the onion and carrot have dissolved into the soup.
2   Taste the chicory. If very bitter, blanch first in lightly salted boiling water to remove some of the bitter flavor. Drain and squeeze out excess water.
3   Heat 30 ml olive oil in a sauté pan over medium flame. Add the garlic. Lightly brown the garlic and add the chicory, then sauté until tender. Remove and discard the garlic and roughly chop the chicory.
4   Add the chicory to the fava mixture and cook for another 5 minutes. Remove from heat.
5   Divide into soup bowls, drizzle with olive oil, and serve with grated pecorino Romano and freshly ground dried chiles.

FARRO PASTA WITH POUNDED WALNUT, PECORINO ROMANO, AND MARJORAM
Serves 6

For this pesto we use our own walnuts and herbs from the garden. It is especially good with farro pasta.

1 clove garlic • pinch of salt • 100 g walnuts • 150 ml olive oil • 3 tbsp chopped marjoram • 3 tbsp chopped parsley • 30 g pecorino Romano, grated • salt and pepper • 460 g farro pasta (*pizzichi pasta di faro*)

1   Remove the interior germ if the garlic has sprouted and put it in a mortar and pestle along with a pinch of salt. Pound to a fine paste.
2   Toast the walnuts in a 350°F (180°C) oven for 8–10 minutes until they are evenly golden. While still warm, wrap them in a clean dish towel and rub off the skins.
3   Add the walnuts to the mortar and pestle and pound to a paste. (If you do not have a mortar and pestle you can do this in a food processor.)
4   Transfer the nut mixture to a bowl. Add the olive oil and smooth out the lumps. Add the herbs to the oil and nuts. Mix in the pecorino and taste for seasoning.
5   Cook the pasta al dente in plenty of boiling salted water. Toss the walnut pesto with the pasta. Thin out the sauce with pasta cooking water if necessary.

CHESTNUT FLOUR CAKE WITH RAISINS AND PINE NUTS
Serves 8–12

I have been told that this used to be a typical treat for children to buy at their neighborhood *forno* (bakery) on their way home from school. We serve it at lunch with fall (autumn) salads and fresh sheep milk ricotta (*ricotta di pecora*).

500 g chestnut flour • pinch of salt • 200 ml olive oil • 800 ml milk • 50 g golden raisins (plumped in warm water if very dry) • 30 g pine nuts • 3 branches of rosemary

1   Preheat the oven to 400°F (200°C).
2   Mix the flour and salt together in a mixing bowl. Combine the olive oil and milk and add to the dry ingredients. Mix well, until no lumps remain.
3   Pour onto a well-oiled 33-cm round pan. Scatter the raisins, pine nuts, and rosemary needles over top. Drizzle the top of the cake with more olive oil.
4   Bake for 30–40 minutes. It will bubble and blister and get crispy on the top and bottom.
5   Serve warm, cut into triangles.

1
Dried fava bean and
chicory soup

2
Farro pasta with pounded
walnut, pecorino Romano,
and marjoram

3
Chestnut flour cake
with raisins and pine nuts

Mona Talbott

Kitty Travers

MENU

Brioche

~

Rhubarb ripple ice cream

~

Trinity burned cream
ice cream

~

Fig-leaf ice cream and
Charentais melon sorbet

~

Blackberry and rose
geranium sorbet

Born in London in 1977, Kitty Travers studied at New York's Institute of Culinary Education. Lionel Poilâne was an early culinary influence during her time at the Poilâne Bakery in London and later Paris. Under his guidance she received an early lesson in creating wonderful taste and texture from just a few essential ingredients. Travers ventured into ice cream at Mario Batali's Otto Enoteca in New York, learning from pastry chef Meredith Kurtzman, and went on to work for Fergus Henderson at St. John Bread & Wine, where she was entrusted with the entire dessert menu. Travers spent time seeking out the best ice cream in Italy, developing the inventive flair for sourcing local ingredients that makes her ice cream so unique. She sells it from a mobile van under her company name, La Grotta, making her ice cream particular to a time and place with its fairylike impermanence, the sense of occasion heralded by the sound of the van arriving.

Apparently we have Gabrielle Hamilton, of Prune in New York, to thank for Kitty appearing at St. John Bread & Wine. It was she who told Kitty to go back to London and get a job with us, where she had her grounding as a pastry chef, making beautiful, intricate sweet things.

Since St. John, Kitty seems to have been on the move, working in Alice Waters's garden in Rome, honing her skills and exploring the possibilities of ice cream. Her fig-leaf ice cream and Charentais melon sorbet is the perfect example of the subtleties that ice cream can capture—it reminds me of Patrick Suskind's *Perfume*, and Grenouille's efforts to bottle the essence of human scent—although, of course, a lot less sinister. At any rate, I can just imagine Kitty messing around with her machines, the different quantities of milk and eggs and sugar, tampering and tweaking and coming up with concoctions that are nothing short of inspired. Kitty is an eccentric in the positive senses—thank goodness that chefs like her have the urge to experiment, making the most of food's lovely mingling of science and art.

Kitty moves about with her ice cream van (a wee Piaggio), once setting up two doors up from St. John—a total treat! Another time we worked together in New York, and I had a chance to try her beautiful stewed fruit. This was the least fusty stewed fruit imaginable—not a prune in sight, a festival of delicate fruits cooked to bursting exuberance. Her ice cream van usually hosts three delicious flavors, including, on my visit, an eye-openingly wonderful kiwi-fruit ice cream, and a creamy rhubarb-and-custard ripple. There was also an intriguing rice pudding flavor, which contained little frozen nuggets of swollen rice. Delicious! A girl at one with her ice cream.

Fergus Henderson

La Grotta Ices, London, UK

1
Rhubarb ripple ice cream

2
Trinity burned cream
ice cream

3
Fig leaf ice cream and
Charentais melon sorbet

4
Blackberry and
rose geranium sorbet

RHUBARB RIPPLE ICE CREAM
Serves 4

This ice cream is made by swirling the clear pink stock from poaching rhubarb into a rich custardy base. It's particularly delicious eaten with those ginger cookies that have chewy chunks of stem ginger in them.

For the ripple
500 g rhubarb • 1 orange • 200 g unbleached granulated sugar • 1 vanilla bean

1   Preheat the oven to 325°F (160°C).
2   Wash the rhubarb and slice into 2.5-cm pieces. Place in an ovenproof dish.
3   Zest the orange, then cut and squeeze both halves, pick out the seeds, and add the juice and zest to the rhubarb.
4   Sprinkle the sugar over the rhubarb, add the vanilla bean, cover the dish with foil, shiny side down, and cook very slowly and gently until the rhubarb is soft and tender and sitting in a pool of beautiful pink juice. This could take up to 40 minutes, but check after 20 minutes and give a little stir to allow the sugar to dissolve, then replace the foil tightly.
5   When ready, let cool with the foil on. Then strain the juice from the fruit and vanilla bean, and taste to check for sweetness—the juice should be just slightly syrupy, and taste both tart and a bit sweet too.
6   Churn until slushy in an ice-cream maker according to the manufacturer's instructions, then store in an airtight container in the freezer.

For the ice cream
1 vanilla bean • 110 g unbleached superfine (caster) sugar • pinch salt • 250 ml whole milk • 5 egg yolks • 250 ml heavy (double) cream

1   Split the vanilla bean and scrape the seeds into a heavy pan, along with the empty bean, half of the sugar, the salt and all of the milk. Bring up to a simmer, whisking occasionally to make sure that the milk doesn't burn, and the sugar dissolves.
2   In the meantime beat the yolks and the rest of the sugar together in a bowl large enough to hold the milk.
3   As soon as the milk reaches a simmer, pour it in a thin, steady stream over your yolk and sugar mixture, beating all the time so as not to cook the yolks.

4 Return all the mixture to the pan, and over very low heat, stirring constantly with a heatproof rubber spatula, cook the custard until thick enough to coat the back of a spoon—or, more reliably, until it reaches 154°F (68°C) on a digital thermometer (this will also pasteurize the egg yolks.) It is most important that this mixture does not get too hot or simmer, or the egg will cook hard and the mixture will split.

5 Take off the heat, and pour the mix through a fine-mesh sieve directly into a clean bowl—a stainless steel one is ideal. Place the bowl into a larger container or sink filled with ice water, and stir until cool, then whisk in the cream (a hand-held stick blender is perfect for this) and refrigerate for at least 4 hours. (This is called the "aging" of the ice cream base and means that the ice cream will have a better structure and texture.)

6 To finish, churn the ice cream according to your machine's manufacturer's instructions, then scrape out into an airtight container, alternating frozen custard with swirls of rhubarb slush. Return to the freezer and freeze hard before serving.

TRINITY BURNED CREAM ICE CREAM
Serves 6

This is a recipe adapted from that of famous French pastry chef Pierre Hermé, who was a good friend of M. Poilâne. I swapped some apple tarts for a copy of his book, which is where I first read about this rather unusual cooking method. It makes the silkiest, richest ice cream base possible and was No. 1 favorite with the staff at St. John Bread & Wine in London—and they really knew what they liked. It's even better after a week in the freezer, when the shattered caramel has just started to go gooey around the edges, making toffee pools in the ice cream.

For the ice cream
1 vanilla bean • 250 ml whole milk • 250 ml heavy (double) cream • 55 g unrefined soft brown sugar • pinch of salt • 5 egg yolks • 55 g unbleached sugar

1 Preheat the oven to 250°F (120°C).
2 Split the vanilla bean and scrape out the seeds, putting them in a pan, along with milk

and cream, unbleached sugar and salt. Bring to a simmer over medium heat, whisking often to prevent scorching.
3 Whisk the yolks and brown sugar together in a bowl large enough to hold the milk-cream mixture, too.
4 Once the milk-cream mixture reaches a simmer, pour it over the eggs in a thin stream, whisking constantly until all is combined.
5 Pour the mix into a shallow baking sheet, ideally around 30 x 23 cm. Carefully transfer to the oven and bake very gently until just set in the middle but still wobbly—don't worry if the edges are a little more cooked—for 15–25 minutes, depending on the depth of your baking sheet.
6 Remove from the oven, pick out the vanilla bean, and scrape the mix into a blender. Mix until smooth and liquid again. Strain the mix through a fine-mesh sieve and refrigerate.

For the caramel
200 g superfine (caster) sugar

This probably makes more caramel than you will need, but it is tricky to work with smaller quantities—and it keeps!

1 Take your heaviest pan and sprinkle the sugar in an even layer. Set over a low–medium heat.
2 Wait for the edges of the sugar to start to melt, then give it a little stir with a heatproof spatula to help it cook evenly and avoid burned pockets of sugar. If it crystallizes into sugary chunks, turn the heat as low as possible and be patient. The sugar will all eventually melt, and get darker and darker in color. You need to cook the caramel for long enough that it loses its sweetness and acquires a delicious dark flavor—usually around 10 seconds after it starts smoking, by which time it is a dark coppery color, but not black!
3 As soon as you reach this stage, pour out the caramel onto a heatproof silicone mat and let cool until set hard.

To serve
1 Churn the ice cream base in an ice-cream maker, and in the meantime put the caramel in a sturdy plastic bag and smash it up with a rolling pin—or give it a quick blast in a food processor.
2 Sprinkle the broken chunks of caramel into your frozen base as you scrape it into an airtight container. Cover with wax (greaseproof) paper and freeze hard.

FIG-LEAF ICE CREAM AND CHARENTAIS MELON SORBET
Serves 8

This is what I want in my breakfast brioche on a summer morning. It instantly evokes that heady feeling of hot-hot heat, long shadows, and holidays…

For the ice cream
500 ml whole milk • 260 ml heavy (double) cream • 3 largish, freshly picked, and washed fig leaves (remove the stem and biggest veins) • 150 g unbleached superfine (caster) sugar • pinch of salt • 7 egg yolks

1 Scald the milk and cream in a heavy pan (to scald is to bring it nearly to a boil, whisking often to prevent the natural sugars and proteins from catching at the bottom of the pan and burning).
2 Toss in the fig leaves, submerge them in the hot liquid, and then turn off the heat. Cover the pan with plastic wrap (clingfilm) to prevent evaporation, and let steep for at least 4 hours.
3 Strain the figgy milk into another pan, really squeezing the leaves to extract all the flavor, and reheat to a simmer with half the sugar and the salt.
4 In a separate bowl, beat together the yolks and the remaining sugar.
5 Make a custard base with the beaten yolks and sugar and figgy milk mixture as described in the rhubarb ripple ice cream recipe.
6 Set the mixture in ice water to cool, chill for at least 4 hours in a refrigerator, and churn as above.
7 Freeze in an airtight container with wax (greaseproof) paper or plastic wrap on top to keep the flavor fresh. It is best eaten within a week, but will still taste good for as long as a month.

For the sorbet
400 ml simple sugar syrup (see method) • 600 g flesh from a very ripe Charentais melon, cut into cubes • juice of 1 lemon (optional)

1 Make a sugar syrup from equal volumes of sugar and water, then mix together until the sugar dissolves in the water. Leftover sugar syrup is useful for making cocktails!
2 Blend the fruit and syrup in a blender until perfectly smooth, taste it, and if you feel it needs it, add the juice of 1 fresh lemon.
3 Chill and churn as above, freeze in an airtight container, covered in wax paper or plastic wrap.

BLACKBERRY AND ROSE GERANIUM SORBET
Serves 4

To this day, the best sorbet I ever made was from some handfuls of blackberries gathered from my mum's railway side allotment by the railroad and a few windowbox geranium leaves. (Shame somebody unplugged the freezer to plug in a kettle and my entire small stock melted and was lost!) It has to be made with wild blackberries—supermarket ones taste of nothing and are a waste of money. And don't confuse the scented geraniums you need here with the somewhat unpleasant-smelling kind of windowbox geraniums that are properly called pelargoniums.

250 g sugar • 300 ml water • 8 or so medium-size rose geranium leaves, rinsed • 500 g blackberries, picked over and rinsed • juice of ½ lemon

1 Bring the sugar and water to a boil together in a stainless steel pan and toss in the geranium leaves. Submerge them in the syrup and turn off the heat. Cover the pan with plastic wrap (clingfilm) and let steep for at least 4 hours.
2 Strain the syrup into another pan, gently squeezing the leaves to extract as much flavor as possible.
3 Bring syrup back up to a simmer and add the blackberries. Turn off the heat and give the berries a stir. Let the syrup warm them through for 10 minutes to heighten their flavor and help to extract as much juice as possible.
4 Blend the entire batch with the lemon juice until as smooth as possible.
5 Strain through a fine-mesh sieve, using the back of a ladle to push as much puree through as possible.
6 Chill, then churn as above. Freeze in an airtight container, covered in wax (greaseproof) paper or plastic wrap.

Kitty Travers

When my friend Carlo Petrini, the founder of Slow Food International, came to San Francisco for the first time, I organized a special dinner in his honor to raise funds for Slow Food Nation (which would become a 60,000-person celebration of American food traditions and producers) at Michael Tusk's wonderful restaurant, Quince. Not only is Quince one of the most beautiful and elegant restaurants in the Bay Area—from its extravagant flower arrangements to its tableware and its classic and luxurious service—the food is prepared with great attention to detail, impeccable ingredients, and pure flavors. The dinner for Carlo was a resounding success.

Michael Tusk did not at first intend to be a cook. He earned a bachelor's degree in Art History from Tulane University in New Orleans, and only began to cook after graduation, first in Europe—Provence, Burgundy, and Barbaresco—and later in the United States. Michael and his wife, Lindsay, opened Quince after years of careful planning. It was an immediate success.

Michael is a purist who understands the importance of his *materia prima*: not only the freshest and best ingredients, but committed and communicative working relationships with his network of farmers and purveyors. He cooks with controlled spontaneity. Whether his dishes are inspired by ideas from colleagues, restaurants he has visited, local foods in season, or the landscapes through which he has travelled, he is constantly striving to refine his culinary technique. His cuisine is surprising without being ostentatious, and his execution is discriminating and graceful. His pastas, for example, are divine. I am always delighted by them, whether I'm eating a perfectly balanced version of spaghetti with sardines or an exquisite dish of ravioli stuffed with sheep's milk cheese and wild nettles.

Alice Waters

Born in New Jersey in 1964, Michael Tusk went to college before migrating to culinary school, which he followed with working stints at restaurants in France and Italy, absorbing the creative and technical aspects of each cuisine. He returned to a range of posts at top US restaurants, including Stars in San Francisco. Under the tutelage of Alice Waters at Chez Panisse, Tusk honed his understanding of sourcing produce and began an association with the Slow Food movement that continues today. The importance of supplier relationships that he learned at Oliveto under Paul Bertolli remains a guiding principle of his restaurant, Quince in San Francisco, which opened in 2003. Here Tusk offers a menu of Italian flavors with the refinement of the French dining experience. He isolates the essence of ingredients while maintaining a respect for process that is evident in his lauded house-made pastas, producing a distinctive cuisine that was awarded a Michelin star in 2006.

MENU

Canederli of rabbit with young Savoy cabbage, Formanova beet, and horseradish

~

Aquarello carnaroli risotto of Pacific sea beans and Santa Barbara sea urchin

~

Porcini mushroom and Romanesco squash tortelloni with Bettelmatt fonduta and squash blossom wafers

~

Roast Paine Farm squab with eggplant in two variations, rapini, tomatoes filled with Taggiasca olives, and orange-Campari sauce

1

Michael Tusk

Quince, San Francisco, CA, USA

For the pasta dough
225 g "00" flour • pinch of salt • 14–16 farm egg yolks

1 Combine the flour and salt on a clean counter.
2 Make a well in the middle of the flour, and add the egg yolks. With your fingertips begin to incorporate some of the flour. Gradually incorporate more flour, moving your fingertips in a circular motion.
3 Start bringing the dough together into a ball, and then knead with the heel of your hand. If the dough is a little dry, moisten your fingertips with a little water. Knead for 8 minutes, then place in plastic wrap (clingfilm) for 1 hour. This dough can also be made in a stand mixer with a paddle attachment.

For the porcini mushroom and Romanesco squash filling
60 g butter • 340 g porcini (cep) mushrooms, cleaned and sliced • 25 ml olive oil • 120 g Romanesco squash, sliced • 120 g Romanesco squash blossoms, sliced • 60 g scallions (spring onions), finely chopped • 1 tsp salt • 125 ml vegetable broth • 1 tsp finely chopped parsley • 1 tsp finely chopped calamint (*nepitella*) • 85 g Parmesan cheese, grated • 60 g fresh ricotta cheese

1 Heat a 30-cm sauté pan over moderate heat and melt the butter.
2 To avoid crowding the pan, add just half the porcini mushrooms and sauté over high heat. Remove the mushrooms when they have browned nicely and are tender. Repeat with the remaining mushrooms, transfer them to a bowl and keep them at room temperature. Reserve 24 of the nicest slices for garnish.
3 Do not clean the pan. The mushroom *fond* on the bottom of the pan is an essential element in the dish.
4 Keep the pan over moderate heat and add the olive oil. Add the squash and turn the heat to high. Quickly sauté, and when tender season and add the squash to the reserved porcini. Set aside.

1
Porcini mushroom and Romanesco squash tortelloni with Bettelmatt fonduta and squash blossom wafers

2
Roast Paine Farm squab with eggplant in two variations, rapini, tomatoes filled with Taggiasca olives, and orange-Campari sauce

5   Add the squash blossoms and the scallions to the pan, and season with salt. Cook quickly until tender and add the mixture to the bowl containing the mushrooms and squash.
6   Turn the heat down a little, then add the vegetable broth and scrape up all the *fond* from the pan. Add to the reserved mushroom mixture, and transfer all the ingredients to a food processor.
7   Blend until smooth, and add seasoning to taste.
8   Fold in the parsley, calamint, and both cheeses. Place in a pastry (piping) bag and hold in the refrigerator until needed.

For the Bettelmatt fonduta
225 ml heavy (double) cream • 120 g Bettelmatt cheese, finely grated • 1 egg yolk

1   Bring the cream to a boil in a 1-liter pan. Add the Bettelmatt cheese and transfer to a blender or a Thermomix. Blend until smooth. Temper the egg yolk with a small amount of the hot cheese mixture.
2   Return the yolk mixture to the blender to finish the sauce, and keep it warm in a bain marie.

For the squash blossom wafers (*cialde*)
1 liter olive oil, for deep-frying • 6 Romanesco squash blossoms • 25 g all-purpose (plain) flour • 125 ml sparkling water

1   Heat the oil to 350°F (180°C) in a fryer or large pan.
2   Clean out the squash blossoms and cut each into 4 pieces. Discard the stem.
3   Put the flour in a small mixing bowl and whisk in the water to make a thin batter.
4   Dip the blossoms in the batter and drain off the excess.
5   Fry 4 blossoms at a time until crispy and translucent. Drain on paper towels and reserve in a warm place. Continue until all the blossoms are fried. Make sure the fryer oil remains at 350°F (180°C). It may be necessary to pause between batches to achieve this.

To fill the pasta
flour, for dusting • semolina, for dusting

1   Remove the pastry bag with the filling from the refrigerator.
2   Roll out the dough on a floured surface and cut into 7.5 x 7.5-cm pieces. Pipe some filling into the center of each piece of pasta. Spray a little water

between the mounds of filling, using an atomizer. If you don't have one, brush a little water between the mounds of filling.
3   Fold the dough in half to form a triangle, and press the edges together to seal. With your thumbs, connect the 2 edges of each pasta triangle to form tortelloni.
4   Make 30 pieces, which will give you some spare in case any of them break.
5   Set on a baking sheet sprinkled with semolina and refrigerate until you are ready to finish the dish.

To finish
salt and pepper • butter

1   Warm 6 (30-cm) plates.
2   Bring a 4–5 liter pan of water to a rapid boil. Season to taste, and boil the tortelloni for 4 minutes or until tender. Reserve in a sauté pan with a little butter.
3   Remove the plates from the plate warmer and divide the Bettelmatt fonduta among them.
4   Place 4 tortelloni on each plate, with a squash blossom wafers between each piece of tortelloni.
5   Garnish each piece of tortelloni with a piece of porcini mushroom, and serve immediately.

ROAST PAINE FARM SQUAB WITH EGGPLANT IN TWO VARIATIONS, RAPINI, TOMATOES FILLED WITH TAGGIASCA OLIVES, AND ORANGE-CAMPARI SAUCE
Serves 6

For the squab
6 Paine Farm squab • 1 sprig summer savory, finely chopped • 1 tbsp olive oil • 1 tbsp red wine • 1 tbsp wildflower honey • 60 ml grapeseed oil • 1 red onion, diced • ½ carrot, diced • ½ stalk celery, diced • ½ head garlic • 1 bay leaf • 1 tbsp preserved tomato • 1 liter orange juice • 225 ml Campari • chicken stock to cover • veal stock to cover

1   Remove the breasts and legs from the squab. Chop up the carcasses into small pieces and reserve.
2   Combine the summer savory, olive oil, red wine, and wildflower honey and marinate the squab for 4 hours. Pat dry.
3   Heat a 3-liter pan and add the grapeseed oil. When hot, add the squab carcasses and brown over high heat. After 10 minutes add the red onion, carrot, celery, and

whole cloves of garlic. Brown the vegetables over moderate heat for another 5 minutes, then add the bay leaf.
4   Add the preserved tomato and cook for another 5 minutes. Deglaze with the orange juice, and reduce until the pan is dry. Add the Campari and reduce until syrupy.
5   Cover with the chicken and veal stocks. Bring to a boil, skimming off any impurities. Simmer for 1 hour and then strain. Reduce until about 225 ml sauce remains and reserve.

For the eggplant in two variations
2 large Tuscan Rose eggplants (aubergines) • 125 ml extra-virgin olive oil, plus a little extra • 7 tsp toasted and ground saffron • 3 sprigs fresh thyme • 3 cloves garlic • salt and pepper • 1 tsp red-wine vinegar • 2 Japanese eggplants (aubergines) • grapeseed oil, for frying

1   Preheat the oven to 425°F (220°C). Lay out enough aluminum foil to hold 2 Tuscan Rose eggplants with a little extra space. Add the olive oil, saffron, thyme, and garlic, and season with salt and pepper.
2   Encase the eggplants in the foil and roast for 45 minutes or until very tender.
3   Cut the eggplants in half lengthwise and scoop out the flesh. Puree this along with the thyme and garlic mixture, adding a little extra-virgin olive oil, if necessary. If any seeds remain, pass through a fine-mesh sieve.
4   If necessary, reduce the puree in a pan, and finish with a splash of red-wine vinegar and seasoning. Keep warm.
5   Preheat a fryer to 350°F (180°C).
6   Cut the Japanese eggplants into 24 (5-cm) sticks (batons), season with salt, and let rest for 1 hour.
7   Rinse under cold water and pat dry.
8   Fry 6 pieces of eggplant at a time until crispy. Reserve and keep warm.

For the rapini
60 ml extra-virgin olive oil • 1 clove garlic • 225 g young rapini (broccoli rabe) • salt and pepper

1   Heat a 30-cm sauté pan over high heat.
2   Add the extra-virgin olive oil and the garlic. When warm, quickly sauté the rapini, remove the garlic when brown, season, and reserve.

For the cherry tomatoes filled with Taggiasca olives
6 sungold cherry tomatoes • 6 sweet cherry tomatoes • olive oil • 120 g Taggiasca olives, chopped • 1 tsp capers • 1 tsp chopped anchovy in oil • 7 tsp chopped summer savory • 7 tsp red-wine vinegar

1   Blanch and peel the cherry tomatoes. Cut off the tops and scoop out the pulp.
2   Toss in olive oil and reserve.
3   Combine the chopped olives, capers, anchovy, savory, and red-wine vinegar. Mix and season if necessary.
4   Fill the tomatoes with the olive mixture and set aside.

To finish
olive oil, for frying • 12 sprigs fino verde basil • fresh black Tellicherry pepper

1   Place 6 large dinner plates in a plate warmer and preheat the oven to 400°F (200°C).
2   Reheat the eggplant puree, rapini, and sauce, and set aside in a warm place.
3   Put the stuffed tomatoes in the oven for 5 minutes and hold with the other vegetables.
4   Heat up a 30-cm sauté pan and add some olive oil.
5   Brown the legs first until crispy on both sides. Hold in the oven while you cook the breasts.
6   Cook the breasts in 2 batches, 6 breasts at a time, skin side down, for about 4 minutes.
7   Self-baste the breasts, and when finished turn them over and remove from the pan and keep in a warm place to rest for 1–2 minutes.
8   Place some rapini in the center of each plate. Place the squab breasts on top of the rapini.
9   Take the crispy legs out of the oven and on each plate place a leg above and below the breasts.
10 Form 2 quenelles of eggplant with teaspoons, and place on the sides of both squab breasts.
11 Refry the eggplant sticks (batons) and form a criss-cross motif over the eggplant quenelles.
12 Place an olive-filled cherry tomato next to each squab leg. Garnish each tomato with a sprig of fino verde basil.
13 Add a little fresh cracked black pepper to the warm sauce, spoon around the plate, and serve immediately.

Michael Tusk

Naoya trained for six years at my restaurant, Kikunoi. After that he worked under his father (who is a renowned chef) for eight years and then left, ignoring the efforts of those who tried to dissuade him from doing so. It has now been five years since he opened his own small restaurant, Gensai. I could not pay a visit until recently, because his restaurant is situated a long distance from my home in the outskirts of the port town of Kobe.

Naoya combines the colorful refinement of Kyoto cuisine that he learned at my restaurant, and the mellow richness of Osaka cuisine, learned from his father, to create Japanese cuisine that can only be prepared by him. His sophisticated skills, which he acquired through years of training, give life to carefully selected local ingredients. His knife skills and his talent at bringing out a mellow yet sharp flavor reminiscent of his father's cuisine are unparalleled. The care he takes to work on the smallest details of any dish is overwhelming.

I was moved to tears as Naoya saw me off the first time I visited his restaurant. I could perceive his earnestness in each and every one of the excellent dishes he had prepared. I was overjoyed to witness the growth of a chef who will lead the future of Japanese cuisine.

Yoshihiro Murata

Naoya Ueno was born in 1970 in Osaka, Japan, and grew up there watching his father, Shuzo Ueno, cook in his restaurant, Naniwa Kappou Kigawa. Shuzo was a major early influence in Ueno's career in food, exposing his son to high-class restaurants and introducing him to *sado*, the tea ceremony. In 1989 Ueno began his culinary career by training at Kyoto's Kikunoi, under Yoshihiro Murata, who became another crucial mentor. Murata taught Ueno a respect for Kyoto's traditional cuisine and for creative development. In 1995 Ueno began working for his father at Naniwa Kappou Kigawa, moving a year later to the branch restaurant of Tenjinzaka Ueno, a tiny eatery with precise serving times to guarantee dishes at the pinnacle of freshness. In 2004 Ueno opened his own restaurant, Gensai, in Kobe, where guests are invited to watch the swift preparation of the best ingredients in Ueno's open kitchen.

MENU

Seared pike conger and blanched golden cuttlefish served cold
Fukunishiki Junmai, Hyogo, Japan, served hot

~

Japanese asari clam dumpling in clear sumashi soup
Oyama, Junmai, Yamagata, Japan, served hot

~

Soy sauce and sugar-basted Tanba red chicken
Nulle Part Ailleurs, L'Anglore, Côtes du Rhône, France, 2007

~

Chrysanthemum greens and mushrooms in white tofu sauce
Le Domaine des Bois Lucas Touraine, Sauvignon Blanc, Loire, France, 2003

~

Assorted small dishes
Le Domaine de Martinolles, Blanquette de Limoux, Languedoc, France, 2006

1
Writing a new menu

2 & 4–6
The chef at work in the kitchen at Gensai

3
Naoya Ueno catching fish from the tank

Naoya Ueno

Gensai, Kobe, Japan

1
Seared pike conger
and blanched golden
cuttlefish served cold

2
Japanese asari clam
dumpling in clear
sumashi soup

3
Soy sauce and
sugar-basted Tanba
red chicken

4
Chrysanthemum greens
and mushrooms in
white tofu sauce

5
Assorted small dishes

SEARED PIKE CONGER AND BLANCHED GOLDEN CUTTLEFISH SERVED COLD
Serves 1

120 g pike conger • salt • ¼ medium-size golden cuttlefish • wasabi, to taste • daikon (mooli), sliced, to serve • kelp-infused soy sauce, to serve • umeboshi paste, to serve

1 Slice the bones of the cleaned pike conger (using the *honegiri* technique), put on metal skewers, and lightly sprinkle the skin with salt.
2 Put iced water into a large bowl, and cover with plastic wrap (clingfilm).
3 Lightly scorch the skin of the pike conger on a flame and place it over the iced water to cool.
4 Clean the golden cuttlefish by removing the quill and guts, slice and spread it open, and place it on a mesh ladle with the outer skin side down. Blanch it in boiling water and immediately cool it down in iced water.
5 Remove the internal thin skin.
6 Slice the pike conger and cuttlefish with a sharp knife and arrange on a plate with a garnish of wasabi and sliced daikon.
7 Serve with a homemade kelp-infused soy sauce (*matsumae shoyu*) and umeboshi paste made by boiling down pickled plums (umeboshi) with sake.

JAPANESE ASARI CLAM DUMPLING IN CLEAR SUMASHI SOUP
Serves 1

0 Japanese asari clams • sake • egg white • 1 tsp grated Japanese mountain yam (*tororo*) • 30 g ground white fish • kuzu root starch • Japanese wild parsley (*mitsuba*), cut into short lengths • yellow nira leek, cut into short lengths • lily bulb, salted and steamed • cloud-ear mushrooms, boiled and shredded • 1 *sayamaki* shrimp (prawn), cooked • bamboo shoots • shiitake mushrooms, simmered in dashi • snow peas, shredded • dashi • salt • pale soy sauce • young leaves of Japanese pepper (*kinome*), to garnish

1 Steam the clams in sake and transfer them to a strainer. Keep the cooking liquid hot.

2 Add the steaming broth, egg white, and grated yam into the ground fish and mix to the right consistency for dumplings.
3 Remove the clam meat from the shells and dredge in kuzu root starch, then add to the ground fish mix with the Japanese wild parsley and yellow nira leek, lily bulb, and cloud-ear mushrooms.
4 Cover a stainless-steel plate with plastic wrap (clingfilm). Place the clams and vegetables on it in small round shapes, and cook in a steamer.
5 Transfer to a wan bowl, and add the shrimp, bamboo shoots, and shiitake mushrooms, then the shredded snow peas.
6 Warm the dashi in a pan, season with salt and pale soy sauce, and pour in the bowl.
7 Garnish with the Japanese pepper leaves, cover with a lid, and serve.

SOY SAUCE AND SUGAR-BASTED TANBA RED CHICKEN
Serves 1

For the tare sauce
sake • mirin • tamari sauce • soy sauce • sugar • kelp

Boil down the sake, mirin, tamari sauce, soy sauce, sugar, and kelp in a pan.

For the chicken
150 g Tanba red chicken • 3 Iwazu leek • 50 g Kawachi lotus root • ½ white radish (daikon) • 8 bulbs on wild yam vines • salt • kuzu root starch • oil, for pan-frying • scallions (spring onions) and mustard leaves, julienned, to garnish

1 Cut the chicken, leek, lotus root, and radish into bite-sized chunks. Steam the yam bulbs in salted water.
2 Dredge both sides of the chicken with kuzu root starch (or ordinary starch).
3 Heat the oil in a pan, fry the vegetables, then remove and set aside.
4 Pour in a good amount of oil in the same pan and fry the chicken, pressing down with a wooden lid.
5 Remove the chicken and wipe away all the oil from the pan, lower the heat, add the cooked vegetables, and stir with the tare sauce.
6 Arrange on a plate and garnish with julienned scallions and mustard leaves.

CHRYSANTHEMUM GREENS AND MUSHROOMS IN WHITE TOFU SAUCE
Serves 1

¹⁄₁₀ konjac • edible chrysanthemum petals • vinegar • 3 chrysanthemum greens • 20 g assorted mushrooms • dashi • pale soy sauce • salt • mirin • ¹⁄₁₀ block tofu • sesame paste • white miso • sugar • pale soy sauce • finely shaved bonito flakes

1 Boil the konjac and cut into thin strips.
2 Boil the chrysanthemum petals in water with a small amount of vinegar, run under cold water, and squeeze tightly to extract the liquid.
3 Simmer the chrysanthemum greens, mushrooms, and konjac in dashi seasoned with pale soy sauce, salt, and mirin.
4 Immerse the chrysanthemum petals in a cold dashi seasoned in the same way and let stand.
5 Sandwich the tofu between paper towels and apply light pressure for 2–3 hours.
6 Strain, then puree the tofu and season with sesame paste, white miso, sugar, and pale soy sauce. Then strain it again to make puree even smoother.
7 Squeeze the water out of the chrysanthemum greens and petals, mushrooms and konjac and mix with the puree.
8 Arrange on a plate and garnish with bonito flakes.

ASSORTED SMALL DISHES
Serves 20

For the mackerel sushi
1 mackerel • salt • rice vinegar • 250 g rice • ginger, finely chopped • sesame seeds, roasted • sliced white kelp • sweet vinegar sauce (amazu)

1 Cut the mackerel into 3 fillets, sprinkle with plenty of salt, and leave to stand for 1–2 hours.
2 Wash away the salt with water and wipe off all the moisture. Immerse in rice vinegar and remove after 5–10 minutes.
3 Cook the sushi rice and gently mix the ginger and roasted sesame seeds into it.
4 Remove all the bones and skin from the mackerel.
5 Wrap the rice with the mackerel.
6 Place the white kelp simmered in sweet vinegar sauce (amazu) on top, slice, and arrange on a plate.

For the deep-fried Kawazu shrimp
40 Kawazu shrimp (prawns) • oil, for deep-frying

1 Cut the heads off the shrimp, dredge with flour, and deep-fry in hot oil.
2 Sprinkle them with salt while hot.

For the rolled persimmon and beans
4 persimmons • 60 common green beans • sesame paste • pale soy sauce • salt • sugar

1 Slice a thin, continuous sheet by cutting around the edge of the persimmon and immerse it in lightly salted water.
2 Simmer the beans and let cool.
3 Cut the beans lengthwise in two and wrap the persimmon around them. Wrap them in plastic wrap (clingfilm) and leave to cool before slicing.
4 Serve them with sauce made by mixing sesame paste, sugar, pale soy sauce, and salt.

For the sweet chestnuts stewed in soy sauce and sugar
tree ash from trees such as oak • 20 chestnuts • dashi • sugar • tamari soy sauce • soy sauce

1 Dissolve the tree ash in water, skim and strain the resulting liquid and set aside.
2 Shell the chestnuts and simmer them in the ash liquid until tender. Leave them to stand for more than half a day to remove the bitterness.
3 Wash them with water and lightly rub with your fingers to remove the fibers of the inner skin.
4 Wipe away the moisture and simmer in the dashi, sugar, tamari soy sauce, and soy sauce.

For the deep-fried gingko nuts
20 gingko nuts • oil, for deep-frying • salt

1 Remove the shell and skin of the gingko nuts.
2 Deep-fry them in medium-hot oil and sprinkle with salt.

Naoya Ueno

Allison Vines-Rushing—part Southern belle, part tough New Yorker—has a great ability to combine her love of the South and its cuisine with the regional ingredients that she finds in New York City. She trained at the Institute of Culinary Education in Manhattan, but purposefully chose to return to her roots in New Orleans to learn more about the local cuisine before coming back to New York.

It takes great dedication and spirit to move from your hometown in the South to the bustling, busy, and competitive culinary scene of New York, but Allison took on the challenge and exceeded our expectations. Having eaten at Jack's Luxury Oyster Bar while she managed the kitchen, executing simple but perfect food, I witnessed what an excellent chef she is. Each dish was beautifully seasoned, always really fresh—as if she had caught it just hours before plating it—and her skilful preparation had me hooked instantly. Allison's take on the New Orleans staple, Oysters Rockefeller, is a deconstructed version calculatedly presented so that each ingredient both stands on its own as well as complementing the others. Yet perhaps her most delicious project has already become a staple at my house all year long: the fried chicken of Dirty Bird To-Go is legendary among my guests and pals alike.

Following her time in New York, Allison returned to New Orleans and opened up a restaurant with her husband, Slade Rushing, just after Hurricane Katrina ravaged the area. Their tenacity and energy kept it alive, and just two years on they have opened up a new restaurant, MiLa, and already made significant waves in the food world. They use local farmers for their produce, which at once inspires their cooking and keeps the cuisine familiar for their clientele. However, familiar is by no means predictable. Their signature dish is Muscadine Wine Gelée. The sweet flavors of the Muscadine remain local, but the treatment as a gelée makes the dish sophisticated and incredibly special.

Allison has not been a chef for long, but she has accomplished more in five years than many chefs do in a lifetime!

Mario Batali

Allison Vines-Rushing was born in 1975 and attended culinary school in New York. She later worked at Brennan's in New Orleans and Gerard's Downtown, training under Gerard Maras, who inspired her with his farm-driven cuisine and love of classic interpretation. Returning to New York, Vines-Rushing held positions at some of the most rigorously competitive kitchens in the city, beginning at the three-Michelin-starred Picholine and moving on to the four-Michelin-starred Essex House. Working in these fast-paced kitchens instilled in Vines-Rushing an attentive eye for detail and a thirst for perfection. She put these skills to work at Jack's Luxury Oyster Bar in New York City, which she opened in 2003 to glowing reviews, quickly joined by her husband, Slade Rushing, as co-chef. Dirty Bird to-Go, with its fresh menu of soulful comfort food, opened shortly afterward. In 2005 the pair returned to the South to open MiLa, where they present cultivated Southern cuisine with a unique twist, showcasing the traditional flavors of the region using local produce.

MENU

Chicory salad with shaved butternut squash, pecan-crusted goat cheese, and fig balsamic vinegar
Foris Gewürztraminer

~

Sweet potato pappardelle with roasted shiitake mushrooms and shaved sheep cheese
Château St Georges Merlot

~

Muscadine wine gelée with tropical fruits, Chantilly cream, and mint chiffonade
Nivole Muscato d'Asti

1
Table settings
2 & 3
Allison Vines-Rushing
in the kitchen

Allison Vines-Rushing

375 MiLa, New Orleans, LA, USA

1

2

3

1
Chicory salad with shaved
butternut squash, pecan-
crusted goat cheese, and
fig balsamic vinegar

2
Sweet potato pappardelle with
roasted shiitake mushrooms
and shaved sheep cheese

3
Muscadine wine gelée with
tropical fruits, Chantilly cream,
and mint chiffonade

376

CHICORY SALAD WITH SHAVED BUTTERNUT SQUASH, PECAN-CRUSTED GOAT CHEESE, AND FIG BALSAMIC VINEGAR
Serves 6

For the pecan-crusted goat cheese
150 g pecan halves • 100 g granulated sugar • 1 tbsp butter • 250 g goat cheese

1   Preheat the oven to 350°F (180°C).
2   Toast the pecans on a baking sheet for 7 minutes. Remove from the oven and let cool.
3   In a medium sauté pan, melt the sugar carefully until it reaches a caramel stage, add the butter and the pecan halves, and stir with a wooden spoon until incorporated. Immediately pour onto a cookie (baking) sheet, spread out evenly, and let cool. Break into pieces and pulse in a food processor to a fine powder. Reserve.
4   Using your hands roll the cheese into 15-g balls. Place the pecan praline in a bowl and drop the goat cheese balls in one at a time. Coat well with the praline and reserve until ready to serve.

For the butternut squash
½ butternut squash, peeled and bottom round section removed • 3 tbsp turbinado (Demerara) sugar

1   Using a mandolin on the thinnest setting, cut the squash into thin strips. Using a knife, square off the squash slices until they are perfect rectangles. For each serving, line about 5 strips of squash side by side in a small pan.
2   Coat each squash strip lightly with turbinado sugar. Using a blowtorch, gently caramelize the squash pieces until the sugar is melted and the squash is brown around the edges.
3   Transfer 5 strips to each of 6 square serving plates a little down-right of center.

To finish the salad
6 heads frisée lettuce, only the small yellow leaves picked, washed well, and dried • salt and pepper • 6 tbsp extra-virgin olive oil • fig balsamic vinegar, for dressing • fresh herb garnish such as chervil sprigs or chive batons

1   Toss the frisée lettuce in a bowl, season well with salt and pepper, and lightly dress with olive oil and fig balsamic.
2   Place a small mound of lettuce in the center of each plate. Place 3 goat cheese balls on each plate around the lettuce, and drizzle around the salad with fig balsamic vinegar.
3   Garnish the salads with chervil sprigs or chive batons.

SWEET POTATO PAPPARDELLE WITH ROASTED SHIITAKE MUSHROOMS AND SHAVED SHEEP CHEESE
Serves 6

For the pasta dough
475 ml sweet potato juice (peel sweet potatoes and push through vegetable juicer) • 120 g durum wheat (hard) flour • 1 tsp salt • 1 tsp olive oil • 1 whole egg

1   Reduce the sweet potato juice by three-quarters to the consistency of paint. Let cool.
2   In a stand mixer with a hook attachment, mix the flour and salt. Add the sweet potato reduction and mix well. Add the olive oil and egg, and mix until the dough comes together in a ball. Continue to work the dough in the mixer for 5 minutes.
3   Remove the dough from the mixer and shape into a ball. Cover in plastic wrap (clingfilm) and place in the refrigerator for an hour to rest.

For the garlic confit
24 cloves garlic, peeled and stem end trimmed • olive oil

1   Place the peeled garlic in a small pan, cover with olive oil, and cook over very low heat until soft.
2   Before using, drain off the oil.

For the mushroom stock
stems from 150 g shiitake mushrooms • 450 g button mushrooms • 1 liter water

1   Wash the mushroom stems and button mushrooms and place in a large pan. Cover with the measured water and bring to a slow simmer.
2   Cook for 1 hour, or until dark and richly flavored. Strain and reserve.

For the finished dish
60 ml olive oil • caps from 150 g fresh shiitake mushrooms, cut into wedges • salt and pepper • 225 g unsalted butter, cut into small cubes • garlic confit • 750 ml mushroom stock • 120 g sheep cheese, such as Thomasville Tomme • fresh herbs for garnish, such as chervil sprigs or chive batons

1   Bring a large pan of lightly salted water to a boil.
2   Heat a large sauté pan over medium heat until smoking. Add the olive oil and the mushroom caps. Immediately season with salt and pepper and caramelize lightly for 1 minute.
3   Reduce the heat to low and add the butter. Once foaming and brown, add the garlic confit. Then add the mushroom stock and bring to a simmer.
4   Once a light sauce has formed in the pan and all the elements are emulsified, drop the pasta in the boiling water and cook for 15 seconds. Drain, and add to the mushroom sauce. Coat the pasta in the sauce carefully and adjust the seasoning.
5   Divide the pasta among 6 serving dishes and top with a few shavings of sheep cheese and fresh herbs.

MUSCADINE WINE GELÉE WITH TROPICAL FRUITS, CHANTILLY CREAM, AND MINT CHIFFONADE
Serves 6

For the Chantilly cream
475 ml heavy (double) cream • 2 tbsp confectioners' (icing) sugar

1   In a stand mixer with a whisk attachment, whip the cream on medium until it begins to ribbon.
2   Add the sugar and continue whipping until you reach stiff peaks, being careful not to overwhip. Refrigerate until serving.

For the gelée
3 sheets gelatin • ½ bottle muscadine wine • 225 ml sugar syrup • pinch salt • 1 mango, skin removed and sliced thinly around the pit

1   Bloom the gelatin sheets in a bowl of ice water until soft.
2   Put the wine, syrup, and salt in a pan and heat on the stove until it is steaming but not boiling.
3   Remove the gelatin from the ice water and squeeze until all water is extracted. Place the gelatin in the wine mixture off the heat and stir until just dissolved.
4   Ladle the mixture into serving dishes and add 3 slices of mango to each. Place in the refrigerator until set (this will take about 4 hours).

To finish
2 kiwis, skin removed and sliced thinly • 2 leaves fresh mint, cut in a chiffonade

1   On each gelée, place 3 slices of kiwi.
2   Top with a quenelle of Chantilly cream and a few strands of mint chiffonade.

Allison Vines-Rushing

Sylvestre has undertaken a labor of love, upholding the tradition of fine cooking at the Oustau de Baumanière since 2005. The Oustau is a skilfully restored 16th-century building that has long been a beacon for all lovers of superb cuisine. But Sylvestre's career is up to the challenge. He earned his stripes in the kitchens of Thierry Marx, Patrick Pagès, and Alain Solivérès before working for five years as sous chef in my Essex House restaurant in New York.

To develop as a chef, first of all you have to immerse yourself in your environment. Sylvestre talks like a Provençal native when he says: "Here, the stones and the light speak to you; you have to listen to them," which is another way of saying that part of the restaurant is its history. Sylvestre also has the wisdom to maintain the ethos that has always made this restaurant work. He pays homage to the lineage of chefs that he follows: Raymond Thuilier and Jean-André Charial. Their two signature dishes, veal sweetbreads and foie gras ravioli, respectively, are still on the menu. But upholding a tradition also means keeping it alive. With tact, he has further developed these two recipes: The sauces and jus have been lightened, while the flavor has stayed the same.

A great chef always cooks for his contemporaries. Sylvestre says with generosity: "My customers help me a lot." Very aware of new ways of eating, he has created a vegetarian menu that puts the spotlight on fabulous Provençal vegetables, many of which come fresh from his own vegetable garden and are grown organically. The interaction with his diners sometimes goes even further, when he prepares dishes on demand for guests who are staying in the hotel for several weeks.

So, by making careful changes, Sylvestre is putting his stamp on the restaurant, while respecting its tradition. Exotic flavors—ginger, lemongrass, perilla—add a contemporary dimension to his dishes, and a personal touch to the carefully evolved menu at the Oustau.

Alain Ducasse

Sylvestre Wahid was born in Pakistan in 1975 and moved to France to train under Thierry Marx at the Cheval Blanc in Nîmes and later with Alain Solivérès at Les Elysées du Vernet in Paris. In 1997 Wahid joined Alain Ducasse at the Plaza Athénée, moving in 2000 to his restaurant Essex House in New York, where he became sous chef to Didier Elena and helped garner the restaurant widespread praise. Returning to France in 2005, Wahid progressed to his current position of head chef at Oustau de Baumanière in Les Baux de Provence. Here he maintains a high respect for the traditional dishes and local produce that made his restaurant's name, without compromising his unstinting curiosity to learn about new ingredients and techniques through travel. Wahid is assisted in maintaining his restaurants enviable reputation by his brother Jonathan, a talented pastry chef.

MENU

Amuse-bouche

~

Lightly cooked duck foie gras, bitter orange, and fruit and nut relish

~

Hens' eggs with green asparagus in a hot or cold black truffle glaze

~

Red mullet

~

Mediterranean sea bass

~

Chocolate mousse

1

Sylvestre Wahid

1
In the kitchen at
Oustau de Baumanière

2–5
Sylvestre Wahid at work

6
A fresh bread basket

379 **Oustau de Baumanière, Les Baux de Provence, France**

LIGHTLY COOKED DUCK FOIE GRAS, BITTER ORANGE, AND FRUIT AND NUT RELISH
Serves 6

For the candied orange zest
1 bitter orange • 30 g sugar

1 Peel the orange to remove all the pith, cut the zest into julienne strips, and blanch 3 times. Set aside.
2 Squeeze the orange, collect the juice, and bring it to a boil with the sugar. Add the zest strips and let them cook on the side of the stove for 1½ hours without boiling. Set aside.

For the bitter orange jelly
1.5 liters bitter orange juice • 25 g superfine (caster) sugar • 10 g agar agar

1 Bring the orange juice and the sugar to a boil, add the agar agar and cook for 5 minutes on the side of the stove.
2 Spread out the jelly so it is about 3 mm thick, reserving a little for the foie gras terrine and let it set in a cold place.

For the dried fruit and nut relish
50 g honey • juice of 6 oranges • 80 g dried figs • 80 g raisins • 50 g almonds, sliced • 50 g hazelnuts, chopped • pinch of fleur de sel • dash of pepper

In a heatproof pan, melt the honey, let it caramelize slightly, deglaze with the orange juice, then add all the dried fruit and nuts. Season with fleur de sel and pepper. Allow them to become candied for 1 hour on low heat, then remove and put in a cool place.

For the foie gras
1 kg preserved foie gras

To finish, place the preserved foie gras in a mold measuring 20 x 20 cm, add a thin layer of orange jelly while it is still liquid, and let it set in a cold place. When about to serve, cut the foie gras into slices and arrange on a plate, accompanied by the dried fruit and nut relish, the candied orange zests, and the jelly.

HENS' EGGS WITH GREEN ASPARAGUS IN A HOT OR COLD BLACK TRUFFLE GLAZE
Serves 4

For the asparagus
12 spears green asparagus

1 Trim the asparagus spears and cut them into three, using the bottom third to make puree, the middle third to dice for a marmalade garnish, and the tops to finish the dish. Blanch and refresh them and set aside.
2 Thinly shave 4 asparagus spears and put the shavings aside in a cool place.

For the asparagus puree
250 g young spinach • 2 scallions (spring onions) • 400 g asparagus • 500 ml white chicken stock • pinch of fleur de sel • dash of pepper • dash of olive oil

1 Trim and wash the spinach.
2 Make an asparagus puree with the scallions, asparagus trimmings, spinach, and white chicken stock.
3 Season with fleur de sel and pepper and gently beat in the olive oil.
4 Divide the puree into two, half to glaze the eggs and half to make the marmalade.

For the lie de vin sauce
1 kg veal trimmings • 100 ml olive oil • 100 g shallots, chopped • 2 cloves garlic • 100 g unsalted butter • a few yellow celery leaves • a few flat-leaf parsley leaves • 1 bouquet garni • 750 ml red wine • 2 liters white chicken stock • 25 g coarse-ground black pepper

1 In a heatproof casserole, brown the pieces of veal in the olive oil, add the butter, shallots, garlic, celery, parsley, and bouquet garni. Sweat it all for a few minutes.
2 Remove some of the fat and pour in three-quarters of the red wine.
3 Reduce by half, and pour in the white chicken stock. Simmer for about 2 hours, until it forms a well-thickened sauce.
4 In the meantime, make the red wine reduction. To do that, gently reduce the remaining red wine without allowing it to boil until all the alcohol has evaporated.
5 Strain the veal juices into the wine reduction through a conical sieve, add the black pepper, and bind the mixture with unsalted butter.
6 Allow to infuse for 30 minutes and strain again. Set aside.

For the garnish
200 g white bread • clarified butter • celery and parsley leaves, to serve

1 Cut the white bread into thin slices, then cut it with a pastry cutter. Place the rounds with some clarified butter between 2 sheets of baking parchment and bake at 250°F (120°C).
2 Cut the rest of the bread into cubes and fry in clarified butter.
3 Fry the celery leaves and the parsley and set them aside.

For the truffle glaze
15 g truffle puree • white stock • dash of olive oil • 100 ml whipped cream • fleur de sel • pepper

Dilute the puree slightly with the white stock, olive oil and whipped cream, season with fleur de sel and pepper and keep in a warm place.

For the marmalade and egg
oil, to taste • pinch of fleur de sel • dash of pepper • 4 whole eggs • 10 g chopped truffles • 10 g chopped chives

1 Add the diced asparagus to half the asparagus puree, beat the mixture with oil, check the seasoning, and keep in a warm place.
2 Separate the eggs and reserve the yolks.
3 Beat the whites until stiff, season with fleur de sel, pepper, and chopped chives, and add the chopped truffle.
4 Line the molds with the beaten egg whites and place the yolks in the center. Season with fleur de sel and pepper, cover with beaten egg white, and bake in a steam oven for 6 minutes at 165°F (75°C).

To serve
1 Pour some asparagus marmalade into the bottom of each plate, arrange the slices of fried bread round it, placing a leaf of fried parsley and a leaf of fried celery between each slice.
2 Decorate the rim of each plate with truffle glaze and asparagus puree. Take the eggs out of the oven, remove them from the molds and glaze them with the remaining asparagus puree.
3 Heat the asparagus tops in the liquid in which they were cooked and arrange them on top of the marmalade.
4 Put a slice of bread under each egg and place it in the center of each plate.
5 Season the asparagus shavings with olive oil, fleur de sel, and pepper, arrange the shavings neatly on the plates, dress with the lie de vin sauce, and serve immediately.

1
Lightly cooked duck foie gras, bitter orange, and fruit and nut relish

2
Hens' eggs with green asparagus in a hot or cold black truffle glaze

Sylvestre Wahid

Tristan Welch won the Gordon Ramsay Scholarship in 2003. We bring together some of Britain's top young chefs and those who get through to the finals have to do a live cook-off against each other, in front of an audience. It's a terrifying feat for any young chef, especially as they have to cook from a black box of unknown ingredients. Tristan was confident, focused, and determined, and was a well-deserved winner. He was already proving to be an extremely talented and promising chef, even at that young age. I knew immediately that I had to snap him up for one of our restaurants.

After several stints working in London and around the UK, he joined us as head chef of Pétrus in 2005 under Marcus Wareing. Before he came to us, he worked for over a year at Le Gavroche, an incredible training ground for any young chef. He learned a lot in that kitchen—techniques, strength, focus. At Pétrus he proved himself in the kitchen, retaining our two Michelin stars while he was there.

As head chef at Launceston Place, Tristan serves the most amazing house-smoked salmon. The flavor of such a simple dish is incredible. Another of my favorites is the rice pudding soufflé with raspberry ripple ice cream, an interesting twist on two classic dishes. His presentation skills are second to none. He serves scallops in their shells with wildflowers, and a pre-dessert of baked vanilla custard in hollowed-out eggshells.

He champions British produce like no one else: ninety percent of the ingredients served at Launceston Place are British. His menu is full of quintessential British classics with a twist. Look at his rhubarb and custard ice cream with a crumble topping—he takes British icons and reinvents them for the modern diner. Absolutely delicious.

Gordon Ramsay

Born in 1979, Tristan Welch began his career with six months of training as a commis chef, followed by stints at the City Rhodes restaurant in 1998 and Aubergine as chef de partie. In 1999 Welch joined the kitchen at Le Gavroche, where he trained for a year and developed tenacity and technical virtuosity. From there he moved to L'Arpège in Paris before an opportunity at the Glenapp Castle in Ayrshire, Scotland, took him north. In 2005 Welch was appointed head chef of Pétrus in London, under the executive guidance of Marcus Wareing. In 2008, Welch relaunched Launceston Place in Kensington, London, where he serves scrumptious British dishes, from smoked salmon and scallops to rice pudding and rhubarb crumble. Welch brings a personal touch and exquisite presentation to each dish, ensuring his menu's unique quality.

MENU

English asparagus
"egg and cress sandwich"

~

West Coast scallops roasted with aromatic herbs and flowers in their shells

~

Drunken quail flambé with hazelnut

~

Hot smoked salmon, with wild herbs

~

Spit-roasted Denham Castle lamb, crackling, and minted peas

~

Rhubarb and custard crumble ice cream

~

Bitter lemon slice

~

Thyme sorbet

Tristan Welch

Launceston Place, London, UK

WEST COAST SCALLOPS ROASTED WITH AROMATIC HERBS AND FLOWERS IN THEIR SHELLS
Serves 4

12 medium scallops in their shells (ask your fishmonger to prepare the scallops for you by taking the top flat shell off, removing the skirt and roe, and leaving the scallop meat intact in shell) • sea salt • olive oil • 25 g butter • 150 ml white wine • 300 ml vegetable stock • selection of fresh flowers, depending on the season

1 Preheat the oven to 350°F (180°C).
2 For the scallops, you will need a hot pan that will fit at least 3 at a time. Scallops cook quickly, and overcooking them will result in very tough and dry scallops. This dish only takes 5 minutes to cook, so you have to be quick.
3 Heat a nonstick frying pan until hot.
4 Take the scallops and dust them lightly with sea salt. Put a tablespoon of olive oil in the pan and place the scallops in the pan with the shell facing up and the meat in contact with the pan's surface. When you cook it this way, you not only brown the scallop but the shell also keeps all the moisture from the scallop and starts to steam it. It gives the scallop a good even, all-round cooking.
5 When the scallop meat is browned, add a piece of the butter and remove the pan from the heat. Take out the scallops and place them meat-side up on a tray.
6 Place the pan back on the heat and add some of the white wine (not all of it, if you are cooking the scallops in batches).
7 Let the wine reduce by half then add some of the vegetable stock (again, not all of it if you are cooking in batches). Stir well and pour the sauce into a small pan, keeping it to one side for the moment.
8 Repeat this until you have all the scallops on the tray, then put them in the oven for 3 minutes. While the scallops are cooking, warm up the sauce and taste it to check the level of salt and acidity. Adjust to taste.
9 To serve, place the scallops on a bed of sea salt to keep them steady, divide the sauce between the 12 scallops, dress the flowers in a little olive oil, place on top of the scallops, and serve.

SPIT-ROASTED DENHAM CASTLE LAMB, CRACKLING, AND MINTED PEAS
Serves 4

For the mint sauce
1 tbsp oil • 500 g lamb bones and trimmings • 6–8 shallots • 2 bulbs garlic • 1 bunch thyme • 1 tsp lavender • 3 bay leaves • 3 white peppercorns • 750 ml white wine • 4 liters brown chicken stock • fresh mint, chopped, to taste • sherry vinegar, to taste

1 Heat the oil in a heavy-based pan and caramelize the lamb. Once brown, add 200 ml water and cook until the liquid has evaporated and the lamb browns again.
2 Add the shallots, and once they have colored add the herbs and deglaze with the white wine.
3 Reduce by four-fifths and add the stock. Bring to a boil and simmer for 1 hour, skimming well.
4 Remove the pan from the stove and let cool for 10 minutes. Pass through a sieve 5 times, until the stock is clear.
5 Pour into a pan and reduce until it has a saucelike consistency. Check the seasoning and add the chopped mint and sherry vinegar to taste.

For the pea puree
300 g frozen small peas • 100 ml heavy (double) cream • salt and pepper

1 Cook the frozen peas in a large pan of boiling water until soft.
2 While the peas are cooking, pour the cream into a pan large enough to accommodate the peas as well. Bring the cream to a boil and keep it warm.
3 Strain the peas and add to the cream, then continue to cook them for a couple of minutes.
4 Blend in a blender then check for seasoning, pass through a fine sieve, and set to one side.

For the pea risotto
300 g fresh small peas • 250 ml fresh pea juice

1 Blanch the fresh peas in a large pot of boiling water, then refresh them in ice water.
2 Season the pea juice and bring to a boil in a pan, whisking constantly. The natural starch in the pea juice will start to thicken and form a loose puree.
3 Add this puree to the fresh peas and warm gently when required.

For the lamb crackling
2 lamb breasts • 300 g salt • 1.4 liter lamb fat • oil, for frying

1 Trim off any loose ends from the lamb, cover it with salt, and keep in the refrigerator for 3 hours to cure it.
2 When cured, wash the lamb thoroughly in cold water, then dry.
3 Warm the lamb fat in a deep roasting pan to melt it, then place the lamb in the fat.
4 Place the pan with the lamb in the oven at 230°F (110°C) and let cook for 2–3 hours or until the lamb is very soft.
5 When cooked, remove from the fat and place skin side down on a flat tray in the refrigerator. Let the fat cool down and keep it for another day in the refrigerator.
6 When the lamb is properly chilled, cut it into 1.5 x 5 cm pieces.
7 To cook the lamb crackling, place the pieces in a hot skillet with a little oil (put aluminum foil on top straight away, as the excess fat might spit), then put the hot pan with the foil in the oven set to 350°F (180°C) for 10–12 minutes or until crispy.

For spit-roasted lamb
1 (1–2-kg) best end of lamb wrapped in lots of thyme and marinated for 3 days • fresh bay leaves • fresh thyme • dried lavender

1 For spit-roasted lamb, light the charcoal and let it burn until the flames have died down and the charcoal is glowing red.
2 Place the lamb on a spit and fasten well. The thyme that is wrapped around the lamb acts as a layer of protection against the fierce heat of the charcoal and gives a great flavor.
3 Set the height of the spit so that the lamb does not cook too quickly and keep the lamb revolving on the spit so it cooks evenly.
4 At regular points throw some of the fresh herbs and lavender onto the fire—they will add a little smoky flavor.
5 The lamb should take no more than 45 minutes to cook. When it is done, remove it from the spit and let rest in a warm oven for 20 minutes or so.
6 While the lamb is resting, warm up the pea risotto, pea puree, lamb crackling, and mint sauce and arrange neatly on 4 warmed plates.
7 Remove the lamb from the bone and slice into 1-cm-thick pieces. Arrange on the pea puree and risotto, and finish with the mint sauce and fresh pea shoots.

BITTER LEMON SLICE
Serves 6–8

2 large sheets or 4 half sheets leaf gelatin • 180 g superfine (caster) sugar • 25 g cornstarch (cornflour) • 4 free-range egg yolks • grated zest and juice of 3 large lemons • 75 ml heavy (double) cream • 3 free-range egg whites

1 Soak the leaf gelatin in a bowl of cold water to cover. When the sheets are floppy, pour off the water and set aside.
2 In a medium heatproof bowl, mix together 30 g sugar, the cornstarch, and egg yolks to a creamy paste. Set aside.
3 Put lemon zest and juice into a pan with 100 ml water and bring to a boil. Then whisk in the cream and return to a boil.
4 Pour the boiling liquid onto the sugar-cornstarch paste, whisking as you pour until blended, then return the mixture to the pan over low heat, and stir with wooden spoon until thickened and smooth.
5 Remove from the heat and stir in the soaked gelatin sheets until dissolved. Scoop into a larger bowl then cover and let cool. (In the restaurant, we would place the bowl in bigger bowl of ice to speed the cooling, stirring often.)
6 When the mixture is cool, whisk the egg whites to the soft-peak stage (you could use an electric mixer) and then gradually beat in the remaining sugar to make a thick meringue. Fold into the lemon cream using a large metal spoon until well blended.
7 Line a 1-kg nonstick loaf pan (tin) with baking parchment and spoon in the mixture, chill until set, then freeze until solid. To serve, dip the frozen loaf pan quickly in a bowl of hot water and loosen the sides with a knife, then turn it over and shake it out. Cut into 6–8 slices with a serrated knife.
8 If you wish to caramelize the slices, pass a cooks' blowtorch over the top before serving.

1
West Coast scallops roasted
with aromatic herbs and
flowers in their shells

2
Spit-roasted Denham Castle
lamb, crackling, and
minted peas

3
Bitter lemon slice

Tristan Welch

1 & 3
Jody Williams in the kitchen

2
Oxtails waiting to be plated

4
Kitchen tools at Gottino

Jody Williams

MENU

**Sanbitter,
Prosecco & orange**

~

Fried whole artichokes
Vino Bianco, Blanc de
Morgex, Valle d'Aosta,
Italy, 2008

~

Walnut pesto

~

**Ancient anchovy bread
soup Genovese**
Ormeasco di Pornassio,
Poggio dei Gorleri, Imperia,
Liguria, Italy, 2007

~

**Steamed eggs and dried
tuna roe on toast**
Refosco dal Peduncolo,
Tenute Aleandre-Fruili,
Italy, 2006

~

**Fresh porcini risotto
with berries**
Insoglio del Cinghiale,
Biserno, Toscana, Italy, 2006

~

**Whole sea bream roasted
with potatoes, rosemary,
and garlic**
Schiava Classico Superiore,
Pfarrhof, Italy, 2006

~

**Oxtails braised in red
wine and bitter chocolate**
Pecoranera, Tenuta Grillo,
Piedmont, Italy, 2003

~

**Quince and heirloom
apples baked in paper
with Vin Santo and served
with walnut bread and
triple-milk cheese**
Isole e Olena, Vin Santo,
Italy, 1997

~

**Torinese chocolate
coffee drink**

Jody Williams was born in northern California in 1962 and began her career in food working at restaurants such as Thomas Keller's three-Michelin-starred Rakel in New York. In 1987 Williams moved to the restaurant Felidia to work under Lidia Bastianich. Next stop, Italy, where she lived and worked for six years, including cooking at a Michelin-starred restaurant in Rome. Returning to New York in 1997, Williams joined Il Buco, turning out authentic and studied Mediterranean dishes, following this with stints at Convivium and at Giorgione under Giorgio DeLuca.
In 2005 she became head chef at Gusto, moving to Keith McNally's kitchen at Morandi the following year. This catalog of success gave Williams the chance to develop and finesse the traditional yet sparky Italian dishes served at Gottino, her "gastroteca" in New York. Her menu is inspired by slow food, boasting favorites such as fried artichokes, bread and anchovy soup, and rosemary-fried rabbit.

I respect and enjoy Jody Williams as a person because of her intelligence and constant curiosity, as well as her inability to accept anything less than what she needs to calm her soul in the kitchen. And I admire her just as much as a chef, for all the perfect things she creates, day in and day out.

Jody is self-taught and educated herself by working and living in Italy, learning how to cook with local chefs, whether it was spanking beets in a sink in Reggio Emilia or tasting culatello at Cavallino Bianco. Being fortunate enough to study Italian cuisine at the source allowed Jody to learn about the culture and language as well. This deeper understanding informs her choices in the kitchen and her presentation of the cuisine.

Her perfectly tiny restaurant in New York's Greenwich Village, Gottino, is charming, real, and hip. It is somewhere between a wine bar and a gastro-pub, so she has labeled it a "gastroteca." For her, this distinguishes it as a gathering place to enjoy food and wine, not just another bar in New York. Her Slow Food–inspired and seasonally dictated dishes are innovative, and yet reminiscent not only of her time in Italy but also of her work at Gusto and Morandi, where her food shone brighter than any movie star who walked through the doors. She focuses on certain ingredients and techniques in every menu, forming a thread that runs through her dishes. Artichokes are favorites, as are sardines.

The character of the restaurant is also captivating. She keeps baskets of walnuts around the bar for a gratis treat, and holds a strict no-reservation policy, which ensures that it remains a neighborhood haunt. These touches carry beyond the running of the restaurant as well—on the Gottino website, she includes links to her sommelier's blog, as well as to other staff members' sites, and she also has a section on how to tie a bow tie and remove red wine stains. She is a constant source of curiosity and confidence in the kitchen, and her food is a permanent reminder of what I aspire to.

Mario Batali

1
Fried whole artichokes

1
Fried whole artichokes

2
Steamed eggs and dried
tuna roe on toast

3
Fresh porcini risotto
with berries

4
Whole sea bream roasted with
potatoes, rosemary, and garlic

5
Oxtails braised in red wine
and bitter chocolate

6
Quince and heirloom apples
baked in paper with Vin Santo
and served with walnut bread
and triple-milk cheese

FRIED WHOLE ARTICHOKES
Serves 4

1 lemon • 4 young medium-size (Romanesco) artichokes • olive oil, for frying • salt

1   Squeeze the lemon into a bowl of cold water.
2   Hold on to the stem of the artichoke and remove, one by one, the dark-green outer leaves to reveal the tender yellow leaves. Turn the artichoke around, and while holding on to the yellow leaves, use a potato peeler to clean away the dark, tough green skin from stem, like peeling a carrot.
3   Using a teaspoon, reach in to remove the hairy choke, which is found deep in the flower between the leaves at base of stem. Be careful not to scoop away the heart—just scratch the choke loose. Place the cleaned artichokes in the bowl of lemon water until ready to fry.
4   To fry artichokes, heat enough olive oil to cover the artichokes in a deep cast-iron pot to 230°F (110°C). Cook slowly until tender. Remove and let rest in a covered container, where they will continue to cook.
5   When cooled, fry the artichokes for a second time at 375°F (190°C) until crisp and golden brown. Season with salt and serve.

STEAMED EGGS AND DRIED TUNA ROE ON TOAST
Serves 2

I steam these eggs in the espresso machine using the steamer attachment and a metal milk pot. Steamed eggs are a Gottino staple, often served with prosciutto, smoked salmon, or Parmesan and sage.

3 organic eggs, seasoned • 2 tbsp chopped parsley • 4 pieces country bread • 1 clove garlic • salt • extra-virgin olive oil • bottarga, to shave

1   Steam the eggs with the parsley. Scrambling the eggs in a sauté pan is a good substitute.
2   Toast the bread and rub with garlic, add salt, drizzle with olive oil, and top with the scrambled eggs. Finish with the shaved bottarga.

FRESH PORCINI RISOTTO WITH BERRIES
Serves 4

4 tbsp butter • 1 shallot, chopped finely • 1 tbsp chopped sage, thyme, and rosemary • 4 firm fresh porcini (ceps), cleaned and sliced (approximately 60–85 g each) • 350 g Carnaroli rice (we use Azienda Agricola Principato di Lucedio rice) • 250 ml dry white wine • boiling water, as needed • 85 g blueberries and blackberries • 50 g Parmesan cheese, grated • salt and pepper

1   In a medium-size heavy pot over high flame, melt the butter, add the shallot, herbs, and sliced porcini, and sauté until golden.
2   Add the rice and continue sautéing for 2 minutes over high heat, then add the white wine and reduce until almost dry.
3   Cover the rice with boiling water and let cook, stirring continuously. Add more water as necessary until it is loose, creamy, and cooked, around 12–15 minutes.
4   Remove from the heat, stir in 2 tablespoons of butter and the berries, followed by half the grated Parmesan. Season with salt and pepper and serve.

WHOLE SEA BREAM ROASTED WITH POTATOES, ROSEMARY, AND GARLIC
Serves 2

1 (700–900-g) sea bream, scaled, trimmed, cleaned, and gutted • 1 head of garlic, crushed • 2 sprigs rosemary • extra-virgin olive oil, for frying • 2 large Yukon Gold potatoes, peeled • pinch of fennel pollen • coarse salt and pepper

1   Prepare the fish for roasting by seasoning generously, and stuffing the cavity with crushed garlic and rosemary.
2   With a mandolin, slice the peeled potatoes thinly, then let them rest on a plate until needed.
3   Heat the olive oil in a sauté pan large enough for the fish, then add the potato slices one by one, creating a single layer like a blanket. Season with salt, pepper, and fennel pollen. Lay the fish on top of the potatoes and fold the potatoes over the fish with a spatula.
4   Bake at 400°F (200°C) for 18 minutes or until cooked, turning once.

OXTAILS BRAISED IN RED WINE AND BITTER CHOCOLATE
Serves 2

700 g oxtails, trimmed and cut into 2 pieces • extra-virgin olive oil, for browning • mirepoix, cut into large pieces • 500 ml dry red wine • 1 liter veal stock 500 ml water • 85 g bittersweet (dark) chocolate • 1 bay leaf • 3 crushed juniper berries • 2 sprigs rosemary • zest of ¼ orange • coarse salt and pepper

1   Season the oxtails generously and brown them in olive oil in a casserole with a tight-fitting lid.
2   Discard the fat and add the mirepoix. Continue cooking, add the red wine and reduce.
3   Add the veal stock and water, chocolate, herbs, spices, and orange zest. Cover and bake at 350°F (180°C) for 2 hours, or until the meat is falling off the bone.
4   Skim off the fat, reduce the juices further if necessary, and serve.

QUINCE AND HEIRLOOM APPLES BAKED IN PAPER WITH VIN SANTO AND SERVED WITH WALNUT BREAD AND TRIPLE-MILK CHEESE
Serves 4

2 quinces • 2 apples • 2 tbsp acacia honey • salt and cracked black pepper • 2 tbsp currants, soaked in Vin Santo • 40 g black walnuts • triple-milk cheese • walnut bread

1   Peel, core, and thinly slice the quinces and apples. Season the fruit with the honey, then add a scant pinch of salt and cracked pepper.
2   Add the currants, black walnuts, and Vin Santo, and toss together all the ingredients.
3   To cook, enclose the macerated fruits in paper. To do this, cut a 20 x 20-cm square of parchment paper. Place 2 heaping tablespoons of fruit in the center of the paper, bring the edges together and fold them over each other, creating a continuous seal.
4   Bake on a sheet pan (baking tray) in the oven at 450°F (230°C) for 10 minutes.
5   Serve with cheese and walnut bread. For the cheese, we recommend La Tur, Caseificio Dell'Alta Langa, Piedmont, Italy.

Jody Williams

One of the most talented young chefs in Scotland, and with a Michelin star under his belt, Martin Wishart has become a dominant face on the British restaurant scene over the last few years.

Scotland is one of the most abundant lands in terms of ingredients, home to some of the world's best produce—from hand-dived scallops to Aberdeen Angus beef, from langoustines and lobster to venison and grouse—a chef's paradise. The rugged landscape and cool, wet climate has made it world-renowned for its meat and fish. These ingredients are of paramount importance to Martin's cooking, and the menus at the restaurant are dependent on the seasonal local produce on offer.

His menu is classical and modern French, but elements of his travels across Europe, Asia, and the Americas creep in, adding twists to dishes and keeping diners on their toes.

During his training, Martin spent time at Le Gavroche, a place where the spirit of Escoffier is alive and kicking, and one of the toughest but most informative training grounds in London. During my years of training, I worked for Albert Roux at Le Gavroche, and it's a restaurant that has seen many of the world's greatest chefs pass through its doors. It is here that Martin will have learned many of the classical techniques that he uses in his cooking to produce such an accomplished and skilful menu.

One of the most striking qualities about Martin is his drive and ambition. He is constantly evolving his menu, soaking up new techniques and skills. He is continuously looking for new suppliers, always searching for the highest-quality produce that is available on the market. I have no doubt that with his amount of talent and determination, Martin will continue to be a huge success.

Gordon Ramsay

Martin Wishart was born in 1969 in Scotland, and the country's culinary heritage has shaped his cooking style to showcase the best of the diverse and delicate local seafood and rich game—venison, mallard, partridge, and grouse. Wishart began to cook at the age of fifteen on a government-sponsored youth training program. After working his way up the kitchen hierarchy, he moved on to work in the kitchens of Marco Pierre White, John Burton Race, Marc Meneau, Charlie Trotter, and Nick Nairn. Of his training placements, his time at Le Gavroche proved particularly critical in the formation of his technique. The highly disciplined environment that Wishart encountered under Michel Roux allowed him to handle a different class of ingredient, from the most perfect vegetables to rich black truffles, and so experience the components of fine cuisine. Wishart continues to develop his menu at Restaurant Martin Wishart in Edinburgh, strengthening Scotland's reputation for good food while developing his culinary school.

MENU

Roasted Kilbrannan scallops, Bellota ham, and Parmesan velouté
Meursault, Clos des Cromin, Olivier Leflaive, France, 2006

~

Presse of foie gras, Blaeberry-cured smoked Orkney beef, beet, and horseradish
Riesling, Langenloiser Steinmassel, W. Bründlmayer, Kamptal, Austria, 2005

~

Lobster croque monsieur with ravioli of braised veal shin
Mornington Peninsula, Chardonnay, Clonale, Kooyong, Australia, 2006

~

Ceviche of halibut, mango, and passion fruit
Vouvray, sec, le Mont, Le Haut Lieu, France, 1995

~

Scottish woodcock, bread sauce, and woodcock giblets on toast
Côte-Rôtie, Cuvée Du Plessy, Domaine Gilles Barge, France, 2001

~

Apricot passion fruit and yogurt lollipop honeycomb
Cabidos, Cuvée Saint Clément, Vin de Nazelle, France, 2005

~

Chocolate and praline Exotic sorbet
Frangelico, Original Hazelnut Liqueur, Italy (served on ice)

Martin Wishart

1–4
Martin Wishart at work
in the kitchen

Martin Wishart, Edinburgh, UK

ROASTED KILBRANNAN SCALLOPS, BELLOTA HAM, AND PARMESAN VELOUTÉ
Serves 6

For the scallops
6 extra-large hand-dived scallops • olive oil • salt • 30 g Parmesan, finely grated

1   Remove the scallops from their shells and discard the skirts and orange roe.
2   Wash and dry the the scallops on paper towels.
3   Heat a little olive oil in a nonstick pan.
4   Season the scallops with a little salt and pan-fry in oil until golden brown on each side and just undercooked.
5   Sprinkle grated Parmesan onto a nonstick baking mat so it is very thinly spread. Cook in the oven until it melts and turns golden brown. Remove from oven and leave to cool until a Parmesan crisp is formed.

For the Parmesan velouté
2 shallots • 50 g unsalted butter • 100 ml white wine • 250 ml chicken stock • 250 ml heavy (double) cream • salt • 50 g Parmesan, finely grated

1   Finely slice the shallots, melt the butter in a pan, and gently sweat the shallots for 1 minute without allowing them to color.
2   Add the white wine and reduce to a glaze.
3   Next add the chicken stock and reduce by two-thirds.
4   Add the cream and bring sauce to the boil for 2 minutes, pass through a fine-mesh sieve, season with a little salt.
5   Finish the sauce to your taste with some finely grated fresh Parmesan.

To serve
6 fine slices Bellota Reserva Jamón Ibérico

1   Place the scallop on a plate and lay a slice of ham on top. Break away a small piece of the Parmesan crisp and place on top of ham.
2   Warm the Parmesan velouté and mix with an electric hand mixer to create a cappuccino froth. Spoon around the scallop and serve.

CEVICHE OF HALIBUT, MANGO, AND PASSION FRUIT
Serves 6

420 g halibut • Maldon salt • 45 ml lemon juice • 15 ml gastrique • 15 g sugar • 5 g salt • juice of lime • tequila (to taste) • 10 g tomato fondue • 1 sprig of fresh cilantro (coriander) • 1 tomato (skinned, seeded, and diced) • 30 g diced mango • 10 g passion fruit curd • cilantro (coriander) oil

1   Cut the halibut into 1-cm squares.
2   Season with Maldon salt.
3   Whisk the lemon juice, gastrique, sugar, and salt together.
4   Add to the halibut along with the lime juice, Tequila, and tomato fondue.
5   Finely chiffonade the cilantro leaves and add to the mixture with the diced tomato.
6   Divide the mixture equally between 6 (6–7-cm) stainless-steel rings in suitable serving bowls.
7   Place the diced mango on top of the halibut.
8   Finish with the passion fruit curd and cilantro oil.

SCOTTISH WOODCOCK, BREAD SAUCE, AND WOODCOCK GIBLETS ON TOAST
Serves 6

For the roast woodcock and giblets
100 g butter • 100 g chicken livers • 6 whole woodcock (with giblets removed, but reserved for the pâté) • 2 sprigs of thyme • 50 ml Armagnac • salt and pepper • oil, for frying

1   Preheat oven to 400°F (200°C).
2   For the pâté, heat a nonstick pan with 50 g of the butter. Add the chicken livers and woodcock giblets. Cook for 1–2 minutes on high heat, then add a few thyme leaves and a tablespoon of Armagnac. Season with salt and pepper.
3   Transfer into a small blender and blend until smooth.
4   For the woodcock, cover the bird with remaining butter and thyme. Season with salt and pepper.
5   Warm a pan on the stove with a little oil. When hot, lay the woodcock in the pan and caramelize until golden on each side.

6   Place the pan in the oven and roast the woodcock for 2–4 minutes, then remove and rest them for 10 minutes.

For the bread sauce
300 ml milk • 1 small onion studded with 3 cloves • 1 bay leaf • 60 g fresh bread crumbs • 30 g unsalted butter • 1 tbsp heavy (double) cream • salt and fresh-ground pepper • 1 tsp English mustard

1   Pour the milk into a pan. Add onion and bay leaf, and simmer for 5 minutes.
2   Stir in the bread crumbs, add butter and cream. Stir on low heat for 5 minutes. Season with salt and pepper.
3   Stir in the English mustard, then remove the studded onion before serving the sauce.

To serve
croutons, for serving

Serve with homemade bread sauce and the pâté on some toasted bread croutons.

APRICOT PASSION FRUIT AND YOGURT LOLLIPOP HONEYCOMB
Serves 6

For the yogurt
10 gelatin leaves • 100 g superfine (caster) sugar • 1 liter natural yogurt • 5 g yogurt powder

1   Soften the gelatin in ice-cold water. Place the sugar and yogurt in a pan. Drain the gelatin of any excess water and add to the pan.
2   Warm to 105°F (40°C) and whisk together until smooth, adding the yogurt powder.
3   Set in a shallow 30 x 20-cm tray and leave to set in the refrigerator.

For the passion fruit
7 leaves of gelatin • 125 ml fresh orange juice • 750 ml passion fruit coulis • 125 ml sugar syrup (half water and half sugar) • 3 g agar agar

1   Soften the gelatin in ice-cold water.
2   Place the orange juice, passion fruit, and syrup into a pan with the agar agar and bring to the boil.
3   Remove the pan from the heat and add the softened gelatin.
4   Pour into a 30 x 20-cm tray and let set in the refrigerator.

For the apricot
7 leaves gelatin • 800 ml apricot puree • 200 ml sugar syrup (half water and half sugar) • 3 g agar agar • 25 ml apricot brandy

1   Soften the gelatin in ice-cold water. Place the apricot puree and the syrup into pan with the agar agar and bring to a boil.
2   Remove pan from heat, add the softened gelatin, and pour into a 30 x 20-cm tray. Let set in the refrigerator.

For the honeycomb
160 g fondant • 25 g honey • 60 g glucose • 20 g water • 7 g baking soda (bicarbonate of soda)

1   Place the fondant, honey, glucose, and water into saucepan over low heat and bring to a light caramel. Whisk in the baking soda (bicarbonate of soda) and pour onto a silicone baking mat. Let cool and set.
2   Place in a food processor and blend the honeycomb to a fine powder.
3   Sift onto a silicone baking mat to create an even and fine layer.
4   Place in the oven at 340°F (170°C) until transparent. While warm, cut into discs.

For the vanilla oil
1 split vanilla bean • 250 ml peanut oil

Scrape the seeds from the bean into the peanut oil, whisk together, and pass through a fine sieve.

To assemble
1   Use a 4-cm round cutter to cut out discs of yogurt, passion fruit, and apricot gelatin.
2   Alternate each flavored gelatin onto a stick that is approximately 15 cm long.
3   Place a honeycomb tuile in between each gelatin disc. Spoon a little of the vanilla oil around the plate.

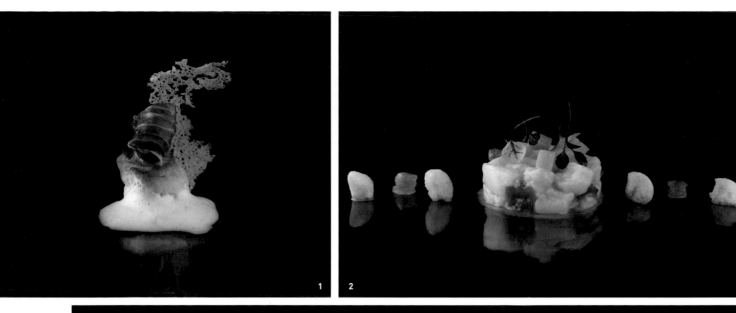

1
Roasted Kilbrannan
scallops, Bellota ham, and
Parmesan velouté

2
Ceviche of halibut, mango,
and passion fruit

3
Scottish woodcock, bread
sauce, and woodcock giblets
on toast

4
Apricot passion fruit and
yogurt lollipop honeycomb

Martin Wishart

Margaret Xu

MENU

Hawker-style
stir-fried clams

~

Yellow earth chicken

~

Red-hot roast baby pig
with kumquat marmalade

~

Lemon chicken

Born in Hong Kong, Margaret Xu found her way into food from a background in design: When she became involved with food styling and recipe development, she realized she had found her calling. From her secluded kitchen, Xu began to explore ancient ethnic Chinese methods of food preparation that continue to inform her menu at Yin Yang in Yuen Long, northwest of Hong Kong. From stone-grinding grains to wood-fired roasting in terra-cotta oven pots, Xu believes the old, slow methods in cooking are the best for preserving taste. This traditional perspective sits alongside lively and modern presentation methods, and attitudes to food production that are ahead of her time. She continues to develop wholesome and exciting dishes that interpret the cuisine of Hong Kong in a refreshing way.

In developing and developed countries in Asia, speed matters in just about everything, from doing business to enjoying the better things in life. That is why Margaret Xu, born and bred in Hong Kong, stands out for her total commitment to the experience of eating, where the process from farm to table is a seamless and integral craft, given due time and undivided passion. Pushing the organic cause a decade ago when little credence was given to such concerns, Margaret was a visionary well ahead of the times. But her attitide had, and still has, a very sound basis: natural food tastes better.

As a kid, curious by nature, Margaret was stealing into the villagers' kitchens, picking up traditional recipes and skills. She was exposed to centuries of experience which had been passed on from generation to generation, experience which reinforces the belief that fresh, natural ingredients lie at the core of simple good food, and a discovery that despite age-old traditions, vernacular dishes do evolve. Margaret was inspired!

Developing upon the foundations of traditional Hong Kong cuisine, Margaret transformed the culinary landscape, her back-to-basics approach galvanizing culture, taste, and art. Through science and experience, ingredients from her organic farm, and traditional methods of preparation, Margaret creates dishes that fully exploit and sharpen flavors, bringing out subtleties that challenge and intrigue the senses. Her creations are astonishing visual feasts as well, incongruent perhaps with the notion of traditional cooking, and yet perfectly at home with her childlike wonder at the infinite possibilities and sensations of taste—an infectious wonder that captures the imagination.

Often described as the queen of organic dining—a misnomer as it doesn't sufficiently describe the depth involved in her work—Margaret epitomizes the passion for eating of the Hong Kong people, where food is an icon of lifestyle, and her contribution, one might say, is iconic.

Jacky Yu

Yin Yang, Hong Kong, China

1
Hawker-style stir-fried clams

2
Yellow earth chicken

3
Red-hot roast baby pig with
kumquat marmalade

4
Lemon chicken

HAWKER-STYLE STIR-FRIED CLAMS
Serves 4

1 kg fresh live clams • 2 tbsp black salted soy beans • 2 tsp light soy sauce • ½ tsp dark soy sauce • 1 tsp sugar • 3 tbsp vegetable oil, for frying • 6 cloves garlic, chopped • 2 red chiles, chopped • 50 g glass noodles, soaked in cold water until transparent (about 20 minutes) • 2 tsp cornstarch (cornflour) dissolved in 60 ml water

1   Heat the clams in their shells in a covered pot over medium heat until half open. Don't add any oil or water—juice will come out from the clams as they open. Drain, and reserve the juice.
2   Lightly mash the black beans and add the light soy sauce, dark soy sauce, and sugar.
3   Heat the oil in a wok, add the garlic and chiles, and stir-fry for 1 minute. Add the clams and noodles, and stir in the mashed black bean mixture.
4   Stir-fry the clams for 1 minute, then pour in the clam juice. Bring to a boil, add the slaked cornstarch and stir until thickened. Serve hot.

YELLOW EARTH CHICKEN
Serves 4

For this dish it might be worth buying one of the special roasting racks for standing chickens upright in the oven. Available in specialty stores, they let the fat drip downward and enable the skin to crisp beautifully.

2 tbsp extra-virgin olive oil • 1 tbsp fresh Kencur ginger, chopped or 1½ tsp dried Chinese ginger powder for chicken • 1 stem curry leaves • 1 tsp sea salt • 1 fresh chicken • 1 tbsp mandarin wine • 1 tbsp rock salt

1   Prepare the marinade by mixing together the olive oil, ginger, curry leaves and sea salt, then let the flavors mingle overnight.
2   Season the inside of the chicken with the marinade and the mandarin wine. Season the outside with the rock salt.
3   Hang the chicken over an enclosed charcoal oven for 1 hour. Alternatively roast it in a preheated rotisserie oven at 440°F (225°C) for 45 minutes.

RED-HOT ROAST BABY PIG WITH KUMQUAT MARMALADE

For the marinade and the pig (preparation)
3 liters water • 225 g rock salt • 60 g natural red Hakka herb, pounded into powder • 60 ml fruit wine or Chinese rosé wine • 1 whole baby pig

1   Bring the water to a boil, add the other marinade ingredients and let cool.
2   Let the piglet stand in the marinade for 24 hours in the refrigerator.
3   Hang the piglet in a smoker over charcoal at 250°F (120°C) for 6–8 hours or until the skin is thoroughly dry and the meat pink and just cooked. Cool thoroughly and store in the refrigerator.

For the kumquat marmalade
175 g fresh kumquats • 120 ml lychee wine • 15 g organic ginger, sliced • juice of 1 organic lemon • 120 g rock sugar • 1–2 liters water • sprig of mint leaves

1   Slice the kumquats and place them together with all the other ingredients except the mint in a heavy nonreactive pan.
2   Bring to a boil, lower the heat to medium, and simmer until reduced by half and thickened.
3   Let cool, and add the mint leaves.

For the pig (to finish cooking)
1   Cut the pig into sections to fit it in the oven.
2   Poach in slowly simmering water for 10 minutes.
3   Cook under a convection broiler (grill) at 425°F (220°C) for 15–20 minutes until the skin is red and crispy.

To serve
Serve the pig on a platter, accompanied by the kumquat marmalade.

LEMON CHICKEN
Serves 2

For the preparation and marinade
400 g corn-fed chicken fillet • 1 tbsp water • 1 tbsp egg white • 2 tsp light soy sauce • 1 egg, beaten • 60 g cornstarch (cornflour)

1   Remove the skin and tendons from the chicken.
2   Carve grooves on the chicken about 2 mm wide, in a criss-cross pattern.
3   Turn the chicken over and repeat step 2.
4   Pound the chicken with a pestle to tenderize and flatten it.
5   Slice it into smaller pieces about 3 cm square and place in a large bowl.
6   Add the water and let stand for 20 minutes.
7   Add the egg white and light soy sauce and mix thoroughly.
8   Add the beaten egg.
9   Place the cornstarch in a container and use it to coat the fillets evenly.

For frying and finishing
2 tbsp cooking oil • 3 shallots, sliced • 225 ml chicken stock • juice and zest of 1 lemon • salt and white pepper, to taste • 120 g rock sugar, crushed • 2 tbsp organic honey • 1 tsp cornstarch (cornflour) dissolved in 1 tbsp water • ½ tsp sesame oil • 1 tsp lemon liquor (optional)

1   Heat 1 tablespoon of the cooking oil in a heavy pan over medium heat.
2   Lay the chicken fillets in the pan, reduce the heat to low, and pan-fry on one side for about 5 minutes until golden.
3   Add the remaining oil, flip over and pan-fry the other side in the same way. Remove the chicken and keep warm.
4   Place the shallots in the pan and pan-fry slowly until translucent.
5   Add the chicken stock and lemon juice, and bring to a boil. Add salt, pepper, sugar, and honey.
6   Add the cornstarch mixture and stir over low to medium heat until thickened.
7   Return the chicken to the pan for a minute. Switch off the heat, and add the lemon zest and sesame oil together with the lemon liquor, if using. Serve hot.

Margaret Xu

Certainly in east Asia, within the culinary world of innovative Chinese cuisine, JinR is a legend. And legend has it that when she opened her first restaurant, Green T. House, in Beijing, upon the unexpected departure of her executive chef she rolled up her sleeves and took the helm at the kitchen. Seized with inspiration, she threw together ingredients with fragrant tea leaves, and her inimitable cuisine was born. The story does not end there; JinR's food is an embarkation upon a journey of holistic proportions, where food is art, and the experience of enjoying her cuisine brings together the entire spectrum of sensory perceptions, taking in the ambience of her restaurants, the flavors of the food, and the touch of her creative genius.

Popularly known as Beijing's Queen of Style, she is China's only female master-chef. And in a culinary world that is dominated by men, where her gender and youth ride head-on against Chinese conventions, she is unique in her role in defining New China. Consummate chef she may be, but first and foremost she regards herself as a musician and artist. This is very telling, because in her food she is a master artist at work, courageously turning out stunning dishes, harnessing the subtleties of tea leaves, and serving up poetic storms that are as hauntingly visual as they are persuasively inspiring. Underlying her creations is her sense of spirituality, which is manifested in the way her dishes are designed and presented—food to be savored, respected, and remembered.

Building upon the foundations of classical Chinese cuisine, JinR brings a refreshingly new approach to how Chinese food could evolve. Yet this approach did not come about from any formal training as a chef. In a seemingly serendipitous way she stumbled into a role which allowed her to discover her innate talent as a chef. The resulting sense of naivety has, contrary to expectations, empowered her to create and deliver beyond the structured confines of Chinese cuisine. In this process she has also found herself.

Jacky Yu

JinR, or Ms. Jin Jie Zhang, was born in 1972 and initially had a successful music career playing the yangqin (Chinese dulcimer). Her multifaceted sense of beauty led her to open the first incarnation of Green T. House in 1997 as a cultural hub for artists and musicians. JinR began to experiment with cuisine after the sudden departure of her chef, creating fresh, exciting dishes that often use tea as an ingredient. When relocating to new premises, she masterminded a conceptual shift for the teahouse in 2002, modernizing its architecture and further refining the presentation and essence of her food. The dining space, tearoom, and gallery now feature diverse dishes, from In the Mood for Fantasy black sesame veal, to fennel dumplings and green tea ice cream. The flavors of JinR's self-dubbed "New China T. Cuisine" are subtle and dynamic, maintaining a vivacious sense of theatre in their presentation. In 2007 JinR launched a new Green T. House at a tranquil rural location in the south of Hong Kong Island.

MENU

Kaffir lime leaf Green T.

~

Green T. pesto and homemade mantao (Chinese steamed bread)

~

Field dreams
Longjing Green T. honey mustard seed sauce on crystal pears sprinkled with Hangzhou pecans, walnuts, and goat cheese

~

Blessed splash
Chilled cucumber orange yogurt soup

~

Green T. wasabi shrimp dancing with mango salsa

~

Autumn sky
Roasted lamb nestled amongst Oolong fennel T. leaves

~

Medley of natural rices

~

Green T. ice cream

JinR. Zhang

1
JinR Zhang with green tea

2
Ingredients at
Green T. House

3
Steamed mantou bread

4
JinR Zhang in the kitchen

5
A sketch for a new dish

Green T. House, Bejing and Hong Kong, China

6

KAFFIR LIME LEAF GREEN T.
Serves 1

2 fresh kaffir lime leaves •
5 g fresh green tea leaves •
250 g hot water at 170°F (80°C)

1   Cut the lime leaves in slivers, put into the cup and add the green tea leaves.
2   Pour the hot water over the leaves and let them steep for 1 minute before serving.

FIELD DREAMS LONGJING GREEN T. HONEY MUSTARD SEED SAUCE ON CRYSTAL PEARS SPRINKLED WITH HANGZHOU PECANS, WALNUTS, AND GOAT CHEESE
Serves 2

12 slices white pear • 80 g Green T. mustard sauce (see method) • 20 g walnuts • 20 g pecans • 80 g fresh goat cheese, crumbled • lettuce leaves, washed and drained

1   To make Green T. mustard sauce, blend yellow mustard, pickled cucumber, honey, onion, garlic, mustard seeds, salt, black pepper, chicken powder and a dash of infused Green T. liquid.
2   Cover the pear slices with Green T. mustard sauce, then sprinkle with the walnuts, pecans and fresh goat cheese.
3   Serve decoratively on lettuce leaves.

BLESSED SPLASH CHILLED CUCUMBER ORANGE YOGURT SOUP
Serves 4

For the soup
350 g plain yogurt • 2 tsp mustard seeds • 2 garlic cloves, finely chopped • 1 tsp green tea leaves, steeped and chopped • 8 g sour pickles • ½ tsp capers • 2–3 drops honey • 3–5 g each of fresh mint, basil, thyme, rosemary, sage and parsley, finely chopped • 5 g black pepper

Blend all the ingredients in a blender until smooth. Pour into a martini glass.

For the garnish
½ medium cucumber, peeled and thinly sliced • ½ medium orange, peeled and thinly sliced • 7–8 fresh mint leaves • orange zest, julienned • 4 small purple onions, thinly sliced into rings

Place the cucumber and orange slices on top of the soup, then decorate with mint leaves, orange zest and purple onion slices.

WASABI SHRIMP DANCING WITH MANGO SALSA
Serves 4

400 g medium shrimp (prawns) • 2 tbsp yellow Huadiao rice wine • salt and pepper • 15 g wasabi mustard • 3 g custard powder • 3 g starch • oil, for frying • 25 g corn flakes • 2 g balsamic vinegar • shredded seaweed • 5 red peppercorns • 15 g mango salsa

1   Peel the shrimp and marinate them with the rice wine, salt and pepper for 3 minutes.
2   Mix the wasabi mustard, the custard powder and starch thoroughly.
3   Heat some cooking oil to 150°F (70°C) and deep-fry the shrimp one by one until golden, then remove from the oil.
4   Mix the shrimp with the wasabi sauce, and cover them with the cornflakes.

5   Pile the shrimp in a plate with the balsamic vinegar, garnish with seaweed, and the red pepper grains. Serve immediately.

AUTUMN SKY ROASTED LAMB NESTLED AMONGST OOLONG FENNEL T. LEAVES
Serves 2

260 g lamb • salt and white pepper • 5 g white rice wine (Er Guo Tou) • 10 g white sesame seeds • 5 g starch • 15 g oolong tea leaves • 45 g cilantro (coriander) leaves • 40 g dry shallot • oil, for deep-frying • 6 g cumin seeds • 6 g fennel seeds • 30 g goat cheese • 10 g yellow Huadiao rice wine

1   Cut the lamb into approximately 1 x 1-cm pieces and marinate them with salt, pepper and white rice wine, then add 3 g white sesame seeds and the starch and mix them well. Set aside.
2   Make the oolong tea and strain.
3   Snip the cilantro and slice the dry shallot.
4   Place the marinated lamb into hot cooking oil to deep-fry until crisp outside and tender inside, then fry the oolong leaves until crisp. Strain off the oil.
5   Heat another pan and add the shallot, cilantro, remaining white sesame seeds, cumin and fennel until fragrant and then mix them with the goat cheese, salt, cooked lamb and oolong tea leaves. Add the white rice wine and serve immediately.

GREEN T. ICE CREAM
Serves 4

1 tsp chopped green tea leaves • 200 g light (single) cream • 3 tsp superfine (caster) sugar • green tea powder (for color) • 200 g milk • 225 ml lemon juice

1   Steep the chopped green tea leaves in hot water.
2   Beat together the cream and sugar until creamy.
3   Add the green tea powder, chopped leaves and 3 teaspoons tea water, milk, and lemon juice. Mix well.
4   Freeze, then serve with fresh pear and honey.

JinR Zhang

1
At the market in the rain

2
Pigs grazing

3 & 4
Grains and fish drying

5
In the kitchen at C'est Bon

Yue-Jiau Zhuang

402

MENU

A spoonful of soft roe

~

Jade summer gourd

~

Golden Kuruma shrimp
with sour creeper sauce

~

Steamed catch of the
season with pickled winter
melon sauce

~

Shiitake mushroom and
heart of mustard greens

~

Dry-pickled mustard
green meatball served
with green tea

~

Pickled cabbage
lion's head

~

Frost red bean
persimmon cake

Born in 1964, <u>Yue-Jiau Zhuang</u> grew up eating food cooked by her mother, sister, and three sisters-in-law, who all hailed from different regions of Taiwan. The family grew their own vegetables and fruit, and raised chickens, ducks, geese, and pigs, giving Yue-Jiau an early understanding of the essence of ingredients. After years of cooking for her family, at 35 she began to sell shrimp stews and *ru rou fan* (pork stewed in soy sauce with rice) from street stalls. In three years her business blossomed into Ah-Jiao's Eatery, her own restaurant in Beitou. At forty she opened C'est Bon, her new restaurant, which is guided by the creative vision of Hsieh Chun-Te, whose long career in the arts is matched only by his knowledge of regional Taiwanese cuisine. Growing its own organic vegetables and rice, the restaurant takes the purest ingredients to create healthy and authentic dishes, each paired with a specific tea.

Three years ago, I came across Yue-Jiau at the Taiwan Porsche Food and Drink Festival. Her passion and intellectual conceptualization of food and drink captivated me, as did her enthusiastic promotion of the spiritual energies behind the culture of "eating slowly." All of this made a deep impression on me. She has gone from being an accountant's clerk to being in charge of a series of small eateries in Taiwan: First shrimp soup and fried-rice stalls, then the private eating rooms now well-known by everyone in Taiwan's food and drink circles as "Yue-Jiau's Shops."

Yue-Jiau's Shops are often hidden away, with old Taiwanese-style place settings and crockery, which together create an atmosphere within of "contemplative meditation." The painstaking layout of the dishes and side orders resembles that of a meticulously executed recipe book, concentrated in its planning. It renders traditional Taiwanese dishes pleasing to the eye without losing their original flavors. With her own hands, Yue-Jiau steeps the coarse meat dishes, smokes the eggs, steams the fish over twigs, braises the pigs' trotters, and dries the crockery.

What made the deepest impression upon me was her way of preparing "kingfisher calabash." First she boils up a thick stock of whole duck, pig bones, and pork, then she strains the liquid until it runs clear. Next the calabash is roasted to enhance the flavor and a Taiwanese soybean paste is added to the sauce, which seeps into incisions made on the surface of the calabash. It is moist without being soggy and both elegant and pure in appearance.

Suffice to say that what seems to be her simple cooking is, like jade, usually both beautiful and drawn from deep experience. I think that many chefs who have spent a lot of years in the kitchen are not yet able to do this. Yue-Jiau's Shops have already become a household name in Taiwanese cuisine, not only in Taiwan itself, but even overseas. Many customers eat there because of their reputation, and they all happily praise Yue-Jiau's handiwork.

Jacky Yu

JADE SUMMER GOURD
Serves 2

For the summer gourd
1 summer gourd • 2 liters vegetable stock • 2 liters water

1   Peel the gourd, slice off the ends, and cut into equal halves.
2   In a pot, combine the vegetable stock and the water, and bring to a boil. Add the gourd, cover, and cook over medium heat for 30 minutes. Turn off the heat and let rest, covered, for 40 minutes.

For the yellow bell pepper sauce
200 g onion • 200 g yellow bell pepper • 2 g salted anchovies • 300 ml vegetable stock • 8 g salt • 10 g egg yolk powder • bamboo leaf, for garnish

1   Finely chop the onion and yellow pepper. Sauté onion in olive oil for a minute, then add chopped yellow pepper and salted anchovies for another minute. Add stock and cook for another 2 minutes.
2   In a blender, blend the pepper mixture, then strain it and reserve the liquid (discarding the solid).
3   Heat the pepper liquid in a pot, then add the salt and egg yolk powder to thicken and finish the sauce.
4   Place the gourd on a white plate and add the sauce to finish the dish. Garnish with bamboo leaf.

GOLDEN KURUMA SHRIMP WITH SOUR CREEPER SAUCE
Serves 6

For the sour creeper sauce
1½ pieces sour creeper • 8 egg yolks • 1 apple • juice of 4 limes • 1 can condensed milk • 200 ml cream • 5 g mustard • custard powder, for thickening • ground black pepper, to taste • limes, cut in half and flesh scooped out, to serve

Blend the first 7 ingredients thoroughly in a food processor. Add custard powder to thicken and black pepper for flavor. Scoop the sauce into halved lime shells until ready to serve.

For the fresh Kuruma shrimp
6 fresh Kuruma shrimp (prawns) • 20 g sea urchin sauce • 2 tbsp cornstarch (cornflour) • 1 (500-g) pack Xinzhu rice noodles • pomegranate seeds, for garnish

1   Clean the shrimp, reserving the heads and tails, then devein and fill the slit with sea urchin sauce. Pat with cornstarch to dry the surface of the sea urchin sauce.
2   Soak the rice noodles in water, then drain. Take enough rice noodles to wrap around the shrimp. Deep-fry the shrimp in 275°F (140°C) oil for approximately 2 minutes until cooked.
3   Garnish with fresh pomegranate seeds and the sour creeper sauce.

PICKLED CABBAGE LION'S HEAD
Serves 7

For the lion's head
600 g pork sirloin and 300 g unrendered lard, or 900 g pork belly • 140 ml pork stock • 20 ml green papaya juice • 2 tsp salt • 1 tsp white pepper powder • 15 g ground ginger • 20 g scallions (spring onions), finely chopped • 1 tsp sesame oil

1   Rinse the meat and pat dry.
2   Dice the lard and sirloin into cubes the size of pomegranate seeds. If using belly, dice slightly less finely. Mix together.
3   In a large mixing bowl, add the stock and papaya juice. Beat the meat mixture while slowly adding it to the juice. Make sure the meat mixture has absorbed the liquid.
4   Add the salt, white pepper powder, and ground ginger to the bowl and mix.
5   Add the finely chopped scallion and sesame oil, stir together, then make approximately 7 meatballs from the mixture.
6   In a pot, heat the water to 175°F (80°C), add the meatballs, and turn off the heat. Cover and let rest for 20 minutes.
7   Steam the meatballs on low heat for 5 hours to complete the lion's head.

For the soup base
14 leaves fresh Chinese cabbage • 20 g salt • 1.4 liters pork stock • 1 (500-g) pack Xinzhu rice noodles • 7 green tea leaves, for garnish

1   For the soup base, clean and pat dry the fresh cabbage slices and cut each slice into 2 long pieces. Rub with salt and allow it to sit overnight at room temperature to pickle.
2   Combine the pork stock with the pickled cabbage and steam over medium heat for 20 minutes to make the pickled cabbage soup base.
3   Soak the rice noodles in water until ready for use.
4   Remove the pickled cabbage from the soup base and cut into shreds. Place some of the cabbage shreds on the bottom of a serving bowl, followed by a layer of rice noodles. Place the lion's head over the rice noodles and surround it with 2 layers of pickled cabbage.
5   Pour in the soup base and steam over medium heat for 15 minutes. Garnish with a green tea leaf on top.

FROST RED BEAN PERSIMMON CAKE
Makes 60 cakes

60 semidried Beipu persimmons • 200 ml lime liquor • 1.2 kg red beans • 8 liters water • 700 g sugar • 700 g superfine (caster) sugar • 600 g fresh rice cake

1   With a paring knife, make an "X" at the bottom of the persimmons. Open up each persimmon by hand into 4 "petals", and spray with lime liquor.
2   Soak the red beans in water overnight and drain.
3   In a stockpot, place the red beans with 8 liters of fresh cold water, bring to a boil, discard the water and repeat the process.
4   The third time, after bringing to a boil, turn down the heat to let the red beans simmer for 40 minutes.
5   Add both sugars and slowly simmer to reduce.
6   Over medium heat, in a large flat pan, evaporate the excess liquid in the red bean mixture to form a paste. Let cool.
7   Divide the red bean paste into 30-g pieces and the fresh rice cake into 10-g pieces.
8   Stuff the rice cake into the red bean paste and shape it into balls.
9   Place the ball onto the persimmon and re-form into the shape of persimmon using plastic wrap (clingfilm).
10   Spray with lime liquor to finish.

1
Jade summer
gourd

2
Golden
Kuruma shrimp
with sour creeper sauce

3
Pickled cabbage lion's head

4
Frost red bean
persimmon cake

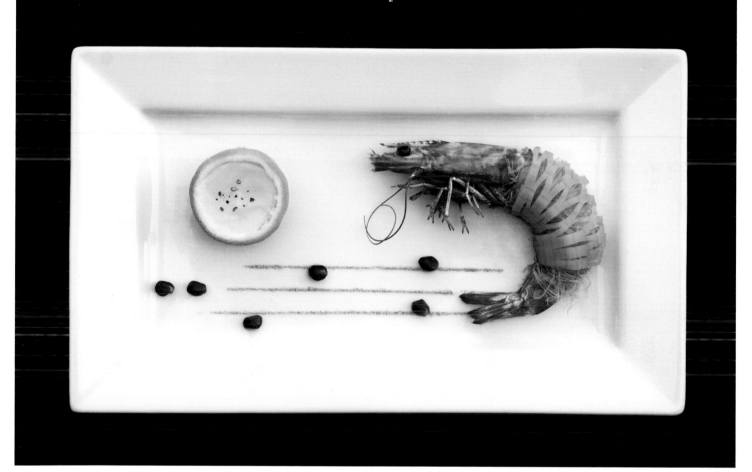

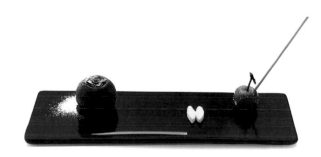

405   **Yue-Jiau Zhuang**

I first came across Eric Ziebold in 2000, when he did a stage at our restaurant in Chelsea, London, as part of a trip to England to gain more experience. He was working at the French Laundry at the time, under Thomas Keller, another incredible chef.

Simplicity is key at CityZen. So many chefs overcomplicate dishes and become carried away with complex techniques while forgetting what is central to the dish—the produce. Ziebold lets the ingredients speak for themselves but showcases them with faultless skill. He doesn't confuse guests with overly fussy plates, and makes food that people understand and can identify with. At the same time, however, he does use techniques that push the boundaries. One of his signature dishes is a *shabu-shabu*, a Japanese variety of our hot pot. The meat is traditionally placed into boiling water, and Ziebold has taken to making a luxurious version of the dish by poaching foie gras tableside.

He is also meticulous when it comes to tasting dishes, which is crucial for a chef. So many chefs don't taste a dish in its various stages of preparation, and it's vital. How can you perfect a dish and season it well if you don't taste it as you prepare it?

Ziebold never forgets the bigger picture. He doesn't just want individual dishes to be perfect—he wants the overall experience to be seamless, from the amuse-bouche to the pre-dessert and from the service to the wines. At the end of the day, we expect more than good food at a restaurant: The whole experience has to blow us away.

His menu at CityZen is constantly evolving—because he's using new ingredients and techniques, but more recently as a result of his travels. He has traveled widely, to Beijing, Tunisia, and France, and brings back new ideas that are reflected ever so subtly on his menu.

Gordon Ramsay

Born in Iowa in 1972, Eric Ziebold began to cook in his mother's kitchen, taking his first restaurant position at the age of 16 before attending culinary school in New York. Ziebold went on to work at Vidalia in Washington, DC, and later Spago in Los Angeles, where executive chef Matt Nichols proved an important source of guidance. Next Ziebold joined the French Laundry, Thomas Keller's restaurant in Yountville, California as chef de partie, working his way up to chef de cuisine in 1999. While at the French Laundry, Ziebold also assisted in the creation of Per Se, Keller's New York restaurant, and completed further training in England and France. In 2004 Ziebold became executive chef at CityZen in Washington, DC. His menu there seeks to tease out the sense of occasion in every meal, serving bread straight out of the oven with his final savory course to construct a communal and accessible experience.

MENU

Shaved sashimi of geoduck clam, marinated English cucumber, scallion, and pickled mushroom salad with toasted sesame vinaigrette

~

Grilled Path Valley Farms green asparagus panisse and sweet pepper salsa, Espelette vinaigrette

~

Crispy-skin Mediterranean branzino, toasted cauliflower, slivered almonds, and green grapes with verjus gastrique

~

Crispy Anson Mills beggar's purse with a fricassee of Marcho Farms sweetbreads and English peas

~

Aiguillettes of Liberty Valley duck breast, duck confit-stuffed squash blossom, and baby zucchini à la paysanne

~

A selection of artisanal cheeses from our trolley

~

Cinnamon bun soufflé, cappuccino ice cream, and steamed milk

Eric Ziebold

1
Eric Ziebold in the kitchen

2
Making the signature Parker
House rolls

3
Sous-chef Rachel Harriman
preparing canapes

4
Macaroons at CityZen

CityZen, Washington, DC, USA

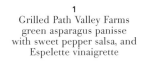

1
Grilled Path Valley Farms
green asparagus panisse
with sweet pepper salsa, and
Espelette vinaigrette

2
Crispy-skin Mediterranean
branzino, toasted cauliflower,
slivered almonds, and green
grapes with verjus gastrique

3
Crispy Anson Mills beggar's
purse with a fricassee of
Marcho Farms sweetbreads
and English peas

4
Aiguillettes of Liberty Valley
duck breast
duck confit-stuffed squash
blossom, and baby zucchini
à la paysanne

GRILLED PATH VALLEY FARMS GREEN ASPARAGUS PANISSE WITH SWEET PEPPER SALSA AND ESPELETTE VINAIGRETTE
Serves 10

For the panisse
1 clove garlic, finely chopped • 10 g olive oil • 670 ml chicken stock • salt, to taste • 150 g chickpea flour • flour, for coating

1   Sweat the garlic in olive oil. Add the chicken stock and salt. Remove from heat before chicken stock gets hot. Pour the stock into a high-speed blender and turn on. Add chickpea flour and puree till smooth.
2   Over medium-high heat, cook the chickpea flour mixture until it boils and thickens. Pour immediately onto a pan and spread evenly 5 mm thick. Cool, then cut to into 1-cm cubes.
3   Next, flour the panisse cubes and sauté in oil over high heat until they are crispy.

For the Espelette vinaigrette
2 tbsp sherry vinegar • 1 tbsp finely chopped shallot • salt, to taste • sugar, to taste • 125 ml red pepper juice • ½ tsp piment d'Espelette • 5 tbsp vegetable oil • 1 tbsp extra-virgin olive oil

Put the sherry vinegar, shallot, salt, and sugar in a bowl. Put the pepper juice and piment d'Espelette in a pot and reduce to 1 tablespoon. Add the pepper juice to the vinegar mixture. Whisk in the vegetable oil, then the olive oil.

For the asparagus
50 pieces of medium asparagus, peeled and lightly blanched olive oil

Toss the asparagus stalks in olive oil and grill. Lay out 5 pieces of asparagus on each plate so they are stacked up.

To serve
60 g roasted red bell peppers, diced 5 mm thick • 60 g roasted yellow bell peppers, diced 5 mm thick

In a bowl, toss the peppers with the panisse and spread out, crossing perpendicularly over the asparagus. Drizzle 125 ml of the Espelette vinaigrette around the plate.

CRISPY-SKIN MEDITERRANEAN BRANZINO, TOASTED CAULIFLOWER, SLIVERED ALMONDS, AND GREEN GRAPES WITH VERJUS GASTRIQUE
Serves 10

For the verjus gastrique
250 ml verjus, reduced by three-quarters • 60 g glucose • 2 tbsp finely chopped tarragon

Combine the reduced verjus, glucose, and tarragon.

For the branzino
30 slices of branzino, 2.5 cm wide by 7.5 cm long • oil, for sautéing • 200 g cauliflower florets, lightly blanched • butter, for sautéing • 125 ml verjus gastrique • 5 tbsp golden raisin puree • 30 peeled seedless green grapes • 2 tbsp tarragon • 5 tsp toasted almonds, finely chopped

1   Season the fish and sauté over medium-high heat to get a crispy skin.
2   While the fish is cooking, sauté the cauliflower in oil until lightly browned, add butter to the cauliflower, and sauté to a rich brown color. Drain the fat from the cauliflower.
3   Using a 5-cm paintbrush, spread a thin layer of gastrique down the center of a plate.
4   Arrange the cauliflower and raisin puree on the plate approximately 3.5 cm apart. Place 1 piece of fish on top of cauliflower, 1 on the raisin puree, and 1 piece on the plate. Put the grapes on one of the ends next to the fish. Sprinkle with tarragon and add a little chopped almond on top of the fish at the top of the plate and also on top of the grapes.

CRISPY ANSON MILLS BEGGAR'S PURSE WITH A FRICASSÉE OF MARCHO FARMS SWEETBREADS AND ENGLISH PEAS
Serves 10

For the grits
275 g cooked Anson Mills white grits • 1 tbsp chopped parsley • 1 tbsp finely chopped chives • 2 tsp finely chopped tarragon • ½ tsp finely chopped chervil • salt and pepper

Mix the grits with all the herbs and season.

For the phyllo dough
1 packet phyllo dough • 175 g butter

Layer 3 sheets of phyllo dough, brushing with clarified butter in between. Cut the phyllo into quarters and put approximately 2 tablespoons grits mixture into the center. Crimp the phyllo dough together at the top to seal the beggar's purse. Bake in a convection oven at 375°F (190°C).

For the sweetbreads
salt and pepper • flour • 40 pieces sweetbread, cut into 1.5-cm cubes • 225 ml chicken stock • white-wine vinegar, to taste • 100 g butter • 350 g cooked English peas • 1 tbsp chopped parsley

Season and flour the sweetbreads, then sauté at medium-high heat until golden brown. In a small pot, bring the chicken stock to a boil. Add a touch of vinegar, then add the butter and cook down until sauce consistency is reached. Add the peas and the chopped parsley.

To serve
Place the beggar's purse in the center of a bowl, arrange the sweetbreads around the purse, and spoon the sauce with the peas around that.

AIGUILLETTES OF LIBERTY VALLEY DUCK BREAST, DUCK CONFIT-STUFFED SQUASH BLOSSOM, AND BABY ZUCCHINI À LA PAYSANNE
Serves 10

For the stuffed squash blossoms
5 legs of duck confit • 1 tbsp finely chopped shallot • 1 tbsp finely chopped thyme • 20 small squash blossoms • 2 tbsp softened butter • flour, for coating • oil, for sautéing

1   Pick the meat off the duck bones and shred well with a fork. Mix into the meat the shallot, thyme, and softened butter.
2   Place approximately 1 tablespoon of the meat mixture inside each squash blossom and close the petals around the meat.
3   Flour the stuffed squash blossoms and sauté in oil over medium heat to a golden brown.

For the duck breasts
5 duck breasts • 175 g butter • 3 tbsp finely chopped shallot • 475 ml white duck stock • 20 baby yellow zucchini (courgettes), sliced 2.5 mm thick • 20 baby green zucchini (courgettes), sliced 2.5 mm thick • 2 tbsp basil puree • lemon juice, to taste • 1 tbsp parsley, chopped

1   Sauté the duck to medium rare, and reserve.
2   In a medium pot, sauté 3 tablespoons shallots gently in a little butter. Add the white duck stock and bring to a boil. Add the rest of the butter and cook down until stock is reduced by half and emulsified.
3   In a separate pan, sauté the baby zucchini until tender. Add the basil puree, lemon juice, and parsley. Add the zucchini.

To serve
40 very thin slices of tomato, with seeds removed

Spoon the squash and sauce into bottom of a bowl. Slice the duck lengthwise into 6 strips. Layer 3 of the strips on top of the squash, slightly overlapping and forming a sort of half-moon. Place the squash blossoms in the center of the half-moon created by the duck breast. Arrange the tomato slices around the duck breast.

Eric Ziebold

IO
Classic Dishes by Master Chefs

Ferran Adrià
Textured vegetable panaché

Mario Batali
Two-minute calamari, Sicilian lifeguard style

Shannon Bennett
Mouton rôti et ris d'agneau

Alain Ducasse
Provençale garden vegetables simmered
with crushed black truffle

Fergus Henderson
Roast bone marrow and parsley salad

Yoshihiro Murata
Yudofu (tofu simmered in hotpot)

Gordon Ramsay
Ravioli of lobster, Norwegian lobster, and
salmon with a lemongrass and chervil velouté

René Redzepi
Vegetable field

Alice Waters
Chicories salad with brandade toast

Jacky Yu
Xi Yan spicy-sauce chicken

TEXTURED VEGETABLE PANACHÉ

Ferran Adrià

The textured vegetable panaché (*la menestra de verduras en texturas*), which we created in 1994, was a milestone dish for elBulli, not only because of what is on the plate, but also because it came at a pivotal moment in the development of our cuisine, and opened up a rich seam of creative potential. The interplay of prepared textures and the use of deconstruction as a creative technique make the dish an expression of some of the best-known characteristics of elBulli's food. Deconstruction is the process by which a dish is inspired by an identifiable external source, but in which every element of that source is modified in the final dish. Although we didn't realize it at the time, it was probably the first example of the use of deconstruction as a creative method.

The dish was created as an homage to Michel Bras's iconic dish *gargouillou de jeunes légumes*, in which thirty different seasonal vegetables are cooked and seasoned separately and presented together in a perfect expression of their inherent qualities. We wanted to create a vegetable dish at the same level, and at the same time we were developing different textures using liquid bases, such as foams, jellies, savory ice creams, and sorbets, all of which went on to play an important role in future dishes. The textured vegetable panaché was the result, and it opened up a new world of possibilities. Each component is an expression of a vegetable through texture: an almond sorbet, a cauliflower mousse, a tomato puree, beetroot foam, raw avocado, basil jelly, and sweet corn mousse. I still consider it to be one of elBulli's most symbolic dishes.

Serves 4

For the almond sorbet
600 ml water • 500 g whole almonds • salt

1 Partially process the almonds and water with a hand blender and refrigerate for 12 hours.
2 Process the mixture in a liquidizer until it forms a thick, smooth paste.
3 Strain through a cheesecloth (muslin) in small amounts, squeezing with your hands to obtain almond milk.
4 Salt 500 ml of the milk to taste and process in a sorbet maker.
5 Keep in the freezer at 14ºF (-10 ºC).

Note: In 1999 we began adding 1 x 2-g gelatin leaf for every 1.15 liters almond milk to stabilize the sorbet.

For the beet espuma
250 g cooked beet • 250 g water • 2 (2-g) gelatin leaves, previously rehydrated in cold water • salt

1 Process the cooked beet and the water in a liquidizer. Strain.
2 Heat 125 g of the beet puree and dissolve the gelatin in it.
3 Remove from the heat and mix in the remaining beet puree. Salt to taste.
4 Strain and fill a siphon with the mixture. Charge the siphon and refrigerate for 2 hours.

For the tomato puree
6 ripe tomatoes, weighing 125 g each • olive oil, 0.4% acidity • freshly ground white pepper • sugar • salt

1 Make 2 cuts to form a cross on the bottom of the tomatoes.
2 Use a sharp knife to remove the stem from the top.
3 Immerse the tomatoes in boiling water for 15 seconds. Use a spider to remove the tomatoes and place them in iced water to cool.
4 Peel the tomatoes, cut them into quarters, and remove the seeds. Cut into 0.5-cm cubes.
5 Heat a nonstick frying pan and sauté the tomato in a little olive oil. Season to taste with the salt, white pepper, and sugar.
6 Process the sautéed tomato in a blender to obtain a puree. Strain through a sieve and leave to drain in a fine-mesh sieve. Set aside before serving.

For the peach water ice
200 ml peach juice

1 Pour the juice into a container ensuring it does not exceed a depth of 1 cm.
2 Seal and freeze at a temperature between 14º (-8ºC) and 18ºF (-10 ºC) for approximately 3 hours.

For the basil gelatin
100 g fresh basil • 100 ml water • ½ (2-g) gelatin leaf, previously rehydrated in cold water • salt

1 Remove the leaves from the stalks.
2 Blanch the leaves for 10 seconds in boiling water and cool in iced water.
3 Process in a blender with the water. Strain before filtering the water through cheesecloth.
4 Heat 25 ml of the basil water and dissolve the gelatin in it.
5 Remove from the heat and mix in the remaining basil water. Salt to taste.
6 Leave to set in the refrigerator for 3 hours in a container that allows for a 1 cm thickness.

For the sweet corn mousse
2 (250-g) cans corn kernels • 45 ml 35% fat light (single) cream • ¾ (2-g) gelatin leaf, previously rehydrated in cold water • salt

1 Drain the liquid from the corn and process up to 3 times in a blender to ensure all of the corn is pureed. Strain.
2 Heat a quarter of the puree and dissolve the gelatin in it. Remove from the heat, add the remaining puree and salt to taste. Cool the puree but do not allow it to set.
3 Half-whip the cream and fold it into the sweet corn puree.
4 Spread in a container which will allow a 2.5-cm thickness. Refrigerate for 2 hours.

For the cauliflower mousse
500 g cauliflower • water • 80 ml 35% fat single cream • 1 (2-g) gelatin leaf, previously rehydrated in cold water • salt

1 Cut cauliflower into florets.
2 Put the cauliflower in cold water in a small pan and place on high heat. When the water comes to a boil, strain, then cover in cold water and boil again.
3 Once cooked, strain and process in a blender to a smooth puree. Salt to taste. Strain through a sieve.
4 Heat a quarter of the puree and dissolve the gelatin in it. Remove from the heat. Add the remaining puree and salt to taste. Cool the puree but do not allow it to set.
5 Half-whip the cream and fold into the cauliflower puree.
6 Spread in a container which will allow a 2-cm thickness. Refrigerate for 2 hours.

For the avocado semicircles
1 avocado weighing 200 g

1 Split the avocado in half, remove the stone, peel, and cut into semicircles 1 cm thick.

To finish
20 peeled fresh almonds • salt

1 Place 2 avocado semicircles in the center of a soup dish to form a circle. Salt to taste.
2 Around the circle and slightly over it, arrange the other preparations in a counter-clockwise direction starting from the bottom. Add 1 level dessertspoon of tomato puree and 1 of cauliflower mousse. Leave a space for the water ice and continue by placing a piece of basil gelatin. Add 1 level dessertspoon of sweet corn mousse and leave space for the espuma. Place an almond between each of the preparations. Place a quenelle of sorbet over the avocado circle.
3 Crack the peach water ice with a spatula and place a spoonful of the ice between the cauliflower mousse. Add the basil gelatin and a beet espuma rosette between the tomato and the sweet corn.

Ferran Adrià

TWO-MINUTE CALAMARI, SICILIAN LIFEGUARD STYLE

Mario Batali

I have actually never met a Sicilian lifeguard, but if one were to cook up a pot of calamari, this is how I imagine he or she might make it.

Since Sicily is much closer to Morocco and the Moorish world than it is to Milan, there is a strong northern African influence in the traditional cooking of the island, and I love the way currants, caper berries, pine nuts, and chiles combine in this dish to create a sweet, hot, and sour Arabic flavor.

When we were developing the menu and ideology for Babbo in early 1998, I made a conscious decision to not only think like an Italian, but also to try to avoid cliché. I rejected classic dishes from my favorite parts of Italy, wanting instead to create new dishes that kept the soul of the different regions without relying on the import of ingredients. Italian cooks and chefs from Liguria would rarely, if ever, use ingredients from Puglia and chefs from the Veneto feel the same way about ingredients from Basilicata or even Le Marche. So I felt that, as an Italian chef in New York, I should behave the same way and use very few ingredients imported fresh from Italy. Of course I use pantry staples such as extra-virgin olive oil from Toscana, or Liguria, and Parmigiano-Reggiano from Emilia Romagna, but the main ingredients and the seasonal produce from local farms are all from well within my 250-mile conceptual limit here on the mid-Atlantic coast.

This dish is considered one of the classics at Babbo and is one of five original dishes that have not changed from the menu created back in June 1998. It makes an excellent antipasto if split between two, three, or four people, and is completely satisfying as a main course in any season. It represents everything I want to say at Babbo and has been a significant part of our success in the world of cephalopods.

Serves 4

For the basic tomato sauce
Makes 950 ml
60 ml extra-virgin olive oil • 1 large onion, cut into 5-mm dice • 4 garlic cloves, thinly sliced • 3 tbsp chopped fresh thyme leaves, or 1 tbsp dried • 1 medium carrot, finely shredded • 2 (700-g) cans peeled whole tomatoes, crushed by hand and juices reserved • kosher salt, to taste

In a 2.8 liter pan, heat the olive oil over medium heat. Add the onion and garlic, and cook until soft and light golden brown, 8–10 minutes. Add the thyme and carrots, and cook for 5 minutes more, until the carrot is quite soft. Add the tomatoes and juice and bring to a boil, stirring often. Lower the heat and simmer for 30 minutes, until as thick as hot cereal. Season with salt. This sauce keeps for 1 week in the refrigerator or up to 6 months in the freezer.

For the calamari
Kosher salt, to taste • 200 g Israeli couscous • 60 ml extra-virgin olive oil • 2 tbsp pine nuts • 2 tbsp currants • 1 tbsp hot red pepper flakes • 40 g caper berries • 500 ml basic tomato sauce (left), or Molto Sugo Pomodoro Sauce • 700 g cleaned calamari, tubes cut into 5-mm rounds, tentacles halved • freshly ground black pepper, to taste • 3 scallions (spring onions), thinly sliced

1 For the couscous, bring 2.8 liters water to a boil and add 1 tablespoon of salt. Set up an ice bath nearby. Cook the couscous in the boiling water for 2 minutes, then drain and immediately plunge it into the ice bath. Once cooled, remove and set aside to dry on a plate.
2 For the calamari, heat the oil in a 30–35-cm sauté pan until just smoking. Add the pine nuts, currants, and red pepper flakes, and sauté until the nuts are just golden brown, about 2 minutes. Add the caper berries, tomato sauce, and couscous, and bring to a boil. Add the calamari, stir to mix, and simmer for 2–3 minutes, or until the calamari is just cooked and completely opaque. Season with salt and pepper, pour into a large bowl, sprinkle with scallions, and serve immediately.

MOUTON RÔTI ET RIS D'AGNEAU

Shannon Bennett

Through lack of knowledge and the narrow range available from supermarkets, mutton is often rejected as a key ingredient by consumers as well as the majority of chefs in Australia.

This is a great pity, because I find lamb, particularly milk-fed lamb, to be boring and inconsistent. It just does not have the flavor I desire from something that is sacrificing its life so prematurely for something so important!

Mutton, on the other hand, has a beautiful texture and a distinctive gamey taste that can only be attributed to maturity. If the animal is allowed adequate time to develop, and proper attention is paid to its diet—which should be mainly grass, with an occasional supplement of grain during droughts to help build intramuscular fat—a skilled chef can really make this ingredient stand out.

I also feel that the conditions under which most meat is currently farmed do not take into account that stress caused to the animals has on quality. The use of mobile abattoirs for slaughter on the land must benefit the quality of the meat produced.

I am very lucky to be situated close to farmers in Victoria and New South Wales who are producing mutton of exceptional quality. These include the Riverina district in southern New South Wales close to the Victorian border and pasture-surrounded small towns such as Junee, Harden, and Goulbourn. On these grassy pastures the lambs develop the resilient characteristics they need to survive the harsh diversities of the southern climate. By the time the animals are slaughtered, they range from 14 to 24 months in age and only need four days to age the whole carcass. They are then broken down into useful cuts such as the rump, front legs, organ meats (offal), and loins. Our butcher, Anthony Puharich, then thoroughly checks the color and firmness of the meat before grading it and sending it to us at Vue de Monde.

The great qualities of this ingredient have enabled me to serve mutton in a way that I would not be able to serve lamb, such as presenting it with stronger flavors like the sweet-and-sour qualities of reduced Pedro Ximénez, which are very similar to vincotto.

At the same time, though, the flavor of the meat is delicate enough to use fresh almonds and for the marzipan to shine through. Fresh almonds from the border of South Australia and Victoria are comparable to those of southern France.

Simplicity must be kept in mind when plating the different components—a sense of comfort and the aesthetic of the dish are vital. The most logical presentation is to place them in a straight line resting on the sauce.

Shannon Bennett

MOUTON RÔTI ET RIS D'AGNEAU

Serves 6

For the mutton loin
1 mutton backstrap •
salt and pepper • olive oil

1 Remove the sinew from the mutton and season it well.
2 Using plastic wrap (clingfilm), roll the mutton tightly into a cylinder shape and refrigerate until set.
3 Remove the mutton from the plastic wrap. Heat olive oil in a pan on high heat and color it all over.
4 Place the pan into the oven and slow-roast at 160°F (70°C) for 10 minutes, then rest for 5 minutes.

For the lamb sweetbreads
6 sweetbreads • salt and pepper •
3 tbsp olive oil

1 Dry the sweetbreads between paper towels. Season well.
2 In a pan on high heat, add the olive oil and cook the sweetbreads until golden. Set aside.

For the potato collar
1 potato, peeled

1 Using a mandolin, slice the potato into long strips.
2 Wrap an 8-cm metal ring or cutter in plastic wrap and carefully wrap the potato around the cutter.
3 Place a ring with potato wrapped around it into a deep fryer and fry until golden. Remove the potato from the ring while still hot, and set aside. Repeat for each serving.

For the mutton rillette

Stage 1
1 mutton leg, seasoned with salt and pepper • 1 liter confit fat • 1 garlic bulb, cut in half • 2 rosemary sprigs

Stage 2
200 g mutton leg confit, picked finely • 10 g shallots, finely diced • 4 g parsley, chopped • 2 g garlic puree • 20 g confit fat • salt • pepper

1 Place the mutton leg in the confit fat with the garlic and rosemary, cover with foil, and cook for 6 hours at 250°F (120°C).
2 Remove the mutton from the fat and take the meat off the bones.
3 To make the rillette, combine the ingredients listed for stage 2 and mix well. Press into a lined mold and set in the refrigerator overnight. Once set, cut the mutton into desired portion size.

For the vinegar reduction
100 ml Pedro Ximénez sherry vinegar • 1 heaping tbsp molasses (dark treacle)

In a heavy pan on medium heat, add the sherry vinegar and reduce by three-quarters. Stir in the molasses. Allow it to cool and set aside until required.

For the pommes mousseline
3 large Sebago potatoes •
250 g butter, finely diced •
2 tbsp warm milk •
2 tbsp sea salt

1 Cook the potatoes for 25 minutes in boiling salted water. Test with a knife—if it slides in without resistance, they are cooked. Immediately mash with 90 g butter. Mix any visible butter into the puree with a wooden spoon.
2 Place the puree in a pan, add 1 tablespoon of the milk, and whisk on low heat for 3–4 minutes.
3 Add remaining butter, a quarter at a time, whisking rapidly. If the butter starts to separate, the puree is too hot. Remove from the heat, beat in 1 tablespoon milk, and whisk like mad to bring it together.
4 When all the butter is incorporated, check the seasoning, add salt if necessary, and serve.

For the frisée
20 g frisée lettuce, picked and washed • 1 tbsp hazelnut vinaigrette • salt and pepper

In a bowl, toss together the frisée and vinaigrette. Season well and serve immediately.

For the truffle sauce
2 tbsp olive oil • ½ tsp garlic puree •
1 tsp finely chopped shallots •
18 fresh whole almonds, blanched (3 per serving) • 1 tsp truffle salsa •
50 ml chicken stock • 50 ml mushroom stock • 40 g French butter • lemon juice

1 In a pan on low heat, add olive oil and sweat the garlic and shallots. Add the almonds and salsa.
2 Add the chicken and mushroom stock and reduce by three-quarters.
3 Whisk in the butter until the sauce is emulsified. Add a squeeze of lemon juice.
4 Toss the sweetbreads through truffle sauce and heat through.

To serve
Murray River salt • sprigs of frisée lettuce

1 Paint vinegar reduction onto a plate with a wide pastry brush.
2 Spoon some pommes mousseline onto each plate. Sit the potato collar on top of the pommes mousseline on a 45° angle. Arrange the sweetbreads and almonds inside the potato collar.
3 Season the mutton with Murray River salt and place on top of the reduction.
4 Arrange 6–7 sprigs of frisée over the sweetbreads.

PROVENÇALE GARDEN VEGETABLES SIMMERED WITH CRUSHED BLACK TRUFFLE

Alain Ducasse

When you have made hundreds of dishes and tasted innumerable products from all four corners of the globe, it is impossible to say why one single recipe should hold a special place in your memory, but that's how it is with this recipe for Provençale garden vegetables. It could be because it evokes the exciting moment when I first arrived at the Louis XV in 1987, or because it is a tribute to the authentic taste of Provençale produce. For seafood, my touchstone is freshly caught striped red mullet, whose briny flavor still excites me every bit as much as it did then. As far as the fruits of the earth are concerned, it's vegetables, with their colors, textures, and tastes. That's one more reason for giving this plant-based recipe a special place in my heart.

And there's another reason: this dish demonstrates a side of the Mediterranean that's less well known—an earthy, I would even say "peasant," side. It's a recipe that speaks of market gardens, small plots of land on which people labor long and hard. It reminds me of the vegetables you pick with great respect, when they're perfectly ready. It's a seasonal recipe, designed for spring in the version presented here, when the scallions are at their tastiest and the carrots crunchiest. But it can be adapted according to what the garden has to offer, like all genuine country recipes for which the rhythms of nature dictate the ingredients.

And then there's the truffle: it gives this commonplace dish a touch of nobility. I like everything about truffles, their powerful flavor, and the mystery surrounding them, even their slightly surly aspect. There are so many reasons to love these Provençale vegetables that I almost forgot the main one: they're as delicious as a spring morning.

Serves 4

The vegetables in this dish can be varied according to season and what is available.

4 baby artichokes • 2 fennel bulbs • 20 small round radishes • 4 baby zucchini (courgettes) • 8 medium turnips with their green tops • 16 small carrots with their green tops • 100 g green (French) beans • 100 g local flat runner beans • 8 pencil-thin leeks • scallions (spring onions) • 1 Little Gem lettuce • white wine, to deglaze the artichokes • lemon juice, for sprinkling • Taggiasca olive oil, to serve • white stock, to moisten 40 g truffle, crushed • 12 g black truffle, peeled and julienned • balsamic vinegar, to serve • vinegar, to serve • 4 zucchini (courgette) flowers • 4 carrot tops • fleur de sel, to taste

1 To prepare the vegetables, trim the artichokes, leaving long stalks, and cut into 4. Remove the choke.
2 Clean each fennel bulb carefully and cut into 6.
3 Clean the radishes, leaving the green top on.
4 Wash the zucchini and cut into 4-cm slices.
5 Wash and trim the turnips and carrots, saving their tops.
6 Top and tail the green beans and runner beans, then cut into 4-cm lengths.
7 Wash the leeks and scallions and cut into 20-cm lengths.
8 Wash the Little Gem lettuce, reserve 8 medium-sized yellow leaves, trim the base, and remove the coarse central rib.

9 To cook the vegetables, plunge the green beans, runner beans, and leeks separately into boiling salted water, then chill in iced water.
10 Cook the artichokes in a pan, deglazing them with white wine, and sprinkle them with a little lemon juice to preserve the color. Chill.
11 Cook the fennel, radishes, turnips, scallions, carrots, and zucchini separately in a pan. Brown each vegetable in hot olive oil to fix the color, add salt, then moisten several times with white stock, covering the pan with a lid
12 When the vegetables are cooked, remove them from the pan and cool rapidly. Keep their cooking juice, except for the liquid from the radishes.
13 To finish the vegetables and to make the sauce, arrange all the cooked vegetables, apart from the radishes, zucchini, leeks, green beans, and runner beans, in a pan large enough for them not to overlap. Moisten with reserved cooking juice.
14 Add the crushed truffle and strips of truffle. Heat gently, taking care to moisten the vegetables well. Cook until the liquids have almost reduced, then add the other vegetables.
15 When the liquid has reached the desired consistency, add the olive oil, check the seasoning, and add both vinegars at the last moment.
16 To serve, place Little Gem leaves in the bottom of a large soup plate and pile the vegetables on top. Finish by coating the vegetables with sauce, then add the flowers and carrot tops, fleur de sel, and strips of raw truffle.

Alain Ducasse

ROAST BONE MARROW AND PARSLEY SALAD

Fergus Henderson

A few weeks before St. John opened in 1994, I had skipped out by myself on Saturday to go to the movies and see *La Grande Bouffe*, a film that I'm sure needs no explanation. For those not in the know, a group of gentlemen gather to kill themselves by overeating, which they do with a certain gastronomic flair. After the first spectacular delivery of meat, there is a scene of very enthusiastic sucking of roast bones. A splendid moment! Here was my dish. It appealed to the architect in me as well as the cook.

A cluster of 5-cm sections of roast marrow bones look like mini cooling towers on your plate. All great architecture should tolerate chaos (my personal theory); you can't design chaos as it will inevitably become trite and annoying, but how fantastic is the formality of a dining room full of people grappling with bones. In an age when people seem happier to buy pink anonymous fillets of meat wrapped in plastic, it's time to celebrate the bone.

Fortunately I already had the parsley salad up my sleeve, which, when paired with the bone marrow, neatly expresses another of my theories, the gastronomic "Naagh." The Naagh is a kind of culinary marker that acts as a counterpoint to the star attraction. It can be a caper, as in this salad, or a pickled walnut with boiled beef. However good something you're eating is, you always need a Naagh; not too much of course, or it will take over, but just enough to keep things buoyant.

Many bones have passed through the kitchen since that Saturday afternoon.

Serves 4

12 x 7–8-cm pieces of middle veal marrowbone • a healthy bunch of flat-leaf parsley, picked from its stems • 2 shallots, peeled and very thinly sliced • 1 modest handful of capers (extra-fine if possible) • juice of 1 lemon extra-virgin olive oil • a pinch of sea salt and pepper • a good supply of toast • coarse sea salt

1 Put the bone marrow in an ovenproof pan and place in a hot oven. The roasting process should take about 20 minutes depending on the thickness of the bone. You are looking for the marrow to be loose and giving, but not melted away, which it will do if left too long (traditionally the ends would be covered to prevent any seepage, but I like the coloring and crispness at the end).
2 Meanwhile, lightly chop your parsley, just enough to discipline it, and mix it with the shallots and capers.
3 Create the dressing by combining the lemon juice, olive oil, and a pinch of sea salt and pepper. Dress the parsley salad just before serving.

Note:
This is a dish that should not be completely seasoned before leaving the kitchen, because you want the eater to add their own; the seasoning, especially in the case of coarse sea salt, gives texture and uplift at the moment of eating. My approach is to scrape the marrow from the bone onto the toast and season with coarse sea salt. Then place a pinch of parsley salad on top of this and eat.

YUDOFU
(TOFU SIMMERED
IN HOTPOT)
Yoshihiro Murata

This story goes back twenty-five years. One day the late Seiko Hirata, then head of the Tenryu-ji temple, told me, "I'd like to invite you for a meal, why don't you come to the temple one of these days?" I eagerly waited for the day to arrive, fantasizing about what magnificent dishes were going to be served.

What was brought to me as I sat in the meditation hall was an earthen nabe pot filled with simmering tofu. Because I had expected to be served some delicacies I had never seen before, or perhaps a secret recipe of the temple, disappointment struck me for a moment.

But, I thought, the master would never serve me just an ordinary *yudofu*. Unable to contain myself any longer, I asked, "Does this *yudofu* convey a teaching?"

"No, it has no particular meaning, I just always wanted to treat you to it. Come, try it," the master answered, and he brought some butterbur sprouts (*fukinoto*) from the garden, chopped them, and sprinkled them over the hotpot. The room was enveloped in the smell of early spring.

The *yudofu* was superb even though no sophisticated skills seemed to be used to prepare it. To this day, I cannot forget the subtle, fulfilling flavor of that tofu and the butterbur sprouts.

At the time, being a young chef who was beginning to receive public attention, I was absorbed in creating dishes that flaunted my skills. I wanted to create special dishes using expensive ingredients. The master's *yudofu* taught me to go back to the basics. I have learned that, in order to cook something truly delicious, it is necessary to give life to the subtle flavors of nature.

Twenty-five years since then, I remember that teaching every time I hold a knife.

Serves 4

For the tofu
1 block silken (*kinugoshi*) tofu, drained • approximately 15 g kombu • 1 liter water

1 Place the kombu in a flat container filled with the water and leave it to soak.
2 Transfer the water and kombu into a nabe pot, place the drained silken tofu in it, and heat without bringing to a boil.

For the dashi sauce
200 ml soy sauce • 100 ml first-brewed (*ichiban*) dashi • 50 ml mirin • 2 g dried bonito flakes • (*katsuobushi*)

1 Bring the soy sauce, dashi, and mirin to a boil.
2 Add the bonito flakes, let cool, and strain.

To serve
scallions (spring onions) • laver seaweed, shredded • fresh ginger • dried bonito flakes (*katsuobushi*) •

1 Slice the scallions into thin circles, wrap in gauze, and wash in water by rubbing lightly.
2 Peel and grate the ginger.
3 Place the scallions, ginger, shredded laver, and bonito flakes in a dish and pour the heated dashi sauce over them. Serve with the tofu in the nabe pot.

Yoshihiro Murata

RAVIOLI OF LOBSTER, NORWEGIAN LOBSTER, AND SALMON WITH A LEMONGRASS AND CHERVIL VELOUTÉ

Gordon Ramsay

Our starter of ravioli of lobster, Norwegian lobster, and salmon with a lemongrass and chervil velouté, which we serve at Restaurant Gordon Ramsay in Chelsea, London, is a long-standing favorite with our diners. The velvety folds of pasta encase handpicked and hand-prepared lobster, Norwegian lobster (langoustine), and salmon that has been carefully combined to preserve the stunning textures and distinctive flavors of the fish. The shellfish drizzle to finish has a strong, robust flavor, while the meat is far more delicate. This finishing touch really lifts the overall flavor of the dish.

At all of the restaurants we are constantly creating new dishes by evolving the old ones. Most often, new ideas come in the middle of service, when you're plating dishes. Sometimes you'll just think, what if I add little of something from one dish onto another or add a little sauce from a dish two menus ago to a new one? Saying that, there are some dishes that we will never change, and the ravioli of lobster is one of them. It demonstrates real skill and technique and is an extremely complex dish to create. We have taken it off the menu occasionally, but there have been so many complaints, we have had to put it straight back on!

Serves 8 as a starter

For the ravioli filling
300 g skinless and boneless salmon fillet • sea salt and black pepper • 50 ml heavy (double) cream • 300 g lobster meat • (from 1 lobster tail and claws) • 150 g Norwegian lobster (langoustine) meat (from 5–6 langoustines) • squeeze of lemon juice • handful of mixed herbs (basil, coriander, and chervil), chopped

1 Put 100 g of the salmon into a food processor with some salt and pepper and whiz to a firm puree. With the motor running, slowly trickle in the cream.
2 Transfer to a bowl, cover with plastic wrap (clingfilm), and chill for 20 minutes. Finely dice the lobster and Norwegian lobster meat and the remaining salmon fillet, mix together in a bowl, and chill for 20 minutes.
3 Fold enough of the salmon puree into the diced lobster mixture to bind it, then add the lemon juice, chopped herbs, salt and pepper. To check the seasoning, blanch a little spoonful of the filling, then taste it.
4 Chill the mixture for 20–30 minutes until firm, then shape into neat balls, about 80 g each. Place on a plate, cover with plastic wrap, and chill again until firm (this can be prepared a day in advance.) Serves 8 as a starter

For the saffron pasta dough
Makes about 900 g

large pinch saffron strands • 1 tbsp boiling water • 500 g Italian '00' pasta flour • ½ tsp fine sea salt • 4 large eggs • 6 egg yolks • 2 tbsp olive oil

1 Soak the saffron in the boiling water for 5 minutes. Sift the flour and salt into a food processor. Add the eggs, egg yolks, and olive oil. Strain in the saffron water.
2 Whiz to combine, stopping twice to scrape down the sides of the machine. The mixture should form small lumps, which will hold together as a smooth, firm paste when pressed with your fingers.
3 Tip onto a lightly floured surface and knead for a few minutes until smooth and slightly springy. Wrap in plastic wrap and leave to rest for at least 30 minutes before using.

For the ravioli

1/3 quantity saffron pasta dough (see above) • 1 egg yolk, beaten with pinch of salt and 2 tsp water (egg wash)

1 Roll out the pasta dough into thin sheets using a pasta machine. Transfer to a lightly floured surface and cut out 12-cm rounds with a pastry cutter.
2 Place a ball of filling in the center of half of the pasta rounds, then brush the edges with egg wash. Press another remaining pasta round on top of each one and press the edges together to seal, stretching the dough slightly and molding it around the filling with your fingers to make sure there are no air pockets.
3 Use kitchen scissors to cut around the ravioli to neaten the edges.
4 Blanch the ravioli in boiling salted water for 3–4 minutes, then refresh in ice-cold water. Drain and chill until ready to serve.

For the fish stock
Makes about 1.5 liters

1.5 k white fish bones (such as turbot, brill, or halibut), washed • 1 onion, peeled and roughly chopped • 1 leek, peeled and roughly chopped • 1 stick celery, roughly chopped • 1 small fennel bulb, roughly chopped • 3 cloves garlic, peeled • 2 tbsp olive oil • 300 ml white wine • 1 bay leaf • sprig of thyme • few parsley stalks • 10 white peppercorns • 1 lemon, sliced • 2 liters cold water

1 If you're using the heads of the fish for the stock, remove the eyes and gills. Chop the bones into smaller pieces. Set aside.
2 Sweat the onion, leek, celery, fennel, and garlic in a little olive oil for 4–5 minutes.
3 Pour in the wine and let boil until reduced to a syrupy glaze. Add the herbs, peppercorns, lemon slices, and fish bones to the pot. Cover with water and bring to a simmer, skimming off the scum that rise to the surface.
4 Gently simmer for 20 minutes then let cool and allow the stock to settle before straining it through a cheesecloth- (muslin-) lined sieve. Set aside for the velouté, and for serving. Freeze remaining stock in small quantities.

For the lemongrass and chervil velouté
Makes about 500 ml

1 shallot, peeled and sliced • ½ tsp white peppercorns • ½ tsp coriander seeds • 1 garlic glove • 1 bay leaf • few thyme sprigs • 2 lemongrass stalks, split • 125 ml Noilly Prat (or other dry vermouth) • 250 ml fish stock (see above) • 250 ml heavy cream • sea salt and black pepper • bunch of chervil, leaves only, chopped

1 Put the shallot, peppercorns, coriander seeds, garlic, bay leaf, thyme, lemongrass, and vermouth in a wide pan and bring to a boil. Let boil until the liquid has reduced down to a syrupy glaze.

2 Add the stock and boil until reduced by half. Add the cream and simmer until the sauce has reduced to a coating consistency.
3 Taste and adjust the seasoning. Strain the sauce through a fine-mesh sieve into a bowl. Just before serving, reheat and stir in the chopped chervil.

To serve
reduced fish stock (see above), to drizzle • buttered leaf spinach • olive oil, to drizzle

1 When ready to serve, warm up the fish stock. Reheat the chervil velouté, adding the chopped chervil as you take the pan off the heat.
2 Add the ravioli to a pan of boiling salted water and reheat for 2–3 minutes, then drain well.
3 Drizzle a spiral of reduced fish stock around each warm plate. Spoon a little buttered leaf spinach into the center of each plate and place a ravioli on top.
4 Drizzle over a little olive oil then top with a neat spoonful of tomato chutney and a basil crisp if you like.
5 Pour over the chervil velouté to serve.

Gordon Ramsay

VEGETABLE FIELD
René Redzepi

When we opened Noma in November 2003, we had promised ourselves that it would be a gastronomic restaurant using only products from our own terroir—the Nordic terroir. Back in 2003 this was still quite an unusual idea. Most high-end restaurants either focused on French cuisine with a touch of Italy, or modern Spanish cooking. And of course these restaurants used mostly products from around Europe rather than the local area.

So when we opened—even though I had been on a two-month produce-discovery journey across the region—I suddenly found myself in a produce shortage. Given our region's weather conditions, it is essential that throughout spring, summer, and fall, you dry, pickle, confit, and salt the best products, such as elderflowers and ramson berries, to create a culinary foundation for the winter season. But as we opened in winter we didn't have this knowledge yet. I started to feel the pressure on my shoulders when I saw we probably didn't have enough produce to show a lot of diversity on our menu.

This made us think outside the box, and the dish I have chosen as of great importance to the restaurant and myself is one that originated in the very early days of Noma. At that time fish and shellfish were in high season but vegetables were scarce. Therefore, because of this lack of produce, I was forced to make dishes that involved only one ingredient. The potato field was born.

I wanted to take the best potatoes and make them taste like…potatoes. I visited my farmer on Lammefjorden and saw these freshly dug-up potatoes, and right there on the field, the dish came to life. A puree of potatoes, smooth, rich in flavor, served on a stone from the same field. On top of the puree, small potatoes cooked in mead and then sprinkled with a "malt soil" to really give it a strong link to the natural environment. Since then our potato field has taken many shapes, forms, and sizes. It is a dish that is always around in our kitchen, and now, in its later years, has developed into a vegetable field.

Serves 4

For the vegetables
The vegetables can be varied throughout the season.

4 orange carrots • 4 yellow carrots 4 radishes • 4 black, green, and red radishes • 1 Jerusalem artichoke 1 baby celery root (celeriac) • 4 baby leeks • 4 baby parsley roots • 60 g water • 50 g butter

1 Peel the carrots, leaving 1 cm of the tops behind, and cut them in half so you keep top and bottom separate.
2 Scrape the radishes and the leeks free of dirt and cut them in half.
3 Scrape the celery root and artichoke and cut them into quarters.
4 Blanch all the vegetables until tender in salted water.
5 Heat the water and whisk in all the butter to make an emulsion.

For the puree
80 g potatoes, peeled • 5 g butter • 15 g cream • 25 g water • horseradish juice

Boil the potatoes and crush with a fork. Add the rest of the ingredients while still warm.

For the malt soil

Day 1
350 g flour • 85 g malt flour • 50 g hazelnut flour • 25 g sugar • 75 g beer

Day 2
40 g flour • 20 g malt flour • 50 g hazelnut flour • 4 g salt • 75 g melted butter

1 Mix all the day 1 ingredients, dehydrate them for 5 hours at 175°F (80°C), and discard all the big, dry lumps.
2 Mix the day 2 ingredients separately and add them to the first batch. Work the batch for a few minutes, and make sure that it is completely homogeneous, without any lumps of raw dough.

To serve
12 leaves from the tops of the carrots used • 4 leaves from the tops of the parsley roots

1 To serve, heat the vegetables in the butter emulsion and heat the puree in a pot by itself, seasoning it with a bit of horseradish juice.
2 Plate a small spoonful on a stone and add all the vegetables to make it look as if they are sticking up from the ground.
3 Sprinkle the malt soil on top and add the picked and rinsed herbs on top of that.

CHICORIES SALAD WITH BRANDADE TOAST

Alice Waters

During my first trip to France in my early twenties, I fell in love with the delicious mesclun salad there—a mix of wild and cultivated, tender and hearty salad greens. When I couldn't find anyone growing those tiny lettuce leaves in this country, I planted a garden in my backyard to supply the restaurant. To this day, we always feature a garden lettuce salad on our daily menu in the café.

When making a salad, start by looking for good colors and textures. In spring, I use radishes—either shaved or quartered—and spring greens. Radishes can go in whole if they're especially tiny. I like fennel in salad; the leaves are beautiful when they're just picked. Chicories are members of the daisy family, closely related to lettuces and dandelions, which they resemble. Escarole, Belgian endive, curly endive, and radicchio are only a few of the many types found in the market. One of the most beautiful sights is a basket of tiny spring radicchios looking like parrot tulip leaves speckled with deep maroon. Their refreshingly bitter flavor and substantial crunchy texture combine well with richer foods in composed salads.

When shopping for chicories, look for salad greens that have just been picked—they should have an aliveness about them. Don't mind if they have a little dirt on them; it means they've just come from the field. Leafy chicories for a salad can be washed and dried ahead of time, like lettuce. Belgian endive and radicchio often need only be wiped with a damp towel.

Brandade, a Provençale specialty, is a mixture of fish, olive oil, milk, and garlic. I like to serve it on grilled toasts alongside a salad of hearty, vinegary greens. This dish can be a rustic first course or a light meal on its own, served with a glass of chilled rosé and followed by a few pieces of the season's perfect fruit.

Serves 4

For the brandade toasts
450 g hake or halibut • salt and pepper • 4 cloves garlic • whole milk • 225 g russet potatoes • 120 ml half-and-half (half milk and half cream) • 120 ml olive oil • 1 baguette • flat-leaf parsley, finely chopped

For the chicories
4 generous handfuls of mixed chicories (radicchio, curly endive, escarole) • 1 garlic clove, pounded to a fine puree • 1 tbsp red wine vinegar • salt • fresh-ground black pepper • 3–4 tbsp extra-virgin olive oil

1 One or two days in advance, very generously season the fish with salt and pepper, and refrigerate, covered, until ready to use.
2 Cook the fish with garlic in lightly simmering milk until soft, about 5–10 minutes. Drain the fish and garlic, reserving the liquid. When it is cool enough to handle, flake the fish, discarding any skin or bones, and pound the garlic to a paste.
3 Peel and boil the potatoes in the fish cooking liquid until soft, then put through a food mill or mash coarsely.

4 In a small pan, warm the half-and-half. Mash the flaked fish with the potatoes, garlic, olive oil and warm half and half, mixing thoroughly. Add more salt and pepper if necessary. The texture of the brandade should be almost like mashed potatoes, but with more body.
5 Carefully wash and dry the greens. Mix together the garlic, vinegar, salt, and pepper. Stir to dissolve the salt, taste, and adjust if needed. Whisk in the olive oil.
6 Using a lettuce leaf, taste the vinaigrette as you add the oil, adding a few drops more vinegar if necessary. Put the lettuce in a large bowl, pour over about three quarters of the vinaigrette, toss, and taste. Add more dressing as needed—chicories can take a bit more vinaigrette than tender young lettuces can.
7 Slice the baguette into 1.25 cm slices, brush with olive oil and toast in a 350°F (175°C) oven for 7–10 minutes. Rub the slices with a split clove of garlic. Spread the brandade thickly on the toast, sprinkling with chopped parsley. Divide the chicories among 4 plates. Garnish each plate with a brandade toast.

Alice Waters

XI YAN SPICY-SAUCE CHICKEN

Jacky Yu

For the chicken
1 chicken • 200 g bean curds •
3 preserved duck eggs • 200 g
cucumber • 80 g Chinese noodles
or mung bean pasta

For the spicy sauce
8 tbsp soy sauce • 2½ tbsp Zhenjiang
vinegar (a sweet brown vinegar) •
4 tbsp cold boiled water • 2 tbsp sugar •
1 tsp ground Szechuan pepper •
1 tbsp finely chopped ginger • 1 tbsp
finely chopped garlic • 1 tbsp finely
chopped cilantro (coriander) •
4 tbsp sesame oil • chili oil to taste

My first taste of real Szechuan cooking was around 1990 in a restaurant that supposedly serves authentic (or as near as we get to it) Szechuan food. The impact of one spicy chicken dish was breathtaking, and I was blown away by the complexity of smell and taste, underlined by the immensely fragrant and numbing sensation of Szechuan peppercorn.

In 2000, when I was developing the concept of Xi Yan and working on creating a cuisine that would modernize the concept of Chinese food, bringing together the many different regional cuisines to present a new perspective to tastes, time and time again I was drawn to the Szechuan chicken dish. It was full of direct and open, in-your-face spices, yet underneath, the nuanced and subtle flavors barely struggled through. I knew I could further the experience of the dish by bringing balance, so that the various tastes could be savored at every level.

My exploration led to a reinvention, which exemplifies Xi Yan's approach to Chinese food: marrying the essentially Szechuan classic dish with touches of Cantonese (southern province in China) and Shanghainese influence. Many complex layers are brought together with four different types of spiciness, combining chile, garlic, ginger, and the distinctive Szechuan peppercorn. The pungent alkaline Cantonese preserved duck egg (also known in the West as "century egg") complements the spiciness, while the Shanghainese mung bean pasta (or noodles) soaks up the delicious sauce to bring balance and texture. And it has all the qualities of a great visual presence, with the ingredients clearly in view and as contrasting as they are colorful.

One of Xi Yan's most renowned signature dishes, it is also known colloquially as "salivating chicken," because simply smelling it makes one salivate in anticipation. For me it is exactly how food should be, where the experience is holistic, like a good story with a beginning and an end.

1 Wash the chicken and blanch it in boiling water for 30 seconds. Remove immediately and soak in ice water for 1 minute. Return to the pot and bring to a boil. Turn the heat off at once, keep the lid on and leave the chicken to poach for another 45 minutes. Remove and leave to cool.
2 Dice the bean curds and preserved duck eggs.
3 Cut the cucumbers into slices.
4 Rinse the noodles, soak in hot water to soften, drain, and immediately soak in ice water.
5 Remove and shred the chicken meat. Transfer to a deep dish.
6 Add the preserved duck eggs, bean curd, cucumber, and Chinese noodles.

1 Mix the sauce ingredients together well and pour the sauce around the chicken.
2 Add 4 tablespoons sesame oil and chili oil (the amount of chili oil depends on personal preference).

To serve
roasted sesame seeds • roasted peanuts • 350 g Chinese celery •
5 large fresh red chiles (12–15 cm long)

To serve, sprinkle the sesame seeds, peanuts, and diced Chinese celery on top. For a stronger flavor, add more ground Szechuan pepper.

Glossary

À la barigoule
A French style of cooking, often used for artichokes or fish, which involves braising with white wine, vinegar, mushrooms, and bacon.

À la ficelle
A French technique in which a piece of meat, often beef fillet, is tied with string (*ficelle*), then roasted or poached.

À la nage
A French technique of poaching food, often seafood, in a flavored liquid that is usually served with the dish.

Absinthium
A bitter-tasting herbaceous plant, also known as wormwood.

Adjika
A paste made from tomatoes and hot red peppers, and flavored with cilantro, dill, and fenugreek, a specialty of Georgia.

Agar agar
A gelling agent derived from seaweed, also known as agar.

Aitchbone
A cut of beef containing the rump or hip bone.

Ajwain
A spice used in Indian cuisine, which has a strong flavor similar to thyme or caraway.

Aleppo pepper
A variety of mild but flavorsome red chile native to northern Syria, commonly found in crushed and dried form.

Algin
An ingredient derived from kelp used as a stabilizer, emulsifier, and thickener; the Algin in the Texturas Ferran y Albert Adrià range of food preparations is often used in the spherification process.

Amazu shoga
The Japanese term for pickled ginger.

Amchur
A tart Indian spice made from the flesh of dried green mangoes, in whole or powdered form.

Amuse bouche
A small appetizer, usually served at the beginning of the meal.

Angelica
An edible plant that can be preserved (the stem) or raw (the seeds and leaves). It is often candied.

Ao nori
A dried green seaweed powder used as a flavoring, mainly in Japanese cuisine.

Argan oil
An oil with a distinctive nutty taste, extracted from the kernels of the argan tree, which grows in northern Morocco.

Assiette
A French term used to describe a dish consisting of several components, often variations on one ingredient.

Bain marie
A vessel used for low-temperature cooking. The ingredients are placed in a heatproof container set in or over a pan of hot water, which is then put in the oven or simmered very gently on the stove.

Ballotine
A meat, fish, or poultry preparation that is boned and sometimes stuffed, then rolled and tied in a long cylinder shape before cooking.

Banyuls vinegar
An aged vinegar made from the fortified wine of the Banyuls-sur-Mer region of France.

Bavarian cream (bavarois)
A dessert based on flavored cream set in a mold with gelatin.

Benton's bacon
A variety of hickory-smoked bacon, made in Madisonville, TN, USA.

Beurre monté
A classic French preparation made by gradually whisking chunks of cold butter into a small amount of boiling water, used as a sauce and as a cooking liquid.

Blanch
To cook food, usually vegetables, briefly in boiling water. Often followed by "refreshing" or "shocking" (plunging the food into ice-cold water to stop the cooking).

Blast chiller
A chilling unit used in the catering industry, which chills food to low temperatures very quickly.

Bloom
To soften gelatin leaves by soaking them for a few minutes in cold water.

Bog stitchwort
A small wild plant with white flowers, related to chickweed.

La Bonnotte de Noirmoutier
A highly prized variety of potato from the island of Noirmoutier, off the western coast of France.

Brix
A unit of measurement for the dissolved sugar-to-water mass ratio of a liquid. It is measured with a saccharometer or refractometer.

Brunoise
To cut an ingredient into small dice.

Caltrop starch
A flour made from a tuber similar to the water chestnut.

Carnaroli rice
A short-grain Italian rice used for risottos.

Carranzana
A variety of sheep from the Basque country.

Cartouche
A circle of wax (greaseproof) paper that covers a dish during cooking, preventing evaporation of liquid while allowing heat to escape.

Cascabel pepper
A variety of round chile from Central America.

Cavolo nero
An Italian variety of cabbage, dark in color with long, thin stems.

Cazuela
A Spanish glazed terracotta dish used for cooking and serving food.

Chawanmushi
A Japanese dish based on savory egg custard.

Chickweed
A flowering plant whose leaves and tender stems are sometimes used in salads.

Chiffonade
To shred vegetables or herbs very finely, often for use as a garnish.

Chinois
A fine-mesh conical sieve.

Chiodini
The Italian name for a variety of small mushrooms which grow in clusters.

Citras
A product in the Texturas Ferran y Albert Adrià range of food preparations, which is used to prevent cut or peeled fruits and vegetables from blackening.

Codium
A variety of seaweed which is bright green and tube-like in appearance, also known as "spaghetti grass".

Colza oil
The oil extracted from colza, a variety of the rape plant.

Coprinus
A variety of mushroom with an elongated feathery cap, also known as "shaggy mane."

Coulis
A smooth liquid preparation, usually made with a puree of vegetables or fruit.

Court bouillon
A flavored liquid, often containing vinegar or wine, traditionally used for poaching fish.

Crépinette
The French term for caul fat, and also the sausage made with it.

Croquant
A food preparation with a crisp, crunchy texture.

Crowdie
A soft, crumbly Scottish cream cheese made from skim milk.

Crumiel
A product in the Texturas Ferran y Albert Adrià range of food preparations. It has the flavor of honey and a crunchy texture.

Cupuaçu
A sweet fruit with a fragrant, white pulp, native to South America.

Daikon
A white radish radish often used in Japanese cuisine, also known as mooli.

Dashi
A Japanese broth or stock made with seaweed (kombu) and dried tuna (bonito).

Deglaze
To add a liquid such as wine to a pan in which food (usually meat) has been cooked, to dissolve any sediment and form a sauce.

Dehydrator
A kitchen appliance that removes the moisture content from food, thereby preserving it and decreasing its volume.

Dendê oil
A thick, dark orange-colored oil extracted from the pulp of the fruit from a palm tree native to Brazil.

Dog cockles
A variety of clam with a brownish shell.

Double boiler
A two-layered pan with an upper section, in which the ingredients are cooked, which fits into a lower pan of boiling water, used to heat delicate sauces on the stove.

Elicoidali
A medium-size tube-shaped pasta, similar to rigatoni.

Emulsify
To mix liquids of different densities together to form a thicker liquid, often with the help of an emulsifying agent.

Espelette
A type of chile pepper grown in Espelette, France. Usually used dried and ground.

Farro
A type of wheat grain, similar to spelt.

Fernet Branca
An Italian bitter, aromatic spirit, made from fruits, herbs and spices.

Feuille de brick
A type of thin, brittle sheets of ready-made pastry, originating in Morocco.

Filé
A Cajun spice made from dried and ground sassafras leaves.

Flat iron
A beef steak cut from the shoulder section of the cow, usually well marbled with fat.

Flat-top
A cooking appliance with a large metal flat surface heated from below, often used in professional kitchens.

Fleur de sel
A type of sea salt harvested by scraping the top layer of crystals from a dried pan of salt. French fleur de sel, particularly from the village of Guérande, is highly regarded.

Fond
A highly flavored liquid created when meat or vegetables are cooked, often incorporated into a sauce by deglazing the sauté pan.

French trim
To clean the meat from the bones of a piece of meat, such as a rack of lamb.

Fresno chiles
A variety of chile pepper, similar to jalapeños, but with a thinner skin.

Fukinoto
Also known as Japanese butterbur, a large-leafed plant native to Japan, of which the stems, flowers and smaller leaves are edible.

Galangal
The root of a plant native to Southeast Asia, with a pungent flavor reminiscent of ginger or pepper, available in fresh or powdered forms.

Galette
A round, flat French biscuit or pastry, or a buckwheat crepe.

Ganache
A thick paste made with chocolate and heavy (double) cream.

Gastrique
A reduction of wine or vinegar, sugar and other ingredients, often fruit.

Gastronorm
A type of deep metal tray used in professional kitchens for food storage and preparation, which are made in a range of standard sizes.

Gelée
The French term for a jelly or aspic.

Gellan
A product in the Texturas Ferran y Albert Adrià range of food preparations that creates a firm gel that slices cleanly.

Ginnan
The Japanese term for gingko nuts.

Girolle
A variety of mushroom with a wide, fan-like shape and yellow color.

Glice
A product in the Texturas Ferran y Albert Adrià range of food preparations which acts as an emulsifier.

Gluco
A product in the Texturas Ferran y Albert Adrià range of food preparations, which is used in the spherification process.

Goma dofu
A type of Japanese tofu made with sesame and kuzu powder.

Gomasio
A Japanese seasoning mixture made with roasted sesame seeds and salt.

Good King Henry
An herb in the spinach family; its leaves have a flavor reminiscent of asparagus and are used like spinach.

Gotlandslimpa bread
A type of sourdough bread from Sweden.

Grits
A thick porridge-like dish made from ground corn, common in the southern parts of North America.

Guar gum
A thickener, texturizer and stabilizer extracted from the guar bean.

Hari nori
Thin, dried strips of Japanese nori seaweed.

Harissa
A hot, spicy North African paste made with chile peppers, caraway seeds, and herbs.

Heart sweetbreads
"Sweetbreads" is the term given to the pancreas and the thymus gland of a young animal. The heart sweetbread is the term used to describe the pancreas, as it is located close to the heart.

Hijiki
A brown sea vegetable that grows on rocky coastlines around Japan, Korea, and China.

Hold-O-Mat
An oven that keeps food at a specific temperature and humidity level, used in professional kitchens.

Homogenize
To break up the fat molecules in a liquid so that they are evenly distributed.

Honegiri
A specialized Japanese cutting technique used in fish preparation.

Inaka miso
A type of red rice-based miso.

Isshi soden
A Japanese tradition of handing down information through the generations.

Iwa nori
A type of seaweed that grows in rock crevices on the Japanese shoreline.

Jicama
The root of a Mexican vine, often used in soups, salads and fruit dishes.

Jinhua ham
A Chinese cured ham named after the city where it is produced.

Jolo
A type of Chinese pickle.

Judas' ear fungus
A jelly-like fungus which grows on wood, also known as wood-ear mushroom.

Julienne
To cut vegetables into very thin matchstick-like strips.

Kaolin
A natural soft, white clay.

Kappa
A product in the Texturas Ferran y Albert Adrià range of food preparations. It is derived from a type of algae, and produces a gel with a firm, brittle texture.

Karasumi
A type of dried Japanese mullet roe.

Kasu
The residue remaining after the final pressing of sake.

Katsuo
The Japanese name for bonito or skipjack tuna.

Katsuobushi
Dried, smoked and fermented Japanese tuna flakes.

Kemangi
A type of Indonesian basil.

Kimchi
A traditional Korean dish of fermented vegetables, often cabbage.

Kinugoshi
A soft, silken type of tofu.

Kirigoma
Crushed, toasted sesame seeds used in Japanese cuisine.

Kombu
The Japanese name for several types of brown seaweed, frequently used in Japanese cooking.

Konjac
The fibrous root of a plant native to tropical Asia.

Krupuk
A type of deep-fried cracker made from shrimp (prawns) and starch.

Kudzu
A starch derived from the root of a vine, used for thickening. Also known as kuzu.

Kurobuta
The Japanese name for a highly prized breed of pork.

Kuruma
A variety of shrimp (prawn) from Japan.

Lactose
A naturally occurring sugar found in milk, used as a sweetening food additive.

Laver
A dried, purple-colored seaweed with a tangy, sweet flavor.

Lavosh
An unleavened Middle Eastern flatbread.

Longan
A fruit similar to a lychee, native to India and China, also known as dragon's eye.

Loquat
A mildly acidic tasting fruit, native to China.

Lukainka
A type of spiced sausage originating in Bulgaria.

Macerate
To soften foods by soaking them, usually in alcohol.

Maitake
A Japanese mushroom, also known as "sheep's head" or "hen of the woods".

Maldon salt
A sea salt harvested in Maldon, Essex, England.

Maltodextrin
A starch-derived sugar, sometimes used to give foods body and texture.

Maltose
A sugar derived from grain and used to sweeten food.

Mandolin
A Japanese kitchen device used for thin and accurate slicing.

Maris Piper
A British variety of main crop potato.

Matcha
A finely powdered green tea used in Japanese cuisine.

Matsutake
A highly prized Japanese mushroom, also known as pine mushroom.

Methylcellulose
A preparation used in baked goods which controls moisture.

Metil
A product in the Texturas Ferran y Albert Adrià range of food preparations. It is made from vegetable cellulose and acts as a thickener when cold and a gelling agent when heated.

Mi-cuit
A term used to describe food that has been partially cooked, often foie gras or dried fruit.

Microherb
Vegetable or herb seedlings, raised and picked when between 6 and 21 days old, and often used for garnishing.

Microplane
A very sharp hand-held grater.

Mignardise
A French term for small dessert bites served at the end of the meal, often with coffee.

Millefeuille
A traditional French puff pastry dessert made up of many layers. Literally translated as "thousand leaves."

Mirepoix
A classic French preparation of diced vegetables and herbs, usually comprising onions, carrots and celery, fried until brown and used as the basis for many sauces.

Mise en place
The food preparation that is done in a restaurant kitchen before the service period begins, such as making sauces and chopping vegetables.

Miso zoni
A Japanese rice soup with miso, traditionally eaten at New Year.

Mitsuba
A Japanese herb with a flavor reminiscent of delicate parsley.

Mojama
A type of Spanish salt-cured and dried tuna.

Monter au beurre
A classic French technique in which a sauce is finished just before service by whisking in chunks of cold butter.

Mycryo
A powdered fat made from cocoa butter, which can be used for frying.

Myoga
A Japanese variety of ginger.

Nabe
A traditional Japanese earthenware cooking vessel.

Nametake
A small yellow Japanese mushroom that grows wild in clusters.

Nepitella
The Italian name for a wild herb reminiscent of mint in flavor, also known as calamint.

Obulato wafer
A thin, transparent Japanese wafer made with potato starch.

Oxalis
A leafy herb, also known as wood sorrel, with a sour and refreshing flavor.

Panko
A type of processed Japanese breadcrumb that has a very crunchy texture.

Pacojet
A machine that blends frozen products to create very fine-textured frozen purees and sorbets.

Pailleté feuilletine
Ready crushed wafers or crepes, often used in sweet preparations.

Panisse
A fried chickpea crepe-like cake originating in the south of France.

Parmentier
The French term for a dish made or served with potatoes.

Perilla
A leafy herb from Asia, in the mint family, known as shiso in Japan.

Pink salt
A rock salt colored with iron oxide or, in charcuterie, a salt mixture used for curing meat.

Plancha
A Spanish term for a very hot flat surface or griddle used for rapid cooking.

Popping candy
A type of candy (sweet) which fizzes and pops in the mouth. Also known as space dust or Pop Rocks.

Puntarella
A variety of Italian chicory, also known as puntarelle.

Quenelle
A small portion of food shaped into an elongated sphere resembling an American football (rugby ball), shaped with two spoons.

Quinoa
An ancient South American grain.

Ramps
A wild onion native to North America, also known as wild leek.

Rapini
A green vegetable with spiked leaves surrounding a green bud, also known as broccoli rabe.

Reduce
To boil or simmer a liquid to evaporate the water it contains, thereby thickening it and concentrating its flavor.

Refractometer
An instrument for measuring a liquid's refractive index, or sugar content.

Refresh
To plunge cooked food into cold water to halt the cooking process quickly.

Roner
A machine used in professional kitchens to poach vacuum-packed foods in liquid for long periods at a low and constant temperature.

Rucola
The Italian term for arugula, or rocket.

Rue
An herb with bitter blue-green leaves and yellow-green flowers.

Sabayon
A traditional French sweet preparation made with whisked eggs and sugar, also known as zabaglione in Italian.

Salamander
A type of broiler (grill) used in professional kitchens, often for browning foods before service.

Salmoriglio
An Italian sauce made with olive oil, lemon juice, garlic, and herbs, often oregano.

Sanguinaccio
An Italian blood pudding or blood sausage. There are sweet and savory varieties.

Sauteuse
A French term for a deep skillet or pan used for sautéing or braising.

Sea buckthorn
A wild shrub with edible fruit.

Serragghia
A variety of Italian caper.

Seviche
A South American dish of raw fish or seafood marinated in citrus juices, also spelled "ceviche."

Shabu shabu
A Japanese dish, similar to a hot pot, in which thinly sliced foods are poached in dashi.

Shaoxing
A Chinese amber-colored rice wine.

Shimeiji
A popular Japanese variety of small brown mushroom.

Shio kombu
A type of kombu which has been simmered slowly with water, soy sauce and other seasonings.

Shock
To plunge cooked food into cold water to halt the cooking process quickly.

Shonai fu
A variety of fu (sticks of dried gluten), combined with shonai (wheat).

Silpat
A nonstick silicone baking mat.

Slake
To mix with water to make a paste. A term often used in relation to cornstarch (cornflour).

Sobrassada
A soft, cured spiced sausage from Spain.

Soy lecithin
A complex fat derived from soy beans and used as an emulsifier.

Speculaas
A type of spiced biscuit traditional in Holland and Belgium.

Spider
A large, flat wire spoon or skimmer used for removing solids from liquids.

Stabilizer
An ingredient used to prevent foods from breaking down. Often used in the preparation of sorbets.

Strascinati
A type of pasta which is ridged on one side, a specialty of the Basilicata region of southern Italy.

Strong flour
A flour with a high protein content.

Succotash
A dish consisting primarily of corn and lima (butter) beans, or other shell beans, which is a specialty of the southern states of the USA.

Sucro
A product in the Texturas Ferran y Albert Adrià range of food preparations, derived from sucrose and fatty acids and used as an emulsifier and for aerating ingredients.

Sudachi
A small, round, green citrus fruit from Japan.

Sultan Ibrahim
A type of red snapper found in the Arabian sea and parts of the Mediterranean.

Sultana grapes
A white grape variety valued for its sweet raisins.

Sumac
The powdered berries of a middle Eastern plant with a tart flavor, used as a spice.

Superbag
A very fine mesh bag through which liquids can be strained and clarified.

Sushi meshi
The Japanese term for sushi rice.

Sushizu
A rice vinegar dressing for sushi rice.

Sweat
To cook foods, often onions, over gentle heat, usually covered or partly covered, until they release their moisture.

Siphon
A pressurized container with which foams can be created by aerating liquids under pressure.

Szechuan buttons
The bud of a plant which, when eaten, produces an "electric" sensation in the mouth.

Talo
A type of flatbread from the Basque country made with cornflour and water.

Tamis
A flat fine-mesh wire sieve.

Thermomix
A food processor that blends foods at specific temperatures.

Thick and Easy
An instant food thickener that adds texture to pureed foods and consistency to liquids.

Togijiru
The Japanese term for the liquid remaining after washing rice in water.

Torrija
A Spanish sweet traditionally eaten around Lent, made from a slice of bread soaked in milk or wine, fried and sprinkled with cinnamon, honey or sugar.

Tsubu miso
A type of miso made with barley.

Turn
To trim a vegetable into a rounded barrel-like shape.

Umami
A Japanese term for one of the major taste categories, alongside sweet, sour, salty and bitter. It is usually described as a savory, meaty flavor.

Umeboshi
A type of Japanese pickled plum.

Umeshu jelly
A jelly made from Umeshu wine, a Japanese plum liqueur.

Uni
The Japanese term for sea urchins.

Vendance roe
The eggs of the vendance fish, popular in Scandinavia.

Ventrèche
A French cured pork product made with pork belly, similar to pancetta.

Verjus
A sour juice obtained by pressing unripe grapes.

Vitaprep
A food processor used for chopping, grinding, or blending.

Wasabi tobiko
A preparation made with tobiko (flying fish roe) and wasabi.

Witch's butter fungus
A jelly-like fungus that grows on wood.

Xanthan gum
A product derived from fermented starch, used as a thickening agent and to maintain solids in suspension within a liquid.

Xarda
The Spanish term for mackerel.

Xiao long bao
A Chinese dumpling or bun, often filled with pork.

Yarrow
A flowering plant with sharp, bitter-tasting edible leaves.

Yuzu
An Asian citrus fruit, which tastes similar to a mandarin or lemon, with an aromatic zest.

Za'tar
A Middle Eastern herb mixture made with wild marjoram, thyme, sesame seeds and salt.

Zwieback bread
A type of crispy, sweetened bread from Germany, made with eggs and twice baked.

Restaurant Directory

Hugh Acheson
Five & Ten
1653 S. Lumpkin Street, Athens,
GA 30606, USA
T +1 7065467300
www.fiveandten.com

The National
232 W Hancock Ave, Athens,
GA 30601, USA
T +1 7065493450

Inaki Aizpitarte
Le Chateaubriand
129 Avenue Parmentier,
75011 Paris, France
T +33 (0)143574595

Victor Arguinzoniz
Acador Etxebarri
1 Plaza San Juan Axpe-Marzana
48291, Alxondo- Bizkaia, Spain
T +34 946583042
www.asadoretxebarri.com

Armand Arnal
La Chassagnette
Le Sambuc, 13200 Arles, France
T +33 (0)490972696

Alex Atala
D.O.M.
Rua Br Capanema, 549 - Jardins,
São Paulo - SP - CEP: 01411-011,
Brazil
T +55 1130880761
www.domrestaurante.com.br

Jason Atherton
Maze
13 Grosvenor Square, Mayfair,
London, W1K 6JP, UK
T +44 (0)2071070000

Eneko Atxa
Azurmendi
Barrio Legina Auzoa,
48195 Larrabetzu, Spain
T +34 944558866
www.azurmendi.biz

José Avillez
Tavares
Rua da Misericórdia 35,
R/C 1200-270 Lisbon, Portugal
T +35 1213421112
www.tavaresrico.pt

Pascal Barbot
L'Astrance
4 Rue Beethoven, 75016 Paris,
France
T +33 (0)140508440

Cédric Béchade
L'Auberge Basque
D 307 Vieille Route de St Jean
de Luz, 64310 Helbarron /
Saint-Pée, France
T +33 (0)559517000
www.aubergebasque.com

Martin Benn
Sepia
201 Sussex St, Sydney,
NSW 2000, Australia
T +61 292831990
www.sepiarestaurant.com.au

Mark Best
Marque Restaurant
4/5 355 Crown Street, Surry Hills,
NSW 2010, Australia
T +61 (0)293322225
www.marquerestaurant.com.au

April Bloomfield
The Spotted Pig
314 W. 11th St,
New York, NY 10014, USA
T +1 02126200393
www.thespottedpig.com

The John Dory
85 10th Ave, New York,
NY 10011, USA
T +1 2129294948
www.thejohndory.com

Robert Owen Brown
The Angel
6 Angel Street,
Manchester, M4 4BQ, UK
T +44 01618334786
www.theangelmanchester.co.uk

Mario Carbone
Aeronuova
Terminal 5,
JFK International Airport,
Jamaica, NY 11430, USA

Wai Man Chan
Tai Woo Restaurant
27 Percival Street, Causeway Bay,
Hong Kong
T +85 228930822
www.taiwoorestaurant.com

David Chang
Momofuku Ko
163 First Ave,New York,
NY 10003, US

Momofuku Noodle Bar
171 First Ave, New York,
NY 10003, US

Momofuku Ssäm Bar
207 Second Ave, New York,
NY 10003, US
www.momofuku.com

Ricky Cheung
Le Mieux Bistro
407-8 Block B,
MP Industrial Centre,
18 Ka Yip Street, Chai Wan,
Hong Kong, China
T +85 225582877

Ryan Clift
Tippling Club
8D Dempsey Road, 249672,
Singapore
T +65 64752217
www.tipplingclub.com

Mauro Colagreco
Mirazur
30 Avenue Aristide Briand,
06500 Menton, France
T +33 (0)492418686
www.mirazur.fr

Chris Cosentino
Incanto
1550 Church Street, San Francisco,
CA 94131, USA
T 11 4156414500
www.incanto.biz

Enrico Crippa
Piazza Duomo
Piazza Risorgimento 4, 12051 Alba,
Cuneo, Italy
T +39 0173366167
www.piazzaduomoalba.it

Mathias Dahlgren
Restaurant Mathias Dahlgren
Grand Hôtel Stockholm,
Södra Blasieholmshamnen 6,
P.O. Box 16424,
S-103 27 Stockholm, Sweden
T +46 (0)86793584
www.mathiasdahlgren.com

Kevin Davis
Steelhead Diner
95 Pine Street, Pike Place Market,
Seattle, WA 98101, USA
T +1 2066250129
www.steelheaddiner.com

Anthony Demetre
Arbutus
63-64 Frith Street,
London, W1D 3JW, UK
T +44 (0)2077344545
www.arbutusrestaurant.co.uk

Wild Honey
12 St. George Street, London,
W1S 2FB, UK
T +44 (0)2077589160
www.wildhoneyrestaurant.co.uk

Kobe Desramaults
In de Wulf
Wulvestraat 1,
8950 Heuvelland (Dranouter),
Belgium
T +32 057445567
www.indewulf.be

Pascal Devalkeneer
Le Chalet de la Forêt
Drève de Lorraine 43,
1180 Brussels, Belgium
T +32 023745416
www.lechaletdelaforet.be

Marcus Eaves
L'Autre Pied
5-7 Blandford Street,
London, W1U 3DB, UK
T +44 (0)2074869696
www.lautrepied.co.uk

Didier Elena
Chateau Les Crayeres
64 Boulevard Henry Vasnier
Reims 51100, France
T +33 (0)326249010
www.lescrayeres.com

Andrew Feinberg
Franny's
295 Flatbush Avenue,
Brooklyn, NY 11217, USA
T +1 7182300221
www.frannysbrooklyn.com

John Fraser
Dovetail
103 West 77th St,
New York, NY 10024, USA
T +1 2123623800
www.dovetailnyc.com

Dani García
Calima
Calle José Melia s/n,
29602 Marbella, Málaga, Spain
T +34 952764252
www.restaurantecalima.com

Cruz Goler
Lupa Osteria Romana
170 Thompson St, New York,
NY 10012, USA
T +1 2129825089
www.luparestaurant.com

Skye Gyngell
Petersham Nurseries
Off Petersham Road, Richmond,
Surrey, TW10 7AG, UK
T +44 (0)2086053627
www.petershamnurseries.com

Tommy Habetz
Bunk Sandwiches and Bar
621 SE Morrison Street, Portland,
OR 97214, USA
T +1 5034779515
www.bunksandwiches.com

Wassim Hallal
Restaurant Frederikshøj
Marselisborg Skov, Odderveg
19-21, DK-8000 Arhus C, Denmark
T +45 86142280
www.frederikshoj.com

Charlie Hallowell
Pizzaiolo
5008 Telegraph Avenue, Oakland,
CA 94609, USA
T +1 5106524888
www.pizzaiolooakland.com

Anna Hansen
The Modern Pantry
47-48 St. John's Sq, London,
EC1V 4JJ, UK
T +44 (0)2075539210
www.themodernpantry.co.uk

Alberto Herráiz
Fogón Restaurant
45 Quai des Grands Augustins,
75006 Paris, France
T +33 (0)143543133
www.fogon.fr

Benjamin Hirst
Necci dal 1924
Via Fanfulla da Lodi,
68 Pigneto, Rome, Italy
T +39 0697601552
www.necci1924.com/site

Jing-long Huang
Long Lai Restaurant
104 No. 1, Alley 11, Lane 147,
Section 2, Minsheng E. Road,
Taipei City 104, Taiwan
T +886 225050891

Jonathan Jones
Anchor and Hope
36 The Cut, SE1 8LP, London, UK
T +44 (0)2079289898

Jacob Kenedy
Bocca di Lupo
12 Archer Street, London,
W1D 7BB, UK
T +44 (0)2077342223
www.boccadilupo.com

Tom Kitchin
The Kitchin
78 Commercial Quay, Leith
Edinburgh, EH6 6LX, UK
T +44 (0)1315551755
www.thekitchin.com

Anatoly Komm
Varvary and *Kommpartiya*
8A Strastnoy Boulevard, Moscow,
Russia
T +7 4952292800

Kupol
Novy Arbat 36, Moscow, Russia
T +7 4952436407

Green.It
30/7 Petrovka Street Moscow, Russia
T +7 4956506887
www.anatolykomm.ru

Filip Langhoff
Feinschmecker
Balchensgate 5, Oslo 0265, Norway
T +47 22129380
www.feinschmecker.no

Ka Lun Lau
Foon Lok Restaurant
2 Sai Tai Street,
Shop 5 G/F Hang Fai Building,
Yuen Long, Hong Kong
T +852 24760883

Alvin Leung
Bo Innovation
Shop 13, 2/f J 60 Johnston Road,
Wan Chai, Hong Kong
T +852 28508371
www.boinnovation.com

Jereme Leung
Jereme Leung Creative Concepts
No 509, Lu Ban Lu,
Luwan Du Shi Hua Yuan, Block 19,
#01-104 Shanghai 200023 PRC
T +86 2163037567
www.jeremeleung.com

Lionel Lévy
Une Table au Sud
2 Quai du Port, 13002
Marseille, France
T +33 (0)491906353
www.unetableausud.com

Ed Lewis
Bank House Hotel
King's Lynn, Norfolk, PE30 1RD, UK
T +44 01553660492
www.thebankhouse.co.uk

Josh Lewis
Vue
Al Bustan Palace Intercontinental
Hotel, PO BOX 1998,
PC 114 Muttrah,
Sultanate of Oman
T +968 24799666
www.intercontinental.com

Kelly Liken
Restaurant Kelly Liken
12 Vail Rd, Suite 100, Vail,
CO 81657, USA
www.kellyliken.com
T + 1 9704790175

Tung-Yuan Lin
Gabee.
No 21 Min Sheng East Road,
Section 3, Alley 113, Taipei City,
Taiwan
T +886 0227138772
gabee-cafe.blogspot.com

Donald Link
Cochon
930 Tchoupitoulas St, New Orleans,
LA 70130, USA
T +1 5045882123
www.cochonrestaurant.com

Herbsaint Bar and Restaurant, 701
St. Charles Avenue, New Orleans,
LA 70130, USA

Paolo Lopriore
Il Canto
Hotel Certosa di Maggiano,
Strada di Certosa 82, Siena 53100,
Italy
T +39 0577288180
www.ilcanto.it

Willin Low
Wild Rocket
Hangout Hotel,
10a Upper Wilkie Road,
Singapore 228119
T +65 63399448
www.wildrocket.com.sg

Relish
#02-01 Cluny Court,
501 Bukit Timah Road,
Singapore, 259760

Robert Marchetti
Icebergs Dining Room and Bar
One Notts Avenue, Bondi Beach,
PO Box 7053, NSW 2026, Australia
T +61 293659000

North Bondi Italian Food
118–120 Ramsgate Avenue
Bondi Beach NSW 2026 Australia

Giuseppe Arnaldo & Sons
Crown, Whiteman Street,
Southbank, Melbourne, Australia
www.idrb.com

Christophe Martin
L'Andana
Tenuta La Badiola, Badiola
58043, Castiglione della Pescaia
(Grosseto), Italy
T +39 0564944800
www.andana.it

Andrew McConnell
Cutler & Co
55-57 Gertrude Street, Fitzroy,
Victoria 3065, Australia
T +61 394194888
www.cutlerandco.com.au

Cumulus Inc
45 Flinders Lane, Melbourne 3000,
Australia

Jakob Mielcke
Mielcke & Hurtigkarl
Frederiksberg Runddel 1,
2000 Frederiksberg, Denmark
T +45 38348436
www.mielcke-hurtigkarl.dk

Russell Moore
Camino
3917 Grand Ave,
Oakland, CA 94610, USA
T +1 5105475035
www.caminorestaurant.com

Marcos Morán
Casa Gerardo
Ctra. AS 19 Gijón - Aviles km.9,
Prendes (Carreño), 33438 Asturia,
Spain
T +34 985888897
www.casa-gerardo.com

Hisato Nakahigashi
Miyamaso
375 Daihizan, Hanaseharachi-cho,
Sakyo-ku, Kyoto 601-1102, Japan
T +81 (0)757460231
www.miyamasou.jp

Motokazu Nakamura
Nakamura
Oike-agaru, Tominokoji,
Chukyo-ku, Kyoto, Japan
T +81 (0)752215511
www.kyoryori-nakamura.com

Akhtar Nawab
Elettaria
33 W. 8th St, New York, NY 10011, USA
T +1 2126773833
www.elettarianyc.com

Davide Oldani
D'O
Via Magenta 10,
San Pietro all'Olmo, Cornaredo,
Milán 20010, Italy
T +39 029362209

Gustav Otterberg
Leijontornet
Lilla Nygatan 5, Gamla Stan,
111 28 Stockholm, Sweden
T +46 (0)850640080
www.leijontornet.se

Scott Peacock
Watershed
406 West Ponce de Leon Ave,
Decatur, GA 30030, USA
T +1 4043784900
www.watershedrestaurant.com

Tom Pemberton
Hereford Road
3 Hereford Road, Westbourne
Grove, London, W2 4AB, UK
T +44 (0)2077271144
www.herefordroad.org

Ricardo Peréz
Yandiola
Paseo del Campo Volantín 15,
48007 Bilbao, Spain
T +34 944134013
www.yandiola.com

Jean-François Piège
Les Ambassadeurs
Hotel de Crillon,
10 Place de la Concorde,
75008 Paris, France
T +33 (0)144711500
www.crillon.com

Glynn Purnell
Purnell's
55 Cornwall Street, Birmingham,
B3 2DH, UK
T +44 (0)1212129799
www.purnellsrestaurant.com

Theo Randall
Theo Randall at the InterContinental
1 Hamilton Place, London,
W1J 7QY, UK
T +44 (0)2073188747
www.theorandall.com

David Rathgeber
l'Assiette
181 Rue du Château, 75014 Paris,
France
T +33 (0)143226486

Albert Raurich
Dos Palillos
Carrer Elisabets 9,
08001 Barcelona, Spain
T +34 933040513
www.dospalillos.com

Lyndy Redding
Absolute Taste Catering
14 Edgel Street, London,
SW18 1SR, UK
T +44 (0)2088705151
www.absolutetaste.com

Mads Refslund
MR
Kultorvet 5,
1720 Kbh K,Copenhagen, Denmark
T +45 33910949
www.mr-restaurant.dk

Chris Salans
Mozaic Restaurant
Jl Raya Sanggingan, Ubud,
Gianyar - Bali 80571, Indonesia
T +62 361975768
www.mozaic-bali.com

Koji Saito
Sushi Saito
Nihon Jitensha Kaikan 1F,
1-9-15 Akasaka, Minato-ku, Tokyo,
Japan
T +81 (0)335894412

Thorsten Schmidt
Malling & Schmidt
Jaegergardsgade 81,
DK-8000 Aarhus C, Denmark
T +45 86177088
www.mallingschmidt.dk

Amaryll Schwertner
Boulette's Larder
1 Ferry Building Marketplace,
San Francisco, CA 94111, USA
T +1 4153991155
www.bouletteslarder.com

Ben Shewry
Attica
74 Glen Eira Road, Ripponlea,
Melbourne, Australia
T +61 95300111
www.attica.com.au

Hidekl Shimoguchi
Chikurin
Byodoin Omotesando,
21 Renge, Uji, Kyoto, Japan
T +81 (0)756110021

Clare Smyth
Restaurant Gordon Ramsay
68-69 Royal Hospital Rd, London,
SW3 4HP, UK
T +44 (0)2073524441
www.gordonramsay.com

Yosuke Suga
L'Atelier de Joël Robuchon Taipei
Bellavita 5F No. 28, Song Ren Road,
110 Hsin Yi Road Taipei, Taiwan
www.joel-robuchon.com

Takuji Takahashi
Kinobu
416 Iwatoyamacho, Bukkoji Sagaru,
Shinmachi-dori, Shimogyo-ku,
Kyoto-shi, Kyoto 600-8445, Japan
T +81 (0)753520001
www.kinobu.co.jp

Mona Talbott
American Academy in Rome
Via Angelo Masina 5, 00153 Rome,
Italy
T +39 0658461
www.aarome.org

Kitty Travers
La Grotta Ices
95B Walcot Square, Kennington,
London, SE11 4UB, UK
www.lagrottaices.com

Michael Tusk
Quince
1701 Octavia, San Francisco,
CA 94109, USA
T +1 4157758500
www.quincerestaurant.com

Naoya Ueno
Gensai
7-5-15 Nakayamate-dori Chuo-ku,
Kobe 6500004, Japan
T +81 (0)783513585

Allison Vines-Rushing
Mila
817 Common St, New Orleans,
LA 70112, USA
T +1 5044122580
www.milaneworleans.com

Sylvestre Wahid
Oustau de Baumanière
13520 Les Baux de Provence,
France
T +33 (0)490543307
www.maisonsdebaumaniere.com

Tristan Welch
Launceston Place
1a Launceston Place, London,
W8 5RL, UK
T +44 (0)2079376912
www.launcestonplace-restaurant.
co.uk

Jody Williams
Gottino
52 Greenwich Ave, New York,
NY 10011, USA
T +1 2126332590
www.ilovegottino.com

Martin Wishart
54 The Shore
Leith, Edinburgh, EH6 6RA, UK
T +44 (0)1315533557
www.martin-wishart.co.uk

Margaret Xu
Yin Yang
18 Ship St, Wan Chai, Hong Kong
T +852 28660868

JinR Zhang
Green T House
No. 6 Gongti Xilu, Chaoyang,
Beijing, China
T +86 1065528310
www.green-t-house.com

Yue-jiau Zhuang
C'est Bon
23 ZhongShan N Rd (Sec 1), Taipei
City, Taiwan
T +886 0225316408

Eric Ziebold
CityZen
Mandarin Oriental Hotel
1330 Maryland Ave SW,
Washington, DC, 20024, USA
T +1 2027876006
www.mandarinoriental.com/
washington/dining/cityzen

Index

Page numbers in *italic* refer to images.

Page numbers in **bold** refer to featured chefs.

Phaidon Press Limited
Regent's Wharf
All Saints Street
London N1 9PA

Phaidon Press Inc.
180 Varick Street
New York, NY 10014

www.phaidon.com

First published 2009
© 2009 Phaidon Press Limited

ISBN: 978 0 7148 4954 6

A CIP catalogue record for
this book is available from
the British Library.

Designed by Change is Good
Printed in China

Acknowledgments
The publisher would like to
thank the 10 curator chefs—
Ferran Adrià, Mario Batali,
Shannon Bennett, Alain Ducasse,
Fergus Henderson, Yoshihiro
Murata, Gordon Ramsay,
René Redzepi, Alice Waters, and
Jacky Yu—and the 100 selected
chefs. We would also like to
thank the following individuals
and organizations for providing
translations into English: from
the French, Imogen Forster and
Angela Bradford; from the Italian,
Irena Hill; from the Japanese,
Naoki Matsuyama; and from
the Spanish, Cillero & De Motta.

Notes

Notes on the recipes

Unless otherwise stated, eggs are
assumed to be large and individual
vegetables and fruits, such as
onions and apples, are assumed
to be medium.

Unless otherwise stated, pepper
is freshly ground pepper.

Cooking times are for guidance
only, as individual ovens vary.

If using a fan oven, follow the
manufacturer's instructions
concerning oven temperatures.

Some words of caution

Some recipes include raw or very
lightly cooked eggs. These should
be avoided particularly by the
elderly, infants, pregnant women,
convalescents, and anyone with
an impaired immune system.

A number of the recipes require
advanced techniques, specialist
equipment, and professional
experience to achieve good results.

Exercise a very high level of
caution when carrying out
recipes involving any potentially
hazardous activity, including the
use of high temperatures, open
flames and when deep frying. In
particular, when deep frying add
food carefully to avoid splashing,
wear long sleeves and never leave
the pan unattended. A number of
recipes include the use of liquid
nitrogen; this substance should
not be handled without training
in how to use it safely.

Picture credits

Picture credits are listed by
page number. Numbers in
parentheses refer to caption
number. Unless otherwise
specified, all photographs have
been supplied courtesy of the
chefs and their restaurants.
Photographic sources are listed
where possible, but the publisher
will endeavor to rectify any
inadvertent omissions.

Christine Alicino: 334–36; Valentina
Ambrosi: 276; Ben Anders: 31–32, 346,
348; Giovanni de Angelis: 167; L'Auberge
Basque: 49; John Autry (styling Charlotte
Fekete): 282–84; Quentin Bacon: 138–39,
141; Lisa Barber: 142–43, 145; Emilie
Baltz: 131, 133; Claes Bech-Paulsen: 250,
252, 331, 333; Stephen Black and Samuel
Chia: 83–84; Mark Blower: 362–64;
Marion Brenner: 368; Matteo Brogi:
231, 232 (2–5); Nicolas Bruant: 378–79,
381; Renaud Callebaut: 122–23; Kelly
Campbell: 413; Mirko Carretta: 169 (1);
Andrew Carter: 383, 385; Greta Caruso:
361 (1–2); Change is Good: 14–16, 42–43,
45; Richard Chen: 224 (4); Nuno Correia:
38–39, 41; Sebastien Cottereau: 47;
Vanessa Courtier: 302–3, 305; Mathias
Dahlgren: 99 (1–2); David Matheson
Photography Inc.: 239–40; Penny Dedel:
254–56; J.-M. Del Moral: 243; Len Depas:
407–8; Jelle Desramaults: 111–12;
Dhamane: 306–8; Alan Donaldson: 391,
393; Will Duke: 174–76; Melanie Dunea:
58–60; Thomas Duval: 244; e & m Eneritz
Mireia: 35, 37; Jerry Errico: 350 (1–3);
Andrew Feinberg: 128 (1–3, 5); Shaun
Fenn: 154–56; Michael Franke: 178–80;
Steven Freeman: 66–67, 69; Jean Pierre
Gabriel: 366, 367 (6); Maki Galimberti:
274 (3); Jeannette Goodrich: 211–13;
John Granen: 102–4; Chris Granger:
226–28; Anna Claudia Grossi: 230
(3); Emily Hall: 10–12; Linus Hallgren:
278–79, 281; Vanina Herräiz: 162–64;
Philippe Heurtault: 326–28; Massimo
Innocenti: 166 (3–4), 169 (2–4); Tim
James: 415; Pablo Jimenez: 134–36;
Jordan Studio: 270–72; P.A. Jorgensen:
421; Glenn Karlsrud: 190–92; Koji Studio/
Patrick Poon: 194, 197, 396 (2, 4); Elena
Koldunova and Vladimir Klyosov: 186–87,
189; Miyuke Kume: 396 (1); Stephan
Langmanis: 287, 289; Joerg Lehmann:
124; Marne Lucas: 147–48; Marcialis:
274 (1–2), 275; Jacqui Melville: 246–47,
249; Gaëtan Miclotte: 114, 116; Marc
Millar: 182–84; Matthew Monteith: 359;
François Moura: 207, 209; Patricia Niven:
417; Bob Noto: 230 (1–2), 232 (1); Jon
Osbourne: 159; Russ Otterwell: 63 (1–2),
65; Colin Page: 338–39, 341; Claudio
Palmieri: 166 (1–2); Edward Park: 106,
107 (3–6), 109; Max Poglia: 386, 388;
Paul Raeside: 420; Viel Richardson:
118, 120; Thomas Schauer: 374–76;
Stuart Scott: 54–55, 57; Neil Setchfield:
107 (2); Zach Shapiro: 361 (3); Tim Shu:
222–23, 224 (1–3, 5–6); Magnus Skoglöf:
100; Francine Stephens: 127; Jack Tan:
234–36; Francesco Tonelli: 74–77; Quist
Tsang/City Magazine: 394, 396 (3);
Michael Harlan Turkell: 90–92; Graham
Uden: 198–200; Jill Ulicney: 126, 128
(4); Richard Van Herckenrode: 292–91;
Cassio Vasconcellos: 26–27, 29; Pär
Wickholm: 99 (3–4); Andy Wijckelsma
and Hsich Chun Te: 402–3, 405; Katie
Wilson: 160; Tim Winter: 315–16; Vadim
Zakharov: 358